# Cost/ Schedule Control Systems Criteria

## The Management Guide to C/SCSC

Quentin W. Fleming

Probus Publishing Company
Chicago, Illinois

Library of Congress Cataloging-in-Publication Data

Fleming, Quentin W.
    Cost/schedule control systems criteria.

    Rev. ed. of: Put earned value (C/SCSC) into your management control system, c1983.
    Includes index.
    1. Cost control. 2. Program budgeting.
3. Production control. 4. United States. Dept. of Defense—Procurement—Cost control. I. Fleming, Quentin W. Put earned value (C/ SCSC) into your management control system. II. Title.
HD47.3.F6 1988        658.1'552        88-19514
ISBN:  1-55738-011-2

Printed in the United States of America

1   2   3   4   5   6   7   8   9   0

# Contents

# List of Figures

# Preface

The C/SCSC concept is celebrating its twentieth birthday. For those of us who have dealt with governmental regulations over the years, a twentieth birthday for any "bureaucratic directive" has to be a milestone of sorts.

Let's face it: governmental regulations have a tendency to be faddish, perhaps even fickle. They are often imposed and then, with the retirement of their sponsors, quietly fade away, soon to be replaced by still other "exciting" new directives. Some of us even find a sort of amusement in reading about a thrilling "new" initiative, which we remember as an earlier directive, which was later discarded, later reincarnated—much like Hollywood remakes the same movies over and over and over again.

But C/SCSC has been around for twenty straight years. Many of our government career people and political appointees have risen to the top of their field, stayed a few years, then retired during this same time period. Perhaps four or five "bureaucratic waves" have come and gone in the two decades since the criteria concept was first introduced. And yet C/SCSC has survived the turnover of people, and is probably stronger today than at any time since it was first introduced. There must be something of substance here.

Of equal or greater significance, however, is the fact that although C/SCSC was initially the product of the United States Department of Defense, the concept was found to be so useful it has now migrated over to the procurement activities at other governmental bodies, to private business, and certain foreign governments. A solid endorsement for any bureaucratic concept.

This book is an updated, expanded version of my 1983 effort, *Put Earned Value (C/SCSC) Into Your Management Control System.* Those sections which were still relevant were left as originally written. Certain of the sections were rewritten to better explain the concept. Seven new chapters and a glossary of C/SCSC terms have been added.

The book is dedicated to those executives who currently use this successful program management concept, and additionally, to those who for some reason have not yet come around to appreciate the full benefit of C/SCSC.

## Acknowledgements

My personal thanks extends to certain individuals who took time from their busy schedules to critique this manuscript.

*From the United States Government*

**Lieutenant Colonel Thomas L. Bowman,** Deputy Program Control, Air Force Wright Aeronautical Laboratory, Wright-Patterson Air Force Base, Dayton, Ohio. Previously for some 8 years, Tom was a professor of Performance Measurement at the Air Force Institute of Technology (AFIT).

**Robert R. Kemps,** Director of Project and Facilities Management, Department of Energy, Washington, D.C., and formerly with the Office of Assistant Secretary of Defense (Comptroller), where he played a key role in the implementation of the C/SCSC concept.

**Dr. Anthony Webster,** Director, Program Cost Management, at the Defense Systems Management College, Fort Belvoir, Virginia.

And two other gentlemen from the Department of Defense, in the Pentagon, who were most heplful in their critique but who have asked to remain nameless.

*From Private Industry*

**Daniel Schild,** presently with The Analytical Sciences Corporation (TASC), Dayton, Ohio, recently retired as Chief, Cost Management Systems Division, Aeronautical Systems Division, Wright-Patterson Air Force Base, Dayton, Ohio.

**Seymour Uberman,** Consultant, formally a professor (retired) at the Defense Systems Managment College, Fort Belvoir, Virginia.

*From Academia*

**Dr. J. Ronald Fox,** Senior Associate Dean and Professor of Business Administration, Harvard University, Graduate School of Business, Cambridge, Massachusetts. In 1963 Dr. Fox received an appointment as Deputy Assistant Secretary of the Air Force, and in 1969 he received an appointment as Assistant Secretary of the Army, where he was instrumental in the implementation of C/SCSC.

**Dr. Francis Webster,** Professor of Business, School of Business, Western Carolina University, Cullowhee, North Carolina.

\* \* \*

Finally, my very special appreciation to **Gary C. Humphreys**, CEO of Humphreys & Associates, Inc., Laguna Hills, California, and to his entire staff, particularly **Lowell Maxwell** (USAF retired) and **Susan J. Palumbo**, who not only helped me with the manuscript, but also contributed much of the material for inclusion in this book.

*Quentin W. Fleming*
*Southern California*

# Introduction

*by Gary C. Humphreys*

The Cost/Schedule Control Control Systems Criteria (C/SCSC) was established in 1967 by the Department of Defense (DOD) to standardize contractor requirements for the reporting of cost and schedule performance on major contracts, and to provide visibility of accomplishments on each contract. Other U.S. Government departments and agencies such as the Department of Energy (DOE), the National Aeronautics and Space Administration (NASA), the Department of Transportation (DOT), the National Security Agency (NSA), as well as some foreign governments and members of NATO, have also adopted similar criteria.

Prior to implementation of C/SCSC (also referred to as "CSPEC," "Earned Value," "CS Squared," "Performance Measurement," and simply "The Criteria"), defense contractors, who often deal simultaneously with more than one customer, were frequently expected to respond to a variety of diverse management requirements from different procuring activities. This imposition made internal and external tracking of performance extremely complex. Therefore, the C/SCSC was established at the DOD level to eliminate the use of multiple sets of requirements. Because of the broad range of contractors, programs, and contract phases, the requirements were written in criteria form intended for broad interpretation and not to be overly restrictive.

It should be emphasized that the C/SCSC do not represent a "system" or "technique." Rather, they are a set of 35 management system requirements, imposed by Government buyers, with which all firms doing business with the Government on contracts of a certain size must comply. The prime objectives of the C/SCSC are to require contractors to employ management control systems for cost/schedule planning and tracking, and to provide timely and auditable data for use by both contractor and customer project/contract management. Procuring managers require assurance that costs and schedule are being managed properly, and that early identification of problems or potential problems is provided. Only then can management actions be taken to reduce the impact of significant variances from original plans. The C/SCSC dictate that the contractor systems used for generating data must replicate internal systems to manage and control cost/schedule performance, thereby eliminating the need for establishment of systems only for the purpose of providing customer reports.

To establish the importance of this book, one must consider the historical perspective of program management systems, which can typically represent approximately eight percent of total progam costs! Earlier program control systems were merely "reporting systems" imposed on contractors by customer managers to satisfy immediate needs for program progress status. Such systems were marginally adequate and had serious defects. The information was not timely for effective management action and was not indicative of actual cost/schedule status. The systems were not a part of the contractor's own internal contract system, were operated by different groups within the organization, and lacked coordination and consistency. Thus, planning and performance data were often not available to reflect effective management of programs.

In 1964 the United States Air Force took action to develop formal requirements dictating that the data from the contractor's own internal management control systems must be the primary source of planned and actual cost/schedule information. Some project managers had already implemented this informally; however, once the decision was made to formalize the requirement, a set of management system characteristics was established. These characteristics formed the basis for establishment of the C/SCSC.

The C/SCSC approach to program management is a significant improvement over the old conventional "budget versus actuals" method. The concept of Earned Value requires the quantification of work progress, using objective indicators of work performed. By focusing on work actually accomplished during a given period, realistic assessments can be made of cost and schedule performance. The very best features of any good management control system (careful planning, baseline establishment, reporting discipline, variance analysis, corrective action, measurement of accomplishments at multiple levels), are all embodied in the C/SCSC. Managers no longer have to guess whether or not contract performance objectives will be met; timely and reliable data are available on which to base decisions. Managers are now able to predict and act on potential problems.

Obviously, a C/SCSC compliant system by itself will not cure all technical problems. Considerable time and effort is still required of managers who deal with the complexities of bringing together large amounts of resources in sufficient quantities and on a timely basis for effective performance on major projects. However, the burden of managers is reduced as a result of early detection of impending cost/schedule problems.

The benefits of improved practices established by the Cost/Schedule Control Systems Criteria have been widely acclaimed by customer and contractor managers alike. Industry executives indicate that Earned Value techniques are now being incorporated on many non-C/SCSC contracts. The reason is obvious—it is clearly an intelligent, efficient and effective approach to successful project management.

*Gary C. Humphreys, CEO*
*Humphreys & Associates, Inc.*
*Laguna Hills, California*

# I

# SOME BASICS

# 1

# SOME BASICS

# 1

# Budgeting
# and Cost Control

*BUDGET.    A balance sheet or statement of estimated receipts and expenditures. A plan for the coordination of resources and expenditures. The amount of money that is available for, required for, or assigned to a particular purpose.*

Black's Law Dictionary[1]

Beginning a book with a series of dry and routine definitions is probably not the most exciting way to start. But face it: people will not pick up a book on cost and schedule control for excitement. However, some of us do have to work for a living and many (perhaps most) of our bosses do expect us to get things done in the time-frame we promised, and within the budgets we were given. And if we think about it further, there are probably few things in life which will alienate the boss/worker relationship quicker than that of being late on finishing a job, or of spending more money to complete it than was originally planned.

In this first chapter we will focus on the subject of budgets, and the control of same, which we typically call cost control. Practically everyone in business uses budgets today but many, when pressed, may not be able to express in words exactly what the term "budget" represents. Therefore, it might be useful if we started with a review of a few of the more understandable descriptions of what this common word actually means. The term "budget" is typically used to describe:

A financial plan...a management tool used for both planning and control.[2]

A budget is a forecast, in detail, of the results of an officially recognized program of operations...[3]

A budget is a quantitative expression of management's plans. Both explicitly and implicitly it represents the intentions and objectives of management to all echelons of the organization and provides a vehicle for monitoring the implementation of plans. In addition, it enables management to assess the adherence of individuals and organizational components to the goals stipulated in the plan and thereby to provide a quantitative basis for measuring and rewarding individual and departmental performance.[4]

Budgets are formal statements of the financial resources set aside for carrying out specific activities in a given period of time.[5]

We will discuss certain aspects of these definitions and just what they might mean for us in our daily work endeavors.

First off, all these definitions of budgets seem to contain a common assumption that a firm is better off when it is operating to a financial plan. This may seem like rather basic stuff, but in fact some firms do attempt or have attempted in the past to function without benefit of a specific direction. Perhaps the past tense is more appropriate to describe such firms—many of them no longer exist, because they attempted to conduct business without a plan. Whatever its form—the annual business plan, the financial plan, short-range, strategic, or long-range—such a plan will contain some type of quantified financial goals, typically referred to as a budget.

Second in these basic assumptions is the notion that a budget or financial plan provides a convenient way for management to monitor ongoing performance. An established budget allows any organization to assess its progress, good or bad, ahead or behind, as it makes its way through the period of performance. With a budget, organizations do not have to wait until the period has ended to determine how well or poorly they have done.

The last characteristic of all budgets is that they provide a means of quantifying the performance of specific individuals and specific organizations, so that they may be rewarded, and in some cases punished, for their performance. While it has become somewhat unfashionable for modern management to actually "punish" individuals for poor performance, the fact of the matter is that there is probably no stronger inducement for people to excel than the knowledge that "management is watching me."

## Some Budgeting Concepts: Top-Down, Bottom-Up, Rolling-Wave

There are a few budgeting terms, used frequently in business settings, which should be generally understood at the outset.

"Top-down" budgets refer to gross, unsupported financial projections, often used to allow the more senior management of an organization to set out the goals or fiscal directions for their firm. Ideally, these top-down budgets should be subsequently reinforced by more detailed "bottom-up" financial estimates, which would serve to verify that the gross plans of management can be met. Bottom-up budgets are, as the term implies, a summarization of the individual budgeting pieces. Both terms, top-down and bottom-up, have their utility in making financial projections.

Top-down budgets, sometimes called "parametric estimates," have their value in the fact that they are easily prepared, easily assessed and easily modified to accommodate a new set of directions or assumptions. They fit in well in a long-range planning exercise, the preparation of a five to ten-year management projection.

Their shortcoming, and a real one, is that such gross projections are not always realistic, or even achievable. When the desired grand plans are subsequently supported with the full financial details from the bottom, the top-level projections are sometimes found to be overly ambitious and sometimes unattainable. Still another drawback with the top-down budgeting approach is that since no detail exists for the gross projections, none of the discrete organizational elements (and individual managers) will know what their piece of the action is expected to be, because only a top parametric summary exists.

"Bottom-up" budgets have their value in that they provide maximum assurances that management's goals are both reasonable and attainable. Typically, they are reinforced with better supporting detail, plus the fact that usually more thought process has gone into their preparation. Each of the performing managers should have had a say regarding their budget needs, and once approved, should know precisely what is expected of them. But bottom-up budgets are by their nature slower to prepare, cumbersome to modify, and take greater effort to monitor. These detailed budgeting estimates often exist under an assortment of titles such as "engineering cost estimates," "detailed cost estimates," "grass roots estimates," and so on.

Both top-down and bottom-up budgets have their own particular utility and both concepts are incorporated into still another technique called a "rolling wave" budget. This approach provides a full-period projection to be made, using a combination of both top-down (unsupported) budgets in conjunction with detailed (bottom-up) budgets. The nearest (often six-month) budget segment would be fully supported with detailed bottom-up plans, and the later periods done with merely top-down projections. As time would pass, the far-term top-down budgets would be progressively defined and superceded with detailed bottom-up budgets (the rolling wave). The detailed plans always would extend perhaps six months into the immediate near-term future.

Thus, each of these budgeting techniques—the "top-down", the "bottom-up," and the "rolling wave"—have their own utility when used at the appropriate time in the budgeting cycle.

## The Budget Window

Every organization experiences the opportunity to establish for itself optimum but realistic budget performance targets. These occasions exist for a very brief period of time, and once passed, will not re-appear again until just prior to the start of the next budgeting cycle. However, not all organizations take advantage of the opportunities and some are not even aware that they exist.

For convenience, these brief time periods will be given a name: "budget window." Such windows occur *prior* to the start of the period planned for a budget (the next quarter, the next calendar year, the next project period, etc.) but are *late* enough to obtain a meaningful commitment from the performing managers, i.e., the people who can make ambitious targets happen. From a purely financial standpoint, it might seem desirable to set all detailed (bottom-up) budgets far into the future. But try to get the attention of line managers too far in advance and you are unlikely to get the type of response or commitment you need to achieve optimum budget performance from them.

The budget window, if allowed to pass without obtaining firm individual commitments, forfeits the opportunity to establish maximum performance goals for an organization. Prior to beginning a period, it is a rather easy task to obtain realistic, but yet ambitious, performance goals from the various operating departments. However, once the budget period starts, the individual performing managers become painfully aware of some of the problems they will have to encounter, and they will then be reluctant to sign up for the same challenging targets. True, upper management could still impose these same aspiring goals. But once the period has started, the personal commitments which were possible earlier, will no longer be accepted by the people who will be making the daily choices, and who can influence, in a meaningful way, the final outcome of the organization's direction. You must get a budget commitment *before* the budget period begins.

The budget window, in addition to having its value in setting maximum performance goals, is also critical to the success of an organization because it is during this brief period that two budget set-asides must be made from the limited resources. These two values must come right off the top of funds being allocated: first a provision for "profits"; and second a provision for "management reserve."

The management reserve is needed to cover any and all adverse contingencies that are likely to occur. Management reserves are expected to be consumed during the period of performance. The management reserve is the buffer which gives an organization assurances that the profit goals it has set for itself will, in fact, survive the performance uncertainties it will face.


## Putting Formality into the Budgeting Process

The scene is the battleship Missouri, in Tokyo Harbor, September 2, 1945, near the end of World War II:

> The weather was so clear that Mount Fuji, the Fortunate Warrior, could be seen sixty miles away. The sun sparkled on the white uniforms of American sailors. Tokyo Bay overflowed with Allied vessels of war—the greatest armada ever assembled. MacArthur delivered an oration and used five pens to sign the surrender instrument. The Japanese signatories walked and talked as stiffly as mechanical dolls. As soon as possible they climbed back down to the launch provided for them and made for shore. They went directly to the palace and reported to the Emperor. The next morning Hirohito and his closest advisors repaired to the Palace Shrine to announce officially the end of the war to his ancestors and the sun goddess.[6]

By the end of that day in 1945, no one in Imperial Japan, no one in the United States, no one in the entire civilized world was *unaware* of the fact that World War II had ended. There is truly something to be said for having "formality."

Now what does this have to do with the subject of budgeting? Well, with somewhat less pompous ceremony, (one pen instead of five; one battleship instead of an armada) when a budget is issued, everyone affected by that action should be absolutely aware of what has taken place. The issuance of budgets, as with the signing of an armistice, should be done with formality.

Too often in the everyday business setting there exists doubt or confusion as to whether or not a given budget was ever issued. Even in those instances where there is general agreement that a budget exists, often there is disagreement on either the *values* contained in the budgets, or on the *statement of work* they were to support. Not only does such confusion often exist with the performing organization, as one might expect, but not infrequently the budgeting people themselves are not sure (or cannot prove) exactly what budgets they have issued. An "ambiguous" budgeting environment creates a worse condition than an environment with no budgets at all. At least in a no-budget environment there can exist an agreement of sorts as to the budget value: zero. It takes less effort to untangle a no-budget situation than it does to correct a condition of budgets issued, but of varying interpretations and values.

There can be no excuse for allowing ambiguity to exist in an organization as to the exact value of budgets. Budgeting is an activity which can be controlled, and it should be controlled by management and the budgeting people, without exception.

## Techniques Used to Elude Budgets

Some of the very smartest people in today's business environment are engineers. Engineers by nature are typically creative people who thrive on new ideas, often pushing the state of the technical arts. By their very nature and educational training, engineers make excellent managers. But engineers also love to elude budgets.

It isn't that engineering managers are deceitful. On the contrary, once they make a commitment to do something they take their obligation as seriously as anyone. But there is sort of an unspoken undercurrent that suggests: "OK business-school person, if you can't do your job and pin me down, you'll get no help from me." Engineers consider themselves professionals, and rightly so, and they expect the budgeting people to be equally professional in the conduct of their jobs. If the budgeters can't define escape-proof budgets, they will get no help from the performing technical managers.

Over the years performing managers have shown incredibly ingenious talents (engineering managers in particular) for circumventing the constraints of budgets. It might be interesting and useful to relate just a few of these techniques in an attempt to better understand the environment, and to suggest a few ways to possibly overcome such conditions.

| Manager's Position | The Symptoms | The Remedy |
|---|---|---|
| 1. "I'm confused." | "Whose numbers are these, where did they come from, who prepared them ?" | Formality. Put the budget in writing, have the recipient sign to acknowledge it, leave a copy. |
| 2. "Things are different now." | "The job has changed, this isn't the same job I agreed to." | Formality. In addittion to numbers, a budget must have a *work statement*, and a schedule. |
| 3. "I don't have the time." | "I'm so busy doing the job I can't stop to fool around with budgets." | Define the budget, get a commitment *before* the period begins. |
| 4. "That's not my commitment." | "I'm the new kid on the block, that budget belonged to my predecessor." | Senior management, when appointing a new person must get a commitment for all aspects of the job, including that of budget performance. |
| 5. "Other areas are causing my budget to overrun." | "The late release of engineering is making me overrun my budget." | Senior management must impress upon all managers a duty to "foresee" events which will adversely affect a budget commitment, so as to be able to stay stay within the committed budget. |

## The Budgeting Process

The functions of budgeting and cost management has been touched on briefly in this chapter. Typically there are five sequential steps to this process as follows:

1. *The Establishment of a Budget Baseline*

   Before the period begins, resources are assigned to the work to be done and to the desired schedule; a profit goal is set, and funds set aside to achieve it. A management reserve is provided to cover the unexpected. All values so allocated are realistic and achievable by the performing departments.

2. *The Formal Issuance of the Budget*

Done in a exacting manner so that there can be no doubt in anyone's mind as to what their particular budget represents. If the full budget period is not released for any reason, the later periods are covered using the rolling-wave budget approach. A commitment to perform within all budgets is agreed to between management and the various performing managers who can make it happen.

3. *The Monitoring of Performance & Analysis of Variances*

Actual costs are compared to the budget for the same work, any differences (+ or -) are analyzed by cost category to help determine why such departures occurred. Performing managers are interviewed, shown their results, and solicited for their reaction to any variances beyond acceptable tolerances.

4. *Projection of the Final Expected Costs*

Actual cost results are compared to the budget plan, an assessment of the value of work accomplished versus work remaining is made, and an educated projection of the expected final financial results is also made.

5. *Management Review & Corrective Actions*

Management's continuing review of the budget performance, and the subsequent actions taken by management to stay within acceptable budget limits: i.e., the de-scoping or delaying of tasks, the issuing of management reserve, the occasional discharge of poorly performing managers, etc., any actions needed to keep the organization on an acceptable budget path.

In order to get the full cooperation and maximum performance by managers, budget goals must be attainable by mortal people. It serves no purpose to issue budgets which can not be achieved under any circumstances, although it is not uncommon for unrealistic budget targets to exist in industry. Further, there are legitimate changes in operating conditions which should be acknowledged and which will sometimes necessitate changes in budgets. When these changes occur, budgets should be modified to accommodate the new conditions, in order to make budgets ambitious, but yet both reasonable and attainable.

## There are Budgets and There are Budgets

All firms today use some type of budgeting methodology to control their destinies, but the essence of the term "budgets" are likely to have different meanings from firm to firm and from industry to industry. For although few managers would likely admit to not using budgets, what constitutes their "budget" would certainly be colored by widely divergent management approaches. Budgeting is accomplished in different flavors. Some approaches are quite sophisticated in that they allow for a high degree of individual management initiative and autonomy. Still other budgeting techniques are, unfortunately, quite archaic and actually stifle the individual manager's initiative.

The most sophisticated budget approach would be expressed in purely monetary terms, e.g., dollars. Ultimate sophistication would provide a monetary budget target for the full period, without setting time-phasing by period. The final time phasing would be done by the performing managers. This approach would give the performing organizations maximum flexibility in the manner in which they run their operations. They could perform their tasks in any way they felt would be best for their operation. For example, they could use their funds to pay for company employees, hire outside consultants, buy or rent robots, and so forth. The approach they take to manage would be purely up to them.

Unfortunately, industry rarely achieves this level of budget sophistication. And by not doing so, industry loses an opportunity to achieve maximum budget performance from the ingenious methods possible when operating managers are allowed to make their own choices. Budgets should be used to stimulate the flow of new ideas, not to inhibit them by imposing artificial and unnecessary controls.

The other extreme of budgeting approaches (the opposite of sophistication) will be referred to as the "archaic." Here a budget is issued, but the budget has little significance. Each time a manager attempts to do something with his or her budget, they must go through additional administrative approval cycles, as if no budget existed. If they want to hire a new employee, they must get additional management approval on a personnel requisition form. The archaic budget approach keeps all organizations tightly in control because each department manager must go through a series of redundant bureaucratic hurdles each time they attempt to take action for their operation. The archaic budgeting approach stifles the operating manager's initiative, and results in something less than optimal performance for the organization.

Unfortunately, in industry today, one too often sees budget approaches more closely aligned to the archaic than to the sophisticated. And by overly controlling the performing organizations with restrictive, little-value budgets, industry loses the benefits and flow of fresh new ideas which can come when personnel are allowed to perform in a manner as they see fit, while of course, still staying within the overall parameters of their agreed to budget goals.

A few years back the young people had an expression about "needing their own space." Too often, financial people when performing the budgeting process, forget that operating managers also need their "own space."

## Who Needs a Budget?

Leaving the world of theory for a moment, how many industry executives can truthfully say that their organization's budget is an accurate representation of the goals they have set for their activities? Further, how many can say that each of their subordinates are rewarded and/or punished with some type of system for performance against these budgets. Those executives who do not bother with the budget process, or who merely pay lip service to this critical task, are missing an opportunity to utilize a proven management tool, one which can maximize the performance of their organization.

The definitions presented at the opening of this chapter were certainly adequate, and no financial executive would likely take issue with them. Inherent in any viable definition of a budget are five basic assumptions:

1. A budget will reflect a financial plan, which in turn reflects the goals set by senior management for their organization.

2. A budget will be expressed in time-phased and measurable terms, with specific elements of work, so that performance along the way can be determined.

3. All individual elements of the organization will be aware of their portion of the overall grand budget.

4. Performance against the budgets will be monitored by management and reviewed periodically with each organizational segment.

5. Good and/or bad performance against the approved budgets will be rewarded and/or disciplined by management.

Who then needs a budget? Answer: Any and all organizations which intend to maximize their firm's performance, and to minimize the "risk" factor in their firm's overall direction.

---

*War Story # 1*

We have been talking about budgeting in a theoretical sense, as if one merely has to issue a value in a formal way and there will be agreement and general harmony thereafter. In fact, the setting of budgets can be one of the more painful but necessary tasks in the management process. Quite often, perhaps most of the time, there is simply not enough money to satisfy everyone's perceived needs.

The following discussion actually took place between a senior manager and a department manager trying to come to an agreement on the proper budget for his department.

Manager:   "I *can't* do the job unless I get more people."

Superior:   "There *isn't* any more budget."

Manager:   "Then I'll have to do a *lesser* job to stay within the budget."

Superior:   "No, you'll have to do the *full* job but with fewer people."

Manager:   "That's an impossibility!"

Superior:   "No, that's management."

Manager:   "I just can't do it!"

Superior:   "Then maybe your replacement *can*."

These two managers did come to an agreement as to the proper budget value, and a formal budget was subsequently issued. And everyone lived happily ever after. Well, almost!

---

## ENDNOTES

[1] *Black's Law Dictionary*, 5th edition (St. Paul, MN: West Publishing Company, 1979).

[2] J. Fred Weston and Eugene F. Brigham *Essentials of Managerial Finance* (Hinsdale, IL: The Dryden Press, 1974), page 112.

[3] John R. Bartizal, *Budget Principles and and Procedures* (New York, NY: Prentice-Hall, Inc., 1940), page 1.

[4] Herbert T. Spire, *Finance for the Non-Financial Manager* (New York, NY: John Wiley & Sons, Inc., 1977), page 110.

[5] James A. F. Stoner, *Management* (Englewood Cliffs, NJ: Prentice-Hall, Inc., 1978), page 593.

[6] David Bergamini, *Japan's Imperial Conspiracy* (New York, NY: William Morrow and Company, Inc., 1971), page 137.

# 2

# Scheduling
# and Schedule Control

*SCHEDULE. Any list of planned events to take place on a regular basis such as a train schedule or a schedule of work to be performed in a factory.*
Black's Law Dictionary[1]

The next subject which is fundamental to the proper understanding of the C/SCSC concept is that of "scheduling",—the second letter in the acronym. Since we all use scheduling in one form or another in our daily lives, the theory is almost innate to each of us. However, there are a few specific terms and concepts which are common in industrial settings, and which should be fully understood by anyone dealing with the topic of C/SCSC. A brief overview of the subject of scheduling is provided in this chapter, in an effort to establish a proper C/SCSC foundation.

## Just What is Scheduling?

To most of us who work for a living, scheduling can best be thought of as that process of simply getting to work each day, at the agreed to time. But if we reflect on this idea for a minute, scheduling is really more than just that. The full process of scheduling includes both the *planning* necessary to get to work on time, as well as the *execution* of such plans. We establish a target goal to arrive at work, say at 9:00 a.m., and we think about doing all those things which must precede our arrival at our place of work, at the expected time.

But in the industrial or business sector the issues often become a little more complex than this simple illustration of simply getting to work on time would suggest. As an example, assume what it would take to plan for the construction and outfitting of a new retail clothing store, our "dream store," to be opened in time for next year's Christmas buying season. And as a side consideration, also assume we know that if we miss the sales at that peak year-end buying period, we may not be able to repay the balloon bank note we had to sign in order to finance construction of our new store. The target opening date must be met.

13

In industrial scheduling care must be taken to incorporate *all* the required tasks which must happen in order to complete a job on time, in this case to open the doors by December 1st of next year. If any of the numerous critical tasks are left out of the plan (like obtaining building permits), or if the times involved for any of the various tasks are poorly estimated (like forgetting about the rainy season), we could miss the critical opening target date, and loose our new store. The Christmas season will not wait for the "I forgots" to eventually happen.

The art of scheduling is nothing more than getting things done on time, according to a plan. It is a full and complicated subject, and we will only touch on it briefly in order to reinforce the C/SCSC concept. However, to do full justice to the subject, there are eight basic terms which must become part of our everyday vocabulary. These terms are:

*Schedule*—A time plan of goals or targets which serves as the focal point for management actions.

*Scheduling*—The act of preparing and/ or implementing schedules.

*Event*—Something that happens at a point or moment in time.

*Milestone*—An event of particular importance, a big event.

*Activity*—Something that occurs over time. The subject of the plan; that which must be accomplished. Also referred to as a "task."

*Sequential*—Things that are done in a sequence, serial, or series; one thing after another.

*Concurrent* or *Parallel*—Two or more tasks that are done at the same time or at times which overlap.

*Dependency* or *Constraint*—Things that cannot happen until something else happens first. Also referred to in scheduling as a "restraint."[2]

## Types of Schedules in Use Today

It is always amusing how ingenious people can be in creating and displaying a variety of schedule formats, as if there were an unlimited supply from which to choose. And to the uninitiated observer the subject must seem unduly complex. But if we cut through the facade, and recognize that scheduling focuses on only three areas, and there are only three generic types of schedules in use, the subject becomes more palatable.

The act of scheduling focuses on three areas:

*Activities*—Most commonly called tasks, things that take place over a period of time and generally consume resources.

*Events*—Points in time, usually called *milestones*, which generally do not consume resources themselves.

*Constraints* or *Dependencies*—The relationships between tasks or milestones which prevent subsequent (downstream) events or milestones from happening according to plan.

The scheduling people take these three areas of emphasis, and develop three types of generic schedules from them:

*Gantt Charts*—Sometimes called *Bar Charts,* which focus on planned tasks or activities.

*Milestone Charts*—Which focus, as one might expect, on milestones or events.

*Network Schedules*—Which tie together activities or events to highlight the relationships between them.

Let us cover each of these schedule types in detail.


## Gantt and Milestone Schedules

Gantt charts are the product of Henry Laurence Gantt, 1861-1919, which he developed in the World War I period. They are sometimes referred to as Bar Charts, but Gantt Charts is the more common title.

The value of the Gantt chart is in its simplicity. No matter how poorly the data might be displayed, the message will likely get through to the audience. Planned activities or tasks are portrayed as (hollow) bars over a horizontal time scale. As progress is made in accomplishing the tasks, the hollow bars are filled in to reflect the progress. When the horizontal progress lines are compared to a vertical "time now" line, the audience can immediately visualize whether the tasks are on, or ahead, or behind schedule. See Figure 2-1 for a display of a simple four task Gantt chart.

The other very commonly used schedule form is that of a milestone chart, which by definition focuses on events, or points in time. See Figure 2-2 for an illustration of a simple milestone chart. Milestone charts are most commonly used by senior management to focus on the "big picture," selected major milestones in a project: did they happen as planned, "yes" or "no"? The buying customers also like to review performance on selected milestones as they monitor a project.

While there are no absolute rules which regulate the symbols used in the preparation of Gantt and milestone charts, there are certain generally accepted forms which are commonly found. See Figure 2-3 for a display of frequently used scheduling symbology.

Gantt charts typically use hollow bars over time to display a plan. As the plans are accomplished, these hollow bars are filled in to reflect progress. Delays to the plan are usually shown with a dotted-line extension to the original line. Some firms will use a single bar to reflect the plan/progress, while others will use a split bar, typically the top reflecting the plan, and the bottom reflecting progress against the plan. These differences are purely ones of personal taste. Either display will convey a clear message to the intended audience, which is the beauty of the Gantt chart—its simplicity.

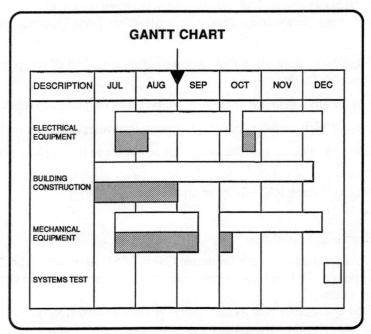

**Figure 2- 1   A Gantt Chart[3]**

### MILESTONE CHART

| EVENT | JAN | FEB | MAR | APR | MAY | JUN | JUL | AUG | SEPT |
|---|---|---|---|---|---|---|---|---|---|
| CONTRACT SIGNED | ▲ | | | | | | | | |
| PROGRAM PLANNED | ▲ | | | | | | | | |
| BILL OF MATERIAL FINALIZED | | | ▲ | | | | | | |
| SUBCONTRACTS SIGNED | | | △▼ | | | | | | |
| SYSTEM SPECIFICATIONS FINALIZED | | | | △ ▽ | | | | | |
| DESIGN REVIEWED | | | | | △ | | | | |
| SUBSYSTEM TESTED | | | | | | △ | | | |
| 1st UNIT DELIVERED | | | | | | | △ | | |
| PRODUCTION PLAN COMPLETED | | | | | | | | △ | |
| PROGRAM PHASE 1 COMPLETED | | | | | | | | | △ |

**Figure 2-2   A Milestone Chart[4]**

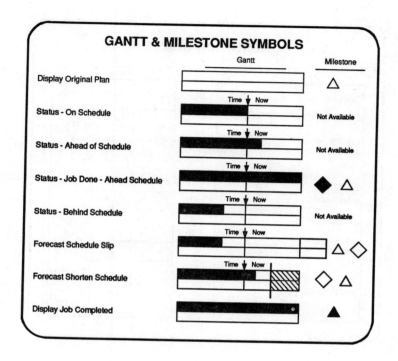

**Figure 2-3  Gantt & Milestone Chart Symbology[5]**

Milestone charts typically use a "triangle" to illustrate the plan, and a "diamond" to reflect changes to the original baseline plan. The "diamond" is used to reflect any change to a baseline, either earlier or later than was originally planned.

Although Gantt charts are expected to display only tasks or activities, and milestone charts are typically expected to reflect only events or milestones, in fact, most of the charts typically found in industry will be an amalgamation of the two concepts. See Figure 2-4 for a "combination chart," reflecting both tasks and milestones in the same display. This illustration is the same four task project as was shown earlier in Figure 2-1. The value in the combination chart is that the longer duration activities/ tasks can be further broken down with intermediate discrete milestones, to better observe a task as it is being performed.

## Network Schedules (aka PERT Charts)

The other technique(s) used to plan and schedule a project is that of network scheduling, sometimes referred to as logic diagramming. This approach attempts to simulate what will be experienced, or is being experienced, in the performance of an actual project.

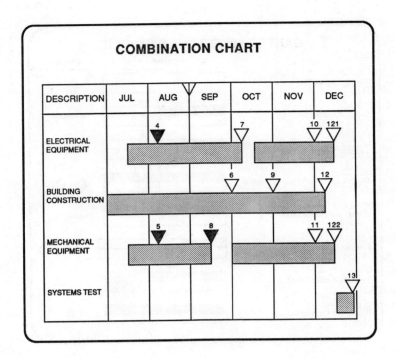

**Figure 2-4  A Combination Gantt/Milestone Chart[6]**

Network schedules simulate a project by taking the planned tasks or events and tieing them together with constraint or dependency lines. Such constraints prevent later tasks or events from occurring until earlier ones are finished. Since they were first introduced in the late 1950s, at least three types of network forms have been used, as shown in the Figure 2- 5.

One such network type, original PERT (Program Evaluation and Review Technique), is shown at the top. It used events to define a project and merely related each event with a dependency line to illustrate that the down-stream events could not happen until the earlier events were accomplished. This approach lasted but a short period, and was replaced by the two other approaches as displayed in the center and bottom of Figure 2-5.

Original PERT was found to be mathematically correct, and the computers quickly accepted the logic inputs without difficulty. But the intended users, the "old guard" managements, had much trouble digesting the logic of original PERT displays. PERT soon merged with another method which came on the scene at the same time but in the construction industry. The Critical Path Method-CPM was more adaptable to management displays and briefings because it was time oriented, and resembled in approximate appearance the popular Gantt chart. Soon PERT and CPM (also known as Arrow Diagram Method-ADM, and IJ Networks), became the most common type of networks in use at the time. The

CPM/ADM/IJ network form is shown in the middle of Figure 2-5. CPM takes the various planned tasks of a project and links them together with dependency lines, somewhat resembling a Gantt chart linked with constraint lines.

Still later, in about 1963, another approach to network scheduling was introduced, the Precedence Diagram Method (PDM). In this concept the focus is also on tasks, but the tasks are displayed as nodes (boxes), also linked together with dependency lines. See the bottom part of Figure 2-5. This approach is the most popular today, likely because it allows the managers of projects considerable flexibility in the *re-planning* of a project as circumstances dictate. The re-planning of a project is perhaps of greater importance to those who schedule than that of preparing the original plan.

The strength of network schedules lies in the assistance they provide in planning or simulating a proposed project. They are also of considerable value in isolating alternate approaches, the "what-ifs", as progress goes poorly, and other ways must be found to accomplish a project.

But networks are not without their faults. Networks typically make very poor displays for presentations to any audience, particularly that of management. Networks are best utilized in the planning process. When the results are to be run by management, it is always wise to convert such network plans into summary form, and present them as a milestone, a Gantt, or as a combination chart.

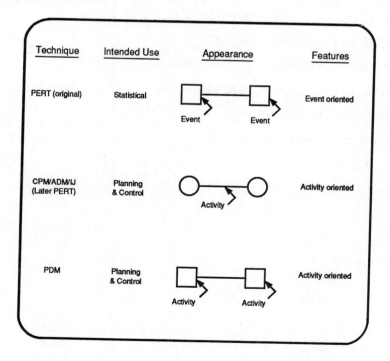

**Figure 2-5 Network Scheduling Types**[7]

## Summary

For those involved in the implementation of C/SCSC, the most important type of schedules will likely be the Gantt or milestone charts. These techniques are most commonly used at lower levels in a cost/schedule control system, in the cost accounts. Network schedules will, to a lesser degree, also be used by the detailed planners to schedule various critical segments of the project.

As was stated in the opening, this chapter was never intended to be a comprehensive treatment of the subject of scheduling. For anyone wishing a more complete discussion of the subject of scheduling, the following book is suggested:

*Project & Production Scheduling,* by Quentin W. Fleming, John W. Bronn, and Gary C. Humphreys, released in 1987 (Probus Publishing Company, 118 North Clinton Street, Chicago, Illinois 60606).

---

## ENDNOTES

[1] *Black's Law Dictionary*, 5th edition (St. Paul, MN: West Publishing Company, 1979).

[2] Fleming, Bronn, and Humphreys, *Project & Production Scheduling* (Chicago, IL: Probus Publishing Company, 1987), pages 4-5.

[3] Fleming, Bronn, and Humphreys, page 39.

[4] Fleming, Bronn, and Humphreys, page 48.

[5] Fleming, Bronn, and Humphreys, page 64.

[6] Fleming, Bronn, and Humphreys, page 49.

[7] Fleming, Bronn, and Humphreys, page 79.

# 3

# Why C/SCSC?

*"The Congress wants what we all want: effective spending and a healthy acquisition system."*

General Lawrence A. Skantze
Commander, Air Force Systems Command[1]

If one could somehow survey all the program managers in the private American industrial/ defense sector with the question: "Do you feel *you* need C/SCSC to manage your contracts?", the overwhelming and truthful answer would likely be a resounding "no." Even those few who might answer in the affirmative would likely be doing so because the concept has been around for so long they have come to accept it as a fact of life in the industry. But the plain truth of the matter is that many (most?) program managers and industrial managements in general do not feel they need the C/SCSC concept to successfully manage their contracts. Such being the case, then why is C/SCSC an absolute requirement on all United States Government contracts of a certain size? The answer is simple: because the buying customers, the United States Government and its various procurement arms, are convinced that *they* need C/SCSC to properly oversee and manage their procurement programs, when the risk of success or failure of a contract is on them.

Perhaps a real-life tale will best illustrate the issue It is a story which took place before C/SCSC came into use, in the late 1950s, a long time ago.

---

## War Story #2

There once was a newly established private firm which had set for itself ambitious growth objectives. It had been bidding on every new job that came its way but without much success. Finally it was given the opportunity to bid on a developmental contract for a new missile system. Their management knew they badly needed a new contract, particularly a "cost plus" type contract, to develop a base of engineers and other specialists, in order to meet their long-term goal of becoming a major aerospace firm in the shortest possible time.

They received the Request for Proposal for the new missile and their pricing people went to work. Pricing established their initial position, indicating that the effort was worth about

$350 million. "Too high to win" was the initial reaction of the management. Pricing got out their sharp pencils and went back to work. The second cut was now down to a little over $200 million. "Still too high to win, show some imagination," was the message which came out of the second price review. At last they had a proposed value they felt would win for them: $99.999 million, with a *one* dollar fee. They submitted their proposal. Surprise surprise—the contractor won the competition. A contract was awarded.

Remember, those were the days when contractors were given cost reimbursable contracts with *fixed* fees, and the buying agencies had no viable means to verify the total (cost) scope of the effort being procured. They had to proceed on trust and the hope that their skills as managers would successfully complete contracts within the funds allotted. Sometimes their approach worked, and other times it didn't. This contract was awarded for $100 million and was to be performed over a 4-year period.

Looking back, at no time during the period of performance did this contractor admit to the buying customer that the contract value would have to be exceeded, or that the four years programmed was insufficient time to complete the effort. At no time, that is, until it became absolutely transparent to all parties that more time and more funds would be needed. Such admissions only came after consuming three-fourths of the funds and three fourths of the allotted time. But in those days it was commonplace for contractors to "buy into" new programs, giving up profit on an initial effort, in exchange for building a long-term resource base for future efforts. Sometimes these "loss-leaders" even went into long-term production runs with corresponding long-term profit returns.

When this contract was finally completed the four years initially programmed extended to six years. But of greater consequence to the paying taxpayers, the $100 million initial effort grew to $550 million, through a combination of added scope, and (much) overrun. A true story, only the values have been updated to reflect the current economic environment.

To set the record straight, this contractor wasn't necessarily deceitful, anymore than most contractors were in that period. And of course the procuring agency, the buyers, had to share at least a part of the responsibility. They had to know that the initial contact value, and the time allowed would not be sufficient to complete the effort. But the governmental buyers during that period had no viable means with which to verify:

*One*—How much money and time a particular job would likely take, before starting it;

*Two*—and once started, what physical work was being accomplished for the funds being spent (what you got for what you spent);

*Three*—and of perhaps greatest importance, once started, what the total bill would likely cost, and how long the total job would likely take in order to finish it.

Remember, those were the days before C/SCSC.

## PERT, PERT/Cost & "Earned Value"

About the same time as this story was taking place there was a related development, although at the time it did not seem to be related.

In the late 1950s (1957-1958) there emerged two network scheduling concepts, one called "PERT" (Program Evaluation and Review Technique) which originated in the defense community, and "CPM" (Critical Path Method), which was started in the construction industry. They both had a similar approach of linking together the planned events and tasks in an attempt to show the relationships and constraints between them. By doing this it was hoped to isolate the longest sequential path of tasks in a project, which they called the critical path. Managements would then focus on this sequential path in order to complete their jobs in the shortest possible time. The networking concept received high acclaim but only moderate success in private industry. However, the management theorists at various universities did accept the concept, more so than did the industrial project managers, and incorporated it into many of their business courses.

In the early 1960s the government attempted to employ the PERT network scheduling concept on all major contracts, and in many cases the technique simply didn't fit. But before the network scheduling concept was even partially accepted by industry, the zealous proponents attempted to take an even more ambitious step: to add resources to the PERT scheduling networks. PERT (later called PERT/Time) thus became PERT/Cost. The concept was ignored by industry, and it quietly faded. But an often overlooked aspect of PERT/Cost was the introduction of a new concept called "earned value" management. It suggested the idea of planning a program and the necessary resources in sufficient detail so as to allow for the precise measurement of performance along the way, and of having the ability to obtain reliable estimates of the total costs, and total times needed to complete various programs.

PERT failed, not because the idea was bad, but because of a number of issues unrelated to the technique itself. The implementation by the government was poor. It was "decreed" to be the single management technique to be used on all major defense contracts, by a young Secretary of Defense and his young, inexperienced staff. Seasoned military officers and seasoned industry project managers quite naturally resented being told what technique to use to manage their contracts, by people not considered to be worthy to make such pronouncements.

But there were also other issues. Computer technology and the computer software programs were not yet available to sufficiently support the new concept. They were perhaps 25 years ahead of themselves.

By the mid 1960s the government procurement people knew that PERT and PERT/Cost were not going to work. But they also knew they had a fundamental requirement to find a way to monitor procurement efforts with a greater degree of visibility and control. They also had learned from their PERT experience that simply directing contractors to use a certain technique would likely not work. Contractors had to see some merit in a concept, or it would be insidiously rejected.

In 1963 the United States Air Force formed a team called the Cost/ Schedule Planning & Control Specification group, and meetings were started by some of the very same people who had been involved in the implementation of PERT/Time and PERT/Cost. By virtue of their PERT experience they quickly agreed they would *not* impose any specific "management control system" on industry. Rather, they conceived the idea of merely requiring that contractors satisfy selected "criteria" with their *existing* management control systems. A subtle difference from the PERT experience, perhaps, but it made the difference between success or failure for the new concept.

## Contract Performance: Often a Question of Priorities

The success of major procurement programs can be measured by three standards of performance: *Cost, Schedule,* and *Technical.* Cost performance is simply the completing of a job, the total job, for the funds originally provided to it. If one is allotted an unlimited amount of money, practically any job can be accomplished. But it takes sharp management skills to complete a given set of involved and complex tasks, for the funds originally agreed to by the contracting parties. Cost or budget performance is often thought of as the first of the three standards of contract performance.

Schedule performance, on the other hand, simply involves completing a job within the time period agreed to by the contracting parties. Meeting ones commitment to time is vital to success in many types of endeavors. To emphasize the importance of this very issue, the lawyers long ago created the phrase "time is of the essence," which they often insert in contracts where one of parties would suffer damages should the other party fail to do their work in the agreed to time period.

The last of the three standards is that of technical performance, which means simply the completion of a job, of a quality and quantity originally agreed to by the parties. While quantity issues do not seem to present much difficulty, perhaps because any deviations are so immediately obvious and measurable, the quality issue often surfaces in contractual disputes. A vendor may contract to deliver the sum of 100 "widgets" and do so. But if shortcuts had been taken in producing the widgets, for cost or time or whatever reason, any deficiencies would likely manifest themselves in the *quality* of the products to arrive. Technical performance is simply providing the services and products of the same caliber, which the parties had in mind when they struck their deal.

But an interesting phenomena or priority of performance standards often takes place in certain of the industries, particularly those industries where the technical people, (engineers and scientists) occupy many of the management positions. These conditions are best exemplified by the defense and aerospace industries.

In these enterprises the standards of contract performance typically thought of as cost (#1), schedule (#2) and technical (#3), are often reversed in priority, and are performed with an emphasis on: technical (#1), schedule (#2), and cost (#3). Most engineers and scientists by education and experience have spent a lifetime with an emphasis on the merits of high technical performance. Most are individuals of high ideals. Therefore, it is almost instinctive to them that they would emphasize those things which seem most natural to them: high technical performance. Thus, when confronted with a choice of setting priorities, they will most likely opt for high technical performance, and if need be, at the expense of both cost and schedule performance. And if pressed further, when given a choice between meeting a cost goal or a schedule commitment, they will most likely meet their commitment to deliver on time. Technical performance comes first, schedule second, and costs come in last.

Therefore, in those industries in which the technical personnel have risen to the top of the management rolls, there will likely exist major philosophical differences of opinion over the priorities of contract performance, with those people who dole out the funds to pay the bills: the accountants. Since all programs must be funded to be viable, and the accountants typically provide the necessary funding, a truce of sorts must exist between the two camps. C/SCSC has provided managements with a tool to answer their basic questions of "how much" and "how long."

## Enter the Criteria Concept

On December 22, 1967, the Department of Defense issued DOD Instruction 7000.2, *Performance Measurement for Selected Acquisitions*. This document defined 35 criteria or standards which the DOD would henceforth impose on all contractors and their management control systems, that is, those firms wishing to do business with the DOD. These same 35 criteria are in place today, essentially unchanged, some two decades later.

The C/SCSC do not represent a "management control system." Rather, the criteria merely specify those minimum requirements which a contractor's management control system must satisfy. The criteria were issued with two primary objectives:

- For contractors to use effective internal cost and schedule management control systems, and

- For the government to be able to rely on timely and auditable data produced by those systems for determining product-oriented contract status.[2]

In 1975, the Department of Energy, then the Energy Research and Development Administration, formally adopted these same criteria and thereafter imposed them on major contractors wishing to do business with the DOE.

Conceptually, there is nothing difficult about understanding the requirements of these criteria. But fully satisfying them with ones management control system is sometimes less than simple.

It is not uncommon for one branch of the U. S. military departments to take the lead in developing new management concepts. In the case of C/SCSC the Air Force took that role.

However, it was recognized early that the criteria concept had to be *universally* applied to all DOD procurement components in order for it to be effective. In their *joint* implementation guide issued in 1976, the military services stressed the need for the criteria concept:

> It is recognized that no single common set of management control systems will meet every DOD and contractor management data need for performance measurement. Due to variations in organizations, products, and working relationships, it is not feasible to prescribe a universal system for cost and schedule controls. DOD has adopted an approach which simply defines the criteria that contractor's management control systems must meet. The criteria provide the basis for determining whether contractor management control systems are acceptable.[3]

Because the Department of Energy implemented the criteria concept subsequent to the DOD, and because some of the same personnel who worked on the concept at the DOD later joined the DOE and implemented it there, the DOE always had benefit of the past experiences from the DOD. Therefore, as one might expect, the DOE has been able to convey the very same requirements on their contractors in a most effective way. In their summary C/SCSC document the DOE stated why they would impose the concept on their contractors:

> The importance and complexity of DOE's outlay programs require the use of project management techniques that promote effective planning, managing, and controlling of contracted work. To the extent to which DOE projects are being accomplished by contractors, DOE needs to ascertain the effectiveness of the cost and schedule control systems applied to this effort. The Criteria approach is used to fill this need. This approach:
>
> • Sets forth the characteristics and capabilities required of a contractor's cost and schedule control system, such as work definition, responsibility assignment, and cost and schedule controls,
>
> • Requires the integration of work organization, planning and budgeting, accounting, analysis, and change incorporation, and
>
> • Requires that a baseline be established and maintained for purposes of performance measurement and that such measurement be on the basis of earned value.[4]

The creators of the 35 criteria divided them into five logical groupings:

*Organization*—To define the contractual effort with use of a work breakdown structure, assign responsibilities for performance of the work, and accomplish all this with use of an integrated contractor management control system.

*Planning and Budgeting*—To establish and maintain a performance measurement baseline for control of the work.

*Accounting*—To accumulate costs of work and materials in a manner which allows for comparison with earned value.

*Analysis*—To measure earned value, to analyze variances of both costs and schedules, and develop reliable estimates of costs at completion.

*Revisions and Access to Data*—To incorporate changes to the controlled baseline as required, and allow appropriate Government representatives to have access to contract data for determining criteria compliance.


## "Conventional" versus "Earned Value" Management

Perhaps if we return once again to "War Story # 2" and provide a couple of similar specific illustrations, it might furnish us with an insight of what the criteria concept was attempting to put in place. Remember, the described program was expected to cost $100 million, and was planned to be accomplished in a four year period. In order to keep the illustration as simple as possible, we will assume that the budget plan for the program called for a constant (straight line) expenditure of $25 million per year, over the four years.

This program plan is displayed in Figure 3-1, using what we will call the "conventional method" of cost control. We have displayed performance at the half way point, after 2 of the 4 years. Note that on this straight line budget plan there should have been completed half of the work, and half of the funds should have been spent. But only $40 of the planned $50 million has been spent. What conclusions should be drawn about contract performance achieved thus far? By use of the conventional method of cost management, there would be the tendency to assume that the program may well be experiencing a cost underrun, and secondly that the allotted funds will be adequate to complete the effort. The cost performance displays do not indicate otherwise. And the procuring customers, using this method to monitor, and sitting in their offices perhaps thousands of miles away from the contractor, would have no basis for challenging the assumption that this program is likely to underrun its costs.

Often, in these circumstances the buying agents would have made frequent trips to the performing contractor's facility in an attempt to determine the "true health" of a given contract. But unless they had an uncanny ability to assess contract performance, they would be limited to the charted facts as illustrated in Figure 3-1, and what the contractors would tell them about program status. They had no method to *objectively* assess program performance, either before or after it was started.

Then came the criteria concept and the requirement for contractors to structure their management control systems so as to allow for the verification of work performed, and to develop reliable and measurable projections of the total contract bill.

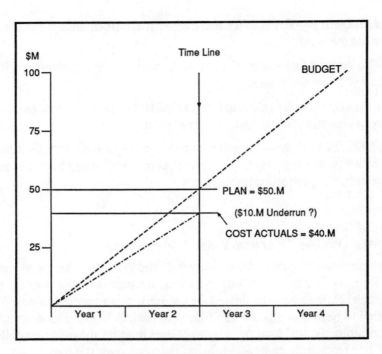

**Figure 3-1   Cost Control (Conventional Method)**

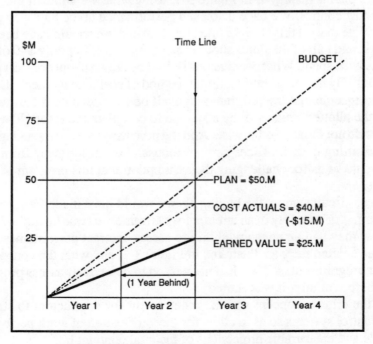

**Figure 3-2   Cost Control (C/SCSC Method)**

Going back once again to our simple example, with an "earned value" (C/SCSC) approach in place, we can assess the true status of this contract as shown in Figure 3-2. While the plan had called for performance of $50 million after two years, of which only $40 million had been spent, we now sadly learn that only $25 million of the physical work (earned value) had actually been accomplished. Thus instead of an underrun, which the earlier performance chart may have lead us to believe, this program is clearly headed for an overrun of costs, and a likely slippage from the target completion date.

In the somewhat extreme example displayed in Figure 3-2, the program at the half-way point of performance has managed to experience a $15 million overrun in costs, and run a full year behind in scheduled physical work accomplished. Thus in this case the buying customer and the performing contractor both have an "opportunity" of major proportions to demonstrate what they can do! But with C/SCSC in place, they both will have a better understanding of the full magnitude of the task at hand.

## Summary

The Criteria Concept came into being because the U.S. Government needed to find a way to reliably quantify the costs of planned procurements before they were started, and once started, what they were getting for what they were spending, while they were spending it. Closely related to how much money projects would cost was the issue of how long they would take to finish, both before they were started, and after they were underway.

Some twenty years after the criteria were implemented the problems of managing major procurements were still present, as was indicated in the headlines of a major American newspaper:

> *"Arms Systems Running Far Over Budget"*
>
> The Pentagon is seeking large funding increases for 20 major weapons programs, many of which have had technical problems and huge cost overruns, according to the draft of a General Accounting Office report.
>
> ...it depicts significant problems in some of the nation's most important weapons programs just as they are to enter full-scale development or production, milestones that will require sharp funding increases.
>
> The report which was leaked to the news media, indicates that overall the 20 weapons systems have experienced cost increases of $20.3 billion.
>
> Thirteen of the 20 programs are behind schedule, nine have posted cost increases...[5]

The Criteria Concept was created to fill a void. No longer were the Governmental procurement agencies, the Congress, the President, and the public in general willing to proceed on only promises and blind faith, as they had been in the past. They wanted, they demanded, a methodology with which to quantify and monitor and control all significant expenditures of public funds. Contractors now wishing to receive major government contracts had to have in place a management control system which satisfied the requirements of these 35 standards or criteria.

The criteria were never expected to *eliminate* cost overruns or schedule slippages, as some individuals have mistakenly suggested. They were, however, expected to provide a tool to the procuring agencies, with which they could better estimate the total costs and the total duration of planned or existing programs. With this knowledge in hand the buying agencies could then make selections of programs it could afford, and have the products in place when they were needed. And, as the news story quoted above would seem to indicate, the C/SCSC are performing their expected mission.

We will cover each of these 35 criteria in some detail in the next few chapters.

---

## ENDNOTES

[1] General Lawerence A. Skantze, "Managing Defense Programs," *Program Manager*, DSMC Publication, November-December, 1986, page 18.

[2] Arthur D. Little, *C/SCSC White Paper*, for the OASD Comptroller, issued 10 July, 1986, page 1.

[3] Departments of the Air Force (AFSCP/AFLCP 173-5), the Army (DARCOM-P 715-5), the Navy (NAVMAT P5240), and the Defense Supply Agency (DSAH 8315.2), *Cost Schedule Control Systems Criterial—Joint Implementation Guide*, 1 October, 1976, page 5.

[4] Department of Energy, DOE/MA-0086, *Cost & Schedule Control Systems Criteria for Contract Performance Measurement—Summary Description*, August, 1979, page 1.

[5] *Los Angeles Times*, 29 March, 1987, page 1.

# II

# INTRODUCTION TO THE CRITERIA

# 4

# Part 1- Organization

The first grouping of the criteria deals, as one might expect, with organization. There are five criteria in this category and they have as their purpose the following objectives:

- To require that a contractor define all work to be accomplished on a given contract, and such definition must be done with use of a single Contract Work Breakdown Structure (CWBS).

- The assignment of the tasks defined with the CWBS to specific contractor organizations for management.

- To require that the contractor plan and measure work performance with use of a management control system which integrates all major activities, for example, planning, scheduling, budgeting, etc., and that all work be planned and measured from a common information data base.

- The identification of those managers who are responsible for the authorization and control of indirect costs.

- To perform on the contract with use of an integrated CWBS and functional organization, so as to allow for the planning, the measuring of performance, and the reporting of such performance from *both* the CWBS, and the contractor's organizational structure.

As many contractors later found, these were not simple requirements to meet. Probably the only way to cover what is actually involved in the process is to discuss each of these 35 criteria—one by one.

## The Organization Criteria

*Criterion number one:*

> *1. Define all authorized work and related resources to meet the require-ments of the contract, using the framework of the CWBS.[1]*

The first Criterion requires that a contractor define all aspects of a given program with use of a work breakdown structure–WBS. A WBS is a product oriented family tree which is used to outline the tasks of a contract covering all hardware, services, and data required by the contract. When a WBS is tailored to a particular contract, the generic WBS becomes a *Contract* Work Breakdown Structure or CWBS.

Such CWBSs must be prepared consistent with governmental guidelines, at least down to level 3 of the structure. Any departures or modifications in the first three levels must be proposed and approved by the procuring customer. Contracts with the DOD are required to follow Military Standard 881, the latest revision. The DOE and NASA each have their own WBS guidelines which must be followed for contracts with those agencies. The WBS provides an excellent vehicle for contractors and the Government to come to an agreement of what constitutes the statement of work in the contract.

Much debate, sometimes heated, has taken place between the government and some contractors, as certain contractors attempt to take "liberties" with the structuring of the first three levels of a given CWBS. Such debates are somewhat pointless, since contractors primarily use their organization structure to manage their contracts, and the government is the primary user of the WBS. From the government's perspective, there must be a consistently patterned WBS down to level 3 in order to be able compare one program to other programs in its historical data base. Without consistency down to level 3, no such comparison can be made. Contractors often overlook (or ignore) the importance of the customer's absolute need for consistency in WBS patterns, and departures from the Government's WBS guidelines run the high risk of being reversed at a later date.

Only one WBS is allowed per contract, which means that any contractor attempting to keep dual books is immediately on weak ground:

> The CWBS is, perhaps, the single most important document—exhibit prepared in support of the C/SCSC...It would be devastating to program management (and performance measurement in particular) if the contractor used one CWBS by which to manage the contract but utilized a different CWBS to report data to the government and satisfy the government's requirements for work control and management. The two-sets-of-books syndrome this would create would kill any effectiveness inherent in the C/SCSC *and would defeat the overall purpose of a common basis for communication.*[2]

The subject of WBS is a fundamental part of the C/SCSC concept and there is a full chapter to follow devoted to this subject alone. While the WBS is primarily the tool of the procuring customer, the technique is most useful to contractors to help them define the work to be accomplished, and in outlining the planned resources. All contract line items and deliverable products should be specified somewhere in the CWBS.

*Criterion number two:*

> 2. *Identify the internal organizational elements and the major sub-contractors responsible for accomplishing the authorized work.*

Here all specific tasks outlined in the CWBS must be relatable to specific departments in the contractor's organization where management and performance will take place. The term "Organizational Breakdown Structure-OBS" is frequently used to describe the contractor's organizational arrangement and to make comparisons of the OBS to the WBS. While the WBS is most often portrayed in a vertical direction, moving downward from top to bottom of the WBS, the OBS is most often depicted as a horizontal chart, going progressively lower from left to right.

All tasks contained in the CWBS must be assigned to a specific organization for performance, even those activities which will be procured outside the company from other sources, i.e., subcontracted to another company for performance. Thus, under this criterion a contractor must have a specific (organizational) performance plan in mind in order to comply with the intent of the requirement. This criterion forces a contractor to decide whether it plans to "make" a particular task by performing it in its own company, or to "buy" the services, hardware, data elsewhere from another firm.

At the point where the CWBS reaches its lowest (vertical) levels, and at the point where the OBS is at its lowest (left to right/ horizontal) organizational level is an *intersection point* which is critical to understanding the C/SCSC concept. At this intersection point is where a "Cost Account" is placed for performance planning and measurement. The cost account is a fundamental building block in C/SCSC theory and is defined as:

> *Cost Account.* A management control point at which actual costs can be accumulated and compared to budgeted costs for work performed. A cost account is a natural control point for cost/schedule planning and control, since it represents the work assigned to one responsible organizational element on one contract work breakdown structure (CWBS) element.[3]

Perhaps there is no more important issue in C/SCSC to understand conceptually than that of the cost account, and just what it represents. Shown in Figure 4-1 is a chart which illustrates the approach. On the top is the WBS (or CWBS if tailored to a contract), and to the left is the Organization (referred to as OBS). At the point at which the CWBS and the OBS intersect is where cost accounts are placed, and these are best thought of as the "building bricks" for all C/SCSC performance measurement.

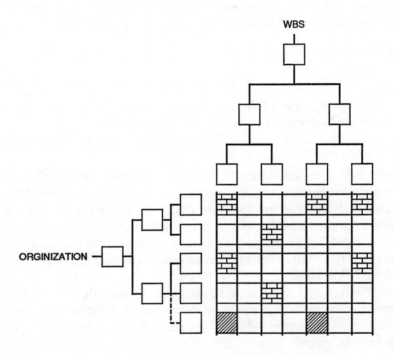

Figure 4-1 Cost Accounts–"Building Bricks" in C/SCSC[4]

Many contractors find it useful in this initial planning process to prepare what is referred to as a "Cost Account Matrix." Such matrices typically list the lowest WBS elements across the top row of the page, and the OBS departments in a vertical column to the left side of the same page. At the point where the WBS/OBS meet is where the cost accounts reside.

Since cost accounts and what they represent are fundamental to C/SCSC, they will be discussed frequently throughout this book.

*Criterion number three:*

---

*3. Provide for the integration of the contractor's planning, scheduling, budgeting, work authorization and cost accumulation systems with each other, the CWBS, and the organizational structure.*

---

The Department of Energy in their C/SCSC requirements *added* "estimating" as an activity to be integrated into the systems:

> Provide for the integration of the contractor's planning, scheduling, budgeting, estimating, work authorization, and cost accumulation systems...[5]

The intent of this requirement is clear; the government wants its contractors to manage their contracts with use of *one* management control system. They insist on a common information data base flowing though all of the contractor's functional disciplines.

The cost account is the key element which permits these various activities to communicate with use of a common data base. A cost account must have four ingredients to be viable: a statement of the work to be done; a planned time-frame for performance; a measurable budget; and a person responsible for its performance.

Contractors, particularly those with large matrix organizations, often have certain problems satisfying this criterion. Each of the various functional organizations have their own performance itineraries, and each wants to manage their own affairs in their own way. Not surprising. It takes some effort to comply with a common data base with which these various functions may co-exist. Master scheduling, project estimating, work authorizations, budgeting, cost accumulating, etc., must all work within the same (traceable) data base. Not an easy task.

The cost account, the fundamental building brick of C/SCSC, made it possible for the various and diverse functional interests to work from the same base of information. It allowed contractors to view programs from either the CWBS, to satisfy the customers demands, or from the OBS, to properly manage its internal affairs.

*Criterion number four:*

> 4. *Identify the managerial positions responsible for controlling overhead (indirect costs).*

Government procurement people are acutely aware that the costs associated with a given contract contain both direct and indirect costs. While there is generally minimal controversy over direct costs, since they are fairly obvious categories, there is much concern over the content and application of indirect or overhead costs which are charged to a given contract. And the known fact that the value of the indirect costs generally exceeds the sum of all direct dollars on a contract further exacerbates the condition.

The government requires that indirect costs as a category be defined, and formally documented. Those individual managers who are responsible for authorizing and controlling overheads must be identified, generally with some type of delegation of authority, which stipulates the limits of such authority. These activities may be centralized or de-centralized, as long as there is consistency, traceability, and a clear assignment of responsibility.

The application of indirect costs to contracts must be consistent for *all* contracts in the organization, and defined somewhere in the firm's procedures. Obviously, such costs may not be arbitrarily applied to a given contract at the whim of a manager. The government is particularly sensitive to the consistency of application of such costs as they are being allotted to different contract *types* within a firm (e.g., cost reimburseable versus fixed price types). Their concern is obvious and somewhat justified: that contractors might be tempted to try to maximize profit returns on fixed price work at the expense of cost (open ended) reimburseable efforts. We sometimes read about such ill advised attempts in the newspapers: "Joe Finance has been sentenced to..."

*Criterion number five:*

> 5.  *Provide for the integration of the CWBS with the contractor's functional organizational structure in a manner that permits cost and schedule performance measurement for CWBS and organizational elements.*

Now we are at the essence of C/SCSC: to provide a means with which a contractor may plan and measure physical performance on a contract, and to do so both from the perspective of the contractor's organization structure (OBS) and the contract work breakdown structure (CWBS). To properly discuss this issue we must understand five very specific C/SCSC terms, the first three of which are as follows:

*Actual Cost of Work Performed (ACWP)*—The costs actually incurred and recorded in accomplishing the work performed within a given time period.

*Budgeted Costs for Work Scheduled (BCWS)*—The sum of budgets for all work packages, planning packages, etc., scheduled to be accomplished (including in-process work packages), plus the amount of level of effort and apportioned effort scheduled to be accomplished within a given time period.

*Budgeted Costs for Work Performed (BCWP)*—The sum of the budgets for completed work packages and completed portions of open work packages, plus the appropriate portion of the budgets for level of effort and apportioned effort.[6]

ACWP is what we typically call "actual costs," but in C/SCSC it only includes those costs relatable with the work performed to date. ACWP does not necessarily include all costs incurred to date, such as those expended for materials purchased, but not yet consumed.

BCWS is best thought of as a conventional "budget or schedule," with one major difference. BCWS is based on the way work is to be performed, not necessarily on the way money is spent or bills are paid.

But "BCWP" is a new and unique term. BCWP is the "earned value," or "performance measurement," or "what we got for what we spent." BCWP is the standard against which all comparisons to actual costs are made to determine the cost performance position, i.e., are we on target, or underrunning, or overrunning (?) the contract. BCWP is also what is compared to schedule to determine whether we are on, or ahead, or behind schedule on a contract.

The Cost Account provides the means with which a contractor may satisfy this requirement for performance measurement because all individual Cost Accounts must, by definition, contain a BCWS, ACWP, and BCWP.

The other two C/SCSC terms which must be added to our vocabulary at this time are:

*Budget At Completion (BAC)*—The sum of all budgets allocated to the contract. It consists of the performance measurement baseline and all management reserves.

*Estimate At Completion (EAC)*—Direct costs, plus indirect costs allocated to the contract to date, plus the estimate of costs (direct and indirect) for authorized work remaining.[7]

The BAC is what we originally planned to spend on the contract. It represents the sum of all BCWSs, plus associated indirect costs, plus all management reserves we had when we started the effort.

The EAC is what we subsequently will estimate will be needed to complete the total effort, after it has started. At the start of a new contract the BAC and EAC will be equal. But as the performance begins, and we continue to measure ourselves along the way, there typically is a spread (plus or minus, good or bad), between the BAC and the EAC.

Program managers, company managements, the buying customer in particular, are all interested in the projected differences between the BAC and the EAC

---

# ENDNOTES

[1] All criteria quoted in this chapter are from DODI 7000.2 and the DOD Joint Implementation Guide, except as noted. U.S. Department of Defense, *Performance Measurement for Selected Acquisition*, DODI 7000.2, June 10, 1987.

[2] Major Thomas L. Bowman, USAF, Interpretive Key To C/SCSC Joint Implementation Guide Checklist," from *Cost Schedule Control Systems Criterial Reference Material*, Wright-Patterson AFB, Ohio: Air Force Institute of Technology, April, 1982, page 275.

[3] DODI 7000.2, enclosure 1, page 2.

[4] U. S. Department of Energy, *Cost & Schedule Control Systems Criteria for Contract Performance Measurement—Information Pamphlet*, DOE/MA-0155, May, 1984, page 12.

[5] U. S. Department of Energy, *Cost and Schedule Control Systems Criteria for Contract Performance Measurement*, DOE 2250.1B, October 25, 1985, Attachment 1, page 1.

[6] DODI 7000.2, enclosure 1.

[7] U. S. Department of Energy, *Cost & Schedule Control Systems Criteria For Contract Performance Measurement—Implementation Guide*, DOE/MA-203, January, 1986, Attachment 3.

# 5

# Part 2 – Planning and Budgeting

In Part 2, the largest section, there are 11 criteria to satisfy, and here it must be demonstrated that the contractor uses an integrated management control system within which it can implement Performance Measurement Baselines (PMB) for all contracts requiring C/SCSC. The total authorized work for these contracts must be planned and budgeted with use of the PMB, and any management reserves must be controlled outside of such performance baselines. All changes or growth to contracts must be tightly controlled, and incorporated into PMBs in an expedient manner, typically on a monthly basis.

*Criterion number one:*

> *1. Schedule the authorized work in a manner which describes the sequence of work and identifies the significant task interdependencies required to meet the development, production and delivery requirements of the contract.[1]*

This criterion requires the contractor to have in place some type of a scheduling system. In particular, a contractor must have issued a "master" program schedule, which set the wide parameters for key contract milestones. The master schedule must be further supported by intermediate level schedules as appropriate, and then by more detailed or functional departmental schedules, as appropriate, going down to the work package level. Shown in Figure 5-1 is a Department of Energy chart which illustrates the scheduling flow from a Project Master Schedule at the top, down to the Cost Account and even Work Package Schedules at the very bottom.

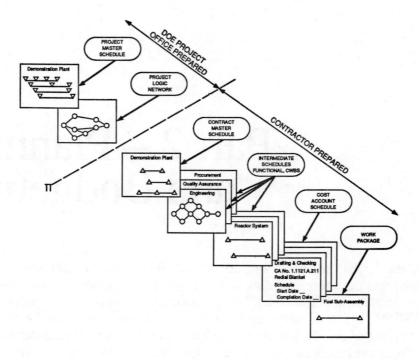

**Figure 5-1 Scheduling Hierarchy in C/SCSC[2]**

The key issues here are the integration of program schedules, and the traceability of key program milestones contained in all such program schedules. Out of the scheduling activity must come the sequence of work to be accomplished, within the framework of the contract period. Each cost account must contain a specific start and stop date, from which a forecast of program completion can be made.

Nowhere in the criteria do they specify that a particular scheduling technique be used. However, here they do require that schedule interdependencies and constraints be shown. As was discussed earlier in the scheduling chapter, only a "network" type schedule will truly show such dependencies and constraints. Therefore, a strict interpretation of this criterion could suggest that C/SCSC requires the use of some type of a PERT or CPM network schedule. However, contractors have been allowed to employ any scheduling technique(s) as long as the intent of the criterion is satisfied. Many contractors across the country have satisfied this criterion without use of network schedules of any variety.

The Department of Energy *added* two words "construction, installation" to the criterion to meet their unique needs:

1. Schedule the authorized work in a manner which describes the sequence of work and identifies the significant task interdependencies required to meet the development, production, construction, installation, and delivery requirements of the contract.[3]

*Criterion number two:*

> 2. *Identify physical products, milestones, technical performance goals, or other indicators that will be used to measure output.*

Here, the contractor must demonstrate that it has in place and will use meaningful indicators to measure physical performance. They must specify what physical products, milestones, technical performance goals will be used to measure work accomplished against a schedule plan. There are numerous methods with which to measure physical work accomplishment, and the contractors must specify which of these methods they will use. The subject of how various contractors provide earned value measurement will be discussed in a later chapter.

*Criterion number three:*

> 3. *Establish and maintain a time-phased baseline at the cost account level against which contract performance can be measured. Initial budgets established for this purpose will be based on the negotiated target cost. Any other amount used for performance measurement purposes must be formally recognized by both the contractor and the Government.*

When this criterion describes "a time-phased baseline" it is talking about a precise C/SCSC term, the "Performance Measurement Baseline." It is important that this new term (PMB) be fully understood. The PMB is defined as:

*Performance Measurement Baseline*—The time-phased budget plan against which contract performance is measured. It is formed by the budgets assigned to scheduled cost accounts and the applicable indirect budgets. For future effort, not planned to the cost account level, the performance measurement baseline also includes budgets assigned to higher level CWBS elements, and undistributed budgets. It equals the total allocated budget less management reserve.[4]

This criterion requires that the contractor take the Contract Budget Base (CBB), defined as the negotiated target costs plus the contractor's estimated cost for authorized but un-negotiated changes, subtract any management reserve they may care to establish for themselves, and produce a top level Performance Measurement Baseline–PMB. Any attempt to budget values greater than the Contract Budget Base is *prohibited* without specific approval of the buying customer. They must then take the gross PMB value and support it with bottom-up, detailed budget plans, at the cost account level. The PMB must consist to the greatest extent possible of short-span *discrete* work packages in the near-term, plus *level of effort* and *apportioned* work packages, all time-phased. These three terms also need to be defined for us:

*Discrete Effort*—tasks which have a specific end product or end result;

*Level of Effort(LOE)*—work which does not result in a final product, that is, liaison, coordination, follow-up or other support activities; and

*Apportioned Effort*—factored effort which can be directly related to other discrete tasks, that is, portions of quality control or inspection.[5]

In those cases where it is inadvisable or impossible to budget far-term effort down to the cost account level, such budgets should be allocated and kept at the higher level CWBS elements. This is simply the rolling-wave budget technique which was discussed earlier. It is very important in C/SCSC that the far-term/gross budgets be tightly controlled to prevent their being reallocated or co-mingled with the near-term budgeted cost accounts.

Generally, cost accounts should be opened based on their scheduled start date, not before. If a situation calls for starting work on cost accounts prior to their planned start date, such work must be authorized on an exception basis. The across-the-board starting of work earlier than planned could adversely impact authorized funding and distort the PMB. Obviously the concern is that overruns might be disguised if budgets were allowed to be shifted back and forth between time periods. Contractor procedures must be specific about how they will control the far-term/gross budgets.

This criterion also requires that indirect costs be allocated to the PMB if they are not included as a part of the individual cost accounts. There is no requirement that indirect costs be included at the cost accounts level, but if outside of cost accounts, they must be allocated in some way so that the full value of the PMB may be established. Through the tight control of bottom-up cost accounts, each one time-phased with a precise start and stop date, the contractor will produce a plan, a PMB, against which contractor performance may be measured.

The establishment of the PMB is a three-step iterative process, in the following sequence:

1. The definition of the work to be done, with use of a CWBS.

2. The identification of the time-frame for the work to be done, i.e., the issuance of program schedules.
3. The issuance of program budgets.

Some people have actually attempted to establish the PMB in different sequences, e.g., issuing the budgets first, then defining the work to be done, then defining the time-frame. It just doesn't work. Best to have some idea of what is expected, and when it is expected, before committing oneself to a budget. This is such basic stuff that it seems foolish to have to mention it, but some have actually tried.

*Criterion number four:*

> *4. Establish budgets for all authorized work with separate identification of cost elements (labor, material, etc.).*

This criterion requires that the total contract be budgeted, which in C/SCSC is referred to as the Contract Budget Base (CBB), representing those contract costs which have been negotiated, *plus* the estimated costs for all changes authorized but not yet priced. Contractor budgets and work authorizations must be issued in a formal (documented) and controlled manner down to the cost account level. All budgets must be expressed in terms of a cost element, example, labor dollars and/or labor hours; or material/ subcontract dollars; or other direct costs (computer costs, etc). Since all authorized work is required to be budgeted, any transfer of work or budget independent of the other, is a violation of this criterion.

*Criterion number five:*

> *5. To the extent the authorized work can be identified in discrete, short-span work packages, establish budgets for this work in terms of dollars, hours, or other measurable units. Where the entire cost account cannot be subdivided into detailed work packages, identify the far-term effort in larger planning packages for budget and scheduling purposes.*

Many of the criteria are interrelated, and at times seem to run together, as does this one which addresses discrete work packages in the near-term, followed by planning packages in the far-term, all of which are time-phased. If the subject seems familiar, it should, for it was generally covered above in Criterion #3, when a time-phased Performance Measurement Baseline was discussed.

Here the contractor must show that it is establishing discrete budgets to the greatest extent possible, in a way which represents the manner in which the job is actually being planned. In the later or far-term periods, the effort may be shown in gross but time-phased planning packages, which will subsequently become definitive work package(s) as they approach the nearer term. Discrete work packages must be of relatively short duration and contain measurable activity to allow for the calculation of work measurement/earned value. The contractor must be able to differentiate between work packages and planning packages, so that work and budget cannot be indiscriminately shifted. All long-term discrete packages must contain some basis to allow for measurement of performance as time passes, and have controls, to prevent a shifting of budgets in either direction.

All budgets must be expressed in measurable units, i.e., dollars or hours or other types of direct costs. Work packages must be assigned to a specific department for performance.

*Criterion number six:*

> 6. *Provide that the sum of all work package budgets, plus planning package budgets, within a cost account equals the cost account budget.*

This criterion requires a reconciliation to show that the sum of all work packages and planning packages within a cost account equals the budget for the cost account, no more no less. All budgets must have an assigned statement of work to be performed, except for management reserve budgets.

*Criterion number seven:*

> 7. *Identify relationships of budgets or standards in underlying work authorization systems to budgets for work packages.*

Some firms which have been in business for a number of years have a fairly consistent product and consistent way of producing it, and have kept good records of such activities over the years; therefore they are able to establish accurate work standards for their firm. If conditions do not vary from one contract to the next, such standards provide an excellent basis for budgeting selected activities. Examples of such standards are the number of hours to produce a typical drawing; to produce a typical tool; to manufacture a typical part; and so forth.

This criterion requires some type of formal relationship to exist between the work performance standards used by the firm and the work package budgets it sets for itself. The issue is how arrived at the budgets they prepared for themselves. Engineered standards, historical standards, industry standards, and geographical standards, are examples of acceptable methods to set ones budgets.

Typically, a published work standard book, directives, procedures, memoranda, or some combination will satisfy this requirement.

*Criterion number eight:*

> *8. Identify and control level of effort activity by time-phased budgets established for this purpose. Only that effort which cannot be identified as discrete, short-span work packages or as apportioned effort will be classified as level of effort.*

Of the three types of work effort to be measured (discrete, level of effort, and apportioned as defined above), the level of effort type is the least desirable one to be used. LOE must be kept to a minimum. Reason: LOE budgets provide nothing with which to measure contract performance, other than the passage of time.

However, as this criterion states, LOE budgets, must be time-phased, formally budgeted, and controlled as with any other effort. Neither budget nor earned value for the LOE account may be shifted in either direction at someone's whim, for such would tend to distort the reported status of a contract. Examples of recognized LOE functions would be the program manager and staff, a field support engineer, (sometimes) a guard, or a scheduler, —each of whom perform activities which are more related to time than to output. Certain functions are justifiable as LOE activities, but they should be kept to a minimum.

The preferred type of cost account budget is the discrete effort, followed by apportioned efforts which relate to some other discrete effort. Contractors are encouraged to plan as much of their activity in discrete and apportioned work packages as is practical to do so.

*Criterion number nine:*

> *9. Establish overhead budgets for the total costs of each significant organizational component whose expenses will become indirect costs. Reflect in the contract budgets at the appropriate level the amounts in overhead pools that will be allocated to the contract as indirect costs.*

The buying customer needs assurances that there is an orderly way to forecast, budget, control, and allocate indirect burdens over all direct cost bases. What cost categories make up the burdens, whether they represent the full plant or only selected parts, and the budgeting cycle for indirect costs must be shown to satisfy this criterion. Each organizational unit that can incur indirect costs should be making commitments only from its own budget, and all elements of overhead expenses should be included in the operating budgets for that organization.

Each company, and frequently each major division or operating unit within a company, must submit a financial disclosure statement to the government outlining the way in which it plans to structure its financial operations. All contractors must subsequently be able to prove that they are conducting operations consistent with the statements made in their disclosure statement. Of particular interest is the makeup of burden costs, including what types and amounts of Independent Research and Development (IR&D) and other such costs will be allotted to the indirect pools. Also of particular interest to the buyers is the makeup of the direct cost base, i.e., the types of firm, non-firm, and potential-only business included in their base. The relationships between the projected direct base and overhead pools must be shown, including what types of costs are being included in the burdens.

Most larger firms have more than one type of indirect pool. Typical of the categories of such pools are: engineering burden, manufacturing burden, material burden, general and administrative, and sometimes even a study or partial burden. The contractor must specify exactly the number of indirect pools it will have, and the types of costs and methods of control which will be imposed on each of these independent burden centers. Costs must be tightly controlled to each of the pools, to preclude the possibility of manipulating such costs by the contractor. How far the burdens and burden bases will be projected into the future, and the rationale behind them, must be shown to satisfy this criterion. When changes in either the direct base or burden pools occur, it must be demonstrated how the contractor will adjust its operation to accommodate such changes.

Lastly, in the event that burdens are not applied to individual cost accounts, and the criteria do not require application of burdens to cost accounts, the contractor must indicate at what point in the CWBS and organizational summaries these burden costs will be added.

*Criterion number ten:*

> 10. *Identify management reserves and undistributed budget.*

Before beginning this discussion, two additional definitions should be provided:

*Management Reserve (Synonymous with Management Reserve Budget)*—An amount of the total allocated budget withheld for management control purposes rather than designated for the accomplishment of a specific task or set of tasks. It is not a part of the Performance Measurement Baseline.

*Undistributed Budget*—Budget applicable to contract effort which has not yet been identified to CWBS elements at or below the lowest level of reporting to the Government.[6]

Undistributed Budget, by definition, is a part of the PMB, whereas Management Reserve, is outside of the PMB until a management decision is made to transfer some portion or all of it into the PMB.

Management Reserve often exists under another title: contingency reserve. Typically MR is taken out of the initial PMB for two reasons:

First is to provide incentives to the lower-level managers to do their jobs as cheaply as possible.

The second use of MR is as a contingency fund, to provide budgeting goals for unanticipated program requirements that will impact the future effort.[7]

However, until the contract is ended, Management Reserve (MR) must be tightly controlled and every transaction which either takes from or adds to the MR budget must be documented and done so with the approval of the program manager. Since MR is by definition outside of the PMB, effort must be made to make sure that no management or contingency reserve is allowed to stay within the PMB, e.g., at cost account levels or within organizational budgets. Typically, MR is expected to be consumed during the term of performance of the contract. If unconsumed at the conclusion of the contract, MR becomes contract underrun, and depending upon the contractual arrangement, might go directly into profits.

Undistributed Budget, by contrast, starts out as a part of the PMB. In all cases, undistributed budget must be allotted to a specific statement of work, time-phased, and tightly controlled so as to not be used for other work. There are three situations in which undistributed budget may be used:

1. For contract changes, authorized but not definitized, where the interim budgets are kept at a higher CWBS level until negotiations are concluded.

2. For definitized changes which, due to time constraints, have not yet been incorporated into cost accounts.

3. For far-term effort where it might prove fruitless to define the planning and budgeting down to the detailed cost account level (rolling-wave budgeting concept).

In those developmental programs which are relatively short in duration, perhaps three to five years in length, the use of undistributed budget would likely be limited to only the first two applications. However, in those developmental contracts that extend eight to ten years or more in duration, the contractor could likely receive approval for the use of undistributed budgets in both situations. The contractor would likely be allowed to define only the near-term effort (three to five years) down to the cost account level, and leave the far-term effort in time-phased, tightly controlled, but higher CWBS levels of undistributed budgets.

*Criterion number eleven:*

> *11. Provide that the contract target cost plus the estimated cost of authorized but unpriced work is reconciled with the sum of all internal contract budgets and management reserves.*

This criterion has introduced another new term so we need one additional definition in order to discuss it:

*Contract Target Cost*—The dollar value (excluding fee or profit) negotiated in the original contract plus the cumulative cost (excluding fee or profit) applicable to all definitized changes to the contract. It consists of the estimated cost negotiated for a cost plus fixed fee contract and the definitized target cost for an incentive contract. The contract target cost does *not* include the value of authorized/unnegotiated work, and is thus equal to the contract budget base only when all authorized work has been negotiated/ definitized.

Here the contractor must demonstrate that its contract budgets add in a precise way, to meet the various C/SCSC definitions covered in this chapter. Three equations will meet this requirement:

1. Cost Accounts + Undistributed Budgets = Performance Measurement Baseline
2. Performance Measurement Baseline + Management Reserve = Contract Target Costs (Excludes Unnegotiated Changes)
3. Contract Target Costs + Authorized/Unpriced Changes = Contract Budget Base

Starting from number 1, the contractor must demonstrate that its cost accounts plus its undistributed budgets add up to the PMB. When the management reserve is added to the PMB the value adds to the new term: Contract Target Costs. Contract Target Costs and Contract Budget Base are the same, until there are changes which have not been negotiated as a part of the CTC. Lastly, when the CTC is combined with the authorized but unpriced work, the result adds to the Contract Budget Base. This subject is covered in more detail in a later chapter on "The C/SCSC Baseline."

All contractors which have a management control system in compliance with the criteria, must define such activity in what is termed a "C/SCSC system description." Once approved by the government, these documents become the baseline definition of all such C/SCSC activity for a contractor. They are usually further supported by detailed working company procedures, most frequently outside of the system description to allow for flexibility. This criterion requires simply that somewhere in the written definition of a contractor's C/SCSC, that the equations cited above be reconcilable from a budgeting methodology.

---

## ENDNOTES

[1] All criteria quoted in this chapter are from DODI 7000.2, except as noted. U.S. Department of Defense, *Performance Measurement for Selected Acquisitions*, DODI 7000.2, June 10, 1977.

[2] U.S. Department of Energy, *Cost & Schedule Control Systems Criteria for Contract Performance Measurement—Implementation Guide*, DOE/MA-0203, January, 1986, page II-13.

[3] U.S. Department of Energy, *Cost and Schedule Control Systems Criteria for Contract Performance Measurement*, DOE 2250.1B, October 25, 1985, Attachment 1, page 2.

[4] DODI 7000.2, enclosure 1.

[5] DOE/MA-0203, January, 1986, page II-6.

[6] DODI 7000.2, enclosure 1.

[7] Thomas J. Bowman, USAF, "Interpretive Key To C/SCSC Joint Implementation Guide Checklist," from *Cost Schedule Control Systems Criteria Reference Manual* (Wright-Patterson AFB, OH: Air Force Institute of Technology, April, 1982), page 317.

# 6

# Part 3 – Accounting

In this third grouping of the criteria, the purpose is to define and reach agreement on the accounting rules governing C/SCSC activity. All firms doing business in the public sector must have some type of accounting system which utilizes acceptable standards of accounting, and which has records available for audit as necessary. Firms doing business with the United States Government must also satisfy the additional requirements of the Cost Accounting Standards, which are overseen by the auditing branch of the DOD, the Defense Contract Audit Agency (DCAA).

With all these rules and standards governing a firm's accounting activity, why is it necessary to require additional practices just for C/SCSC? The answer is simple: because C/SCSC requires a contractor to be able to record costs at the cost account level and summarize the same costs through both the WBS and the OBS. C/SCSC requires a "performance measurement" plan (BCWS) against which actual contractor performance (BCWP) may be measured. Such activity does not typically exist in other public management control or accounting systems, where they normally focus on a broad plan and actuals, but do not concern themselves with this thing called "earned value."

In order to accept existing financial systems from public firms, and to add the performance measurement dimension, the criteria needed to define certain additional operating rules which would apply to contractor's accounting systems. Hence, the requirement for a group of seven criteria which focus on accounting, and require agreement with contractors on the accounting methodology to be used.

*Criterion number one:*

> *1. Record direct costs on an applied or other acceptable basis in a formal system that is controlled by the general books of account.[1]*

Here the criteria insist on an agreement as to the acceptable method of accounting for direct costs. They will allow for any conventional method of accounting to be used, but the preferred technique is the "applied direct cost" method. Since this term is not a "household word" in the accounting world, and since it is so critical to the proper recording of costs to satisfy C/SCSC, two definitions of Applied Direct Costs will be provided, a long one from the DOD and a shorter version from the DOE:

**Applied Direct Costs**—The amounts recognized in the time period associated with the consumption of labor, material, and other direct resources, without regard to the date of commitment or the date of payment. These amounts are to be charged to work-in-process in the time period that any one of the following takes place:

1. When labor, material and other direct resources are actually consumed, or
2. When material resources are withdrawn from inventory for use, or
3. When material resources are received that are uniquely identified to the contract and scheduled for use within 60 days, or
4. When major components or assemblies are received on a line flow basis that are specifically and uniquely identified to a single serially numbered end item.[2]

**Applied Direct Costs**—The amounts charged to work in process in the time period associated with the consumption of labor, material, and other direct resources, without regard to the date of commitment or the date of payment.[3]

In simple terms, this criterion requires firms to account for items when they are *consumed,* which works well for labor and associated indirect costs. In the case of materials, firms are restricted to accounting for them not earlier than physical receipt of such goods. Firms cannot account for materials when they are requested with a commitment, or when they are ordered, or when the bills are paid. Direct costs must be budgeted and actual costs accumulated, in a manner consistent with each other, and take place at the cost account level. When the appropriate burdens are added to the direct costs, the values must reconcile with the contract total.

Further, it requires that all C/SCSC accounting be done within the framework of a firm's general books of account, i.e., their official defined accounting system.

*Criterion number two:*

> *2. Summarize direct costs from the cost accounts into the WBS without allocation of a single cost account to two or more WBS elements.*

*Criterion number three:*

> 3. Summarize direct costs from the cost accounts into the contractor's functional organizational elements without allocation of a single cost account to two or more organizational elements.

Criteria 2 and 3 are related, the only difference between them is the direction of the summation of the detailed cost accounts. Number 2 requires the ability to sum cost accounts upward into the WBS total. Criterion number 3 requires the summation of cost accounts by functional organization, the OBS, to a higher organizational grouping—engineering, manufacturing, material, and such—to also match the contract total. Both criteria prohibit the allocation of a single cost account to more than one WBS element, or more than one organizational unit.

*Criterion number four:*

> 4. Record all indirect costs which will be allocated to the contract.

Once again, a criterion addresses the issue of indirect costs. Here the requirement is that the contractor be able to sum indirect costs from the point where they are incurred, allocated to specified pools if multiple pools are used and, charged upward to contract totals; and that actual overhead costs be relatable to the planned budgets. There must be a formal documented relationship between those persons who have responsibility for control of indirect budgets, and those persons who are able to incur costs against such budgets.

The government is always concerned that the allocation of indirect costs from point of accumulation to final source be equitably applied over all contracts, both government and commercial work. Here the contractor must demonstrate that no manipulation in the allocation of such costs can take place between contracts, and that both the commercial work and government contracts are treated properly in the allotment of burden costs.

Lastly, the contractor must show the methods it uses to allocate indirect costs to the final source. Whether the method chosen calls for a monthly adjustment of indirect actuals against a yearly plan, or a constant rate applied and adjusted at year-end for actuals, whatever, the procedures governing such activity must be formally documented, in place, and be auditable by the DCAA. Any practices so chosen which would permit severe year-end adjustments to happen are discouraged.

*Criterion number five:*

> 5. *Identify the bases for allocating the cost of apportioned effort.*

Under C/SCSC, there are three types of work effort: Discrete, Level of Effort, and Apportioned, as defined in the previous chapter. Apportioned effort is that which has some rational/ historical direct relationship to discrete work packages. This criterion requires that the relationships between apportioned versus their discrete (base) effort be defined.

The concept is that the same methodology of earning value on the discrete work packages  may be used to accurately measure the earned value of the apportioned effort. For example, the function of quality inspection will often have a direct relationship to the function of manufacturing assembly (depending upon the business of course). Each firm will have its own unique situations. The point is that apportioned effort (quality inspection here) need not be measured for its own performance. All that is needed is that the primary base cost account (manufacturing assembly) be measured, and the progress of the base will accurately represent the progress of the apportioned effort.

This criterion requires that the discrete bases (cost accounts that have a direct relationship to apportioned functions) against which apportioned effort will be measured, be defined and justified in specific terms.

*Criterion number six:*

> 6. *Identify unit costs, equivalent unit costs, or lot costs as applicable.*

A new product will generally go through two distinct phases: one to develop it, and one to produce it over and over again. The developmental phase will often go under several titles: research and development; development; full scale development; nonrecurring effort; and so forth. Included in these activities will be the tasks necessary to engineer and produce one or more units for testing, and to test the units until management is satisfied with the product created.

Subsequent to the developmental phase will be the recurring phase, which also goes by various titles: production; manufacturing; recurring effort; and such. One important distinction between these two sequential phases is the importance of the per unit costs of the article produced in the recurring phase. In the nonrecurring/ developmental phase, tasks generally happen only once, and do not occur again. The costs of a single task are therefore not that significant to the total costs of producing the article in a developmental mode.

But by contrast, in the recurring production phase, the same tasks will repeat themselves again and again. Therefore, in order to determine the efficiency of manufacturing performance, the costs associated with producing subsequent (recurring) units must be known. To do this, one must have the ability to isolate the unit costs for labor, material and other direct costs of producing article 1, versus article 10, versus article 100, versus article 1,000, and so on. This type of cost tracking allows performance to be analyzed and displayed on a learning or experience curve.

Under this criterion, the contractor must be able to distinguish between nonrecurring (developmental) effort, and the recurring (production) effort, and have such methods documented in its procedures. At what point does an endeavor (such as engineering) go from nonrecurring to recurring effort? These types of questions must be covered procedurally by the contractor.

The criterion also requires that the contractor be able to establish unit, or equivalent unit, or lot costs for articles produced in the recurring phase. Unit costs may be developed by hours, labor dollars, material dollars, or total unit price.

Unit costs may be established by isolating the individual costs of one unit, or by equivalents of units, or by lot costs. Under lot costs, a block of selected units will be produced in a batch, all at one time. The contractor must fix the actual average cost of one unit in a given block to satisfy this criterion. The average cost of units in block 1 are then equated to the average unit costs in subsequent blocks 10, 100, 1,000, and so on, to determine if the costs per unit are being reduced, and efficiency being increased, as the articles being produced increase.

*Criterion number seven:*

> 7. *The contractor's material accounting system will provide for:* (**a**) *Accurate cost accumulation and assignment of costs to cost accounts in a manner consistent with the budgets using recognized, acceptable costing techniques.* (**b**) *Determination of price variances by comparing planned versus actual commitments.* (**c**) *Cost performance measurement at the point in time most suitable for the category of material involved, but no earlier than the time of actual receipt of material.* (**d**) *Determination of cost variances attributable to the excess usage of material.* (**e**) *Determination of unit or lot costs when applicable.* (**f**) *Full accountability for all material purchased for the contract, including residual inventory.*

The subject of "material" is a big and often painful one for contractors attempting to satisfy C/SCSC, and here only those aspects related to meeting this criterion will be covered. A separate chapter will be devoted later to the subject of material and C/SCSC.

Standing back, material costs may be tracked at several distinct points in time:

1. When an article is requested or, a purchase requisition is issued say by engineering.
2. When the purchase order is placed, i.e., commitments made by procurement.
3. When the purchased articles are received.
4. When the units received have passed inspection.
5. When the articles are placed into a stockroom.
6. when the articles are paid for, i.e., expenditures recorded in the accounting books.
7. When articles are withdrawn from the stockroom (if previously put into stock).
8. When articles are taken from the stockroom and incorporated into an assembly or final product.
9. When a purchased article is received, inspected, and placed directly into an assembly or final product (generally reserved for large, serially numbered items).
10. When an end item is delivered to a customer.

This criterion requires that whatever point in the material process is tracked, that the budget plan (BCWS) and the actual costs (ACWP) and the earned value (BCWP) all use the same point in time, or be able to precisely adjust the accounts to reflect the same point of reference.

If budgets are set on one basis—say, when materials are received—and actual costs relate to expenditures, a distortion in reporting the program's status will occur. The contractor must either use the same basis to report BCWS, BCWP, and ACWP, or be able to make a precise accounting adjustment in one or two of these points, so that the C/SCSC performance status will relate to the same point in time. The criterion also requires that performance for C/SCSC purposes not be done earlier than receipt of material, which eliminates the first two material tracking points stated above.

The contractor's system must be able to identify material cost variances in both material quantities used, as well as differences in material prices. Merely because there is no variance at the top summary level does not mean that a variance has not taken place at lower levels. For example:

BCWS for 15 units at $10.00 = $150 total

ACWP for 10 units at $15.00 = $150 total

The contractors's material system must be able to reflect any differences in either quantities used or in unit prices.

Lastly, the procurement system must have a documented way to determine unit or lot prices of materials purchased, including how it will account for any residual material inventory, if appropriate.

## ENDNOTES

[1] Except as noted, all criteria quoted in this chapter are from U. S. Department of Defense, *Performance Measurement for Selected Acquisitions,* DODI 7000.2, June 10, 1977.

[2] DODI 7000.2, Enclosure 1.

[3] U. S. Department of Energy, *Cost & Schedule Control Systems Criteria for Contract Performance Measurement-Implementation Guide,* DOE/MA-203, January, 1986, page A3-1.

# 7

# Part 4 –Analysis

This fourth grouping of the criteria assumes that a C/SCSC foundation has been laid which allows "performance measurement" to take place during the period of a contract. If during the life of a contract everything would go exactly as planned, then this fourth group would not be needed, for its main purpose is to analyze any departures from the plan. If there were no variances, then obviously no analysis would be needed, and this fourth criteria group could be eliminated.

However, it is doubtful that in the history of the civilized world a project of any consequence has ever been undertaken and completed exactly as it was originally planned. Therefore, it is probably wise to allow for some provision, in a formal way, for the analysis of what has happened and is presently happening, and for forecasting what might happen, if one desires to monitor the health of a contract during the term of its performance.

To provide the necessary tools to allow for performance measurement, the criteria in this group require that five types of data be accessible from a contractor's management control system. These terms were previously covered in Chapter 4:

1. **BCWS**—Budgeted Cost for Work Scheduled (i.e., the cost/schedule budget).
2. **ACWP**—Actual Cost for Work Performed (i.e., cost actuals).
3. **BCWP**—Budgeted Cost of Work Performed (i.e., work physically accomplished, or earned value).
4. **BAC**—Budget At Completion (i.e., the sum of all cost accounts budgeted for the contract.
5. **EAC**—Estimate At Completion (i.e., the estimated costs required to actually complete the total contract).

With these five data elements available and procedurally controlled, the contractor has the basis with which to determine and report status during the term of a contract.

As a prerequisite, the Analysis section requires that a contractor have specified "Variance Thresholds" against which plan versus actuals may be compared. Anytime such established thresholds are penetrated, some type of formal analysis must take place, and a corrective plan must be implemented.

And now for a review of the six criteria in this group.

*Criterion number one:*

> *1. Identify at the cost account level on a monthly basis using data from, or reconcilable with, the accounting system:* [1] **(a)** *Budgeted cost for work scheduled and budgeted cost for work performed.* **(b)** *Budgeted cost for work performed and applied (actual where appropriate) direct costs for the same work.* **(c)** *Variances resulting from the above comparisons classified in terms of labor, material, or other appropriate elements together with the reasons for significant variances.*

The Department of Energy made three changes to this first criterion.[2]

1. They added "and budgeting" to the required systems:

   *Identify at the cost account level on a monthly basis using data from, or reconcilable with, the accounting and budgeting systems.*

2. They added a new (c) paragraph:

   *(c) Budgets at completion and estimates at completion.*

3. They added "including technical problems" to the previously designated DOD (c) paragraph:

   *(d) Variances resulting from the above comparisons classified in terms of labor, material, or other appropriate elements together with the reasons for significant variances, including technical problems.*

Here the criterion requires a monthly comparison to take place at the cost account level, showing the results of:

1. **BCWP** (earned value) versus **BCWS** (cost/schedule plan), to determine the Schedule Variance (SV).
2. **BCWP** (earned value) versus **ACWP** (cost actuals), to determine the Cost Variance (CV).

Note that all performance comparisons in C/SCSC are from "earned value," which is an important distinction from a conventional approach, which typically only compares actual costs to a plan.

When either the SV or CV exceeds a previously established outer parameter, called in C/SCSC a variance threshold, the contractor must perform a variance analysis to determine precisely why the established threshold was broken. The analysis must specify the types of costs involved, e.g., labor, material, other direct costs, and provide a discussion of the reasons for any variances. A plan for recovery must be provided, if recovery is possible, and the future impact on cost/schedule projected. All variance analysis must take place in accordance with defined procedures.

When the contractor has a major part of the work effort performed by another company, a subcontractor, and when the value of the subcontract exceeds a specific dollar value, the prime contractor must impose C/SCSC on the subcontracted effort and have the same capability to measure and report progress as is contained in the prime contract effort. The requirement of flow down of C/SCSC to subcontractors will be covered in detail in a later chapter.

*Criterion number two:*

2. *Identify on a monthly basis, in the detail needed by management for effective control, budgeted indirect costs, actual indirect costs, and variances along with the reasons.*

The contractor must have the ability to perform an analysis of any variances of indirect expenses to the budget. The analysis must cover the types of costs involved, and the indirect pool or pools involved, as may be appropriate.

Indirect expenses will vary from what is originally planned for two principal reasons:

1. Because indirect effort and/or expenses incurred varied (up or down) from the original budgeted amounts.

2. Because the direct business base over which the indirect costs were to be allocated changed (up or down), and the indirect costs being incurred were not altered in a corresponding manner, resulting in a change in planned values allocated to a given contract.

The changes which are of primary concern to management are *increased* indirect costs over those originally planned, or a *lesser* direct base to absorb such costs, resulting in an adverse impact to all contracts affected by these overhead costs. Managements don't generally get excited, except perhaps for a slight smile, when indirect budgets are under-run, direct forecasted bases are exceeded, resulting in less burdens allocated to contracts, and increased profit margins realized.

The contractor's analysis must specify exactly what caused the variances, what elements of cost were involved, and what steps will be taken to correct the condition.

*Criterion number three:*

> 3. *Summarize the data elements and associated variances listed in (1) and (2) above through the contractor organization and WBS to the reporting level specified in the contract.*

Although contractors are required to analyze (internally) all significant variances at the cost account level, normally by contractual agreement, they are not required to *report* all such variances to the customer. Rather, formal customer reporting usually takes place at a higher level, for example WBS level 3, sometimes at level 2, or at a higher organizational tier. This concept of higher level formal reporting allows contractors some flexibility in managing their contract. Many variances which happen at the cost account level are never actually reported to the customer, simply because there are offsetting variances at the same levels of the WBS or OBS which offset/cancel out differences at the reporting levels. Through internal corrective actions, contractors are able to bring most variances back on track without involvement by the customer. There is nothing wrong with this concept, which gives contractors the opportunity to manage their programs without undue customer involvement.

This criterion requires that a contractor have the ability to summarize variances upward through the WBS, as well as horizontally by organization unit, and be reconcilable with any reports submitted to the government. Both contractors and the government must track contract performance from the same database.

*Criterion number four:*

> 4. *Identify significant differences on a monthly basis between planned and actual schedule accomplishment, and the reasons for them.*

While it is the purpose of this book to describe the many merits of C/SCSC, and they are considerable, it would be naive and misleading to present the criteria concept as being totally foolproof. The technique provides an excellent means of systematically ascertaining both cost and schedule status of an activity throughout its life. But there are shortcomings, and one is in the ability of C/SCSC to precisely measure the *true* schedule position of a program.

Schedule Variances (SV) reflect the differences between the work scheduled (BCWS) versus work physically accomplished (BCWP). What this really reflects is the dollar value of work accomplished versus work scheduled, which may or may not necessarily reflect the critical schedule position. Some effort may be accomplished ahead of schedule, or out of sequence, representing considerable dollar amounts, but still leaving critical program milestones unfinished, thereby adversely affecting the overall schedule condition of the effort. Therefore, Schedule Variances (SV) must be viewed as a general indicator of the overall schedule position of a program, but SV should *not* be used as a substitute for intelligent scheduling management, either with the contractor or with the customer.

This criterion requires the contractor to integrate into its C/SCS activity, a scheduling system which focuses on tangible and measurable milestones, (such as Preliminary Design Reviews (PDR); Critical Design Reviews (CDR); test completions; and so on.) and not simply on the summation of BCWP results for all cost accounts, which could present a misleading picture. The contractor, with whatever scheduling system it uses, must be alert to meeting all key milestones as scheduled, and to integrate these into C/SCSC activities.

*Criterion number five:*

> 5. *Identify managerial actions taken as a result of criteria items* (1) *through* (4) *above.*

This criterion deals with the issue of whether or not C/SCSC performance information is disseminated throughout the organization, from top management down to the lowest level cost account managers, and what if anything is done with such information once received. It requires that there be a system in effect which initiates certain corrective actions, when established cost/schedule performance parameters (variance thresholds) have been penetrated, or when milestone realization has deviated from the scheduled milestone plan.

Unless otherwise directed, each contractor may establish its own variance thresholds which, when approved by the procuring customer, serve to trigger certain internal actions when exceeded. There are three primary points at which thresholds are typically established:

1. At the *cumulative* total to date position.
2. With the *current month* reporting period.
3. At the *estimate to complete* totals.

Most contractors will use a combination of two or all three points for monitoring performance.

Variances in either direction, either over or under a standard, can indicate a problem of sorts, although positive parameters are often allowed to be set at a greater percentage level than negative ones before corrective action is required. For example, if a negative (over-run) parameter is set at $100,000, a positive (underrun) parameter might be set at twice that value, $200,000. The thinking here is that a negative variance reflects a potentially more serious problem, although there is no universal agreement on this concept.

Variances in excess of a percentage of a base, and/or in excess of an absolute value, require management action to be taken.

The most common type of management action is the requirement to prepare a variance analysis report, which exists by several titles in the industry, e.g., Problem Analysis Report (PAR); Variance Analysis Report (VAR); and so on. Such reports must reflect the cost account manager's statement of the problem causing the variance, and what actions will be taken to remedy the problem. At a minimum, the next level of management must sign the report to indicate a concurrence with the corrective actions proposed. Sometimes, by procedure, the program manager must also concur on the PAR/VAR report. These reports are reviewed internally, and top level WBS summaries are submitted to the customer monthly as one part of the Cost Performance Report (CPR).

One of the biggest complaints of the government is the *quality* of PAR/VAR reports they receive. Most do not focus on the root problem which caused the variance in the first place, or on a meaningful corrective plan to overcome the condition in the future.

When such corrective actions are required of all organizations, and documented through formalized procedures, this criterion is normally met.

*Criterion number six:*

> 6. *Based on performance to date and on estimates of future conditions, develop revised estimates of cost at completion for WBS elements identified in the contract and compare these with the contract budget base and the latest statement of funds requirements reported to the Government.*

There are many "official" reasons given for why C/SCSC is imposed on private contractors, but the one that really matters is that the government insists on receiving accurate contractor projections of the total costs for all jobs. They want reliable, measurable, verifiable estimates of costs to complete their jobs, when the risk of cost is on the government.

The last criterion in the Analysis section focuses on the contractor's projection of the final costs to complete the total job, the Estimate At Completion (EAC). While distorted information at times exist in the cost/schedule performance data, the EAC is where the contractor could (if it so desired) mislead a customer into an unrealistic expectation of the value of the final bill. Call it being optimistic, call it being unrealistic, call it deliberately lying; whatever the term, some firms have established for themselves a reputation of consistently making poor projections of the total bill, particularly when under cost-reimbursable type contracts. Therefore, an essential ingredient in any management control system must be the ability to make reasonably accurate forecasts of the final costs on jobs, the EAC.

This criterion insists that an EAC be based on performance to date and an assessment of the work remaining to complete all contract tasks unfinished, starting from the point of physical work performed to date (BCWP). Such estimates must be relatable to original estimates for each WBS element, the Contract Budget Base, and functional estimates. In effect, the government insists that contractor EACs be based on what was referred to earlier as bottom-up estimates of the remaining effort, as contrasted with gross, top-down parametric type projections.

Once again, because of their magnitude, overhead or indirect costs are emphasized as being an essential part of an EAC, even though such costs are shared with all contracts in an organization. Historical performance of the indirect pools should be examined to see if there is some obvious pattern which must be considered in the EAC. Example, adjustments in indirect charges rarely take place in concert with adverse changes in direct bases over which overhead costs must be allocated. Actually, many of the overhead costs will be essentially fixed (e.g., an engineering building) and are not easily modified as the direct bases go down.

Normally, direct bases go up or go down, and there is usually a time delay before burden costs adjust proportionately. Thus, if a firm's direct base trend is downward, one must be alert to a possible increase in burden rates, no matter what the experts forecast. Why? Because history has shown that changes in indirect costs seldom take place with the same speed as a reduced direct base. Most people are optimistic by nature, and they refuse to believe company projections of a downturn in business. Therefore, managers often do not take the necessary painful actions to cut out indirect costs with the same speed that the direct base may be reducing.

The opposite condition can also take place: the direct base may increase faster than indirect expenses, and result in reduced burden rates. Such conditions must also be considered when making the EAC.

There are a series of issues with respect to the EAC preparation, which can be best handled through documented internal procedures. An example is the frequency with which *detailed* EACs must be prepared from the bottom-up, comparing cost account estimates with functional estimates and WBS elements, including incorporating inputs from major subcontractors. Whether or not the latest EAC is coordinated with plant-wide management, to make certain that all critical resources are available when needed is also an important factor. Procedures which specify broad management approval of an EAC is one way to require such plant-wide coordination.

Lastly, any contract calling for full C/SCSC implementation will usually require at least three types of reports to be submitted, which will be discussed in more detail in a later chapter:

1. Cost Performance Report (CPR), normally due monthly, reporting cost and schedule and earned value progress.
2. Contractor Cost Data Reports (CCDR), due quarterly or semiannually, or annually, for the purpose of inputting data to the government's historical cost data base.
3. Contract Funds Status Report (CFSR), normally due quarterly, providing a forecast of funds required to complete the program, displayed at the price level (costs with fee).

This criterion insists that all contractor EACs be consistent with data contained in the CPR, the CCDR, and the CFSR, certainly not an unreasonable requirement.

---

## ENDNOTES

[1] Except as noted, all criteria quoted in this chapter are from U. S. Department of Defense, *Performance Measurement for Selected Acquisitions,* DODI 7000.2, June 10, 1977.

[2] U. S. Department of Energy, *Cost and Schedule Control Systems Criteria for Contract Performance Measurement,* DOE 2250.1B, October 25, 1985, Attachment 1, pages 3 & 4.

# 8

# Part 5 – Revisions and Access to Data

This last of the five sections of criteria deals with revisions to the contract or a Performance Measurement Baseline resulting from either external customer redirection, or internal management redirection. No program of any consequence ever runs its full course without encountering some change, and it is incumbent upon a contractor, in order to comply with the criteria, that it accommodate such changes in an orderly and controlled and documented manner, consistent with its written procedures.

*Criterion number one:*

> *1. Incorporate contractual changes in a timely manner, recording the effects of such changes in budgets and schedules. In the directed effort before negotiation of a change, base such revisions on the amount estimated and budgeted to the functional organizations.[1]*

Since all major programs encounter changes, both external and internal, in order to maintain some relationship between the work authorized and the physical work going on, a contractor must by necessity incorporate authorized work changes into its budgets and schedules in a timely manner. Just what constitutes "timely" is a question of fact. In some cases "timely" could represent minutes, as when stopping work at the direction of the customer. In other situations "timely" might allow for days or weeks to pass before incorporation. The outer limit of "timely" would likely be dictated by the monthly reporting cycle of the Cost Performance Report (CPR). There must be consistency on what is being reported to the customer and what is being worked.

Changes to the working budgets and schedules must be accommodated in an expeditious manner and reflected in the Performance Measurement Baseline (PMB). Work which has been authorized, but not negotiated with the customer, must be folded into the PMB based on the estimated value of the new work, and once negotiated, adjusted to reflect the final settlement with the customer. Authorized but unpriced work must be planned and controlled as tightly as definitized work. Obviously, all changes must be tightly controlled to allow for a complete understanding of what is in and what is outside of the PMB.

*Criterion number two:*

> *2. Reconcile original budgets for those elements of the work breakdown structure identified as priced line items in the contract, and for those elements at the lowest level of the DOD Project Summary WBS, with current performance measurement budgets in terms of* **(a)** *changes to the authorized work and* **(b)** *internal replanning in the detail needed by management for effective control.*

Many government contracts contain selected articles in the statement of work which must be priced as "contract line items," and which must be tracked throughout the life of the effort to determine the final actual costs for such articles. As changes occur in the total effort, the contractor must provide sufficient traceability for all changes to be able determine the actual final price of these contract line items.

Closely related to this requirement is the customer's interest in knowing the costs of selected hardware it is buying, as reflected in the lower WBS elements of its Project Summary Work Breakdown Structure (PSWBS). For example, if the Air Force were procuring multiple aircraft systems, it might desire to know the costs of the navigation systems on each aircraft, as a way of determining whether or not it is procuring these articles at fair prices. To accomplish this goal, a PSWBS is typically established for all aircraft, with a standardized breakout of the WBS elements isolating hardware of particular interest, e.g., the navigation system.

Through its Contractor Cost Data Reports (CCDR), the DOD customers will require cost actuals to be presented in a prescribed WBS format, to allow for incorporation of these statistics into their historical cost databank. With the databank, costs of similar hardware are relatable by the DOD, system by system and article by article.

This criterion requires traceability of changes, down to the lowest level PSWBS, to reflect the final costs of PSWBS elements.

## Criterion number three:

> *3. Prohibit retroactive changes to records pertaining to work performed that will change previously recorded amounts for direct costs, indirect costs, or budgets, except for correction of errors and routine accounting adjustments.*

Perhaps the single most unique feature of C/SCSC is the earned value aspect (Budgeted Costs for Work Performed BCWP), i.e., the value of the work actually accomplished. When BCWP is compared to actual costs (ACWP), the Cost Variance is known; when BCWP is related to work scheduled (BCWS), the Schedule Variance is known. Given the significance of earned value, it should be no surprise that the rules would prohibit after-the-fact changes in performance measurement by contractors. This prohibition restricts the shifting of both direct and indirect costs into other periods.

Two exceptions to this rule are allowed: correction of errors in calculations, and correction of legitimate routine accounting adjustments. Both types of corrections should be done with DCAA approval, and be consistent with internal accounting procedures.

## Criterion number four:

> *4. Prevent revisions to the contract budget base except for Government directed changes to contract effort.*

The precise C/SCSC term "Contract Budget Base (CBB)" was defined earlier, and is nothing more than the Performance Measurement Baseline (PMB), plus Management Reserve, if any, plus the estimated value of authorized but unpriced work. This criterion emphasizes the importance of the CBB:

> *Intent:* The Contract Budget Base (CBB) represents two things on a contract: (1) the total amount of work authorized on the contract and (2) the amount of budget targeted to accomplish this work. When this criterion requires a prohibition against changes to the CBB it is addressing both of these facets. The contractor may not arbitrarily change the amount of work authorized on the contract and the contractor may not arbitrarily alter the amount of budget targeted to accomplish this amount of work. Only the government shall have the authority to change the CBB and this shall only be done by specific government direction through contract change notification.[1]

Sometimes a program will experience difficulties in staying within the total limits of its Contract Budget Base (CBB), and after careful analysis of the work remaining, determines it would make no sense to continue to measure progress against unrealistic and unattainable cost goals. When such conditions occur, this criterion permits the contractor to budget the work beyond the CBB, but only with strict approval of the customer. Such remaining activity should have at least six months to run after the authority to proceed, and generally it is not to occur more than once during the life of a contract, but there are exceptions.[2]

The contractor must have procedures which prevent proceeding with the remaining effort until approval is received from the customer. Often, the Limitation of Government Funds clause in contracts provides the strongest inducement to not proceed with effort beyond the CBB, until authorized by the customer.

*Criterion number five:*

> *5. Document, internally, changes to the performance measurement baseline and, on a timely basis, notify the procuring activity through prescribed procedures.*

Maintenance of the Performance Measurement Baseline (PMB) is fundamental to C/SCS, and a later chapter will be devoted to the subject. This criterion requires that the contractor have in place the necessary procedures to preclude unauthorized changes to the PMB, and that all such changes be traceable. The status of the PMB must be provided each month as one of the five formats of the Cost Performance Report (CPR).

While contractors are prohibited from making retroactive changes to work behind them, as was described in an earlier criterion, they are given certain latitude in the "internal replanning" of the authorized work remaining on a contract. But all such internal replanning activity must be controlled and reported to the government. Strict rules govern what is allowed and what is not allowed under such activity, as is displayed in the "Internal Replanning" table on the following page.

There is another condition which can happen to the PMB, when the remaining funds are simply not sufficient to complete the work. It is referred to by a few amicable terms such as "formal reprogramming," and "over target baseline," but in fact it is nothing more than "overrun," that unspoken word on cost-reimbursable type contracts. Face it, overruns do occur, and when they do they should be quantified and budgeted and managed as with any other type of program effort.

The result of the customer authorizing effort over the original PMB is to "re-baseline" the work. However, the customer will still want to continue to monitor such effort until it is successfully concluded. Customer cognizance, tight controls, and procedures are all required to satisfy the incorporation of an overrun into the PMB.

# Internal Replanning[3]

| A Contractor *May:* | A Contractor *May Not:* |
|---|---|
| 1. Use Management Reserve to change cost account budgets. | 1. Make retroactive changes to budgets or costs of completed work. |
| 2. Replan *unopened* work packages within confines of cost account budgets. | 2. Rebudget in-process work packages. |
| 3. Transfer work and associated budget between cost accounts | 3. Transfer work or budget independently of each other. |
| 4. Conduct other replanning actions with cognizance of procuring activity. | 4. Reopen closed work packages. |

*Criterion number six:*

> 6. *Provide the contracting officer and his duly authorized representatives access to all of the foregoing information and supporting documents.*

Undoubtedly, sometime in the past a contractor must have refused to provide supporting data to the customer—not a wise move. Hence, this criterion insists on such data being made available to the contracting officer and other customer representatives. Any wise contractor would normally do so, even without this criterion.

In the early years of C/SCSC, there was some confusion as to whether or not C/SCSC applied to firm fixed-price contractual efforts, where the cost risks were clearly on the contractor. Procuring customers asked for detail on firm fixed-price efforts, where they did not need such information, and they were refused. As of this writing, C/SCSC clearly does not apply to firm fixed price contracts, and the previous ambiguity has been eliminated with specific language incorporated into all DOD and DOE government documents.

However, there are some in the government who feel that the criteria have proven to be a useful tool in the management of contracts, and there is discussions underway to expand the application of C/SCSC to all contracts of a certain size, even firm-fixed-priced contracts.

## Summary

The 35 C/SCSC criteria have been scrutinized in the last five chapters, and although it has been a lengthy exercise, it was absolutely necessary. The criteria form the foundation for a C/SCSC compliant management control system, and it would not be possible to fully understand the concept without having first visited these criteria.

Other aspects of C/SCSC will now be covered, building upon the understanding of these criteria.

---

## ENDNOTES

[1] Except as noted, all criteria in this chapter are from U. S. Department of Defense, *Performance Measurement for Selected Acquisitions*, DODI 7000.2, June 10, 1977.

[2] Major Thomas L. Bowman, USAF, "Interpretative Key To C/SCSC Joint Implementation Guide Checklist," from *Cost Schedule Control Systems Criteria Reference Material* (Wright-Patterson AFB, Ohio: Air Force Institute of Technology, April, 1982) page 360.

[3] Robert R. Kemps, "The Cost and Schedule Control Systems Criteria for Contract Performance Measurement," page 49. Paper presented at the conference on *Cost/Schedule Control Systems,* sponsored by the Project Management Institute and Institute for the Advancement of Engineering, Washington, D.C., November 28-30, 1984.

# III

# THE IMPLEMENTATION OF C/SCSC

# 9

# The Work Breakdown Structure

*War Story # 3*

There once was a young man who was given his first "cost/schedule assignment," although at the time he thought he was an administrative assistant. Being an administrative assistant to a program manager has its inherent dangers. His company had just won a large (for them) contract from the Air Force, and his boss was named as program manager.

The program manager handed this young man a copy of their new contract with instructions to go out and set up budgets for the effort. He had had no special training for such an endeavour, so he started with the newly issued organizational charts for the program. He contacted the manager of design, the manager of systems engineering, the manager of test, the manager of manufacturing and so on and carefully made his way through the organization. He reached agreements with each of them on their budget needs, and when finished, he had budgeted the entire contract with little left over for a management reserve (that has never happened again to this young man!). He was quite proud of himself, and so was his boss the program manager.

A few weeks later the Air Force came in for their periodic review of the program, and the young man was asked to present the budgets to them. In his presentation he traced through the budgeting approach, relating cost actuals to the plan. To his surprise and chagrin, instead of the accolades he was expecting, the Air Force officers were upset with what they were shown. "Why are you budgeting the program against your internal organizational structure?" "Don't you know you have a contract with us which has a detailed statement of work which is important to us?" These were some of the kinder remarks sent in his direction that morning.

On that day this young man made an important discovery, one which he has never since forgotten. The social scientists have a word for what had transpired that morning: *Egocentrism*. It means, simply, viewing the world in relationship to oneself. The Air Force had awarded his firm a contract with a statement of work. They felt (and rightfully) that everything that was done by that company on their contract should be done in relation to the statement of work. By contrast, the company/project also had an organization, and each of the department managers felt (also rightfully) that what they did should be done in relationship to their internal organization structure. What could be done to achieve his primary goal of controlling contract costs in the organization, as well as satisfying an apparently conflicting customer demand?

The young man continued to internally control the program costs with budgets structured around the organization, to satisfy the needs of the department managers. However, just prior to each customer review, he would stay up late into the night and restructure the budget and actuals to present the very same data the way the Air Force wanted: by the contract tasks.

No one should misunderstand the point being made here: both the Air Force customer and the company department managers had valid reasons to look at the same data (the effort to be budgeted) from their own, but differing perspectives. Nowadays the young man's dilemma is satisfied routinely. It is done with two important tools not available to him back in the late 1950s: (1) improved computers, and (2) a management technique called the *Work Breakdown Structure (WBS)*.

---

## Enter the WBS Concept

By the mid-1960s, there was no such thing as a WBS concept; rather, there were *multiple* WBS concepts in existence. A given statement of work could be, and often was, displayed:

- by the contractor's functional organization;

- by contract phase;

- by contract tasks;

- by a PERT/Cost network;

- by financial reporting requirements;

- by demands from configuration management, and others;

- and so forth.

Displays, all under the broad banner of a "work breakdown structure," were being influenced by the perceived needs and demands of particular special interests or individuals in the organization, each with their own "exciting ideas" on how things should be done.

In order to establish some semblance of consistency between various major system acquisitions, and to create a historical database to improve their future procurements, the defense establishment had to take steps to standardize the collection of costs according to some common language. Thus, in August 1965, the Department of Defense initiated a special study with the stated purpose:

> to develop guidelines for the preparation and application of a WBS for a single project that would satisfy multiple user needs in DOD and industry...and to develop a practical minimum of uniform WBSs that could be applied to the widest possible variety of both large and small system/projects.[1]

The result of this special study was the issuance of Department of Defense Directive 5010.20 on July 31, 1968, and later of Military Standard 881 on November 1, 1968, both bearing the same title: "Work Breakdown Structures for Defense Materiel Items." The DOD Directive set forth the policy, and the Military Standard was the detailed implementing document, the latter containing specific instructions as to the preparation of all future DOD generated WBSs. Both DOD documents included identical definitions of a WBS, as follows:

> A work breakdown structure is a product-oriented family tree composed of hardware, services and data which result from project engineering efforts during the development and production of a defense materiel item, and which completely defines the project/program. A WBS displays and defines the product(s) to be developed or produced and relates the elements of work to be accomplished to each other and to the end product.[2]

The Department of Energy always has had the benefit of trailing the DOD's C/SCSC implementation activities, so it is no wonder that their definition of the same terms would be similar, but perhaps a little more palatable. The DOE defined a WBS as:

> A WBS is a product-oriented family tree subdivision of the hardware, services, and data required to produce the end product... The WBS is structured in accordance with the way the work will be performed and reflects the way in which project costs and data will be summarized and eventually reported to DOE. Preparation of the WBS also considers other areas which require structured data, such as scheduling, configuration management, contract funding, and technical performance parameters.[3]

With the creation of a standard WBS format, the DOD was able thereafter to be in a position to compare the cost proposals of all new procurements, or sub-tasks therein, to those of previous similar buys, to test such values for reasonableness, and to test the final estimates for existing programs against their historical database, again to test the reasonableness of such estimates. Henceforth, with the implementation of a common WBS format, the DOD was able to independently assess the validity of the costs for future and existing buys. Thereafter, it became more difficult—but still not impossible—for contractors to "buy into" individual procurements, and to keep their cost overruns hidden until it was too late to do anything about them.

## Just What is a WBS?

When one sees a WBS on a wall it looks like an organization chart, but it is definitely not an organization chart although some have attempted to use it as such. But there are similarities between the methodology of both organization chart displays and WBS displays.

Whereas an organization chart will graphically portray a given company's management reporting arrangement, a WBS will likewise graphically display a given contract's statement of work, specifically calling out the hardware, software, and services to be performed, and their relationship to each other.

The single most important DOD document to assist in the preparation of the WBS is Military Standard 881, other related WBS documents will apply depending on the buying customer. And although all new program managers feel that their activity is "unique" and different from anything that has come along before, all new DOD contracts can be, should be, and must be portrayed in a WBS according to Military Standard 881. Certainly, a given new system may have unique features, such as the "swing wing" aspect of the F-111 Fighter. But the basic system and its unique features will fit within a standard WBS in conformance with the requirement. They all have in the past, they all will in the future.

A WBS will start out with a single box at the top, into which everything below will flow. This single box represents the total system and is referred to as WBS level 1. Lower levels are appropriately numbered levels 2, 3, 4, and so on. Figure 9-1 displays a WBS down to level 3, for a complete aircraft system. A level 3 display is significant in that most contracts will call for cost/ schedule status reporting in detail down to level 3, although actual cost collection on most large programs may go to lower WBS levels, perhaps down to levels 5, 6, or 7. Typically, hardware legs go to lower levels, versus non-hardware items, e.g., training data, program management, and such, which are usually limited to levels 3 or 4. A display of a WBS down to level 5 is shown in Figure 9-2 for an aircraft system. A separate WBS may be used to reflect a single subsystem only—i.e., a fire control unit or wing structure. Or, on commercial work, it will reflect something completely unrelated to military hardware; for example, a hotel, shopping center, factory, a new city, a harbor, utility plant, a training program, and so forth, to mention just a few.

The lowest levels of a WBS are important because each box (or element, as they are called) represents a discrete segment of work identifying hardware, data, or the services to be performed therein. It is into these lowest WBS elements, where a performing contractor must provide for a given departmental budget, and create a detailed standard against

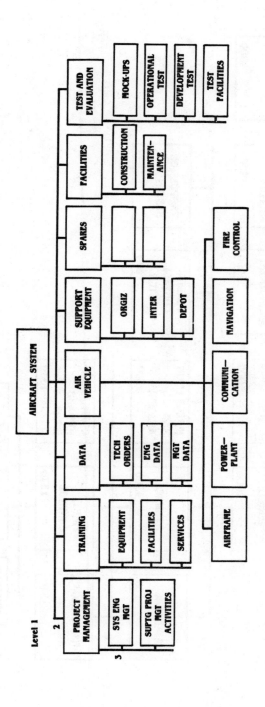

Figure 9-1 A Summary Work Breakdown Structure[4]

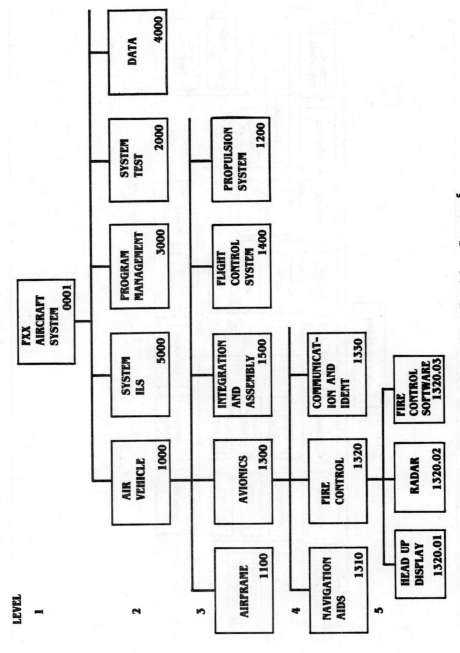

Figure 9-2 A Project Work Breakdown Structure[5]

which future performance may be measured. These detailed, low level efforts are referred to in C/SCSC as "cost accounts," and were defined earlier.

By providing for work definition, budgets, schedules, cost accumulation, and work measurement in detail at the lowest level of the WBS, a contractor may, with the aid of the computer processing equipment presently available, sort the same data in two directions: vertically to reflect WBS displays and satisfy the customer needs, or horizontally to reflect organizational breakouts and thereby satisfy the interests of individual department managers. This approach is reflected in Figure 9-3, which illustrates the pivotal point of the cost account, and the subordinate work packages within the cost accounts.

## WBS Terminology

The collection of costs by the WBS breakout is primarily of interest to the buying customer, and the contractor is normally only interested in looking at costs by its functional organization, but there are exceptions. One such exception could exist where there are known subsystem "risks" on a program, and management, therefore, would want to focus closely on how well those risk areas are being worked and eliminated.

For example, perhaps the development of the fire control unit is felt to be a high risk area of a new aircraft system's design. Management will want to closely follow the performance of the fire control unit. By an organizational display, the fire control unit cannot be tracked exclusively because multiple departments in the contractor's plant would likely be involved in the development of the unit. Under these circumstances, contractor management may want to review the performance (earned value performance against plan and actual costs) of the WBS element on the guidance unit, in addition to their normal review of functional departmental costs. In Figure 9-2, the fire control unit is shown as WBS element 1320, at level 4. In such a case, the contractor may on its own call for special review of this level 4 item, as a part of its risk management effort.

Another example of where a contractor might have a definite interest in a WBS display could exist where there were severe funding constraints in the development of, say, a new aircraft system. Under these (hypothetical) circumstances, management may feel it desireable to accelerate the design of the aircraft structure, but since the radar, navigation system, and other equipment may be standard shelf-item units, work on them could be deferred to later periods in order to preserve near-term funds. In this situation management would want to focus its attention of performance by WBS at level 3, in addition to its normal review of functional cost categories.

In the last five chapters, the C/SCSC criteria were discussed in detail one by one. Of the 35 such criteria which a contractor must meet in order to comply with the C/SCSC requirement, the number one criterion required that there be only one WBS on any given program. This means clearly that a contractor may not use one WBS to report to the customer, and another WBS for its internal management, or for any other purpose. Only one WBS is al-

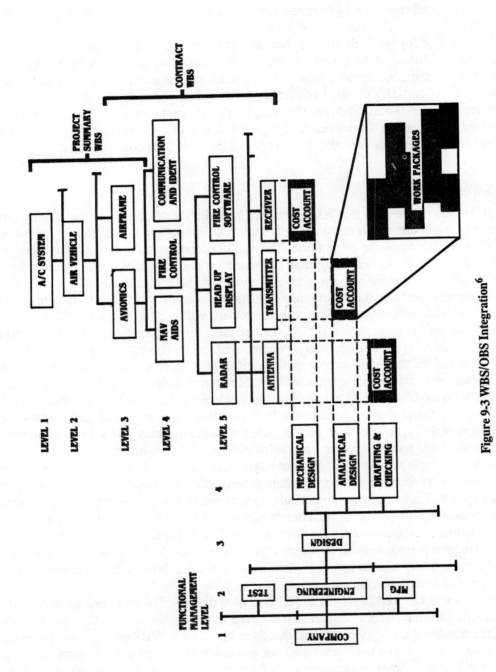

Figure 9-3 WBS/OBS Integration[6]

lowed, and if multiple charts are found to exist by the customer, the violation is serious enough to withdraw validation of the contractor's C/SCSC compliance.

Now, having said that only one WBS is allowed on any program, shown below are four definitions of unique WBSs, all of which may exist on a given program at the same time, as defined in Military Standard 881. Confusing? Not really. As one reviews these four definitions it becomes apparent that each is but a special purpose derivative from a single WBS concept.

1. *Summary Work Breakdown Structure (Summary WBS)*

   The upper three levels of a full WBS represent the Summary WBS. Figure 9-1 represents a Summary WBS. It has primary significance in that the first three levels usually represent the formal cost/schedule reporting levels for a given contract. In order to allow the DOD to make comparisons of one program to others, uniform definitions, terminology, and structuring must be strictly followed down to level 3, as defined in Military Standard 881.

   The first three levels of a WBS represent:

   **Level 1**—The entire materiel item, or project, or system.

   **Level 2**—Major subsections of the total project.

   **Level 3**—Elements subordinate to Level 2 major subsections.

2. *Project Summary Work Breakdown Structure (Project Summary WBS)*

   A special purpose WBS prepared by the customer, for its exclusive use. A Project Summary WBS is used when the customer desires to define a conceptual design of a total system that may have unique configuration elements or unique features.

3. *Contract Work Breakdown Structure (CWBS)*

   Normally prepared by a contractor in accordance with Military Standard 881 to reflect the statement of work in a specific contract and/or a request for proposal. A CWBS describes the total product and work to be done to satisfy a specific contract, going to levels below level 3.

4. *Project Work Breakdown Structure (Project WBS)*

   Used by the customer to define a total program and is made up by merging all the Contract WBSs with all other in-house WBSs to form one consolidated Project WBS.

From an individual contractor's standpoint, the Contract WBS above is of primary concern, for here the particular contractor extends the WBS down to the appropriate levels for cost budgeting and tracking. However, everyone should be aware that the customer may be looking at derivations and extensions of several WBSs on any particular program.

Before leaving the subject of WBS, the following three additional definitions are needed in order to fully appreciate the daily workings of the WBS concept.

**WBS Index**—An indented listing of WBS elements. Taking Figure 9-2, the WBS Index would look something like this:

| WBS Level 1 2 3 4 5 | WBS Element |
|---|---|
| 0001 | Aircraft System |
|   2000 | System Test |
|   3000 | Program Management |
|   4000 | Data |
|   5000 | System ILS |
|   1000 | Air Vehicle |
|     1100 | Airframe |
|     1200 | Propulsion System |
|     1400 | Flight Control System |
|     1500 | Integration & Assembly |
|     1300 | Avionics |
|       1310 | Navigation Aids |
|       1330 | Communication & Ident |
|       1320 | Fire Control |
|         1320.01 | Head Up Display |
|         1320.02 | Radar |
|         1320.03 | Fire Control Software |

**WBS Dictionary**—A book which takes each WBS element and describes the statement of work associated with the element, showing its relationship within the total WBS. The various pages will often also specify the affected functional organizations responsible for performance of the WBS element. See Figure 9-4, for a single sheet from a WBS Dictionary, which is used to define a single CWBS element.

**Responsibility Assignment Matrix—RAM (aka Cost Account Matrix)**—A summary one-page chart or conversion table which relates the functional organizations (OBS) to the work breakdown structure (WBS) elements. If one would take Figure 9-3, and list the WBS Elements horizontally across the top, list the functional departments vertically in the left column, then place an "x" at the intersection of the two, one would have a RAM, sometimes also referred to as a Cost Account Matrix. The RAM will sometimes get quite large on certain programs, but it does provide a useful summary of the work contained in the WBS dictionary, and helps to place responsibility for performance of all tasks. A RAM is a most helpful device when used early in a program, during the proposal phase, and updated after award.

| PROJECT/PROGRAM FXX | | | | | | CONTRACT WORK BREAKDOWN STRUCTURE DICTIONARY | DATE | | |
|---|---|---|---|---|---|---|---|---|---|
| CONTRACT NO. | | | | | | | SHEET 1 | OF | 1 |

| WBS LEVEL | | | | | | ELEMENT TITLE |
|---|---|---|---|---|---|---|
| 1 | 2 | 3 | 4 | 5 | 6 | |
| | | 1000 | | | | AIR VEHICLE |

**ELEMENT DESCRIPTION**

**AIR VEHICLE**

The complete flyaway FXX for delivery to the U.S. Government. The flyaway FXX constitutes the structural airframe, installed engines and subsystems, including mission peculiar equipments, as defined by the Detail Specification for Model F-XX Aircraft Weapon System including all attendant addendums and the Avionic Specification.

| WBS LEVEL | | | | | | ASSOCIATED LOWER LEVEL ELEMENTS |
|---|---|---|---|---|---|---|
| 1 | 2 | 3 | 4 | 5 | 6 | TITLE |
| | | | 1100 | | | AIRFRAME |
| | | | 1200 | | | PROPULSION |
| | | | 1300 | | | AVIONICS SUBSYSTEM |
| | | | 1400 | | | FLIGHT CONTROL SYSTEM |
| | | | 1500 | | | INTEGRATION AND ASSEMBLY |

Figure 9-4 Contract WBS Dictionary[7]

## The Production WBS

When a contractor is fortunate enough to have a program which is about to transcend from full-scale development into production, one of the first things it must do is examine the work breakdown structure it used during FSD. Planning with use of a WBS will have started in the FSD phase, or sometimes earlier in the pre-FSD study phase. While the WBS for a given program will stay essentially constant as it goes from study to FSD to production, there are likely to be minor changes required in the WBS.

> The planning, execution and control of the production phase activities requires that the work be divided into manageable tasks that are compatible with the existing manufacturing and performance measurement systems. Often, the work breakdown structure used during the development phases will not be appropriate for the production phase. Consequently, the contractor should, as a basis for production planning, identify the WBS which will be used. While this WBS may differ from the FSD structure, the two should be such that production phase costs can be related to the development WBS. This is especially critical for those programs which have utilized a design to unit production cost management approach during development.[8]

The two WBSs (FSD versus Production) must be relatable, but are likely to have minor differences tailored to the phase of the effort. The two WBSs are likely to be 95% common with each other. Figure 9-5 illustrates the subtle but important differences between the two WBSs.

| Development | Production |
|---|---|
| 1. Emphasis on Design/ Development | 1. Emphasis on Manufacturing/ Material |
| 2. Subsystem Orientation —Engineering —Testing —Change Incorporation | 2. Flow/Buildup Orientation —Fabrication —Assembly —Test Inspection |
| 3. Labor Intensive-Low Level Responsibility Assignment | 3. Material Intensive-High Level Responsibility Assignment |

**Figure 9-5  Work Breakdown Structure Differences**[9]

## Summary

The WBS technique is important to the buying customer because it aids in the definition of work to be done in total, and it allows the supplier to break the total effort down into manageable pieces for purposes of defining specific procurement packages. Once under contract, a standardized WBS reporting format allows the buying customer to compare proposals for new efforts and estimates to completion on existing jobs against its historical databank, and to independently assess the reasonableness of such forecasts. It is also a useful tool for the contractor to help develop a product cost database and cost models for future pricing activities.

A WBS is important to individual contractors because it helps them to plan a new project and to fully demonstrate to the buying customer that it is completely knowledgeable about the proposed new job.

Lastly, the WBS concept allows contractors to take the same data, and sort it vertically by WBS to satisfy the buying customer, or horizontally to satisfy the needs for internal management control.

There is an important distinction which needs to be made between the WBS approach used by the Department of Defense (DOD) versus that used at the Department of Energy (DOE). At the DOD they use a WBS to display both the initial development of the program, through what they call the non-recurring phase, and continue with a modified version of that same WBS through all production work, the recurring phase of that same product. The DOD guide for such activity is the Military Standard 881, the latest version.

By contrast, the DOE has essentially *all* non-recurring type programs, that is, one-of-a-kind programs, with particular emphasis on system engineering and one-time construction. The DOE has no comparable "standardized" WBS, as with the DOD and defined in their Military Standard 881. The most comparable DOE book covering WBS activity is their *Work Breakdown Guide,* document DOE/MA-0295, dated February 6, 1987.

---

*War Story # 4*

There once was a great and strong warrior whom everyone in the land respected. Because of his personal strength and constant source of new ideas, this great warrior was named program manager for his company's most important new business endeavour.

He personally handled all aspects of the new program, he challenged every old or set way of doing things. He wanted, he demanded the very best for his new program.

He took personal charge of the development of the work breakdown structure for his new program. He didn't care what his advisors said about having to conform to this thing called Military Standard 881. He had a better idea about how to structure a WBS.

Everyone in the land who had anything to do with the WBS met with him to try to persuade him to conform to the military standard. But he would have no part of it. He had a better idea. Truly he did have a better idea. But this was over a decade since the DOD had established their ground rules on the structuring of a WBS, and his better idea did not conform to that standard.

The proposal was submitted and it contained his "unorthodox" WBS. The company won the program and everyone was pleased with the result. C/SCSC was implemented consistent with the non-standard Military Standard 881.

A few months later the customer came in and gave the company a "debriefing" on the proposal they had submitted, which later resulted in their win. Overall, the proposal was described as an exceptional package. The proposal was considered better than all of the competition, in all aspects—except for the WBS! The company had lost evaluation points on its WBS submittal. The people who were evaluating the proposal were comparing the WBS submittal against MIL-STD 881, and the two didn't match. The firm had won the program, in spite of its proposed WBS.

A Performance Measurement Baseline was established, aligning costs to the "un-orthodox" WBS. The customer, those persons who monitor the submittal of C/SCSC reports recommended that this contractor change its cost structure, to conform to MIL-STD 881, but the program manager would have no part of it.

Since this new contract was a "major" new effort, the customer advised the contractor that it would be performing what they called a SAR, a Subsequent Applications Review to assure that this contractor was using its "approved" C/SCSC management control system.

The customer arrived at the plant and immediately took notice of the unusual looking WBS. After all, the use of a standard WBS is a requirement of the first of the 35 criteria. They didn't like what they saw. They immediately asked for a meeting with the person responsible for this unusual WBS approach, and they met with the great warrior. For two days they met, in closed session they met. Finally, they emerged from their meeting.

The customer carefully explained their position. While they did not feel they could tell the contractor how to conduct its internal business affairs, and they clearly acknowledged that the great warrior's ideas on a WBSs were excellent, responsibility for approving this contractor's C/SCSC SAR was theirs to make. If this contractor did not conform to Military Standard 881, they would *not* pass their SAR. They would loose their approved C/SCSC management control system.

The next day a directive went out to all areas to restructure the C/SCSC activities so that they would conform to Military Standard 881.

---

## ENDNOTES

[1] J. Nucci and A. L. Jackson, Jr., "Work Breakdown Structures for Defense Material Items," in *Defense Industry Bulletin*, February, 1969, reprinted in J. Stanley Baumgartner, *Systems Management*, (Washington, D. C.: The Bureau of National Affairs, 1979) page 198.

[2] U. S. Department of Defense, *Work Breakdown Structure for Defense Material Items*, DODD 5010.20, July 31, 1968, page 2.

[3] U. S. Department of Energy, *Cost & Schedule Control Systems Criteria for Contract Performance Measurement—Summary Description*, DOE/MA-0195, October, 1985, page III-1.

[4] Defense Systems Management College, *Program Manager's Notebook*, article by G. A. Kristensen, "Work Breakdown Structure (WBS)" (Fort Belvoir, VA: August, 1985), page 4.2c.

[5] DSMC, *Program Manager's Notebook,* page 4.2e.

[6] DSMC, *Program Manager's Notebook,* page 4.2d.

[7] DSMC, *Program Manager's Notebook,* page 4.2g.

[8] Defense Systems Management College, *Department of Defense Manufacturing Management Handbook for Program Managers* (Fort Belvoir, VA: July, 1984), pages 3-20.

[9] Table courtesy Humphreys & Associates, Inc., from their course: "Work Measurement/Production Performance Measurement."

# 10

# The C/SCSC Baseline

Now that the criteria have been reviewed in detail, and the importance of the Work Breakdown Structure, (WBS) covered, it is time to take the next logical step in discussing performance measurement: the subject of "baseline management." In C/SCSC, the baseline has particular importance because of what the technique attempts to do. C/SCSC is nothing more than conventional budgeting and cost/schedule control, but with one important addition: earned value measurement. Thus, if one is attempting to assess work performance, on a periodic (monthly) basis, one must know in precise terms what one is attempting to measure. Therefore, one absolutely needs a baseline in order to measure performance.

Almost as important as knowing what one is measuring is knowing what one is *not* measuring, i.e., what is outside of an established baseline. Hence, in C/SCSC, it is of paramount importance to know how to establish a baseline, how to maintain the baseline, and how to monitor departures from it. In C/SCSC vernacular the "baseline" is referred to as the Performance Measurement Baseline, or PMB.

This chapter will cover three large but interrelated subjects:

- The C/SCSC Baseline—What it is, how it is established, why it is needed, and how it is maintained.

- Variances from the C/SCSC Baseline—When they occur, how to recognize, how to analyze, what corrective actions are required.

- Estimate at Completion (EAC)—The C/SCSC bottom line, i.e., what the project is likely to cost when it is over.

## The C/SCSC Baseline

The following pages will cover material in very specific detail, using terms which have definite meanings in C/SCSC. Thus, there is no choice but to present fourteen precise definitions, all from the glossary in this book, some of which may be new to the reader, and some that have been discussed earlier.

1. *Contract Target Price (CTP)*—The negotiated estimated cost (CTC) plus profit or fee.
2. *Fee/Margin/Profit*—The excess in the amount realized from the sale of goods, minus the cost of goods.
3. *Contract Budget Base (CBB)*—The negotiated contract cost plus the estimated cost of authorized but unpriced work.
4. *Contract Target Cost (CTC)*—The negotiated cost for the original definitized contract and all contractual changes which have been definitized, but excluding the estimated cost of any authorized, unpriced changes. The CTC equals the value of the BAC plus management reserve, when there is no authorized, unpriced work.
5. *Authorized Unpriced Work*—The effort for which definitized contract costs have not been agreed to, but for which written authorization has been received by the contractor.
6. *Management Reserve (MR)*—A portion of the Contract Budget Base that is held for management control purposes by the contractor to cover the expense of unanticipated program requirements. It is not a part of the Performance Measurement Baseline.
7. *Performance Measurement Baseline (PMB)*—The time-phased budget plan against which project performance is measured. It is formed by the budgets assigned to scheduled cost accounts and the applicable indirect budgets. For future effort, not planned to the cost account level, the Performance Measurement Baseline also includes budgets assigned to higher level CWBS elements. The PMB equals the total allocated budget less management reserve.
8. *Undistributed Budget (UB)*—Budget applicable to contract effort which has not yet been identified to CWBS elements at or below the lowest level of reporting to the government.
9. *Cost Account (CA)*—An identified level at the natural intersection point of the work breakdown structure (WBS) and organizational breakdown structure (OBS) at which functional responsibility for the work is assigned, and actual direct labor, material, and other direct costs are compared with earned value for management control purposes. Cost accounts are the focal point of cost/schedule control.
10. *Work Packages* (WP)—Detailed short-span jobs, or material items, identified by the contractor for accomplishing work required to complete a contract.
11. *Discrete Effort*—Tasks which have a specific end product or end result.

12. *Apportioned Effort*—Effort that by itself is not readily divisible into short span work packages, but which is related in direct proportion to some other measured effort.

13. *Level of Effort (LOE)*—Work that does not result in a final product, e.g., liaison, coordination, follow-up, or other support activities, and which cannot be effectively associated with a definable end product process result. It is measured only in terms of resources actually consumed within a given time period.

14. *Planning Package*—A logical aggregation of far-term work within a cost account that can be identified and budgeted but not yet defined into work packages. Planning packages are identified during the initial baseline planning to establish the timing of the major activities within a cost account and the quantity of the resources required for their performance. Planning packages are placed into work packages consistent with the rolling wave concept prior to the performance of the work.

These fourteen definitions are all an integral constituent in the establishment of the PMB. They are displayed graphically in Figure 10-1, "The Performance Measurement Baseline (PMB)", with each of these definitions referenced by number in the diagram.

Note that to get to the PMB, one first takes the contract (#1), subtracts the planned fee (#2), further subtracts any management reserve (#6) set by the program manager, to arrive at the value to be measured during contract performance, the PMB.

Earlier, when the criteria were discussed, the second of the five criteria groupings was entitled "Planning and Budgeting." This is simply another name for describing the process of establishing a Performance Measurement Baseline, (PMB) against which all actual work accomplishment will be measured. The effort can be best thought of as a three-step, iterative process, as is displayed in Figure 10-2.

Step 1 in the process reflects the definition of the contract work, with use of the Contract Work Breakdown Structure, (CWBS). Step 2 is the scheduling task, which takes the lowest level CWBS elements and schedules them down to cost accounts, within the framework of all program milestones. The sequence of work to be done is set and the interrelationships between tasks shown. Step 3 allocates the budget, which takes program resources and earmarks them down to the cost account and work package levels, consistent with the work specified for each cost account task.

Once completed, the time-phased PMB is created, as reflected in Figure 10-3. One important point concerning the C/SCSC baseline:

> To be effective, both the scheduling and the budgeting systems must be formal and disciplined, mainly to prevent inadvertent or arbitrary budget or schedule changes. This does not mean that the baseline is static or inflexible, simply that changes must be controlled and result only from deliberate management actions.[1]

The process of creating the PMB looks simple enough and in theory it is. However, the establishment of a good performance baseline takes time—much time. Few people fully understand how much time is required. As one person who was on the customer side of

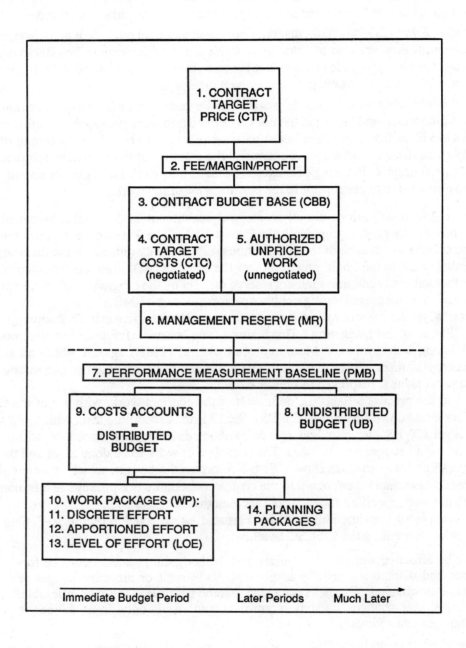

Figure 10-1  The Performance Measurement Baseline (PMB)

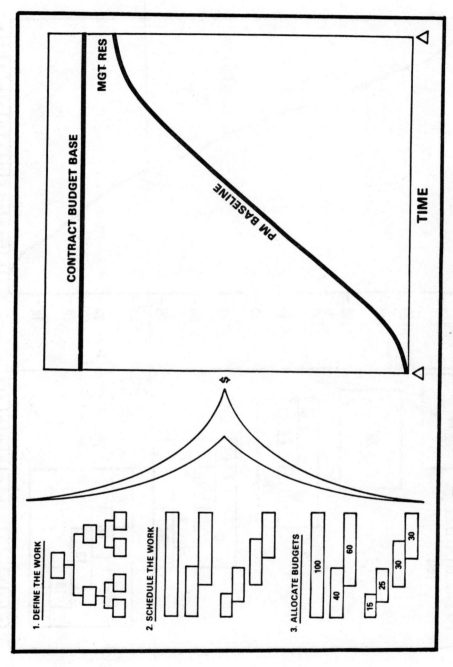

Figure 10-2 Establishing the PMB—A 3-Step Iterative Process[2]

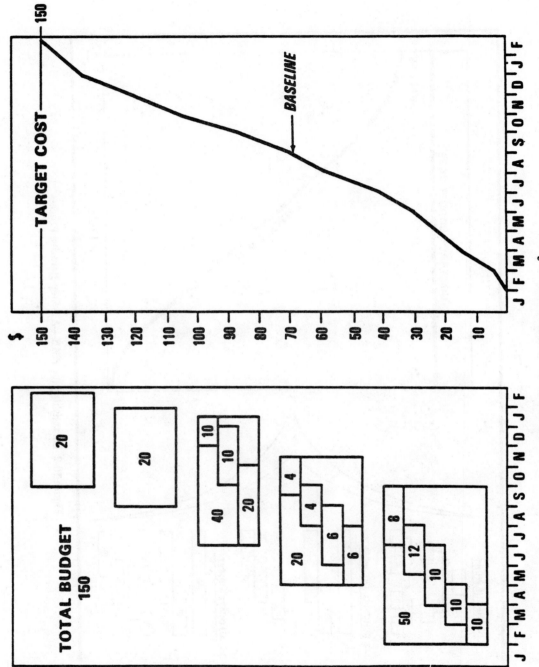

Figure 10-3 Baseline Establishment[3]

the house for many years and had witnessed many such baselines taking place once described the process:

It normally takes anywhere from 9 to 12 months after a contract go-ahead to get a good budget baseline established on a *major* effort.[4]

It would be easy to take issue with this 9 to 12 month forecast, particularly if one has never been through the process. That does seem like an excessive amount of time. But anyone who has ever experienced the excitement (and confusion) of a new program award, and particularly a major one, knows well that it takes time for things to come together. Engineers demand to start engineering "immediately." Manufacturing wants to start cutting chips "now." Buyers want to start buying "at once."

What a good program manager has to do in these cases is to say "hold it," and keep all start-up activity to a minimum until a definitive program plan is established and approved. An essential component of any viable program plan is the PMB, which defines down to the very lowest levels the tasks and schedules and budgets to be used in performing the effort.

Realistically, no matter how adamant the program manager may be about slowing down the initial activity until a program plan is established and approved, certain activities will start—spontaneously. Therefore, an initial budget is typically issued to authorize work which will start anyway. The initial budget is usually issued for three to six months, and iterated until agreements are reached. Shown in Figure 10-4 are eight steps which normally must take place in various form on most major programs after award. The planning of the program becomes progressively more specific until all areas understand what they are to do and are all marching in step with the authorized program plan (and PMB).

Thus, it takes until step 8 (Figure 10-4), going through a series of work definitions, schedule exercises, and budget "discussions," to have in place a PMB on a major program. No matter how detailed the original proposal may have seemed, no matter how long one's firm may have had a cadre of people working on pre-contract activity, "day one" happens when the contract is awarded, not before. And after award (day one), there is a definite sequence of activities and events which must happen before the program is fully underway as a cohesive team. Therefore, the above expert's statement of it taking "9 to 12" months to reach a good PMB is quite accurate, and representative, even though the length of time involved might seem on the surface to be unduly long.

Once the budget and schedule baseline (PMB) is established, to a degree which allows for earned value measurement and customer reporting to take place, an equally difficult task, and one which will last for the duration of a program, will be that of maintaining the baseline. Programs in their developmental or nonrecurring phase are dynamic in nature. Changes are the rule, not the exception. That is precisely what makes the early establishment of the PMB so very essential: to define a budget baseline for the original work, *before* the changes to the original work hit. There have been cases where contracts were

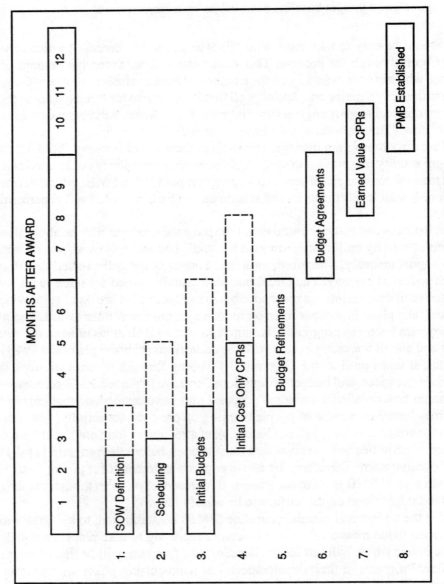

**Figure 10-4  Steps from Contract Award to PMB**

awarded on one day, and contract changes issued the very next day. There have been construction contracts which have had in excess of 1,000 changes over the duration of the effort! Without the creation of an original baseline, and the positive control of changes to that baseline, performance measurement and program management in general becomes insurmountable.

Changes to a contract, and thus to the PMB, will come essentially from two sources: internal and external. Internal changes result from the engineers finding a better way, manufacturing finding the initial design impossible to build, test failures, and so forth. When these changes happen, it is critical that they be managed. Such work should not be started until specifically authorized by the customer, and then subsequently authorized internally by the program manager. Sometimes a contractor will not be able to wait for customer authorization and *must* start a change on its own authority. Obviously there is considerable "risk" involved in proceeding with a change prior to customer approval, but sometimes it is necessary. These types of efforts must be isolated and controlled with particular regard. The value of all such change work must be estimated and folded into the PMB under the category of "authorized unpriced work."

External changes are normally straightforward, from a program control standpoint, and result from the customer's requirement for something different from that which is presently under contract. In all cases, however, it is mandatory that any work coming from outside of the PMB be logged and tightly monitored. An example of a typical budget baseline log is shown in Figure 10-5. Each individual contract change is listed and tracked until it becomes a part of the approved PMB.

During the life of a program, changes to the baseline (PMB) will take place almost continuously, and it is vital to the integrity of C/SCSC activity that such changes be managed and traceable to their origin. Without the tight discipline of managing changes, any established baseline will be lost. Shown in Figures 10-6 through 10-10 are a series of examples of the various changes which commonly take place to an established PMB.

Figure 10-6 shows the graphic display of an initial PMB, with Management Reserve overlaid on top of the PMB, resulting in a top level curve equating to the Contract Target Cost (CTC).

All programs are planned with success in mind, which is quite reasonable. However, it is always prudent to set aside some "just in case" funds in the form of a Management Reserve, in the (likely) event that everything doesn't go exactly as planned. Thus, if a program is planned with the assumption that all testing will be a success, and test failures do occur, there obviously will be some additional budget required. These values come from the shifting of Management Reserve, which by definition is outside of the PMB, into the baseline. Customer approval is not required in these cases, but traceability and reporting of the changes to the MR is and must be described in the CPR.

This condition is illustrated in Figure 10-7. Note that no changes are made to either the Contract Target Costs or program duration. Only Management Reserves is shifted, and this is used for approved statement of work, not for hiding poor performance.

## BUDGET BASELINE LOG

| DATE | CHANGE TITLE | TARGET COST | AUTH UN-PRICED | CBB | MGMT RE-SERVE | PMB | UNDIST BUDGET | DIRECT BUDGET | O/H BUDGET | G & A BUDGET |
|------|-------------|-------------|----------------|-----|---------------|-----|---------------|---------------|------------|--------------|
| 1/14 | ABC CONTRACT | 120 | -- | 120 | 10 | 110 | 10 | 40 | 40 | 20 |
| 1/31 | JANUARY 79 SUMMARY | 120 | -- | 120 | 10 | 110 | 10 | 40 | 40 | 20 |
| 2/5 | CONTRACT CHANGE NO. 001 | -- | 45 | 45 | 5 | 40 | -- | 16 | 16 | 8 |
| 2/15 | P.O. LTR-ADDITIONAL MGMT RPTS | -- | 30 | 30 | -- | 30 | -- | 12 | 12 | 6 |
| 2/25 | P.O. LTR-MOTOR REDESIGN | -- | 30 | 30 | -- | 30 | -- | 12 | 12 | 6 |
| 2/28 | FEBRUARY 79 SUMMARY | 120 | 105 | 220 | 15 | 210 | 10 | 80 | 80 | 40 |
| 3/11 | P.O. LTR-6 MO. SCHEDULE EXTEN | -- | 40 | 40 | 10 | 30 | -- | 12 | 12 | 6 |
| 3/20 | ECP 10-3 ENGR STUDIES | -- | 10 | 10 | -- | 10 | -- | 4 | 4 | 2 |
| 3/26 | CONTRACT CHANGE NO. 001 | 42 | (45) | (3) | (3) | -- | -- | -- | -- | -- |
| 3/31 | MARCH 79 SUMMARY | 162 | 110 | 272 | 22 | 250 | 10 | 96 | 96 | 48 |
| 4/3 | P.O. LTR-DELETION GFP | -- | 20 | 20 | 2 | 18 | -- | 12 | -- | 6 |
| 4/10 | CONTRACT CHANGE NO. 002 | -- | 90 | 90 | 10 | 80 | -- | 32 | 32 | 16 |
| 4/19 | SUBCONTRACT ENVIRONMENTAL TESTING | -- | -- | -- | -- | -- | (10) | 7 | -- | 3 |
| 4/30 | APRIL 79 SUMMARY | 162 | 220 | 382 | 34 | 348 | -- | 147 | 128 | 73 |
| 5/7 | CCN NO. 3-REDUCED SUPPORT | -- | (50) | (50) | (4) | (46) | -- | (19) | (19) | (8) |
| 5/31 | MAY 79 SUMMARY | 162 | 170 | 332 | 30 | 302 | -- | 128 | 109 | 65 |
| 6/4 | ECP 14 - ALTERNATE MATERIAL | -- | 10 | 10 | -- | 10 | -- | 7 | -- | 3 |
| | | | | | | | | | | |
| | | | | | | | | | | |
| | | | | | | | | | | |
| | | | | | | | | | | |

Figure 10-5  A "Budget Baseline Log" [5]

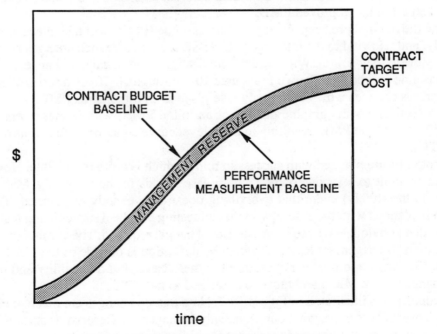

Figure 10-6  The PMB + MR = CTC[6]

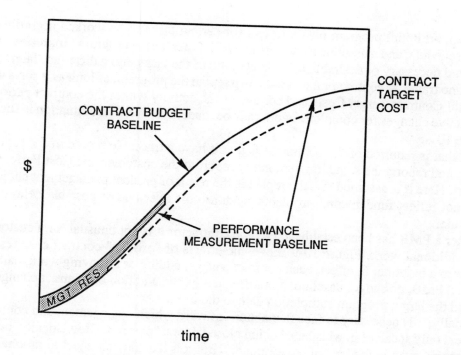

**Figure 10-7 Use of Management Reserve[7]**

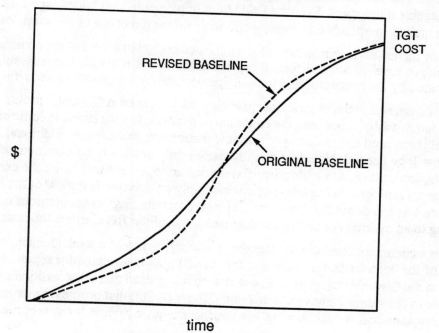

**Figure 10-8 Internal Replanning of the PMB[8]**

Often, an initial program plan will call for certain tasks to be worked according to a given schedule, and a baseline is thus established. Later, as the program progresses, it may be found necessary or desirable to replan certain of the tasks into a different (later or earlier) time frame. A contractor may on its own replan the program, as long as it stays within the total Contract Target Costs and completes the activity within the contract period. No retroactive changes for completed work may be made, however. This situation is shown in Figure 10-8.

All that is required of the contractor is that it have a traceable record of the replanned effort, and reports the same in the monthly report to the customer, the Cost Performance Report. Here it is assumed that the replan is the result of prudent management choice and does not reflect fundamental problems, such as cost overruns or possible delays in the schedule.

After a PMB has been established by the contractor it is not unusual for a customer to add additional work. Figure 10-9 shows the effects of "official" contract changes being added to a baseline. In effect, each contract change, adding or removing work, calls for a revised PMB, or budget baseline. Not infrequently, the addition of contract changes will extend the target program completion date to the right.

Finally, it is necessary to face that abhorrent word which management and contracting officers only speak of in whispers, behind closed doors: "overrun." Realistically, overruns do happen, even in the best of enviornments. But it is a difficult subject to rationally discuss, because an overrun connotes a previous flaw in the plan, or in the approach taken, or in a management judgment. Even the DOD Joint Implementation Guide (page 3-12) which has been quoted so often in this work, seems to avoid the direct use of the word "overrun."

> Any increase which results in a total allocated budget in excess of the contract budget base constitutes formal reprogramming and must be formally submitted by the contractor and formally recognized by the procuring activity.

In this case, and in the chart shown in Figure 10-10, the term "formal reprogramming" is just a fancy way of describing the condition of overrun. In such cases, specific customer approval is required for a number of reasons, particularly since some additional contract funding will be needed. Note that this discussion only applies to cost-reimbursable type contracts, any cost growth under firm-fixed price arrangement will be on the contractor. Also, formal reprogramming does not *always* imply an overrun, just most of the time.

If there was any doubt that the term "formal reprogramming" in the previous quote was referring to an overrun condition, the next paragraph of the JIG clarifies the issue:

> When a contractor formally notifies the procuring agency of a total allocated budget in excess of the contract budget base and the revised plan is accepted for reporting performance to the Government, then it should also be recognized that this condition may be an indicator to the Administrative Contracting Officer (ACO) that progress payments, liquidation rates, or cost reimbursement fee vouchers require review for appropriate adjustment.

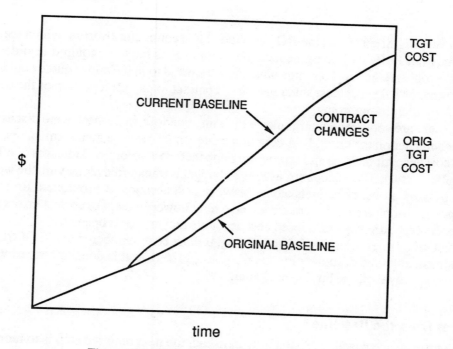

**Figure 10-9  Effects of Contract Changes on the PMB[9]**

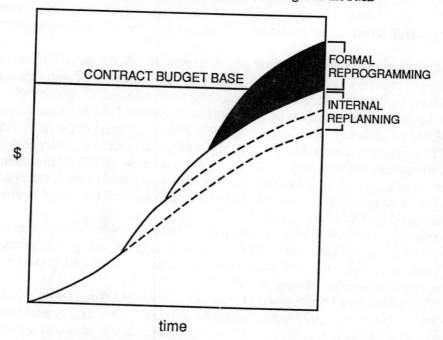

**Figure 10-10  Formal Reprogramming or "Overrun"[10]**

Thus, in very dignified terms, the JIG has alluded to a contractor overrun, which means that the approved PMB will be exceeded. Additional funds may be required in order to complete the job, and the "appropriate adjustment" referred to in the above quote could affect the contractor's fee on a cost share incentive contract to pay for a portion of the overrun, i.e., "formal reprogramming."

Finally, there are some replanning rules which must be followed (these were discussed in an earlier chapter on the criteria). A contractor may on its own use management reserve to change cost account budgets and reprogram unopened cost accounts. Transfers of effort may take place between cost accounts, as long as budget is transferred along with the work. Transfers of work alone, or budgets alone, between cost accounts is prohibited. Retroactive changes to completed cost accounts are also not allowed, except to correct errors and routine accounting adjustments. Closed cost accounts may not be reopened.

If this last set of rules seems unduly confining, it must be remembered that C/SCSC allows for almost any type of replanning to take place, as long as it is done in concert with, and with the approval of, the buying customer.

## Variances from the Baseline

Once the performance baseline (PMB) is established, the next required step is to monitor and report progress against the plan. While it might seem fitting to do a comprehensive review of all approved budgets and schedules each month, a more efficient way to monitor performance is to do so on an "exception basis," commonly referred to as management by exception.

In C/SCSC, performance variances cause particular attention to be focused only on those areas which have exceeded reasonable, and previously set, limitations. These reasonable limits are called "variance thresholds," and are nothing more than outer limit cost/schedule parameters. Anytime such parameters or thresholds are exceeded, C/SCSC procedures call for a special type of analysis to take place, and for the formal reporting of the results to the customer. These special examinations are typically referred to as variance analysis reports (VARs), or sometimes problem analysis reports (PARs). Thus in a C/SCSC management control system, when a performance threshold has been penetrated beyond a previously agreed-to value, a sort of "buzzer" goes off, and certain actions must take place in order to comply with the rules of C/SCSC.

The customer, by agreement, usually sees only a portion of these variance analyses reports, only the more significant ones. But internally, company managements may go through a comprehensive review of such variances to assess their full impact to the program and to take corrective actions, as needed.

Variance thresholds may be expressed in either *absolute* terms (for example, $10,000 over or under a budget value; or 10 work days ahead or behind schedule); or as *a percentage* of some particular base, (for example 10 percent ahead or behind a cost value or a schedule date). Positive variances—an under budget or ahead-of-schedule condition, are sometimes allowed to persist at twice the value of a negative condition—simply because positive variances are more likely to be related to a poor plan than to poor performance. However, there is no universal agreement on this issue, and many organizations set the same threshold values for both positive and negative variances. A chronic positive performance condition could, however, be reflecting a more fundamental problem, as for example one's basic method of planning for the work (BCWS) in the first place.

During the term of performance on a contract, C/SCSC variance thresholds may be tracked at three distinct points of reference, as displayed in Figure 10-11:

1. The "Cumulative to Date" position, reflecting performance on a cumulative or total basis, through the current reporting period.

2. The "Current Month" period, focusing only on the last month (30 days) of performance.

3. The "Estimate at Completion," which incorporates all actuals to date, and makes a projection to the end (EAC).

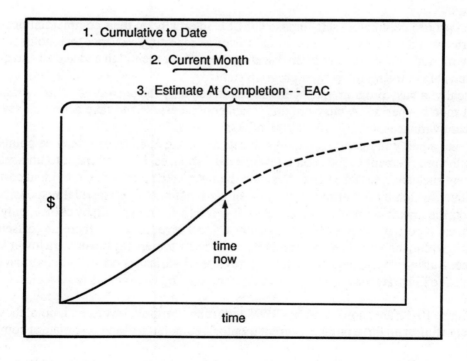

**Figure 10-11 Variance Threshold Points**

It is not uncommon for the buying customers to impose variance thresholds at *all three points,* (cumulative/current month/EAC), although there is a certain group of C/SCSC people who consider such reporting requirements to be "excessive." This group takes the position that the "cumulative to date" thresholds are all that is needed for good performance monitoring. They claim that the "current month" threshold is too prone to accounting fluctuations to measure progress, and results only in excessive paperwork (PAR/VAR reports).

There is mixed opinion on the value of setting "EAC" thresholds. Some claim that the EAC is too subjective. However, since one of the primary purposes of imposing C/SCSC is to obtain a reliable EAC, it seems a weak argument to claim that the EAC is not worth monitoring.

To pause on this issue for a minute, the C/SCSC concept can be an excellent program management tool. But it is not, and was never intended to be, a substitute for sound management. It merely complements and assists good program management. If a customer or contractor program manager fails to spot a potential problem from data reflecting variances to the baseline at the "cumulative to date" position, chances are likely they will also miss any adverse signals from data reflecting the "current period" and "EAC" points also. But the data and the PAR/VAR reports resulting from the monitoring of all three points will be oppressive. And when PAR/VAR reports become excessive, they are seldom read.

When private contractors self-impose C/SCSC internally on their commercial or firm-fixed price work, which require no external customer reporting, variance thresholds for the "current month" and "EAC" are often discarded because of their high added cost and questionable value in the monitoring of program status.

Typically, a busy program manager will ask to see only the *ten most critical variances* for that month—period. A busy program manager can assess and take action on say ten significant variances, but not 50, or 100, or 500!

Whether a particular contract requires formal reporting at all three reference points, or relaxes the requirement to focus on a few critical variances, it is important to understand just where such analyses take place. Variance analyses take place at the individual cost account level, which by definition is where a single functional departmental responsibility intersects the lowest element of the CWBS. However, a customer will, by choice, only see a summary report at a higher level, typically CWBS level 3. When there are offsetting variances within the same CWBS summary level, the customer may never see a lower level variance. But internally, the contractor will review all variances down to individual cost accounts. To illustrate these points, two charts (supplied by Humphreys & Associates) will be used.

In Figure 10-12 are shown typical *CWBS* reporting threshold levels, and, note, they require reporting at all three points: "current month," "cumulative," and "estimate at completion."

By contrast, Figure 10-13 shows the variance thresholds at the *cost account* level. One important point to notice is that the thresholds shown for cost accounts specify different values by department or function. The variance at which engineering labor must perform

## Threshold Values at the Reporting Levels of the WBS

|  | Favorable | Unfavorable | Minimum Values |
|---|---|---|---|
| *Current Month* | $20,000 or 15%, whichever is greater | ($10,000) or (15%), whichever is greater | $10,000 |
| *CUM to Date* | $100,000 or 10%, whichever is less | ($50,000) or (10%), whichever is less | $50,000 |
| At Completion | $200,000 | ($100,00) | |

**Figure 10-12 WBS Thresholds[11]**

## Threshold Values at the Cost Acount Level

| | Minimum Value | Cost -% | Cost +% | Schedule -% | Schedule +% |
|---|---|---|---|---|---|
| *Current Month* | | | | | |
| Engineering Labor | 100 Hrs | 15 | 20 | 15 | 20 |
| Manufacturing Labor | 250 Hrs | 15 | 20 | 15 | 20 |
| Production Material | $2,500 | 15 | 20 | 15 | 20 |
| Tooling Material | $1,200 | 15 | 20 | 15 | 20 |
| Subcontractors | TO BE DETERMINED*** | | | | |
| *CUM to Date* | | | | | |
| Engineering Labor | 250 Hrs | 10 | 15 | 10 | 15 |
| Manufacturing Labor | 500 Hrs | 10 | 15 | 10 | 15 |
| Production Material | $5,000 | 10 | 15 | 10 | 15 |
| Tooling Material | $2,500 | 10 | 15 | 10 | 15 |
| Subcontractors | TO BE DETERMINED*** | | | | |
| *At Completion* | | | | | |
| Engineering Labor | 250 Hrs | 10 | 10 | 10 | 10 |
| Manufacturing Labor | 500 Hrs | 10 | 10 | 10 | 10 |
| Production Material | $5,000 | 10 | 10 | 10 | 10 |
| Tooling Material | $2,500 | 10 | 10 | 10 | 10 |
| Subcontractors | TO BE DETERMINED*** | | | | |

$$-\% = \frac{BCWP - ACWP}{BCWP} \qquad +\% = \frac{BCWP - BCWS}{BCWS}$$

***Based on Subcontractor Dollars and Criticality.

**Figure 10-13 Typical Thresholds for Cost Accounts[12]**

a problem analysis report is different from manufacturing labor, which is different from production materials, and so on. Also note the different thresholds for positive and negative variances, with a wider tolerance allowed for positive variances.

At present, there is no such thing as a "standard" variance threshold at the customer (CWBS) reporting level. Each customer sets the values at which it will require formal variance reporting from a contractor, and imposes these in the contractual document. If a customer insists on reports in excess of a contractor's normal reporting level, as reflected in its validated C/SCSC systems description and internal procedures, then the customer will likely have to pay additional costs for these added C/SCSC reporting requirements.

Shown in Figure 10-14 are thresholds specified in an actual contract. Compare this with Figure 10-12, which outlines typical *CWBS* reporting thresholds.

Note in Figure 10-14 that the cumulative thresholds decrease from 10 percent initially, down to 2 percent as the program moves toward completion. Also note, that the decreasing EAC threshold stays constant at a 2 percent floor throughout the balance of the contract.

To keep such thresholds from inundating program personnel with variance analysis reports, often a *percentage* is combined with an *absolute* value, say $100,000, so that the threshold is 10 percent *and* $100,000, which reduces the preparation of PARs/VARs to worthwhile levels.

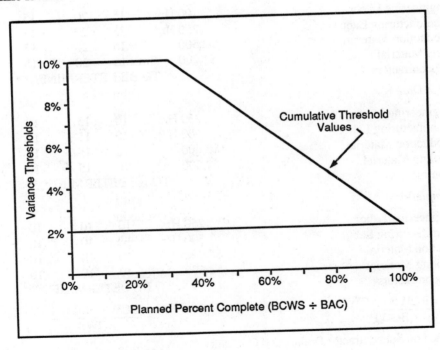

**Figure 10-14 Cost/Schedule Variance Thresholds**

The formula used to set the values in Figure 10-14 are listed as follows and are slightly different from those shown in in Figure 10-13:

1. *Program Completed %*  $=$  $\dfrac{\text{Budgeted Cost Work Performed}}{\text{Budget at Completion}}$  $=$  _____%

2. *Cost Variance %*  $=$  $\dfrac{\text{Cum. BCWP less Cum. ACWP}}{\text{Budgeted Costs Work Performed}}$  $=$  _____%

3. *Schedule Variance %*  $=$  $\dfrac{\text{Cum. BCWP less Cum. BCWS}}{\text{Budgeted Costs Work Scheduled}}$  $=$  _____%

4. *Estimate at Completion Variance %*  $=$  $\dfrac{\text{BAC less EAC}}{\text{BAC}}$  $=$  _____%

In addition to there being no set standard customer variance thresholds, there are also no standard cost account thresholds for the industry. Each contractor may set its own threshold levels by function, which must be defined in its C/SCSC procedures, and approved by the validation team in its demonstration review. It is up to the contractor to propose threshold levels, by function, which in turn must be approved by the customer. Hopefully such thresholds will achieve a balance between providing adequate visibility to the customer, while doing so at a reasonable cost to the program.

Once a variance threshold has been penetrated, certain formal actions must take place in order to meet the spirit of the criteria contained in the fourth grouping on "Analysis." These formal actions are the preparation and review and submittal of VAR/PAR reports. The PAR/VAR is a brief one-page summary of the analysis of a variance to the budget/schedule plan. The exact reporting formats will vary by contractor. See Figure 10-15 is an example of a typical PAR (aka VAR).

All PAR/VAR reports should meet four requirements:

1. They should be prepared by the responsible cost account manager, the one closest to the variant condition, and not by an outside planner/scheduler/or budgeter.
2. They must explain separately each cost and schedule variance and its present and potential impact to the program.
3. They should state the actions taken/or to be taken to resolve the variance.
4. The PAR should be reviewed with, and approved by, the next higher level of management.

What the formalization of the variance analysis process does in effect is to require that a contractor go through a series of defined steps any time its performance is outside of the plan by a previously set tolerance. It also requires that such analysis be documented, so

PMB PROBLEM ANALYSIS REPORT

PROGRAM _____

COST ACCOUNT _____

SALES ORDER _____

WBS _____

DATE _____

AS OF _____

| IMPACT: | SCHED. | COST |
|---|---|---|
| RECOVERABLE | ☐ | ☐ |
| IRRECOVERABLE | ☐ | ☐ |

VARIANCES

| | SCHEDULE | | COST | |
|---|---|---|---|---|
| | $ | HOURS | $ | HOURS |
| CURRENT | | | | |
| CUM TO DATE | | | | |
| AT COMPLETION | | | | |

A. PROBLEM

B. CORRECTIVE ACTION

| | CUM TO DATE | MONTHLY | | | | | | | | | | | CUM AT COMPLETION |
|---|---|---|---|---|---|---|---|---|---|---|---|---|---|
| BCWS | | | | | | | | | | | | | |
| BCWP | | | | | | | | | | | | | |
| ACWP | | | | | | | | | | | | | |
| RECOVERY PLAN | | | | | | | | | | | | | |

RESPONSIBLE ANALYST _____

COST ACCOUNT MANAGER _____

Figure 10-15  A Problem Analysis Report (PAR)

that a contractor's program manager and, if need be, the customer may trace through each problem area at a subsequent date.

The PAR/VAR is an essential part of the monthly Cost Performance Report (CPR) and is specifically called out as Format 5 of DOD Instruction 7000.10, which sets forth the requirements for the Cost Performance Report (CPR) (see the appendix to this book).

## Estimate at Completion (EAC)

Some might take issue with the placement of the subject of Estimate At Completion (EAC) at this point in a book on a C/SCSC. One could argue that the EAC represents a final forecast of the total costs of a program; therefore, the subject properly belongs in a final chapter. Others might quarrel with the co-mingling of the subject of baseline management with that of the Estimate at Completion, in a single chapter.

But the EAC has been intentionally included with the subject of baseline management to emphasize the point that in C/SCSC, the estimated costs at completion of a program is but a logical *extension* of the effort to establish and manage the Performance Measurement Baseline (PMB). If one thinks of the preparation of the Estimate at Completion as a 4-step continuing process, the concept will be clearly understood:

1. Establish a baseline position, which is referred to in C/SCSC as the Performance Measurement Baseline (PMB).
2. Manage the baseline, i.e., control changes into and out of the PMB, and incorporate all authorized changes in a timely manner.
3. Measure performance as the work is accomplished, i.e., understand what work was realized from the plan for what was spent. Determine the efficiency factor for the work done.
4. Assess what is left to be accomplished from the approved plan (BCWS), and make an estimate of the costs (ETC) to do this effort. Add the estimated costs to complete (ETC), to the costs to date (ACWP), to establish the total estimated costs (EAC) for the program.

These four steps, taken in a logical manner, and continuing for the period of the contract, should produce a reliable estimate of the total costs of a given contract, and thus meet the primary purpose of imposing C/SCSC on a given program.

Before getting into a discussion of the EAC, one point needs to be made. A new program, *prior* to its start, is typically represented by a plan. The plan is symbolized by four C/SCSC terms used throughout this book, which are essentially synonymous prior to starting the program:

$$BCWS = PMB = BAC = EAC$$

The Budgeted Costs for Work Scheduled (BCWS) will equal the Performance Measurement Baseline (PMB), which will equal the Budget at Completion (BAC), which will equal the Estimate at Completion (EAC). See Figure 10-16.

Unfortunately, a program only experiences this condition for a brief moment, and only *before* starting performance.

However, as performance begins against the plan, what was originally a common projection line quickly separates into multiple curves, as departures from the plan start to take place. Thus, the program which was displayed in Figure 10-16, might now start to resemble the one shown in Figure 10-17.

What this hypothetical example displays is a program behind schedule (BCWP less BCWS), and a program overrunning its costs (BCWP less ACWP). In order to forecast the ending costs (Estimate At Completion), one must quantify the value of the work done, and the costs of the remaining work (Estimate To Complete) to go.

Question: When doing an EAC projection, which of the three performance curves shown in Figure 10-17 should be considered: the BCWS, or the BCWP, or the ACWP? Answer: All three, plus other factors.

The BCWS curve to the end represented the PMB, or all the work required to complete the job. When one subtracts the BCWP (work accomplished), from the BCWS, the result isolates the balance of the work necessary to finish the job. When one adds a cost estimate to the work remaining to finish the job, one has forecasted the estimate to complete (ETC). When one adds the ETC to the ACWP, (cost actuals), one has established the EAC (Estimate At Completion). Thus all three curves shown in Figure 10-17 above must be considered when estimating the final costs of a program.

Four factors should always be considered when making an estimate to complete a given job:

1. The performance to date, the BCWP, as related to the original plan, the BCWS. What was the efficiency factor of the work planned versus the work physically accomplished?

2. The actual costs to date, the ACWP, which includes the direct costs on the program, as well as the indirect costs added to the direct charges. What was the efficiency factor of the costs incurred versus the work accomplished?

3. A projection of future performance. What will the future hold? Are there additional tasks which are within the work statement but beyond what was originally planned, still to be accomplished? Are there uncertainties regarding the schedule?

4. An estimate of the cost of the remaining work. What is likely to happen to escalation costs, to future overhead rates, to the economy in general, to the efficiency factors achievable in future performance?[13]

Some firms take pride in making a determined effort to achieve a balanced forecast of the total funds required to finish a job. It might be worthwhile to review the techniques used by a certain firm in the preparation of their EACs.

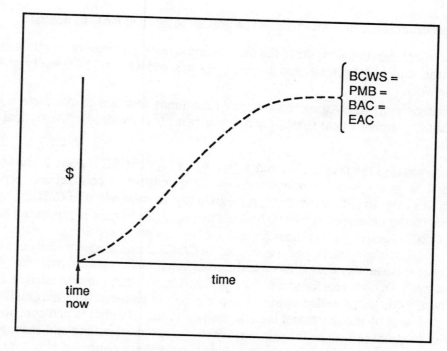

**Figure 10-16  Conditions *Before* a Program Starts**

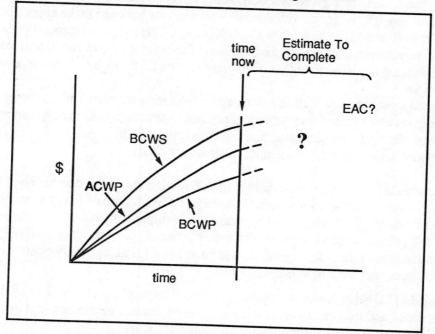

**Figure 10-17  Conditions *After* a Program is Underway**

Their procedures require two factors to be present in all such EAC forecasts:

1. Balanced organizational inputs to the final estimate (EAC), representing all functional organizations which have a vested interest in the job, and who will be actually performing the work.
2. Two independent forecasting techniques of the funds required to complete a job: a monthly "Mathematical EAC," and a periodic (as required) "Analytical EAC Override."

Organizationally, the preparation and submittal of all C/SCSC reports is the responsibility of one group, which remains constant from contract to contract and period to period. In this firm, as with many firms in the industry, the placement of C/SCSC responsibility is with the finance department. And within the firm's finance organization are two separate C/SCSC activities: (1) those assigned to assist a given specific *program*, to represent that program's interests, and consolidate all C/SCSC data related to that contract for reporting to the customer; and (2) those assigned to *functional* organizations, who typically support multiple contracts for that particular function. A classic matrix relationship.

As a routine practice, detailed estimates to complete are gathered from the detailed cost account managers by the functional organization only, for submittal to and consolidation by a given program. Program finance personnel manage the baseline and management reserve and assemble the data in report form for transmittal to a customer. However, when there is any indication that a given function is either overestimating a job, or underestimating it for some reason, the program financial person has authority to make an independent forecast of the effort and to use it in the C/SCSC report. The program financial person has final say on the estimate used unless the functional financial person or functional manager insists on elevating the issue to higher management for a final resolution of the proper estimate to be used.

The process seems to work well and recognizes the diverse interests and pressures which exist on program managers versus functional performing managers, each of whom are supported by specific financial personnel assigned to support them.

With respect to the—EAC, two distinct methods are used:

**Mathematical EAC**—is derived (monthly) by subtracting the work accomplished to date (BCWP) from the total work scheduled to date (BCWS), both of which have costs allocated by detailed sub-tasks, and by making an estimate of the costs for the remaining work (ETC), and adding this value to the actual costs to date (ACWP). This approach assumes that the original detailed estimates for all currently opened and future cost accounts are still valid.

**Analytical EAC Override**—is derived (periodically as required) by review of detailed performance and trend analysis of the work completed and in process, and by preparing a detailed estimate to complete for all remaining work.

The mathematical EAC method is probably typical of most estimating approaches used in the industry. It is the method which typically is included in the EAC forecast of the monthly CPR. There is nothing inherently wrong with the method, as long as the original planning estimates were valid when prepared and nothing has happened since the program began to alter these original premises—two big "Ifs." Unfortunately, few programs (perhaps none) ever finish exactly as first planned. Tests fail, requirements change, better ideas are conceived, and soon the current modified plan hardly resembles the original plan. Also, hopefully, people do get smarter as they work on a program. Thus, the Analytical EAC Override method takes on real significance as experience and knowledge is gained through trial and error.

The Mathematical EAC is mechanical in form, and thus lends itself nicely to computer applications. By contrast, the Analytical EAC Override is not, and the approach requires more seasoned C/SCSC personnel working closely with a program manager and functional management to give the method meaning. The use of both of these EAC techniques, in conjunction with balanced organizational estimates, plus frequent and very critical internal management reviews, does add confidence to the forecasting of final estimates (EAC) with at least one company in the industry.

If the above illustration gives the impression from that all is peace and tranquility in the preparation of EACs for programs, the following two quotes, representing the customer side, quickly disillusion us:

> If the cumulative BCWP is less than the cumulative BCWS this means a behind-schedule situation. If the BCWP is less than the cost actuals for that same work, then this means a cost overrun situation. These are *facts*. The contractor may claim the ability to catch up, or to become more efficient, but these are *opinions*. There should be no quibbling between facts and opinions.[14]

> EACs have a habit of reflecting optimism, an optimism based on the realities of the negotiated contract cost (NCC). It would be foolish for a contractor to project an overrun on the first month's CPR; the government might terminate the contract or accuse them of 'buying into' a government job. Further, the EAC's are a primary input into the Selected Acquisition Reports (SARs) which go to the major acquisition commands and eventually end up in Congress. The political sensitivity of the EAC can be far-reaching.[15]

The establishment of the C/SCSC baseline (PMB), the management of that baseline, and the projection of the final results (EAC) of that baseline, represent the very essence of the criteria concept.

---

## ENDNOTES

[1] Robert R. Kemps, Office of the Assistant Secretary of Defense (Comptroller), *Cost Performance Reporting and Baseline Management,* circa 1975, page 9.

[2] Robert R. Kemps, Office of The Assistant Secretary of Defense (Comptroller), *The DOD Cost/Schedule Control Systems Criteria,* circa. 1978, Page 30.

[3] Ibid, Kemps, page 10.

[4] Interview with Lloyd L. Carter, March 19, 1981, retired from the United States Air Force, later a Director with Humphreys & Associates, Inc.

[5] Chart courtesy Humphreys & Associates, Inc.

[6] Ibid, Kemps, page 24.

[7] Ibid, Kemps, page 26.

[8] Ibid, Kemps, page 28

[9] Ibid, Kemps, page 30.

[10] Ibid, Kemps, page 62.

[11] Chart courtesy Humphreys & Associates, Inc.

[12] Chart courtesy Humphreys & Associates, Inc.

[13] Major Thomas L. Bowman, USAF, "Interpretive Key to C/SCSC Joint Implementation Guide Checklist," from Cost Schedule Control Systems Criteria Reference Manual (Wright-Patterson AFB, OH: Air Force Institute of Technology, April, 1982) page 349.

[14] Major Thomas L. Bowman, USAF, and George A. Neyhouse, *Estimates at Completion (EAC)* (Wright-Patterson AFB, OH: Air Force Institute of Technology, November, 1982) page 251.

[15] Major Thomas L.Bowman and George Neyhouse, page 227.

# 11

# Earned Value Techniques

There are numerous government publications dealing with the subject of C/SCSC. However, nowhere in any of these documents do they give any clue as to *how* one is to measure earned value. With something as fundamental to the integrity of the entire concept as the "how" the performance is to be measured, is not the government somewhat remiss in leaving this critical issue up in the air? Answer: not really. Their approach of not telling contractors how they must measure earned value is consistent with the criteria concept itself. The government merely defines what it needs from the private sector, it is up to the private contractors to find a way to satisfy the requirement.

The government documents on C/SCSC merely set forth the requirements for work measurement as a part of meeting the 35 criteria. The "how to" is strictly up to the contractors to propose in their (modified?) management control systems description, and for the government to approve, or to modify, or to reject while reviewing (validating) the contractor's cost/schedule management control system.

Fundamental to making an assessment of the BCWP (earned value) is that previously a BCWS (plan/PMB) had been established, against which performance could be measured. Without a baseline plan (BCWS/PMB) in place there can be no basis for ascertaining earned value. And during the performance period, it is also fundamental that the BCWP (earned value) methodology be consistent with the methodology used to establish the BCWS (plan) in the first place.

In C/SCSC the Performance Measurement Baseline (PMB) is made up of the sum of cost accounts, and cost accounts come in three distinct flavors:

"Discrete/Work Package," "Level of Effort," and "Apportioned". While the main thrust of C/SCSC and work measurement is intended to focus on discrete/work-package type cost accounts, there are instances where the other two are appropriately used, and their performances must also be quantified.

There are three rules which apply to the calculation of earned value:

1. Performance measurement must take place at the lowest possible level, at the cost account or down to the subordinate work package level. Exceptions may be allowed.

2. The calculation of the earned value (BCWP) must be done using methods consistent with the way the plan (BCWS) was established in the first place, and the manner in which the cost actuals (ACWP) are being accumulated.

3. Once the BCWP is determined and reported to management and the government, no retroactive changes may take place, except for the adjustment of legitimate accounting errors.

## "Level of Effort (LOE)" Work Packages

LOE activities are those which are necessary to a program, but which are more *time*-oriented than *task*-related. Examples of these activities are program management, scheduling, contract administration, field engineering support, security guards,and so on. When these functions are charged directly to a contract, they will continue for the full term of a program, but they will have no measurable outputs. In these cases work performance (BCWP) is always assumed to equal the work planned (BCWS), no more, no less. Therefore, by definition, LOE activities can experience no schedule variances (BCWP less BCWS always equals zero). But they can have cost variances (BCWP less ACWP), when more or less resources are consumed than was planned. And when LOE work packages show positive cost variances, the condition show be examined because it may indicate problems in implementation, e.g., staffing.

For LOE, the BCWP, monthly and cumulative, always matches the BCWS, up to 100 percent of the budget, or BCWS. BCWP can never exceed 100 percent of BCWS. With respect to cost actuals (ACWP), any differences between BCWP and ACWP will cause a positive or negative cost variance.

## "Apportioned" Effort

Apportioned efforts are those which have a direct intrinsic performance relationship to some other discrete activity, often called their reference base. An example of this type of relationship might be that of "factory inspection," which normally would have a direct time and value relationship to the "factory" labor, but at a fraction (perhaps 8 percent) of its related base, factory labor. When the (apportioned) effort for factory inspection is issued, it must state in writing that the earned value for it will be set as a relationship to the BCWP established for its base work package, factory labor. Thus if the cumulative BCWP for factory labor is set at 47.87%, factory inspection will have likewise earned a cumulative BCWP of 47.87%.

When determining either the monthly or cumulative BCWP for the apportioned effort, the value will always reflect the same percentage BCWP as its related base (the discrete work package). In this example, if the factory labor cost account is experiencing a negative schedule variance (BCWP less BCWS), likewise, the inspection effort will reflect the identical negative schedule variance condition.

Cost variance relationships are different, however. Any cost variance for the apportioned effort (inspection), will reflect the actual costs (ACWP) for the inspection work, and not that of the base work package of factory labor. The cost variance position of the (apportioned) inspection effort will be the difference between the ACWP for its own activity versus its derived BCWP. Thus, if the manager of inspection were to double the inspectors from the 8 percent budgeted rate, to say 16 percent, the inspection (apportioned) work would reflect a negative cost variance, even if the base effort for factory labor might be reflecting a positive cost variance.

With respect to schedule variances, apportioned effort always reflects the position of the related base work package. With respect to cost variances, however, they reflect their own cost performance, as related to the BCWP (as a percentage) of their related bases.

## "Discrete/Work Package" Cost Accounts

The techniques for measuring performance (BCWP) of both LOE and apportioned efforts are generally consistent throughout the industry. However, these two types of tasks by the very rules of C/SCSC are intended to represent only a small portion of all work. The majority of the cost accounts are expected to consist of discrete/work packages, and the methodology for measuring performance of the discrete/work packages is, by no means, uniform throughout the industry.

While establishing the earned value position each month, discrete/work packages may be thought of as being in three distinct categories, as illustrated in Figure 11-1:

1. Those which are completed, and thus have earned 100 % of their BCWS.
2. Those which were not yet started, and thus have earned 0 % of their BCWS.
3. Those which are in-process, started but not yet completed, and which have earned some value (?) of their BCWS.

The work packages which are completed will earn 100 % of their BCWS, easy. Those which are not yet started will earn 0%-also easy. But those work packages which are opened and in process as of the reporting—period are not always easy to assess in a meaningful way, particularly those which are delinquent to their planned completion date. The DOD Joint Implementation Guide states:

> The major difficulty encountered in the determination of BCWP is the evaluation of in-process work (work packages which have been started but have not been completed at the time of cutoff for the report).[1]

Therefore, most of the attention of those attempting to determine the earned value position will be focused on the open, active, in-process discrete work packages.

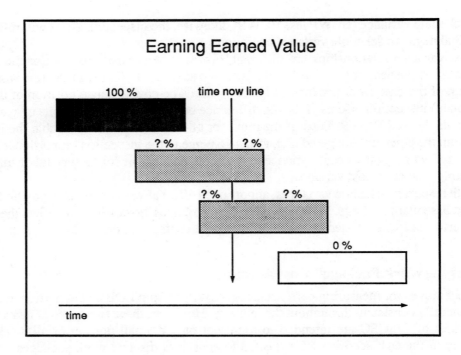

**Figure 11-1  Earned Value on Discrete Work Packages**

While the government did leave the issue entirely up to the private contractors to decide, and the techniques used to measure performance do vary in the industry, there are essentially only six distinct methods used to measure the BCWP, the earned value—"what you got for what you spent":

1. *The 50/50 Technique*—This approach was popular in the early days of C/SCSC, but its use has diminished in recent times. The 50/50 technique is used for work packages with a duration of not more than three accounting periods, preferably two maximum. Fifty percent of the planned value is earned when the activity starts, and the balance is earned when the effort is completed. Some contractors use a modified approach which allows the cost account manager to set (in advance) the percentage values to something other than 50/50, say 25/75, or 40/60, etc.

2. *The 0/100 Technique*—This approach is best applied to those work packages which are scheduled to start and complete within one accounting month. Nothing is earned when the activity starts, but 100 percent is earned when completed.

3. *Milestone Method*—This approach works well when work packages exceed three or more  months in duration. Objective milestones are established, preferably one or more

each month, and the assigned budget for the work package is divided up based on a weighted value assigned to each milestone. In those instances where there are no milestones in a given month, an estimate of the value of work completed during the month may be allowed, as long as the original plan called for such estimates to be made.

4. *Percent Complete*—This approach allows for a monthly estimate of the percentage of work completed to be made, usually on a cumulative basis, by the manager of the work package. Typically such estimates are on a "subjective" basis, but some firms have established guidelines by function, which assists their managers in assigning a percentage value for the work accomplished. By providing these guidelines to their managers, (examples: lines released, drawings issued, materials ordered, parts received, etc.) some measure of "objectivity" is placed into the percent complete estimate.

Over the years, the percent complete method has received increasingly wide industry favor. There is nothing inherently wrong with this direction as long as the work packages stay short in duration, and internal company managements go through periodic reviews where each work package manager must justify the completion estimates they have assigned to their activities. Many a heated discussion has taken place between work package managers and their next level of supervision (and even from their colleagues) when they feel work package managers were claiming too much or too little completion value for their work tasks.

If a company is genuinely utilizing the C/SCSC approach in the performance of a program, the professional integrity of employees and supervision will often provide a sort of unwritten "check and balance" on the accuracy of the monthly percent complete estimate. Conversely, if a firm is giving lip service only to C/SCSC, the monthly BCWP can have wide *manipulated* distortions using the percent complete method to set earned value, since this approach allows for, in effect, a "subjective" assessment of performance status to be made.

One approach used to minimize the subjectivity factor in the percent completion methods to set earned value is to limit the maximum amount allowed to be earned in any work package until it is 100 percent completed. While the percentages allowed do very from company to company, 80 percent to 90 percent maximum is typical of most firms. Thus, a given work package may earn only up to say 80 percent of the manager's estimate, until the task is 100 completed, at which time the balance is earned.

The four methods listed above to measure performance, apply well to engineering type activity, effort which is said to be of the non-recurring type. There are two additional techniques that apply best to manufacturing efforts, that which is considered to be of the recurring type:

5. *Equivalent and/or Completed Units*—This method places a given value on each unit completed, or fractional equivalent unit completed, say $25, or 25 hours per unit, as

the basis for setting both the budget value and earned value. The equivalent unit approach works best when the fabrication or assembly periods are of a longer duration, say in excess of two accounting periods. If the fabrication or assembly periods are of a lesser duration, the completed units approach works well.

6. *Earned Standards*—This approach to budgeting and measuring performance is the most sophisticated and requires the most discipline on the part of the contractor. It requires the prior establishment of standards for the performance of the tasks to be worked. Historical cost data, time and motion studies, etc., are all essential to the process of setting work standards. This approach may well be the one increasingly used in the future, based on the requirements of Military Standard 1567, on work measurement, which will be discussed in a later separate chapter.

There is no single method of setting earned value which works best in all types of activity. Probably the best approach for a firm to take is to allow for several different methods to be used, and the one employed for individual work packages will be based on the collective judgments of the cost account managers, working closely with their C/SCSC specialists and the customer.

To assess the methods actually being used in the defense industry, a survey of five major contractors was made, and the results are summarized in Figure 11-2. The five contractors are listed across the top, "A" to "E", and the six earned value methods listed down the left side.

| Earned Value Technique | A-1 | A-2 | A-3 | A-4 | B | C | D | E |
|---|---|---|---|---|---|---|---|---|
| **Contractor** | | | | | | | | |
| 1. 50/50 | No | No | Yes | Yes | Yes | Yes | Yes | No |
| 2. 0/100 | No | No | Yes | Yes | Yes | No | Yes | No |
| 3. Milestone | Yes | Yes | Yes | Yes | Yes | Yes | Yes | Yes |
| 4. Percent Complete | Yes | Yes | Yes | Yes | Yes | Yes | Yes | Yes |
| Maximum EV allowed until 100 % Complete | 85% | 80% | 80% | 80% | 100% | 85% (95% LOE) | 100% | 90% |
| 5. Equivalent Units | Yes | Yes | No | Yes | Yes | No | No | No |
| 6. Standards | Yes | Yes | Yes | Yes | No | Yes | No | No |

**Figure 11-2  Survey of Earned Value Techniques**

Notice that Contractor "A" has four major divisions, each with its own approved C/SCSC activity. Notice also that each division of Contractor "A" has been allowed to select different techniques to measure earned value, which emphasizes the autonomy of C/SCSC applications. Each of the five firms listed is a major defense contractor, and all have their own validated C/SCSC management control systems, with Contractor "A" having four separate validated management control systems.

Observe that no two of these five contractors have used exactly the same combination of techniques. Each has some unique feature. Since all have approved C/SCSC systems, a safe conclusion is that the government, when validating a given contractor's C/SCSC approach, will allow the contractor to determine its own choice of methods, as long as they meet the intent of the criteria. The one consistent pattern, however, is the frequent use of the milestone and percent complete methods. All contractors surveyed use these methods.

To illustrate just how the earned value (BCWP) is actually determined using four of the six techniques, Figure 11-3 shows the approach used to set the earned value using the "50/50," "Equivalent Unit," "Percent Complete," and "Milestone" techniques.

Work Package # 1 uses the "50/50" technique. In month 1 the WP was started, so 50 percent of the plan (BCWS) was earned, i.e., the BCWP was 100 in month 1. In month 2, the scheduled completion date was slipped to month 4. Therefore, the BCWP status at the end of months 2 and 3, was still only 100 since the balance of the BCWP, the other 50 percent, cannot be earned until the WP is completed, which is planned to happen in month 4.

Likewise, in WP # 2, using the equivalent units method, the planned (BCWS) values are shown on the above portion of each month, and the earned (BCWP) values are shown below. In month 2, the BCWS was 6 units, or $150, as compared with the performance (BCWP) of just 2, or $50. In the 3rd month, the BCWP was increased to 6 units, or $150, a nice recovery.

One can trace through WP's # 3 and # 4 and compare planned (BCWS) versus earned value (BCWP) for each approach shown.

## Other Direct Costs (ODC)

Other Direct Costs (ODC) covers such things as travel, computer usage, and a host of other activities chargeable directly to a contract, but excludes materials, which is generally treated as a separate subject. The BCWP (earned value) for ODC is usually set when either costs for these items are *incurred,* or when costs are *recorded.*

If the cost incurred method is used, the ACWP must be shifted to the earlier time frame to match the BCWS and BCWP, which is sometimes accomplished by use of a commitment report. If the cost-recorded method is used, the BCWS must be placed into a later time frame, to be in concert with the time delay (normally about two months), between when costs are incurred until payment is actually made. Since Other Direct Costs are normally relatively small compared to the major categories of labor and materials with their respective burdens, ODC rarely presents a major problem to contractors.

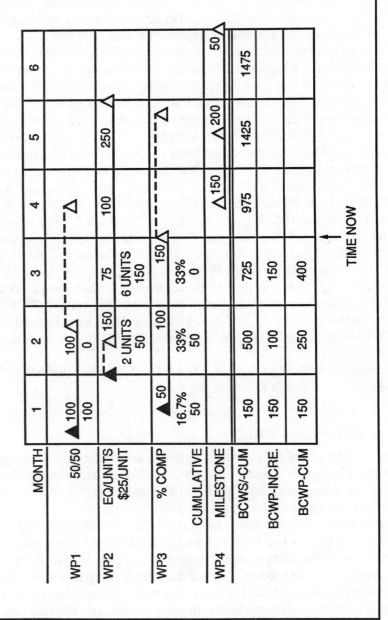

# SAMPLE COST ACCOUNT
## EARNED VALUE CONCEPT
### BUDGETED COST FOR WORK PERFORMED (BCWP)

| MONTH | | 1 | 2 | 3 | 4 | 5 | 6 |
|---|---|---|---|---|---|---|---|
| WP1 | 50/50 | 100 | 100 | | | | |
| | | 100 | 0 | | | | |
| WP2 | EQ/UNITS | | 150 | 75 | 100 | 250 | |
| | $25/UNIT | | 2 UNITS | 6 UNITS | | | |
| | | | 50 | 150 | | | |
| WP3 | % COMP | 50 | 100 | 150 | | | |
| | | 16.7% | 33% | 33% | | | |
| | | 50 | 50 | 0 | | | |
| WP4 | CUMULATIVE | | | | | | |
| | MILESTONE | | | | 150 | 200 | 50 |
| | BCWS/-CUM | 150 | 500 | 725 | 975 | 1425 | 1475 |
| | BCWP-INCRE. | 150 | 100 | 150 | | | |
| | BCWP-CUM | 150 | 250 | 400 | | | |

TIME NOW

Figure 11-3  Earned Value Techniques[2]

## Earned Value on "Buy" Items and "Overhead"

The subject of determining earned value on those items which are purchased by a contractor is perhaps *the* thorniest path on the road to an approved performance management system. Therefore, the subject of material and subcontracting and inter-divisional work will be covered separately in the next two chapters covering the "buy items."

Equally as difficult and complex as the subject of those items which are bought from the outside, is the subject of indirect cost management. Therefore, this subject will also be covered in a separate chapter later in this book. Suffice it to say, while earning earned value, that the totals would be incomplete without the application of indirect costs on top of the direct cost bases. However, just what constitutes the appropriate value of the overheads is a complicated matter, and will also be covered separately.

## How Earned Value is Established on a Contract

The earned value position (BCWP) for a given contract is simply the summation of all its cost accounts, those which are completed or in-process or unopened, expressed in either hours or dollars including the appropriate burdens. It is a derived estimate. Each cost account must be assessed individually, and the summation of all cost accounts represents a contract's earned value or BCWP position.

---

### ENDNOTES

[1] Department of Defense, *Cost/Schedule Control Systems Criteria—Joint Implementation Guide*, October 1987, page 3-14.

[2] Chart courtesty Humphreys & Associates, Inc.

# The "Buy Items" – Part I:
## Major Subcontracts

*The typical buyer is a man past middle life, spare, wrinkled, intelligent, cold, passive, noncommittal, with eyes like a codfish, polite in contact, but at the same time, unresponsive, cool, calm, and damnably composed as a concrete post or a plaster of Paris cat; a human petrification with a heart of feldspar and without charm, or the friendly germ, minus bowels, passions, or a sense of humor. Happily they never reproduce, and all of them finally go to hell.[1]*

It ain't easy finding really great buyers these days. Because of their complete dedication to their jobs, and through a general lack of use, they have lost their capacity to reproduce and are now on the endangered species list. Such being the case, what is management to do when a particular job calls for the work of a really great buyer? Simple. Management merely takes an average buyer and gives him an exciting tool called C/SCSC. That seems to make the difference.

Up to this point the discussion has centered on having the criteria imposed downward on us from a customer. Now, *we* are the customer, and have assumed our rightful role as that of the "imposer." Out there somewhere are thousands of "imposees", just waiting for our instructions. Exciting isn't it!

But prior to addressing the subject of flowing the criteria downward to our subcontractors, it might be wise to stand back and examine the function of subcontract management. What is it, how significant is it to the total prime contractor's effort, and is there a proper role for C/SCSC in this process?

## The Importance of Subcontract Management

Starting sometime in the 1960's, there began a subtle, almost unnoticed shifting in the amount of effort prime government contractors were keeping for themselves. More and more they were asking other firms (some prime contractors themselves) to perform significant portions of their contracts.

There were numerous reasons for this change. The "pay dirt" in prime contracting work is not represented by the research and development contracts. They are merely a necessary means to an end. The real objective and value of prime contracting is the possibility of securing the long-term production run. And the competition for the very few new production runs was becoming progressively more severe. Not only were there fewer production runs being started, but the cost of competing for them, i.e., the costs of the specialized assets, professional staff, long-time commitments of facilities, etc., was making it a high risk business. Private industry does not enjoy high risks unless, that is, there are correspondingly high profit potentials. Subcontracting selected portions of the action was a way of spreading these costs to compete, and of diluting the associated business risks over several firms.

In addition to the advantages of diluting the business risks associated with the new but often delayed competitions, prime contractors found they could actually enhance their chances of success by the formation of strong prime/subcontractor teams which complemented obvious weaknesses in any individual firm's technical and manufacturing capability.

While it is unlikely that one could ever determine exactly how much of the prime contract's efforts are being sent outside for performance, there is general agreement that it is well in excess of half of the prime contractor's effort:

> Few people realize that since 1970, 50 percent or more of every defense dollar eventually ends up going to a subcontractor. All evidence indicates that this trend will not only continue but probably increase. Thus, through subcontracting, a prime contractor is becoming a manager of resources rather than a producer of goods.[2]

Still others place the value of subcontracting even higher:

> On almost every defense system acquisition program, subcontracts account for more than half of the prime contractor's costs. One prime contractor, for example, subcontracts 66 percent of a missile program while two others have subcontracted 60 to 70 percent of aircraft and destroyer programs, respectfully.[3]

The importance of subcontracting, which as a broad category includes all items purchased from the outside, will likely increase to as much as 80% or more of prime contracting effort as we go into the 1990s.

The increased amount of work going to other firms for performance brought with it certain challenges to management. Instead of work being accomplished inside where one could keep a close surveillance on the activity and easily exert pressures on fellow employees, now the required tasks had to be precisely defined, in advance, and all monitoring was restricted to that authorized in the subcontracting document. Managers who once prided themselves on their effectiveness in getting work done in their own company, suddenly got all entangled in such things as terms and conditions, statements of work, authorities and responsibilities, when trying to get the same job done by way of a subcontract with another company. Just who in the prime contractor's company was responsible for what, opened a whole new set of territorial disputes, as this illustration reveals:

> Sometimes the fault for loss of subcontractor's control of costs is traceable to the prime contractor and, more specifically, to the matter of who in the prime's organization has responsibility for what. On a large aerospace program a few years ago a company's program engineer for propulsion assumed that he had full responsibility for both in-house and subcontract propulsion work because a documented company policy assigned this responsibility to the program engineer. At the same time a subcontract administrator in the prime contractor organization assumed he had full responsibility for propulsion subcontracts on the program because another numbered company policy assigned responsibility for subcontracts to the procurement organization. Company management was (and may still be) unaware of these conflicting directives.

> The net result was that, although it was clear to the individuals involved who was responsible for strictly technical and subcontract administration aspects, neither was directly responsible for cost or schedule management and neither took effective steps to control the two propulsion subcontractors. The company's program manager, more interested in technical aspects than in cost and controls, assumed no direct responsibility for subcontract management. Costs galloped out of control while progress inched along on subcontractor's work.[4]

In addition to the organizational issue of who does what with respect to subcontract management is a related concern of which is the best vehicle to define the prime/subcontractor relationship. While there are multiple types of contractual arrangements available, most are derivatives of two diverse types: the cost reimbursable and the fixed price contract type.

Under the various fixed price type contracts available, the most stringent is the Firm Fixed Price, commonly referred to as FFP. This type of contract is the most desirable to use, *as long as* one knows exactly what one wants to buy from the subcontractor. If the definition of work is vague or is apt to change, for whatever reason, a fixed price contract is not a good vehicle to use. Under FFP contracts, the subcontractor agrees to perform services and/or to deliver hardware according to an agreed to price which is fixed. However, in the defense industry, as we all know only too well, many a low-bidding subcontractor "got well" through negotiated re-directions in the statement of work and/or in delays in the official subcontract schedule. Under FFP subcontracts one has to know exactly what one wants, and be able to define it in a legal document, or one might want to consider another contracting arrangement.

The opposite of the FFP subcontract is the cost reimbursable type, of which there are several varieties, the most common of which are the Cost-Plus-Fixed-Fee (CPFF) and Cost-Plus-Incentive-Fee (CPIF) types. Here, the subcontractor agrees to perform for a cost which can vary, but with a fee which is fixed within a range, unless the statement of work changes. Such an arrangement accommodates the incorporation of changes and redirection without causing a major disruption of the effort. The CPFF and/or CPIF subcontract is appropriate when the activity purchased cannot be precisely defined, and when there is little or no performance history with which to establish a fair firm price. However, a cost type subcontract places the risks of cost performance, not on the subcontractor, but directly back on the prime contractor.

What is the overall significance to a prime contractor of fixed price versus cost type subcontract arrangements? Studies have shown that although fixed price subcontracts represent the largest number of procurements, conversely, they represent a lesser percentage of the total subcontracted dollars. And although cost reimbursable type subcontracts are used less frequently than are fixed price types, they do represent the largest dollar volume.[5] Hence, in terms of prime contractor risk exposure, the high value cost risks of performance still remain with the prime contractor, represented by just a few cost type subcontracts. Thus, if the prime contractors are able to find a way to properly manage their few cost type subcontracts, they may reduce their overall exposure on any given program.

But what has history shown about the ability of a prime contractor to control its subcontractors and, thus, to minimize program risks? As two gentlemen with over 50 years of collective subcontract management experience point out:

> ...statistically, subcontracts invariably will overrun more, in percent, than the prime contract. Analysis of a selective sample of major defense contracts shows that work done in-house is more likely to be accomplished at the cost predicted than work done through subcontracts.[6]

In its broadest sense, the role of subcontract management includes the administration of all activity which goes outside of a firm for performance. Realistically, however, the activity should be focused on where the risks to the program lie:

> Subcontract management is primarily the management of cost-plus contracts. The principal characteristic of a cost-plus contract is that it provides for work that carries a substantial degree of risk. The risk results from an inability to define the requirement or from an effort involving very advanced technology. Were these risks not present, a no-risk, firm, fixed-price contract could and should have been used.[7]

Going one step beyond the cost type subcontracts, which would appear to represent the primary business risks associated with major procurements, these two experts further emphasized where they feel the heart of most subcontract problems will lie:

Although cost, schedule, and technical achievement are involved in sub-contract management, the principal problem is one of cost. This is not to minimize either delivery to schedule or achievement of the technical goals, but when one raises the subject of subcontract problems, he is usually talking about a cost overrun.[8]

If one were to take what these two seasoned experts in the field of subcontract management say literally, and there is no reason to dispute their positions, the primary risk associated with major subcontracting is a cost risk, resulting from a few cost type procurements. And with some understanding of the utility of a management concept which uses "earned value" to control subcontractor performance, can there be any doubt but that one of the most valuable tools available to any prime contractor's procurement organization would be in the selected application of C/SCSC on just a few of its critical subcontract buys, where the risk of cost performance remains with the prime contractor.

## Imposing C/SCSC on Subcontractors

The requirement for contractors to flow-down C/SCSC on purchases of a selected size is defined in DODI 7000.2, Appendix B to this book. The instruction further requires that prime contractors employ C/SCSC on those "critical" subcontractors, as agreed to between the government and prime contractor, on all but firm fixed price subcontracts. On the smaller subcontracts, which do not warrant the use of a full C/SCSC implementation, the requirement is to impose C/SSR type reporting, which will be covered below.[9]

Although the DOD requires prime contractors to impose C/SCSC on selected major subcontractors, the government must take care not to interfere with the prime/subcontractor relationship. In law there is a thing called "privity", which means there is a legal relationship between two bodies. Privity of contract exists between the government and the prime contractor, and between the prime contractor and its subcontractors. Privity of contract does *not* exist between the government and the subcontractors, and the government must take care to honor this relationship:

> The program manager, and all representatives of the program office, must respect the privity of the contracting relationship between the prime and subcontractor to ensure that the prime contractor remains responsible for the total system. If the program manager directs specific action by a subcontractor, the government may become responsible and the prime may be entitled to an equitable adjustment in the prime contract terms and conditions.[10]

The program manager described here refers to the government's program manager, generally called the SPO, System Program Office, in DOD program offices.

Within the defense establishment, there are two organizations whose role it is to monitor the procurement activities of the various military departments: the Defense Contract Audit

Agency, commonly referred to as DCAA, and the Contract Administration Offices, CAO, represented by the AFPRO, ARPRO, NAVPRO, etc. These groups have their own C/SCSC manual entitled *C/SCSC Joint Surveillance Guide*. In it, the requirement to use the criteria on selected purchases is also specified:

> **Surveillance of Subcontractors.** Subcontracts, excluding those that are firm-fixed-price, or fixed price with economic price adjustment, may be selected for C/SCSC application by mutual agreement between the prime contractor and the procuring activity based upon dollar value and/or criticality of the subcontract to which C/SCSC will be extended. Subcontracts selected should be identified in the prime contract.[11]

In earlier chapters the necessity for contractors to define all of their contractual effort with use of a Work Breakdown Structure-WBS was covered. This is an absolute requirement, whether the work is to be performed in-house by its own departments, or purchased outside from a subcontractor.

Returning once again to Military Standard 881 which defines the WBS requirement, there is the following statement:[12]

> The prime contractor shall be responsible for traceable summarization of subcontractor data supporting his prime contract WBS elements. The prime contractor may negotiate any WBS with a subcontractor that permits the prime contractor to fulfill his contract WBS requirements and which provides adequate control of the subcontractor.[12]

Thus, when the very first of the 35 criteria states that "all" of the work must be defined within the framework of the WBS, it means *all* of the work, including that which goes outside of the prime contractor's plant for performance.

All major subcontractors are expected to develop their own Subcontract WBS (SWBS), and it is important that all such subordinate WBSs be relatable to the prime contractor's WBS. This requirement is necessary in order for all cost data to be compatible on a given total military system. There are at least three approaches possible for subcontractors when preparing their SWBS:

1. Prepare a separate SWBS, independent of the prime contractor's WBS.
2. Take a single WBS element from the prime contractor's WBS and develop a full subcontractor SWBS, going down several levels from the single prime contractor WBS element.
3. Take the prime contractor's full WBS and select those elements from it in which the subcontractor has work, and develop a mini-tailored version of the prime contractor's WBS.

*Method #1* is likely not a viable approach. There is too much temptation for a subcontractor to innovate, to come up with a SWBS which is not compatible with the WBS of the prime contractor.

*Method #2* is generally acceptable, and is the easiest to administer for the prime contractor. The cost performance reports are easily assimilated into the cost reports of the prime contractor, as a single WBS entry. This approach works well when there are multiple subcontractors with C/SCSC or C/SSRs supporting a single prime contractor.

*Method #3* is an acceptable approach and is recommended when the subcontractor has a major portion of the prime contractor's effort. In this case the subcontractor takes the prime contractor's WBS and isolates those elements on the prime WBS in which it has effort. Under this approach the prime contractor can either assimilate the subcontractor's cost data into its own cost reports, or more likely, add the totals to a single prime WBS element, and include the subcontract WBS cost report as an addendum to the prime contractor cost report.

In a later chapter, the subject of validation of C/SCSC activities will be covered. If a major subcontractor is performing under a requirement for C/SCSC, it too must have an approved system or go through some type of a validation, either an initial demonstration review, or more likely a Subsequent Application Review to verify that it is properly using its earned value system on the new subcontract. The Joint Implementation Guide specifies who may perform these reviews:

> Subcontractor selection for application of the C/SCSC will be by agreement between the prime contractor and the Government. The prime contractor will contractually require the selected subcontractors to comply with the criteria. However, demonstrations and reviews of these selected subcontractor's management systems may be performed by the procuring authority when requested by either the prime or subcontractor.[13]

Thus, it is apparent from this language that a subcontractor's demonstration or SAR may be performed by any of four teams made up of:

1. A government team exclusively.
2. A government team, assisted by prime contractor personnel.
3. The prime contractor exclusively.
4. The prime contractor, assisted by government personnel.

Opinion: prime contractors should always insist on options 2 or 4; under no circumstances should a prime contractor ever allow option number #1 to be used, to have others do their vital work for them.

There is too much at stake, too much vital subcontractor information to be gained in the reviewing process, information which is vital to the long-term management of the prime/

subcontract relationship. While a subcontractor may rightfully take the position that certain of the information surfacing in a review is proprietary, particularly overhead rates if the prime and subcontractor are competitors on other programs, that type of subcontractor data may rightfully be withheld from prime contractor personnel and only be discussed with the government team members. However, most of the demonstration/SAR activity will focus on the planning and performance of direct costs (with overheads applied as a rate) and conformance to C/SCSC procedural matters. That type of data cannot be considered proprietary to the prime contractor.

There is a great deal of critical information to be gained from either an initial demonstration or SAR, and, therefore, the prime contractor must insist on its own personnel taking an active part of any review activity. The most appropriate makeup for reviewing teams are likely the joint government/prime contractor teams, options #2 or #4 above. And from the subcontractor's point of view, a review team which includes government personnel, but with prime contractor's personnel also participating, (#2 or #4 above) may be useful in other DOD or DOE work.

## Subcontractor C/SCSC Reporting

The full implementation of C/SCSC with a subcontractor must include the formal submittal of certain standardized reports, as a necessary part of the process. The full discussion of C/SCSC reports will be covered in a later chapter, and the review here will merely emphasize how these structured reports, plus certain other status reports coming from a subcontractor, may assist the prime contractor in the management of its subcontracts.

C/SCSC reports from selected subcontractors will allow the prime contractor to:

1. Receive the subcontractor's own monthly assessment of its cost/schedule status position.
2. Observe and forecast any adverse trends in subcontractor performance.
3. Be in a position to make an independent (from the subcontractor's position) estimate of what the final cost and schedule position is likely to be, based on performance to date.

Before discussing what type of data might be required from the subcontractor, it is important to stress the point that such data does not come free. There is a cost to prepare and submit reports and such costs—directly or indirectly—will be included in the price of the subcontract. Therefore, it is imperative that any "I'll take one of each" mentality in selecting such data be avoided. Only those reports which are needed for sound management reasons should be requested. The risk of doing without the data should be weighed against the costs and benefits of having the visibility, and, hopefully, a proper balance will be struck. The dollar value of certain procurements (C/SCSC thresholds) or the critical nature of certain buys will sometimes automatically dictate the reporting requirements for the prime contractor. Subcontractor reporting specifications are normally contained in a document titled an Subcontractor Data Requirements List (SDRL).

Three cost reports are typically an essential part of any C/SCSC implementation with a major subcontractor:

1. *Contract Funds Status Report (CFSR)*—Due quarterly on cost reimbursable contracts to forecast the funding requirements, normally, only those contracts over $500,000 in value.

2. *Cost Performance Report (CPR)* or the *Cost/Schedule Status Report (C/SSR)*—For any cost reimbursable contract in excess of $2 million in value and 12 months in duration, the C/SSR should be imposed, and any cost type subcontracts reaching the value of $40 million or more should require a full CPR. Critical subcontracts may lower the CPR thresholds to $25M.

3. *Contractor Cost Data Reporting (CCDR)* —Provides inputs to a DOD historical cost data base, and is useful to prime contractors when attempting to project future costs, e.g., costs of a planned production run. The CCDR is also useful to help maintain a competitive position between multiple subcontractors by providing comparative cost data. The CCDR normally applies to cost reimbursable contracts, but may also apply to fixed price efforts if the equipment is deemed critical to the prime contractor's total effort.

In addition to these cost/schedule reports, there are certain scheduling reports which should be considered on critical procurements:

4. *Subcontractor Schedules*—Sometimes these schedules will be represented by milestone schedules, included as a part of the subcontract document itself. Other times such schedules will be those which are used by the subcontractor in the normal course of its business. By merely requesting a copy of the subcontractor's "routine" schedules the costs associated with this requirement will be kept to a minimum.

5. *Network Schedules (PDM/ADM)*—Are useful when a cost reimbursable development subcontract calls for a series of complex tasks, and the final product is required by the prime contractor on a specific need date. Network schedules provide good visibility and are complementary to CPR or C/SSR reports.

6. *Line of Balance (LOB)*—Provides good visibility on equipment buys where large repetitive quantities are involved, and are useful on both cost type and fixed price subcontracts.

One of the most overlooked and under-used reports in the C/SCSC arsenal, one which can provide excellent cost/schedule status in a structured format and do so with a minimal impact on the supplier, is that of the "mini-CPR", the C/SSR-Cost/Schedule Status Report.

One major military command requires the submittal of the C/SSR reports at *seven* times the level as they receive a full CPR report. This command receives over 200 C/SSRs each month from their smaller suppliers.[14] By contrast, very few private contractors require C/SSR reporting, even though they often have cost type procurements representing millions of dollars. Why is there such a disparity between private contractors and the military?

The Cost Performance Report-CPR came into being along with the introduction of the criteria in the late 1960s. Many procurement personnel with private firms reviewed the criteria and the CPR at the time and decided, probably rightfully, that the imposition of these requirements on their small suppliers, even on cost type buys, would place an undue hardship on them. Some seven years later (1974) when the C/SSR was introduced, it went largely unnoticed by most buyers with these private firms.

The joint military guide which covers the C/SSR described its purpose:

> The Cost/Schedule Status Report (C/SSR) was established in 1974 to meet the needs of all managers within the Military Departments for cost and schedule information on non-major contracts in which the Government shares or assumes all of the cost risk.[15]

If one would substitute the words "prime contractor" for "Military Departments," the C/SSR might be considered useful even to a private contractor when it "assumes all of the cost risk," i.e., anytime a cost reimbursable type contract is used.

The C/SSR guide goes on to state:

> ...the C/SSR requirement does not establish any minimum requirements (standards) with respect to the contractor's management systems, nor does it involve, the evaluation, acceptance, or rejection of the contractors' internal management procedures, except where compliance with contractual provisions relative to the report is in question.[16]

Thus the C/SSR, which is used extensively by the military buyers, but rarely used within private industry, may well constitute an excellent device to increase visibility on selected minor procurements in which the prime contractor has assumed the cost risk on the activity, i.e, a cost type contract. The DOD imposes the C/SSR on all cost type contracts in excess of $2 million and over 12 months in duration, which would likely be an appropriate threshold for private firms as well.

Specific instructions for the preparation of the C/SSR are contained in DODI 7000.10, Appendix C to this book.

One issue which any prime contractor imposing either full C/SCSC or minimal C/SSR activity on a subcontractor must settle is that of who in the organization is best suited to act as cost account manager (CAM) for a given subcontract. Related issues are what are the responsibilities of the CAM, and whether one or multiple cost accounts will be used to represent a single subcontract effort.

With respect to the issue of a single versus multiple cost accounts used for a given subcontract, a *single* cost account is normally advisable. Unless a justification can be made, there does not appear to be any sound reason to separate a single subcontract into multiple cost accounts. The analysis of subcontractor data can become cumbersome when multiple cost accounts are used to represent a single subcontract.

Next is the issue of who in the organization is best equipped to act as cost account manager (CAM) for a given subcontract. A strong case can be made for any of the functions existing within a prime contractor organization: engineering, manufacturing, the program office, or procurement personnel. In an R & D type subcontract the use of an engineer is sometimes advisable, since most of the difficult problems will likely be technical in nature. Obviously, as a program matures into a production effort the use of a manufacturing person might make the ideal candidate. However, a strong argument can also be made for a procurement person to act as CAM since they must administer the subcontract anyway, and usually have the "ear" of subcontractor's management in their other dealings. The important point is that some one person be appointed and held responsible to act as CAM for all major subcontracts.

The responsibilities of a cost account manager (CAM) for a subcontract typically include the implementation and monitoring of C/SCSC performance at the subcontractor. During any validation reviews the CAM would likely play the major role in such activities, perhaps lead the reviewing team. As performance reports are received the CAM would take the lead in the analysis of such data. In any subcontractor status reviews this person would be in attendance.

In many cases, the procurement personnel with private firms will be unfamiliar with the Criteria, the CPR, CFSR, CCDR, and the C/SSR in particular. In such cases, it might be advisable for such private firms to consider some type of special training effort, similar to that used when they prepared for their initial C/SCSC validation review. Often there are experienced C/SCSC people within a company who could prepare specialized training sessions. Sometimes it might be advisable or necessary to go outside to one of the management consultant firms which specialize in such C/SCSC training.

## Conclusion

In the opening of this chapter certain frivolous remarks were made about typical buyers, their physical presence, and the demise of certain of their vital parts. Also, the statement was made that management could simply take an average buyer, give them C/SCSC, and make them into a super-star. Such statements should have been taken in the spirit in which they were given—complete nonsense. But there was one important message that was intended in all this triviality.

Coming to grips with the proper control of subcontractors, which now represents 50 to perhaps 80 percent of most prime contracts efforts, and perhaps an even higher percentage of the prime contractor's absolute cost risk exposure, is an important part of the process of prime contract management. The successful control of the subcontractor's performance is the collective result of several functions in the prime contractor's organization, but two people in particular are vital to the process: the prime contractor's program manager and its subcontract manager/buyer.

The program manager must set forth the policy, the direction, and the performance targets for all aspects of a given program, including that portion which goes outside for execution. The buyer must take this direction, define it in a way to be understood all participants, and monitor compliance as some other firm performs the contracted work.

The theme of this chapter has been that these two essential players (program manager and buyer), plus the implementation of C/SCSC to its proper level, will provide an awesome triad in the management of the largest segment of the prime contractor's work today: the "buy items."

In the next chapter we will continue the subject of "buy items," focusing on the other types of procurements: materials, and inter-divisional work. We will also cover the issue of earning earned value on the buy items.

---

## ENDNOTES

[1] Elbert Hubbard in *Plant Production Control,* by Charles A. Loepke, (New York, NY: John Wiley & Sons, Inc., 1941) page 104.

[2] Reprinted by permission of the publisher, from George Sammet, Jr., and Clifton G. Kelly, *Subcontract Management Handbook,* (New York, NY: AMACOM, a division of American Management Association, 1981), page 2.

[3] J. S. Baumgartner, "The Program Manager and Subcontractor: Hands On or Hands Off?" in *Systems Management,* edited by J. S. Baumgartner, (Washington, D.C.: The Bureau of National Affairs, Inc., 1979), page 160.

[4] Ibid, pages 162-163.

[5] Sammet and Kelly, *Subcontract Management Handbook* (New York, NY: AMACOM, 1981), page 11.

[6] Ibid, page 3.

[7] Ibid, page 1.

[8] Ibid, page 10.

[9] DODI 7000.2, paragraph D.3, page 2.

[10] Defense Systems Management College, *Program Manager's Notebook,* article by Paul O. Ballou, "Subcontract Management" (Fort Belvoir, VA: July,1985), page 6.2.8b.

[11] Department of Defense, C/SCSC Joint Survillance Guide, October, 1984, page 2-5.

[12] Military Standard 881AA, 1975, paragraph 5.5.6, page 15.

[13] Department of Defense, Cost/Schedule Control Systems Criteria-Joint Implementation Guide, October, 1987, Appendix A-1.

[14] Interview with Daniel Schild, Chief of the Cost Management Systems Division, United States Air Force Aeronautical Systems Division (Wright-Patterson Air Force Base, OH: July, 1982).

[15] Department of Defense, Cost/Schedule Managment of Non-Major Contracts-Joint Guide, 1978, page 3.

[16] Ibid, page 3.

# 13

# The "Buy Items" – Part II:
## Materials and Interdivisional

In the last chapter we reviewed one aspect of those items to be bought from the outside—major subcontracts. Major subcontracts, because of their sheer relative size, will receive much attention from the various functional components of the prime contractor organization. Major subcontracts, in a sense, sort of take care of themselves. Many people in the organization will concern themselves with the "care and feeding" of major subcontractors.

But the other side to the procurement picture is the efficient buying of those hundreds or thousands of items which are also a critical part of the overall process of producing the "item" the customer has contracted to receive from *you*. These are the items which, because of their large quantities and relatively small values, can get "lost" in the hustle of daily business.

This chapter will focus on the other part of the buy items: materials and interdivisional work.

## C/SCSC and the Contractor Procurement System

It is doubtful if there is any single issue which has given the people implementing C/SCSC more headaches or difficulty than that of materials. Many a contractor has failed to pass its initial validation review because it could not demonstrate an ability to comply with the material accounting requirements as specified in the criteria. At least one contractor lost its existing validation because of material problems. With anything as straightforward as the buying of a few parts, why should it be so tough to account for materials under C/SCSC? In order to answer this question, one must step back and compare the requirements imposed by C/SCSC with the normal way a contractor manages its material activity. Perhaps the answer will be obvious.

Under a typical contractor procurement system, management will normally set three primary objectives for such activities:

1. To accommodate the efficient purchase of the required buy items, with consideration of both the short-term needs (getting the best price) and long-term needs (the development of a supplier base which provides adequate but fair competition between suppliers).
2. The availability of all required parts in the time-frame needed to support an efficient manufacturing operation.
3. The compliance with governmental regulations dealing with procurement matters, which typically manifests itself in what is called a "CPSR," a Contractor Procurement System Review.

The very first thing one must recognize is the satisfaction of the above three goals of providing for an efficient contractor procurement system has little, perhaps *nothing,* to do with satisfying the C/SCS criteria dealing with materials. The C/SCS Criteria impose requirements generally beyond those needed to provide for an efficient contractor procurement system. The criteria on materials impose requirements beyond those needed to provide an effective contractor procurement activity. Harsh but true realities.

The subject of an effective and efficient contractor procurement activity is beyond the scope of this book. Therefore, all of what follows will address the more focused issue of how contractors satisfy the C/SCS Criteria dealing with the subject of materials—not an insignificant issue, in and of itself.

## The Material Accounting Criterion

Most of the criteria issues which have been discussed up to this point have related to labor, with is associated indirect burdens. This is quite natural since at the time the criteria were conceived in the mid-1960s, labor was "the" big cost driver. But, as was mentioned in the last chapter, since that time contractors for a host of reasons began to "buy" progressively greater portions of the end products than they had previously been "making" with their own people. While many of the criteria issues which relate to labor also apply to material, there is one which specifically addresses the subject of material, and accounting for materials.

We should again study Criterion III, #7 to fully understand its impact on a contractor:

The contractor's material accounting system will provide for:

(a) Accurate cost accumulation and assignment of costs to cost accounts in a manner consistent with the budgets using recognized, acceptable costing techniques.

(b) Determination of price variances by comparing planned versus actual commitments.

(c) Cost performance measurement at the point in time most suitable for the category of material involved, but no earlier than the time of actual receipt of material.

(**d**) Determination of cost variances attributable to the excess usage of material.

(**e**) Determination of unit or lot costs when applicable.

(**f**) Full accountability for all material purchased for the contract, including residual inventory.[1]

This criterion, addressing material accounting, has thus laid down six very precise requirements on a contractor wishing to comply:

1. That its material cost actuals (ACWP) must equate to its material plans (BCWS), and do so down at the *cost account* level.
2. Material price variances must be determinable by comparing planned commitments (estimated material value) to actual commitments (actual cost of the material).
3. Physical work progress or earned value (BCWP) must be determinable, but *not* before the materials have been received by a contractor.
4. Usage cost variances must be determinable from excess material usage.
5. Material unit costs and/or lot costs must be determinable, as applicable.
6. There must be full accountably of all materials bought, including any residual material inventory.

Most firms attempting to satisfy their material requirements in an efficient manner will typically focus on only two areas:

1. *The Material Plans* (BCWS), which frequently starts at the point at which engineering or manufacturing or others have provided a definition sufficient to initiate an order for the items, regardless of when such items are actually ordered or received.
2. *The Material Actuals* (ACWP), which is ordinarily the point at which the costs of the parts are recorded on the firm's accounting books, i.e., when the bill is paid.

Those firms which have a material commitment system in use are usually able to establish and update the estimated liability for their purchased goods at multiple points: at the point at which engineering or manufacturing defines the requirement, where someone initiates the request, updated to an accrued liability when an order is placed by purchasing, later updated to an actual liability when parts are received and accepted, and finally updated when the bill is paid and the costs recorded on the accounting books. While a material commitment system will show the relationship of the plan with actuals at the point at which orders for parts are initiated and processed, such systems ordinarily do *not* meet the specific language of the material accounting criterion. Under C/SCSC requirements, a third reference point must also be incorporated into the above two areas of focus:

3. *The Material "Earned Value," or physical performance, or BCWP, Budgeted Costs for Work Performed.*

With the addition of this third dimension, the BCWP, the work of those attempting to manage an effective procurement system has increased significantly.

The criteria themselves do not directly specify the requirement for the synchronization of BCWS/ACWP/BCWP in the same reporting month. But the DOD's Joint Implementation Guide is quite clear on what it requires for the earned value measurement of materials:

> 10. Material BCWS and BCWP are intended to permit measurement of events which reflect progress in contract performance, not for measurement of administrative or financial events (e.g., booking of actual costs or invoice payment). Therefore, BCWS should normally be scheduled in accordance with a contract event and BCWP should be earned when the event occurs.
>
> **(a)** To avoid distortion, actuals should be recorded when BCWP is earned. In situations where BCWP is earned and the invoice has not been paid, estimated actual cost may be incorporated into ACWP from purchase order information.
>
> **(b)** Administrative or financial events may be used as indicators for contract events when such indicators occur in the same reporting period as the contract events. However, it is not generally acceptable to use administrative or financial events as indicators when they would depict performance past the actual material use or need dates.[2]

This criterion (and related interpretations) tells a contractor what it must do, and also what it must not do, regardless of the contractors other requirements of providing an efficient procurement system. For example, while all contractors will want to monitor the systematic flow of their materials to meet the criteria, they cannot measure performance until the materials have been physically received. Thus, the point which creates a material accrued liability, the material commitment, is immediately eliminated as an option to plan and measure BCWP, since that point is *prior* to physical receipt of materials.

The criterion also requires that budgets (BCWS) and cost accumulation (ACWP) be consistent, which is easy, by and of itself. It also requires that price variations be isolated between BCWS and ACWP, which adds a further complexity. But the real difficulty comes with the full accountability requirement, the setting of both unit and lot costs, and the isolation of any residual inventory purchased under the contract. These are no small tasks, for now such factors as handling attrition, machine scrappage, and surplus inventory must all be considered in the full accounting for all materials.

The distinction between what is required in the prior accounting criterion and what is required under this material criterion is important. In criterion #6 of the accounting group, the contractor is required to identify the type of costs associated with each unit and each lot, by major category of costs involved. This means that costs must be isolated by: (1) labor costs, (2) material costs, and (3) other direct costs. The material accounting criterion

7 further requires that all material costs for production or recurring work be identified by unit and lot, to demonstrate in detail what is contained in the "material" category, by unit and by lot. In other words the contractor must:

> ...identify the number of units of each type of material that went into each unit on a given contract. Instead of just requiring the identification of that part of the unit cost which was due to materials, this standard requires a tabulation identification capability of the contractor's accounting system, to tell which materials were used in each end item produced, and how many units of each type of material was used per end item.[3]

And if this does not present enough of a challenge for any mortal contractor, they must further account for *all* materials purchased under a contract, including any residual material inventory. The contractor's material accounting system must be able to:

> ...reflect the acquisition, issue to cost accounts, return of unused materials from cost accounts, scrap quantity and disposition, and residual material inventory.[4]

This single criterion covering material accounting thus laid out requirements which taxed contractor systems to their fullest.

## Material Control Points

In order to properly analyze the subject of materials, one might want to examine the various points in the acquisition process at which materials can be monitored, from the point where they are first defined, until they are consumed into the final end-item for delivery to the customer.

Shown in Figure 13-1 are twelve control points at which materials may be tracked by a contractor. Admittedly, the distinction between some of these points may seem quite fine, but each may be used as a discrete point of reference. Points 1 through 6 are classified as the "cost control phase." These points are significant because here "earned value" may *not* be measured by a contractor. Points 7 through 12 are referred to as the "applied direct cost phase," the points at which "earned value" may take place on materials.

A typical contractor planning a material procurement system, without considering C/SCSC requirements, would likely focus most of its plans on points 1 through 6, from the point where materials are first defined, until an order has been placed with a supplier. Not only are these the natural points for the setting of the procurement plans, but they are the points where contractors may exert some *control* over the costs of their buy items. But while points 1 through 6 are natural for purposes of planning and of controlling costs, they are *not* allowed to be considered in a C/SCSC earned value approach. Reason: in C/SCSC material performance may not be measured any earlier than "receipt of materials."

## MATERIAL CONTROL POINTS

### Cost Control Phase

| *Activity* | *Organization* |
|---|---|
| 1. Define the requirements. | 1. Design engineering: issue a Bill of Materials. |
| 2. Request to purchase. | 2. User department: initiate a Purchase Requisition. |
| 3. Management authorization to buy. | 3. User functional manager: sign Purchase Requisition. |
| 4. Price quotes obtained. | 4. Purchasing department. |
| 5. Negotiate a price. | 5. Purchasing department. |
| 6. Issue an order to buy. | 6. Purchasing department. |

### Applied Direct Cost (Earned Value) Phase

| | |
|---|---|
| 7. Materials received. | 7. Receiving department. |
| 8. Materials inspected/approved; or rejected/returned. | 8. Quality inspection. |
| 9a. Materials put in stockroom. *or* | 9a. Inventory control. |
| 9b. Materials placed on line. | 9b. Inventory control. |
| 10. Invoice paid. | 10. Accounting. |
| 11. Stockroom materials issued. | 11. Inventory control. |
| 12. Materials consumed in article. | 12 Manufacturing. |

**Figure 13-1 Material Control Points**

Thus what might be best for contractors in the management of their procurement activities does not necessarily comply with the material criterion, which requires firms to measure the acquisition of parts, the placement of planning (BCWS), the recording of cost actuals (ACWP), and the measurement of work performance (BCWP) in a consistent manner, and all in the same reporting period. In order to comply with the criteria, firms must also focus their procurement activities in the "applied direct cost phase," points 7 through 12 in Figure 13-1.

Additionally, the most natural point for the tracking of cost actuals (ACWP) is point 10, when the bills are actually paid and costs recorded in the accounting ledgers. Commercial firms in particular have always been concerned with their cash flow. But to satisfy the criteria, the ACWP must often be adjusted to the left or to the right so as to coincide with the BCWS and BCWP.

To further complicate the matter, as anyone involved in scheduling knows only too well, when commercial firms have to address the issue of having all parts available to support the production lines, they will generally focus on item 7, when the materials are physically received. For purposes of schedule management, point 7 has primary significance. Scheduling is one of those activities in a contractor's total management control system which has to be "integrated" into one system.

In short, many firms had to create a new or substantially modified material accounting system in order to comply with the criteria. Meeting these requirements shifted the contractor's primary focus from the "cost control phase" to the "applied direct cost phase." Not all firms understood that fact initially, and it took the harsh lessons of a failed C/SCSC demonstration review to cause some to eventually modify their material accounting systems to meet the criteria.

## Material Categories

To further examine and analyze the broad subject of materials, it should be recognized that materials are not a homogeneous category. Rather, there are a variety of material types, each with a peculiar set of characteristics, all of which must be considered when attempting to satisfy the materials criteria. Shown in Figure 13-2 is a display which attempts to place the various material types into five broad category groupings, which are summarized as follows:

*Category I: Production Materials*—Which are relatively low-value items, but large in quantity. These items are generally stored in open bin areas, and will typically represent perhaps 80% of the total parts in the deliverable end-item, but perhaps only 20% of the bill of material costs. These items are usually bought on a firm fixed-price arrangement.

*Category II: Subcontracted Purchases*—These are items of a relatively higher value, and are more complex in design. They are often bought from a contractor's design or product specification, and frequently tailored to such specifications. These items typically represent 80% of the costs of the bill of materials, but perhaps only 20% of the required part numbers. Because these parts can be definable in precise terms, they are usually bought on a firm fixed price basis. These items will be stored in controlled stock room areas and disbursed to work in process on demand orders from the shop.

## MATERIAL CATEGORIES

I. **Production Materials**—(low-value/shelf items/open bin storage)

(80% of the parts/20% of the costs)
—Metallic raw stock
—Purchased shelf parts (fasteners/bearings/etc.)
—Non-metallic (composites material)
—Tooling materials (NR) (for in-house & outside buys)
—Shipping materials

II. **Subcontracted Purchases**—(FFP/high-value/controlled storage)

(20% of the parts/80% of the costs;end-item specific)
—Castings, forgings, extrusions
—Tooling items (NR) (built per product specification)
—Major parts or assemblies
—Electrical/electronic components
—Diverted planned manufacturing

III. **Non-production Purchased Items**

—Purchased labor
—Time and material
—Engineering or manufacturing R & D materials (NR)
—Vendor services (NR) (e.g., qualification testing)

IV. **Major Subcontracts** (Cost type with full C/SCSC or C/SSR)

V. **Interdivisional Work/Procurements**

---

**Figure 13-2  Categories of Materials**

*Category III: Non-Production Purchased Items*—These make up the "all other" category of materials. They are such items as purchased labor, contracts for time and material support, non-recurring engineering or non-recurring manufacturing materials, vendor services for such items as qualification testing, and so forth.

*Category IV: Major Subcontractors*—Of a "cost reimbursable" type, in which full C/SCSC or lesser C/SSR is flowed downward to the subcontractor. (This subject was covered in the last chapter.) Because of the magnitude of each of these few major subcontractors, they will normally receive adequate attention from the prime contractor and the buying customer.

*Category V: Interdivisional Work/Procurements*—Represent those items which a given prime contractor will buy from other divisions of the same company.

The grouping of these various material types into five separate categories will be useful when we later cover the subject of how contractors measure the earned value of their materials.

## Material Variances: Price and Usage

One of the requirements of the C/SCSC material accounting criterion which is generally consistent with that of normal procurement practices is the matter of determining just why material budgets are exceeded, called variance analysis. When the actual costs exceed a material budget the fault can normally be traced to two causes:

1. The articles purchased cost more than was planned, called a "price variance."
2. More articles were consumed than were planned, called a "usage variance."

When material budgets are exceeded, typically, some combination of these two has happened.

Price variances (PV) occur when the budgeted price value (BCWS) of the material items was different than what is actually experienced (ACWP). This condition can arise for a host of reasons: poor initial estimates, inflation, different materials used than were planned, too little money available to budget, and so on.

The formula for price variances (PV) is:

$$PV = (\text{Budgeted Price - Actual Price}) \times (\text{Actual Quantity})$$

Price Variance is the difference between the budgeted cost for the bill of materials, and the price paid for the bill of materials.[5]

By contrast, usage variances (UV) happen when a greater quantity of materials are consumed than were planned. The formula for usage variances (UV) is:

$$UV = (\text{Budget Quantity - Actual Quantity}) \times (\text{Budgeted Price})$$

Normally, usage variances are the resultant costs of materials used over and above the quantity called for in the bill of materials.[6]

Perhaps a specific example will best illustrate the differences between a price variance (PV) and a usage variance (UV).[7]

Condition: the material budget (BCWS) was set at $1,000, and the material actuals (ACWP) came in at $1,320, or $320 over budget. What happened?

The budget (BCWS) was established as follows: 100 articles (including attrition) times $10 per item, resulting in a budget of $1,000. Actual costs (ACWP) showed an actual price paid for the materials of $12 per unit, and a total of 110 items consumed.

Taking the formula from the previous page we can determine that the following variances occurred:

$$Price\ Variance\ (PV) = (BCWS\ price - ACWP\ price) \times Actual\ Quantity;$$
$$PV = (\$10 - \$12 = -\$2) \times 110$$
$$PV = -\$2 \times 110$$
$$PV = -\$220$$

$$Usage\ Variance\ (UV) = (BCWS\ Qty - ACWP\ Qty) \times BCWS\ Price;$$
$$UV = (100 - 110 = -10) \times \$10$$
$$UV = -10 \times \$10$$
$$UV = -\$100$$

Thus, we have determined that the material budget (BCWS) versus material actual costs (ACWP) variance of -$320 was caused by a combination Price Variance of -$220, and Usage Variance of -$100.

Good business practices would dictate that such variance analyses take place, to determine why the actual material costs exceeded the authorized budget values.

## Interdivisional Work

The last category to be discussed under the broad subject of the buy-items is that of "interdivisional work." This effort is sometimes referred to as "IDWA," and defined by one segment of the Department of Defense as:

> Interdivisional Work Authorization (IDWA) is any portion of a contract... which is performed by any segment of the same corporation other than the segment having overall responsibility for management of the prime contract.[8]

Interdivisional work presents a dichotomy of issues and perceptions to a prime contractor.

First off, just what is interdivisional work: is it a "make" or is it a "buy" item? Answer: it is both, depending on who you talk to.

From a prime contractor's perception, interdivisional work generally represents a "buy item". It is work which someone other than "our division" is to perform. The fact that it is being done by another unit of the same company has little bearing. It is work to be performed by an outside organization. The formal process of using a "make or buy" committee must usually pass judgement on the outside purchase of articles, even those purchased from another sister division.

And yet, when the work is to begin, the very same person who might have made the deliberate make or buy decision to send the work "outside" of their shop for performance wants to pick up the phone and call his old buddy at the other division and say: "Hey Jack,

I've got a little job for you to do." Why bother with all those things called terms and conditions needed to buy something from the outside: "We're all part of the same family."

When things go *right* at the performing sister division—as they sometimes do—that division wants its fair share of the prime division's profits. After all it did perform the job in a responsible way, as any other outside subcontractor would have performed that same work. This will cause a little internal discussion because IDWA tasks do not create additional profit in the prime contract. Any fee which might flow to the performing sister division represents a reduction in fee to the prime contractor division. However, when things go *wrong*—as they sometimes do—with cost overruns, schedule slips, poor workmanship, and such, that same performing sister division wants now to be treated, not as an "arms-length" outside subcontractor, but as a part of "our big family."

From the buying customer's perspective, the United States Government, interdivisional work is viewed a little differently:

> IDWAs are "Prime Work" and Government has privity to directly require contractor management control/ visibility.[9]

Thus while the government is generally careful to respect the "privity of contract" issue and not deal directly with a prime contractor's subcontractors, they have no such reluctance in dealing directly with a performing sister division. After all, "it's all one company" from the government's perspective, and all entities of the corporation are subject to the terms and conditions contained in the prime contract.

But while the government considers interdivisional work to be part of one prime contract effort, they also expect that such tasks be handled in a formal procedural way, and treated as if they were an outside buy:

> The contractor is expected to manage intra-company transactions the same as subcontracts relative to performance, schedule and cost, and maintain visibility commensurate with complexity or cost of work transferred.[10]

Interdivisional work is often handled differently by various companies in the same industry. Some firms treat IDWA as strictly a buy item, and the same organization and people who are responsible for the procurement of other items are also charged with the management of IDWA. This would seem to be a logical approach, because after all the debate and philosophical discussion ends, interdivisional work is really a buy item to the prime contractor. The same personnel who procure other articles would seem to be in the best position to also manage IDWA.

But other approaches work well also. Some firms charge their program offices, or their contracts departments with the task of managing IDWA. Others treat IDWA essentially as a make item, and such work is managed by the functional department transferring the tasks/work to the sister division: engineering to engineering, manufacturing to manufacturing. The dichotomy of interdivisional work goes on and on.

## Measuring the Earned Value of Materials

This chapter has addressed the subject of materials and has progressively divided it into elements in order to best deal with the question: how should contractors measure the earned value (BCWP) of their materials? One of the quickest ways to understand how best to accomplish an unfamiliar task is to find out what others in the industry have done or are doing to accomplish the same chore. In other words, survey what other companies are doing.

Displayed in Figure 13-3 are the results of a survey of six major contractor organizations, each having a separately approved C/SCSC activity. Note that Contractor "A" has three autonomous operating divisions (A-1, A-2, A-3), each with its own approved C/SCSC management control system. Note also that all of these organizations have placed their material cost accounts into the three conventional classifications of "discrete"; "apportioned"; and "level of effort" activity.

All six of these organizations use discrete material cost accounts to plan and measure the earned value on what each classifies as "high value" items. What will constitute a "high-value" versus a "low-value" item will likely be different at various organizations, depending on the circumstances and thresholds set at each firm.

By contrast, only two of the six organizations use a manager's "percent completion" estimate to set a value on their lower valued discretely measured cost accounts. This is somewhat surprising, since the "percent completion" estimating method is considered by some to be one of the more viable approaches to plan and measure earned value on material items. Some even suggest that all contractors designing a new C/SCSC material system consider incorporating this method in their C/SCSC systems description, to provide flexibility in handling difficult material categories.

Four of the six firms use an "apportioned" type material cost account to relate performance based on what is accomplished on another activity. The related base cost account is generally a labor or another high value material item. Finally, five of six organizations set performance of low value material items using a "level of effort" method.

What conclusions can be drawn from this survey of material earned value techniques actually used in the industry? Probably the message is similar to that which was discussed in Chapter 11, which covered earned value methods on labor type activities. Each firm should plan to tailor its own system, based on the peculiar circumstances which exist at that firm. There are no absolute patterns which can or should be followed. Each company should make its own assessment of its peculiar requirements and create a system which best satisfies those needs. As indicated in the survey findings in Figure 13-3, companies are given considerable latitude by the government to satisfy their own unique requirements, but while still complying with the intent of the criteria.

One of the most important considerations in placing the BCWP on material cost accounts is determining the proper time frame for such activities. On those tasks which are of a non-recurring nature, e.g., engineering design, the timing is usually determined by following the master program schedule, assuming that it contains sufficient detail. Certain ground-rules can be applied to placing the BCWP on non-recurring tasks, for example:

## EARNED VALUE METHODS

| Technique | Contractor | | | | | |
|---|---|---|---|---|---|---|
| | A-1 | A-2 | A-3 | B | C | D |
| 1. Discretely Measured: Milestones (High-Value Items) | Yes | Yes | Yes | Yes | Yes | Yes |
| 2. Discretely Measured: Percent Completion (Low-Value Items) | No | No | No | Yes | No | Yes |
| 3. Apportioned to Discrete Effort | Yes | Yes | Yes | No | No | Yes |
| 4. Level of Effort-LOE | Yes | Yes | No | Yes | Yes | Yes |

**Figure 13-3 Survey of "Material" Earned Value Methods**

1. *Engineering Design*—Placed at the point of planned drawing delivery and approval.
2. *Testing Services*—Placed as a function of planned test report acceptance.
3. *Special Tooling*—Placed at planned acceptance of tools.
4. *SDRL Items*—Placed at planned receipt and approval of data items.
5. *Technical Services*—Earned as a result of discrete milestone accomplishment, or completion of short span tasks, or as a part of other labor account accomplishment.[11]

For activities of the recurring type, one usually needs some type of a manufacturing build schedule, which is referred to by various names in industry, such as manufacturing set-back schedule, factory water-fall chart, and so on.

Shown in Figure 13-4 is a display of what we will refer to as a "Manufacturing Build Schedule." This type of display is critical to the setting of the proper time frame on production articles. Working backwards from a delivery date, the manufacturing phase is typically divided into a fabrication phase and an assembly phase. As a further division, the assembly period is often further separated into a "sub-assembly" and a "final assembly" span. In a recurring type effort, each material item is carefully planned to be available to support the production work specified in the manufacturing build schedule. Raw materials must be available in the proper quantities to support the fabrication phase, components and fasteners must be available to support the assembly work, and so forth.

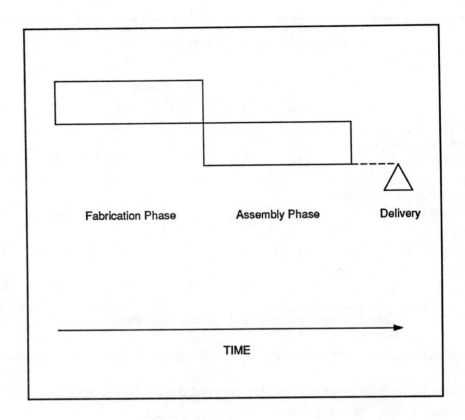

**Figure 13-4 Manufacturing Build Schedule**

Shown earlier in Figure 13-1 the flow of materials was separated into 12 discrete pieces, called "material control points." Also displayed in this figure in the far right column are the organizations or functions which generally are responsible for these 12 material control points. Points 1 through 6 are typically used to plan and to control procurement costs, but do not satisfy the requirements of the material accounting criterion because earned value cannot be taken earlier than physical receipt of materials. That leaves points 7 through 12 in which to measure earned value. But it does more than that. It can also be used to *eliminate* certain organizational functions from being in a position to plan and to measure physical performance (BCWP) on materials.

Generally, there are six functions which are primarily involved with the processing of materials in any contractor organization:

1. Those who define the requirements—engineering.
2. Those who buy the items—purchasing/material.
3. Those who accept/approve the items—quality control.

4. Those who pay the bill—accounting/finance.
5. Those who store the items—inventory control.
6. Those who consume the items—manufacturing.

Surprising perhaps, is the fact that the "one" organization which is most often thought of as being responsible for materials in any firm, those who buy the material items, usually called purchasing or materials or procurement, are *not* in a good position to plan and measure the earned value (BCWP) of the very materials they buy. Why? Because their effort occurs prior to the receipt of the materials, control point 7, the earliest point at which BCWP can be measured.

Generally, those functions which are in the best position to plan and set the earned value on materials are the groups which store the items as a part of the work-in-process management, usually called "inventory control," and/or those who actually consume the materials, e.g., "manufacturing." Most firms rely on these two functions to plan and set the BCWP for material items on their contracts. These two functions are in the best position to satisfy the criterion which requires that material BCWP be based on "physical progress," not on what the government calls an "administrative/financial" event. These two functions also are in a good position to be assigned the task of being "Cost Account Manager" (CAP) for this group of material buy items.

Progress payments represent a constant source of confusion on the subject of earned value (BCWP) measurement of material items. Progress payments are often included as a part of a firm fixed-price contractual arrangement, whereby the buyer authorizes the release of funds to a supplier based on some pre-determined schedule, often time phased over the duration of contract period. Progress payments *per se*, by themselves, do not represent physical work accomplishment, and therefore, may *not* be used to set the earned value (BCWP) on buy items.

Having said that, some words of qualification are needed. If progress payments are made to a supplier for the sole purpose of assisting the supplier with its cash flow, they would not qualify as physical work accomplishment, and could not be used to set earned value. If however, progress payments were tied to specific planned physical work accomplishment, such as is the common practice in the construction industry, and such progress were measurable, then it could serve as physical work realization, and could be used to set the BCWP for the effort.

Perhaps the best way to fully cover this complex subject is to take the display of Figure 13-2, which grouped the broad subject of materials into five distinct categories, and discuss how best to plan and determine earned value for each of these material categories.

*Category I: Production Materials*—Generally represents perhaps 80% of the total parts to be used in the end-items. But because these are relatively low value items, they will not usually be controlled by individual part number. These are the raw material stock items, the fasteners, washers, lubricants, and such. One of the more critical issues concerning the management of these items is the *availability* of such parts to support the smooth flow of the manufacturing cycle.

These items are usually bought and disbursed to the shop floor to support the manufacturing plans as defined in the build schedule, illustrated by Figure 13-4. Raw metallic stock will support the fabrication phase, and fasteners, washers, etc., will support the assembly phases. Historical company experience will determine the appropriate setback from the planned delivery date.

Contractors usually plan for the earned value to occur using one of three distinct methods: (1) "apportioned" to some labor cost account or major material item cost account; (2) as a "percent completion estimate" determined from a shop manager; or (3) simply as a "level of effort" cost account, over the particular manufacturing phase.

*Category II: Subcontracted Purchases*—These are the items which, because of their individual higher value, will be tightly controlled and only disbursed to the shop floor when it is ready to consume the item. These items will include high-value metallic raw materials, expensive composite materials, part assemblies in various forms, components made to a specification, castings and forgings—anything which is of sufficient value to warrant individual control.

These material items are typically "discretely" measured based on either disbursements from a controlled stock room, or at the estimated point of incorporation into the deliverable end-item.

*Category III: Non-Production Items*—Includes a wide array of items from purchased labor, to time and material contracts, to qualification testing contracts, engineering materials, manufacturing R & D materials, and so forth. These items more closely resemble the category of "Other Direct Cost" items than materials, but because they are purchased from the outside they are generally classified with materials.

Earned value for purchased labor is most often included as a part of the labor of the functional department receiving the labor support; that is, whatever method the organization using the purchased labor uses to measure its BCWP will be used to also measure performance of the purchased labor. Purchased labor is considered to be a part of the department's labor base which uses the support.

Both engineering materials and manufacturing R & D materials are a form of nonrecurring activity which can be set in place based on the program master schedule and BCWP earned by either using a manager's "percent completion estimate," or simply "apportioned" against the labor cost account which consumes such materials.

Contracts for such things as qualification testing can be "discretely" measured based on the dates contained in the program master schedules. But the setting of the BCWS in accordance with the master schedules, versus the earning of BCWP can be a little tricky in practice. The BCWP for a qualification test will normally take place only when the "Qualification Test Plan" has received final approval. The test could take place in say January as planned (BCWS), and actual costs (ACWP) recorded in the same period, but because of some minor wording disagreement in the final test document, the plan itself may not be approved for several months. Thus the BCWP may not hit the records until months after the BCWS and ACWP were recorded, showing both a negative cost and a negative schedule variance for several months until the BCWP is recorded.

*Category IV: Major Subcontracts*—Of a cost type of sufficient size to warrant the flow-down of either a full Cost Performance Report (CPR) or a more limited Cost/Schedule Status Report (C/SSR). The subcontractor sets its own earned value based on its approved C/SCSC management control system. The values reported in the CPR or C/SSR are simply appended or integrated into the prime contractor's CPR for submittal to the government.

*Category V: Interdivisional Work/Procurements*—Those items which are purchased from a sister division are placed into one of two categories based on whether or not the sister division has its own approved C/SCSC activity. In those cases where the other division has an approved C/SCSC activity, the performing division is asked to measure the BCWP of its effort in conformance with its system.

In those cases where the performing division has no approved C/SCSC activity, then the items purchased must be placed into one of the first three categories listed above, (Category I, II, III) and earned value set as with any of these material types.

## Conclusions

From this examination of the very broad and complex subject of materials, one conclusion should be obvious: each company wishing to comply with the criteria must tailor its own material system to accommodate the C/SCSC. It is appropriate to look around and see what others have done to satisfy the criteria. But what has worked for someone else does not necessarily mean that it will work for another firm. Each firm has its own unique requirements and circumstances, and it is this uniqueness which must be considered when formulating the system to satisfy the criteria.

It should have also been apparent from the above discussion that there is very little relationship between what is required to provide for an efficient contractor procurement system, and the satisfaction of those criteria which impact materials.

Another important fact to understand is that those organizations and individuals who purchase the materials are *not* the ones who likely should be charged with the task of planning for the BCWS and later determining the BCWP. These tasks are best performed by those functions which control a contractor's work-in-process. Typically, the material planning or inventory control or manufacturing departments can best handle these C/SCSC tasks on material categories, major subcontracts excluded.

The final point to be made is that in order to satisfy the criteria, all of the issues which deal with the "buy items" and have been discussed in these past two chapters must be documented in some fashion, in either the internal company procedures or in a separate document called a C/SCSC systems description. These are a critical part of the process of getting a company's management control system "validated," which is the subject of our next chapter.

---

## ENDNOTES

[1] DODI 7000.2, June 10, 1977.

[2] Department of Defense, *Cost/Schedule Control Systems Criteria—Joint Implementation Guide*, October, 1987, page 3-13.

[3] Thomas J. Bowman, USAF, "Interpretive Key To C/SCSC Joint Implementation Guide Checklist", from *Cost Schedule Control Systems Criterial Reference Manual* (Wright-Patterson AFB, OH: Air Force Institue of Technology, April, 1982) page 334.

[4] Bowman, page 334.

[5] Bowman, page 332.

[6] Bowman, page 333.

[7] Illustration provided by Humphreys & Associates, Inc., *Z-Best Company: Model System Description for Full C/SCSC Applications,* July 16, 1986, section 9.3.4.

[8] Department of the Air Force (AFCMD Regulation 70-31) *Management of Interdivisional Work Authorizations* (IDWAs) (Headquarters, Air Force Contract Management Division, Kirkland AFB, NM: March 13) 1981 page 1.

[9] AFCMD 70-31.

[10] AFCMD 70-31.

[11] List provided by Mr. William J. Schmidt, Northrop Corporation, Aircraft Division.

# 14

# The Validation Process: Demonstration and Documentation

An expression used in the legal community seems to fit nicely with our next subject. The expression is "condition precedent." In very simple terms, a condition precedent is something that must happen before a second something can take place. Up to this point the discussion has focused on the implementation of a C/SCSC compliant management control system. However, before the C/SCSC can be considered fully operational, there is something which must happen beforehand. That something is validation. The proposed C/SCSC management control system must be validated or verified by the customer before earned value measurement and Cost Performance Reporting can have any meaning. Hence, the process of customer validation should be viewed as a condition precedent to a contractor having an operational C/SCSC management control system.

## The Validation Process: "Company is Coming"!

When you win a contract requiring compliance with the criteria you get many visits from people you hitherfore did not know existed. They are the C/SCSC specialists whose job is to verify that you are employing a management control system which satisfies the criteria. If you like having company and visits from strangers, you're going to love the validation process.

In this chapter we will be using the term "review" to describe a multitude of processes. In order to avoid confusion, it might be useful if we define the various types of customer "reviews" that can and will take place, all associated with the overall C/SCSC validation of your management control system.

1. *Demonstration Review (DR)*—The formal review of a contractor's management control system to determine whether or not it satisfies the requirements of the 35 C/SCS Criteria.

2. *Subsequent Application Review (SAR)*—A visit by government personnel (and/or prime contractor and/or both) to a contractor's facility to determine whether the contractor has properly applied the management control system which had been previously accepted as meeting the requirements of C/SCSC, to a *new contract*.

3. *Extended Subsequent Application Review (ESAR)*—A formal review performed in lieu of a full C/SCSC demonstration review when contractor conditions have changed: (1)when programs transcend from *one phase to another* (e.g., R & D into production); (2)when contractors move programs from *one facility to another;* (3)when contractors make significant *changes to their C/SCSC systems description*.

4. *Baseline Review*—A customer review conducted to determine with a limited sampling that a contractor is continuing to use the previously accepted performance system and is properly implementing a baseline on the contract or option under review. A baseline review is particularly applicable to follow-on contracts, where key C/SCSC knowledgeable contractor personnel are retained from previous efforts.

5. *Implementation Review/Visit*—An initial visit by selected members of the customer C/SCSC review team to a contractor's plant, to review the contractor's plans for implementing C/SCSC on a new contract. Such visits should take place within 30 days after contract award.

6. *Readiness Review/Assessment*—A meeting or series of meetings by selected members of the customer C/SCSC review team to a contractor's plant, to review contractor plans and progress in implementing C/SCSC in preparation for a full demonstration review. Such visits are expected to happen about 30 days after the initial implementation review/visit, or about 60 days after contract award.

7. *Combination Implementation Review/Readiness Assessment*—A meeting with a contractor which has an *approved* C/SCSC activity, which must now pass either a SAR or ESAR.

For the first two decades of C/SCSC existence, the process of validating compliance went by two commonly used terms. The "first time" validation activity was (and is still) referred to as a Demonstration Review (DR), which is a comprehensive *initial* examination of a contractor's management control system to verify that it has satisfied the 35 criteria. The second term that was (and is) used is called a SAR, or Subsequent Application Review. Note, the C/SCSC term "SAR" should not be confused with another DOD SAR term meaning "Selected Acquisition Report," which is unrelated, but was also imposed in a closely numbered document DODI 7000.3. The Selected Acquisition Report is not a contractual requirement; rather, it is a summary report on major programs for the Congress.

In a SAR, the reviewing team understands that the contractor has an existing validated C/SCSC management control system, but it wants verification that the system which was previously approved is in fact being used, either on a newly awarded contract or on the same contract after some lapse of time. A different application, such as moving from one program phase to another, from one location to another, generally require another *full* Demonstration Review.

But there was some ambiguity as to whether a customer had to conduct merely a brief SAR, or insist on another full DR when contractors 1) formed a new organizational unit, a new division, or a new subsidiary which performed on existing contracts; 2) moved their operations to a new location or plant in which some/many new personnel or new/modified procedures were put into place; 3) the contractor had made substantial changes to their approved C/SCSC system description and/or related procedures. In these circumstances the customer would sometimes insist on a SAR, and other times would require a full Demonstration Review. The customer's concern was that the changed environment could have an adverse effect on the previously approved control techniques and procedures.

In order to remove the confusion as to whether a full DR or more limited SAR was appropriate, the DOD in their 1987 Joint Implementation Guide update approved a new type of review called an "Extended SAR," or "ESAR," which would be used when:

1. Programs moved from one phase to another, e.g., R & D into production,
2. Contractors moved existing programs from one facility to another,
3. Contractors made substantial changes to an approved C/SCSC system description or procedures.

A summary of these various reviews is displayed in Figure 14-1. The precise timing, review team size, and durations shown are only approximate, and will vary from customer to customer. These data are displayed as a guideline for planning and to better understand what is involved with each type of review. Each customer may define the reviews in a slightly different manner, which becomes the "official" definition for a given application.

If a contractor expects to both develop and produce a given new product, and it currently has both engineering and production efforts underway, it is wise to request a simultaneous review of its systems and procedures as they apply to both developmental and production activities. To do otherwise, the contractor must later pass a second major review for the recurring or production effort. However, the production activity must exist in the plant in order to be examined, that is, it cannot simply be a plan in someone's mind. When a contractor has or anticipates multi-service contracts (Army, Navy, Air Force), it should also request a multi-service review team so it will have what is called a "tri-service validation."

In the validation and subsequent revalidation process the burden of proof necessarily rests with the contractor. It is up to the contractor to demonstrate that its management control system, the supporting procedures, and its staff have implemented their system in full compliance with the criteria.

**Summary of Review Types**

| Review | Timing | Review Team | Duration |
|---|---|---|---|
| Implementation Review/Visit | +30 Days After Award | 4-5 People | 2-3 Days |
| Readiness Review/Assessment | +60-90 Days After Award | 5-15 People | 5 Days |
| Demonstration Review | +90-120 Days After Award | 10-25 People | 15-20 Days |
| Extended SAR | +90 Days After Award | 10-25 People | 10-15 Days |
| SAR | +90 Days After Award | 6-10 People | 5 Days |
| Baseline Review | +90-120 Days After Award | 4-6 People | 3 Days |

**Figure 14-1 Review Types/Timing/People/Duration[1]**

The principal difference between the full demonstration review and the ESAR, SAR, and BR is one of degree. In simple pragmatic terms, the team arriving at a contractor's facility to conduct a demonstration review is likely to be made up of anywhere from 10 to 25 people, and they are likely to stay three to four weeks reviewing every policy and procedure, and interviewing most cost account managers. The Joint Implementation Guide describes the demonstration review process well:

> The C/SCSC review team will examine the contractor's working papers and documents to ascertain compliance and document their findings. For this purpose, the contractor will be required to make available to the team the documents used in the contractor's management control systems; for example, budgeting, work authorization, accounting, and other functional documents which apply to the specific contracts being reviewed. The documentation must be current and accurate.[2]

The goal of the demonstration review is to verify that the contractor's management control system meets the criteria and is in fact being used.

In the case of the SAR (Subsequent Application Review), the goal is simply to show that the previously validated system is still being used. Back to pragmatic terms, the reviewing team is usually much smaller, 6 to 10 people, and their stay is normally shorter, about one week. The SAR is less formal, and the team merely makes spot checks on the system. They are not trying to prove that a compliant system exists, for that is a basic assumption. Rather, they are verifying that the approved system is still in use:

> The objective of a subsequent application review is to ensure that, on a new contract, the contractor is properly and effectively using the accepted system, revised in accordance with approved changes. It is not the purpose of the review to reassess the contractor's previously accepted system.[3]

The "approved changes" referred to above are those evolutionary modifications which take place from time to time in any management system. One company received a tri-service validation for both development and production contracts in 1971. Over the following years there were numerous minor changes made to the original system. In every case, the proposed C/SCSC modification resulted in a documented procedural change which was coordinated with and approved by the local government representative (typically represented by an AFPRO; or ARPRO; or CAO; or DCAS; or NAVPRO-see Glossary of Terms) prior to implementing the change. The government's on-site representatives are usually delegated the authority to monitor and to approve on-site changes to a validated C/SCSC management control system.

From a contractor standpoint it should be obvious that it is highly desireable to satisfy the intent of the criteria, do so early, pass the demonstration review on the first try, and maintain the approved management control system in a consistent manner. By so doing the contractor saves much grief, both for themselves and for the procuring customer. Nobody enjoys altercations. When a contractor demonstrates that it is using C/SCSC as the founders had envisioned, there develops a certain confidence level between the customer and contractor. In such cases a second DR becomes merely an ESAR, or an ESAR is reduced to a SAR, or a SAR is reduced to a BR. The ongoing relationship and confidence level between the contractor and customer can tilt subsequent reviews in either direction.

Baseline reviews are the easiest type of review to accommodate from a contractors standpoint. BRs are appropriate when it has been less than a year since the successful passage of a DR/ ESAR/ SAR; there are no outstanding C/SCSC discrepancies between the contractor and the local government plant representatives; and the minimum review can be "justified" by the customer.

> The baseline review is not intended to be a routine replacement for more comprehensive reviews. It should be utilized only where there is a firm basis (e.g., historical evidence) to propose that a more comprehensive review is not warranted.[4]

There is considerable latitude on the part of the customer as to the precise type of review to conduct.

In the above descriptions, the demonstration review has been referred to as a larger task than that of the SAR or intermediate ESAR. This is the norm, but there are exceptions. One example is the contractor which failed to pass its SAR after two attempts, going for some 18 months without receiving approval of its management control system. The team which arrived for the third SAR attempt, interviewed *all* cost account managers, and traced through their *entire* management system in a totally comprehensive way. In this case there was no fundamental difference between the typical demonstration review and their third attempted SAR. The customer was justifiably concerned that the system under review had experienced fundamental changes in its operation. Instead of simply working off the discrepancy list from the previously failed SAR, the customer's team performed a comprehensive review of their total C/SCSC compliance, much in the spirit of a full formal demonstration review.

## Preparation for a Review

According to the standard clause inserted in the language of contracts requiring C/SCSC, one must be prepared to demonstrate compliance "...within ninety (90) calendar days after contract award, (or as otherwise agreed to by the parties)."[5] The 90-day period has likely never happened, and the norm for demonstration review is more like 9 to 12 months after contract award. ESARs and SARs will likely happen sooner. Sometimes a SAR for follow-on options to the same contract will happen in the 90-day period. The customer also has a vested interest in successful passage and will not be unreasonable in reaching an agreement as to the exact timing of their arrival.

Before they arrive to examine the system, certain activities must be accomplished. The best tangible proof of one's preparation for a review, and a general rule of thumb, is the submittal of a complete Cost Performance Report (CPR). After a firm has submitted two successive CPRs which include earned value measurement, and they look acceptable, and all procedures, bulletins, manuals, and such, have been issued defining the compliant system, a firm is normally considered ready to receive the team that will examine C/SCSC management control system.

Generally, two events will prior to the demonstration or ESAR/SAR, take place preparatory to the actual review. The first is the implementation visit by the customer team that will monitor C/SCSC compliance and performance. In this initial visit, the customer will impress on the contractor the importance of cost/ schedule reporting, if this is an unsettled issue. Usually the contractor will provide a presentation of its management control system, as it is being used on other contracts. The specific reports which are due, their frequency, and variance thresholds are normally discussed. Typically, prior to leaving, the customer will provide a list of documents it will want to review in a later visit, illustrated by the Figure 14-2.

The next visit by the customer C/SCSC team will usually take place about four weeks prior to the actual demonstration review or ESAR or SAR date. This visit is called a

## Review Documentation

1. Organization charts.

2. Listing of burdens pools, and their content.

3. List of major vendors, and their dollar value.

4. Work Breakdown Structure/Index/Dictionary.

5. Work authorization methods, for each functional area, i.e., engineering, manufacturing, etc., including the review of actual documents and their flow.

6. Budget methods, as per #5.

7. Cost accumulation methods, as per #5.

8. Variance Analysis procedures.

9. Baseline Management; change control; undistributed budget procedures; and associated logs.

10. Cost Account Matrix, listing the WBS across the top, the organization along the side, and reflecting which intersect with which, and the dollar values of each.

11. Master Schedule.

12. Intermediate Schedules associated with the work authorization, as per #5.

13. Detailed Schedules associated with work authorization, as per #5.

14. Most recent Cost Performance Report (CPR).

15. Specific examples of engineering and manufacturing cost accounts reflecting discretely measured effort, apportioned effort, and Level of Effort (LOE).

16. Management Reserve Log.

17. List of cost account managers, by function.

18. Statistical summaries of measured cost account/work package time-spans.

**Figure 14-2 Typical Review Documentation** [6]

readiness review or assessment. Such visits usually take three to five days, and the purpose is to assess whether or not the contractor will be in a position to support a demonstration review, or ESAR, or SAR.

This is a serious effort, and the documents listed in Figure 14-2 will be examined in considerable detail. Selected interviews will also be conducted with a few cost account managers to determine the preparedness of the contractor, and to give it an idea of what to expect in the forthcoming review. Prior to leaving, the customer team will debrief the contractor on its findings and will list obvious deficiencies. If the contractor is significantly unprepared for the readiness review, or the list of deficiencies is extensive, by mutual agreement the planned demonstration or ESAR or SAR date is usually delayed, and another readiness review is normally scheduled in its place. This is not a good omen for a contractor.

In preparation for the actual demonstration or ESAR or SAR, two essential ingredients are needed: there should be a broad company team formed to support the activity, and there must be genuine support from all levels of management, especially top management. The C/SCSC review cannot be done by a handful of people, working *outside* of the mainstream of program activity. If the program manager and other functional management do not view the validation effort in a serious way and are not fully committed to giving C/SCSC their complete support, then the best advice for anyone associated with it is to seek another assignment—soon!

Failure to pass the review has an adverse effect on a program, as will be discussed later. If the management is only partially committed to C/SCSC and intends to give only lip-service to the system and to the review, a graceful exit for participants is suggested. If one's contract calls for full C/SCSC in accordance with DODI 7000.2, management has no alternative but to fully support the effort. Unfortunately, such realization is sometimes delayed until the first or second demonstration or ESAR or SAR failure has gotten the attention of a firm's management.

The demonstration review and/or SAR is a major exercise, not too dissimilar from a major proposal. An initial step, therefore, is, the preparation of an outline and plan of action. The Joint Implementation Guide (JIG) [Appendix E] is an excellent starting point, and it contains much information on the review process. Of particular significance is the fact that the reviewing team will use the JIG as their outline for the review. Three of the appendices in the JIG pertain directly to the review process. (Note, these three appendices are a part of the JIG, which is copied in total in Appendix E to this book.)

*Appendix C: C/SCSC Review Reports*—Provides a suggested format for the report to be submitted by the team conducting the review. The outline provides a glimpse of what the team must cover.

*Appendix E:Evaluation/Demonstration Review Checklist*—A listing of the 35 criteria and supporting questions. This checklist provides blank spaces to the right of each question, which should be used to make reference to one's specific procedures, schedules, budgets, documents, etc., which will be cited as being in compliance with the requirement of the criteria. Prior to the team arrival this checklist is frequently displayed across a blank wall, with referenced documents, and is discussed by the internal team which will ask the question: Does this satisfy the intent of the criterion? Much of the review discussion will be focused on Appendix E.

Appendix E is used to support a DR or ESAR, but is generally not appropriate for a SAR, and certainly not for a BR.

*Appendix F:C/SCSC Review Worksheets and Exhibits*—Contains 12 separate formats for reviewing the C/SCSC in very specific detail. Example: Format 3 aids the team with the reconciliation of the total budget, to allow traceability up the WBS. Considerable time should be spent with Appendix F prior to the arrival of the reviewing team.

Just as with a major proposal, the team preparing for the demonstration or ESAR/SAR will find a large conference room dedicated to its exclusive use to be most helpful. On the blank walls can be displayed the JIG appendices discussed above. In addition, one wall should display a flow diagram of all company documents which form an integral part of the C/SCSC compliance, including delegations of authority, procedures, organization charts, and other related documents.

Such displays are useful both to the contractor team preparing for the review, as well as providing a quick overview for the customer team itself, which hopefully will understand C/SCSC, but likely not be familiar with a given firm's systems or particular approach. Space permitting, the WBS, organization charts, and a Cost Account Matrix of WBS elements versus the organization should be displayed.

Training is an essential part of the C/SCSC validation process. One's organization, particularly the cost account managers and management at all levels, must be familiar with the system being demonstrated. In addition to knowing how to use the system, as a practical matter, all personnel should be able to recite C/SCSC "buzz-words" and must know how to respond to questions they will be asked from the reviewing team.

Many firms find it useful to prepare a list of most likely questions their managers are probably going to be asked during the process. Many a SAR deficiency item has been listed because someone failed to use the proper term to describe the workings of C/SCSC, and conversely, many a "snow job" has been performed by those who don't actually know or use the system, but do know the critical C/SCSC jargon. Whether one intends to genuinely implement C/SCSC in the firm, and hopefully that is the case, or merely put on a show for the reviewing team, a listing of most likely questions will be beneficial.

Listed in Figure 14-3 are some 20 questions found to be frequently used by reviewing teams when interviewing members of the contractor's organization. Obviously, no single list will be absolutely complete or foolproof. Review teams have been known to innovate!

It is always important to know the make-up of the team about to descend on a firm and to prepare to answer questions likely to be asked from them, based on their experiences and backgrounds. While no two teams are exactly alike, there is a pattern which is generally followed:

*Team Director* appointed from the respective DOD headquarters command of AFSC, AMC, ASN (S & L), or the DOE headquarters, is the expert on C/SCSC. This person may head up more than one team at the same time and will provide "policy guidelines" and the interpretation of criteria to members of the team.

*Team Chief* may come from the lead DOD command headquarters or a subordinate command, or from the DOE field operation office. This person is responsible for the organization of the team, for the conduct of the review, for preparing the written report,

## Typical Review Questions

1. What is your job and where do you fit in the organization?
2. Do you use C/SCSC in your job?
3. What is your role with C/SCSC?
4. Do you understand the need for C/SCSC?
5. Are you a cost account manager, and if so, how many cost accounts do you manage?
6. From whom do you receive your budget, and in what form?
7. Do you presently have a copy of your budget?
8. How do you plan your work?
9. How is work performance measured (earned value), and who does it?
10. How is your plan revised?
11. What schedules do you use in your job, and where do they come from?
12. What is a work package, and do you use them?
13. Do you provide inputs to the CPR, and do you ever see a full CPR document?
14. How is your performance to your BCWS?
15. Do you have variance thresholds, what are they?
16. What happens when you exceed a variance threshold, describe the process.
17. Do you prepare variance reports, who must see them, what happens to them?
18. Do you do an ETC and EAC, or is it done for you? By Whom? How often?
19. What C/SCSC procedures do you use, do you have a copy?
20. Do you like C/SCSC?

**Figure 14-3 Typical Review Questions**

and for reporting the findings to the team director, who may or may not take an active part in the review itself. Most team chiefs have been through several reviews prior to being designated chief.

*Team Members* generally represent a balanced mix of backgrounds including engineering, testing, manufacturing, accounting (DCAA), program control, cost/price analysis, contract administration, and customer plant representatives (AFPRO).

Once assembled, the reviewing teams generally take one of two approaches in the conduct of the review, and sometimes a third composite approach. Depending upon the backgrounds of the team members, they normally structure the review process either along the lines of the criteria or on the functions to be reviewed. Probably the most effective approach is the criteria, but the approach requires highly experienced C/SCSC team members, who are not always available. This approach simply focuses on the five criteria groupings: organization; planning and budgeting; accounting; analysis; and revisions. These teams are usually smaller in size, and their review methods and findings are usually well-integrated.

When criteria-experienced team members are unavailable, the approach is usually along functional lines, out of necessity. The team size will be larger than the criteria approach, simply because each team member will cover a particular specialty. Integration of their findings is more difficult because of the size of the team. The third approach, the mixed review team, is a composite of the two, depending upon the availability of experienced C/SCSC members. Most C/SCSC review teams use the mixed approach.

Prior to the arrival of the reviewing team, certain homework will have to be done by the contractor, such as analyzing the initial budget baseline, examining in detail the distribution of all cost accounts issued. Contractors should have some "just-in-case" statistics available, or they may want to actually include such data in their initial presentations. Of particular interest will be statistical data covering:

- The total number of cost accounts planned/used;

- Cost account lengths, maximum/minimum/average lengths;

- Average dollar size, maximum and minimum; and

- Percent of discrete, apportioned, and LOE activities.

Shown in Figure 14-4, A Summary of Cost Accounts, is a representative display of these types of cost account data, in this case displayed as a bar-type chart. (Pie charts will also work nicely.)

When defense industry contractors were preparing for their initial C/SCSC reviews two decades ago, there was little outside help available. Today all is different, and there is considerable advisory talent available. In most larger firms, sister divisions frequently have experienced personnel who have worked with C/SCSC and have been through the validation process. Unfortunately, these same experts who might be available in any given firm also have their own jobs and responsibilities, and are thus not always available when one needs the help, or for as long a duration as they are needed.

While as a general rule the author has never been a proponent of the use of outside management consultants, there are certain exceptions. One of these exceptions is in the use of outside consultants to critique a proposed C/SCSC management control system, and to assist in preparation for the demonstration process. Not only is one able to get the support when it is needed, but the assistance is available for the duration of one's needs. The outside consultant will be the "expert" in the validation process, and is often used to convince the internal company management to act or not act in a certain critical way. They can also be used to structure a training course unique to a company's particular needs.

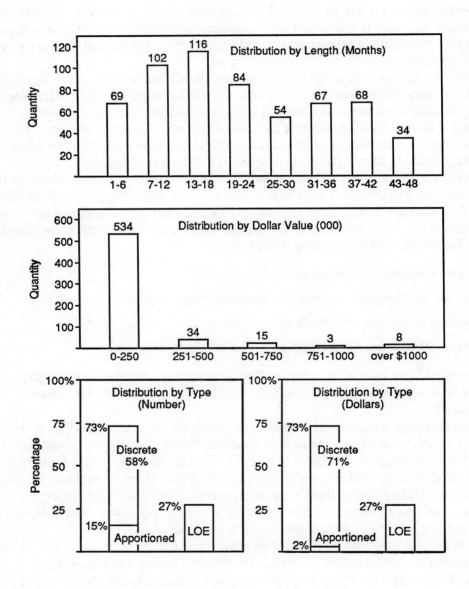

**Figure 14-4  A Summary of Cost Accounts (954 total)**

Perhaps the most appropriate use of the outside consultant is in the "mock C/SCSC review," which should take place sometime prior to the actual government review, but with sufficient time to correct any deficiencies uncovered. Such mock reviews are done for the readiness assessment, the review itself, or often for both. The mock review is somewhat analogous to a dress rehearsal. However, in the mock review the team will want to review the proposed organization, the management system, and the individual responses to questions in sufficient time to be able to correct deficiencies the internal review might expose. As early as eight weeks prior to the customer's arrival, or as late as three weeks, is generally the best time for a mock review to take place.

## The Consequences of Failure

When a contractor fails to pass a demonstration review, a SAR or ESAR, there is little tangible impact in a contractual sense. There may be suggestions of adverse actions from the contracting officer, say the implied threat of the withholding of progress payments. However, that rarely happens. In one case, an eastern firm did have progress payments withheld, coinciding with a failure of their SAR. But in that particular case the payments were withheld as much due to discrepancies in their material accountability, as to the failure of their SAR itself.

Probably one of the most effective techniques which could be used to put incentives into the C/SCSC validation process would be in the use of award fees in contracts, to encourage implementation and passage of the review on the first try. An award fee is a relatively new form of contractual incentive which places a portion of a contract's fee in a pool, and makes the earning of such fees dependent on the occurrence of certain program events, as determined solely by the customer's program manager. Perhaps the future will see more of this concept used to put "muscle" into the C/SCSC enforcement. There is probably no better way to get the attention of a contractor's "top management" than to incorporate the earning of fee into a process.

Repeated contractor failures of a SAR/ESAR, suggesting that fundamental adverse changes have happened to a contractor's management control system, could result in a total withdrawal of a previous C/SCSC validation. A contractor can actually lose an approved C/SCSC validation. But does that matter? Without a contract clause stipulating a penalty for failure, why should a contractor be concerned?

The first thing that happens after a SAR/ESAR failure is the *immediate drain* on the effective use of all program personnel, i.e., engineering, manufacturing, and other human resource talent needed to perform the contract statement of work. Suddenly, everyone is working on that "damned C/SCSC!" and how to work off the discrepancy list left by the customer's reviewing team. Management at all levels suddenly becomes interested in C/SCSC. And furthermore, the customer comes around more often to "help" in the process.

But the most profound and devastating effect of a failed DR, ESAR, or SAR is in the political realm. Government programs must be approved by, and funded by, the United

States Congress, and the Congress is a political body. No program can ever expect to have total Congressional support if for no other reason than the fact that company plants are located in specific states, and particularly in specific Congressional districts.

It probably would not be possible to precisely quantify the negative political impact which resulted when the contractor of a new aircraft system failed to pass a C/SCSC demonstration review for its newly formed division. However, it may safely be assumed that the failed C/SCSC review did give the opponents of the new aircraft the means to impugn the overall program, and the company, and thereby contributed in some way to its subsequent cancellation in the late 1970s. No company needs a reputation of failure with respect to its internal management systems.

The reasons for failures are numerous. Quite often failures occur because company management simply does not believe in the C/SCSC concept. They may feel they can have both their preferred management control approach and C/SCSC. In these cases all the planning, work measurement, estimates to complete, and such, are done, not by the cost account managers as it should be, but rather by personnel brought in to perform such tasks for them, with the instruction: "Do not bother my engineers." The customer reviewing teams are not stupid, and they quickly see through such a facade when interviewing cost account managers and other company personnel. In such cases, failure of the DR/ ESAR/ SAR is preordained.

## The Fruits of Passage

Passage of a C/SCSC review creates an immediate organizational high. The most tangible result of passage will be the signing of a Memorandum of Understanding (MOU) by the contractor. The Joint Implementation Guide defines the MOU as:

> **(1)** The memorandum of understanding is not a contract clause, but it may be incorporated in any contract by appropriate reference when the contract includes a requirement for compliance with the criteria.

> **(2)** This document serves to clarify intent of the contractor and DOD components relative to implementation of the criteria. It contains reference to a description of accepted systems and subsystems; it identifies facilities and locations; and provides for Government access to pertinent contractor records and data for surveillance purposes. Provision is also made to permit accepted changes to accepted systems.[7]

A sample MOU is contained in Appendix D to the JIG (Appendix E of this book).

Also resulting from the successful passage of the validation process will be the approval of the contractor's *C/SCSC System Description*, mentioned in the above quote. The system description provides a defined baseline against which all future C/SCSC compliance will be measured, and it gives the customer a reference point for continued contract surveillance.

will be measured, and it gives the customer a reference point for continued contract surveillance.

The only negative aspect of successfully passing the C/SCSC review, particularly on the first try, is that the "company," the strangers you so eagerly hoped would be visiting you, will now be elsewhere, "helping" others in their validation process. But such is life.

---

## ENDNOTES

[1] Types of Reviews & Timing per: Department of the Air Force, *Interim Policy #83-1, Guidelines for C/SCSC Reviews,* 10 December, 1982; Review Team Size and Duration per: Charles R. (Chuck) Sell, "The Review Process," paper presented at the conference on *Cost/Schedule Control Systems and Performance Measurement Systems,* sponsored by The Institute of Cost Analysis, Atlanta, Georgia, October 26, 1987.

[2] Department of Defense, *Cost/Scheduel Control Systems Criteria—Joint Implementation Guide,* October, 1987, page 5-4.

[3] DOD JIG, October, 1987, page 7-1.

[4] DOD JIG, October, 1987, page 7-6.

[5] DOD JIG, October, 1987, page B-1.

[6] List provided by Daniel Schild, formerly Chief, Cost Management Systems Division, United States Air Force Aeronautical Systems Division, Wright-Patterson AF Base, Ohio (retired); presently with TASC, The Analytic Sciences Corporation, Dayton, Ohio.

[7] DOD JIG, October, 1987, page 5-5.

# IV

# SPECIAL C/SCSC ISSUES

# 15

# The Meaning of Schedule Variances

*A C/SCSC schedule variance is stated in terms of dollars of work and must be analyzed in conjunction with other schedule information such as provided by networks, Gantt charts, and line-of-balance.*

*By itself, the C/SCSC schedule variance reveals no "critical path" information, and may be misleading because unfavorable accomplishment in some areas can be offset by favorable accomplishment in others.*

Arthur D. Little, White Paper
for the OASD Comptroller,
Issued 10 July, 1986, page 3

It often comes as a surprise to many that the "schedule" portion of C/SCSC may not indicate the true schedule position on a given program. And to make matters worse, the "schedule variance" position as reported in the monthly Cost Performance Report (CPR) may actually be reflecting a *distorted* picture of a program's true schedule condition. After having said this, the next obvious question has to be: then who needs it? But before we "toss out" the schedule portion of C/SCSC, perhaps we should review what the SV does and does not do for the criteria concept.

Repeatedly in this book we have stated that the "foundation" for C/SCSC is the creation and maintenance of a Performance Measurement Baseline, referred to as the PMB. The establishment of the PMB is an iterative process and consists of three steps taken in the following order:

1. Define the work to be done.
2. Time phase/ schedule the work to be done.
3. Allocate the budgets to accomplish the work to be done.

Earlier, in Figure 10-2, we displayed a DOD chart which illustrated the concept. Shown in Figure 15-1 is a DOE chart which shows the same process: define the work; time the work; and allocate the resources.

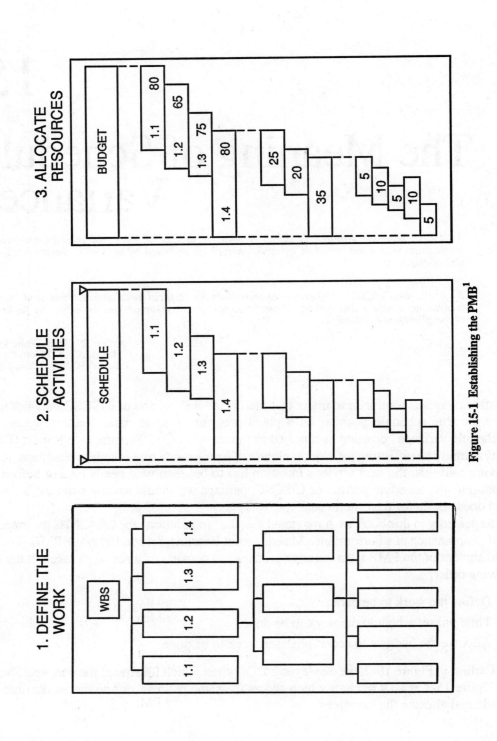

Figure 15-1 Establishing the PMB[1]

Step 2 in this process represents the timing or scheduling of the work to be done. It represents choosing the appropriate time periods in which the defined work tasks are planned to be done. Subsequent performance against these tasks in these selected time zones may or may not reflect the true schedule condition of the program, as related to meeting contractual commitments. That statement may sound contradictory but it is not. In C/SCSC the "schedule" part of the acronym represents the "planned" time period for the defined work tasks, which may or may not precisely coincide with the program's schedule plan required to meet the contractual obligation. Perhaps a few specific examples will help this concept to be understood.

## Schedule Variances in the Cost Performance Report (CPR)

To illustrate the point, we will assume three hypothetical scenarios of schedule variances as they might be reported in a monthly Cost Performance Report (CPR):

*Scenario #1*—The CPR indicates a condition of being "minus three months behind schedule," while in fact the program is *on schedule* to meet its contract commitment.

*Scenario #2*—The CPR reflects an "on schedule" position, while in fact the program is *three months behind* schedule to meet the contract commitment.

*Scenario #3*—The CPR reflects an "on schedule" position, while in fact the program is *three months ahead* of schedule to meet its contract commitment.

Let us discuss each of these assumed conditions, which can and do happen in the real C/SCSC world.

*Scenario #1—The CPR reflects a "-3 months behind schedule" condition, (while in fact the program is on schedule)*

Someone somewhere, after having worked in the defense industry for a long time, made the following "tongue-in-cheek" observation about engineers:

- engineers are always optimistic; and

- engineers are always late.

We do not necessarily endorse this concept, but if one did it could have far reaching consequences to those implementing a C/SCSC Performance Measurement Baseline (PMB).

Let us assume that we are under contract to design and develop, deliver one large cargo aircraft to the Air Force. The initial part of our PMB will consist of those design activities necessary to engineer this new aircraft. Our C/SCSC specialists are bright young people who will work with the seasoned engineers to put these thousands of design tasks (Work Packages) into the proper time frame in order to create the PMB, and then to measure performance against the PMB.

Our young C/SCSC specialists have never heard the theory that design engineers may have a certain "bias" in their attitudes and performance which could affect the precise placement of Work Packages for purposes of performance measurement. And in defense of the engineers, remember it is the engineers who are hired to do creative and innovative work, and almost by nature one who does this type of work must be confident and optimistic about things in general, including their ability to finish something by a certain point in time. Let us review one specific design task, which we will call "Task A," see Figure 15-2.

"Task A," is estimated to be a 30 day activity, and consists of the design of a certain test article. According to our master schedule, this particular test must be performed late next year, sometime after the June time-frame. Assume that independent of the PMB exercise, the schedulers had performed a "critical path analysis" of all design activities for our new airplane. They didn't bother to let the C/SCSC specialists know about the critical path analysis—they assumed it wouldn't be of interest to them. They know (but the C/SCSC specialists do not know) that "Task A" has six months of total float, that is, it can happen anywhere in the January to June time-frame and it will *not* impact the ability to deliver the airplane on time.

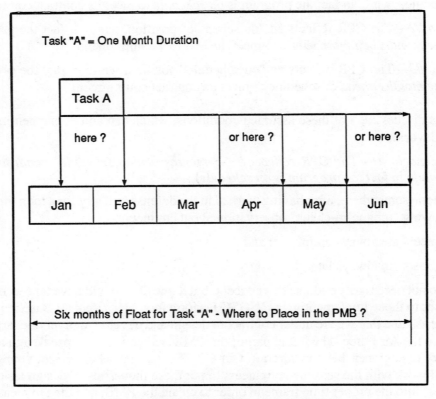

**Figure 15-2  Placing "Task A" in the PMB**

The C/SCSC specialist goes to the engineer who is the Cost Account manager for Task A and solicits the planned time-frame for this effort. The engineer considers for a moment, and being the optimistic type, sets this effort in the most ambitious time period: 15 January to 15 February. He could have just as easily selected April or May or even June, but he set the earlier time period because he was confident of his work.

Now what happens when the actual performance takes place in April or May or even in June? The CPR, that portion dealing with Task A, will reflect a "behind schedule" condition. But we also know that this task doesn't need to complete until as late as June, and it will have no impact on our contractual commitment to deliver the airplane on time.

Imagine that our PMB is made up of thousands of similar design tasks, and that each of these tasks was placed in the "most optimistic," or earliest, time-frame for performance. And then the subsequent performance against the plan actually happened *later* than that called for in the PMB. However, this condition did not impact our ability to meet our contractual commitment to the Air Force, because the PMB was established without knowledge that a critical path study had been done, which showed that many of these thousands of tasks could and perhaps should have been placed in a later time frame, consistent with the true contractual needs of the program. The "optimistic" bias of the engineers was actually *incorporated* into the Performance Measurement Baseline.

Later, our Program Manager picks up the Cost Performance Report (CPR) and reads that his contract is "-3 months behind" schedule. He calls in the scheduling people and confronts them with this information. Their comment is "No Sir, we are on schedule to ship the airplane on time to meet the contractual delivery." They trace through their critical path analysis and prove the point.

In his next meeting with the C/SCSC manager the PM comments: "Can't you C-Spec people ever give me accurate schedule status on this program?"

*Scenario #2—The CPR is reflecting an "on schedule" condition, (in fact the program is three months behind schedule)*

Assume for the moment that we are under contract to design and develop and deliver that same large cargo aircraft. Everything seems to be going very well. The design was done on or even ahead of our internal schedules. All ground tests worked just fine. It is indeed a pleasure to work on this type of "model" program. Then to our chagrin we find that in the final assembly of the aircraft we have lost—scrapped—one small but critical titanium landing gear part. Replacing this single part will take three months. Our schedule to meet our contractual delivery commitment will slip by three months!

Our Program Manager has been on a two week vacation in Hawaii, and comes into work late Sunday afternoon to catch up on his reading material. The first document he reads is the CPR which shows that his program is "on cost" and "on schedule." He mumbles to himself, "Good." The very next document he picks up is a "Red Flag" report which notified the Air Force that we will be *three months late* in the delivery of the airplane.

In our "emergency" staff meeting later that night we try to tell the PM how terrific he looks with his newly acquired suntan, but all he wants to discuss is our questionable heritage and the unfortunate circumstances of our births.

Let us examine what has happened. When we created the PMB we carefully listed all the tasks to be done, then we placed them into the planned time-frames for performance. The planned work was then accomplished as planned, or even ahead of plan. It was quite natural that the CPR would reflect an "on schedule" condition because the "bulk" of the planned work effort was done on schedule, as planned. A C/SCSC Schedule Variance is by definition:

$$SV = \begin{array}{l} BCWP \quad \text{(actual earned value expressed in dollars)} \\ \underline{- BCWS} \quad \text{(planned earned value expressed in dollars)} \\ SV \qquad \text{(+ = favorable; - = unfavorable} \end{array}$$

The CPR indicated that the performance had essentially no SV, an "on schedule" condition, as expressed in dollars in the PMB.

However, then came the issue of the small titanium part which was scrapped, but nevertheless was critical to the delivery of the airplane. The costs associated with this small titanium part while individually quite expensive, was nevertheless insignificant in relation to all of the work which was done on or ahead of the planned tasks in the PMB. Therefore, the negative impact of this one titanium part was more that offset by work done according to, or ahead of plan, and the CPR quite properly reflected an "on schedule" condition.

However, the Program Manager read that the program was on schedule according to the CPR, and expected that the "Cost/ Schedule Control Systems Criteria" management control system would give him the precise schedule position on his contract. Wrong.

More on this later.

*Scenario #3—The CPR is reflecting an "on schedule" condition (while in fact the program is three months ahead of schedule)*

Some of the cagiest people you will ever come in contact with in the defense industry are likely to be in manufacturing. Often they have risen to their present management jobs as a result of dedicated long-term commitment to their professions; having started at the very bottom of the organization, worked their way upward to important positions. They know their business. They also know how to sign up to a commitment to senior management—with a "just-in-case" safety pad built into all such commitments.

Most manufacturing people learn early in their careers of the importance of meeting one's commitment to finish a particular job "as agreed." Management will not generally complain about a job finishing a few days or even a couple of weeks early. But all Hell will break loose when jobs run behind schedule. Therefore, most manufacturing commitments to meet a particular deadline come from people with years of experience, who are aware of what can happen to a particular job as it travels through the factory. Throughout history (defense industry history that is), when manufacturing commitments are made, they generally will have a contingency or safety pad built into them, to cover those things that for some reason, just might go wrong.

Therefore, when things do go right in the factory—and they sometimes do—jobs will be finished *ahead* of schedule. The "positive" float that was intentionally built into the manufacturing commitment will distort the true schedule position, as reported in the monthly Cost Performance Report.

Assume that this time our same contract to build the large cargo aircraft is into its manufacturing phase, and everything is going perfectly. The CPR reflects an "on schedule" position, and we simultaneously notify the Air Force that the airplane will be delivered three months early. The PM again complains: "Can't you people ever give me an accurate schedule position with that C/S crap!"

It should be obvious from these three examples that our hypothetical Program Manager was expecting to get schedule visibility from the C/SCSC Cost Performance Report which it was not able, nor ever intended to provide. Is that untypical of what many people expect from C/SCSC? Probably not. The Deputy Secretary of Defense addressed this very issue nicely when he released the DOD C/SCSC white paper to the public:

> When dissatisfaction was expressed, it almost universally was based on expectations that C/SCSC could provide information it was never designed or expected to produce...[2]

## Why We Need the "Schedule" in C/SCSC

The word "schedule" in C/SCSC is almost a misnomer. When the criteria were being conceived and debated in the mid-1960s, there were some who felt a term other than "schedule" should be used. But no other term was found to better represent the intended concept. They founders did demand that cost and schedule people must be working together from one management control system base, so they finally settled on "schedule." But terms like "planned work time-frame," and a resulting "work variance," might have better described what was desired from the concept.

However, "schedule" and "schedule variances," or whatever better term might have been used, are essential elements to the C/SCS Criteria concept.

While it is true that a schedule variance as reflected in a CPR may or may not reflect the true schedule position on a contract, a long-term chronic schedule variance can be a most reliable indicator of the long-term trend on a contract. Assume that a given contract has been performing with a negative schedule position for half of its planned contract period. At some point in the life of this contract schedule recovery will become impossible, and a schedule slip becomes an irrefutable fact. Negative schedule variances indicate that planned work did not get done. A negative schedule variance is likely to be the first indicator of problems on a contract.

Schedule variances, in the longterm, are one of the more tangible and reliable indicators of performance trends on a contract. SV is a "stand back" indicator of contract performance trends.

But perhaps of greater importance is the fact that the schedule position is vital in determining what the total cost will be on a given contract. What C/SCSC refers to as the Estimate at Completion (EAC) is really made up of two components once a contract has been started: "Actual Costs To Date" and the "Estimate to Complete." Schedule status and the physical work accomplished/to be accomplished, are essential ingredients to making a valid estimate to complete a job.

For example, if a certain contract was planned to be done in a 12 month period, but because of prolonged performance to plan the effort required 18 months to finish, the overall program costs must go up. Even if all the discrete tasks don't change and don't increase in cost, all "level of effort" tasks will take longer. They will incur additional costs by virtue of a longer period of performance. The total cost bill will be higher.

The criteria do not require that any particular scheduling technique or method be used. But this statement should not be construed as meaning that the criteria do not expect—indeed demand a very sophisticated scheduling approach to be used by contractors, in conjunction with the 35 criteria. The DOD JIG is quite specific about what it expects from a contractor's scheduling system:

1. Provide for all specified work to the lowest defined element of the CWBS.
2. Provide schedules so actual progress can be related.
3. Identify key milestones and activities.
4. Interface with other planning and control systems.
5. Provide current status and forecasts of completion dates for scheduled work.
6. Enable a comparison of planned and actual status of program accomplishment based on milestones or other indicators.
7. A master schedule and related subordinate schedules (intermediate and/or cost account), consistent with and supportive of the master schedule.
8. Show interdependencies from the master schedule to the detailed work package levels.
9. Vertical traceability.
10. A scheduling system which is formal, complete, and consistent.[3]

Program managers cannot ascertain their precise schedule position from simply reviewing the monthly CPR, although that fact isn't always understood. Too much is read into the "Schedule" word of C/SCSC. But one can gain a good understanding of a long-term schedule trend from the SV as reflected in the CPR. However, the scheduling system which is a required adjunct to a fully operational C/SCSC activity will provide interested management with the precise schedule position at any given point in time.

Schedule considerations must be a part of any valid estimated costs to complete a job. Conversely, without knowing one's schedule position, ones cost projections to complete a given job will be of questionable validity. The founders of C/SCSC rightly insisted on "schedule" being a part of the concept.

---

## ENDNOTES

[1] Department of Energy, DOE/MA-0160, *Contract Performance Measurement Reporting and Baseline Management,* (Washington, D.C.: June, 1984), Page 7.

[2] William H. Taft, IV, Deputy Secretary of Defense, when issuing the DOD C/SCSC white paper, Washington, D.C., 10 July, 1986.

[3] Paraphrased from the DOD JIG, October, 1987, pages 3-9 and 3-10.

# 16

# Indirect Cost Management

*(a) An indirect cost is any cost not directly identified with a single, final cost objective, but identified with two or more final cost objectives or an intermediate cost objective. After direct costs have been determined and charged directly to the contract or other work, indirect costs are those remaining to be allocated to the several cost objectives.*

*(b) Indirect costs shall be accumulated by logical cost groupings with due consideration of the reasons for incurring such costs. Each grouping should be determined so as to permit distribution of the grouping on the basis of the benefits accruing to the several cost objectives.*

*(c) Once an appropriate base for distributing indirect costs has been accepted, it shall not be fragmented by removing individual elements.*

*(d) The contractors method of allocating indirect costs shall be in accordance with standards promulgated by the CAS Board, if applicable to the contract; otherwise, the method shall be in accordance with generally accepted accounting principles which are consistently applied.*

*(e) A base period for allocating indirect costs is the cost accounting period during which such costs are incurred and accumulated for distribution to work performed in that period.*

Federal Acquisition Regulation
31.203 (abridged)

There is another group of costs that are not exclusive to any single contract or program, but which apply to all contracts within a given company. These costs represent the largest single category of expenses to contracts, and are referred to as indirect costs. They are also called overhead costs or burden expenses or general and administrative costs. The government makes a fine distinction between such costs, as follows:

> In the government contracting environment, indirect costs are usually divided into two sub-categories; overhead and general and administrative (G & A). Overhead costs are indirect costs that support a specific part or function of the company, but not the whole company.

> The G & A costs, on the other hand, cannot logically be associated with any particular group of cost objectives, but are required to support the business as a whole.[1]

Such indirect costs are collected in accounting pools for subsequent distribution over the direct cost base by some approved method. The treatment of these costs by contractors must be consistent, fair, and apply to all programs in an equitable way. Costs which are charged into indirect pools (or burden centers), as with direct costs, must be well defined, approved by the government, and applied thereafter in accordance with the financial disclosure statement for the company.

Smaller firms may have only a single such indirect pool. Larger companies often have multiple pools. Six or seven (or more) such indirect pools are not uncommon, and charges going into each pool must be approved by category, and consistently applied to a specific pool in a manner similar to the distinction between direct and indirect costs. To allow the uncontrolled judgmental shifting of costs between indirect pools, or between direct and indirect categories, would allow contractors to manipulate costs between different types of contracts (firm types and cost types), obviously a practice which must be prohibited.

Indirect costs are those which, by definition, are impossible or at least cumbersome to identify to any one contract, and are also of benefit to multiple programs. A firm with only one contract might be able to charge everything directly to their single contract. However, the minute they get a second contract, or start to pursue additional business, it would no longer be appropriate to charge everything to the one contract only. Hence, at the point at which two or more programs/activities exist in a given firm, there is a need for some type of indirect accounting approach, to equitably allocate the non-direct activity over the multiple contract direct base.

The allocation of the costs of indirect activity is generally provided for as a "percentage rate" of total direct activity. For example, for every dollar of direct costs the plan may call for, indirect costs would be allocated at, say, 110 percent based on the following:

$$\text{Indirect Rate} = \frac{\text{Indirect Pool}}{\text{Direct Base}} = \frac{\$110,000}{\$100,000} = \text{Indirect Rate of } 110\%$$

The difficulty of forecasting such burdens is that indirect costs must be relatable to direct costs, and indirect pools are made up of two types of costs:

1. *Fixed Indirect Costs* (e.g., facility rental/depreciation; company president; etc.) which will not vary in amount with changes in the direct base.
2. *Variable Indirect Costs* (e.g., fringe benefits; telephone use; accounting personnel; office supplies; etc.) which will vary with changes in the direct base.

A given program has virtually no control over fixed indirect costs (one rarely fires a company president to save money) and only limited influence over the variable indirect costs. While fringe benefit expenditures may go down roughly proportionate to the number of people on the indirect payroll, it is not an absolute relationship. In a declining business environment, it is a simple known truth that the first people to be cut are those who are the lowest paid, and with only limited seniority. Thus, if the indirect work force is cut from 1,000 to 500 people to adjust to a 50 percent loss of direct base, the indirect cost savings will never reach the same proportion as the absolute reduction in people. The high-priced company officers and senior people are still on the payroll, as are the employees with the extra weeks vacation because of long-term service with the company.

Another difficulty of forecasting indirect burden rates is accurately forecasting the direct base, over which indirect costs will be allocated. A direct base forecast will usually be made up of two categories of business: (1) firm business (contracts in hand); and (2) new or follow-on business (with a high likelihood of capture). Low probability contracts are excluded from a forecasted direct base, until such time as they are won.

The new or follow-on business opportunities sometimes do not materialize, or they fall short of the forecast, in which case the indirect rates must go up on existing contracts because indirect expenses are (never) adjusted with the same speed or in exactly the same proportions as a declining direct base. Admittedly, "never" is a strong word, but if there has ever been a situation in which indirect costs were able to be reduced in the same proportions and with the same speed as the loss of a direct base, we know of no one who has witnessed the event. Thus, changes in a direct base will have the following impact on a given contract:

1. When the total forecasted direct base goes down—the indirect burden rates will increase (always).
2. When the total direct base goes up—the burden rates will come down (ever so slowly).

When a given contract establishes a Performance Measurement Baseline (PMB) which calls for indirect costs at the 110 percent planned rate, and indirect actuals reflect a higher percentage, say 200 percent of direct costs, the contractor must be in a position to describe what took place. Assuming that cost actuals reflected the cost plan, i.e., that there was no arbitrary shifting of costs between direct and indirect, and between the various indirect pools, a change in burden percentage rates must be the result of two factors, or a combination of the two:

1. A change in the direct base (up or down).
2. A change in the indirect pool costs (up or down).
3. Some combination of the two.

A contractor must be in a position to trace and explain the reasons why indirect burdens deviated from the plan, and adversely impacted all contracts in the company. Was there a change in the direct base over which indirect costs were allocated; or was there a change in the amount of indirect costs charged to the burden pools; or was it a combination of both (which is generally the case).

Surveillance of a given contractor's indirect activity is typically delegated by the procuring military department to the local in-plant governmental representative. This approach makes sense based on the complexity of most overhead activities:

> The evaluation of a contractor's indirect cost control system is within the purview of the cognizant plant representative and the DCAA; the responsibility for ensuring that these systems are in compliance with the C/SCSC is normally assigned to their representatives on the demonstration review team.[2]

The DCAA is quite specific about what it expects from a contractor in the way of indirect cost management.

> The contractor should charge indirect costs to appropriate overhead pools by methods acceptable to DCAA. Controls of indirect costs are required and should include:
>
> (a) Establishment of realistic time-phased budgets or forecasts by organizations; for example, department or cost center.
>
> (b) Placement of responsibility for indirect costs in a manner commensurate with a person's authority.
>
> (c) Variance analyses and appropriate action to eliminate or reduce costs where feasible.
>
> (d) Review of budgets at least annually and when major unforeseen variations in workload or other factors affecting indirect costs become known.[3]

## Categories of Indirect Costs

So much for indirect accounting basics. To forecast a position and assess C/SCSC performance, one must understand that indirect rates fall into four precise categories:

1. *Bidding Rates* (a long-term forecast) often referred to as "Forward Pricing Rates," are those burdens negotiated with the government to be used for the pricing of new business, based on a reasonable projection of estimated business volume, of a direct base forecast as related to a projection of indirect costs, usually set annually and projected perhaps three years into the future.

2. *Applied Rates* (for the current year) are those used by internal management for the budgeting and reporting for the current period. These rates do not have to match the negotiated bidding rates, and conservative management will often set them slightly above the bidding rates.

3. *Actual Incurred Rates* (for the current year) are those which reflect actual direct and indirect cost expenditures as they appear on the company books. Each firm is likely to use a slightly different approach because of its accounting system. For example,

some firms might use a running monthly cumulative adjustment, while others might make adjustments only periodically, but always at year end. Whatever method is used, it is important that actual overhead rates approximate the approved negotiated bidding rates.

4. *Negotiated Final Rates* (for prior periods) are the actual rates which are agreed to between the company and the government after the fact, sometimes years after the fact. Actual costs recorded on the books are adjusted to exclude those items which the government refuses to allow, such as entertainment costs. Adverse disallowances to the indirect pools impact company profits, but not individual contracts.

There are valid reasons why the government insists on making certain distinctions in the types and applications of rates contractor's use in their overhead projections:

> First, rates are developed for pricing and negotiating new contracts or modifications. These rates are estimates of anticipated future overhead costs. The second primary utilization is the billing rate used by the contractor to obtain reimbursement for costs incurred during the performance of the contract. Third, rates are developed at the conclusion of the contractor's fiscal year to determine the final allowable cost on all cost reimbursement type contracts.[4]

## Performance Measurement and Indirect Costs

With at least four categories of possible indirect rates available to programs (Bidding; Applied; Incurred; Final), a reasonable question would be: which rates should be used to set the BCWS, BCWP, ACWP, BAC, and EAC on a given contract?

Four general rules are recommended:

1. The rate and methodology used should be amenable to performance measurement and should not be administratively cumbersome.
2. The rates used for BCWS and BCWP should be identical.
3. The applied rate should be reconcilable with the bid rate.
4. The rate used for ACWP should liquidate the burden (overhead) pool on a current period basis and avoid significant year end adjustments.[5]

In order to measure C/SCSC performance on a given contract, it is necessary that in all cases the BCWS (work scheduled) use the same category of indirect burdens as that of the BCWP (earned value), and that no retroactive revisions be allowed to either the BCWS or BCWP. The recommended category to use for the work scheduled and earned value is the Applied Rate, #2 above, less the estimated (historical) value of disallowed costs in overheads.

With respect to ACWP (actual costs) it is appropriate to also use applied rates even though the actual incurred rates may be running above or below that rate, as long as one has confidence that the applied rates will be achieved. In such cases, any adjustments to the actual incurred rates are allowed for customer reports with a careful explanation in the Cost Performance Report. If, however, one has reason to suspect that indirect rates will go up or down for any of the various reasons discussed earlier, the ACWP should reflect the latest updated forecasts and allow any resulting cost variances (BCWP less ACWP) to show.

Since the Budget at Completion (BAC) and Estimate at Completion (EAC) projections can extend over several years into future periods on major long-term contracts, both such projections must out of necessity use a combination of indirect cost categories to make these forecasts. In the immediate near-term period, the Applied Rates #2 should be used to set the BCWS and BCWP for the BAC/EAC.

For those far-term periods, both the BAC and EAC should use the same indirect category in the forecast, and revert back to the contractor's approved Bidding Rate #1. However, if there are changes which may have happened in the long-term indirect rate projections since the contract award, and these changes leave in question the validity of a contractor's approved bidding rates, then that contractor has a fundamental problem to settle with the government before any reliable BAC and EAC can be provided on a contract. An approved bidding rate is obviously a condition precedent to a contractor being in a position to provide a reliable BAC and EAC forecast to the government.

Exactly where indirect costs are to be applied in the C/SCSC Performance Measurement Baseline (PMB) is a matter for the individual contractor to decide:

> After indirect costs are accumulated and allocated to contracts, they are applied at the level selected by the contractor. There is no requirement in the criteria to apply indirect costs at either the work package or cost account levels, although some contractors may choose to do so. However, it must be possible to summarize indirect costs from the applied level to the contract level without the need for further divisions.[6]

Earned value in C/SCSC refers to the performance measurement of a single contract. The performance of a firm's indirect activity affects all contracts in the company and is normally beyond the ability of a single program to control or influence. Nevertheless, as deviations to the plan occur, a firm must have the ability to analyze and explain just what happened to their indirect costs, and to do so on an individual contract basis.

## Summary

The above discussion covers only briefly the important subject of indirect cost management, but at no time did we touch on the very critical issue of what might constitute a "proper" indirect rate, or combination of indirect rates, for contractors to use. That delicate matter has historically been left up to individual contractors to sort out and then for the marketplace to either reward or eliminate firms based on the prices they quoted for new business. That had been the practice up to now.

However, the Department of Defense has recently conceived the new innovation of the "Indirect Should Cost Study." Under this concept, a sizeable DOD team will physically descend on a selected contractor's plant and for several months they will study, scrutinize and finally make suggestions and/or recommendations as to the "proper" values for contractors to use for their indirect expenses. This is a most interesting new development—in our "free enterprise" system.

---

## ENDNOTES

[1] Defense Systems Management College, *Program Manager's Notebook*, article by E. M. Dworin, LTC, USA, and Dr. B. C. Rush, "Indirect Cost Management" (Fort Belvoir, VA: July, 1985) page 6.12c.

[2] Department of Defense, *Cost/Schedule Control Systems Criteria-Joint Implementation Guide,* October, 1987, page 5-4.

[3] DOD JIG, October, 1987, page 3-14.

[4] DSMC, *Program Manager's Notebook*, page 6.12d.

[5] From the Humphreys & Associates, Inc., course, *Cost/Schedule Control Systems and Performance Measurement Systems*, Chart #09-120.

[6] DOD JIG, October, 1987, page 3-14.

# 17

# Co-Existence with Military Standard 1567: Work Measurement

At a recent joint government/industry meeting on C/SCSC, a representative from the Defense establishment was asked what he thought would be the final outcome in the relationship between C/SCSC and Military Standard 1567. The person was quick to respond: "There is no relationship between the criteria and 1567." Well, that settles that. Or does it?

If there is no relationship between these two governmental directives, then why are there many people in private industry, familiar with both the criteria and MIL-STD-1567, who believe that there is some relationship? Why does the standing "Management Systems Subcommittee" of the NSIA (National Security Industrial Association) keep the subject of the MIL-STD-1567 on their agenda for discussion at each of their bimonthly meetings? Why are there successful commercial C/SCSC seminars held across the United States, in which one of the continuing topics for discussion is "MIL-STD-1567A: Coping With Implementation."

With all due respect to the gentleman from the DOD, no discussion of the Cost/Schedule Control Systems Criteria would be complete without some mention of Military Standard 1567, covering the subject of work measurement.

## Background on MIL-STD-1567

The work measurement initiative is the product of the United States Air Force and resulted in the issuance of their formal directive MIL-STD 1567 on 30 June 1975. A military standard (sometimes referred to as a DOD Standard) would typically be expected to apply to all

197

branches of the defense establishment, not just one. Although initially only the interest of the USAF, ten years after the Air Force issued their directive, the other branches of the DOD committed to the cause and issued the "Joint Agreement on Support of MIL-STD-1567A, Work Measurement."[1] With this senior level of military command endorsement, it becomes important that everyone fully understand what the DOD may be demanding from the private sector on future contracts.

Military Standard 1567A is intended to apply to all DOD contracts which fit the following criteria:

- Full-scale acquisition program developments which exceed $100 million.

- Production, which may include some types of depot level maintenance repair or overhaul, that exceeds $20 million annually or $100 million cumulatively.

- Related subcontracts and/or modifications which exceed $5 million annually or $25 million cumulatively.[2]

Excluded from MIL-STD-1567A application will be contracts or subcontracts for construction, facilities, off-the-shelf commodities, time and materials, research, study, and most ship construction efforts.

One very important point: the original 1975 USAF issue of MIL-STD-1567 specifically *excluded* all "firm fixed-price contracts." That logical and reasonable exclusion was surgically removed from the DOD 1983 MIL-STD-1567A update. By definition, all contracts which now meet the dollar levels stated above can be made subject to MIL-STD-1567A, *including firm fixed-price contracts!*

The application of Military Standard 1567 requires contractors to prepare and submit for customer approval some type of a generic *Work Measurement Plan*, which will typically define:

1. The contractor's organizational responsibilities for implementing Military Standard 1567A.

2. The company's internal procedures required to be added or modified, in order to comply with MIL-STD-1567A.

3. An agreement by the contractor to establish and maintain engineered labor standards of known accuracy for all the "touch labor" functions of machining, welding, fabricating, cleaning, painting, assembling, and production functional testing. At least 80% of these hours must be covered by type 1 standards of a +/-10% accuracy level, and with a 90% or more confidence level.

4. An agreement by the contractor to establish a time-phased plan to achieve 80% coverage with type 1 standards.

5. An agreement by the contractor to continue to improve work methods associated with the established labor standards.

6. An agreement by the contractor to use the approved labor standards in their budgeting, estimating, production planning, and "touch labor" performance evaluations.

7. An agreement by the contractor to internally report progress to standards on a weekly basis.

8. An agreement by the contractor to conduct annual internal audits of the compliance of Military Standard 1567, and to make the results of such audits available to the cognizant government representative

9. An agreement by the contractor to allow the government to review the initial implementation of work measurement and to continuously survey the contractor's efforts.

If the government surveillance personnel determines that the contractor's system does not meet the MIL-STD-1567A requirements, they can mandate implementation of a corrective action plan which would be subject to their approval. Should the contractor then fail to meet the corrective action plan, their approved manufacturing work measurement system can be "invalidated" by the government. Sounds much like the C/SCSC implementation and surveillance, doesn't it?

## Evolution of the MIL-STD-1567 Documentation

Over the brief decade or so since the Air Force first introduced MIL-STD-1567 to the public in 1975, there have been certain important releases of documentation which dictate the work measurement requirement. It might be beneficial to trace this evolution and briefly describe what each of these work measurement documents covered:

1. *MIL-STD-1567 Work Measurement*: 30 June, 1975 (7 pages) (USAF)—In this initial USAF document the concept of work measurement was introduced. Certain very precise definitions were provided to contractors. Some of the more significant were:

    3.1.1 *Earned Hours*—The time in standard hours credited to a workman or group of workmen as the result of successfully completing a given task or group of tasks: usually calculated by summing the products of applicable standard times multiplied by the completed work units.

    3.1.2 *Labor Efficiency*—The ratio of earned hours to actual hours spent on a prescribed task during a reporting period. When earned hours equal actual hours, the efficiency equals 100%.

    3.1.7 *Touch Labor*—Production labor which can be reasonably and consistently related directly to a unit of work being manufactured, processed, or tested. It involves work affecting the composition, condition, or production of a product; it may also be referred to as "hands-on labor" or "factory labor."

*Note:* As used in this standard, touch labor *does not include* the functions of engineering, production control and production planning. It does include such functions as machining, welding, fabricating, cleaning, painting, assembling and functional testing of production articles.

3.1.9   *Type I Engineered Labor Standards*—These are standards established using a recognized technique such as time study, work sampling, standard data, or a recognized predetermined time system to derive at least 90% of the total time associated with the labor effort covered by the standard.

3.1.10  *Type II Labor Standards*—All labor standards not meeting the criteria established in paragraph 3.1.9, above.

In this initial document firm fixed-price contracts were *excluded* from the requirement, as was described earlier. Later they were included, a significant change. In addition, the requirement to employ Type I standards was specified in 1975 as: "...to statistically support an accuracy of plus or minus 25%, with at least a 90% confidence level." With the 1983 issuance the 25% requirement was tightened to "+ or -10% with a 90% or greater confidence at the operating level". Again, a significant change.

2. *MIL-STD-1567A Work Measurement*: 11 March, 1983 (7 pages) (DOD)—The update of the document contained the definitions above, and additionally, prescribed certain new/expanded definitions of importance as follows:

3.1   *Actual Hours*— An amount determined on the basis of time incurred as distinguished from forecasted time. Includes standard time properly adjusted for applicable variance.

3.7   *Realization Factor*—

(a) A ratio of total actual labor hours to the standard earned hours.

(b) A factor by which labor standards are multiplied when developing actual/projected manhour requirements.

3.14  *Touch Labor Normal/Standard Time*—Normal time is the time required by a qualified worker to perform a task at a normal pace, to complete an element, cycle or operation, using a prescribed method. The personal, fatigue and unavoidable delay allowance added to this normal time results in the standard time.

3. *MIL-STD-1567A Work Measurement Notice 1*: 3 March, 1986—In this first change notice a new 19-page *Appendix* was added to MIL-STD-1567A. This document further defined and interpreted requirements for implementing a work measurement system which would:

Apply these engineered standards to 80 percent of the direct manufacturing touch labor hours. Apply estimated standards to the remaining work.[3]

Additionally the Appendix defined the application of MIL-STD-1567A:

1. *Contracts in the Conceptual or Validation Phase*—In this phase contractors may be asked to describe their existing work measurement systems, and/or when they will be complying with MIL-STD-1567A.

2. *Full Scale Development (FSD) Contracts*—The government's intent is to require that work measurement be developed and used to the maximize extent during FSD.

3. *Production Contracts*—Type I standards should be applied to 80% of touch labor hours.

The Appendix specifies the flow-down requirements of MIL-STD-1567A to subcontractors: "Prime contractors are responsible to see that their subcontractors comply with the requirements of MIL-STD-1567A..." Interdivisional (IDWA) work is considered to be "make" work, i.e., part of the prime contractor's effort.

4. *MIL-STD-1567A Work Measurement Notice 2*: 21 November 1986 (3 pages)—In this second change notice to MIL-STD-1567A, selected pages were updated, but the most significant addition was the inclusion of a 3-page Data Item Description (DID) on work measurement. This DID requires contractors to formally report performance to goals by contract end-item, including: quantity of units completed, total manufacturing hours including hours not contractually required to be covered, performance factor, performance index, variance analysis by end-item.

There is probably no single step that the government can take to "institutionalize" a requirement than to put an approved DID in the hands of a procuring officer. The DID (#DI-MISC-80295) on *Work Measurement Labor Performance Report* was approved for release on 12 February, 1987.

5. *MIL-STD-1567, Work Measurement Verification and Audit Plan*, AFSCP 84-1: 20 April, 1987—This 38-page Air Force document was issued as an internal guide for Air Force implementing commands, but did add additional requirements. It contains a basic section and three appendices covering:

1. Verification Review and Compliance Audit.
2. Time Study Standard Accuracy Determination (step by step).
3. Work Sampling Standard Accuracy Determination (step by step).

However, the most permanent aspect is likely two new definitions contained in the basic section:

**(1)** *Verification Review*—A work measurement system review by the government to determine if an offeror's (i.e., contractor's) documented policies and procedures adequately address MIL-STD-1567 contractual requirements. Normally the review is performed prior to contract award.

**(2)** *Compliance Audit*—An annual work measurement study by the government, normally performed by the cognizant Contract Administration Service (CAS) organization, to confirm that a contractor is following the policies and procedures determined satisfactory through verification review.[4]

Sounds a little like "C/SCSC *deja vu*," doesn't it?

Thus, in a period of twelve years the documentation covering work measurement grew from 7 pages in 1975, to over 67 pages in 1987.

With all this DOD documentation there can be little doubt that all branches of the military will soon be requiring MIL-STD-1567 on selected contracts. However, as late as 1986 it was still primarily an Air Force show:

> The Air Force continues to be the lead agency requiring aerospace contractors to use work measurement systems on government contracts. In FY 85, the Air Force included the MIL-STD in 136 contracts, whereas the other services included it on only 4 contracts.[5]

## The Relationship of MIL-STD-1567 to C/SCSC

No matter how often people repeat their "official" position that there is no overlap or relationship between MIL-STD-1567 and the C/SCSC, there is a growing awareness that certain of the C/SCS Criteria and work measurement requirements do cover the same territory. Selected examples of the C/SCSC requirements:

*Criterion I, #3*—Provide for the integration of the contractor's planning, scheduling, budgeting, work authorization and cost accumulation systems with each other...

*Criterion II, #7*—Identify relationships of budgets or standards in underlining work authorization systems to budgets for work package budgets.

*Criterion IV, #1*—Identify at the cost account level on a monthly basis...(c)Variances resulting from the above comparisons classified in terms of labor,...

These are but three of the more obvious examples of the encroachment of MIL-STD-1567 into the area covered by the C/SCS Criteria.

However, the two regulations do have divergent philosophies and objectives, as the following comparison illustrates:[6]

| MIL-STD-1567A | C/SCSC |
|---|---|
| 1. Management of touch labor. | 1. Management of total contract. |
| 2. Labor reduction through methods improvement | 2. Management through goal setting and baselining. |
| 3. Dynamic baseline. | 3. Static baseline for reporting consistency. |
| 4. Detail by part number (hours) | 4. Detail by Work Packages (hours or dollars). |
| 5. Control at work center. | 5. Control at cost account. |
| 6. Maintenance is dynamic retroactive. | 6. Maintenance is restricted to the future, in unopened work packages. |
| 7. Acceptance by individual contract only. | 7. Acceptance by Tri-Services on all contracts of certain dollar thresholds. |

In terms of status reports going to the government, it is not inconceivable that a given contract with both C/SCSC and MIL-STD-1567 requirements could be reporting at the same time:

- Good MIL-STD-1567 performance and bad C/SCSC performance.
- Bad MIL-STD-1567 performance and good C/SCSC performance.

While industry considers both requirements to cover much the same effort, the DOD and USAF continues to insist that the two requirements are separate and distinct:

> The two (C/SCSC and MIL-STD-1567) are different and separate. C/SCSC validated contractor management systems provide cost and schedule performance, whereas the MIL-STD-1567's purpose is to help increase discipline in contractor work measurement programs with the objective of improved productivity and efficiency in contractor industrial operations. In this sense, MIL-STD-1567's disciplined approach is a management tool. The C/SCSC system receives the benefits from a number of management tools, from a multitude of functional disciplines. Implementation of C/SCSC would not stop if there were no MIL-STD-1567, nor would the reverse ever happen. The two purposes, separately, are vitally important to current and future weapon systems acquisitions. AFSC manufacturing and comptroller personnel agree that it would benefit neither purpose for the work measurement program to become a mandated part of C/SCSC.[7]

## Summary

The aggressive implementation of Military Standard 1567 to its fullest will likely have an impact on C/SCSC by virtue of their overlapping interests, although interestingly, nowhere in the various MIL-STD-1567 documents is reference made to C/SCSC. Conversely, no place in any C/SCSC documents is there mention of MIL-STD-1567. One thing is certain, however: MIL-STD-1567 will likely have a very profound impact on the various private contractors and the way they do business in the future, not too dissimilar from the impact felt by these contractors as they implemented C/SCSC in the 1970s.

There is an important distinction between the implementation approach used by Military Standard 1567 and that taken by the C/SCS Criteria. Under the criteria approach, the government merely indicated that they needed certain data, and the contractors were allowed considerable flexibility in choosing the specific method to satisfy the criteria. Hence, over the years different firms have used different methods to satisfy the requirements of C/SCSC. Nowhere does C/SCSC documentation tell industry "how" to provide such data.

Military Standard 1567, on the other hand, not only specifies the requirement for certain data, but it also essentially provides the "how" to do it. It assumes that its way is *the best way* and allows little flexibility to the private firms. In this regard, the implementation approach is not too dissimilar from the one used two decades earlier to impose PERT and PERT/Cost on industry.

One of the principal concerns of private industry is the critical issue of who will pay the costs for implementing and maintaining MIL-STD-1567. From their perspective the idea of cost benefits is still unproven. Some people from the government have suggested that such costs be charged into contractor overhead pools, and applied over all contractor contracts. Industry generally objects to this approach. Such implementation costs, if clearly beneficial to a given contract, should be charged directly to the contract requiring such effort.

But the USAF is adamant that the cost benefits are there:

> We expect minimum added costs associated with work measurement system implementation resulting from contractual application of this DID. We also expect that the long-term benefits from work measurement systems implementation (DID included) will greatly exceed the costs.[8]

There are some who are not concerned about the issue of work measurement. They feel that "touch labor" will be on the decline in the future as robotics and automation start to take over. Others cite the decreasing content of in-house effort on most new contracts and the increasing significance of the purchased portion. However, touch labor is touch labor, whether performed in-house or purchased from a supplier. The central issue is still present and poses a challenge to industry.

What the final impact Military Standard 1567 will have on the defense procurement business is anybody's guess. If the MIL-STD-1567 approach turns out to be a viable, efficient way for all contractors to conduct their business, then it will certainly survive the test of time. The recent developments of the U.S. Congress incorporating work measurement requirements into their authorization legislation, and the development of FAR (Federal Acquisition Regulations) clauses specifically requiring work measurement by contractors will certainly contribute much to the longevity of the applications.

At the very least, MIL-STD-1567 would appear to be a distant cousin, a logical extension of the C/SCSC concept. Perhaps some day the two camps, the industrial engineers and the program controllers, will see the relationship.

Although not presently cross-referenced or required by any governmental document, the Military Standard 1567 personnel and the C/SCSC personnel may well start "bumping" into each other in the corridors of contractor's plants, as both teams vigorously implement and monitor their respective missions—which have "no relationship to each other"!

---

## ENDNOTES

[1] "Joint Agreement on Support of MIL-STD-1567A, Work Measurement," dated 08 January, 1985, signed by the Commanders of the U.S. Army Materiel Command, the USAF Logistics Command, the USAF Systems Command, and the Chief of Naval Material, Naval Material Command.

[2] U.S. Department of Defense, *Work Measurement MIL–STD-1567,* 11 March, 1983, Page 1.

[3] MIL–STD–1567A, Notice 1, 3 May, 1986, page 10.

[4] AFSCP 84–1, 20 April, 1987, page 2.

[5] Major General Bernard L. Weiss, USAF, Commander of Air Force Contract Management Division, in a paper intitled "Report Card 86," delivered to the National Contract Management Association meeting, Los Angeles, 17 July, 1986.

[6] Dan Pifer, from material he used entitled "MIL-STD-1567A Implementations," presented at The Technical Marketing Society of America  (TSMC) seminar: *Performance Measurement Conference,* Los Angeles, California, 9 March, 1987.

[7] Brigadier General James C. Dever, Jr., USAF, Air Force Systems Command, in a letter to the Editor of *Industrial Engineering Magazine,* 29 April, 1984.

[8] Major General Monroe T. Smith, USAF, in a letter to the Aerospace Industries Association of America, Inc., dated 12 January, 1987.

# 18

# Coping with Overruns
# and Schedule Slips

This will come as no surprise to anyone, but we live in a less than perfect world. One merely has to open the daily newspaper to get the latest update on who's business is in trouble because of what they did or did not do in their business affairs. The issues are getting so exciting that they are starting to move from the business sections right on to the front pages of our newspapers. To put it bluntly, life's a mess. And the one thing all these evils have in common, is that nobody (except the newsmedia) ever wants to talk about them. We will be an exception.

The ethical/moral issues are clearly beyond the intended scope of this book. But such problems as cost overruns and schedule slippages on government contracts are things that we ought to discuss, as unpleasant a topic as it might be for some of us.

An interesting fact: as one reads through the thousands of pages of governmental publications on C/SCSC, rarely do they ever use the word "overrun" in their documents. Rather, they consistently substitute that unspoken word with such nebulous terms as "Unfavorable cost variances," "over the target baseline," "formal reprogramming," and "contracts with cost growth," to avoid the terrible utterance "overrun." This condition is not by accident. Rather, it was by deliberate direction. In the early days of C/SCSC the people who were implementing the concept were specifically directed (from above) not to use the term "overrun," since technically "an overrun is not an overrun until a contract is over."

Again, we will be an exception and frequently use those repugnant terms, "overruns" and "schedule slips" on the pages to follow. Such conditions, as bad as they may be for those involved, do happen, even in the best of families.

## Cost Overruns

In order to disscuss cost overruns and the C/SCSC, certain precise definitions may be beneficial to the discussion:

*Performance Measurement Baseline (PMB)*—The time-phased budget plan against which project performance is measured. It is formed by the budgets assigned to scheduled cost accounts and the applicable indirect budgets. For future effort, not planned to the cost account level, the Performance Measurement Baseline also includes budgets assigned to higher level CWBS elements. The PMB equals the total allocated budget less management reserve.

*Replanning*—A change in the original plan for accomplishing authorized contractual requirements but stays within target costs. There are two types of replanning effort:

(a) *Internal Replanning*—A change in the original plan that remains within the scope of the authorized contract. It is caused by a need on the part of the contractor to compensate for cost, schedule, or technical problems which have made the original plan unrealistic.

(b) *External Replanning*—(Government directed changes to the contract) can be in the form of a definitized change order or an unpriced change order that calls for a change in the original plan. While this change may remain within the scope of the original contract it most often exists as a change in the scope of the contract in terms of cost, schedule, technical parameter or a combination thereof.

*Reprogramming*—Also called "Formal Reprogramming,"this is a comprehensive replanning of the effort remaining in the contract resulting in a revised total allocated budget which will exceed the current contract budget base.

*Over Target Baseline (OTB)*—A baseline which results from formal reprogramming with the approval of the customer, which will exceed target costs.

*Overrun*—Costs incurred in excess of the contract target costs on an incentive-type contract, or the estimated costs on a on a fixed-fee contract.

The three terms "reprogramming" "over target baseline", and "overrun" are generally considered to be synonymous within C/SCSC terminology.

The management of cost overruns is nothing more than the management of the PMB, the Performance Measurement Baseline which we discussed earlier. Cost overruns are simply an anomaly that sometimes happens to the PMB. Two of the more common conditions which can and do happen with the formation and subsequent maintenance of the PMB have been given names by the C/SCSC practitioners: the "Front Loading" of the PMB, and a PMB with a "Rubber Baseline." We should cover both of these possible conditions.

The "Front Loading" of the PMB is a situation which happens while the baseline is in formation by a contractor. The condition can happen intentionally or unintentionally on the part of the contractor, but the result is the same. A PMB is established with adequate budget allocated at the front-end, for near-term work, but the contract is left with inadequate funds for the later, far-term effort. A latent overrun is thus solidly incorporated into a baseline plan.

When contractors *intentionally* front load a baseline they do so with the belief or hope that subsequent changes in the statement of work will be sufficient to avoid an eventual overrun condition from surfacing. In effect, they hope—they pray—to "get well" on contractually directed changes.

When contractors *inadvertently* front load a contract they are in effect inadequately planning for the far-term contractual effort.

A "Front Loading" condition is displayed in Figure 18-1.

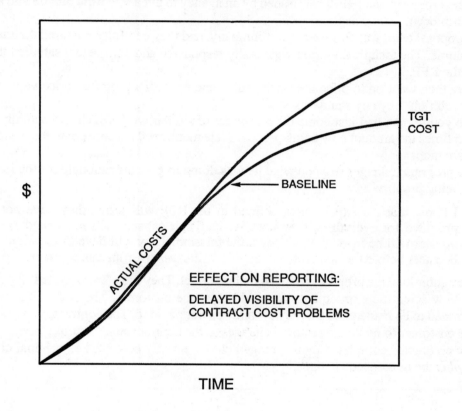

TIME

**Figure 18-1  "Front Loading" the PMB[1]**

One senior government official described the condition of front loading as follows:

> Front loading occurs most frequently in situations where the negotiated contract target cost is unrealistic at the outset. In such cases, the contractor may budget the first part of the contract effort realistically and underbudget the far term effort, hoping to "get well" on contract changes along the way. If this does not happen, the project manager will encounter a surprise overrun on a contract which may otherwise have appeared to be in good shape.[2]

---

*War Story # 5*

This story illustrates how some contractors have intentionally maneuvered themselves to avoid exposing an overrun condition in the belief that they could prevent it from eventually happening. Sometimes they were successful, and sometimes they were not.

In the early years of the space program, years before the manned space program was undertaken, most of the effort was directed at simply putting scientific packages into space. A request for proposal (RFP) was issued by an agency to put a scientific bundle into a shallow earth orbit.

A proposal team was formed by one company, and they carefully prepared their technical volume. The technical section was totally responsive and completely satisfied the letter of the RFP.

They then went on to price the effort, and came up with a proposed price value which was "ambitious" by any standards.

One young man had just come off a contract of similar work which had actually spent some 5 times the amount now being proposed. He mentioned his concern to the designated program manager.

The program manager stopped what he was doing to give his rationale for the low cost value being proposed:

> I know that the experiments defined in the RFP will grow, they have not provided for everything they hope to do. Their capsule will grow, and the booster will be inadequate to cover the mission. They will have to substitute boosters before the contract is over. We will *never* overrun this contract.

They submitted the proposal and won their contract. They then "front loaded" the budget plan. New scientific experiments were added by the customer. The rocket booster was determined to be inadequate for the new and heavier payload. The contractor was directed by the customer to make the required changes to the contract statement of work.

The contractor completed their arrangement essentially on cost, i.e., original contract costs *plus* the negotiated changes.

---

The second condition which sometimes happens on contracts is termed a "Rubber Baseline." It happens after the PMB is in place, usually during the early phases of contractor performance.

As cost problems start to appear in performance, the contractor will attempt to shift allocated down-stream budget to the left, back into the current period in order to cover the current cost problems. The effect, if allowed to happen, is the same as a "front loaded" baseline. Inadequate budget will later be available to cover down-stream effort, and the contract will eventually overrun the costs. However, a "rubber PMB baseline" will disguise the latent overrun because negative cost variances will not be appearing in the early cost reports.

The criteria do specifically prohibit the shifting of budget alone, without also shifting the accompanying statement of work. However, some contractors have shown themselves to be quite clever (if not absolutely ingenious) in shifting funds to the left, but with an *inadequate* or *lesser-valued* shifting of corresponding work tasks to the left, which has the same effect as front loading: the inadequate provision of down-steam budget.

The graphical display of a rubber baseline condition is shown in Figure 18-2.

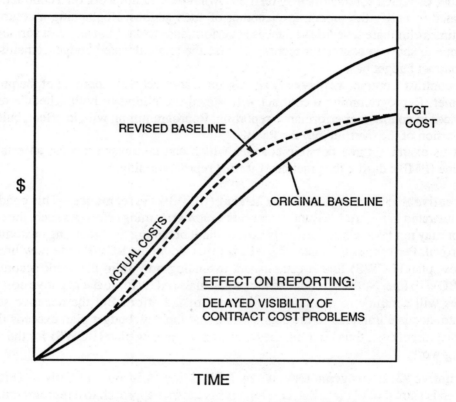

**Figure 18-2  A PMB with a "Rubber Baseline"**[3]

In both these situations the procuring customer, whether it be the government or a private contractor, has a responsibility to take an active role in overseeing the formation and maintenance of the contractor's Performance Measurement Baseline, in order to preclude the tendency by some contractors to "front load" or "rubber baseline" their Performance Measurement Baseline.

Overruns, once they become obvious to the contractor and the procuring customer, beg the question: what do we do now? When a contractor is experiencing either cost or schedule problems, or probably both, the contractor at some point is likely to suggest "wiping the slate clean" and start over with a new plan. Such requests have no performance or surveillance value to a contract. Rather, they are usually done for the "psychological" well-being of the program involved. People do not like to be held accountable for performance against unachievable goals.

The new plan can take one of two forms, depending on the desired results. Contractors can "replan" the contract, or they can "reprogram" the contract. These two terms have precise meanings in C/SCSC parlance, as were defined above.

Under C/SCSC, contractors may on their own *replan* future work on a contract, but are obligated to notify the procuring customer of such actions. Replanning a contract will sometimes eliminate schedule variances in performance to date, but any cost variances will continue to show in contractor reporting, since the total allocated budget remains tied to the contract budget base.

By contrast, contractors may only *reprogram* a contract with approval of the procuring customer. Reprogramming a contract will sometimes eliminate both schedule and cost variances in contractor performance reporting. Reprogramming will, in effect, build in all or a portion of the overrun into the PMB.

Let us examine three possible changes which can take place against an established baseline (PMB), during the practice of formal reprogramming.

**Alternative # 1: Reprogram from Current (BCWP) Performance**—This condition is illustrated in Figure 18-3, and represents a reprogramming effort. As such, the contractor may not take this action on its own without obtaining the procuring customer's approval. Performance to date (BCWP) is reflected by the BCWP time-now line, and a new plan (BCWS) line is established, extending now from the work accomplished (BCWP) line. Nothing is done to the cost actuals (ACWP), so the negative cost variances will continue to show for the balance of the effort. But the negative schedule variance is eliminated in the action. Note that the new budget plan exceeds the contract target cost, thus building the overrun into the new plan (BCWS) for the remaining work.

**Alternative #2: Reprogram from a new BCWS line: Add Budget Only**— This condition is shown in Figure 18-4, and represents another approach to a reprogramming action. Budget is added to eliminate the negative cost variances to date, but in this case nothing is done to eliminate the negative schedule variances.

Performance to date (BCWP) is reset at the cost actuals (ACWP) value line, and a new plan line (BCWS) is set above the BCWP level, in order to continue the actual negative schedule variance condition in the new plan.

This type of reprogramming action is somewhat rare, but may take place when the item being procured is "time critical," and although the procuring customer is willing to provide additional funding in order to set more realistic cost targets, they want *no* more loss of schedule. They deliberately choose to let the behind-schedule position continue to show on performance charts.

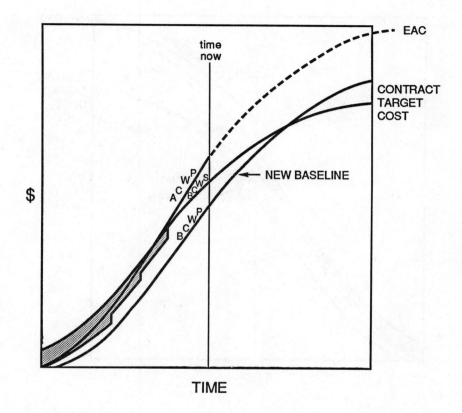

**Figure 18-3 Partial Reprogramming: Eliminate the Schedule Variance** [4]

**Alternative #3: Reprogram from the ACWP line: Add Budget and Reschedule**—This action is a total reprogramming effort and eliminates both the negative cost and schedule variances to date. It is shown in Figure 18-5, page 215.

The performance to date line (BCWP) is re-positioned at the cost actuals (ACWP) line, and a new plan (BCWS) is set, extending now from intersection of the combined ACWP/BCWP point on the time-now line.

Earlier it was said that the government in its treatment of cost overruns seemed to be avoiding calling, a "spade a spade" and an "overrun an overrun." This may be true, but by no means were the government managers unaware of this critical problem.

In fact, overruns and the early exposure of them were the very reason why, initially, the Air Force in the mid-1960s—and later the other services—all combined their positions to endorse the criteria concept. They knew they had a dilemma, and they took the unified positive action of issuing the C/SCSC to help manage this difficult problem.

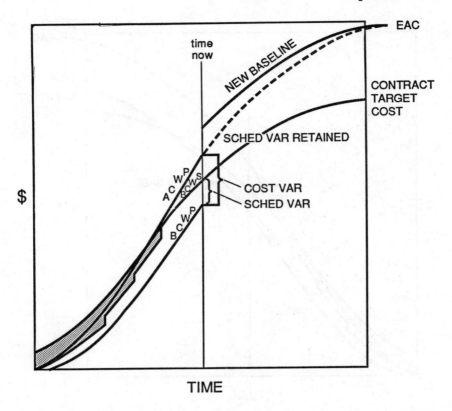

**Figure 18-4  Partial Reprogramming: Eliminate the Cost Variance**[5]

Often throughout this book, and particularly in this chapter, we have relied on work done by one government official to illustrate the C/SCSC concept. Years after he departed the DOD and went on to the DOE to implement the criteria concept at that agency, he made the following remarks concerning overruns and the criteria concept:

> To the extent possible, emphasis should be placed on keeping the measurement baseline oriented to the contractual cost and schedule targets; i.e., the budgets should add up to the negotiated contract cost plus the estimated cost for authorized, unnegotiated work, and the schedule plan should conform to the contractual schedule provisions.

> There may be exceptional situations, however, where it makes more sense to budget to some other goal in order to provide increased budgets for remaining contract work. Such situations result from technical problems or other difficulties which obviously dictate a significant overrun on the contract. C/SCSC provisions are available to accommodate these situations on a carefully controlled, highly visible and formal basis.[7]

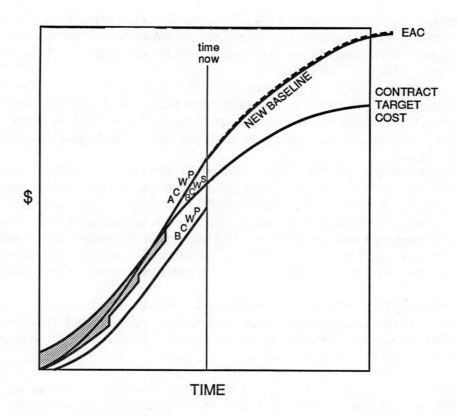

**Figure 18-5  Total Reprogramming:  Eliminate Both Cost and Schedule Variances** [6]

Allowing the budget baseline to exceed the contract value (contract budget base) is called Formal Reprogramming in C/SCSC parlance. It is also commonly referred to as "over-target baselining." It occurs, usually at the request of the contractor, when a contract is in an unfavorable cost position and the budget remaining to complete the work is decidedly insufficient. In effect, it constitutes a formal declaration of an overrun, and results in a new baseline which "builds in" that overrun. Formal recognition by the procuring agency is required before a contractor may employ an over-target budget, since the Cost Performance Report is adversely affected by this action.

## The "Nunn-McCurdy Amendment" [8]

This is serious stuff!

Anyone who heretofore may have been cavalier about cost overruns should probably review in detail a subtle amendment inserted into the FY1983 Authorization Act, common-

Department of Defense Instruction DODI 7220.31 on "Unit Cost Reports" has put "teeth" into the reporting requirements of the Department of Defense to the United States Congress. By law the DOD must report to the Congress anytime a program exceeds its baseline values by pre-established thresholds.

For some time, the Defense Secretary has had to submit annual reports to the Congress on all programs of a sufficient value, currently representing about 100 such candidates. These reports take the form of a "Selected Acquisition Report," or SAR, and the governing document is DODI 7000.3 (not to be confused with the C/SCSC SAR, Subsequent Applications Review).

What is new and different about "Nunn-McCurdy" is that the amendment contains very precise definitions of exactly what constitutes a "unit cost" (of two types), what constitutes a reporting threshold, what constitutes a breach of the threshold, and what actions must be taken and when by the DOD in submittal of their reports to the Congress. Failure to take the required reporting actions within the required time-frame also requires that specific actions must be taken by the DOD, including the "suspension" of further obligations to the affected contracts. Suspension of obligations has happened twice since the amendment was passed.

Nunn-McCurdy requires baseline "cradle to grave" estimates to be made of the value for all SAR level reporting programs, beginning with the first SAR submittal. These baseline values reflect the estimated worth of the program in the President's budget, and are expressed in two types of "unit cost" estimates:

> **(1)** *Program Acquisition Unit Cost (PAUC)*—Representing the sum of *all* RDT&E, production, and weapon system specific military construction costs for the total acquisition program, divided by the total program acquisition quantity; and/or
>
> **(2)** *Current Procurement Unit Cost (CPUC)*—Representing the total of all procurement funds appropriated for the program for a given year, divided by the number of end items to be procured in that same year.

Thus, a given program will have *on record* with the DOD and the Congress a baseline of "total program unit cost" (PAUC), and a "yearly unit cost" value (CPUC), both of which will be monitored for the life of the program.

With both total program (PAUC) and annual procurement unit costs (CPUC) set as parameters for cost thresholds, overruns cannot be hidden by simply reducing the total units procured under a given contract. Two threshold parameters are prescribed: a 15% and a 25% level. Both these levels require specific reporting actions by the Department of Defense when they are exceeded.

The Nunn-McCurdy requirements provide for report submittals at progressively higher organizational levels. Normally, reporting is quarterly from the various DOD program managers to their respective service secretary (e.g., USAF). This keeps the service secretary informed of the program unit costs on a regular basis. Exception reporting to the service secretary is required at any time when a program breaches a threshold, or when the program manager believes a threshold is likely to be breached.

If the service secretary determines from the program manager's report that a breach exceeding 15% has occurred, or will likely occur, the service secretary must submit a report to the Congress along the lines of that displayed in Figure 18-6. If the breach exceeds 25%, then the Secretary of Defense becomes involved and must *certify* certain facts on the program, with information as displayed in Figure 18-7.

When the service secretary's report goes to the Congress, it must contain the *identities* of the responsible individuals, by name—a fact which in itself has to have some effect on any ambitious career officer. Also identified by name are the *contractors* involved, and the status of the contract as reported in their CPR or C/SSR submittals. Nunn-McCurdy leaves no room for innovation on the part of those preparing the reports to Congress.

The 15% threshold value applies only the first time a breach occurs. Any additional increases of 5% or more over those breaches, once reported, require still another round of reporting to the United States Congress.

---

## Unit Cost Reports
## Procedures for a 15% Breach

- If Service Secretary agrees with the Program Manager that there is a breach, he must "promptly" notify Congress and submit a report within 30 days:

  — Explanation of the reasons for the increase.

  — Identities of the Military and Civilian Officers responsible for program management and cost control of the major defense system.

  — Action taken or proposed to control future cost growth of the system.

  — Any changes made in the performance or schedule milestones of the major system, and the degree to which such changes have contributed to the increase in total program acquisition cost or procurement unit cost.

  — Identities of the principal Contractors and status of each major contract.

- *If the report is not submitted within 30 days, the Service Secretary must take immediate action to suspend obligations.*

---

**Figure 18-6  Procedures for a 15% Breach [9]**

Any contractor breaking through the 25% barrier runs some risk of program termination, unless the program is on very solid technical ground and has friends in high places, particularly at the Department of Defense. But any enemies of given programs—and they all have them—are also given devastating information.

As a part of the certification process by the Defense Secretary, those previous contractor/customer C/SCSC activities and resulting cost reports come into direct play as the following quotations from the certification procedure illustrates:

**(c)** Discuss Cost/Schedule Control Systems Criteria (C/SCSC) requirements and status of system validation and subsequent application reviews.

**(d)** Describe type of contract cost reporting, such as CPR, C/SSR, Contract Funds Status Report (CFSR), and Contractor Cost Data Reporting (CCDR), and frequency of each.

**(h)** What differences exist in the program office's estimate-to-complete and the prime and associate contractor's estimates? Explain the differences. [10]

---

### Unit Cost Reports
### Procedures for a 25% Breach

- If the increase is more than 25%, the Secretary of Defense must "certify" within 60 days:

  — The System is essential to National Defense.

  — There are no alternatives to the System which will provide equal or better capability at less cost.

  — The new estimates of the total program acquisition unit cost or procurement unit cost are reasonable.

  — The management structure for the major system acquisition is adequate to manage and control total program acquisition unit or procurement unit cost.

- *If report is not submitted within 60 days, the Service Secretary must take immediate action to suspend obligations.*

---

**Figure 18-7  Procedures for a 25% Breach** [11]

To repeat: *"This Is Serious Stuff!!"*

## Schedule Slips

The subject of schedules and slippages to established schedules is also related to the subject of baseline management in C/SCSC. One of the three essential elements of the PMB is that of the "time-frame" for the placement of a program work packages and cost accounts. It is a simple fact that without a program schedule in place the baseline (PMB) cannot be established.

Contractors are given more leeway with respect to making changes to an established schedule position than they are to corresponding changes to their cost baseline. This feature of C/SCSC is both a good and bad. Anytime a contractor chooses to replan its program, to set more realistic schedule targets for itself, the effect may eliminate all schedule variances in performance to date. Thus, a certain amount of prudent judgement needs to be exercised in the replanning or resetting a contract's schedule baseline, with a contractor and customer working closely.

A stable time-frame, a stable program schedule, is an essential prerequisite to setting a C/SCSC PMB. Why? Because it takes time to establish a PMB, to set in place the thousands of work packages which will constitute a baseline on any major contract. About four schedule changes per year, or about one change each quarter, is the upper limit of what can be absorbed in C/SCSC without losing control of one's baseline. Sometimes, in a period of severe schedule replanning, it is necessary for C/SCSC personnel to simply wait for the schedule to stabilize, before attempting to set the PMB in place.

While there is sometimes a tendency on the part of program managers to accommodate a revised schedule, or "work-around plan," more often than some would like, prudent schedule management dictates that at least the original schedule baseline be kept in place as a constant point of reference. Without a reference point one cannot determine with any certainty how far one has come, how far one has yet to go, and perhaps even where one is presently at on a contract. In short, to do its job properly, C/SCSC is dependent on a competent schedule management system being in place.

As one astute corporate executive was once heard to remark: "My best cost control system is my schedule control system."

## Early Indicators

While there are various "official" reasons given for justifying the imposition of C/SCSC on programs, the primary justification is that the procuring customer actually is in a better position to forecast overruns with the criteria imposed than without them. It is not a perfect tool—just better than anyone has thought of thus far.

Probably one of the earliest indicators of potential future cost and schedule problems is a given contractor being unable to get a Performance Measurement Baseline (PMB) in place, for whatever reason or excuse. While no contractor is likely to fess up to an inability to set a PMB because "there are not adequate funds to do the job," they will likely come up with a thousand excuses for not getting their baseline in place.

Many, perhaps most, large firms today are organized in some type of functional "matrix" arrangement, as compared to a "projectized" organization in which everyone is direct line reporting to the program manager. A matrixed organizational arrangement provides a certain amount of independence to the participants in that the various managers are often able to "respectfully" refuse to accept budgets or schedules which are unrealistic and cannot be achieved.

When a reasonable amount of time has passed after the contract award, and there is no definitive progress toward getting agreed-to budgets and schedules in place, the procuring customer had better take a hard look at the reasons causing this condition. It might signal a potential cost or schedule problem in the contract, regardless of trite contractor statements like "We're too busy getting the important job done..."

Unilaterally issued budgets or schedules, in which the functional departments have been given but have *not* been accepted, are also points which need close examination by a procuring customer. An arbitrary PMB can also signal potential down-stream difficulties.

Other good indicators of potential cost/schedule problems are "front loaded" PMBs, and or attempts at "rubber baselining" an established PMB. Large amounts of "undistributed budget," i.e., funds not placed in planning packages, can also be an indicator of future cost growth.

Another reasonably reliable indicator of potential cost/schedule difficulties requires somewhat of an "intuitive," or perhaps a "seat-of-the-pants," assessment of the *shape* of the cumulative PMB curve. Remember a couple of summers (decades?) ago when you took that Business Statistics course? One of the things you studied were "bell-shaped" or what typically are called "S-shaped" curves. Remember?

Well, any PMB when plotted on a cumulative basis should resemble in form roughly one-half of a "bell-shaped" curve, or something close to it. The baseline projection should start out slowly, accelerate in the middle, then slow down as it nears program completion. If the plotted cumulative PMB curve doesn't take this "S- shaped" form, or something close to it, and particularly if it shows a high rate of initial acceleration near or above the straight-line plot, the baseline may well be "front loaded."

See Figure 18-8 for an example of an "S-shaped" curve, representing a cumulative PMB projection, and its relationship to the straight-lined projection.

According to the wisdom of one senior C/SCSC official, any contract which will likely experience cost/schedule problems will doubtless send out definite *sequential* indicators, which will follow a fairly set pattern:

1. *Schedule Variances*—Are the first indication of problems. The schedule variance simply tells one that the planned work is not getting done, whether it is on the critical path or not. Eventually, that work has to be done and it usually costs more to do it later.

2. *Management Reserve*—Usage is often the second indicator of problems as efforts to recover schedule may require overtime, the application of additional resources, etc. Cost variances may not yet be appearing since what work is getting done may be done for the budget originally assigned.

3. *Cost Variances*—Eventually, if schedule problems persist, cost variances will start to appear.

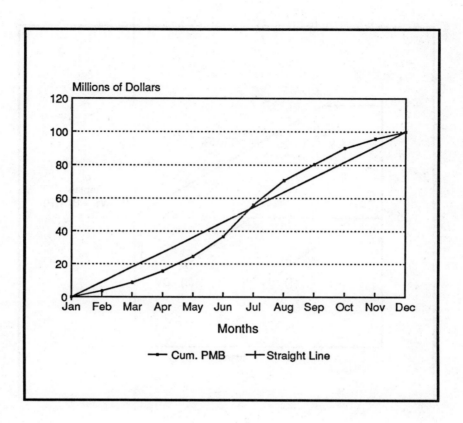

**Figure 18-8  An "S-Shaped" Cumulative PMB Curve[12]**

4. *Replanning*—At some point, management will decide to replan, (not reprogram, which involves an over-the-target baseline). Replanning will probably eliminate the schedule variances as BCWS is set equal to BCWP, but the cost variances should remain. Resetting BCWS means that tracking of the Schedule Variance starts over and the cumulative schedule variance (and cumulative SPI) becomes virtually meaningless.[13]

This condition is illustrated graphically in Figure 18-9.

## Summary

With industry often denying the very existence of overruns, and the government frequently avoiding the use of the term "overrun," it is no wonder that this is one of the more delicate and controversial C/SCSC subjects—never to be discussed in polite circles.

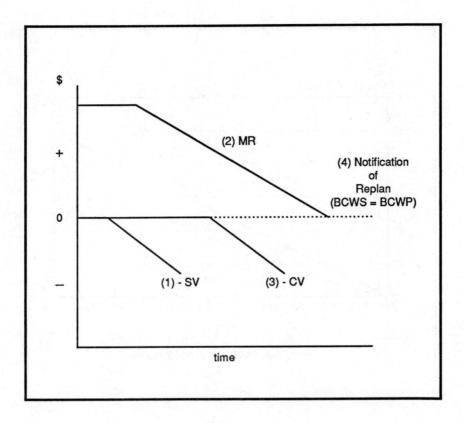

**Figure 18-9 Indicators of Cost/Schedule Problems**

In defense of the contractors, while it may be sound theory that contractors are not to proceed on an over-the-target baseline until specifically approved by the procuring customer, the plain fact of the matter is that such approval takes time, a lot of time. The sound theory often breaks down in practice.

The following scenario describes steps toward obtaining customer approval of an OTB:

1. The cost/schedule control people realize that a cost overrun is inevitable on their contract. They estimate the new EAC, which is over the contract target costs.
2. The cost/schedule people convince their program manager and other appropriate company management that an overrun is a certainty.
3. The procuring customer is "unofficially" notified of the possible overrun.
4. The contractor "officially" notifies the ACO of the potential overrun, for transmittal to the PCO.

5. The ACO transmits the data to the PCO.

6. The PCO transmits the request to the Field Command.

7. The Field Command transmits the request to the Service Headquarters.

8. Sometimes, depending on the amounts involved, the Service Headquarters must go to the DOD for funding.

9. Funding is approved by the DOD, transmitted to the Service Headquarters, transmitted to the Field Command, transmitted to the PCO for approval, and finally transmitted to the contractor.

10. The contractor implements the approved over-the-target baseline, only to now find that the EAC and requested funds are inadequate to fully complete the effort! The cycle starts again.

Question: can anyone imagine how long it takes to go from step 1 to step 10? This is a real problem. And while approval of an over-the-target baseline is separate from approval of funding, the two are essentially inseparable.

There are some people who have been with the criteria concept from the beginning who feel the issue of overruns and C/SCSC implementation could best be dealt with if the practitioners consistently broke programs into two parts: a beginning phase, and some later phase when all parties have a better understanding of what is actually involved in a given program. The program would thus be "baselined" at two points, at the start and after the completion of a key milestone:

> Maybe, we ought to consider a re-baselining requirement at some key milestone, like the Critical Design Review, i.e., make it *mandatory* that the baseline be re-assessed through a formal contractor/customer review process at that point.[14]

The DOD has essentially done just this as we see more programs going through a "Demonstration/Validation/Risk Reduction" phase, prior to being committed to a full-scale development. Both the Dem/Val and FSD phases have their own established baselines.

One word of caution is sounded by our senior government official as he comments on the use of over-the-target baselining:

> C/SCSC is intended to reflect *contract* performance measurement. Theoretically, it makes no difference whether the target cost is realistic or not in an earned value system. When the contract is complete, it is the "contract value" which is earned.

> The minute you baseline to something other than target cost, you are no longer measuring *contract* performance. You are measuring something else. It's important for people to understand this.

When we agree to go to an over target baseline, we introduce certain distortions into the Cost Performance Report, no matter how hard we try to keep track of variance adjustments, etc. The portion of the overrun budget that gets distributed to future work becomes "invisible" since it is buried in the new baseline; consequently, the BCWP is always overstated and the cost variances are all understated, subsequent to the reprogramming, in terms of contract performance.

Of all the possibilities available, formal reprogramming is probably the *worst* solution because of the complications, distortions and confusion it generates.

Unfortunately, most reprogramming is done to get rid of variances that people are tired of looking at and explaining. The main message to get across is: focus on the work remaining, the best way to get it done and the minimum resources required to do it. Adding more budget to cancel out variances is just icing on the cake, but the effect is to make people forget exactly where the problems were.[15]

Nobody could have said it better.

---

## ENDNOTES

[1] Department of Defense, Office of the Assistant Secretary of Defense (Comptroller), *Cost Performance Reporting and Baseline Management,* circa 1975, page 36.

[2] Robert R. Kemps, "Cost and Schedule Control Systems Criteria for Contract Performance Measurement," page 72. Paper presented at the conference on *Cost/Schedule Control Systems,* sponsored by the Product Managment Institute and Institute for the Advancement of Engineering, Washington, D.C., November 28-30, 1984.

[3] Department of Defense, ibid, page 34.

[4] Department of Defense, ibid, page 42.

[5] Department of Defense, ibid, page 44.

[6] Department of Defense, ibid, page 46.

[7] Robert R. Kemps, ibid, page 54.

[8] Gary E. Christle, Office of the Assistant Secretary of Defense (Comptroller); data for this section is summarized from a paper presented by Mr. Christle entitled the "Nunn-McCurdy Amendment" at the conference on *Cost/Schedule Control Systems and Performance Measurement Systems*, sponsored by the Institute of Cost Analysis, Atlanta, Georgia, October 26, 1987.

[9] Gary E. Christle, ibid.

[10] U.S. Department of Defense, *Unit Cost Reports*, DODI 7220.31, January 17, 1986, page 3-2.

[11] Gary E. Christle, ibid.

[12] Curve drawn with "Harvard Presentation Graphics," a product of Software Publishing Corporation, Mountain View, California.

[13] Robert R. Kemps, Director of the Office of Project and Facilities Managment, Department of Energy, in an interview, December 2, 1987.

[14] Robert R. Kemps, interview, December 2, 1987.

[15] Robert R. Kemps, interview, Janary 4, 1987.

# 19

# C/SCSC Reporting

No management control system would be complete without containing some provision for the formal reporting of program status, both to its internal management and to the procuring customer. C/SCSC is no exception.

Now the C/SCSC "traditionalists" will be quick to point out that: (one) the criteria are not a "system" per se, and (two) *nowhere* in the criteria do they require formal reporting of any kind. True. They are technically correct on both points.

However, the 35 criteria, once applied to a given firm's management control system, do result in a modified "criteria compliant" management control system, which will be different than what had existed before application of the criteria. And without providing reports to management, telling management how well or poorly things are going, there would be no purpose or justification for having C/SCSC imposed on contracts.

There are four distinct C/SCSC reports which, while technically not a part of the criteria, are nevertheless an important adjunct to it. However, not more than three reports will be required on any contract, and they will be applied based on contract size.

These four C/SCSC reports were designed to satisfy the diverse needs for information by the procuring customer, recognizing that when the customer is the defense or energy arm of the United States government, that multiple uses will be made from the same data. For example, the actual procurements will be made by a given governmental department, as will be for example the Department of the Air Force. This procuring group will need current information on the cost/schedule status of the contract in order to perform their role as program manager.

The next higher level management at Air Force headquarters will want the same information, as assurances that the program is going well. They will also need an accurate projection of the funding requirements for the program in order to submit their funding needs to the Department of Defense.

At the DOD, they will also need current status and funding information on all contracts, and, additionally, they will want to obtain "historical cost data" to compare the costs of one program against other similar programs. At the DOD, further cost analysis by program will take place as an added check that the funding projections being reported are adequate to complete all aspects of the programs. And as programs depart from their established baselines, the DOD is obligated to report such conditions to the United States Congress, as was mentioned in the last chapter.

All data submitted in conjunction with C/SCSC must therefore be in a sufficiently standardized format to allow for the comparison of one program with another, and with all other programs of the various procuring services. The costs of a Navy fighter aircraft must be relatable to the costs of an Air Force fighter. The Work Breakdown Structure (WBS) as specified in Military Standard 881 is the vehicle used to standardize the cost reporting format at the DOD. At the DOE they have their own standardized WBS format as specified in their DOE/MA-0295 document.

The four reports due in concert with the C/SCSC are listed in Figure 19-1. Each will be discussed individually in this chapter. Also shown in the table are the approximate frequencies of report submittals, the purpose of the reports, the applicable DOD Instruction, and the approximate dollar thresholds for imposing such reports.

| Report | Frequency | Purpose | DOD Instruction | Dollar Threshold* |
|---|---|---|---|---|
| Contract Funds Status Report (CFSR) | Quarterly | Forecast Funding Requirements, including Fee & Term. Liability | DODI 7000.10 | $ .5M |
| Cost Performance Report (CPR) | Monthly | Summary of Cost/ Schedule Position (5 Formats) | DODI 7000.10 | $40.M FSD; $160.M Production |
| Cost/ Schedule Status Report (C/SSR) | Monthly | mini-CPR on smaller Programs (3 Formats) | DODI 7000.10 | $2.M |
| Contractor Cost Data Reporting (CCDR) | Quarterly or Semi-Annual or Annually or at End | Historical Data Base on critical items (4 Reports) | DODI 7000.11 | $75.M FSD; $300.M Production  Any size on critical items |

*Dollar thresholds may vary from service branch.

**Figure 19-1 C/SCSC Reports (DOD)**

## Contract Funds Status Report (CFSR)

On all cost reimbursable type contracts a funding profile is normally established at the time of award. However, the very conditions which make a cost type contract appropriate (i.e., the likelihood of changes and redirection) will also most probably cause the funding profile to change during the course of the program. Therefore, on all DOD cost type contracts of six months duration or more and over $500,000 in value, a CFSR is required quarterly to forecast the necessary program funding required. Firm-fixed price contracts do not generally call for a CFSR because their funding is usually provided for in a separate delivery or billing schedule.

In these days of high interest rates, it is particularly important that a contractor give adequate attention to the projections in the CFSR. The funding projection must be properly balanced to keep a firm's cash flow adequate on a contract, but it must do so without requesting funds excess to programs needs. In Figure 19-2, this concept is illustrated.

Figure 19-2A reflects the contractor projection of expenditures on a hypothetical program. Such funding projections must also include the estimated value of all termination liabilities and estimated contract fee at any point in time.

The center box, Figure 19-2B, illustrates a program which has been adequately funded by the customer. At no time does the contractor have to fund its own expenditures, i.e., wait for reimbursement for costs incurred, because all funds have been sufficiently allocated to cover forecasted expenditures.

The last box, Figure 19-2C, reflects an undesirable funding condition. Here the contractor has assumed the role of financing most of the contract. Since the government does not recognize interest as an element of reimbursable cost, all costs of funding the deficit funding, i.e., expenditures ahead of reimbursements, will come out of contractor profits. With the high cost of borrowing money, the costs of deficit funding could conceivably exceed profits on a given contract.

But perhaps of greater importance to a contractor is the fact that when a contractor exceeds the funding of a program, it does so at its own risk. Should the contract be terminated for any reason while the contractor has exceeded the authorized funding, the government is under no legal obligation to cover such exposure. One of the most common causes of deficit funding, however, is that unmentionable problem of "overrun," particularly prior to the government's formal recognition of the over-target condition which often takes months to happen. In these cases, the contractor must assume at least part of the blame.

The precise format for the CFSR is specified in DOD Instruction 7000.10 (Appendix C to this book), and in more exact detail by DID (Data Item Description) DI-F-6004-B, a part of 7000.10. Those interested in the report can read the instructions contained in that Appendix. All categories of costs are tightly structured in the CFSR, illustrated in Figure 19-3, page 231.

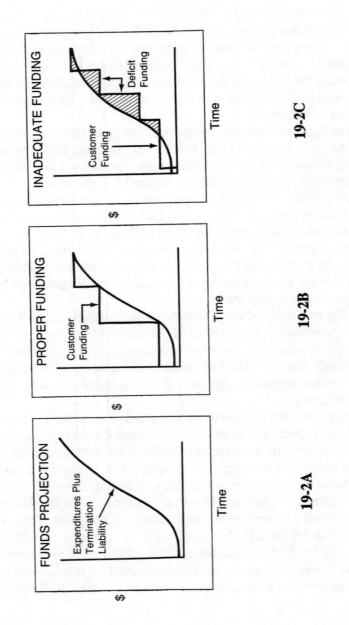

**Figure 19-2  Customer Funding**

## CONTRACT FUNDS STATUS REPORT (DOLLARS IN ----000------)

| 1. CONTRACT NUMBER | 3. CONTRACT FUNDING FOR | 5. PREVIOUS REPORT DATE | 7. CONTRACTOR (NAME, ADDRESS AND ZIP CODE) | 9. INITIAL CONTRACT PRICE |
|---|---|---|---|---|
| FPIF #1 | FOR FY  N/A | APRIL | MEGA HERTZ ELECTRONICS | TARGET $22,459.9K CEILING $26,200.0K |
| 2. CONTRACT TYPE | 4. APPROPRIATION | 6. CURRENT REPORT DATE | 8. PROGRAM | 10. ADJUSTED CONTRACT PRICE |
| FPIF | XXXX | JUNE | MOH-2 | TARGET $22,459.9K CEILING $26,200.0K |

### 11. FUNDING INFORMATION

| LINE ITEM/WBS ELEMENT (a) | APPROPRIATION IDENTIFICATION (b) | FUNDING AUTHORIZED TO DATE (c) | ACCRUED EXPENDITURES PLUS OPEN COMMITMENTS TOTAL (d) | CONTRACT WORK AUTHORIZED DEFINITIZED (e) | NOT DEFINITIZED (f) | SUBTOTAL (g) | FORECAST NOT YET AUTHORIZED (h) | ALL OTHER WORK (i) | SUBTOTAL (j) | TOTAL REQUIREMENTS (k) | FUNDS CARRY-OVER (l) | NET FUNDS REQUIRED (m) |
|---|---|---|---|---|---|---|---|---|---|---|---|---|
| TOTAL CONTRACT | XXXX | 22459.9 | 9959.6 | 22459.9 | ------- | 22459.9 | ------- | ------- | ------- | 22459.9 | ------- | ------- |

### 12.

| | ACTUAL TO DATE | CONTRACT WORK AUTHORIZED (WITH FEE/PROFIT) ACTUAL OR PROJECTED | | | | | | | | | AT COMPLETION |
|---|---|---|---|---|---|---|---|---|---|---|---|
| | | JUL | AUG | SEP | OCT | NOV | DEC | JAN | FEB | MAR | |
| a. OPEN COMMITMENTS | 107.4 | -0- | -0- | -0- | -0- | -0- | -0- | -0- | -0- | -0- | -0- |
| b. ACCRUED EXPENDITURES | 9852.2 | 11844.6 | 13856.8 | 15924.4 | 17879.7 | 19610.9 | 21068.5 | 22211.5 | 22405.1 | 22459.9 | 22459.9 |
| c. TOTAL (12a 12b) | 9959.6 | 11844.6 | 13856.8 | 15924.4 | 17879.7 | 19610.9 | 21068.5 | 22211.5 | 22405.1 | 22459.9 | 22459.9 |
| 13. FORECAST OF BILLINGS TO THE GOVERNMENT | 8616.4 | 2112.2 | 2128.0 | 2172.2 | 2082.7 | 1903.2 | 1724.2 | 1509.4 | 163.6 | 48.0 | 22459.9 |
| 14. ESTIMATED TERMINATION COSTS | N/A | 600K | 600K | 600K | 500K | 500K | 500K | 400K | 400K | 400K | -0- |

REMARKS

**Figure 19-3 Contract Funds Status Report (CFSR)** [1]

## Cost Performance Report (CPR)

Probably one of the most important and frequently used acronyms in C/SCSC is "CPR," which stands the Cost Performance Report. It should not be confused with the medical term "CPR," which stands for Cardio Pulmonary Resuscitation, a technique used on critically ill patients who denote:

> ...the absence of any clinical signs of consciousness and pulse, and who if not treated immediately, will experience permanent neurological damage.

Well perhaps—just perhaps—the creators of the C/SCSC Cost Performance Report knew exactly what they were doing when they also used the term "CPR" to describe contractor performance!

The CPR is a monthly report which is used by the customer and company management to monitor and assess cost/schedule status of a given program. It displays the typical subjects normally contained in such reports, i.e., the plan (BCWS) and actual costs (ACWP) incurred. But in addition, the CPR requires an assessment of the physical work actually performed (BCWP), and a continuing forecast of the ultimate resulting estimate of costs at completion (EAC) compared to the budget at completion (BAC).

The requirements for the CPR is also shown in DODI 7000.10 (Appendix C to this book), and the precise guidelines are specified in DID DI-F 6000C, contained therein. Five precise reporting formats are called out:

*Format 1*—Work Breakdown Structure
*Format 2*—Functional Categories
*Format 3*—Baseline
*Format 4*—Manpower Loading
*Format 5*—Problem Analysis Report

*CPR Format 1—Work Breakdown Structure:*

Early in any new program, usually 30 days after contract award, a WBS (Work Breakdown Structure) will be required. Typically, this WBS will merely be an update of the WBS submitted with the proposal, and if all things are perfect, the contractual Statement of Work (SOW) will be a close reflection of the WBS, item by item. Once approved by the customer, the WBS will serve to define the categories of costs required under CPR Format 1.

Although a Contractor WBS will likely go down to levels 5, 6 or 7, customer reporting under Format 1 is usually held to level 3 only, (level 4 on primary hardware items, e.g., air vehicle), as instructed in DODI 7000.10. However, there have been instances where the customer has required Format 1 reporting down to the very lowest level of the CWBS. Not only does this type of requirement provide more data than is humanly possible to assimilate, but it is costly, and certainly not required for proper program management. Since the contractor must be collecting costs at the lowest level of the CWBS anyway, summary reporting at WBS level 3 or even 2 is generally adequate, because anytime a variance threshold is penetrated, the contractor must describe what caused it as required under Format 5 (Problem Analysis Reporting).

Contractors normally manage their programs through their functional organizations, not by any WBS arrangement. The WBS reports were a customer idea, and are used almost exclusively by the customer. Therefore, if contractors were to be given a free choice, the WBS reports required by Format 1 would likely be the first to go. But there are exceptions. An important exception is in the area of "risk management."

In defense of the WBS report, is what can and perhaps should be done with it. Every new program, particularly those pushing the technological state of the art, face certain risks. Management, both with the procuring customer and contractor, will want to have such program risks defined and isolated, and once so identified, will find that one of the best places to monitor progress toward the elimination of such risks is with the CPR Format 1-WBS report. For example, a new radar development may represent "the" major risk on a new aircraft program. Functional organizational displays will only partially isolate and focus on the radar issue. But the combination of functional sorting and a WBS breakout would likely provide concentrated focus on the program risk areas, as determined by management.

But to stay with the radar as an example, under a typical WBS the radar would likely be identified at levels 4 or 5. If management makes the determination that the radar is a high program risk area, there is nothing improper with having the monthly WBS format routinely contain summaries at level 3, and in addition, require that the radar WBS element be shown as a special line item. Such an approach would reflect the intelligent use of CPR requirements, and this seems to be the direction of both industry and the government. Rather than monitor every nut and bolt in a system, the trend is toward higher level summaries, but with special focus on potential program risks areas, i.e., the radar.

Contained in Figure 19-4 is Format 1, covering the WBS. There are special government forms which may be used by the contractor. However, a contractor may substitute a photo/copy of a computer report printout, in lieu of these special forms, as long as all of the same data are included.

## CPR Format 2—Functional Categories

The data contained in the columns of both CPR Format 1 (WBS), and CPR Format 2 (Functional Categories), must summarize to the same bottom line values. The same data is thus provided in both formats, but with a different sorting. Prior to the introduction of computers, this requirement often kept certain young men at work all night long preparing for a customer review, since the customer always wanted to see the data by hardware/statement of work, and the normal practice in industry was, and still is, to manage contracts by the functional organization structure. This issue was covered earlier in Chapter 9 on "The Work Breakdown Structure."

COST PERFORMANCE REPORT – WORK BREAKDOWN STRUCTURE

| CONTRACTOR: Newton Aerospace, Inc. Missile Division | LOCATION: Sunnyvale, MA | RDT&E [ ] PRODUCTION [X] |
|---|---|---|
| QUANTITY 50 Missiles 10 Launchers | NEGOTIATED COST 292420 | |

| CONTRACT TYPE/NO: CPIF-A00019-73-C-0157 | PROGRAM NAME/NUMBER: Boomerang/MGM-89A | TGT PROFIT/FEE % 8.2 | EST COST AUTH. UNPRICED WORK 0 | REPORT PERIOD December | SIGNATURE, TITLE & DATE / PROGRAM DIRECTOR — January | FORM APPROVED OMB NUMBER 22R0280 |
|---|---|---|---|---|---|---|
| | | | TGT PRICE 316398 | EST PRICE 307507 | SHARE RATIO 85/15 | CONTRACT CEILING | EST CONTRACT CEILING |

| LEVEL 2 ITEM | CURRENT PERIOD — BUDGETED COST — WORK SCHEDULED | BUDGETED COST — WORK PERFORMED | ACTUAL COST WORK PERFORMED | VARIANCE — SCHEDULE | VARIANCE — COST | CUMULATIVE TO DATE — BUDGETED COST — WORK SCHEDULED | BUDGETED COST — WORK PERFORMED | ACTUAL COST WORK PERFORMED | VARIANCE — SCHEDULE | VARIANCE — COST | REPROGRAMMING ADJUSTMENTS — COST VARIANCE | BUDGET | AT COMPLETION — BUDGETED | LATEST REVISED ESTIMATE | VARIANCE |
|---|---|---|---|---|---|---|---|---|---|---|---|---|---|---|---|
| (1) | (2) | (3) | (4) | (5) | (6) | (7) | (8) | (9) | (10) | (11) | (12) | (13) | (14) | (15) | (16) |
| **WORK BREAKDOWN STRUCTURE** | | | | | | | | | | | | | | | |
| **MISSILE SYSTEM** | | | | | | | | | | | | | | | |
| AIR VEHICLE | 3387 | 3655 | 3880 | (232) | (225) | 28159 | 23877 | 30531 | (4282) | (6654) | | | 71005 | 71327 | (322) |
| COMMAND & LAUNCH EQUIPMENT | 5076 | 5064 | 5147 | (12) | (83) | 24772 | 23506 | 26008 | (1266) | (2502) | | | 82494 | 83255 | (761) |
| TRACKED VEHICLE | 1080 | 1055 | 1055 | (25) | 0 | 6399 | 6164 | 6496 | (235) | (332) | | | 23026 | 23239 | (213) |
| TRAINING | 72 | 75 | 80 | 3 | (5) | 274 | 271 | 285 | (3) | (14) | | | 1930 | 1930 | 0 |
| PECULIAR SUPPORT EQUIPMENT | 24 | 23 | 23 | (1) | 0 | 119 | 115 | 114 | (4) | 1 | | | 2386 | 2386 | 0 |
| SYSTEMS TEST & EVALUATION | 760 | 665 | 768 | (75) | (103) | 6487 | 5855 | 6975 | (632) | (1320) | | | 26661 | 26995 | (314) |
| PROJECT MANAGEMENT | 630 | 642 | 624 | 12 | 18 | 7670 | 7380 | 7470 | (190) | (90) | | | 18636 | 18636 | 0 |
| DATA | 136 | 140 | 140 | 4 | 0 | 886 | 904 | 911 | 18 | (7) | | | 8362 | 8062 | 300 |
| REPAIR PARTS | 0 | 0 | 0 | 0 | 0 | 0 | 0 | 0 | 0 | 0 | | | 6699 | 6699 | 0 |
| COST OF MONEY | 253 | 246 | 254 | (7) | (8) | 1616 | 1471 | 1704 | (145) | (233) | | | 5229 | 5257 | (28) |
| GENERAL & ADMINISTRATIVE | 1632 | 1591 | 1643 | (41) | (52) | 10449 | 9504 | 11028 | (945) | (1524) | | | 33790 | 33974 | (184) |
| UNDISTRIBUTED BUDGET | | | | | | | | | | | | | 0 | 0 | 0 |
| SUBTOTAL | 13550 | 13176 | 13634 | (374) | (450) | 86731 | 78847 | 91522 | (7884) | (12675) | | | 280436 | 281960 | (1522) |
| MANAGEMENT RESERVE | | | | | | | | | | | | | 11982 | 0 | 11982 |
| TOTAL | 13550 | 13176 | 13634 | (374) | (450) | 86731 | 78847 | 91522 | (7884) | (12675) | | | 292420 | 281960 | 10460 |
| **RECONCILIATION TO CONTRACT BUDGET BASE** | | | | | | | | | | | | | | | |
| VARIANCE ADJUSTMENT | | | | | | | | | | | | | | | |
| TOTAL CONTRACT VARIANCE | | | | | | | | | | | | | | | |

Figure 19-4 CPR Format1-Work Breakdown Structure

Format 2 reports reflect the contractor's normal organizational structure or functional categories, usually those that were reviewed at the time of validation. However, if a given program manager prefers a different organizational breakout, the government would likely consent to the request because, typically, Format 2 reports are used by the contractor for their internal management of a contract. Once again, a photocopy of a computer printout may be substituted for this government form if it contains the same data. Format 2 is displayed in Figure 19-5.

### CPR Format 3—Baseline

A couple of chapters ago there was a discussion on baseline management and control of same, which in C/SCSC is called the Performance Measurement Baseline (PMB). As a way of review, included in the PMB are all the budgets issued, plus the assigned but undistributed budget. Outside of the PMB will be the management reserve. The purpose of this Format 3 report is to tell the government precisely what is included in the current PMB and, by elimination, what is not included in the baseline.

Format 3, as shown in Figure 19-6, starts with the original target costs and traces all changes made thereto. Particular detail is provided by line item, for all changes which might have occurred to the PMB during the month.

### CPR Format 4—Manpower Loading

This report uses the same functional organizational categories as those contained in Format 2. But while Format 2 expressed costs in dollars, this report will reflect equivalent manpower in man months (MM). For those who might have forgotten what constitutes an equivalent man month, such represents a value equal to one month's equivalent work, regardless of how many persons it took to achieve it. For example, two people working half-time equals 1.0 man month. Two people working 50 percent overtime, or 60 hours per week, would equal 3.0 man months. The format requires the rounding off of values, for example 11.6 MM would be rounded to 12 MM.

Figure 19-7 illustrates a specific format for Format 4. This type of report also lends itself nicely to a computer printout, which may be substituted for the government form. The report calls for a display of actual man months for the current period, total man months to date, a six-month projection, and the total man months forecasted at completion (EAC). If there are significant differences between a previous and the current EAC, the differences must be explained in a Problem Analysis Report.

### CPR Format 5—Problem Analysis Report

This report, sometimes called a VAR (Variance Analysis Report) contains a narrative summary of what went wrong in CPR Formats 1 through 4. Each PAR should address the following issues:

**COST PERFORMANCE REPORT – FUNCTIONAL CATEGORIES**

| CONTRACTOR: Newton Aerospace, Inc. Missile Division | CONTRACT TYPE/NO: CPFF-A00019-73-C-0157 | PROGRAM NAME/NUMBER: Boomerang/MGM-99A | REPORT PERIOD December | SIGNATURE, TITLE & DATE |
|---|---|---|---|---|
| LOCATION: Sunnyvale, MA | EST COST AUTH. UNPRICED WORK 0 | TGT PROFIT/FEE % 8.2 | TGT PRICE 316398 | PROGRAM DIRECTOR January |
| RDT&E [X] PRODUCTION [ ] | | | EST PRICE 30750Z | |
| QUANTITY 50 Missiles 10 Launchers | NEGOTIATED COST 292420 | | SHARE RATIO 65/15 | |

| ORGANIZATIONAL OR FUNCTIONAL CATEGORY | CURRENT PERIOD | | | | | CUMULATIVE TO DATE | | | | | REPROGRAMMING ADJUSTMENTS | | AT COMPLETION | | |
|---|---|---|---|---|---|---|---|---|---|---|---|---|---|---|---|
| | BUDGETED COST | | ACTUAL COST WORK PERFORMED | VARIANCE | | BUDGETED COST | | ACTUAL COST WORK PERFORMED | VARIANCE | | CONTRACT CEILING | | EST CONTRACT CEILING | | |
| | WORK SCHEDULED | WORK PERFORMED | | SCHEDULE | COST | WORK SCHEDULED | WORK PERFORMED | | SCHEDULE | COST | COST VARIANCE | BUDGET | BUDGETED | LATEST REVISED ESTIMATE | VARIANCE |
| (1) | (2) | (3) | (4) | (5) | (6) | (7) | (8) | (9) | (10) | (11) | (12) | (13) | (14) | (15) | (16) |
| ENGINEERING | 6098 | 5908 | 6410 | (192) | (504) | 35633 | 32001 | 38751 | (3632) | (6750) | -- | -- | 101862 | 102872 | (1010) |
| TOOLING | 12 | 11 | 13 | (1) | (2) | 88 | 76 | 83 | (12) | (7) | -- | -- | 4257 | 4257 | 0 |
| QUALITY CONTROL | 16 | 15 | 16 | 0 | (1) | 162 | 162 | 170 | 0 | (8) | -- | -- | 876 | 876 | 0 |
| MANUFACTURING | 526 | 524 | 532 | (2) | (8) | 3005 | 2997 | 3119 | (8) | (122) | -- | -- | 27463 | 27463 | 0 |
| PURCHASED EQUIPMENT | 231 | 230 | 232 | (1) | (2) | 1874 | 1870 | 1901 | (4) | (31) | -- | -- | 13729 | 13729 | 0 |
| MATERIAL OVERHEAD | 12 | 12 | 12 | 0 | 0 | 94 | 94 | 95 | 0 | (1) | -- | -- | 686 | 686 | 0 |
| SUBCONTRACT | 3933 | 3784 | 3878 | (149) | 106 | 25080 | 22117 | 26005 | (2963) | (3888) | -- | -- | 63418 | 64018 | (600) |
| OTHER: TRAINING | 72 | 75 | 80 | 3 | (5) | 274 | 271 | 285 | (3) | (14) | -- | -- | 1930 | 1930 | 0 |
| PROJECT MANAGEMENT | 630 | 642 | 624 | 12 | 18 | 7870 | 7380 | 7470 | (190) | (90) | -- | -- | 18636 | 18636 | 0 |
| DATA | 136 | 140 | 140 | 4 | 0 | 886 | 904 | 911 | 18 | (7) | -- | -- | 8362 | 8062 | 300 |
| | | | | | | | | | | | | | | | |
| COST OF MONEY | 253 | 246 | 264 | (7) | (8) | 1616 | 1471 | 1704 | (145) | (233) | -- | -- | 5229 | 5257 | (28) |
| GENERAL & ADMINISTRATIVE | 1632 | 1591 | 1643 | (41) | (52) | 10449 | 9504 | 11028 | (945) | (1524) | -- | -- | 33790 | 33974 | (184) |
| UNDISTRIBUTED BUDGET | | | | | | | | | | | | | 0 | 0 | 0 |
| SUBTOTAL | 13550 | 13176 | 13634 | (374) | (458) | 86731 | 78847 | 91522 | (7884) | (12675) | -- | -- | 280436 | 281960 | (1522) |
| MANAGEMENT RESERVE | | | | | | | | | | | | | 11982 | 0 | 11982 |
| TOTAL | 13550 | 13176 | 13634 | (374) | (458) | 86731 | 78847 | 91522 | (7884) | (12675) | -- | -- | 292420 | 281960 | 10460 |

Figure 19-5 CPR Format 2-Functional Categories

**COST PERFORMANCE REPORT - BASELINE**

CONTRACTOR: Newton Aerospace, Inc. / Missile Division / LOCATION: Sunnyside, MA / RDT&E [X] PRODUCTION [ ]

CONTRACT TYPE/NO: CPIF-A00019-73-C-0157

PROGRAM NAME/NUMBER: Boomerang/MGM 69A

REPORT PERIOD — PROGRAM DIRECTOR: December

FORM APPROVED OMB NUMBER 22R0280

| (1) ORIGINAL CONTRACT TARGET COST | (2) NEGOTIATED CONTRACT CHANGES | (3) CURRENT TARGET COST (1)+(2) | (4) ESTIMATES COST OF AUTHORIZED, UNPRICED WORK | (5) CONTRACT BUDGET BASE (3)+(4) | (6) TOTAL ALLOCATED BUDGET | (7) DIFFERENCE (5)−(6) (SEE PAGE 5) |
|---|---|---|---|---|---|---|
| 228900 | 63520 | 292420 | None | 292420 | 292420 | 0 |

(8) CONTRACT START DATE: January
(9) CONTRACT DEFINITION DATE: January
(10) LAST ITEM DELIVERY DATE: September
(11) CONTRACT COMPLETION DATE: December
(12) ESTIMATED COMPLETION DATE: December

**BUDGETED COST FOR WORK SCHEDULED (NON-CUMULATIVE)**

| ITEM | BCWS CUM TO DATE (2) | BCWS FOR REPORT PERIOD (3) | +1 JAN (4) | +2 FEB (5) | +3 MAR (6) | +4 APR (7) | +5 MAY (8) | +6 JUN (9) | 3 QTR (10) | 4 QTR (11) | 2 YR (12) | 3 YR (13) | (14) | UNDIST. BUDGET (15) | TOTAL BUDGET (16) |
|---|---|---|---|---|---|---|---|---|---|---|---|---|---|---|---|
| PM BASELINE (BEGINNING OF PERIOD) | 73181 | 13550 | 10940 | 12763 | 14587 | 14587 | 14587 | 14587 | 18233 | 18233 | 47407 | 16414 | | | 269069 |
| (LIST BASELINE CHANGES AUTHORIZED DURING REPORT PERIOD) | | | | | | | | | | | | | | | |
| MANAGEMENT RESERVE APPLIED | | | + 100 | +1100 | +2300 | +2300 | +2300 | +2300 | + 900 | 0 | 0 | 0 | | | 11300 |
| PM BASELINE (END OF PERIOD) | 80731 | | 11040 | 13863 | 16887 | 16887 | 16887 | 16887 | 19202 | 18233 | 47407 | 16414 | | | 280436 |
| MANAGEMENT RESERVE | | | | | | | | | | | | | | | 11982 |
| TOTAL | | | | | | | | | | | | | | | 292420 |

Figure 19-6 CPR Format 3-Baseline

# COST PERFORMANCE REPORT – MANPOWER LOADING

| CONTRACTOR: Newton Aerospace, Inc. Missile Division | CONTRACT TYPE/NO: | PROGRAM NAME/NUMBER | REPORT PERIOD | FORM APPROVED |
|---|---|---|---|---|
| LOCATION: Sunnyside, MA | CPIF-A00019-73-C-0157 | Boomerang/MGM-99C | PROGRAM DIRECTOR   December | OMB NUMBER 22R0280 |
| RDT&E ☐   PRODUCTION ☒ | | | | |

| ORGANIZATIONAL OR FUNCTIONAL CATEGORY | ACTUAL CURRENT PERIOD | ACTUAL END OF CURRENT PERIOD (CUM) | SIX MONTH FORECAST BY MONTH (ENTER NAMES OF MONTHS) | | | | | | FORECAST (NON-CUMULATIVE) (ENTER SPECIFIED PERIODS) | | | | | AT COMPLETION |
|---|---|---|---|---|---|---|---|---|---|---|---|---|---|---|
| | | | Jan | Feb | Mar | Apr | May | Jun | 3 QTR. | 4 QTR. | 2 YR. | 3 YR. | | |
| (1) | (2) | (3) | (4) | (5) | (6) | (7) | (8) | (9) | (10) | (11) | (12) | (13) | (14) | (15) |
| ENGINEERING | 2861 | 15066 | 2734 | 2812 | 2972 | 2972 | 2972 | 2972 | 5468 | 2550 | 7236 | 78 | | 47852 |
| TOOLING | 8 | 42 | 15 | 15 | 15 | 315 | 315 | 315 | 945 | 52 | 123 | 0 | | 2152 |
| QUALITY CONTROL | 10 | 98 | 17 | 17 | 17 | 17 | 17 | 17 | 54 | 54 | 177 | 9 | | 492 |
| MANUFACTURING | 519 | 2754 | 608 | 608 | 608 | 608 | 608 | 608 | 1824 | 1824 | 6936 | 315 | | 17301 |
| OTHER: TRAINING | 28 | 96 | 25 | 60 | 60 | 60 | 50 | 50 | 150 | 150 | 43 | 0 | | 744 |
| PROJECT MANAGEMENT | 151 | 1821 | 158 | 158 | 158 | 158 | 158 | 158 | 474 | 474 | 1500 | 263 | | 5480 |
| DATA | 49 | 320 | 107 | 107 | 107 | 107 | 107 | 107 | 662 | 662 | 2735 | 289 | | 5310 |
| TOTAL DIRECT | 3426 | 20215 | 3664 | 3777 | 3937 | 4237 | 4227 | 4227 | 9577 | 5766 | 18750 | 954 | | 70931 |

(ALL FIGURES IN WHOLE NUMBERS)

Figure 19-7 CPR Format 4-Manpower Loading

1. It should be prepared by the lowest responsible manager of the work package, and not by an outsider unfamiliar with the problem, and not in a position to resolve it.
2. Each cost and/or schedule variance must be explained with a separate PAR, and its full impact described.
3. A plan for recovery must be specified.
4. The next higher level of supervision must review and sign the PAR.

Figure 19-8 illustrates a PAR.

The CPR is the heart of the C/SCSC activity and provides demonstrative proof to a customer that the intent of DODI 7000.2, which imposes the criteria on a contract, has been properly implemented. It provides the customer with a status position which can be tangibly verified on site at the contractor's plant.

The CPR is typically used by the customer to:

• Provide reliable and structured cost/schedule information.

• Monitor and evaluate contract/contractor performance.

• Isolate long-term trends and the early identification of cost/schedule problems.

• Quantify the size of potential cost/schedule problems.

• Use in concert with other program management techniques.

The inability of a contractor to submit a CPR for whatever reason, and to consistently track performance to it, sends out a clear signal to the customer that something is wrong. In such cases a detailed management probe might be in order.

The CPR is an extremely important document for management, both with the contractor and with the procuring customer. Also, the CPR is the document which forms the basis for reporting to the Congress, whenever contractors break the 15% or 25% thresholds.

## Cost/Schedule Status Report (C/SSR)— The Poor Man's CPR

There is another report that is used on those contracts which are not of sufficient size to warrant requiring a full CPR. This report is called a Cost/Schedule Status Report (C/SSR).

The present threshold at which a C/SSR is generally required is $2 million and have contract periods in excess of 12 months. With continuing inflation, a more reasonable dollar value may well be $5 or $10 million in the future. However, any program determined to be of a critical nature in the defense community may well warrant a full CPR or the less demanding C/SSR, no matter what the contract size.

| COST PERFORMANCE REPORT – PROBLEM ANALYSIS | | | |
|---|---|---|---|
| CONTRACTOR: | CONTRACT TYPE/NO: | PROGRAM NAME/NUMBER: | REPORT PERIOD: |
| LOCATION: | | | FORM APPROVED OMB NUMBER 22R0280 |
| RDT&E PRODUCTION | | | |

EVALUATION

SECTION 1 – TOTAL CONTRACT: PROVIDE A SUMMARY ANALYSIS, IDENTIFYING SIGNIFICANT PROBLEMS AFFECTING PERFORMANCE. INDICATE CORRECTIVE ACTIONS REQUIRED, INCLUDING GOVERNMENT ACTION WHERE APPLICABLE.

SECTION 2 – COST AND SCHEDULE VARIANCES: EXPLAIN ALL VARIANCES WHICH EXCEED SPECIFIED VARIANCE THRESHOLDS. EXPLANATIONS OF VARIANCES MUST CLEARLY IDENTIFY THE NATURE OF THE PROBLEM, THE REASONS FOR COST OR SCHEDULE VARIANCE, IMPACT ON THE IMMEDIATE TASK, IMPACT ON THE TOTAL PROGRAM, AND THE CORRECTIVE ACTION TAKEN. EXPLANATIONS OF COST VARIANCES SHOULD IDENTIFY AMOUNTS ATTRIBUTABLE TO RATE CHANGES SEPARATELY FROM AMOUNTS APPLICABLE TO MANHOURS USED: AMOUNTS ATTRIBUTABLE TO MATERIAL PRICE CHANGES SEPARATELY FROM AMOUNTS APPLICABLE TO MATERIAL USAGE: AND AMOUNTS ATTRIBUTABLE TO OVERHEAD RATE CHANGES SEPARATELY FROM AMOUNTS APPLICABLE TO OVERHEAD BASE CHANGES AND AMOUNTS APPLICABLE TO CHANGES IN THE OVERHEAD ALLOCATION BASIS.

    WITHIN THIS SECTION, THE FOLLOWING SPECIFIC VARIANCES MUST BE EXPLAINED:

      a. SCHEDULE VARIANCES (BUDGETED COST FOR WORK SCHEDULED vs. BUDGETED COST FOR WORK PERFORMED)
      b. COST VARIANCES (BUDGETED COST FOR WORK PERFORMED vs. ACTUAL COST OF WORK PERFORMED)
      c. COST VARIANCES AT COMPLETION (BUDGETED AT COMPLETION vs. LATEST REVISED ESTIMATE AT COMPLETION)

SECTION 3 – OTHER ANALYSIS: IN ADDITION TO THE VARIANCE EXPLANATIONS ABOVE, THE FOLLOWING ANALYSIS ARE MANDATORY:

      a. IDENTIFY THE EFFORT TO WHICH THE UNDISTRIBUTED BUDGET APPLIES.
      b. IDENTIFY THE AMOUNT OF MANAGEMENT RESERVE APPLIED DURING THE REPORTING PERIOD, THE WBS AND ORGANIZATIONAL ELEMENTS TO WHICH APPLIED, AND THE REASONS FOR APPLICATION.
      c. EXPLAIN REASONS FOR SIGNIFICANT SHIFTS IN TIME–PHASING OF THE PM BASELINE SHOWN ON FORMAT 3
      d. EXPLAIN SIGNIFICANT CHANGES IN TOTAL MAN–MONTHS AT COMPLETION SHOWN ON FORMAT 4.
      e. EXPLAIN REASONS FOR SIGNIFICANT SHIFTS IN TIME–PHASING OF PLANNED OR ACTUAL MANPOWER USAGE SHOWN ON FORMAT 4.

SECTION 4 – OVER–TARGET BASELINE: IF THE DIFFERENCE SHOWN IN BLOCK (7) ON FORMAT 3 BECOMES A NEGATIVE VALUE OR CHANGES IN VALUE, PROVIDE:

      a. PROCURRING ACTIVITY AUTHORIZATION FOR THE BASELINE CHANGE WHICH RESULTED IN NEGATIVE VALUE OR CHANGE .
      b. REASONS FOR THE ADDITIONAL BUDGET IN THE FOLLOWING TERMS:

          (1) IN–SCOPE ENGINEERING CHANGES
          (2) IN–SCOPE SUPPORT EFFORT CHANGES
          (3) IN–SCOPE SCHEDULE CHANGES
          (4) ECONOMIC CHANGE
          (5) OTHER (SPECIFY)

      c. THE AMOUNT (BY WBS ELEMENT) FOR ADDED IN–SCOPE EFFORT NOT PREVIOUSLY IDENTIFIED OR BUDGETED.

**Figure 19-8 CPR Format 5-Problem Analysis Report**

It is generally inappropriate to require either a CPR or C/SSR under a firm-fixed price contractual arrangement, since the cost risk rests with the contractor in these situations. This could change in the future. There are some who feel the procuring customer's requirements are absolute, and that such cost reports should be imposed on all government contracts, even those which are firm-fixed price. This is exactly the situation that happened on MIL-STD 1567 in the period from 1975 to 1983, when it was later approved for application to *all* contracts, even firm-fixed price efforts.

While the total dollar value of contracts covered by CPRs may be greater, the vast number of C/SSR applications has had a broader impact on the industry. As one Air Force official remarked about the importance of the C/SSR:

> Here at ASD for every CPR we impose, we receive over seven C/SSRs from contractors.[2]

Under the rules which govern the C/SSR, a contractor must be in a position to describe how the work was measured (BCWP), and most of the same definitions which govern C/SCSC activity, as specified in DODI 7000.2, also apply to the C/SSR. Reporting of costs is typically at WBS level 3, but a contractor must be in a position to trace deeper if variance parameters are exceeded. Therefore, cost segregation must be at the lowest WBS Levels, as with the CPR.

No initial validation demonstration or subsequent application reviews are required of contractors under the C/SSR approach. While the rules covering the CPR are quite rigid, on the C/SSR they are typically negotiable between the customer and contractor or subcontractor.

The C/SSR has three sections:

1. The C/SSR summary form-by WBS (see Figure 19-9).
2. A brief narrative on status.
3. Problem Analysis Reports (PARs), if thresholds are exceeded.

Note that the C/SSR summary, as shown in Figure 19-9, reflects only the cumulative to date position and the Estimate at Completion (EAC). It does *not* require the current period (monthly) status, as is required with the CPR. Considerable contractor preparation costs are thus saved by discarding the monthly status period. All work authorized, both priced and unpriced, must be included in the C/SSR, as with the CPR.

The C/SSR was devised by the DOD in an attempt to improve the management of small contracts, but without the imposition of excessive reporting requirements (i.e., full CPRs). By standardizing the format, the proliferation of unique reports has been somewhat avoided. The very nature of the C/SSR allows for flexibility, as the joint service guide which covers the report states:

| | COST/SCHEDULE STATUS REPORT ($000) | | | SIGNATURE, TITLE & DATE | FORM APPROVED |
|---|---|---|---|---|---|
| CONTRACTOR: KENDOOIT, INC. | | | | I. R. A. DROAN | OMB NUMBER |
| LOCATION: YELLOW SPRINGS, OH | PROGRAM NAME/NUMBER: RVP-2 | REPORT PERIOD: OCT | | PRESIDENT | 22R8327 |
| RDT&E    PRODUCTION | CONTRACT TYPE/NO.: FPIF #1 | | | | |

**CONTRACT DATA**

| (1) ORIGINAL CONTRACT TARGET COST | (2) NEGOTIATED CONTRACT CHANGES | (3) CURRENT TARGET COST (1) + (2) | (4) ESTIMATED COST OF AUTHORIZED, UNPRICED WORK | (5) CONTRACT BUDGET BASE (3) + (4) |
|---|---|---|---|---|
| $12,926.0 | | $12,926.0 | | $12,926.0 |

**PERFORMANCE DATA**

| WORK BREAKDOWN STRUCTURE | CUMULATIVE TO DATE | | | | | AT COMPLETION | | |
|---|---|---|---|---|---|---|---|---|
| | BUDGETED COST | | ACTUAL COST WORK PERFORMED | VARIANCE | | BUDGETED | LATEST REVISED ESTIMATE | VARIANCE |
| | WORK SCHEDULED | WORK PERFORMED | | SCHEDULE | COST | | | |
| (1) | (2) | (3) | (4) | (5) | (6) | (7) | (8) | (9) |
| AIR VEHICLE | 3,349.5 | 2,946.8 | 3,179.2 | (402.7) | (232.4) | 3,364.6 | 4,649.9 | (1,285.3) |
| COMMAND & LAUNCH | 738.4 | 664.1 | 826.3 | (74.3) | (162.2) | 957.8 | 1,000.3 | (42.5) |
| TRAINING | 7.9 | 8.0 | 9.4 | .1 | (1.4) | 10.0 | 10.6 | (.6) |
| PECULIAR SUPT. EQUIP | 32.3 | 28.7 | 23.9 | (3.6) | 4.8 | 37.4 | 37.1 | .3 |
| SYSTEM TEST & EVAL. | 247.3 | 208.1 | 278.9 | (39.2) | (70.8) | 921.7 | 1,194.2 | (272.5) |
| SYSTEM PROGRAM MGMT. | 936.8 | 907.8 | 1,070.6 | (29.0) | (162.8) | 1,268.9 | 1,864.3 | (595.4) |
| DATA | 191.4 | 179.8 | 172.6 | (11.6) | 7.2 | 458.2 | 462.7 | (4.5) |
| SUBCONTRACT | 4,122.6 | 3,806.0 | 3,878.3 | (316.6) | (72.3) | 4,189.0 | 5,130.3 | (941.3) |
| SUBTOTAL | 9,626.2 | 8,749.3 | 9,439.2 | (876.9) | (689.9) | 11,207.6 | 14,349.4 | (3,141.8) |
| GENERAL AND ADMINISTRATIVE | 1,144.2 | 1,032.4 | 1,166.9 | (111.8) | (134.5) | 1,620.1 | 1,831.9 | (211.8) |
| UNDISTRIBUTED BUDGET | | | | | | | | |
| MANAGEMENT RESERVE | | | | | | 98.3 | | 98.3 |
| TOTAL | 10,770.4 | 9,781.7 | 10,606.1 | (988.7) | (824.4) | 12,926.0 | 16,181.3 | (3,255.3) |

**Figure 19-9 Cost/Schedule Status Report (C/SSR)**

For CPR reporting, BCWS and BCWP must be the result of the direct summation of work package budgets. The C/SSR permits the determination of these values through any reasonably accurate, mutually acceptable means... Thus, the C/SSR allows the contractor greater flexibility in the selection of internal performance measurement techniques than does the CPR.[3]

In addition to the C/SSR, the smaller contracts may well require the submission of the Contractor Funds Status Report (CFSR), mentioned earlier, as well as the CCDR, to be covered next.

## Contractor Cost Data Reporting (CCDR)

The fourth and last report used in conjunction with C/SCSC goes by the title of Contractor Cost Data Reporting (CCDR), a generic title actually covering four distinct cost reports. The purpose of the CCDR is to provide the procuring military command and, likely more importantly, the Department of Defense with the means to prepare an "independent cost estimate" of all their major acquisitions, and the means to compare one system (e.g., aircraft) with all other related systems. The CCDR provides the defense establishment with information for its historical cost data bank.

The CCDR is a requirement defined in DODI 7000.11, (Appendix D to this book) and is implemented under a joint service approach with a guide entitled: *Contractor Cost Data Reporting (CCDR)*, dated 5 November 1973. The CCDR supercedes two earlier DOD reports entitled the Cost Information Reports (CIR) and Procurement Information Reports (PIR).

Contracts with a value of less than $2 million are not generally required to prepare a CCDR, but all programs which exceed that value are placed into two categories for purposes of specifying reporting requirements:

- *Category 1* are acquisitions estimated to require in excess of $75 million for research, development, test, and evaluation; or production in excess of $300 million. All four CCDR reports are required.

- *Category 11* are selected contracts, or specific line items from Category 1 above. Only two of the four CCDR reports are required (1921-1 and 19121-1) in this category, and generally only at contract completion.

Contrary to the normal rules which generally exclude the requirement of contractor cost reporting on firm-fixed-price contracts, Category 1 type procurements often require the submittal of CCDRs whenever the effort is deemed to be of particular importance to the DOD. The CCDR applies to both prime and subcontracted efforts.

Since the primary purpose of the CCDR is to provide the defense establishment with the ability to make an independent cost estimate, and to compare the costs of one system against all other similar systems, the data must obviously be reported in a standardized format to be useful. The WBS concept as specified under Military Standard 881 provides the definition of reporting format for the CCDR.

While the responsibility for implementing the CCDR on contracts rests with the major command procuring the system (e.g., the Air Force Systems Command), they must do so in accordance with a *Contractor Cost Data Reporting Plan,* submitted for approval to the Department of Defense, and more specifically to the Cost Analysis Improvement Group (CAIG) of the Office of the Secretary of Defense. One of the principal reasons for the CAIG review and approval is to assess the compatibility of reporting format being proposed in the CCDR plan with other elements of its historical data base, using the proposed WBS as the standardized report format. Figure 19-10 illustrates the CCDR plan.

And now for a brief description of each of the four parts of the CCDR, which are:

1. Cost Data Summary Report (DD Form 1921).
2. Functional Cost-Hour Report (DD Form 1921-1).
3. Progress Curve Report (DD Form 1921-2).
4. Plant-Wide Data Report (DD Form 1921-3).

*The Cost Data Summary Report (1921):*

This report provides cost data by WBS element, separating the nonrecurring (NR) from recurring (R) costs, displaying total costs to date, and the EAC. Costs by WBS element normally go to level 3, but they may by agreement go to lower WBS levels on selected elements of particular interest to the government, e.g., program risk areas. Costs for each WBS element represent total burdened costs, but without G & A and profit. On the last page of the report, the subtotal of WBS element costs are shown, then management reserve, G & A, and profits are added to reach a total price for the contract. Form 1921 is shown in Figure 19-11.

A report on a contract with perhaps 75 WBS reporting elements will run about three pages in length. This report is typically due annually, and may be quarterly or semiannually depending upon the critical nature of the program.

*The Functional Cost-Hour Report (1921-1):*

In this report, each of the WBS elements shown as a one-line entry in the Cost Data Summary Report (1921) above, are further broken down into a one-page summary by detailed cost element, and then further subdivided into a separate page covering both the nonrecurring and recurring costs. Therefore, a program reporting on 75 WBS elements will run at least 225 pages in length.

Any of the CCDRs may be submitted with use of a photocopy of a contractor's computer report, as long as the same data and format are used. Because of the size of this report, the use of computer reporting is almost a necessity. The Functional Cost-Hour report format is shown in Figure 19-12, using a computer printout to comply with the requirement.

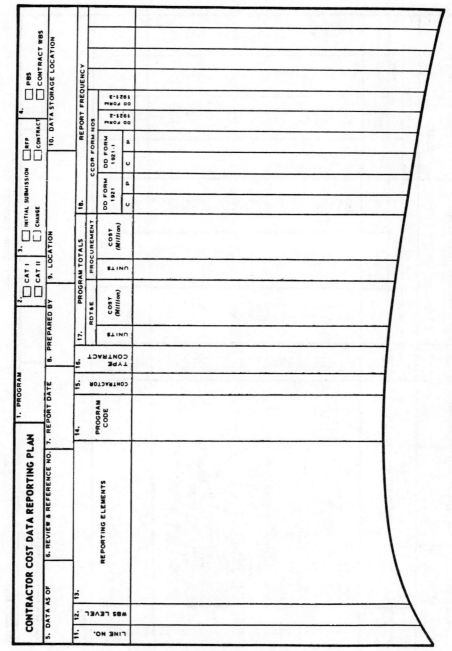

Figure 19-10 Contractor Cost Data Reporting Plan

Form Approved OMB No. 22R0322

## COST DATA SUMMARY REPORT
(Dollars in _Thousands_ )

| 1. PROGRAM | 8. CONTRACT PRICE | 9. CONTRACT CEILING |
|---|---|---|
| XYZ    FSD | N/A | N/A |

2. ☒ CONTRACT ☐ RFP ☐ PROGRAM ESTIMATE

3. ☒ RDT&E   ☐ PROCUREMENT

4. MULTIPLE YEAR CONTRACT ☒ YES ☐ NO

5. REPORT AS OF: 26 June 1981

6. FY FUNDED: 1981

7. CONTRACT TYPE: CPIF/AF

10. ☒ PRIME/ASSOCIATE ☐ SUBCONTRACTOR (Name and Address, include ZIP Code): Ajax Aircraft

11. NAME OF CUSTOMER (Subcontractor use only): USAF

| CONTRACT LINE ITEM | REPORTING ELEMENTS | ELEMENT CODE | TO DATE COSTS INCURRED | | | AT COMPLETION | | | |
|---|---|---|---|---|---|---|---|---|---|
| | | | NON-RECURRING | RECURRING | TOTAL | UNITS | NON-RECURRING | RECURRING | TOTAL |
| 314 | AIR VEHICLE/SUBSYSTEM GROUND TESTS | 2114 | 18003 | - | 18003 | - | 18556 | - | 18556 |
| 355 | ARMAMENT/WEAPON DELIVERY INTEG. TESTS | 2117 | 10 | - | 10 | - | 10 | - | 10 |
| 358 | FLIGHT SIMULATION PROGRAM | 2118 | - | - | - | - | - | - | - |
| 361 | CONTRACTOR FLIGHT TESTS | 2119 | 8452 | - | 8452 | - | 8712 | - | 8712 |
| 376 | MISCELLANEOUS TEST PROGRAM | 2190 | 4181 | - | 4181 | - | 4310 | - | 4310 |
| 390 | DROP AND ACCELERATED LOADS TEST PROGRAM | 2191 | 4337 | - | 4337 | - | 4470 | - | 4470 |
| 395 | TECHNICAL EVALUATION | 2200 | - | - | - | - | - | - | - |
| 396 | FLIGHT TEST SUPPORT SYSTEM | 2220 | - | - | - | - | - | - | - |
| 402 | MOCKUPS | 2400 | 4621 | - | 4621 | - | 4625 | - | 4625 |
| 406 | TEST AND EVALUATION | 2500 | 3243 | - | 3243 | - | 3270 | - | 3270 |
| 423 | SYSTEM ENGR./PROJECT MGMT. (Other than ILS) | 3XXX | 27228 | - | 27228 | - | 27231 | - | 27231 |
| 424 | SYSTEM ENGINEERING (Other than ILS) | 3100 | 11508 | - | 11508 | - | 11508 | - | 11508 |
| 440 | PROJECT MANAGEMENT (Other than ILS) | 3200 | 6466 | - | 6466 | - | 6469 | - | 6469 |
| 457 | SYSTEM ENGINEERING (ILS) | 5100 | 7154 | - | 7154 | - | 7154 | - | 7154 |
| 458 | LOGISTIC SUPPORT ANALYSIS PROCESS | 5110 | 6594 | - | 6594 | - | 6594 | - | 6594 |
| 467 | ILS FOR ENGINEERING CHANGE PROPOSALS | 5120 | - | - | - | - | - | - | - |
| 468 | DEPOT AND INTERMEDIATE REWORK ANALYSIS | 5130 | - | - | - | - | - | - | - |
| 472 | FACILITIES REQUIREMENTS ANALYSIS | 5140 | - | - | - | - | - | - | - |
| 473 | GROUND SUPPORT EQUIP. REQMTS. PROGRAM | 5150 | 55 | - | 55 | - | 55 | - | 55 |
| 474 | SPARE AND REPAIR PARTS PROGRAM | 5160 | 310 | - | 310 | - | 310 | - | 310 |
| 475 | TRAINING SYSTEM DEVELOPMENTS | 5170 | 195 | - | 195 | - | 195 | - | 195 |
| 476 | PKG. HANDLING STORAGE & TRANSP. (PHS & T) | 5180 | - | - | - | - | - | - | - |
| 477 | PROJECT MANAGEMENT (ILS) | 5200 | 2100 | - | 2100 | - | 2100 | - | 2100 |
| 478 | ILS PLANNING | 5210 | 1396 | - | 1396 | - | 1396 | - | 1396 |
| 480 | ILS, DEMO & EVALUATION PROGRAM | 5220 | 9 | - | 9 | - | 9 | - | 9 |
| 485 | SITE/UNIT ACTIVATION PROGRAM | 5230 | - | - | - | - | - | - | - |
| 486 | PREOPERATIONAL (INTERIM) SUPPORT | 5240 | 695 | - | 695 | - | 695 | - | 695 |
| 446 | DATA (Other than ILS) | 4XXX | 2401 | - | 2401 | - | 2428 | - | 2428 |
| 447 | ENGINEERING (Other than ILS) | 4100 | 938 | - | 938 | - | 937 | - | 937 |
| 451 | MANAGEMENT DATA (Other than ILS) | 4200 | 1121 | - | 1121 | - | 1149 | - | 1149 |

REMARKS

NAME OF PERSON TO BE CONTACTED

SIGNATURE

DATE: 23 July 1981

DD FORM 1921, AUG 73

**Figure 19-11 CCDR Cost Data Summary Report (1921)**

FUNCTIONAL COST-HOUR REPORT
DOLLARS IN: THOUSANDS
HOURS IN: THOUSANDS

PROGRAM: **XYZ**

REPORT AS OF: 26 JUNE 1981
X CONTRACT    PROGRAM ESTIMATE    REP

RDT&E  X  PROCUREMENT  OTHER

MULTIPLE YEAR CONTRACT:  YES  X  NO
MULTIPLE YEAR CONTRACT:

FY FUNDED: 1979

X  SUBCONTRACTOR: **Ajax Aircraft**

NAME OF CUSTOMER: USAF
REPORTING ELEMENT: TOTAL WBS 1100 **AIRFRAME RECURRING**

| FUNCTIONAL CATEGORIES | ADJUSTMENTS TO PREVIOUS REPORTS | CONTRACTOR | | SUBCONTRACT OR OUTSIDE PROD- AND SERV- | | TOTAL | |
|---|---|---|---|---|---|---|---|
| | | TO DATE | AT COMPL. | TO DATE | AT COMPL. | TO DATE | AT COMPL. |
| DIRECT LABOR HOURS | 0 | 369 | 370 | 11 | 11 | 380 | 381 |
| DIRECT LABOR DOLLARS | 0 | 4480 | 4486 | 136 | 136 | 4616 | 4622 |
| OVERHEAD | 0 | 7392 | 7401 | 203 | 204 | 7595 | 7605 |
| MATERIAL | 0 | 72 | 72 | 10 | 10 | 82 | 82 |
| OTHER DIRECT CHARGES | 0 | 2284 | 2278 | 35 | 35 | 2319 | 2313 |
| TOTAL ENGINEERING DOLLARS | 0 | 14228 | 14237 | 384 | 385 | 14612 | 14622 |
| DIRECT LABOR HOURS | 0 | 238 | 238 | 9 | 9 | 247 | 247 |
| DIRECT LABOR DOLLARS | 0 | 2405 | 2406 | 81 | 81 | 2486 | 2487 |
| OVERHEAD | 0 | 4109 | 4111 | 115 | 115 | 4224 | 4226 |
| MATERIALS AND PURCHASED TOOLS | 0 | 1483 | 1489 | 28 | 28 | 1511 | 1517 |
| OTHER DIRECT CHARGES | 0 | 191 | 190 | 6 | 6 | 197 | 196 |
| TOTAL TOOLING DOLLARS | 0 | 8188 | 8196 | 230 | 230 | 8418 | 8426 |
| DIRECT LABOR HOURS | 0 | 222 | 223 | 23 | 23 | 245 | 246 |
| DIRECT LABOR DOLLARS | 0 | 2140 | 2141 | 214 | 214 | 2354 | 2355 |
| OVERHEAD | 0 | 3667 | 3665 | 299 | 299 | 3966 | 3964 |
| OTHER DIRECT CHARGES | 0 | 222 | 228 | 16 | 16 | 238 | 244 |
| TOTAL QUALITY CONTROL DOLLARS | 0 | 6029 | 6034 | 529 | 529 | 6558 | 6563 |
| DIRECT LABOR HOURS | 0 | 1412 | 1412 | 162 | 162 | 1574 | 1574 |
| DIRECT LABOR DOLLARS | 0 | 13280 | 13276 | 1393 | 1394 | 14673 | 14670 |
| OVERHEAD | 0 | 22830 | 22816 | 1949 | 1950 | 24779 | 24766 |
| MATERIALS AND PURCHASED PARTS | 0 | 7076 | 7241 | 503 | 505 | 7579 | 7746 |
| OTHER DIRECT CHARGES | 0 | 1387 | 1393 | 100 | 104 | 1487 | 1497 |
| TOTAL MANUFACTURING DOLLARS | 0 | 44573 | 44726 | 3945 | 3953 | 48518 | 48679 |
| PURCHASED EQUIPMENT | 0 | 4894 | 4933 | 0 | 0 | 4894 | 4933 |
| MATERIAL OVERHEAD | 0 | 1961 | 1979 | 57 | 58 | 2018 | 2037 |
| OTHER COSTS NOT SHOWN ELSEWHERE | 0 | 0 | 0 | 0 | 0 | 0 | 0 |
| TOTAL COST LESS G&A | 0 | 79873 | 80105 | 5145 | 5155 | 85018 | 85260 |
| G&A | 0 | 0 | 0 | 411 | 413 | 411 | 413 |
| TOTAL PLUS G&A | 0 | 79873 | 80105 | 5556 | 5568 | 85429 | 85673 |
| FEE OR PROFIT | 0 | 0 | 0 | 499 | 501 | 499 | 501 |
| TOTAL OF LINES 29 and 30 | 0 | 79873 | 80105 | 6055 | 6069 | 85928 | 86174 |

DD 1921-1

**Figure 19-12 CCDR Functional Cost-Hour Report (1921-1)**

*The Progress Curve Report (1921-2):*

This report is prepared to reflect the hours and costs required to manufacture the production units/lots on a contract. It measures progress toward the reduction in hours/costs to build a given article. The data from this report are displayed on a report which is relatable to a learning curve format to highlight how well, or poorly, a contractor is doing to reduce the hours required to produce a unit. It is an important report used by the DOD to prepare parametric cost estimates by program, costs per pound, etc., and to compare one system against other systems.

These reports are due at the completion of each production lot, but not less frequently than annually. Actual costs for units completed are shown, plus a projection of estimated future performance. Figure 19-13 reflects the report format.

*The Plant-Wide Report (1921-3):*

This is a report that reflects the indirect costs for all activity in a contractor's plant, with particular emphasis on any differences between the commercial and government programs. While the other three CCDRs are program specific, this one deals with *all* contracts and business in a given firm.

The reports are due annually, and if submitted on one contract, a photocopy will generally suffice for other program requests. The report covers the current period, and projects two years into the future. Figure 19-14 illustrates the format for this report.

Because the Plant-Wide Data Report will contain a company's proprietary or business sensitive data, these reports are normally only submitted to the government, i.e., a prime contractor (a private firm) is not usually a recipient of these company private reports.


## Consistency and Reconciliation Between C/SCSC Reports

Without belaboring the subject of cost reporting, it must be mentioned that when multiple reports are due on a given contract, the data contained therein must be consistent with each other, or at least be reconcilable with each other. This particularly true when reports are reflecting data as of the same time period, e.g., June 30th or December 31st of a given year.

While any given contract with C/SCSC will likely have three reports due (CFSR, CPR *or* C/SSR, and CCDR), the primary difficulty in reconciliation seems to be between the quarterly CFSR submittals and the monthly CPR or C/SSR. Two issues seem to cause the problem: Profit/Fee and Termination Liability.

If one understands that the primary purpose of the CFSR is to forecast the government's total liability at any point in time, *including* the contractor's profit and estimated termination liabilities, and that the CPR is a monthly status report which focuses on the Performance Measurement Baseline (PMB) which *excludes* both profit and termination liability, much of the confusion goes away.

SECURITY CLASSIFICATION

| PROGRESS CURVE REPORT (Recurring Cost Only) | 1. PROGRAM | Form Approved OMB No. 22R0322 |
|---|---|---|

**SECTION A**

| 2. DOLLARS IN | 3. HOURS IN | 5. CONTRACT | 6. REPORT FOR ____ MONTHS |
|---|---|---|---|
| 4. TOTAL UNITS ACCEPTED PRIOR TO THIS REPORT | | | ENDING: ____ |

7. MULTIPLE YEAR CONTRACT ☐ YES ☐ NO

8. FY FUNDED:

9. ☐ PRIME/ASSOCIATE ☐ SUBCONTRACTOR (Name and address; Include ZIP Code)

10. NAME OF CUSTOMER (Subcontractor use only)

11. REPORTING ELEMENT(S)

**SECTION B**

| ITEM | UNITS/LOTS ACCEPTED | | | | | ESTIMATE OF NEXT UNIT/LOT TO BE ACCEPTED | TO COMPLETE CONTRACT |
|---|---|---|---|---|---|---|---|
| | a | b | c | d | e | f | g |
| 1. MODEL AND SERIES | | | | | | | |
| 2. FIRST UNIT OF LOT | | | | | | | |
| 3. LAST UNIT OF LOT | | | | | | | |
| 4. CONCURRENT UNITS | | | | | | | |
| CHARACTERISTICS 5. | | | | | | | |
| 6. | | | | | | | |
| 7. | | | | | | | |
| CONTRACTOR DATA (PER UNIT/LOT) | | | | | | | |
| 8. DIRECT QUALITY CONTROL MAN-HOURS | | | | | | | |
| 9. DIRECT MANUFACTURING MAN-HOURS | | | | | | | |
| 10. QUALITY CONTROL DIRECT LABOR DOLLARS | $ | $ | $ | $ | $ | $ | $ |
| 11. MANUFACTURING DIRECT LABOR DOLLARS | $ | $ | $ | $ | $ | $ | $ |
| 12. RAW MATERIAL & PURCHASED PARTS DOLLARS | $ | $ | $ | $ | $ | $ | $ |
| 13. PURCHASED EQUIPMENT DOLLARS | $ | $ | $ | $ | $ | $ | $ |
| 14. TOTAL DOLLARS | $ | $ | $ | $ | $ | $ | $ |
| SUBCONTRACT/OUTSIDE PROD. & SERV. | | | | | | | |
| 15. DIRECT QUALITY CONTROL MAN-HOURS | | | | | | | |
| 16. DIRECT MANUFACTURING MAN-HOURS | | | | | | | |
| 17. TOTAL MAN-HOURS | | | | | | | |
| 18. QUALITY CONTROL DIRECT LABOR DOLLARS | $ | $ | $ | $ | $ | $ | $ |
| 19. MANUFACTURING DIRECT LABOR DOLLARS | $ | $ | $ | $ | $ | $ | $ |
| 20. RAW MATERIAL & PURCHASED PARTS DOLLARS | $ | $ | $ | $ | $ | $ | $ |
| 21. PURCHASED EQUIPMENT DOLLARS | $ | $ | $ | $ | $ | $ | $ |
| 22. TOTAL DOLLARS | $ | $ | $ | $ | $ | $ | $ |
| UNIT TOTAL ☐ AVERAGE ☐ | | | | | | | |
| 23. DIRECT QUALITY CONTROL MAN-HOURS | | | | | | | |
| 24. DIRECT MANUFACTURING MAN-HOURS | | | | | | | |
| 25. TOTAL MAN-HOURS | | | | | | | |
| 26. QUALITY CONTROL DIRECT LABOR DOLLARS | $ | $ | $ | $ | $ | $ | $ |
| 27. MANUFACTURING DIRECT LABOR DOLLARS | $ | $ | $ | $ | $ | $ | $ |
| 28. RAW MATERIAL & PURCHASED PARTS DOLLARS | $ | $ | $ | $ | $ | $ | $ |
| 29. PURCHASED EQUIPMENT DOLLARS | $ | $ | $ | $ | $ | $ | $ |
| 30. TOTAL DOLLARS | $ | $ | $ | $ | $ | $ | $ |
| 31. % SUBCONTRACT OR OUTSIDE PROD. & SERV. | | | | | | | |
| MFG FLOW TIME | | | | | | | |
| 32. START | | | | | | | |
| 33. FINISH | | | | | | | |
| 34. | | | | | | | |
| 35. | | | | | | | |
| 36. | | | | | | | |
| 37. | | | | | | | |
| 38. | | | | | | | |
| 39. | | | | | | | |

(left margin: MOS OR QTRS)

DD FORM 1 AUG 73 1921-2

SECURITY CLASSIFICATION

**Figure 19-13 CCDR Program Curve Report (1921-2)**

Figure 19-14 CCDR Plant-Wide Data Report (1921-3)

Perhaps a specific illustration displaying specific CFSR and CPR forms will eliminate the difficulty. Shown in Figure 19-15, pages 252–53, are the forms used in the CFSR and a CPR Format 1 covering the WBS. The five circled letters shown in Figure 19-15 relate specific comparable sections of each report to the other.

So much for C/SCS reporting. Should anyone need additional information on the subject, the specific report requirements may be reviewed in full in the DOD documents contained in DODI 7000.10 and 7000.11 (Appendices C and D to this book).

---

## ENDNOTES

[1]All charts in Figures 19-3 through 19-9 and 19-15, are courtesy of Humphreys & Associates, Inc., from their 5 day course entitiled "Cost/Schedule Control Systems and Performance Management Systems."

[2]Interview with Dan Schild, Chief of the Cost Management Systems Division, USAF Aeronautical Systems Division, Wright-Patterson Air Force Base, OH, July 7, 1982.

[3]Department of Defense, *Cost/Schedule Managment of Non-Major Contracts (C/SSR)*, 1978, page 1-5.

**CFSR**

- A. CURRENT REPORT DATE
- B. CONTRACT WORK AUTHORIZED DEFINITIZED
- C. CONTRACT WORK AUTHORIZED NOT DEFINITIZED
- D. ACCRUED EXPENDITURES ACTUAL TO DATE
- E. FORECAST OF BILLINGS TO THE GOVERNMENT AT COMPLETION

---

**CONTRACT FUNDS STATUS REPORT** (DOLLARS IN ............ )

FORM APPROVED
OMB NUMBER 22-R0180

| 1. CONTRACT NUMBER | 3. CONTRACT FUNDING FOR FOR FY | 5. PREVIOUS REPORT DATE | 7. CONTRACTOR (NAME, ADDRESS, AND ZIP CODE) | 9. INITIAL CONTRACT PRICE TARGET ............ CEILING ............ |
| 2. CONTRACT TYPE | 4. APPROPRIATION | 6. CURRENT REPORT DATE (A) | 8. PROGRAM | 10. ADJUSTED CONTRACT PRICE TARGET ............ CEILING ............ (F) |

11. FUNDING INFORMATION

| LINE ITEM/WBS ELEMENT | APPROPRIATION IDENTIFICATION | FUNDING AUTHORIZED TO DATE | ACCRUED EXPENDITURES PLUS OPEN COMMITMENTS TOTAL | CONTRACT WORK AUTHORIZED | | | FORECAST | | | | TOTAL REQUIREMENTS | FUNDS CARRY-OVER | NET FUNDS REQUIRED |
| | | | | DEFINITIZED (B) | NOT DEFINITIZED (C) | SUBTOTAL | NOT YET AUTHORIZED | ALL OTHER WORK | SUBTOTAL | | | |
| a | b | c | d | e | f | g | h | i | j | k | l | m |
| | | | | | | | | | | | | |

12. CONTRACT WORK AUTHORIZED (WITH FEE/PROFIT) ACTUAL OR PROJECTED

| | ACTUAL TO DATE | | | | | | | | | | AT COMPLETION |
| a. OPEN COMMITMENTS | | | | | | | | | | | |
| b. ACCRUED EXPENDITURES (D) | | | | | | | | | | | |
| c. TOTAL (12a 12b) | | | | | | | | | | | |
| 13. FORECAST OF BILLINGS TO THE GOVERNMENT | | | | | | | | | | | (E) |
| 14. ESTIMATED TERMINATION COSTS | | | | | | | | | | | |
| REMARKS | | | | | | | | | | | |

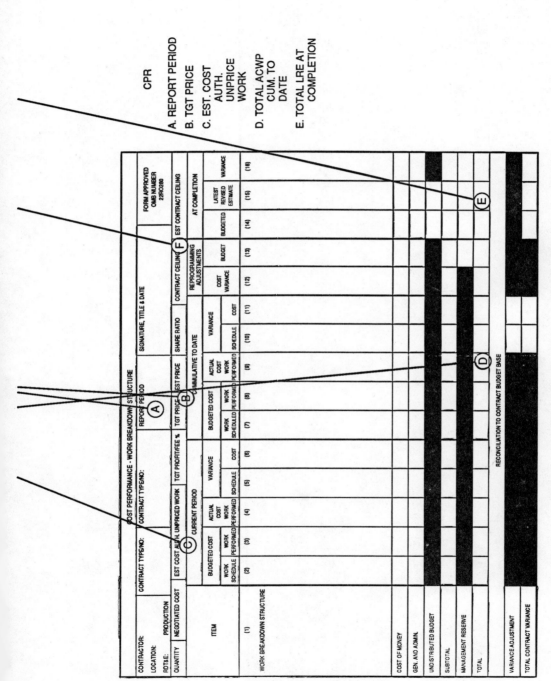

**Figure 19-15 Reconciliation between C/SCSC Reports**

# 20

# Analysis of C/SCSC Data

We have arrived at a point in our discussion where we have established the Performance Measurement Baseline (PMB) against which our planned work accomplishments may be measured; the customer has paid us a visit and has approved our C/SCSC compliant management control system; and we are dutifully submitting Cost Performance Reports (CPRs) monthly to the customer. What do we do next? Perhaps we should actually look at the data we have been sending to the customer each month in our CPR submittals.

Up to this point we have been doing C/SCSC things because we had to do them in order to comply with the letter of our contract. The PMB and the Demonstration Review and the CPRs were all *required* actions, dictated by the contract or related governmental directives. But the "analysis" of our performance measurement data is not specifically required anywhere. So why should we do it?

Perhaps the very best reason for us to look at the performance data contained in the CPRs is the fact that our customer will be analyzing our data. And so will their next higher level bosses, and their bosses, and their bosses, and so forth, all the way up the line to the United States Congress, who will be deciding whether to put money aside to fund *our* contract next year.

And to make matters worse, our customer(s) will be comparing our contract performance against other programs of a similar nature in an attempt to "independently" predict where our contract will likely end up, both in funds spent and in time required. Perhaps we should look at our data for no other reason than for our own "self-defense," to be in a position to answer queries from the people who must allocate the funds to keep our program alive.

But before starting a discussion on the various methods used in the industry to analyze and display C/SCSC data, it would likely be beneficial for us to review five specific terms, for these terms will be used often in the illustrations which will follow. These five terms are:

1. *BCWS*—Budgeted Costs for Work Scheduled, is the plan against which performance will be measured.
2. *BCWP*—Budgeted Costs for Work Performed, is the earned value of the work accomplished against the plan.
3. *ACWP*—Actual Costs of Work Performed, are the cost actuals.
4. *BAC*—Budget at Completion, is the value of the sum of the budgeted plans (BCWS), at the end of the effort.
5. *EAC*—Estimate at Completion, is the latest projected value of what the effort will actually cost (ACWP) at the end.

The assessment of contractor performance data can be viewed from at least three vantage points:

- From the government's perspective, examining contractor submitted CPR data;

- From a private contractor's perspective, examining their own internal performance, as reflected in their CPRs; and

- From the a prime contractor's perspective, examining subcontractor provided CPR data.

There are likely hundreds of techniques used by various C/SCSC practitioners to analyze performance data. One could probably fill a book with nothing but the countless ways people assess the well-being of a given program. We will limit ourselves to just ten of the more conventional ways to ascertain the "health" of a contract, based on data contained in contractor submitted CPRs, and other related program performance indicators.

## Determining Current Status and the Performance Trends
Seven analytic techniques will be examined.

*Technique #1: Cumulative Plan/Status Display*—The most common display method in C/SCSC is simply the cumulative curve, showing dollars over time. A cumulative curve is best represented by an "S-shaped" curve, which usually portrays a slow build-up, faster acceleration near the middle, and a slow tapered-down ending. Any cumulative program curve which does not approximate an "S" shape is highly suspect of displaying a faulty plan.

To illustrate a typical C/SCSC cumulative curve, Figure 20-1 reflects a hypothetical program which runs for two years, and which has a cost value for performance purposes of $2.5 million. The chart reflects performance at 14 months of its planned 24 month duration.

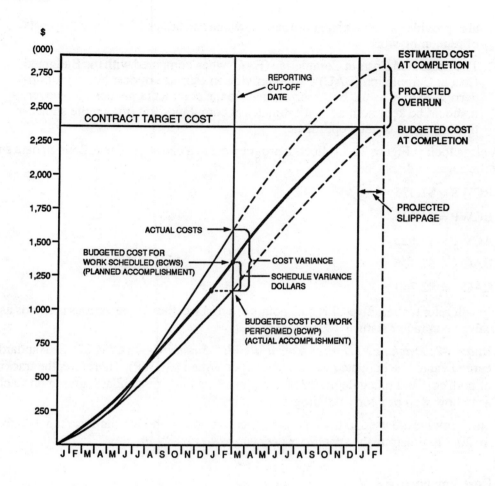

**Figure 20-1  Cumulative Plan/Status Display [2]**

This curve illustrates nicely the concept that C/SCSC focuses principality on physical work accomplishment (BCWP), and its relationship to the work planned (BCWS) and funds spent (ACWP). As one senior government official described the process:

> In order to properly evaluate contract cost performance, the information reported must relate directly to the work accomplished. The Budgeted Cost for Work Performed (BCWP) is the most important data element required since, when compared with the Budgeted Cost for Work Scheduled (BCWS), a schedule variance results and, when compared with the Actual Cost of Work Performed (ACWP), a cost variance is obtained. BCWS, BCWP and ACWP provide a clear depiction of contract status at a point in time. A graphic plot of these elements, or of the cost and schedule variances emanating therefrom,

also provide valuable trend information which can be used for projecting costs of remaining work.

The Estimated Costs at Completion (EAC) when compared with the Budgeted Cost at Completion (BAC) should provide an estimate of cost overrun or underrun, so long as the BAC corresponds to the contract target cost. However, it should be kept in mind that estimates at completion are often quite subjective in nature; usually optimistic.[1]

A close look at Figure 20-1 reflects a program off to a bad start. The following data support the curve as displayed:

- BCWS = $1,375
- BCWP = $1,125
- ACWP = $1,625
- BAC   = $2,375
- EAC   = $2,750

We will refer to these five CPR data points often as we discuss the various methods used to analyze contractor status.

*Technique #2: Tracking Variances from a "BCWP" Standard*—In C/SCSC the standard is earned value, the budgeted value of work performed (BCWP). Therefore, the tracking of both cost and schedule performance is made against the standard, giving one a clue as to how well or poorly the program is doing.

Four formulae are used to track performance variances, and we shall use the data from Figure 20-1 to illustrate the specific concepts:

- **Cost Variance** = CV
  CV = BCWP less ACWP = $1,125 less $1,625 = ($500)

- **Cost Variance Percentage** = CV%
  $$CV\% = \frac{CV}{BCWP} = \frac{(\$500)}{\$1,125} = (44\%)$$

- **Schedule Variance** = SV
  SV = BCWP less BCWS = $1,125 less $1,375 = ($250)

- **Schedule Variance Percentage** = SV%
  $$SV\% = \frac{SV}{BCWS} = \frac{(\$250)}{\$1,375} = (18\%)$$

When the CV and CV% and SV and SV% are displayed graphically, they resemble the chart shown in Figure 20-2. These data can be shown in dollar variances, or in percentage variances, and they can be plotted representing the monthly or cumulative values. To be above the zero BCWP line is good, and represents either an underrun of costs or an ahead-of-schedule condition. To be below the line represents a poor condition, cost overruns or a behind-of-schedule condition.

This type of display normally represents variances in the contract total dollar values. But such displays may also represent the program at any WBS level (levels 2, 3, 4, etc.) or any functional area, or even areas designated as program risk areas, e.g., a "radar unit."

It is also a good statusing approach to display both the "Cumulative Plan/Status Chart" along side a "Performance Trend Chart" to get a full indication of the direction of the program. Figure 20-3 presents such a display. On the left is a chart similar to that shown Figure 20-1, and on the right is a chart similar to that shown in Figure 20-2. The display on the right shows not only the Cost and Schedule Variances, but also the use of Management Reserve (MR), which is a good indicator of performance trends in and of itself. MR monitoring will be covered shortly.

*Technique #3: Determining the Efficiency Factor of Work Performed*—In addition to an absolute or a percentage variance from the BCWP standard, one would likely want to know how "efficient" the cost and schedule performance of the work accomplished to date has been.

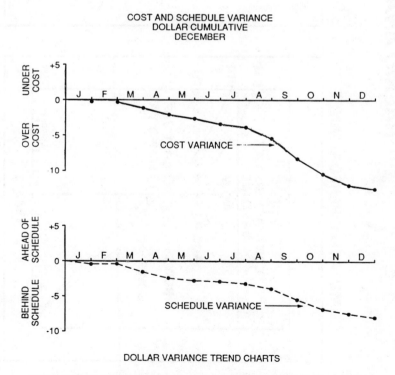

Figure 20-2  Cost Variances (CV) and Schedule Variances (SV) [3]

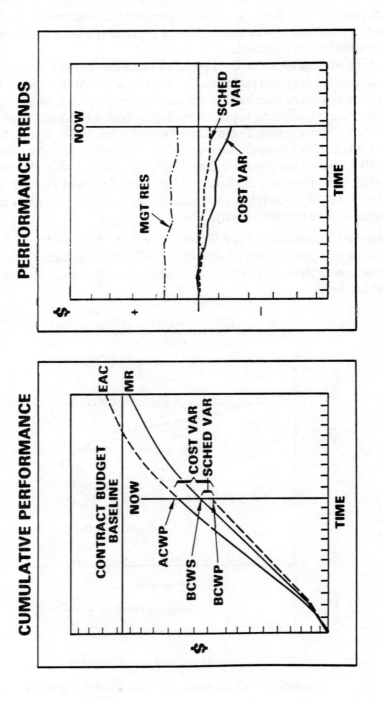

Figure 20-3    Side by Side Performance Charts[4]

Three formulae are available to isolate performance efficiency as a percentage of meeting the standard BCWP:

- **Cost Performance Index (e)**  =  CPI (e)

  CPI (e) = $\dfrac{BCWP}{ACWP}$  =  $\dfrac{\$1,125}{\$1,625}$  =  .69% cost efficiency

- **Schedule Performance Index (e)** = SPI (e)

  SPI (e) = $\dfrac{BCWP}{BCWS}$  =  $\dfrac{\$1,125}{\$1,375}$  =  .82% schedule efficiency

- **Cost Performance Index (p)**  =  CPI (p)

  CPI (p) = $\dfrac{ACWP}{BCWP}$  =  $\dfrac{\$1,625}{\$1,125}$  =  1.44% actual costs for each dollar planned

Note that there are two cost performance indicators shown above: the CPI(e) reflects the *efficiency* of performance, and the CPI(p) reflects how much one dollar of *planned* work actually cost. The CPI(e) is the more popular indicator of cost performance, and will be used throughout this chapter. The CPI(p) formula is shown for information only, to provide a complete description of the subject.

Graphically, the CPI and SPI may be plotted using a display similar to that used earlier to show the absolute or percentage variances from the BCWP standard. Figure 20-4 is a plotting of the CPI and SPI, not at WBS level 1 which is the generally the case, but at WBS level 4, to reflect the development of perhaps the "radar unit," which might be of special interest to management because it has been designated a risk item to the program. These types of charts may be plotted to reflect either the monthly position, or the cumulative to date position.

The CPI(e) will be used later to prepare an independent (from what a contractor may be forecasting) estimate of what the program will likely cost (EAC), and how long it will probably take to complete.

*Technique #4: Tracking Manpower*—One of the most important indicators to watch on all programs is that of labor, usually expressed as manpower loading, and may be displayed in dollars, or hours, or equivalent people. Format 4 of the monthly CPR reflects manloads by function, actuals to date, a six-month projection, and the latest estimate at completion. Shown in Figure 20-5, page 263, is a typical manpower display, with a supporting data table reflected at the bottom. This particular figure reflects the original plan (BCWS) as compared with what has been spent (ACWP). Some displays also add the earned value (BCWP) for the manloads charted.

In addition to tracking total manpower, as reflected by Figure 20-5, the tracking of all major functions should also be done. In the early phases of all programs engineering is a logical function to monitor closely, and later in the program manufacturing will take on

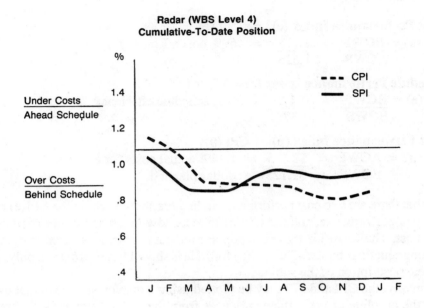

**Figure 20-4 Plotting of the Cumulative CPI and SPI**

increased importance. Shown in Figure 20-6, page 264, is a display of six major functions, typically those functions listed in Format 4 of the CPR, manpower loading. Note that all six functions are displayed over the same time scale to compare the phasing of the various functions. Both the original plan (BCWS) and current end projection (EAC) phasing are shown.

Looking ahead once again to having an ability to do an independent EAC, the manload planning data by specific function may be used to make such estimates.

*Technique # 5: Tracking the Use of Management Reserve (MR)*—One of the most important indicators of program condition and therefore something which should be watched closely, is that of the use of management reserve (MR) over the life of a contract.

Management Reserve is a type of "budget" which is set aside in the beginning of a program to cover contingencies, i.e., in-scope problems as they surface. Management Reserve is expected to be completely exhausted before the end of a contract; however, if it is utilized too early in a program, that condition could reflect some type of difficulty which should be examined by the customer.

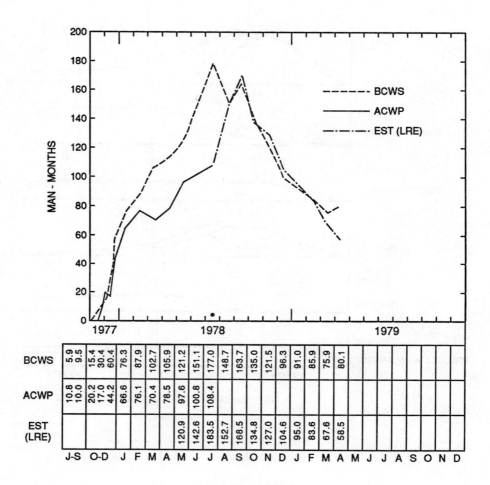

| | J-S | O-D | J | F | M | A | M | J | J | A | S | O | N | D | J | F | M | A | M | J | J | A | S | O | N | D |
|---|---|---|---|---|---|---|---|---|---|---|---|---|---|---|---|---|---|---|---|---|---|---|---|---|---|---|
| **BCWS** | 5.9 / 9.5 | 15.4 / 30.4 / 60.4 | 76.3 | 87.9 | 102.7 | 105.9 | 121.2 | 151.1 | 177.0 | 148.7 | 163.7 | 135.0 | 121.5 | 96.3 | 91.0 | 85.9 | 75.9 | 80.1 | | | | | | | | |
| **ACWP** | 10.8 / 10.0 | 20.2 / 17.0 / 44.2 | 66.6 | 76.1 | 70.4 | 78.5 | 97.6 | 100.8 | 108.4 | | | | | | | | | | | | | | | | | |
| **EST (LRE)** | | | | | | | 120.9 | 142.6 | 183.5 | 152.7 | 168.5 | 134.8 | 127.0 | 104.6 | 95.0 | 83.6 | 67.6 | 58.5 | | | | | | | | |

**Figure 20-5  Manpower Loading [5]**

One of the most useful displays of Management Reserve (MR) is to compare on a single chart both the Cost Variance and Schedule Variance and their relationship in dollars to the use of MR. Figure 20-7, page 265, contains such a display. This display reflects a substantial depletion of MR in December, which should be explained in either the CPR, or in person at the contractor's plant.

Another approach used to monitor the reasonable consumption of Management Reserve is to relate its usage against a "straight line plot," going from the MR established at the start, down to zero at the end of the planned contract period. This type display tracks the usage of MR in proportional usage over the expected life of the contract.

*Technique #6: Tracking Technical Performance*—The monitoring of the cost and schedule status of a program, even if one could determine with absolute certainty the true con-

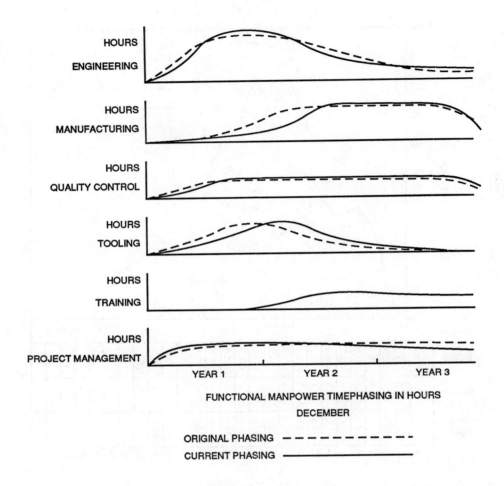

**Figure 20-6 Manpower Loading by Function**

ditions, tells only part of the story. There are technical performance goals for every developmental program which are of equal, and likely of *greater* importance than either the cost or schedule status.

For example, it would be of small comfort to have a program end exactly within its target costs and on schedule, only to have it perform at a fraction of the required operating levels. A fighter aircraft that must have a flight range of say 1,000 miles would be of little value if it came in within its cost and schedule targets, but with a flight range of only 500 miles, half the required range. Technical performance targets must be met, and few would argue on the criticality of achieving them.

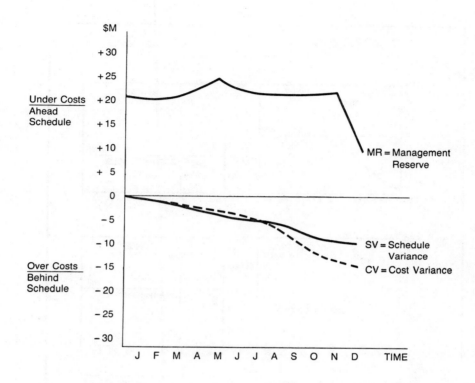

**Figure 20-7 Management Reserve Consumption[6]**

The technical performance goals of all programs are unique and must be specifically tailored jointly by the customer and contractor. Shown in Figures 20-8 is a display of four technical indicators used to monitor a U.S. Army developmental program. Shown in Figure 20-9, page 267, is a display of reliability performance indicators. Reliability performance goals exist on most programs.

When these technical indicators are used in concert with cost and schedule indicators provided from C/SCSC reporting data, both the contractor and customer will have good visibility on the factual status of the program.

*Technique #7: Analyzing What the Contractor Is Saying*—Format 5 of the monthly Cost Performance Report (CPR) is a section entitled Problem Analysis Report (PAR). A PAR is required anytime either a cost or schedule variance has exceeded a previously set threshold level. For instance, if the radar development WBS element experiences a negative cost variance of 12%, as compared with a 10% threshold, the subcontractor is required to submit a PAR each month which sets forth:

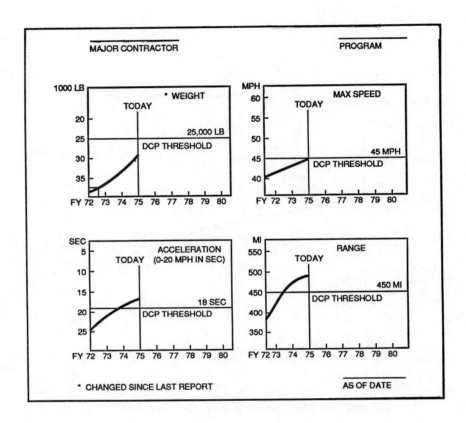

**Figure 20-8  Technical Performance Indicators** [7]

- A description of the problem and what caused it, etc.; and the impact it has on cost, schedule and technical performance; and

- The planned corrective action to eliminate the variance, including an estimate of when it will be corrected.

PARs are intended to enlighten, and if there are questions lingering after a review of the reasons given for the variances, and the proposed recovery plan doesn't make sense to a reader, a procuring customer has two options available. The performing contractor can be informed that the PAR write-ups are uninformative and must be resubmitted in order to better describe what is actually happening. Or, the customer may call for an on-site review at the contractor's plant to discuss in person the reasons causing the variances.

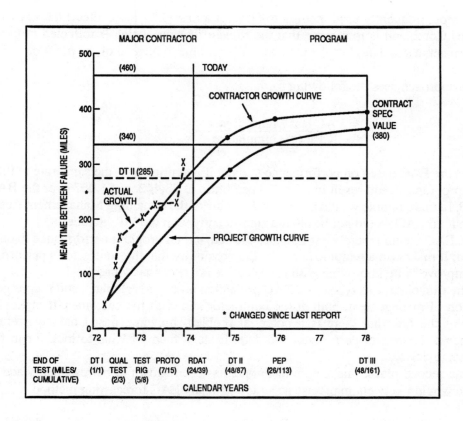

**Figure 20-9  Reliability Performance Indicators[8]**

## Forecasting the Position at Program Completion (EAC)

Now that some of the methods used to monitor performance and performance trends have been reviewed, the next logical question is, What will it all mean at the end? In C/SCSC, the forecasted costs to complete the program are termed the EAC, the Estimate at Completion. What impact will the contractor's performance to date have on the EAC? Three forecasting techniques will be reviewed to answer this question.

*Technique #8: EAC Projection Based on the CPI (e)*—Earlier, the Cost Performance Index-CPI(e) was discussed. It is an indictor of cost efficiency of the work accomplished to date.

The CPI(e) for the program shown in Figure 20-1 after the first 14 months was said to be:

$$\text{EAC CPI (e)} = \frac{\text{BCWP}}{\text{ACWP}} = \frac{\$1,125}{\$1,625} = .69\% \text{ cost efficiency}$$

The most frequently used method to forecast an EAC by the United States Air Force Systems Command is to assume that the *same* efficiency which is reflected in the total program actuals to date, i.e., the CPI (e), will continue to the end of the program.

This approach uses the following formula:

$$EAC = \frac{BAC \text{ less Mgmt. Reserve}}{CPI \ (e) \text{ Cumulative}} = \frac{\$2,375}{.69\%} = \$3,442$$

Thus the EAC based on performance to date, if it continued at the same rate to the end of the program, would result in a total expenditure of $3,442, or $1,067 over the BAC of $2,375. In this example we did not know the value of the remaining Management Reserve, but the total EAC would not be altered significantly with the MR included.

This EAC method merely extrapolates the actual total program performance to date, to the end. It makes no attempt to consider the possibility that the contractor's performance may improve or be improving with time. This is not necessarily bad.

In the first place, this type of an EAC projection is easy to calculate, and it *does* get the attention of management, both at the contractor and with the customer. It makes them aware of the fact that there is a potential problem brewing, based on the irrefutable evidence of contractor performance to date. It alerts them of what to look for in future program reviews.

In the second place, this simple technique has been shown to be reasonably accurate. No one would likely claim precise accuracy with any EAC forecasting method.

*Technique #9: EAC by Function*—Probably a more precise and sophisticated method of forecasting the ending cost result would be to take the same technique discussed above (CPIe forecast to end) and apply it individually to *each* of the contractor's major functional organizations. In the monthly CPR, Formats 2 and 4 indicate performance by major function, and a CPI (e) may be established for each of these functions.

In all developmental programs certain functions will happen prior to other functions. The most obvious example of this phasing by function is that of the relationship between engineering and manufacturing. The engineers must create the design before the factory can build it. An example of the historical phasing of the various functions was shown back in Figure 20-6. Each firm with its unique product lines will have a slightly different phasing of their functions, which will be reflected in their historical performance records.

A CPI (e) forecast to the end is thus done for each function, which is another way to extrapolate a forecast to the end based on contractor performance to date. This type of forecast is shown in Figure 20-10. Engineering's BAC of $108,798 is thus divided by its CPI (e) of .828, to forecast their EAC of $131,399.

| Function | ACWP | BCWP | CPI | BAC | EAC |
|----------|------|------|-----|-----|-----|
| Engineering | 40455 | 33493 | .828 | 108798 | 131399 |
| Manufacturing | 3119 | 2997 | .961 | 27463 | 28578 |
| Quality Control | 170 | 162 | .953 | 876 | 919 |
| Tooling | 83 | 76 | .916 | 4257 | 4647 |
| Training | 285 | 271 | .951 | 2386 | 2509 |
| Project Mgt. | 7470 | 7380 | .988 | 18336 | 18559 |
| Subcontract | 26005 | 22117 | .850 | 63418 | 74609 |
| Other | 2907 | 2875 | — | 21114 | 21114 |
| Mgt. Reserve | — | — | — | 10538 | — |
| G & A | 11028 | 9504 | — | 35234 | 38680 |
| **Total** | 91522 | 78875 | — | 292420 | 321014 |

**Figure 20-10  EAC Forecast by Function** [9]

*Technique #10: Determine What "Efficiency Factor" it will Take to Stay Within the Original Budget at Completion (BAC) or Latest Estimate at Completion (EAC)*—This last method takes the cost efficiency experienced to date, as reflected in the CPI(e), and determines what level of performance efficiency will be required for "every day" remaining in the program, in order to stay within either the original budget at completion (BAC); or the latest estimate at completion (EAC).

Throughout history, contractors have taken the position that in spite of all the facts, in spite of their actual performance thus far, "we expect to stay within the present authorized funds." This forecasting technique attempts to "quantify" exactly what it will take to achieve that noble goal. The results sometimes make even the most optimistic individuals humble. Sometimes.

This technique goes by two titles, both using the same formula. In some instances it is referred to as the "CPItg," meaning the "Cost Performance Index to go." In other cases it is called the "TCPI," meaning the "To Complete Performance Index." They are the same method and both use the same formula:

$$\text{CPItg or TCPI} = \frac{\text{Work Left}}{\text{Money Left}} = \begin{array}{l}\text{Performance factor needed} \\ \text{stay within authorized funds}\end{array}$$

The "authorized funds" can be either the original BAC or the latest EAC.

Going back again to the program displayed in Figure 20-1 for an example, the CPI (e) achieved for the first 14 months of the 24 month effort was .69%—not very impressive. If the contractor takes the position that it will stay within its "present authorized funds," they would have to perform all remaining work with an efficiency factor as follows:

$$\text{TCPI (BAC)} = \frac{\text{BAC - BCWP}}{\text{BAC - ACWP}} = \frac{\$2,375 - \$1,125}{\$2,375 - \$1,625} = \frac{\$1,250}{\$750} = 1.67\%$$

$$\text{TCPI (EAC)} = \frac{\text{BAC - BCWP}}{\text{EAC - ACWP}} = \frac{\$2,375 - \$1,125}{\$2,750 - \$1,625} = \frac{\$1,250}{\$1,125} = 1.11\%$$

Thus, the contractor for all remaining effort on the program would have to achieve a performance efficiency of 1.67%, to stay within the original Budget at Completion, or a factor of 1.11% to stay within the latest EAC. The 1.67% is highly unlikely, but the factor of 1.11% is possible, although still ambitious.

A comparison chart reflecting the "TCPI" versus the cumulative "CPI (e)" is displayed in Figure 20-11. Notice how the continued performance of the CPI (e) below the 1.0 line increases the TCPI indicator for the work remaining.

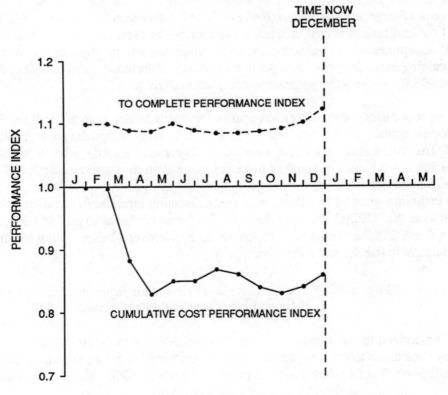

Figure 20-11 A Comparison of "CPI (e)" versus "TCPI"

C/SCSC is a technique which can show the cost and schedule position of a given contract, but only in gross dollar terms. True, by tracing down the WBS levels, problems can be isolated. But as a forecasting tool, a 10-percent overrun of costs typically has more significance than is reflected in a 10 percent behind-schedule condition. The reasons for this result were discussed in Chapter 15, on "The Meaning of Schedule Variances (SV)."

In the foregoing pages only a small sampling of the many techniques available to analyze and assess C/SCSC data have been covered, with emphasis on CPR data. Additional analyses may be made from the Contract Funds Status Report (CFSR) and the four separate reports from the Contractor Cost Data Reporting (CCDR), particularly the performance learning curves which may be prepared from the 1921-1 forms.

But no matter how much information is made available from any management control system, the limiting factors usually turn out to be the quality of the analysis of the data, the quality of the displays of the data, and the quality of the management reviews. In short, a C/SCSC compliant management control system will provide the monitoring structure and information, but only intelligent management can put it to effective use.

## Summary

Far too often contractors fail to analyze the very data they compile each month and obligingly submit to their waiting customers. Far too often the first time contractors take the necessary actions to assess what they have been saying all along, is when that customer confronts them with a series of unfavorable conclusions the customer has made on their own, from the very data the contractor has been providing. As strange as this may seem, one finds this situation over and over again in the C/SCSC environment.

We have reviewed ten specific techniques out of the countless methods used in the industry to forecast the final results on a given contract. By contrast, one senior government official has uncovered a unique method to quantify the final position of contracts, based on simply the "empirical" performance of contractors during the first 15% of a contract period. His observations cover the very largest contracts issued by the DOD over the past decade. The method is worth nothing, because it may well represent a dependable approach to forecasting the final results of any major program.

This individual has found that programs, once they have created a performance footprint of at least 15% on a contract, have established a predictable pattern as to what they are likely to achieve in the end. His findings are summarized in Figure 20-12.

In his formal presentation this official updated the number of actual contractor candidates in his findings from 200 to 300 over the past ten years. But whether the actual sample is 200 or 300, these empirical findings are certainly impressive, and could be significant both to the government and to private contractors, as we find ourselves drifting in the direction of increasing emphasis on the use (misuse?) of firm-fixed price contracting arrangements, and of contractor cost participation during demonstration/validation phase of new program competitions.

**Estimates at Completion**

- Given: Contract more than 15% complete.

  1. Overrun at completion will not be less than overrun to date.

  2. Percent overrun at completion will be greater than percent overrun to date.

- Conclusion: You can't recover!!

- Who says: More than 200 major DOD contracts since 1977.

- Why: If you underestimated the near, there is no hope that you did better on the far term planning.

**Figure 20-12  Projecting EACs [10]**

# ENDNOTES

[1] Robert R. Kemps, Office of the Assistant Secretary of Defense (Comptroller), *Cost Performance Reporting and Baseline Management,* circa 1975, page 13.

[2] Robert R. Kemps, page 14.

[3] Charts 20-2, 20-6, and 20-11 were provided courtesy of Humphreys & Associates, Inc.

[4] Department of Energy, DOE/MA-0184, *Analyzing Performance of Small Projects,* March, 1985, page 33.

[5] United States Air Force Systems Command, *Guide to Analysis of Contractor Cost Data,* August, 1979, page 4-21.

[6] United States Air Force Systems Command, *Guide to Analysis of Contractor Cost Data,* August, 1979, page 4-10.

[7] George Sammet Jr., Major General, U.S. Army, from an article appearing in "*Army Research and Development News Magazine,*" November-December, 1974, appearing in J. S. Baumgartner, *Systems Management,* (Washington, D.C.: The Bureau of National Affairs, Inc., 1979), page 284.

[8] George Sammet Jr., Major General, U.S. Army, page 285.

[9] United States Air Force Systems Command, *Guide to Analysis of Contractor Cost Data,* August, 1979, page 4-27.

[10] Gary E. Christle, Office of the Assistant Secretary of Defense (Comptroller), in a paper entitled "Contractor Performance Measurement-Projecting Estimates at Completion," at the conference *Cost/Schedule Control Systems & Performance Measurement Systems,* sponsored by the Institute of Cost Analysis, Atlanta, Georgia, October 26, 1987.

# V

# SUMMARY

# 21

# The Arthur D. Little Study

On the surface, and without really looking into the reasons behind the original requirement, one obvious area where the DOD could immediately save money on all major procurements would be to abandon the C/SCSC concept. Many seasoned executives both in government and in private industry have advocated just that over the past 20 years.

It was in this environment that the Department of Defense, some 15 years after originally establishing the criteria concept in 1967, decided to go to an outside source to perform an independent inquiry into the utility of C/SCSC, and determine whether it was worth the added costs to its major procurements. This type of review had been done before internally, but never by an independent source completely outside of the government.

The management consulting firm of Arthur D. Little Company (ADL), with its impeccable reputation for objectivity, was selected to perform a study. Their findings, good or bad, might just convince even the most ardent critics of the concept.

## Background

The ADL study contract was awarded in 1982. It had as its stated purpose to:

- Determine the degree of acceptance and use of the C/SCSC by defense contractors and government program managers;

- Identify problems and issues, the resolution of which could lead to improvements in the C/SCSC and contract performance measurement reporting requirements; and

- Recommend policy changes that will lead to these improvements and could be implemented by the Assistant Secretary of Defense (Comptroller).[1]

The study was to be conducted in two phases. Phase I was to consist of a mail-out questionnaire and would be conducted in June, 1983. Phase II would consist of field interviews and would take place from April through June, 1984. The interviews in Phase II would be from twenty-four sources: four contractors and four DOD program offices, one from each of the three military service branches (Army, Navy, Air Force).

275

Although the ADL study was done exclusively for the DOD, their findings and certain of their recommendations for improvements are purely generic, and could well apply to any branch of government which imposes the C/SCSC (DOE, NASA, etc.). We will outline the seven specific areas of focus and their findings, and then the ten specific recommendations for improvements in C/SCSC made by Arthur D. Little.

## ADL Study Findings (7)

**1. *Cost and Benefit:* ** *Do the benefits of C/SCSC outweigh its costs?*

There was a general endorsement of the criteria concept, both from government and private industry. Both groups considered C/SCSC to be effective and to outweigh the costs involved. However, most of the respondents had their own ideas for improvements in the concept, and it was in these suggested changes that the differences between the government's perspective and that of the private contractor became apparent.

Most contractors wanted less "documentation" of cost account variances at all levels of reporting. In particular, they felt that detailed variance analysis for the current reporting period was unnecessary for their own internal management of the contract and was unlikely to be read at any level of the government. "Their point was that there were more timely methods to keep abreast of near real-time events, and that documented monthly reporting did not have a substantive purpose for them."[2] *(Author's comment: This is a valid point.)*

Contractors felt that there should be fewer cost accounts. They would raise the intersection points of both WBS and organization levels, which sets the numbers of cost accounts on a contract. They pointed out that when C/SCSC developmental contracts later went into a firm fixed price production mode and they (on their own) continued the concept, this was the first thing that they did to reduce costs without degrading the quality of management control. In particular, contractors suggested raising the level of WBS reporting to higher levels, since their internal management control focused on organization, not on WBS. *(Author's comment: A valid point, but many contractors shoot themselves in the foot in this area. Contractors frequently set these levels excessively low for themselves.)*

The third area where contractors had suggestions for changes was in the replanning of contracts to reflect "work around" or changed schedule conditions. They felt that the requirement to maintain the original baseline was overly restrictive in C/SCSC. *(Author's comment: Be careful of this issue—an original "baseline" as a constant reference point is critical to the fundamental C/SCSC concept.)*

Suggestions for changes from government personnel were not as cohesive as those from industry. Some wanted lower costs associated with C/SCSC, with less contractor personnel involved, and more timely data. Some wanted weekly or biweekly data reporting. Some wanted results which the C/SCSC concept never intended to provide. *(Author's comment: These types of scattered suggestions reflect a lack of understanding for what is practical, and achievable, and the intended purpose of C/SCSC.)*

One area where there was genuine concern was the issue of schedule variances as reported in CPRs. Quite often the CPR will reflect a contractors internal baseline plan for producing something, which will contain a positive slack condition. As slips occur the CPR would be reflecting a negative schedule condition, yet deliveries would be made on time, according to contract schedule. *(Author's comment: A valid criticism of the schedule variance part of the CPR. See Chapter 15.)*

The ADL study seemed to put things into proper prospective with this statement:

> In summary, effective internal management does not in itself require detailed reporting to the government. However, reporting to the government should be expected as a reality of doing business with the government, particularly when the work entails cost risk to the government. This government need for information is not always taken into account by contractors.[3]

ADL made two recommendations for improvements: 1) Prepare a "White Paper" on C/SCSC, and 2) Certification process for C/SCSC practitioners. All ten of the ADL recommendations are covered in the next section of this chapter.

**2.  *Criteria Concept and Approach:*** *Are the criteria concept, approach, and the criteria themselves appropriate; and are the DOD practices effective?*

Some four out of five people surveyed indicated that they felt the criteria approach is sound. They felt the criteria as presently defined is effective in evaluating a contractor's management control system.

One issue which surfaced was contractor dissatisfaction with the required planning and control of material, in order to satisfy the criteria. The concern, related to the WBS, was having to plan and measure material costs by several WBS elements whenever material was common to multiple elements. Another dissatisfaction was the time period in which earned value must be credited for materials. *(Authors comment: "Materials" is perhaps the most difficult area for the criteria. In order to satisfy the material criterion, contractors must treat materials in a manner which is cumbersome and unnatural for most contractors.)*

**3. *C/SCSC Review Process:*** *Is the government review process effective?*

This area dealt with the governments responsibility to verify that contractors have properly implemented C/SCSC. This process takes the form of Demonstration Reviews (DRs) on new efforts and Subsequent Application Reviews (SARs) and Extended SARs (ESARs) once validated.

While there was agreement on the necessity for conducting the various C/SCSC reviews, certain contractor complaints surfaced regarding the competency of the teams performing such reviews. Some felt that as many as three-fourths of the reviewing team were lacking in both related work experience and in general knowledge of C/SCSC principles. Their concerns focused on:

...perceptions of personal views in interpreting C/SCSC, resolution of issues by team opinion, inadequate understanding of real-world processes, a textbook-rulebook-formula-inflexible approach, inadequate preparation in terms of understanding the system they are going to review, and personalities.[4]

ADL responded with three recommendations specifically addressing the issues: 2) Certification for all C/SCSC practitioners; 3) A C/SCSC manpower pool; and 4) Centralization of C/SCSC responsibility. *(Authors comment: There will always be personality conflicts. Our experience with reviewing teams has been quite positive. They are directed by qualified and experienced persons, and supported by various specialists, who are not expected to have the same level of experience as that of the team chief or director. Every team member does not need to be a C/SCSC expert.)*

### 4. Consistency of C/SCSC Interpretation: *Are C/SCSC consistently interpreted?*

Concerns from contractors on this issue centered on "how" the criteria were being interpreted by government representatives rather than on the "consistency" of interpretation. It is related to issue 3) (C/SCSC Review Process—see above) because most of any disputed interpretations would likely come out of demonstration reviews and SARs.

The issue of WBS levels and the resulting excessive numbers of cost accounts was given as a problem for contractors. *(Authors comment: Our experience would indicate that C/SCSC "experts" in both industry and government have a tendency to make interpretations which result in an "excessive" number of cost accounts.)*

Another specific example was cited. At two contractor locations where ADL interviewing manufacturing personnel, they were told that these contractors had been required to create a "manufacturing cost account plan" in order to comply with the criteria. Such plans were duplicating information contained in other company documents, and were superfluous to their needs and costly to maintain. *(Authors comment: Sounds like a bad interpretation of the criteria, such information would rightly belong in either the C/SCSC systems description or company procedures.)*

The ADL recommendations made for issue 3) On the review process, applied equally to this issue.

### 5. Time Allowances for Implementing C/SCSC: *Are the time allowances for certain C/SCSC actions realistic?*

According to Federal Acquisition Regulation (FAR), a contractor is to demonstrate compliance with the C/SCSC requirements within 90 days after contract award, or as otherwise agreed to by the parties. Unfortunately, few people remember the "or as otherwise agreed to by the parties," and some have expected contractors to establish their Performance Measurement Baselines (PMBs) and be ready for a demonstration visit three months after contract award. Ninety days is totally unrealistic for anything but the most simple contracts, which are fully definitized at time of award and for which there has been an ongoing C/SCSC activity in place at a contractors facility.

There was general agreement that it would be preferable to have C/SCSC in place at the earliest possible date. Many contractors are able to demonstrate compliance within 6 months of award, but most run 12 months to a SAR, and demonstration reviews took as long as 18 months to achieve. Also, there was agreement that a "quality" PMB is preferable to an "early" PMB. *(Authors comment: Establishing a PMB is a big job, and 12 months is not excessive for a large contract. Also, few people understand that "definitization" of the contract is an absolute prerequisite to establishing a PMB.)*

Another real-life issue facing most contractors at contract award is the lack of manpower, combined with the overabundance of initial work to do. And as some contractors pointed out, functional people have no "natural" inclination to support C/SCSC, may even feel it conflicts with their primary mission for the company.

One suggested method to get contractors to establish their PMB at the earliest possible time is to set up tangible incentives for them to do so. An example of such an incentive is a contract fee of some type, either an incentive fee or even an award fee. Some government people have a philosophical concern (or block) about giving contractors another fee for work they are being paid to do anyway. Realistically, award fees do work and do have a tendency to "get the head guy's attention."[5]

ADL made two recommendations for improving the time necessary to establish the PMB: 5) Use of incentives, and 6) Initial high-level contacts for the review process. *(Authors comment: these are sound and realistic recommendations which should be seriously considered by the government).*

### 6. Cost/Schedule Performance Reporting: *Are Cost Performance Reports (CPRs) and internal contractor cost/schedule data timely and useful?*

This issue emphasized the different perspectives of the government and the contractor. Government personnel were concerned about the timeliness of the CPRs and the quality of variance analysis reporting contained therein. Contractors were critical of excessive reporting requirements due to inappropriate variance thresholds and unnecessarily low WBS levels. Contractors also felt that the variance analysis for the current month was superfluous and most often reflected a temporary condition which would correct itself the following month, in most cases.

Government personnel felt that the CPR variances levels were about right, but that the quality of variance reporting in CPRs was poor, particularly the analysis of schedule variances. Contractors stated that their pacing item for the timely submittal of CPRs was the requirement for variance analysis. Contractors consistently wanted less variance analysis reporting, particularly at low WBS levels.

ADL made four recommendations from these almost conflicting complaints, which were the result of the differing perspectives of the government and the private contractor. Recommendation 7) Dealt with a suggested change to the CPR requirement which would clarify schedule variance reporting; 8) Proposed clarification of CPR terminology; 9) Suggested separating the CPR into two parts, one for raw data submitted first, and the later submittal of variance reports; and 10) Which suggested an automated data link for transmittal of CPRs.

**7. *C/SCSC Surveillance:* *Is government C/SCSC surveillance by agencies having contractor plant cognizance effective in ensuring that the contractor's system continues to operate as accepted?***

The "agencies" which this issue addresses are the Contract Administration Offices (CAOs) and the various armed forces plant representatives, e.g., Air Force Plant Representative Office (AFPRO). Once a C/SCSC activity has been validated these offices act as sort of a delegated extension of the governmental body which approved the contractor's system.

There was a general acknowledgement, even among private contractors, that there was a genuine requirement for some type of system surveillance by the government. However, there was also a complaint by some contractors that the function of C/SCSC surveillance did not appear to be a high priority by the CAOs and plant representative offices. Also there was the observation that the people who were performing such tasks were lacking expertise in C/SCSC knowledge, and that there seemed to be a high turnover of personnel who performed these tasks.

ADL made three suggestions for improvements, which had been made before: 2) Certification process; 3) Contracting-out for manpower; and 4) Centralization.

## The ADL Recommendations for Improvements (10)

### 1. *White Paper-Purpose and Value of C/SCSC*

A brief "white paper" of no more than five pages in length was suggested, which would describe the objectives of C/SCSC and discuss some of the more relevant issues.

*Note*: ADL did prepare a brief "white paper" for the DOD, which was formally released by William H. Taft IV, Deputy Secretary of Defense on 10 July, 1986. This well-written document is important, and is now included as a "Preface" to the newly issued *Joint Implementation Guide,* Appendix E to this book.

### 2. *Certification Process for Practitioners*

A process for establishing a centralized method of identifying and training practitioners in C/SCSC was suggested. Such a method would include not only formal training, but also address the issue of minimal experience requirements of such personnel. The certification would focus on those who would make up the reviewing teams as well as those who would later survey the validated management control systems as a part of the CAOs and PROs.

### 3. *Contracting-out For Manpower Pool*

There should be a central manpower pool of persons with C/SCSC expertise, available as needed to the three services. Such efforts would be funded by the three services receiving the benefits of the pool. These personnel would only be supportive of the teams and would *not* be expected to fill leadership positions. Excluded from the pool would be persons intended as the Review Director, the Team Chief, and the CAO C/SCSC monitor. *(Authors comment: This is an excellent suggestion, particularly if the pool included those "retired" C/SCSC experts who might welcome a short-term assignment on occasion.)*

### 4. *Centralization of Focal Points Under Joint Logistics Commanders*

There should be a jointly manned C/SCSC group formed under the Joint Logistics Commanders (JLC). All personnel from the various services and the Defense Logistics Agency working with C/SCSC would be transferred administratively to this centralized group.

Problems associated with tri-service coordination and validation reviews and final reports would be expected to be minimized under such an arrangement. Additionally, any problems of mixed or inconsistent criteria interpretation would be kept to a minimum.

### 5. *Use of Incentives*

There should be a *realistic* DOD position established with respect to the time necessary to implement the C/SCSC Performance Measurement Baseline (PMB), and to establish the steps leading up to the PMB. (Ninety days after contract award is not considered realistic). Once this position is established, the use of incentive fees or award fees to contractors to make the C/SCSC PMB happen as planned should be considered.

### 6. *Initial High-level Contacts for Review Process*

Approximately 30 days after the award of a contract, there should be an initial service "flag rank" contact with senior management at the selected contractor, which would stress the importance of C/SCSC compliance. The contact may be a personal visit, a phone call, or correspondence—whatever is appropriate to obtain a commitment from the company to seriously implement the C/SCSC concept on the new contract award.

### 7. *Schedule Event Discussion on CPR Problem Analysis Format*

That section of the Cost Performance Report (CPR) which deals with the details of why schedule variances (SVs) are happening, should be expanded to require better descriptions from contractors.

Schedule variances should be related to specific tasks, events, or milestones and be correlated to other data items which cover the issue of scheduling on a contract. *(Authors comment: in total agreement, the government should get reporting from an "integrated" cost/schedule management system, as they intended, not from a "fragmented" approach, which is too often the case.)*

### 8. *Clarification of Terminology in DOD Guidance*

In the Department of Defense (DOD) Instruction 7000.10 which defines the purpose of the CPR, there is a term which is subject to varying interpretations and which is causing unrealistic expectations on the part of certain people. The issue is the "timeliness" of the CPR. Should the CPR be a near real-time indicator of contract performance as some have insisted, or what. *(Authors comment: This is not a big issue. The same people who expect the PMB to be in place within 90 days, will likely want CPRs to reflect near "real-time" conditions. They will be disappointed in both instances.)*

### 9. *Separate Submittal of CPR Formats*

Those who have prepared a Cost Performance Report (CPR) know there are two somewhat separate activities involved in the effort: (1) the pulling together and summarization of raw financial data, and (2) the analysis and detailed write-ups focusing on the variances. This recommendation would split the CPR submittal into two phases in an attempt to speed up the overall submittal. Financial data would be sent in first, followed later by the detailed variance write-ups.

### 10. *Data-Nets for CPRs*

This recommendation is similar to the one above in that its intent is to speed-up the CPR submittal process. Under this approach CPR submittals would be made via a data-net or data-link from contractor to the government.

## Summary

The ADL study was a useful endorsement of the validity of the C/SCSC concept. The fact that it was performed by a body outside of the government made its findings all the more valid. Of the numerous findings contained in the 219-page Phase I report and later in the 65-page Phase II report, these four points seem to stand out from the rest:

1. The C/SCSC concept is perceived to be useful, and to outweigh the costs involved.
2. There is room for improvements in the C/SCSC.
3. People using C/SCSC need to better understand its purpose, capability, and limitations.
4. The qualifications of C/SCSC practitioners needs to be improved.

## ENDNOTES

[1] Arthur D. Little Company, *Survey Relating to the Implementation of Cost/Schedule Control Systems Criteria Within the Department of Defense and Industry-Phase I*, (Washington, D.C.: Department of Defense, December 5, 1983), p. I-1.

[2] Arthur D. Little Company, *Survey Relating to the Implementation of Cost/Schedule Control Systems Critera Within the Department of Defense and Industry-Phase II*, (Washington, D.C.: Department of Defense, Ausgust 15, 1984), p.III-3.

[3] Phase II, p. III-6.

[4] Phase II. p. III-11.

[5] Phase II, p. III-19.

# 22

# Employee Training and Professional Organizations

This chapter will address the issue of the preparation of an organization and its people to comply with a contract requiring C/SCSC. It will discuss the major task of C/SCSC implementation, which must also include the matter of employee and management training for doing business in a slightly different way, including the strict compliance with all documented rules.

In some cases such efforts will consist of the *initial* training of personnel, which is a fairly straightforward task. But in other cases, the effort will involve the *re-training* of personnel in an organization after a certain lapse of time. The re-training of an organization is often a more difficult task than simply initial training. Reason: no one has yet devised a method to accomplish an "organizational lobotomy" with any degree of success. It takes time and effort and energy to the reverse stubborn "mind-sets" of personnel, including senior management, in any established organization.

Another factor which bears heavily on the ability of an organization to comply with the criteria is the organization's past history with C/SCSC. Did they previously have a fully compliant activity, and then let it deteriorate? What is the present relationship with the customer, particularly those from the customer whose job it is to monitor C/SCSC? Have they alienated their customer? Have they recently failed a review, and how many times? What does company management really think of C/SCSC? Does management truly support the criteria concept, or simply pay "lip-service" to it, "sandbagging" the efforts of those whose job it is to work on the criteria? These important factors will determine the extent of training required by an organization to successfully prepare its personnel to pass a customer reviewing team.

This chapter will also review selected professional organizations which exist and which present opportunities for employees to discuss C/SCSC problems with their peers, and to keep current with the latest directions of the criteria.

285

## C/SCSC Implementation and Employee Training

The issue of employee training for C/SCSC is but one segment of the larger issue facing an organization which has just won a new contract requiring compliance with the criteria: the full implementation of C/SCSC. What follows, therefore, is a review of *one* generic model devised by one consulting firm in the field, as interpreted by the author. [1]

This generic model, as it will be described, will perhaps fit certain environments and likely miss in others. A word of caution is thus in order to anyone who might expect that the model could be immediately applied to any and all situations. Also, it should be pointed out that this model addresses full C/SCSC compliance. A lesser requirement for C/SSR applications would likely involve considerably less time and effort.

This model also assumes that internal company management has made the decision to seek external assistance, either from an outside management consultant firm or from a sister division, to assist them in the implementation and training of their organization.

The model will outline seven tasks which are typically involved in the full implementation of a criteria compliant management control system. The big variable in costs will be what the company presently does versus what it must do to fully comply with all 35 criteria. Since it is generally regarded (in some educated circles) that most firms typically comply with perhaps up to 75% of the requirements of the criteria in their normal good business practices, what's the "big deal" in going the other 25% ? The "big deal" is a considerable step for firms to take. It requires assessment; documentation; dedication; discipline; and a strong management commitment. Big steps for any established firm to take, as the following will illustrate.

*Task 1-Team Organization and Start-Up*—This task begins subsequent to the decision by management to implement (or re-institute) a C/SCSC-compliant management control system. Typically, such decisions are made shortly after the award of a contract requiring same, or the failure to successfully pass a SAR or ESAR on an existing C/SCSC activity.

As a first step, it is recommended that a "management review committee" be formed to advise and monitor the implementation of the criteria until the customer has actually given approval of the modified management control system. The management review committee will likely want to immediately establish a *dedicated* multi-disciplined C/SCSC "design and implementation team" to carry out the work of actual execution of the plans. It is critical to the success of the task to be undertaken that the management review committee and the design and implementation team reach an agreement on a charter and methodology plan, prior to starting the actual work of compliance.

Some of the initial work of the newly formed design and implementation team will be to set the operating rules which will govern the process and hopefully minimize confusion factors. They will want to specify the standard writing formats for all documentation, and the documentation of the effort will be considerable. They will want to set up a control method to record problems as they are uncovered, and then work through them to a successful conclusion.They will probably want to start on an initial glossary of internal C/SCSC terms and acronyms in use at their company, which might be slightly different than that used by the rest of the industry.

One of the first things the team will want to do is to review the appropriate C/SCSC (JIG) or C/SSR checklists and initiate the effort of creating systematic "story-board" flowcharts which will graphically display their existing management control system to better assess what modifications might be in order to satisfy the criteria. They will want to assign initial responsibilities for developing subsystem tasks. A responsibility assignment matrix can be an invaluable aid in helping to decide who does what in this process (see Figure 22-1).

Notice that in addition to the management review committee and the design and implementation team, a third category of activity has been included in Figure 22-1, that of the management consultant. This category of assistance is optional to the team, depending on the C/SCSC resources available to work on the endeavor from within the company. The outside management consultants do have a few things in their favor. They are generally "experts" in the subject, or they don't stay in business long. They can be contractually required to work full-time on this particular endeavor, as compared to sister division help, which often gets pulled off the job for "more pressing work." And lastly, the management consultant can be "excused" from the job when no longer needed, with little effort.

| | Responsibility | | |
| Implementation Task | Design & Implementation Team | Management Review Committee | Outside Consultant |
|---|---|---|---|
| 1. Team Organization | — | Primary | — |
| 2. System Assessment | Assist | Review | Primary |
| 3. Develop Subsystems | Primary | Review | Assist |
| 4. Document System | Primary | Review | Assist |
| 5. Implement System | Primary | Review | Assist |
| 6. Train Personnel | Primary | Review | Assist |
| 7. Evaluate Compliance | Assist | Review | Primary |

Figure 22-1 C/SCSC Implementation Responsibility Matrix[2]

*Task 2-System Assessment*—The design and implementation team will want to continue the process of scrutinizing their existing management control system by expanding the visual displays of story-board flow charts, with the addition of narratives, to identify any gaps, over-laps and missing-links in their system. They will want to collect and incorporate samples of all documentation related to their current system, and make an initial assessment of what parts might need revision in order to comply with the criteria.

Another part of this effort will be to take a close look at their existing automation capability to start the process of deciding what supplements and/or changes might be needed in hardware or software. Although C/SCSC does not require any form of automation, and many fine systems have been approved with little or no automation, it is generally concluded that life is better with automation, than without it.

The team will want to start looking at requirement deficiencies which need to be addressed with computer upgrades. A survey of software packages should be undertaken by a subgroup of the design and implementation team. Automation can be a big cost driver, depending on the approach selected. A micro/PC approach could cost as little as perhaps $100,000, while the mini or mainframe approaches could go as high as perhaps a $1 million or more—Quite a difference.

The design and implementation team will want to start identifying deficiencies and problems with the current system, to isolate which forms, procedures, etc., will need enhancement. If C/SCSC is new to them they will need new forms to cover such things as Cost Account Plans, Work Packages, a Work Breakdown Structure Index & Dictionary, Budget Transfers, Problem Analysis Reports, and other precise forms. They will want to establish a preliminary set of design criteria and review their findings with the management review committee as a continuing process throughout the full term of the implementation. The story-boards and flow charts generated here will serve to define the subsystem development which will then need to be developed.

*Task 3-Subsystem Development*—It is in this activity that the root of compliance with the criteria will start to take place. All of the issues/problems which were identified under system assessment will need to be addressed, manifesting themselves in initial documents for evaluation by the management review committee. The story-board wall-chart displays will be modified as appropriate to reflect the altered but now more closely compliant C/SCSC system. A cross reference of each box on the story-board should be prepared which relates in narrative procedural form the flow of the system.

The outline of a C/SCSC systems description which will describe the compliance approach will start to take shape, along with an initial listing of the required C/SCSC specific procedures. Each step in the process will be reviewed with the management committee overseeing the team activities.

The systems description document can and has taken various forms over the years. Initially many firms found it convenient to structure such documents along their internal organization, as related by function to the criteria. More and more the trend now seems to be to structure the systems description along the five criteria groupings—organization, planning and budgets, accounting, etc.—as they relate to the specific company's internal organization.

Among the procedures to be developed will be work authorization, work breakdown structures, the scheduling system, budgeting control, the procurement activities (material/ subcontract/ interdivisional), indirect cost control, manufacturing control including work measurement, and so forth. Special topics such as the methodology for performing earned values, doing estimates at completion, controlling revisions to the baseline, analysis of findings, all need to be covered in either the systems description or in related procedures.

*Task 4-System Documentation*—In this task , a description of the modified management control system must be put on paper. A C/SCSC systems description and related procedures must all be created.

Unique special-purpose pamphlets covering critical subjects relating to a particular team member or function will often emerge. A typical example of these documents might be *A Guide for Cost Account Managers,* packaged in convenient pocket-size form. The final glossary of C/SCSC terms will be issued.

*Task 5-System Implementation*—Everything required for a full C/SCSC compliance must be covered in this phase. Selected formats from the DOD Joint Implementation Guide or DOE Systems Review/Surveillance Guide, as appropriate, need to be prepared here.

A CWBS, WBS Index, and Dictionary will be put in place. A program organization chart and responsibility assignment matrix should be available. Schedules will need to be integrated and milestones will be traceable from the master schedule down to detailed work package schedules. A complete time-phased Performance Measurement Baseline will need to be in place, and all changes to it tightly controlled.

The best proof of this task being accomplished is the ability of the organization to compile a Cost Performance Report which actually measures earned value on the contract being implemented. The total organization must be capable of *demonstrating* its ability to perform the respective portions of the now fully compliant C/SCSC management control system. Any variances from performance thresholds must be explained by use of a variance analysis report. An EAC must be included based on that described in the VARs/PARs. In short, the established C/SCSC compliant system must be in force and capable of passing an internal audit.

*Task 6-System Training*—Finally, we come to the issue of employee and management training. The total organization must be assessed to determine its training needs.

Training outlines, specific training plans, course outlines, and formal presentations will need to be created which will cover that which is contained in the C/SCSC systems description document and the related procedures.

One of the special purpose guides which might be appropriate is a summary of the more common C/SCSC terms. Often during a customer review, personnel will understand the workings and concept of the revised system but may get tripped up because they have forgotten one of the particular C/SCSC terms.

Special one-on-one training sessions are usually advisable for the more critical functions (cost account managers). Additional training sessions of a more general nature will be needed for all managers, and summary overviews for the very senior members of management, who must be involved in the overall process. Lastly, the internal C/SCSC trainers themselves will have to be trained and knowledgeable in the detailed workings of the system, so that there is a continuing network of training capability in the organization.

*Task 7-System Compliance Evaluation*—The last essential step in this overall implementation process is to verify, within the company, that the newly compliant system is working as planned. A series of internal "mock" reviews should be conducted by persons independent of the implementing team. The consultants, particularly some "fresh faces," serve this role well in the mock customer reviews.

Three types of internal reviews are generally recommended: a mock "Implementation Visit", a mock "Readiness Review," and lastly, a mock "Demonstration Review." These internal mock reviews need to be performed sufficiently in advance of the planned customer reviews to allow time for correcting problems uncovered during the internal mock reviews.

*A Generic C/SCSC Implementation Cost Model*—A famous lawyer (the author's son) once remarked: "Anything is possible—particularly if you don't know what you are talking about."

Well, much in the same vein that people, particularly the uninformed, cannot possibly fathom that it could take 9 to 12 months to establish an initial PMB on a major contract, will also be shocked at the costs of fully implementing C/SCSC so that a contractor can successfully pass a customer review. And there is an inverse relationship to the total costs of training an organization, and the total *lack* of management support which exists for the criteria concept. An additional significant cost driver is the necessary retraining, or reorientation of personnel "set" in doing things in their accustomed way.

Shown in Figure 22-2 is a generic cost model for implementing *full* C/SCSC in a company. The model has been intentionally set with wide values (350 to 700 person weeks) to cover a variety of possible situations. Factors which impact the costs required are the size of the company, the size and length and complexity of the contract, and particularly the

| Implementation Task | Equivalent Person Weeks |
|---|---|
| 1. Implementation Team Organization & Start-up | 8 to 12 weeks |
| 2. System Assessment | 45 to 85 weeks |
| 3. Subsystem Development | 80 to 170 weeks |
| 4. System Documentation | 22 to 28 weeks |
| 5. System Implementation | 140 to 300 weeks |
| 6. Training | 15 to 45 weeks |
| 7. System Evaluation | 40 to 60 weeks |
| **Total** | 350 to 700 weeks |

**Figure 22-2  The Cost Range of Full C/SCSC Implementation[3]**

number of cost accounts for the contract. A C/SSR application will be considerably less expensive to implement than full C/SCSC, and less than that displayed in Figure 22-2.

Sixty to seventy percent of the necessary effort will be consumed in just two tasks: development and implementation of C/SCSC. Of the values shown in Figure 22-2, over 90-plus percent should be utilized by internal company personnel. Somewhere between 5% to 8% should be planned for the outside help, a sister-division or management consultant. But, the bulk of the implementation effort should be performed by internal company personnel, or the system will likely revert back to its old form once the customer departs the plant. Should that happen, a contractor will have to start the process all over when the customer discovers the relapse to the old ways. And customers generally do discover any and all relapses.

*A Generic C/SCSC Implementation Schedule Model*—Assuming that it properly takes 9 to 12 months for the implementation of a full Performance Measurement Baseline, an accompanying implementation and training schedule is shown in Figure 22-3. The seven tasks described above is shown with an approximate time-frame displayed for each. Just as with the cost model, the required time-frame will be determined by the actual conditions in place at the given contractors location. With a requirement for a C/SSR, the time period and total resources needed could likely be reduced significantly. By contrast, a major contractor experiencing difficulties, both with its management system and in performance on the contract itself, could take longer to complete.

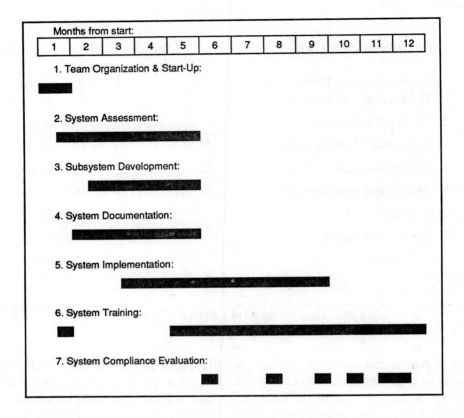

**Figure 22-3  A C/SCSC Implementation & Training Schedule[4]**

## Professional Organizations

There are various professional organizations, available to both individuals and corporations, which offer opportunities to persons interested in the subject of C/SCSC. They keep track of what may be changing in the criteria, or in applications of the criteria. These organizations are listed below in descending order, based on their focus on the subject of C/SCSC.

### I. Individual Membership Organizations (6)

Performance Management Association (PMA)
P.O. Box 272
Lionville, PA  19353-0272
(215) 873-8987

This association was started in 1985 to provide a forum and organization for persons interested in project management and performance measurement with criteria applications. It is made up primarily of practitioners from private industry and from the government who work daily with C/SCSC. Its main focus is on C/SCSC and criteria applications.

PMA holds an annual national meeting at rotating locations, regional conferences, and local chapter gatherings. It publishes a quarterly journal entitled *In Control*. Membership fees run $35.00 per year.

\* \* \*

Institute of Cost Analysis (ICA)
8101 Hinson Farm Road
Suite 201
Alexandria, VA 22306
(703) 360-9581

This organization was formed in 1981 to further the effectiveness of cost and price analysis in government and industry. It holds national and local chapter meetings on various cost subjects, and periodic national seminars devoted exclusively to the subject of C/SCSC.

ICA publishes various informational documents including a *Newsletter of the Institute* and *The Journal of Cost Analysis*, which contains articles from practitioners in the industry. They offer education assistance leading to the designation of "Certified Cost Analyst (CCA)" to members. Membership fees run $35.00 per year.

\* \* \*

American Association of Cost Engineers (AACE)
308 Monongahela Building
Morgantown, WV 26505
(304) 296-8444

AACE is a professional organization founded in 1956 to advance the science and art of cost engineering. Through publications and meetings at international, national, and a local chapters, AACE and their affiliated AACE-Canada, endeavor to keep members and the pubic informed on problems affecting costs.

AACE makes available to members a series of related cost publications including their monthly journal *Cost Engineering*. They offer educational certifications as: "Certified Cost Engineer (CCE)" and "Certified Cost Consultant (CCC)." Annual membership runs $70.00 per year.

Project Management Institute (PMI)
P.O.Box 43
Drexel Hill, Pennsylvania 19026
(215) 622-1796

PMI is a professional organization formed in 1967, dedicated to advancing the state-of-the-art in the management of projects. Their membership encompasses a broad range of persons whose common thread is an interest in project management.

PMI holds national, regional, and local chapter meetings, and offers various selected publications for practitioners in project management. Their main publication is the *Project Management Journal,* a large magazine issued five times per year containing articles submitted by PMI members and specialists in the field. They offer various educational activities and special seminars, including a certification program leading to the designation of a "Project Management Professional (PMP)."

PMI has an affiliation with the School of Business, Western Carolina University, Cullowhee, North Carolina, which reviews their educational materials and offers advanced degree programs in project management. Annual membership is $60. per year plus local chapter dues.

* * *

National Contract Management Association (NCMA)
6728 Old McLean Village Drive
McLean, Virginia 22101
(703) 442-0137

NCMA was started in 1959 to foster professional growth and the educational advancement of members involved in the management of contracts of various types: public, private, prime, subcontract, grant, lease, and so on.

They offer a series of national and local meetings and educational seminars on subjects related to contract management. Their monthly magazine *Contract Management* contains a wide range of articles and announcements on the subject of contract and program management. NCMA offers two certification programs: the "Certified Professional Contracts Manager (CPCM)" and the "Certified Associate Contracts Manager (CACM)." Annual membership dues run $45.00 per year plus a one-time initiation fee of $15.00

* * *

American Production and Inventory Control Society (APICS)
500 West Annandale Road
Falls Church, Virginia 22046-4274
(703) 237-8344

An organization founded in 1957 to develop recognition of the profession, and to increase efficiency of production and inventory management through education, research and applications of scientific methods.

They offer national, regional and local meetings, as well as educational seminars. They also offer a wide range of documents including their monthly magazine *Production & Inventory Management Review*. APICS has a professional educational program leading to the designation: "Certification in Production & Inventory Management (CPIM)." Annual membership dues run $40.00 per year plus local chapter dues as appropriate.

## II. Corporate Membership Organizations (3)

National Security Industrial Association (NSIA)
1025 Connecticut Avenue, NW, Suite 300
Washington, DC 20036
(301) 775-1440

NSIA was organized in 1944 to foster a close working relationship and effective two-way communication between the government, primarily the defense segment, and the industry which supports it. It is an association made up of about 400 industrial and associated firms, with representatives of the member firms serving as working participants on standing committees of particular interest to their organization. NSIA has direct communication links to all key segments of the government, both the executive and legislative branches.

Of particular interest to the C/SCSC practitioners is the standing committee on "Procurement," with its special subcommittee on "Management Systems." This subcommittee is made up of representatives of firms dealing with defense, aeronautics, space, energy, transportation, and management and support services.

The Management Systems subcommittee typically meets six times per year, to discuss and formulate an industry position with respect to government laws, directives and implementation of same. Meetings are sometimes conducted with senior government representatives in attendance to stimulate a two-way discussion between industry and government.

NSIA is perhaps *the* most important vehicle for private industry to maintain discussions with the government (particularly the PMJEG) and to establish a unified position on government regulations, of particular interest is the C/SCSC. Virtually every subject contained in this book has been discussed at some time in one of the open NSIA forums. Membership in NSIA is limited to corporate firms.

\* \* \*

Aerospace Industries Association of America (AIA)
1725 DeSales Street, NW
Washington, D.C. 20036
(202) 429-4620

The AIA is a trade association representing some 48 companies engaged in research, development, and manufacturing of aerospace products. It serves as a medium for presenting the consensus positions of its members to the U.S.government, on broad policy matters of interest to its members. Working members of AIA are the senior executives of its corporate members. Membership of AIA is limited to selected corporations.

* * *

Council of Defense and Space Industry Associations (CODSIA)
1620 Eye Street, NW
Suite 1000
Washington, D.C. 20006
(202) 659-5013

CODSIA is a council of organizations with interest in government procurement of defense and space items. It was established in 1964 to represent the broad policy interests of its members in the areas of U.S. government procurement regulations, policies and procedures. Currently the council is made up of eight members, including the AIA and NSIA.

---

## ENDNOTES

[1] This generic C/SCSC implementation model was provided by Humphreys & Associates, Inc., Laguna Hills, CA.

[2] Humphreys & Associates., Inc.

[3] Humphreys & Associates, Inc.

[4] Humphreys & Associates, Inc.

# 23

# Future Directions

On the foregoing pages, we have discussed the C/SCSC concept and its impact on all firms which have been subject to the requirement. Everything we have covered up to this point has been addressed in the past and present tenses. Now it might be appropriate to stand back from it all and ask ourselves: Where does the criteria concept go from here? What changes might the future hold for C/SCSC?

We will examine four issues which appear to represent possibilities for changes in the criteria concept. Some offer opportunities for improvements, others are simply more of the same."

## 1. *"Work Team" Cost Accounts*

Any individual who has worked on contracts requiring both full C/SCSC implementation *and* the lesser C/SSR, knows only too well that there is an important difference between the two. The distinction is perhaps only one of degree, but it is an important difference nevertheless.

Under the full implementation of C/SCSC, a performance baseline must be developed representing a summation of detailed cost accounts, which constitute the intersection point of the Work Breakdown Structure (WBS) with the Organizational Breakdown Structure (OBS). The result on any large contracts is literally the formation of *thousands* of cost accounts, each of which must be separately managed, measured, and reported on during the course of performance under the contract. The difference between a contract with 1,000 cost accounts and another with 2,000 cost accounts is an important concern for those involved in the management of the criteria concept.

By contrast, those smaller contracts ($2 to $40 million) which are subject to the lesser C/SSR requirements, are able to take certain "liberties" with the number and content of measurable cost accounts they must create in order to satisfy the requirement. Thus, if a firm on a given contract would be able to satisfy the intent of the criteria with just 1,000 cost accounts, instead of 2,000, they would have less to do to achieve the same performance measurement goals.

But a word of caution is in order in the above illustration. The very foundation of C/SCSC was in the establishment of a baseline of *detailed* cost accounts/work packages, which allowed for the precise measurement of physical work accomplishment during performance of a contract. Simply combining the detailed cost accounts/work packages and making them larger to reduce their quantity is *not* the intent of this "work team" initiative. Rather, the purpose of this approach is to combine cost accounts into larger management units only where it makes sense to do so. And to do so only in those cases where the original purpose of providing detailed work measurement units is not compromised by such actions.

Under the "work team" concept, cost accounts would be allowed to be *grouped* to better represent a logical amalgamation of various multi-functional/ multi-discipline activities, which all share a common goal to produce a specific end product or service. Such common tasks would continue to be authorized by formal work authorizations, as with all C/SCSC effort. But the larger cost account grouping would include *all* people who contribute to the specific common goal, irrespective of their organizational placement, and would include all of the supporting personnel and related subcontractors in the same cost account.

The placement of specific management responsibility for the work team cost account would continue to be an essential ingredient, but the team leader responsibility could actually rotate along with its phasing, depending on the nature of the task involved. The team leader would be comparable to the cost account manager and would be responsible for providing a "consolidated" variance analysis, should such be required. The team leader under this concept is perhaps better referred to as a "WBS element manager."

The expected result of the work team cost account approach would be to reduce the quantity of cost accounts on a given contract by allowing for larger resource quantities and longer duration cost accounts to be used. But the concept would do so *without* a degradation in the quality of C/SCSC implementation. In this regard, the C/SCSC activity would effectively be taking a step in the direction of C/SSR activities, in that the lesser cost account numbers contained in a baseline would typically constitute a larger "grouping" of WBS related elements into a single cost account, while crossing multiple organizational lines and functions.

The cost savings under this approach could be significant. The key is not to diminish the quality of the performance measurement. One of the major unresolved issues is the support the approach will receive from the Government reviewing teams, who must ultimately approve any such changes in the implementation of C/SCSC.

## 2. *Problem Analysis Reporting*

One of the major differences of opinion which has always existed between the Government managers and contractor managers involved in C/SCSC is in the value each places in Format 5 of the Cost Performance Reports, the "Problem Analysis Reports" (PARs). Contractors view PARs as useful, up to a point, but far too often PAR requirements become overwhelming. The minute a given contract experiences a broad, across-the-board cost/schedule difficulties, PAR requirements tend to become excessive, as individual thresholds are breached and each variance requires a separate and formal write-up. Not infrequently PARs represent more pages and space in the CPR than do the balance of the CPR formats. The quality of PARs goes down in direct proportion to their increases in quantity, in the opinion of many.

The result is often a massive paperwork generation requirement, which results in a major drain of energy on those same people trying to get the contract back where it should be. Not only are the PAR pages excessive, but there exists in the minds of those who prepare and submit the PARs, serious doubts that these PARs are ever read or analyzed by the receiving customer.

By contrast, some Government managers can't seem to get enough of these PARs, as was pointed out in the Arthur D. Little study. They seem to feel that the PARs represent a vital part of their surveillance needs as to what may be happening with contracts they have authorized.

The National Security Industrial Association's (NSIA) management system subcommittee has made a recommendation that the Government managers consider authorizing a limit on the number of Problem Analysis Report submittals each month. Three PARs is their recommendation, which would be based on the contractor's assessment of the most critical problems facing a contract. The intent is to allow contractors to focus on the more critical issues of what is going wrong on a given contract. Instead of submitting a "stack" of paper which is of questionable value, the contractor would focus on a set number of what it considers are its critical problems, and describe how it will fix them.

The reception to the NSIA proposal was quite positive. While the Government felt that three may be few, they countered with a suggesting number of ten. Whatever might be the proper number, three or five or ten, this could be a step in the right direction and actually improve the quality content of Format 5, PAR reports.

Perhaps of more significance, however, is the fact that in real life situations, the *involvement* of both the contractor and customer program managers actually *decreases* directly in proportion to the increase in the quantity of PARs generated each month. However, if there were a set limit on the number of PARs required, and the burden was placed on a contractor to focus the discussion on the major problems confronting the contract, the quality of the submittals and contract recovery might just be vastly improved, as suggested by the proponents of this approach. It is certainly worth a try.

### 3. C/SCSC and Firm Fixed Price Contracts

In the early days of C/SCSC there was a certain amount of confusion which centered around the issue of whether or not the criteria should or should not be applied to firm fixed-price type contracts. Remember the basic principles: under a cost reimburseable type contract, the Government underwrites the risk of any cost growth; by contrast, under a firm fixed-price contractual arrangement the performing private contractor assumes any and all risk of cost growth.

The issue seemed to be settled at the time, and C/SCSC was not to be applied to firm fixed-price contractual arrangements, where the private contractor had assumed the risk of any cost growth. It was up to the private contractor to internally self-impose C/SCSC if it so desired. And many private contractors do just that: when they assume the risk of cost growth on firm fixed-price contracts they have self-imposed a "relaxed" model of the criteria concept.

It was also a generally accepted concept that there was a place in Government contracting for both types of contractual arrangements, the cost type and the firm fixed-price type, depending upon the circumstances. Cost-type arrangements were recommended when the end product was not sufficiently definable at the time of award. But if the Government knew precisely what it wanted to buy, and could define the requirement, a firm fixed price contract should always be used.

Then we seemed to get away from the basics. Certain people joined the Government (in high places) with the conviction that "more bang for the buck" could be obtained if only more firm fixed-price contracts were issued by the Government. Thus, there was an emphasis toward the greater use of fixed-price contracts, even in those areas where the buyers were not able to define with sufficient precision, exactly what they needed to buy. The result: certain firm fixed-price contracts started to experience cost growth, not dissimilar to that typically experienced with cost-type contracts, because of contract changes and redirection in the fixed priced efforts.

Some Government program managers, in an effort to control cost growth problems now being experienced in their fixed price contracts, fell back on their proven management approach which had provided a method of early exposure of cost and schedule problems. The Government started to impose full C/SCSC requirements on contracts of a firm fixed-price type, a highly questionable practice, in most instances.

However, it should be mentioned that there are at least two situations in which C/SCSC might be appropriate on firm fixed-priced contracts:

- When the item being procured is of a "critical" nature and the Government must out of necessity closely manage the contract.

- When the "financial" condition of the contractor is (how do we say this delicately), in a questionable condition.

These are circumstances which could reasonably justify the flow-down of full C/SCSC to a contractor.

For a multiplicity of reasons, we are likely to see a continued, perhaps an expanded, requirement for C/SCSC even on contracts of a firm fixed-price type. What the Government (DOD) is expected to do is to raise the authorization level at which C/SCSC can be applied on firm fixed price contracts. Perhaps in the future, approval of a two-star command officer will be needed before C/SCSC can be imposed on firm fixed price contracts. This would likely reduce, but not necessarily eliminate, the flow-down of the C/SCSC requirement to such contracts.

### 4. *Government Demands on Contractor Management Control Systems*

Starting in the 1960s, the Government took steps to satisfy its need for accurate estimates of the final costs and total duration required to complete their contracts, which later gave rise to the criteria concept. The result has been described in the previous chapters.

Then, independent of what had been already imposed on contractor management control systems by the C/SCSC, the industrial engineers in the early 1970s started to define their own demands for work measurement applications, an additional requirement on contractor management control systems. The result: MIL-STD 1567, which is now firmly established as a requirement on selected contracts.

More recently, in the late 1980s, a new requirement is starting to take shape: Material Requirements Planning (MRP I), and Manufacturing Resource Planning (MRP II). Position papers are emerging which describe MRP I and MRP II as a *single* concept—a frightening thought in and of itself! MRP I and MRP II are related, but vastly different, concepts.

This time the focus is on the contractor's purchasing and inventory control methodology. As with both C/SCSC and work measurement, the supporters of "MRP" are also convinced that this requirement, when imposed on contractors, quite possibly will produce positive results for the American taxpayer.

However, it is also possible that this third major requirement placed on the contractor's management systems could actually have the effect of eliminating what might be left of private contractor initiative. Remember, we are supposed to be functioning under a "free-enterprise" type of industrial system. Private contractors are supposed to be given some latitude in the way they manage their own company's affairs. It is one thing to protect taxpayers funds and to eliminate fraud and abuse, but it quite another to be telling contractors precisely "how" to manage their private businesses.

A suggestion: it just might be in the best interests of an endangered species, the "free-enterprise system," if all those with new demands—requirements on the various private contractor management control systems, were to be sent to the "top of the mountain" to decide once and for all what they want, what they will require from the private contractors. Perhaps instead of just "35 C/SCSC criteria," that there should be "50 management control system criteria", to be applied to all private contractor systems. Then, with these 50 management criteria imposed, programs could be fairly competed, and the private contractors could be allowed to do their jobs without the imposition of additional and potentially costly "improvements," every few years.

Let us give private business initiative another chance at survival. End of sermon.

# APPENDIX A
# Summary of Government C/SCSC Documents

**DEPARTMENT OF DEFENSE**
**C/SCSC DOCUMENTS**

| REFERENCE NUMBER/ DATE | TITLE | PURPOSE |
|---|---|---|
| DODI 7000.2<br><br>June 10, 1977 | *Performance Measurement for Selected Acquisitions* | C/SCS Criteria for uniform DOD applications. |
| DODI 7000.3<br><br>April 4, 1979 | *Selected Acquisition Reports (SARs)* | Standardized formats for reporting on the cost/schedule/ units/technical data to the Congress. |
| DODI 7000.10<br><br>Dec. 3, 1979 | *Contract Cost Performance, Funds Status and Cost/ Schedule Status Reports* | C/SCSC reporting requirements. |
| DODI 7000.11<br><br>March 27, 1984 | *Contractor Cost Data Reporting (CCDR)* | C/SCSC historical cost data reporting requirements. |
| DODI 7220.31<br><br>Jan. 17, 1986 | *Unit Cost Reports* | Defines unit cost thresholds for DOD reporting to the Congress. |
| AFSC P173-5<br>AFCC P173-5<br>AFLC P173-5<br>AMC-P 715-5<br>NAVSO P3627<br>DLAH 8400.2<br>DCAAP 7641.47<br>Oct. 01, 1987 | *Cost/Schedule Control Systems Criteria-Joint Implementation Guide* | The "JIG", working C/SCSC procedures for all DOD services. |

**DEPARTMENT OF DEFENSE
C/SCSC DOCUMENTS**

| REFERENCE NUMBER/ DATE | TITLE | PURPOSE |
|---|---|---|
| AMC-P 715-10 NAVMAT P5243 AFLC P173-6 AFSC P173-6 DLAH 8315.1 DCAAP 7641.46 Oct. 01, 1984 | *C/SCSC Joint Surveillance Guide* | Guidance procedures for administration and surveillance of contracts. |
| DARCOMP715-13 NAVMAT P5244 AFLCP 173-2 AFSCP 173-3 DLAH 8315.3 Nov. 01, 1978 | *Cost/Schedule Management of Non-Major Contracts (C/SSR Joint Guide)* | The joint service procedure for small contracts. |
| NAVMAT P-5241 AMCP 715-8 AFLCP 800-15 AFSCP 800-15 Nov. 05, 1973 | *Contractor Cost Data Reporting System (CCDR)* | The joint service procedure for the historical cost data reporting. |
| DODD 5000.1 March 29, 1982 | *Major System Acquisitions* | DOD policy for major systems acquisitions or modifications. |
| DODI 5000.2 March 19, 1980 | *Major System Acquisition Procedure* | The procedure for DODD 5000.1. |
| DODD 5000.4 Oct. 30, 1980 | *OSD Cost Analysis Improvement Group* | Authorizes the CAIG for creation of a historical cost data base within the OASD. |

## DEPARTMENT OF DEFENSE
## C/SCSC DOCUMENTS

| REFERENCE NUMBER/ DATE | TITLE | PURPOSE |
|---|---|---|
| DODD 5010.20<br><br>July 31, 1968 | *Work Breakdown Structures For Defense Material Items* | Sets the policy for use of WBS. |
| MIL-STD 881A<br><br>Apr. 25, 1975 | *Work Breakdown Structures For Defense Material Items* | Implements the DOD policy on WBS. |
| MIL-STD 1567A<br><br>March 11, 1983 | *Work Measurement* | Defines DOD policy on measurement of touch labor. |
| AFSC<br><br>Jan. 22, 1979 | *C/SCSC Team Handbook* | Provides guidance to USAF review teams. |
| USAF ASD<br><br>Sept., 1981 | *C/SCSC Demonstration Review Checklist* | Provides a C/SCSC functional checklist for review teams. |
| AFWLP 173-2<br><br>Oct., 1981 | *Guide for the Conduct of CPR/No Criteria Review* | Provides guidance for non-criteria reviews. |
| AFSC<br><br>Aug. 01, 1979 | *Guide to Analysis of Contractor Cost Data* | Selected techniques for the analysis of cost data by USAF. |
| AMETA<br><br>Sept., 1975 | *Status, Trends, and Projections: For Use With Cost and Schedule Measurement Data* | Selected techniques for the analysis of cost data by USA. |

**DEPARTMENT OF ENERGY**
**C/SCSC DOCUMENTS**

| REFERENCE NUMBER/ DATE | TITLE | PURPOSE |
|---|---|---|
| DOE 2250.1B<br><br>Oct. 25, 1985 | *Criteria for Contract Performance Measurement* | Establishes policy for DOE C/SCSC. |
| DOE/MA-0195<br><br>Oct., 1975 | *Summary Description* | An overview of DOE contract performance measurement. |
| DOE/MA-0203<br>Jan., 1986 | *Implementation Guide* | Provides uniform guidance to assist DOE and contractor personnel. |
| DOE/MA-0221<br><br>Mar., 1986 | *Data Analysis Guide* | Suggested techniques for analysis of cost and schedule data. |
| DOE/MA-0229<br><br>June, 1986 | *Systems Review/Surveillance Guide* | Guidance for conduct of DOE personnel in validation reviews. |
| DOE/MA-0262<br><br>Feb., 1987 | *Checklist Handbook* | Listing of criteria questions for DOE and industry. |
| DOE/MA-0155<br><br>May, 1984 | *C/SCSC Information Pamphlet* | Overview of basic C/SCSC concept. |
| DOE/MA-0160<br><br>June, 1984 | *Reporting and Baseline Management Information Pamphlet* | Covers reporting and baseline management concepts. |

**DEPARTMENT OF ENERGY**
**C/SCSC DOCUMENTS**

| REFERENCE NUMBER/ DATE | TITLE | PURPOSE |
|---|---|---|
| DOE/MA-0184<br><br>Mar., 1985 | *Analyzing Performance of Small Projects Using URS and PMAS-Information Pamphlet* | Discusses the DOE Uniform Reporting System and Performance Measurement Analysis System. |
| DOE/MA-0191<br><br>June, 1985 | *Uniform Reporting System-Information Pamphlet* | Illustration of the DOE URS. |
| DOE 1332.1A<br><br>Oct., 1985 | *Uniform Reporting System* | Implementing formats, forms, instructions, and procedures URS. |
| DOE/MA-0197<br><br>Nov., 1985 | *Project Status Reporting and Performance Data Analysis* | Basic concepts and general requirements on reporting and data analysis. |
| DOE/MA-0295<br><br>Feb., 1987 | *Work Breakdown Structure Guide* | All new guide on the DOE WBS requirements. |
| N/A<br><br>Oct., 1985 | *Performance Measurement Analysis System for Microcomputers-Users Manual* | DOE PMAS manual for microcomputers. |

# APPENDIX B
# DODI 7000.2:
# Performance Measurement for
# Selected Applications

*NUMBER*  7000.2
*DATE*  June 10, 1977

# Department of Defense Instruction

ASD(C)

*SUBJECT*            Performance Measurement for Selected Acquisitions

References:      (a)  DoD Directive 7000.1, "Resource Management Systems
                      of the Department of Defense," August 22, 1966
                 (b)  DoD Directive 5000.1, "Major System Acquisitions,"
                      January 18, 1977
                 (c)  DoD Directive 5000.2, "Major System Acquisition
                      Process," January 18, 1977
                 (d)  through (i), see enclosure 2.

## A.  REISSUANCE AND PURPOSE

This Instruction reissues reference (f) and sets forth objectives and
criteria for the application of uniform DoD requirements to selected defense contracts.  The provisions of this Instruction specifically require
the use of Cost/Schedule Control Systems Criteria (C/SCSC) in selected
acquisitions.  Reference (f) is hereby superseded and cancelled.

## B.  APPLICABILITY AND SCOPE

1.  The provisions of this Instruction apply to all Military Departments and Defense Agencies (hereafter referred to as "DoD Components") which
are responsible for acquisitions during systems development and production.

2.  The acquisitions governed by this Instruction are in selected contracts and subcontracts within programs designated as major system acquisition programs in accordance with reference (b).  Firm-fixed-price and firm-
fixed-price-with-economic-price-adjustment contracts are excluded.  Application of the C/SCSC to major construction projects is also encouraged where
appropriate.

## C.  OBJECTIVES

1.  To provide an adequate basis for responsible decision-making by
both contractor management and DoD Components, contractors' internal management control systems must provide data which (a) indicate work progress,
(b) properly relate cost, schedule and technical accomplishment, (c) are
valid, timely and auditable, and (d) supply DoD managers with information
at a practicable level of summarization.

2.  To bring to the attention of, and encourage, DoD contractors to
accept and install management control systems and procedures which are
most effective in meeting their requirements and controlling contract performance.  DoD contractors also should be continuously alert to advances
in management control systems which will improve their internal operations.

D. **POLICY**

1.  It shall be the general policy to (a) require applications of the C/SCSC as stated in enclosure 1 to programs that are within the scope of section B., above, (b) require no changes in contractors' existing cost/ schedule control systems except those necessary to meet the C/SCSC, and (c) require the contractor to provide to the Government performance data directly from the same system used for internal management.

2.  The policies and criteria contained herein will not be construed as requiring the use of specific systems or changes in accounting systems which will adversely affect (a) the equitable distribution of costs to all contracts, or (b) compliance with the standards, rules, and regulations promulgated by the Cost Accounting Standards Board.

3.  Subcontracts within applicable programs, excluding those that are firm-fixed-price, may be selected for application of these criteria by mutual agreement between prime contractors and the contracting DoD Component, according to the criticality of the subcontract to the program. Coverage of certain critical subcontracts may be directed by the Department of Defense, subject to the changes article of the contracts. In those cases where a subcontractor is not required to comply with the criteria, the Cost/Schedule Status Report (C/SSR) approach to performance measurement set forth in DoD Instruction 7000.10 (reference (g)) will normally be used. The limitations in reference (g) apply.

4.  The applicability of C/SCSC and provisions concerning the acceptability and use of contractor's cost/schedule control systems shall be (a) included in the Decision Coordinating Papers (DCP) leading to the decisions for full-scale development and production, (b) addressed in procurement plans, (c) set forth in Requests for Proposal (RFP), and (d) made a contractual requirement in appropriate procurements.

   a.  Reviews of Systems.  To ensure compliance with the Cost/ Schedule Control Systems Criteria, contractors' systems will be reviewed during various phases of the contracting process.

      (1) Where the C/SCSC are included as a requirement in the RFP, an Evaluation Review will be performed as an integral part of the source selection process.

      (2) After contract award, an in-plant Demonstration Review will be made to verify that the contractor is operating systems which meet the criteria.

      (3) Upon successful completion of the Demonstration Review, contractors will not be subjected to another Demonstration Review unless there are positive indications that the contractor's systems no longer operate so as to meet the criteria.

(4) Subsequent contracts may require a review of shorter duration and less depth to ensure the appropriate and effective application of the accepted systems to the new contract.

(5) Detailed procedures relating to contractual application, interpretative guidance, interservice relationships, and conduct of systems reviews are contained in the Cost/Schedule Control Systems Criteria Joint Implementation Guide (reference (h)).

b. Memorandum of Understanding. After determination that a management system meets C/SCSC, a Memorandum of Understanding may be established between the Department of Defense and the contractor to apply to future contracts.

(1) The use of a Memorandum of Understanding contemplates the execution of a written instrument which references the C/SCSC and negotiated provisions which (a) reflect an understanding between the contractor and the DoD of the requirements of the DoD criteria, and (b) identify the specific system(s) which the contractor intends to use on applicable contracts with DoD Components.

(2) The Memorandum of Understanding will include or make reference to a written description of the system(s) accepted in a Demonstration Review. The system description should be of sufficient detail to permit adequate surveillance by responsible parties. The use of a Memorandum of Understanding is preferred where a number of separate contracts between one or more DoD Component(s) and the contractor may be entered into during the term of the Memorandum of Understanding. It contemplates the delegation of authority to the DoD Component negotiating the Memorandum of Understanding with the contractor to make the agreement on behalf of all prospective DoD contracting components.

(3) Action to develop a Memorandum of Understanding may be initiated by either the contractor or the DoD Component, but will usually be in connection with a contractual requirement. In a proposal, reference to a Memorandum of Understanding satisfies the C/SCSC requirement in RFP's and normally obviates the need for further Evaluation Review during source selection. Procedures for executing Memorandums of Understanding are included in the Cost/Schedule Control Systems Criteria Joint Implementation Guide (reference (h)).

c. Surveillance. Recurring evaluations of the effectiveness of the contractor's policies and procedures will be performed to ensure that the contractor's system continues to meet the C/SCSC and provides valid data consistent with the intent of this Instruction. Surveillance reviews will be based on selective tests of reported data and periodic evaluations of internal practices during the life of the contract. Guidance for surveillance is set forth in the C/SCSC Joint Surveillance Guide (reference (i)).

E.   RESPONSIBILITIES

Pursuant to authority contained in DoD Directive 7000.1 (reference (a)):

1.   The Assistant Secretary of Defense (Comptroller) will establish policy guidance pertaining to the Cost/Schedule Control Systems Criteria and will monitor their implementation to ensure consistent application throughout the Department of Defense.

2.   The Secretaries of the Military Departments will issue appropriate instructions which promulgate the policies contained herein and which assign responsibilities for accomplishing the actions required to validate contractors' compliance with the C/SCSC.

3.   The Joint Logistics Commanders will develop and issue joint implementing instructions which outline the procedures to be used in applying, testing and monitoring the C/SCSC on applicable contracts and will ensure that adequate reviews of contractors' systems are performed.  The joint implementing procedures and their revisions will be coordinated among all affected DoD Components and submitted to the Assistant Secretary of Defense (Comptroller) for review prior to publication.

4.   The Defense Contract Audit Agency and the appropriate Contract Administration Service office will participate in reviews of contractors' systems under their cognizance and will perform required surveillance, collaborating with each other and with the procuring DoD Component in reviewing areas of joint interest.

F.   EFFECTIVE DATE AND IMPLEMENTATION

This Instruction is effective immediately.  Forward two copies of the implementing documents to the Assistant Secretary of Defense (Comptroller) within 60 days.

*Fred P. Wacker*

Assistant Secretary of Defense
(Comptroller)


Enclosures - 2
1.   Cost/Schedule Control Systems Criteria
2.   List of additional references

7000.2 (Encl 1)
Jun 10, 77

## COST/SCHEDULE CONTROL SYSTEMS CRITERIA

1. <u>GENERAL</u>

a. Any system used by the contractor in planning and controlling the performance of the contract shall meet the criteria set forth in paragraph 3., below. Nothing in these criteria is intended to affect the basis on which costs are reimbursed and progress payments are made, and nothing herein will be construed as requiring the use of any single system, or specific method of management control or evaluation of performance. The contractor's internal systems need not be changed, provided they satisfy these criteria.

b. An element in the evaluation of proposals will be the proposer's system for planning and controlling contract performance. The proposer will fully describe the system to be used. The prospective contractor's cost/schedule control system proposal will be evaluated to determine if it meets these criteria. The prospective contractor will agree to operate a compliant system throughout the period of contract performance if awarded the contract. The DoD will agree to rely on the contractor's compliant system and therefore will not impose a separate planning and control system.

2. <u>DEFINITIONS</u>

a. <u>ACTUAL COST OF WORK PERFORMED (ACWP)</u>. The costs actually incurred and recorded in accomplishing the work performed within a given time period.

b. <u>ACTUAL DIRECT COSTS</u>. Those costs identified specifically with a contract, based upon the contractor's cost identification and accumulation system as accepted by the cognizant DCAA representatives. (See Direct Costs.)

c. <u>ALLOCATED BUDGET</u>. (See Total Allocated Budget.)

d. <u>APPLIED DIRECT COSTS</u>. The amounts recognized in the time period associated with the consumption of labor, material, and other direct resources, without regard to the date of commitment or the date of payment. These amounts are to be charged to work-in-process in the time period that any one of the following takes place:

(1) When labor, material and other direct resources are actually consumed, or

(2) When material resources are withdrawn from inventory for use, or

(3) When material resources are received that are uniquely identified to the contract and scheduled for use within 60 days, or

(4) When major components or assemblies are received on a line flow basis that are specifically and uniquely identified to a single serially numbered end item.

e. APPORTIONED EFFORT. Effort that by itself is not readily divisible into short-span work packages but which is related in direct proportion to measured effort.

f. AUTHORIZED WORK. That effort which has been definitized and is on contract, plus that for which definitized contract costs have not been agreed to but for which written authorization has been received.

g. BASELINE. (See Performance Measurement Baseline.)

h. BUDGETED COST FOR WORK PERFORMED (BCWP). The sum of the budgets for completed work packages and completed portions of open work packages, plus the appropriate portion of the budgets for level of effort and apportioned effort.

i. BUDGETED COST FOR WORK SCHEDULED (BCWS). The sum of budgets for all work packages, planning packages, etc., scheduled to be accomplished (including in-process work packages), plus the amount of level of effort and apportioned effort scheduled to be accomplished within a given time period.

j. BUDGETS FOR WORK PACKAGES. (See Work Package Budgets.)

k. CONTRACT BUDGET BASE. The negotiated contract cost plus the estimated cost of authorized unpriced work.

l. CONTRACTOR. An entity in private industry which enters into contracts with the Government. In this Instruction, the word may also apply to Government-owned, Government-operated activities which perform work on major defense programs.

m. COST ACCOUNT. A management control point at which actual costs can be accumulated and compared to budgeted costs for work performed. A cost account is a natural control point for cost/schedule planning and control, since it represents the work assigned to one responsible organizational element on one contract work breakdown structure (CWBS) element.

n. DIRECT COSTS. Any costs which can be identified specifically with a particular final cost objective. This term is explained in ASPR 15-202.

o. ESTIMATED COST AT COMPLETION OR ESTIMATE AT COMPLETION (EAC). Actual direct costs, plus indirect costs allocable to the contract, plus the estimate of costs (direct and indirect) for authorized work remaining.

p. INDIRECT COSTS. Costs, which because of their incurrence for common or joint objectives, are not readily subject to treatment as direct costs. This term is further defined in ASPR 3-701.3 and ASPR 15-203.

Appendix B: DODI 7000.2                                      319

7000.2 (Encl 1)
Jun 10, 77

q.  INITIAL BUDGET.  (See Original Budget.)

r.  INTERNAL REPLANNING.  Replanning actions performed by the contractor for remaining effort within the recognized total allocated budget.

s.  LEVEL OF EFFORT (LOE).  Effort of a general or supportive nature which does not produce definite end products or results.

t.  MANAGEMENT RESERVE.  (Synonymous with Management Reserve Budget). An amount of the total allocated budget withheld for management control purposes rather than designated for the accomplishment of a specific task or set of tasks.  It is not a part of the Performance Measurement Baseline.

u.  NEGOTIATED CONTRACT COST.  The estimated cost negotiated in a cost-plus-fixed-fee contract, or the negotiated contract target cost in either a fixed-price-incentive contract or a cost-plus-incentive-fee contract.

v.  ORIGINAL BUDGET.  The budget established at, or near, the time the contract was signed, based on the negotiated contract cost.

w.  OVERHEAD.  (See Indirect Costs.)

x.  PERFORMANCE MEASUREMENT BASELINE.  The time-phased budget plan against which contract performance is measured.  It is formed by the budgets assigned to scheduled cost accounts and the applicable indirect budgets.  For future effort, not planned to the cost account level, the performance measurement baseline also includes budgets assigned to higher level CWBS elements, and undistributed budgets.  It equals the total allocated budget less management reserve.

y.  PERFORMING ORGANIZATION.  A defined unit within the contractor's organization structure, which applies the resources to perform the work.

z.  PLANNING PACKAGE.  A logical aggregation of work within a cost account, normally the far term effort, that can be identified and budgeted in early baseline planning, but is not yet defined into work packages.

aa.  PROCURING ACTIVITY.  The subordinate command in which the Procuring Contracting Office (PCO) is located.  It may include the program office, related functional support offices, and procurement offices. Examples of procuring activities are AFSC/ESD, AFLC/OC-ALC, DARCOM/MIRADCOM, and NMC/NAVAIRSYSCOM.

bb.  REPLANNING.  (See Internal Replanning.)

cc.  REPROGRAMMING.  Replanning of the effort remaining in the contract, resulting in a new budget allocation which exceeds the contract budget base.

7000.2 (Encl 1)
Jun 10, 77

dd.  RESPONSIBLE ORGANIZATION.  A defined unit within the contractor's organization structure which is assigned responsibility for accomplishing specific tasks.

ee.  SIGNIFICANT VARIANCES.  Those differences between planned and actual performance which require further review, analysis, or action. Appropriate thresholds should be established as to the magnitude of variances which will require variance analysis.

ff.  TOTAL ALLOCATED BUDGET.  The sum of all budgets allocated to the contract.  Total allocated budget consists of the performance measurement baseline and all management reserve.  The total allocated budget will reconcile directly to the contract budget base.  Any differences will be documented as to quantity and cause.

gg.  UNDISTRIBUTED BUDGET.  Budget applicable to contract effort which has not yet been identified to CWBS elements at or below the lowest level of reporting to the Government.

hh.  VARIANCES.  (See Significant Variances.)

ii.  WORK BREAKDOWN STRUCTURE.  A product-oriented family tree division of hardware, software, services, and other work tasks which organizes, defines, and graphically displays the product to be produced, as well as the work to be accomplished to achieve the specified product.

(1)  Project Summary Work Breakdown Structure.  A summary WBS tailored to a specific defense materiel item by selecting applicable elements from one or more summary WBS's or by adding equivalent elements unique to the project (MIL-STD-881A).

(2)  Contract Work Breakdown Structure (CWBS).  The complete WBS for a contract, developed and used by a contractor within the guidelines of MIL-STD-881A, and according to the contract work statement.

jj.  WORK PACKAGE BUDGETS.  Resources which are formally assigned by the contractor to accomplish a work package, expressed in dollars, hours, standards, or other definitive units.

kk.  WORK PACKAGES.  Detailed short-span jobs, or material items, identified by the contractor for accomplishing work required to complete the contract.  A work package has the following characteristics:

(1)  It represents units of work at levels where work is performed.

(2)  It is clearly distinguishable from all other work packages.

(3)  It is assignable to a single organizational element.

(4)  It has scheduled start and completion dates and, as applicable, interim milestones, all of which are representative of physical accomplishment.

7000.2 (Encl 1)
Jun 10, 77

(5) It has a budget or assigned value expressed in terms of dollars, man-hours, or other measurable units.

(6) Its duration is limited to a relatively short span of time or it is subdivided by discrete value-milestones to facilitate the objective measurement of work performed.

(7) It is integrated with detailed engineering, manufacturing, or other schedules.

3. CRITERIA

The contractors' management control systems will include policies, procedures, and methods which are designed to ensure that they will accomplish the following:

a. Organization

(1) Define all authorized work and related resources to meet the requirements of the contract, using the framework of the CWBS.

(2) Identify the internal organizational elements and the major subcontractors responsible for accomplishing the authorized work.

(3) Provide for the integration of the contractor's planning, scheduling, budgeting, work authorization and cost accumulation systems with each other, the CWBS, and the organizational structure.

(4) Identify the managerial positions responsible for controlling overhead (indirect costs).

(5) Provide for integration of the CWBS with the contractor's functional organizational structure in a manner that permits cost and schedule performance measurement for CWBS and organizational elements.

b. Planning and Budgeting

(1) Schedule the authorized work in a manner which describes the sequence of work and identifies the significant task interdependencies required to meet the development, production and delivery requirements of the contract.

(2) Identify physical products, milestones, technical performance goals, or other indicators that will be used to measure output.

(3) Establish and maintain a time-phased budget baseline at the cost account level against which contract performance can be measured. Initial budgets established for this purpose will be based on the negotiated target cost. Any other amount used for performance measurement purposes must be formally recognized by both the contractor and the Government.

7000.2 (Encl 1)
Jun 10, 77

(4) Establish budgets for all authorized work with separate identification of cost elements (labor, material, etc.).

(5) To the extent the authorized work can be identified in discrete, short-span work packages, establish budgets for this work in terms of dollars, hours, or other measurable units. Where the entire cost account cannot be subdivided into detailed work packages, identify the far term effort in larger planning packages for budget and scheduling purposes.

(6) Provide that the sum of all work package budgets, plus planning package budgets within a cost account equals the cost account budget.

(7) Identify relationships of budgets or standards in underlying work authorization systems to budgets for work packages.

(8) Identify and control level of effort activity by time-phased budgets established for this purpose. Only that effort which cannot be identifed as discrete, short-span work packages or as apportioned effort will be classed as level of effort.

(9) Establish overhead budgets for the total costs of each significant organizational component whose expenses will become indirect costs. Reflect in the contract budgets at the appropriate level the amounts in overhead pools that will be allocated to the contract as indirect costs.

(10) Identify management reserves and undistributed budget.

(11) Provide that the contract target cost plus the estimated cost of authorized but unpriced work is reconciled with the sum of all internal contract budgets and management reserves.

c. Accounting

(1) Record direct costs on an applied or other acceptable basis in a formal system that is controlled by the general books of account.

(2) Summarize direct costs from cost accounts into the WBS without allocation of a single cost account to two or more WBS elements.

(3) Summarize direct costs from the cost accounts into the contractor's functional organizational elements without allocation of a single cost account to two or more organizational elements.

(4) Record all indirect costs which will be allocated to the contract.

(5) Identify the bases for allocating the cost of apportioned effort.

7000.2 (Encl 1)
Jun 10, 77

(6) Identify unit costs, equivalent unit costs, or lot costs as applicable.

(7) The contractor's material accounting system will provide for:

(a) Accurate cost accumulation and assignment of costs to cost accounts in a manner consistent with the budgets using recognized, acceptable costing techniques.

(b) Determination of price variances by comparing planned versus actual commitments.

(c) Cost performance measurement at the point in time most suitable for the category of material involved, but no earlier than the time of actual receipt of material.

(d) Determination of cost variances attributable to the excess usage of material.

(e) Determination of unit or lot costs when applicable.

(f) Full accountability for all material purchased for the contract, including the residual inventory.

d. Analysis

(1) Identify at the cost account level on a monthly basis using data from, or reconcilable with, the accounting system:

(a) Budgeted cost for work scheduled and budgeted cost for work performed.

(b) Budgeted cost for work performed and applied (actual where appropriate) direct costs for the same work.

(c) Variances resulting from the above comparisons classified in terms of labor, material, or other appropriate elements together with the reasons for significant variances.

(2) Identify on a monthly basis, in the detail needed by management for effective control, budgeted indirect costs, actual indirect costs, and variances along with the reasons.

(3) Summarize the data elements and associated variances listed in (1) and (2) above through the contractor organization and WBS to the reporting level specified in the contract.

(4) Identify significant differences on a monthly basis between planned and actual schedule accomplishment and the reasons.

7000.2 (Encl 1)
Jun 10, 77

(5) Identify managerial actions taken as a result of criteria items (1) through (4) above.

(6) Based on performance to date and on estimates of future conditions, develop revised estimates of cost at completion for WBS elements identified in the contract and compare these with the contract budget base and the latest statement of funds requirements reported to the Government.

e. Revisions and Access to Data

(1) Incorporate contractual changes in a timely manner recording the effects of such changes in budgets and schedules. In the directed effort prior to negotiation of a change, base such revisions on the amount estimated and budgeted to the functional organizations.

(2) Reconcile original budgets for those elements of the work breakdown structure identified as priced line items in the contract, and for those elements at the lowest level of the DoD Project Summary WBS, with current performance measurement budgets in terms of (a) changes to the authorized work and (b) internal replanning in the detail needed by management for effective control.

(3) Prohibit retroactive changes to records pertaining to work performed that will change previously reported amounts for direct costs, indirect costs, or budgets, except for correction of errors and routine accounting adjustments.

(4) Prevent revisions to the contract budget base (paragraph 2.k.) except for Government directed changes to contractual effort.

(5) Document, internally, changes to the performance measurement baseline (paragraph 2.x.) and, on a timely basis, notify the procuring activity through prescribed procedures.

(6) Provide the contracting officer and his duly authorized representatives access to all of the foregoing information and supporting documents.

7000.2 (Encl 2)
Jun 10, 77

REFERENCES

(d) Armed Services Procurement Regulation (1976 Edition)
(e) MIL-STD-881A, "Work Breakdown Structures for Defense Material
      Items," April 25, 1975
(f) DoD Instruction 7000.2, "Performance Measurement for Selected
      Acquisitions," April 25, 1972 (hereby cancelled)
(g) DoD Instruction 7000.10, "Contract Cost Performance, Funds
      Status and Cost/Schedule Status Reports," August 6, 1974
(h) AFSCP/AFLCP 173-5, DARCOM-P 715-5, NAVMAT P5240, DSAH 8315.2
      "Cost/Schedule Control Systems Criteria Joint Implementation
      Guide," October 1, 1976
(i) DARCOM-P 715-10, NAVMAT P5243, AFLCP/AFSCP 173-6, DSAH 8315.1,
      DCAAP 7641.46, "C/SCSC Joint Surveillance Guide," July 1, 1974
      and Change 1, October 1, 1976

# APPENDIX C
# DODI 7000.10:
## C/SCSC Reports—
## CPR; CFSR; C/SSR

REPRINT - Change 1 has been incorporated.

December 3, 1979
**NUMBER** 7000.10

# Department of Defense Instruction <sup>ASD(C)</sup>

SUBJECT          Contract Cost Performance, Funds Status and Cost/Schedule
                 Status Reports

References:   (a)  DoD Instruction 7000.10, "Contract Cost Performance,
                   Funds Status and Cost/Schedule Status Reports,"
                   August 6, 1974 (hereby canceled)
             (b)  DoD Directive 7000.1, "Resource Management Systems
                   of the Department of Defense," August 22, 1966
             (c)  DoD Directive 5000.1, "Major System Acquisitions,"
                   January 18, 1977
             (d)  through (j), see enclosure 1

## A.  REISSUANCE AND PURPOSE

This Instruction:

1.  Reissues reference (a) to revise the Cost Performance Report
(CPR), the Contract Funds Status Report (CFSR), and the Cost/Schedule
Status Report (C/SSR);

2.  Assigns responsibilities and provides uniform guidance for
implementation of the CPR, the CFSR, and the C/SSR; and

3.  Provides procedures for collecting summary level cost, and
schedule performance and funding data from contractors for program
management purposes, pursuant to references (b), (c), and DoD Directive
5000.2 (reference (d)), and for responding to requests for program
status information on major system acquisitions, primarily by means
of DoD Instruction 7000.3 (reference (e)).

## B.  APPLICABILITY AND SCOPE

The provisions of this Instruction apply to the Office of the
Secretary of Defense, the Military Departments, the Defense Agencies,
and the Unified and Specified Commands (hereafter referred to
as "DoD Components") responsible for (1) managing acquisition
contracts falling within the scope of section C., and (2) determining
fund requirements for contracts and managing the flow of such funds.
Application of the provisions of this Instruction to construction contracts is encouraged where appropriate.

## C.  POLICIES

1.  In concert with the policies established in DoD Directive
5000.2 (reference (d)), utilization of the CPR, CFSR, and C/SSR shall

be limited by system managers to that necessary to achieve essential management control.

      a.  Contractors are encouraged to substitute internal reports for CPR, CFSR, and C/SSR provided that (1) data elements and definitions used in the reports are comparable to CPR, CFSR and C/SSR requirements, and (2) the reports are in forms suitable for management use.

      b.  As applicable, provisions of DoD Directive 5000.19 (reference (f)) concerning the tailoring of management systems may be employed by system managers in the implementation of CPR, CFSR, and C/SSR.

    2.  Instructions regarding levels of detail and frequencies of reporting are contained in the Data Item Descriptions (DD Forms 1664) in enclosures 2, 3, and 4 of this Instruction.  Local reproduction of formats contained in these enclosures is authorized.

    3.  The Cost Performance Report (CPR):

      a.  Provides (1) contract cost/schedule status information for use in making and validating management decisions, (2) early indicators of contract cost/schedule problems, and (3) effects of management actions taken to resolve problems affecting cost/schedule performance.

      b.  Applies to selected contracts within those programs desig-nated as major system acquisitions in accordance with the criteria of DoD Directive 5000.1 (reference (c)).  CPRs will be applied to all con-tracts which require compliance with the Cost/Schedule Control Systems Criteria (C/SCSC) of DoD Instruction 7000.2 (reference (g)).

      c.  Will not be required on firm fixed-price contracts (as defined in Section 3-404.2 of the Defense Acquisition Regulation (ref-erence (h)), unless those contracts represent the development or production of a major defense system or a major component thereof and circumstances require cost/schedule visibility.

      d.  Applies to ongoing contracts only in those cases where the procuring agencies consider it necessary to support program management needs and DoD requirements for information.  Some of the factors which may affect applications to ongoing contracts are anticipated time to contract completion, anticipated program deferrals, and the relative importance of subcontracts.

      e.  Is assigned OMB Approval No. 22-R0280.

4.  The Contract Funds Status Report (CFSR):

a.  Supplies funding data that, with other related inputs, provides DoD management with information to assist in (1) updating and forecasting contract fund requirements, (2) planning and decision-making on funding changes, (3) developing fund requirements and budget estimates in support of approved programs, and (4) determining funds in excess of contract needs and available for deobligation.

b.  Applies to all contracts greater than $500,000.

c.  Will not apply to firm fixed-price contracts unless the contract represents the development or production of a major defense system or a major component thereof and specific funding visibility is required.  CFSR may be applied to unpriced portions of firm fixed-price contracts that individually or collectively are estimated by the Government to be in excess of 20 percent of the initial contract value.  In such cases, the contract will delineate the specific CFSR requirements, if any, to be imposed on the contractor to fit the circumstances of each particular case.

d.  May be implemented at a reduced level of reporting for (1) those contracts with a dollar value between $100,000 and $500,000; (2) time and material contracts; and (3) contractual effort for which the entire CFSR report is not required by the procuring activity, but limited funding requirements information is needed.

e.  Will not be required on:

(1)  Contracts with a total value of less than $100,000, or

(2)  Contracts expected to be completed within 6 months.

f.  Is assigned OMB Approval No. 22-R0180.

5.  The Cost/Schedule Status Report (C/SSR):

a.  Provides summarized cost and schedule performance status information on contracts where application of the CPR is not appropriate.

b.  Applies to contracts of $2,000,000 or over and 12 months' duration or more which do not use the CPR.  (DoD Instruction 7000.11 (reference (i)) provides for application of Contractor Cost Data Reporting (CCDR) to Category II contracts.  To avoid the possibility of duplicative reporting, those elements of cost which are provided by the C/SSR will not be required by CCDR.)

c. Will not be required on firm fixed-price contracts unless those contracts represent the development or production of a critical component of a major defense system, and circumstances require cost/schedule visibility.

d. Is assigned OMB Approval No. 22-R0327.

D.  RESPONSIBILITIES

1. The Heads of DoD Components will assure that:

a. Contractor reports are timely and submitted in accordance with the instructions contained in enclosures 2, 3, and 4.

b. Submitted data are checked for discrepancies and necessary corrections are furnished by contractors.

c. Application of the CPR, CFSR, and C/SSR to ongoing programs or firm fixed-price contracts is held to the minimum essential to support program management needs and DoD requirements for information.

d. Appropriate members of the Performance Measurement Joint Executive Group (reference (j)) provide a forum to arbitrate misapplications of CPR or C/SSR requirements that cannot be resolved amicably through focal points established in the headquarters of the procuring commands.

2. The Director of the cognizant Defense Contract Audit Agency (DCAA) office shall:

a. At the request of a DoD Component, provide advice at the time of preaward evaluations as to whether the contractor's accounting and control systems are adequate and reliable for CPR, CFSR, and C/SSR reporting purposes.

b. Review selected CPR, CFSR, and C/SSR reports when it is considered necessary to assure the continuing adequacy and reliability of procedures and the validity of reported data.

c. Review selected individual CPR, CFSR, and C/SSR reports when requested by the Procuring Contracting Officer (PCO) or Administrative Contracting Officer (ACO) and submit a report thereon.

E.   EFFECTIVE DATE AND IMPLEMENTATION

This Instruction is effective immediately.  Forward two copies
of implementing documents to the Assistant Secretary of Defense
(Comptroller) within 120 days.


                                        Fred P. Wacker
                                Assistant Secretary of Defense
                                        (Comptroller)


Enclosures - 4
   1.  References
   2.  DD Form 1664, DI Number DI-F-6000C,
         Cost Performance Report (CPR)
   3.  DD Form 1664, DI Number DI-F-6004B,
         Contract Funds Status Report (CFSR)
   4.  DD Form 1664, DI Number DI-F-6010A,
         Cost/Schedule Status Report (C/SSR)

References, continued

(d)  DoD Directive 5000.2, "Major System Acquisition Process,"
     January 18, 1977

(e)  DoD Instruction 7000.3, "Selected Acquisition Reports (SARs),"
     April 4, 1979

(f)  DoD Directive 5000.19, "Policies for the Management and Control
     of Information Requirements," March 12, 1976

(g)  DoD Instruction 7000.2, "Performance Measurement for Selected
     Acquisitions," June 10, 1977

(h)  Defense Acquisition Regulation (1976), Section 3-404.2

(i)  DoD Instruction 7000.11, "Contractor Cost Data Reporting (CCDR),"
     September 5, 1973

(j)  AFSCP/AFLCP 173-5, DARCOM-P 715-5, NAVMAT P5240, DSAH 8315.2,
     "Cost/Schedule Control Systems Criteria Joint Implementation Guide,"
     October 1, 1976

Dec 3, 79
7000.10 (Encl 2)

| DATA ITEM DESCRIPTION | 2. IDENTIFICATION NO(S). | |
|---|---|---|
| | AGENCY | NUMBER |

**1. TITLE**

COST PERFORMANCE REPORT (CPR)

| | |
|---|---|
| AGENCY | NUMBER |
| DOD | DI-F-6000C |

**3. DESCRIPTION/PURPOSE**

3.1  This report is prepared by contractors and consists of five formats containing cost and related data for measuring contractors' cost and schedule performance.  Format 1 provides data to measure cost and schedule performance by summary level work breakdown structure elements.  Format 2 provides a similar measurement by organizational or functional cost categories.  Format 3 provides the budget baseline plan against which performance is measured. Format 4 provides manpower loading forecasts for          (Continued on page 2)

**4. APPROVAL DATE**

1 December 1979

**5. OFFICE OF PRIMARY RESPONSIBILITY**

OASD(C)MS

**6. DDC REQUIRED**

**8. APPROVAL LIMITATION**

**7. APPLICATION/INTERRELATIONSHIP**

7.1  The CPR normally will be required for selected contracts within those programs designated as major programs in accordance with DoD Directive 5000.1, "Major System Acquisitions."  It will be established as a contractual requirement as set forth in the DD Form 1423 Contract Data Requirements List (CDRL), and DD Form 1660, Management System Summary List.

7.2  If the CPR supports a contractual requirement for contractor compliance with the Cost/Schedule Control Systems Criteria (C/SCSC), the CPR data elements will reflect the contractor's implementation in accordance with DoD Instruction 7000.2, "Performance Measurement for Selected Acquisitions." If compliance with the C/SCSC is not contractually required,

(Continued on pages 2 and 3)

**9. REFERENCES (Mandatory as cited in block 10)**

DoD 4120.3M, Aug 78
DoDD 5000.1, 18 Jan 77
DoDD 5000.19, 12 Mar 76
DoDD 5000.32, 10 Mar 77
DoDI 7000.2, 10 Jun 77
DoDI 7000.10, 6 Aug 74
Cost Accounting
    Standard 414, 1 Sep 76

**MCSL NUMBER(S)**

00934

**10. PREPARATION INSTRUCTIONS**

10.1  Unless otherwise stated in the solicitation, the effective issue of the document(s) cited in the referenced document(s) in this block shall be that listed in the issue of the DoD Index of Specifications and Standards (reference of DoD 4120.3M) and the supplements thereto specified in the solicitation and will form a part of this data item description to the extent defined within.

10.2  Hard copy printouts from contractors' internal mechanized reporting systems may be substituted for CPR formats provided the printouts contain all the required data elements at the specified reporting levels in a form suitable for DoD management use.  Where data are furnished which require mechanized processing, narrative remarks should accompany tapes or cards and identify pertinent items to which they apply, and a listing of the tape or card data should be included to expedite processing.  CPR formats will be completed in accordance with the following instructions:

10.2.1  Heading Information - Formats 1 through 5

10.2.1.1  CONTRACTOR NAME AND LOCATION :  Enter the name, division, if applicable, plant location and mailing address of the reporting contractor.

10.2.1.2  RDT&E ▱  PRODUCTION ▱:  Check appropriate box.  Separate reports are required for each type of contract.

10.2.1.3  CONTRACT TYPE/NUMBER:  Enter the contract type, contract number and the number of the latest contract change or supplemental agreement applicable to the contract.

(Continued on pages 3 through 13)

DD FORM 1664 JUN 68

DI-F-6000C (Continued)
3.   DESCRIPTION/PURPOSE (Continued)

correlation with the budget plan and cost estimate predictions.
Format 5 is a narrative report used to explain significant cost and
schedule variances and other identified contract problems.

3.2  CPR data will be used by DoD system managers to:  (a) evaluate
contract performance, (b) identify the magnitude and impact of actual
and potential problem areas causing significant cost and schedule
variances, and (c) provide valid, timely program status information
to higher headquarters.

---

7.   APPLICATION/INTERRELATIONSHIP (Continued)

the data elements to be reported on the CPR will be as specified in
the solicitation document or as subsequently negotiated.

7.3  Unless otherwise provided for in the contract, the CPR normally
will be required on a monthly basis and submitted to the procuring
activity no later than 25 calendar days following the reporting
cutoff date.  Reports may reflect data either as of the end of the
calendar month or as of the contractor's accounting period cutoff
date.

7.4  Data reported in the CPR will pertain to all authorized contract
work, including both priced and unpriced effort.  The level of detail
to be reported normally will be limited to level three of the Contract
Work Breakdown Structure (WBS) or higher.  If a problem area is
indicated at a lower level of the WBS, more detailed data will be
provided until the problem is resolved.  Functional data normally
will be reported at the total contract level rather than by individual
WBS elements.  Certain aspects of the report are subject to negotiation between the Government and the contractor, such as:

7.4.1  The specific variance thresholds which, if exceeded, require
problem analysis and narrative explanations.

7.4.2  The specific organizational or functional categories to be
reported on Formats 2 and 4.

7.4.3  The specific time increments to be used for the baseline and
manpower loading projections required by Formats 3 and 4.

7.4.4  The reporting provisions which apply to the COST OF MONEY line
on Formats 1 and 2.

7.4.5  The reporting provisions which apply if compliance with C/SCSC
is not contractually required.

DI-F-6000C (Continued)
7.   APPLICATION/INTERRELATIONSHIP (Continued)

7.5  In all cases, the CPR is subject to "tailoring" to require less
data in accordance with the provisions of DoD Directive 5000.19,
"Policies for the Management and Control of Information Requirements,"
and DoD Instruction 5000.32, "DoD Acquisition Management Systems and
Data Requirements Control Program."  All negotiated reporting provisions
will be specified in the contract, including the reporting frequency,
specific variance thresholds, and the WBS elements to be reported.

7.6  The prescribing document which generates this reporting requirement is DoD Instruction 7000.10, "Contract Cost Performance, Funds
Status and Cost/Schedule Status Reports."

7.7  This Data Item Description supersedes DI-F-6000B.

---

10.  PREPARATION INSTRUCTIONS (Continued)

10.2.1.4  PROGRAM NAME/NUMBER:  Enter the program name, number,
acronym and/or the type, model and series or other designation of the
prime items purchased under the contract.

10.2.1.5  REPORT PERIOD:  Enter the beginning and ending dates of the
period covered by the report.

10.2.1.6  SECURITY CLASSIFICATION:  Enter the appropriate security
classification.

10.2.2  FORMAT 1 - WORK BREAKDOWN STRUCTURE:

10.2.2.1  SIGNATURE, TITLE AND DATE:  The contractor's authorized
representative will sign the report and enter his title and the date
of signature.

10.2.2.2  QUANTITY:  Enter the number of prime items to be procured on
this contract.

10.2.2.3  NEGOTIATED COST:  Enter the dollar value (excluding fee or
profit) on which contractual agreement has been reached as of the
cutoff date of the report.  For an incentive contract, enter the
definitized contract target cost.  Amounts for changes will not be
included in this item until they have been priced and incorporated
in the contract through contract change order or supplemental agreement.  For a fixed-fee contract, enter the estimated cost negotiated.
Changes to the estimated cost will consist only of amounts for changes
in the contract scope of work, not for cost growth.

DI-F-6000C (Continued)
10.  PREPARATION INSTRUCTIONS (Continued)

10.2.2.4  ESTIMATED COST OF AUTHORIZED, UNPRICED WORK:  Enter the
amount (excluding fee or profit) estimated for that work for which
written authorization has been received, but for which definitized
contract prices have not been incorporated in the contract through
supplemental agreement.

10.2.2.5  TARGET PROFIT/FEE %:  Enter the fee or percentage of profit
which will apply if the negotiated cost of the contract (paragraph
10.2.2.3, above) is met.

10.2.2.6  TARGET PRICE:  Enter the target price (negotiated contract
cost plus profit/fee) applicable to the definitized contract effort.

10.2.2.7  ESTIMATED PRICE:  Based on the latest revised estimate of
cost at completion for all authorized contract work and the appropriate
profit/fee, incentive, and cost sharing provisions, enter the estimated final contract price (total estimated cost to the Government).
This number normally will change whenever the estimated cost at
completion is revised.

10.2.2.8  SHARE RATIO:  Enter the cost sharing ratio(s) applicable to
costs over/under the negotiated contract cost.

10.2.2.9  CONTRACT CEILING:  Enter the contract ceiling price applicable to the definitized effort.

10.2.2.10  ESTIMATED CONTRACT CEILING:  Enter the estimated ceiling
price applicable to all authorized contract effort including both
definitized and undefinitized effort.

10.2.2.11  COLUMN (1) - ITEM

10.2.2.11.1  WORK BREAKDOWN STRUCTURE:  Enter the noun description of
the WBS item for which cost information is being reported.  WBS items
or levels reported will be those specified in the contract.

10.2.2.11.2  COST OF MONEY:  Enter in Columns (2) through (16) the
Cost of Money associated with the Cost of Facilities Capital applicable to the contract (see Cost Accounting Standard 414 for guidance).

10.2.2.11.3  GENERAL AND ADMINISTRATIVE (G&A):  Enter in Columns (2)
through (16) the appropriate G&A costs.  If G&A has been included in
the total costs reported above, G&A will be shown as a nonadd entry
on this line with an appropriate notation.  If a G&A classification
is not used, no entry will be made other than an appropriate notation
to that effect.

DI-F-6000C (Continued)
10. PREPARATION INSTRUCTIONS (Continued)

10.2.2.11.4 UNDISTRIBUTED BUDGET: Enter in Columns (14) and (15) the
amount of budget applicable to contract effort which has not yet been
identified to WBS elements at or below the reporting level. For
example, contract changes which were authorized late in the reporting
period should have received a total budget; however, assignment of
work and allocation of budgets to individual WBS elements may not
have been accomplished as of the end of the period. Budgets which can
be identified to WBS elements at or below the specified reporting
level will be included in the total budgets shown for the WBS elements
in the body of the report and will not be shown as undistributed budget.
All undistributed budget will be fully explained in the narrative
analysis section of the report (Format 5).

>        NOTE: The provisions made in this report for undis-
tributed budget are primarily to accommodate temporary situations
where time constraints prevent adequate budget planning or where
contract effort can only be defined in very general terms. Undistributed budget should not be used as a substitute for adequate
contract planning. Formal budgets should be allocated to contract
effort and functional organizations at the earliest possible time,
normally within the next reporting period.

10.2.2.11.5 SUBTOTALS: Enter the sum of the direct, indirect, Cost
of Money, and G&A costs and budgets in Columns (2) through (16). In
Columns (14) and (15) also add the undistributed budget.

10.2.2.11.6 MANAGEMENT RESERVE: An amount of the overall contract
budget withheld for management control purposes rather than for the
accomplishment of a specific task or set of tasks. In Column (14)
enter the total amount of budget identified as management reserve as
of the end of the current reporting period. In Column (15) enter
the amount of management reserve expected to be consumed before the
end of the contract. In Column (16) enter the difference between
Columns (14) and (15). Amounts of management reserve applied to
WBS elements during the reporting period and the rationale for the
figure in Column (15) will be explained in the narrative analysis on
Format 5. (The entry in Column (15) is discretionary and may be zero
if the contractor does not wish to make an estimate.)

>        NOTE: Negative entries will not be made in Column (14).
There is no such thing as "negative management reserve." If the
contract is budgeted in excess of the Contract Budget Base (the negotiated contract cost plus the estimated cost for authorized-unpriced
work), the provisions applicable to formal reprograming and the
instructions in paragraphs 10.2.2.11.8, 10.2.2.12.6 and 10.2.2.12.7
apply.

DI-F-6000C (Continued)
10.  PREPARATION INSTRUCTIONS (Continued)

10.2.2.11.7  TOTAL: Enter the sum of all direct, indirect, Cost of
Money, G&A costs, undistributed budgets and management reserves in
Columns (2) through (16).

10.2.2.11.8  VARIANCE ADJUSTMENT: In exceptional cases, the procuring
agency may authorize the contractor to establish baseline budgets
which in total exceed the Contract Budget Base.  If the contractor
uses a portion of the additional budget to eliminate variances applicable to completed work, the total adjustments made to the schedule
and cost variances will be shown on this line.  The total cost variance
adjustment entered on this line in Column (11) will be the sum of the
individual cost variance adjustments listed in Column (12).

10.2.2.11.9  TOTAL CONTRACT VARIANCE: In Columns (10) and (11), enter
on this line the sum of the cost and schedule variances shown on the
TOTAL line and on the VARIANCE ADJUSTMENT line.  In Column (14) enter
the sum of the negotiated contract cost plus the estimated cost for
authorized, unpriced work.  In Column (15) enter the latest revised
estimate of cost at completion.  In Column (16) enter the difference
between Columns (14) and (15).

10.2.2.12  Cols (2) through (16): If compliance with the C/SCSC is
contractually required, Columns (2) through (16) will contain information developed by the contractor's system implemented in accordance
with the definitions and criteria contained in DoD Instruction 7000.2.
If compliance with C/SCSC is not contractually required, the data
elements in these columns will be negotiated using the definitions of
DoD Instruction 7000.2 for guidance.

10.2.2.12.1  Col (2) and Col (7) - BUDGETED COST-WORK SCHEDULED: For
the time period indicated, enter the Budgeted Cost for Work Scheduled
(BCWS) in these columns.

10.2.2.12.2  Col (3) and Col (8) - BUDGETED COST-WORK PERFORMED: For
the time period indicated, enter the Budgeted Cost for Work Performed
(BCWP) in these columns.

10.2.2.12.3  Col (4) and Col (9) - ACTUAL COST-WORK PERFORMED (ACWP):
For the time period indicated, enter the actual direct and indirect
costs for work performed without regard to ceiling.  In all cases,
costs and budgets will be reported on a comparable basis.

10.2.2.12.4  Col (5) and Col (10) - VARIANCE - SCHEDULE: For the time
period indicated, these columns reflect the differences between BCWS
and BCWP.  For the current period, Col (5), schedule variance is
derived by subtracting Col (2) (BCWS) from Col (3) (BCWP).  For the
cumulative to date, Col (10), schedule variance is derived by subtracting Col (7) (BCWS) from Col (8) (BCWP).  A positive figure

DI-F-6000C (Continued)
10. PREPARATION INSTRUCTIONS (Continued)

indicates a favorable variance. A negative figure (indicated by
parentheses) indicates an unfavorable variance. Significant variances
will be fully explained in the problem analysis on Format 5.

10.2.2.12.5 Col (6) and Col (11) - VARIANCE - COST: For the time
period indicated, these columns reflect the differences between
BCWP and ACWP. For the current period, Col (6), cost variance is
derived by subtracting Col (4) (ACWP) from Col (3) (BCWP). For
cumulative to date, Col (11), cost variance is derived by subtracting
Col (9) (ACWP) from Col (8) (BCWP). A positive figure indicates a
favorable variance. A negative figure (indicated by parentheses)
indicates an unfavorable variance. Significant variances will be
fully explained in the problem analysis on Format 5.

10.2.2.12.6 Col (12) REPROGRAMING ADJUSTMENTS - COST VARIANCE:
Formal reprograming results in budget allocations in excess of the
Contract Budget Base and, in some instances, adjustments to previously
reported variances. If such variance adjustments have been made, the
adjustment applicable to each reporting line item affected will be
entered in Col (12). The Total of Col (12) will equal the amount
shown on the Variance Adjustment line in Col (11).

10.2.2.12.7 Col (13) REPROGRAMING ADJUSTMENTS - BUDGET: Enter the
total amounts added to the budget for each reporting line item as the
result of formal reprograming. The amounts shown will consist of the
sum of the budgets used to adjust cost variances (Col (12)) plus the
additional budget added to the WBS element for remaining work. Enter
the amount of budget added to management reserve in the space provided
on the Management Reserve line. The Total of Col (13) will equal the
amount the contract has been budgeted in excess of the Contract Budget
Base. An explanation of the reprograming will be provided in the
Problem Analysis Report.

NOTE: Cols (12) and (13) are intended for use only in
situations involving formal reprograming (over-target baselines).
Internal replanning actions within the Contract Budget Base do not
require entries in these columns. Where contractors are submitting
CPR data directly from mechanized systems, the addition of Cols (12)
and (13) as shown may not be practical due to computer reprograming
problems or space limitations. In such cases, the information may
be provided on a separate sheet and attached as Format 1a to each
subsequent report. Contractors will not be required to abandon or
modify existing mechanized reporting systems to include Cols (12)
and (13) if significant costs will be associated with such change.
Nor will contractors be required to prepare the report manually
solely to include this information.

**DI-F-6000C** (Continued)
10. <u>PREPARATION INSTRUCTIONS</u>  (Continued)

10.2.2.12.8 <u>Col (14) - AT COMPLETION - BUDGETED</u>: Enter the budgeted
cost at completion for the WBS items listed in Col (1). This entry
will consist of the sum of the original budgets plus or minus budget
changes resulting from contract changes, internal replanning, and
application of management reserves. The total should be equal to
the negotiated contract cost plus the estimated cost of authorized
but unpriced work except where special exception has been made
resulting in formal reprograming.

10.2.2.12.9 <u>Col (15) - AT COMPLETION - LATEST REVISED ESTIMATE</u>:
Enter the latest revised estimate of cost at completion including
estimated overrun/underrun for all authorized work.

10.2.2.12.10 <u>Col (16) - AT COMPLETION - VARIANCE</u>:  Enter the difference between the Budgeted - At Completion (Col 14) and the Latest
Revised Estimate at Completion (Col 15) by subtracting Col (15) from
Col (14).  A negative figure (indicated by parentheses) reflects an
unfavorable variance.  Significant variances will be fully explained
on Format 5.

10.2.3 <u>FORMAT 2 - FUNCTIONAL CATEGORIES</u>:

10.2.3.1 <u>Col (1) - ORGANIZATIONAL OR FUNCTIONAL CATEGORY</u>:  Under this
item list the organizational units or functional categories which
reflect the contractor's internal management structure in accordance
with Contractor/Government agreement.  This format will be used to
collect organizational or functional cost information at the total
contract level rather than for individual WBS elements.  The level
of detail to be reported will normally be limited to the organizational
level immediately under the operating head of the facility except
when there is a significant variance.  If a problem area is indicated
at a lower level of the organization, more detailed data will be
provided until the problem is resolved.

10.2.3.2 <u>COST OF MONEY</u>:  Enter in Columns (2) through (16) Cost of
Money applicable to the contract (CAS 414).

10.2.3.3 <u>GENERAL AND ADMINISTRATIVE</u>:  Enter in Columns (2) through
(16) applicable G&A costs.  (See paragraph 10.2.2.11.3).

10.2.3.4 <u>UNDISTRIBUTED BUDGET</u>:  Enter in Cols (14) and (15) the budget
applicable to contract effort which cannot be planned in sufficient
detail to be assigned to a responsible organization or functional
area at the reporting level.  The amounts shown on this format may
exceed the amounts shown as undistributed budget on Format 1 if
budget is identified to a task at or below the WBS reporting level

DI-F-6000C  (Continued)
10.  PREPARATION INSTRUCTIONS  (Continued)

but organizational identification has not been made; or may be less
than the amount on Format 1 where budgets have been assigned to
functional organizations but not to WBS elements.

10.2.3.5  SUBTOTAL:  Enter the sum of the direct, indirect, Cost of
Money, and G&A costs and budgets in Cols (2) through (16).  In Cols
(14) and (15) also add the undistributed budget.

10.2.3.6  MANAGEMENT RESERVE:  In Col (14) enter the amount of budget
identified as management reserve.  In Col (15) enter the amount of
management reserve forecasted to be consumed before the end of the
contract.  In Col (16) enter the difference between Cols (14) and (15).
The MANAGEMENT RESERVE entries will be identical to those shown on
Format 1.  (The entry in Col (15) is discretionary and may be zero if
the contractor does not wish to make an estimate.)

10.2.3.7  TOTAL:  Enter the sum of all direct, indirect, Cost of Money,
and G&A costs and budgets, undistributed budgets and management
reserves in Cols (2) through (16).  The totals on this page should
equal the TOTAL line on page 1.

10.2.3.8  COLS (2) THROUGH (16):  The instructions applicable to these
columns are the same as the instructions for corresponding columns on
Format 1 (see paragraphs 10.2.2.12.1 through 10.2.2.12.10).  All
significant variances will be fully explained in the problem analysis
on Format 5.

10.2.4  FORMAT 3 - BASELINE:

10.2.4.1  BLOCK (1) - ORIGINAL CONTRACT TARGET COST:  Enter the dollar
value (excluding fee or profit) negotiated in the original contract.
For a cost plus fixed-fee contract, enter the estimated cost negotiated.
For an incentive contract, enter the definitized contract target cost.

10.2.4.2  BLOCK (2) - NEGOTIATED CONTRACT CHANGES:  Enter the cumulative cost (excluding fee or profit) applicable to definitized contract
changes which have occurred since the beginning of the contract.

10.2.4.3  BLOCK (3) - CURRENT TARGET COST:  Enter the sum of Blocks
(1) and (2).  The amount shown should equal the current dollar value
(excluding fee or profit) on which contractual agreement has been
reached and should be the same as the amount shown as NEGOTIATED COST
on Format 1.

10.2.4.4  BLOCK (4) - ESTIMATED COST OF AUTHORIZED, UNPRICED WORK:
Enter the estimated cost (excluding fee or profit) for contract

DI-F-6000C  (Continued)
10.  PREPARATION INSTRUCTIONS  (Continued)

changes for which written authorizations have been received, but for
which contract prices have not been negotiated, as shown on Format 1.

10.2.4.5  BLOCK (5) - CONTRACT BUDGET BASE:  Enter the sum of Blocks
(3) and (4).

10.2.4.6  BLOCK (6) - TOTAL ALLOCATED BUDGET:  Enter the sum of all
budgets allocated to the performance of the contractual effort.  The
amount shown will include all management reserves and undistributed
budgets.  This amount will be the same as that shown on the TOTAL
line in Col (14) on Format 1.

10.2.4.7  BLOCK (7) - DIFFERENCE:  In most cases, the amounts shown
in Blocks (5) and (6) will be identical.  If the amount shown in
Block (6) exceeds that shown in Block (5), the difference should be
reflected as a negative value and explained in the narrative analysis
on Format 5 at the time the negative value appears and subsequently
for any change in the value.

10.2.4.8  BLOCK (8) - CONTRACT START DATE:  Enter the date the contractor was authorized to start work on the contract, regardless
of the date of contract definitization.  (Long lead procurement
efforts authorized under prior contracts are not to be considered.)

10.2.4.9  BLOCK (9) - CONTRACT DEFINITIZATION DATE:  Enter the date
the contract was definitized.

10.2.4.10  BLOCK (10) - LAST ITEM DELIVERY DATE:  Enter the date the
last major item of equipment is scheduled to be delivered to the
government as specified in the contract.  The date shown should
represent the completion of the significant effort on the contract
(approximately 95% of the total contractual effort in most cases).

10.2.4.11  BLOCK (11) - CONTRACT COMPLETION DATE:  Enter the contract
scheduled completion date in accordance with the latest contract
modification.

10.2.4.12  BLOCK (12) - ESTIMATED COMPLETION DATE:  Enter the latest
revised estimate of contract completion.

10.2.4.13  COL (1) - ITEM:

10.2.4.13.1  PM BASELINE (BEGINNING OF PERIOD):  The time-phased
performance measurement baseline (including G&A) which existed at
the beginning of the current reporting period.  Most of the entries

Dec 3, 79
7000.10 (Encl 2)

DI-F-6000C  (Continued)
10.  PREPARATION INSTRUCTIONS  (Continued)

on this line are taken directly from the PM BASELINE (END OF PERIOD)
line on the previous report.  For example, the number in Col (4) on
the PM BASELINE (END OF PERIOD) line from last month's report becomes
the number in Col (3) on the PM BASELINE (BEGINNING OF PERIOD) line
on this report.  The number in Col (5) (end of period) last report
becomes Col (4) (beginning of period) this report, etc.  This rule
pertains through Col (9) where the time increments change from monthly
to some other periods of time.  At this point, a portion of Col (10)
(end of period) would go into Col (9) (beginning of period) and the
remainder of Col (10) (end of period) would go into Col (10) (beginning
of period).  Cols (11) through (16) simply move directly up to the
(beginning of period) line without changing columns.

10.2.4.13.2  BASELINE CHANGES:  List by number, the contract changes
and supplemental agreements authorized during the reporting period.
All authorized baseline changes should be listed whether priced or
unpriced.  The amount of management reserve applied during the period
should also be listed.

10.2.4.13.3  PM BASELINE (END OF PERIOD):  The time-phased performance
measurement baseline as it exists at the end of the reporting period.
The difference between this line and the PM BASELINE (BEGINNING OF
PERIOD) should represent the effects of the authorized changes and
allocations of management reserves made during the period.  Significant differences should be explained in Format 5 - Problem Analysis
Report, in terms of reasons for necessary changes to time-phasing
due to replanning, and reasons for the application of Management
Reserve.

10.2.4.13.4  MANAGEMENT RESERVE:  Enter the total amount of management
reserve remaining as of the end of the reporting period.

10.2.4.13.5  TOTAL:  Enter the sum of the PM BASELINE (END OF PERIOD)
and the management reserve in Col (16).  This amount should be the
same as that shown on the TOTAL line in Col (14) on Format 1.

10.2.4.14  COL (2) - BCWS - CUM TO DATE:  Enter the cumulative BCWS
for the periods indicated.  The entry on the PM BASELINE (BEGINNING OF
PERIOD) line should be the same number reported as BCWS - CUM TO DATE
(Col (7)) on the TOTAL line of Format 1 of the previous month's CPR.
On the PM BASELINE (END OF PERIOD) line, enter the cumulative BCWS
as of the last day of the reporting period.  (This should be the
same number which appears on the TOTAL line in Col (7) of Format 1 for
this reporting period.)

DI-F-6000C  (Continued)
10.  PREPARATION INSTRUCTIONS  (Continued)

10.2.4.15  COL (3) - BCWS FOR REPORT PERIOD:  On the PM BASELINE
(BEGINNING OF PERIOD) line, enter the BCWS planned for the reporting
period.  (This should be the number in Col (4) on the PM BASELINE
(END OF PERIOD) line on the preceding month's report.)

10.2.4.16  Cols (4) through (14):  In the Blocks above Columns (4)
through (9), enter the appropriate months for the next six report
periods.  Enter the projected BCWS (by month for six months and by
other specified periods, or as negotiated with the procuring activity)
for the remainder of the contract.

10.2.4.17  COL (15) - UNDISTRIBUTED BUDGET:  On the PM BASELINE
(BEGINNING OF PERIOD) line, enter the number from Col (15) on the PM
BASELINE (END OF PERIOD) line from the preceding report.  On the PM
BASELINE (END OF PERIOD) line, enter the Undistributed Budget shown
in Col (14) on Format 1 of this report.

10.2.4.18  COL (16) - TOTAL BUDGET:  On the PM BASELINE (BEGINNING
OF PERIOD) line enter the number from Col (16) on the PM BASELINE (END
OF PERIOD) line from the preceding report.  In the section where baseline changes (priced and unpriced contract changes and changes in
management reserve) which occurred during the period are listed in
Col (1), enter the amount of each of the changes listed, (negotiated cost for priced changes not previously reported as authorized,
unpriced changes; difference between estimated cost and negotiated
cost for priced changes previously reported as authorized, unpriced
changes; and estimated cost for authorized, unpriced changes).  On
the PM BASELINE (END OF PERIOD) line, enter the sum of the amount in
the preceding columns on this line.  On the MANAGEMENT RESERVE line,
enter the amount of management reserve available at the end of the
period.  On the TOTAL line enter the sum of the amounts in this column
on the PM BASELINE (END OF PERIOD) line and the MANAGEMENT RESERVE
line.  (This should equal the amount in Block (6) on this Format and
also the amount of the TOTAL line in Col (14) of Format 1.)

10.2.5  Format 4 - Manpower Loading:

10.2.5.1  General:  For those organizational or functional categories
shown in Col (1) equivalent man-months will be indicated for the
current reporting period, cumulative through the current period, and
forecast to completion.  Direct man-months will be shown for each
organizational unit or major functional category for the contract.
An equivalent man-month is defined as the effort equal to that of one

Dec 3, 79
7000.10 (Encl 2)

DI-F-6000C  (Continued)
10.  PREPARATION INSTRUCTIONS  (Continued)

person for one month.  Figures should be reported in whole numbers,
(Partial man-months, .5 and above, will be rounded to 1; below .5 to
0.)  When mutually agreed by the contractor and the Government, manpower loading may be reported in terms of man-days or man-hours.

10.2.5.1.1 ORGANIZATIONAL OR FUNCTIONAL CATEGORY:  List the organizational or functional categories which reflect the contractor's
internal management structure in accordance with Contractor/Government
agreement.  Categories shown should coincide with those shown on
Format 2 of the report.

10.2.5.1.2 TOTAL DIRECT:  The sum of all direct man-months for the
organizational or functional categories shown in Col (1).

10.2.5.2 COL (2) - ACTUAL - CURRENT PERIOD:  Enter the actual equivalent man-months incurred during the current reporting period.

10.2.5.3 COL (3) - ACTUAL END OF CURRENT PERIOD (CUM):  Enter the
actual equivalent man-months incurred to date (cumulative) as of the
end of the report period.

10.2.5.4 COLS (4) THROUGH (14) - FORECAST (NONCUMULATIVE):  Enter a
forecast of manpower requirements by month for a six-month period
following the current period and by periodic increment thereafter,
such increment to be negotiated with the procuring activity.  The
forecast will be updated at least quarterly unless a major revision
to the plan or schedule has taken place, in which case forecasts will
be changed for all periods involved in the report submitted at the
end of the month in which the change occurred.

10.2.5.5 COL (15) - FORECAST AT COMPLETION:  Enter the estimate of
equivalent man-months necessary for the total contract in Col (15)
by organizational or functional category.  Any significant change in
the total number of man-months at completion of the contract (i.e.,
Col (14) Total) should be explained in Format 5 - Problem Analysis.

10.2.6 FORMAT 5 - PROBLEM ANALYSIS REPORT:  The Problem Analysis
Report is a narrative report prepared to supplement the other pages
of the Cost Performance Report as well as other reports which identify
significant problems.  The report should be prepared as specified on
Format 5.

Figure 1

Figure 2

Page 15 of 18 Pages

CLASSIFICATION _____

## COST PERFORMANCE REPORT — BASELINE

FORM APPROVED
OMB NUMBER
22R0260

| CONTRACTOR: | | CONTRACT TYPE/NO.: | PROGRAM NAME/NUMBER | REPORT PERIOD: | PAGE ____ OF ____ |

LOCATION:

RDT&E [ ]    PRODUCTION [ ]

| (1) ORIGINAL CONTRACT TARGET COST | (2) NEGOTIATED CONTRACT CHANGES | (3) CURRENT TARGET COST (1) + (2) | (4) ESTIMATED COST OF AUTHORIZED, UNPRICED WORK | (5) CONTRACT BUDGET BASE (3) + (4) | (6) TOTAL ALLOCATED BUDGET | (7) DIFFERENCE (5) − (6) (SEE PAGE 5) |

| (8) CONTRACT START DATE | (9) CONTRACT DEFINITIZATION DATE | (10) LAST ITEM DELIVERY DATE | (11) CONTRACT COMPLETION DATE | (12) ESTIMATED COMPLETION DATE |

BUDGETED COST FOR WORK SCHEDULED (NON-CUMULATIVE)

| ITEM | BCWS CUM TO DATE | BCWS FOR REPORT PERIOD | SIX MONTH FORECAST | | | | | | (ENTER SPECIFIED PERIODS) | | | | | | UNDIST BUDGET | TOTAL BUDGET |
|---|---|---|---|---|---|---|---|---|---|---|---|---|---|---|---|---|
| | | | +1 | +2 | +3 | +4 | +5 | +6 | | | | | | | | |
| (1) | (2) | (3) | (4) | (5) | (6) | (7) | (8) | (9) | (10) | (11) | (12) | (13) | (14) | (15) | (16) |
| PM BASELINE (BEGINNING OF PERIOD) | | | | | | | | | | | | | | | |
| (LIST BASELINE CHANGES AUTHORIZED DURING REPORT PERIOD) | | | | | | | | | | | | | | | |
| PM BASELINE (END OF PERIOD) | | | | | | | | | | | | | | | |
| MANAGEMENT RESERVE | | | | | | | | | | | | | | | |
| TOTAL | | | | | | | | | | | | | | | |

COST PERFORMANCE REPORT — MANPOWER LOADING

Figure 4    Page 17 of 18 Pages

CLASSIFICATION

## COST PERFORMANCE REPORT — PROBLEM ANALYSIS

PAGE ___ OF ___

FORM APPROVED OMB NUMBER 22R0280

CONTRACTOR:

LOCATION

RDT&E ☐    PRODUCTION ☐

CONTRACT TYPE/NO.:

PROGRAM NAME/NUMBER:

REPORT PERIOD:

## EVALUATION

**Section 1 — Total Contract:** Provide a summary analysis, identifying significant problems affecting performance. Indicate corrective actions required, including Government action where applicable.

**Section 2 — Cost and Schedule Variances:** Explain all variances which exceed specified variance thresholds. Explanations of variances must clearly identify the nature of the problem, the reasons for cost or schedule variance, impact on the immediate task, impact on the total program, and the corrective action taken. Explanations of cost variances should identify amounts attributable to rate changes separately from amounts applicable to manhours used; amounts attributable to material price changes separately from amounts applicable to material usage; and amounts attributable to overhead rate changes separately from amounts applicable to overhead base changes and amounts applicable to changes in the overhead allocation basis.

Within this section, the following specific variances must be explained:

a. Schedule variances (Budgeted Cost for Work Scheduled vs Budgeted Cost for Work Performed)
b. Cost variances (Budgeted Cost for Work Performed vs Actual Cost of Work Performed)
c. Cost variances at completion (Budgeted at Completion vs Latest Revised Estimate at Completion)

**Section 3 — Other Analysis:** In addition to the variance explanations above, the following analyses are mandatory:

a. Identify the effort to which the undistributed budget applies.
b. Identify the amount of management reserve applied during the reporting period, the WBS and organizational elements to which applied, and the reasons for application.
c. Explain reasons for significant shifts in time-phasing of the PM Baseline shown on Format 3.
d. Explain significant changes in total man-months at completion shown on Format 4.
e. Explain reasons for significant shifts in time-phasing of planned or actual manpower usage shown on Format 4.

**Section 4 — Over-Target Baseline:** If the difference shown in block (7) on Format 3 becomes a negative value or changes in value, provide:

a. Procuring activity authorization for the baseline change which resulted in negative value or change.
b. Reasons for the additional budget in the following terms:
(1) In-scope engineering changes
(2) In-scope support effort changes
(3) In-scope schedule changes
(4) Economic change
(5) Other (specify)
c. The amount (by WBS element) for added in-scope effort not previously identified or budgeted.

Dec 3, 79
7000.10 (Encl 3)

| DATA ITEM DESCRIPTION | 2. IDENTIFICATION NO(S). | |
|---|---|---|
| | AGENCY | NUMBER |

| 1. TITLE | |
|---|---|

CONTRACT FUNDS STATUS REPORT (CFSR)         DOD     DI-F-6004B

**3. DESCRIPTION/PURPOSE**

3.1  The Contract Funds Status Report (CFSR), DD Form 1586, Figure 1, is designed to supply funding data about Defense contracts to system managers for:  (a) updating and fore-casting contract fund requirements, (b) planning and decision-making on funding changes in contracts, (c) developing fund requirements and budget estimates in support of approved programs, and (d) determining funds in excess of contract needs and available for deobligation, and (e) obtaining rough estimates of termination costs.

**4. APPROVAL DATE**

1 November 1979

**5. OFFICE OF PRIMARY RESPONSIBILITY**

ASD(C)

**6. DDC REQUIRED**

**7. APPLICATION/INTERRELATIONSHIP**

7.1  The CFSR is applicable to contracts over $100,000 in value and 6 months in duration.  It is not normally applicable to firm-fixed price contracts (as defined in DAR 3-404.2) except for unpriced portions of such contracts that are estimated to be at least twenty (20) percent of the initial contract value, and except for firm-fixed price contracts which represent a major system acquisition or a major component thereof.

7.2  _Contractual Application_.  ONLY THOSE PARTS OF THE CFSR ESSENTIAL TO THE MANAGEMENT OF EACH ACQUISITION WILL BE RE-QUIRED.  The DoD system manager will determine the need for contract funds information and apply only those portions of the CFSR deemed appropriate.  (Continued on pages 2 and 3)

**8. APPROVAL LIMITATION**

**9. REFERENCES (Mandatory as cited in block 10)**

DAR 3-404.2
DAR 7-104.35
DAR 7-108.3
DAR 7-203.4
DAR 15-205.42
DAR Section III,
  Part 4
DoD 5000.12M, 1 Mar 70

**MCSL NUMBER(S)**

70934

**10. PREPARATION INSTRUCTIONS**

10.1  _Specific Instructions_

10.1.1  _Item 1 - CONTRACT NUMBER_.  Enter the assigned contract number and the latest modification number on which contractual agreement has been reached.

10.1.2  _Item 2 - CONTRACT TYPE*_.  Enter the type of contract as identified in DAR, Section III, Part 4; e.g.,

        Cost Plus Fixed Fee (CPFF)
        Fixed Price Incentive (FPI), etc.

10.1.3  _Item 3 - CONTRACT FUNDING FOR*_.  Enter the applicable type as follows:

        Multi-Year Procurement (MYP)
        Incrementally Funded Contract (INC)
        Contract for a Single Year (SYC)

10.1.3.1  _For FY_.  For contracts which are financed with funds appropriated in more than one fiscal year, a report is required for each fiscal year's funds where the separate year's funds in the contract are associated with specific quantities of hard-ware or services to be furnished.  The fiscal year(s) being reported will be shown this block and that year's share of the total target prices (initial and adjusted) will be shown in Items 9 and 10.

*Items marked with an asterisk (*) have been registered in the DoD Data Element Dictionary.
                                            (Continued on pages 4 through 10)

DI-F-6004B (Continued)
7.   APPLICATION/INTERRELATIONSHIP (Continued)

7.2.1  Level of Reporting.  If a contract is funded with a single
appropriation, a single line entry at the total contract level should
be considered for CFSR reporting.  Reporting by line item or WBS
element will be limited to only those items or elements needed to
suppport funds management requirements and will normally not include
items funded for less than $500,000 or elements below level two of the
contract WBS.  Contracts which have a dollar value between $100,000
and $500,000 will require reporting at the total contract level only.

7.2.2  Multiple Appropriations.  Where two or more appropriation
sources are used for funding a single contract, contractors will
segregate funds data by appropriation accounting reference.  The procuring agency will supply the appropriation numbers applicable to individual line items or WBS elements.  If a single line item or WBS
element is funded by more than one appropriation, methods for segregat-
ing and reporting such information will be negotiated and specified
in the contract.

7.2.3  Mechanized Data Submissions.  Computer products may be substituted for the DD Form 1586 provided all data elements are available
in a form suitable for DoD management use.  Otherwise data should be
submitted in the attached form.  Where data are furnished which require
mechanized processing, narrative remarks should accompany tapes or
cards and identify pertinent items to which they apply, and a listing
identifying tape or card data should be included to expedite processing.
In the event that more than one procuring agency desires mechanized
data processing from a single contractor, the procuring agencies will
provide the contractor with a uniform and mutually agreed upon set of
data processing instructions.

7.3  Frequency and Submission.  The Contract Funds Status Report, DD
Form 1586 (Figure 1), will be a contractual requirement as set forth in
the DD 1423, Contract Data Requirements List (CDRL) and DD 1660, Management System Summary List.  Unless otherwise provided for in the
contract, the CFSR will be prepared as of the end of each calendar
quarter or contractor accounting period nearest the end of each quarter.  The required number of copies of the CFSR will be forwarded
to the Administrative Contracting Officer (ACO) within 25 calendar
days after the "as of" date of the report, or as otherwise specified
in the contract.  In the event of exceptional circumstances which
call for increased frequency in reporting, such frequency will not be
more often than monthly and will be specified in the contract or will
be mutually agreed upon.

Dec 3, 79
7000.10 (Encl 3)

DI-F-6004B (Continued)
7. APPLICATION/INTERRELATIONSHIP (Continued)

### 7.4 Explanations of Terms

7.4.1 <u>Open Commitments</u>. For this report, a commitment represents the estimated obligation of the contractor (excluding accrued expenditures) to vendors or subcontractors (based on the assumption that the contract will continue to completion).

7.4.2 <u>Accrued Expenditures</u>. For this report, include recorded or incurred costs as defined within the Allowable Cost, Fee and Payments Clause (DAR 7-203.4) for cost type contracts or the Progress Payments Clause (DAR 7-104.35) for fixed price type contracts, plus the estimated fee or profit earned. Such costs include:

7.4.2.1 Actual payments for services or items purchased directly for the contract.

7.4.2.2 Costs incurred, but not necessarily paid, for storeroom issues, direct labor, direct travel, direct other in-house costs and allocated indirect costs.

7.4.2.3 Progress payments made to subcontractors.

7.4.2.4 Pension costs provided they are paid at least quarterly.

7.4.3 <u>Termination Costs</u>. Although this report is prepared on the basis that the contract will continue to completion, it is necessary to report estimated termination cost by Government fiscal year and generally more frequently on incrementally funded contracts. The frequency will be dependent on the funding need dates (i.e., quarterly) and should be compatible with the contract funding clauses, Limitation of Funds clause (cost type contracts) or Limitation of Obligation clause (fixed price type contracts). Termination costs include such items as loss of useful life of special tooling, special machinery and equipment; rental cost of unexpired leases; and settlement expenses. The definition of termination costs is included in DAR 15-205.42. In the event the Special Termination Costs clause (DAR 7-108.3) is authorized, then costs defined in this clause will be eliminated from the estimated termination costs.

7.5 This Data Item Description (DID) implements requirements of DoD Instruction 7000.10 for contract funds status reporting.

7.6 This DID supersedes DI-F-6004A.

DI-F-6004B (Continued)
10.  PREPARATION INSTRUCTIONS (Continued)

10.1.4  Item 4 - APPROPRIATION.  Enter the appropriation and Service source in this block.

10.1.5  Item 5 - PREVIOUS REPORT DATE.  Enter the cut-off date of the previous report.  (Year, Month, Day)

10.1.6  Item 6 - CURRENT REPORT DATE.  Enter the cut-off date applicable to this report.  (Year, Month, Day)

10.1.7  Item 7 - CONTRACTOR.  Enter the name, division (if applicable), and mailing address of the reporting contractor.

10.1.8  Item 8 - PROGRAM.  Identify the program (if known) by name or enter the type, model and series or other military designation of the prime item or items purchased on the contract.  If the contract is for services or a level-of-effort (research, flight test, etc.), the title of the service should be shown.

10.1.9  Item 9 - INITIAL CONTRACT PRICE.  Enter the dollar amounts for the initial negotiated contract target price and contract ceiling price when appropriate.  For contracts which are financed with funds appropriated in more than one fiscal year, only the share of the total initial target and ceiling associated with the fiscal year shown in Item 3 will be entered.

10.1.10  Item 10 - ADJUSTED CONTRACT PRICE.  Enter the dollar amounts for the adjusted contract target price (initial negotiated contract plus supplemental agreements) and adjusted contract ceiling price or estimated ceiling price where appropriate.  For contracts which are financed with funds appropriated in more than one fiscal year, only the share of the total adjusted target and ceiling associated with the fiscal year shown in Item 3 will be entered.

10.1.11  Item 11 - FUNDING INFORMATION

10.1.11.1  Col. a. - LINE ITEM/WORK BREAKDOWN STRUCTURE (WBS) ELEMENT.  Enter the line item or WBS elements specified for CFSR coverage in the contract.

10.1.11.2  Col. b. - APPROPRIATION IDENTIFICATION.  Enter the appropriation number supplied by the DoD for the contract or, if applicable, each line item or WBS element.

10.1.11.3  Col. c. - FUNDING AUTHORIZED TO DATE.  Enter dollar amounts of contract funding authorized under the contract from the beginning through the report date shown in Item 6.  This entry should contain funds applicable to the fiscal year(s) shown in Item 3.

Dec 3, 79
7000.10 (Encl 3)

DI-F-6004B (Continued)
10. PREPARATION INSTRUCTIONS (Continued)

10.1.11.4 Col. d. - ACCRUED EXPENDITURES PLUS OPEN COMMITMENTS TOTAL.
For contract work authorized, enter the total of (a) the cumulative -
accrued expenditures incurred through the end of the reporting period,
and (b) the open commitments on the "as of" date of the report. Enter
the total applicable to funds for the fiscal year(s) covered by this
report as shown in Item 3.

   Note a.: On selected contracts, the separation of open commitments and accrued expenditures by line item or WBS element may be a
negotiated requirement in the contract. Utilization of this provision
should be held to the minimum essential to support information needs
of the procuring agency. In the event this separation of data is not
available in the contractor's accounting system or cannot be derived
without significant effort, provision should be made to permit use of
estimates. The procedures used by the contractor in developing estimates should be explained in the Remarks section of the report.

   Note b.: When a Notice of Termination has been issued, potential
termination liability costs will be entered in this column. They will
be identified to the extent possible with the source of liability
(prime or subcontract).

10.1.11.5 Col. e. - CONTRACT WORK AUTHORIZED - DEFINITIZED. For the
fiscal year(s) shown in Item 3, enter the estimated price for the
authorized work on which contractual agreement has been reached, including profit/fee, incentive and cost sharing associated with projected
over/underruns. Amounts for contract changes will not be included in
this item unless they have been priced and incorporated in the contract
through a supplemental agreement to the contract.

10.1.11.6 Col. f. - CONTRACT WORK AUTHORIZED - NOT DEFINITIZED. Enter
the contractor's estimate of the fund requirements for performing
required work (e.g., additional agreements or changes) for which firm
contract prices have not yet been agreed to in writing by the parties
to the contract. Report values only for items for which written orders
have been received. For incentive type contracts, show total cost to
the Government (recognizing contractor participation). Enter in Narrative Remarks a brief but complete explanation of the reason for the
change in funds.

10.1.11.7 Col. g. - SUBTOTAL. Enter the total estimated price for
all work authorized on the contract (Col. e. plus Col. f.).

DI-F-6004B  (Continued)
10.  PREPARATION INSTRUCTIONS  (Continued)

10.1.11.8  Col. h. - FORECAST - NOT YET AUTHORIZED.  Enter an estimate of fund requirements, including the estimated amount for fee or
profit, for changes proposed by the Government or by the contractor,
but not yet directed by the contracting officer.  In the Narrative
Remarks state each change document number and estimated value of each
change.

10.1.11.9  Col. i. - FORECAST - ALL OTHER WORK.  Enter an estimate
of fund requirements for additional work anticipated to be performed
(not included in a firm proposal) which the contractor, based on his
knowledge and experience, expects to submit to the Government within
a reasonable period of time.

10.1.11.10  Col. j. - SUBTOTAL.  Enter an estimate of total requirements for forecast funding (the sum of Col. h. plus Col. i.).  Specific
limitations on the use of the forecast funding section may be a part
of the contract.

10.1.11.11  Col. k. - TOTAL REQUIREMENTS.  Enter an estimate of total
fund requirements for contract work authorized and forecast (the sum
of Col. g. plus Col. j.).

10.1.11.12  Col. l. - FUNDS CARRYOVER.  For incrementally funded
contracts only, report the amount by which the prior Federal fiscal
year funding was in excess of the prior year's requirement.  If there
is no carryover, report zero.  Specific instructions for the use of
this item may be made a part of the contract.

10.1.11.13  Col. m. - NET FUNDS REQUIRED.  Enter an estimate of net
funds required, subtracting funds carryover in Col. l. from total
requirements in Col. k.

10.1.11.14  Column Totals.  Totals should be provided for Columns c.
through m. for all line items or WBS elements reported.

10.1.12  Item 12 - CONTRACT WORK AUTHORIZED (WITH FEE/PROFIT) - ACTUAL
OR PROJECTED.  Data entries will be as follows:  In the first column,
actuals cumulative to date; in all other columns except the last,
projected cumulative from the start of the contract to the end of the
period indicated in the column heading; in the last column, the projected cumulative from the start to the end of the contract.

DI-F-6004B   (Continued)
10.  <u>PREPARATION INSTRUCTIONS</u>   (Continued)

Columns 2 through 10 will be headed to indicate periods covering the
life of the contract and may be headed to show months, quarters, half
years and/or fiscal years as prescribed by the procuring agency.
Projected data should include all planned obligations, anticipated
accruals, anticipated over/under targets (total cost to the Government
recognizing contractor participation), G&A, and fee/profit.

10.1.12.1  <u>OPEN COMMITMENTS</u>.  In the first column enter commitments
open as of the date of the report.  In subsequent columns enter the
projected commitments which will be open as of the end of each period
indicated by the column headings.  The amount entered will be the
projected cumulative commitments less the planned cumulative expenditures as of the end of time period indicated.  At the end of the contract, the amount will be zero.

10.1.12.2  <u>ACCRUED EXPENDITURES</u>.  In the first column enter actuals
to date.  In subsequent columns enter the projected cumulative accrued
expenditures as of the end of each period indicated by the column
headings.

10.1.12.3  <u>TOTAL (12.a. & 12.b.)</u>.  In the columns provided, enter the
total contract work authorized - actuals to date (column 1) or projected (columns 2 through 10).  This total is the sum of open commitments and accrued expenditures through the periods indicated by the
column headings.

10.1.13  <u>Item 13 - FORECAST OF BILLINGS TO THE GOVERNMENT</u>.  In the
first column enter the cumulative amount billed to the Government
through the current report date, including amounts applicable to
progress or advance payments.  In succeeding columns enter the amount
expected to be billed the Government during each period reported
(assuming the contract will continue to completion).  Amounts will
not be cumulative.

10.1.14  <u>Item 14 - ESTIMATED TERMINATION COSTS</u>.  In the columns provided, enter the estimated costs that would be necessary to liquidate
all Government obligations if the contract were to be terminated in
that period.  Applicable fee/profit should be included.  These entries
may consist of "rough order of magnitude" estimates and will not be
construed as providing formal notification having contractual significance.  This estimate will be used to assist the Government in
budgeting for the potential incurrence of such cost.  On contracts
with Limitation of Funds/Obligation clauses, where termination costs
are included as part of the funding line, enter the amounts required
for termination reserve on this line.

DI-F-6004B   (Continued)
10.   PREPARATION INSTRUCTIONS   (Continued)

10.2   Narrative Remarks

10.2.1   A separate sheet will be used to submit any additional information or remarks which support or explain data submitted in this
report.   Information on changes, as specified in the next two paragraphs, will also be reported in the remarks section.

10.2.2   General.   The contractor will use the Remarks section of the
Contract Funds Status Report to submit information regarding changes,
as indicated below.   A change in a line item will be reported when the
dollar amount reported in Item 11, Col. k. of this submission differs
from that reported in the preceding submission.   The movement of
dollar amounts from one column to another (Item 11, Cols. e. through
j.), indicating a change in the firmness of fund requirements, need
not be reported in this section.   Change reporting should include the
following:

10.2.2.1   The location of the changed entry (page, line, and column);

10.2.2.2   The dollar amount of the change;

10.2.2.3   The coded identification of the cause (see classification
below); and

10.2.2.4   A narrative explanation of the cause of each change.

10.2.3   Change Categories.   The contractor will use the categories
shown in this paragraph for identifying the reasons for changing
fund requirements.   The System Manager will assist the contractor in
assigning change categories to assure the assignment of the proper
category in relation to the total program.   These categories identify
two basic causes for changes in funds requirements - change in the
scope of the contract (identified simply as "Scope" changes) and
changes in the price with no change in the scope ("Price" changes).
Categories will be used as shown unless the contractor is advised of
specific alternatives through contractual channels.   While the general
intent in providing categories for use is that one category will
describe one change, it is recognized that more than one category may
be required in selected cases of changes in estimates of fund requirements.   In such cases reporting contractors should identify changes
using more than one change category and utilize the Remarks section
to describe the circumstances of overlap or duplication.   The reasons
for change are broken down as follows:

DI-F-6004B   (Continued)
10.   PREPARATION INSTRUCTIONS   (Continued)

10.2.3.1  "Scope" Changes.  There are four categories for this class
of reasons for change in estimates.  Report Total Funds Requirements
changes (Item 11, Col. k.) due to:

10.2.3.1.1  Engineering Change*.  An alteration in the physical
or functional characteristics of a system or item delivered, to be
delivered, or under development, after establishment of such characteristics.  Specific changes must be separately identified and
quantified.  Code A1.

10.2.3.1.2  Quantity Change*.  A change in quantity to be procured,
the cost of which is computed using the original cost-quantity relationships, thereby excluding that portion of the current price
attributable to changes in any other category.  Code A2.

10.2.3.1.3  Support Change*.  A change in support item requirements
(e.g., spare parts, training, ancillary equipment, warranty provisions,
Government-furnished property/equipment, etc.).  Code A3.

10.2.3.1.4  Schedule Change*.  A change in a delivery schedule,
completion date or intermediate milestone.  Each change must separately
be identified as Government responsibility or contractor responsibility
and quantified as to amount.  Code A4.

10.2.3.2  Price Changes.  There are three categories for this class.
Report Total Funds Requirements changes (Item 11, Col. k.) due to:

10.2.3.2.1  Economic Change*.  A change due to the operation of one
or more factors of the economy.  This includes specific contract changes
related to economic escalation and the economic impact portion of quantity changes not accounted for by the original cost-quantity relationships used to calculate quantity change variance.  This category also
includes changing constant or current dollar amounts in program estimates to reflect (1) altered price levels, or (2) definitized contract
amounts.  Code B2.

10.2.3.2.2  Estimating Change*.  A change in cost due to correction
of error or refinements of the base estimate.  These include mathematical or other errors in estimating, revised estimating relationships, etc.  Excluded from this category should be revisions of cost
estimates that occur because of other change categories, i.e.,
engineering, support, schedule, etc.  For example, a cost change which
occurs because of the addition of a new warhead is an engineering

DI-F-6004B  (Continued)
10.  PREPARATION INSTRUCTIONS  (Continued)

change, and not an estimating change; a revised production schedule
is a schedule change, not an estimating change.  Code B3.

10.2.3.2.3.  Other Changes*.  A change in contractual amount for
reasons not provided for in other change categories.  The reason for
the change should be stated.  Code B4.

10.3  General note for ADP personnel processing this report:

10.3.1  Coding must be as indicated in the instructions.  In cases
where specific coding instructions are not provided, reference must
be made to the Department of Defense Manual for Standard Data
Elements, DoD 5000.12M.  Failure to comply with either the coding
instructions contained herein or those published in referenced
manual will make the noncomplier responsible for required concessions
in data base communication.

Dec 3, 79
7000.10 (Encl 3)

Figure 1

Page 11 of 11 Pages

Dec 3, 79
7000.10 (Encl 4)

| DATA ITEM DESCRIPTION | 2. IDENTIFICATION NO(S). | |
|---|---|---|
| | AGENCY | NUMBER |

**1. TITLE**

COST/SCHEDULE STATUS REPORT (C/SSR)

OSD      DI-F-6010A

**3. DESCRIPTION/PURPOSE**

3.1  This report is prepared by contractors and provides summarized cost and schedule performance information for program management purposes.

**4. APPROVAL DATE**

1 November 1979

**5. OFFICE OF PRIMARY RESPONSIBILITY**

ASD(C)

**6. DDC REQUIRED**

**8. APPROVAL LIMITATION**

**7. APPLICATION/INTERRELATIONSHIP**

7.1  The Cost/Schedule Status Report (C/SSR), Figure 1, is applicable to contracts of $2,000,000 or over and 12 months' duration or more which do not use the Cost Performance Report (DI-F-6000).  It will be established as a contractual requirement as set forth in the Contract Data Requirements List, DD Form 1423, and Management System Summary List, DD Form 1660.

7.2  Data reported on the C/SSR will pertain to all authorized contract work, including both priced and unpriced effort. Data reported will be limited to level 3 of the contract work breakdown structure or higher.  However, if a problem area is indicated at a lower level, more detailed data will be provided on an exception basis until the problem is resolved.
(Continued on page 2)

**9. REFERENCES (Mandatory as cited in block 10)**

DoD 4120.3M, Aug 78
MIL STD 881A, 25 Apr 75
DoDI 7000.2, 10 Jun 77

**MCSL NUMBER(S)**

71559

**10. PREPARATION INSTRUCTIONS**

10.1  Unless otherwise stated in the solicitation, the effective issue of the document(s) cited in the referenced document(s) in this block shall be that listed in the issue of the DoD Index of Specifications and Standards (reference DoD 4120.3M) and the supplements thereto specified in the solicitation and will form a part of this data item description to the extent defined within.

10.2  Heading Information

    10.2.1  CONTRACTOR:  Enter the name and division (if applicable) of the reporting contractor.

    10.2.2  LOCATION:  Enter the plant location and mailing address.

    10.2.3  RDT&E ▱  PRODUCTION ▱:  Check appropriate box.  Separate reports are required for each type of contract.

    10.2.4  CONTRACT TYPE AND NUMBER:  Enter the contract type, contract number and the number of the latest contract change order or supplemental agreement applicable to the contract.

    10.2.5  PROGRAM NAME/NUMBER:  Enter the name, number, acronym and/or the type, model and series, or other designation of the prime items purchased under the contract.

(Continued on pages 2 through 5)

DD FORM 1664      PAGE 1 OF 6 PAGES

DI-F-6010A   (Continued)
7.   APPLICATION/INTERRELATIONSHIP   (Continued)

7.3  Frequency of reporting will be specified in the contract but will
not exceed a monthly requirement.  Reports will be submitted to the
procurement activity no later than 25 calendar days following the
reporting cut-off date.  Reports may reflect data as of the end of the
calendar month or as of the contractor's accounting period cut-off date.

7.4  The definitions of terms contained in the Cost/Schedule Control
Systems Criteria (C/SCSC) of DoD Instruction 7000.2, "Performance
Measurement for Selected Acquisitions," may be used as guidance in
completing Columns (2) through (9) of the C/SSR with the exception of
the definitions for Budgeted Cost for Work Scheduled and Budgeted
Cost for Work Performed (see paragraphs 10.4.2 and 10.4.3, below).
However, application of the C/SSR does not in any way invoke unique
requirements or disciplines of the C/SCSC, such as applied direct
costs or use of work packages for determining Budgeted Cost for Work
Performed, unless these methods constitute the contractor's normal
way of doing business.  The derivation of Budgeted Cost for Work Performed to satisfy C/SSR requirements will be left to the discretion
of the reporting contractor and subject to negotiation and inclusion
as a part of the contract.  While the contractor must be in a position
to explain the method used for determining Budgeted Cost for Work Performed, the in-depth demonstration review referred to in DoD Instruction
7000.2 is not a requirement of C/SSR.  If compliance with C/SCSC is
required, the provisions of DAR 3-501 and 7-104.87 must be used.

7.5  The variance thresholds which, if exceeded, require problem analysis
and narrative explanations, will be as specified in the contract or as
otherwise mutually agreed to by the contracting parties.

7.6  This Data Item Description supersedes DI-F-6010.

---

10.   PREPARATION INSTRUCTIONS   (Continued)

10.2.6  REPORT PERIOD:  Enter the beginning and ending dates of the period
covered by the report.

10.2.7  SIGNATURE, TITLE AND DATE:  The contractor's authorized representative will sign the report and enter his title and the date of
signature.

10.3  Contract Data:

10.3.1  Item (1) - ORIGINAL CONTRACT TARGET COST:  Enter the dollar value
(excluding fee or profit) negotiated in the original contract.  For a

Dec 3, 79
7000.10 (Encl 4)

DI-F-6010A  (Continued)
10.  PREPARATION INSTRUCTIONS  (Continued)

cost plus fixed-fee contract, enter the estimated cost negotiated.  For
an incentive contract, enter the definitized contract target cost.

10.3.2  Item (2) - NEGOTIATED CONTRACT CHANGES:  Enter the cumulative
cost (excluding fee or profit) applicable to definitized contract changes
which have occurred since the beginning of the contract.

10.3.3  Item (3) - CURRENT TARGET COST:  Enter the sum of Items (1) and
(2).  The amount shown should equal the current dollar value (excluding
fee or profit) on which contractual agreement has been reached.

10.3.4  Item (4) - ESTIMATED COST OF AUTHORIZED, UNPRICED WORK:  Enter
the estimated cost (excluding fee or profit) for contract changes for
which written authorization has been received but for which contract
prices have not been negotiated.

10.3.5  Item (5) - CONTRACT BUDGET BASE:  Enter the sum of Items (3)
and (4).

10.4  Performance Data:

10.4.1  Col. (1) - WORK BREAKDOWN STRUCTURE:  Enter the noun description of the work breakdown structure (WBS) elements for which cost
information is being reported.  WBS elements or levels required will
be those specified in the contract.

10.4.2  Col. (2) - BUDGETED COST - WORK SCHEDULED:  Enter the numerical
representation of the value of all work scheduled to be accomplished as
of the reporting cut-off date.

10.4.3  Col. (3) - BUDGETED COST - WORK PERFORMED:  Enter the numerical
representation of the value of all work accomplished as of the reporting
cut-off date.

        NOTE:  Specific methods used to derive the Budgeted Cost for
Work Scheduled and the Budgeted Cost for Work Performed will be deline-
ated in the proposal and explained on the initial report.  If methods
used should change during the contract, explain the new method and the
reason for the change in procedure.

10.4.4  Col. (4) - ACTUAL COST WORK PERFORMED:  Enter the cumulative
actual costs (direct and indirect) applicable to work accomplished as
of the reporting cut-off date.  Actual costs and budgeted costs will be
reported on a comparable basis.

DI-F-6010A   (Continued)
10.   PREPARATION INSTRUCTIONS   (Continued)

10.4.5  Col. (5) - SCHEDULE VARIANCE:  Enter the difference between the
Budgeted Cost for Work Scheduled and the Budgeted Cost for Work Performed
by subtracting Col. (2) from Col. (3).  A negative figure indicates
an unfavorable variance and should be shown in parentheses.  Variances
exceeding established thresholds must be fully explained.

10.4.6  Col. (6) - COST VARIANCE:  Enter the difference between the
Budgeted Cost for Work Performed and the Actual Cost for Work Performed
by subtracting Col. (4) from Col. (3).  A negative figure indicates
an unfavorable variance and should be shown in parentheses.  Variances
exceeding established thresholds must be fully explained.

10.4.7  Col. (7) - AT COMPLETION - BUDGETED:  Enter the total budget
identified to each WBS element listed in Col. (1).  Assigned budgets
will consist of the original budgets plus or minus budget adjustments
resulting from contract changes, internal replanning, and application
of management reserves.

10.4.8  Col. (8) - AT COMPLETION - LATEST REVISED ESTIMATE:  Enter the
latest revised estimate of cost at completion including estimated overrun/
underrun for all authorized work.  The estimated cost at completion
consists of the sum of the actual cost to date plus the latest estimate
of cost for work remaining.

10.4.9  Col. (9) - AT COMPLETION - VARIANCE:  Enter the difference between the Budgeted Cost at Completion, Col. (7), and the Estimated Cost
at Completion, Col. (8), by subtracting Col. (8) from Col. (7).  A
negative figure indicates an unfavorable variance and should be shown in
parentheses.  Variances exceeding established thresholds must be fully
explained.

10.4.10  GENERAL AND ADMINISTRATIVE (G&A):  Enter in Columns (2) through
(9) the appropriate G&A costs.  If G&A has been included in the costs
reported above, G&A will be shown as a non-add entry on this line with
an appropriate notation.  If a G&A classification is not used, no entry
will be made other than an appropriate notation to that effect.

10.4.11  UNDISTRIBUTED BUDGET:  Enter in Cols. (7) and (8) the amount of
budget applicable to authorized contract effort which has not been identified to WBS elements at or below the reporting level.  All undistributed
budget will be fully explained.

10.4.12  MANAGEMENT RESERVE:  Enter in Col. (7) the amount of budget
identified as management reserve as of the end of the reporting period.
Enter in Col. (8) the amount of management reserve expected to be consumed before the end of the contract.  Enter in Col. (9) the difference

DI-F-6010A   (Continued)
10.  PREPARATION INSTRUCTIONS   (Continued)

between Cols. (7) and (8).  Amounts of management reserve applied during
the reporting period and the rationale for the figure in Col. (8) will be
explained in the Narrative Analysis.  (The entry in Col. (8) is discretionary and may be zero if the contractor does not wish to make an
estimate.)  Application of management reserve during the reporting period
will be explained in terms of amounts applied, WBS elements to which
applied, and reasons for application.

10.4.13  TOTAL: Enter the sum of the direct, indirect and G&A budgets
and costs in Cols. (2) through (9).  In Cols. (7), (8) and (9), also
add the Undistributed Budget and Management Reserve.

10.5  Narrative Explanations:

10.5.1  Provide a summary analysis of overall contract performance, including significant existing or potential problems and identify corrective actions taken or required, including Government action where required.

10.5.2  Explanations of significant variances must be explicit and
comprehensive.  They must clearly identify the nature of the problems
being experienced, the impact on the total contract, and the corrective
actions taken or required.

10.5.3  Normally, the amount shown on the Total line in Col. (7),
Budgeted at Completion, will equal the amount shown in Item (5), Contract
Budget Base.  This relationship is necessary to insure that the Budgeted
Cost for Work Scheduled and the Budgeted Cost for Work Performed provide
meaningful indicators of contractual progress.  Therefore, if the amount
shown on the Total line in Col. (7), Budgeted at Completion, exceeds the
amount shown in Item (5), Contract Budget Base, fully explain the reasons
for the additional budget allocation and identify by WBS element the
specific amounts added to each element.

COST/SCHEDULE STATUS REPORT

Figure 1

# APPENDIX D
# DODI 7000.11:
## Contractor Cost
## Data Reporting (CCDR)

## Department of Defense
# INSTRUCTION

March 27, 1984
**NUMBER** 7000.11

SUBJECT:  Contractor Cost Data Reporting                          ASD(C)/PA&E

References:  (a)  DoD Instruction 7000.11, "Contractor Cost Data Reporting
                  (CCDR)," September 5, 1973 (hereby canceled)
             (b)  "Contractor Cost Data Reporting System," AMCP 715-8,
                  NAVMAT-5241, AFSCP/AFLCP 800-15, November 5, 1973
             (c)  DoD Directive 5000.1, "Major System Acquisitions," March 29,
                  1982
             (d)  DoD Directive 5000.4, "OSD Cost Analysis Improvement Group,"
                  October 30, 1980
             (e)  through (h), see enclosure 1

## A.  REISSUANCE AND PURPOSE

1.  This Instruction reissues reference (a) to update policy, procedures,
and responsibilities for collecting projected and actual cost data on acquisition
programs from contractors and government facilities through a single integrated
system for DoD cost analysis and procurement management purposes.

2.  Data from this system assist the Department of Defense in preparing
cost estimates for acquisition programs reviewed by the Defense Systems
Acquisition Review Council (DSARC); in developing independent government cost
estimates in support of cost-effectiveness studies, budgeting to most likely
costs, and contract negotiations; and in tracking actual versus contractor
negotiated costs.

## B.  APPLICABILITY AND SCOPE

1.  This Instruction applies to the Office of the Secretary of Defense
(OSD), the Military Departments, and the Defense Agencies (hereafter referred
to collectively as "DoD Components") having acquisition programs covered by
the criteria established herein.

2.  As used herein, the term "contractor" refers both to industrial
contractors and government facilities.

## C.  POLICY

It is DoD policy that projected and actual costs and related data shall be
reported on selected contracts within acquisition programs through the Contractor
Cost Data Reporting (CCDR) System (reference (b)).  CCDR coverage shall be in
accordance with the procedures described herein from the point of commitment
to full-scale development through the completion of production (reference (c)).
CCDR also shall be required on large advanced development prototype programs.

**D.   PROCEDURES**

1.   The CCDR Plan and CCDR forms (DD Forms 1921 series) ("Contractor Cost
Data Reporting System," reference (b)) shall be used as the basis for
contractor responses in applicable Requests for Proposals (RFPs) and resulting
contracts meeting the CCDR criteria in subsection D.2., below.  CCDR also
shall be included in equivalent documents when the supplier is a government
facility.

2.   For purposes of CCDR, two categories of procedures are established.
Category I procedures apply to all acquisition programs that are designated as
major system acquisitions by the Secretary of Defense or that are estimated to
require an eventual total research, development, test, and evaluation expenditure of more than $200 million in constant fiscal year (FY) 1980 dollars or an
eventual total procurement expenditure of more than $1 billion in constant FY
1980 dollars.  Category II procedures apply to selected contracts or to specific
line items within Category I requirements; generally, the data will not be
required on contracts below $2 million.

3.   All aircraft, electronic, missile, ordnance, ship, space, and surface
vehicle acquisition programs and their related components that meet the
criteria of Category I, above, shall be covered by CCDR requirements unless
specifically waived by the OSD Cost Analysis Improvement Group (CAIG) (DoD
Directive 5000.4, reference (d)).

a.   .Acquisition programs not meeting Category I criteria may be
covered by Category I procedures (including appropriate review and approval
procedures) at the discretion of the DoD Component concerned or the OSD CAIG.

b.   Other acquisition programs not covered by Category I procedures
may collect cost data using the Category II procedures described herein at the
discretion of the DoD Component concerned.  This determination shall consider
contract type, complexity, or criticality of the item as it pertains to the
overall structure of the national defense, future procurement plans, contract
value, and the need for a historical data base to support cost analysis and
procurement management objectives.

4.   For Category I acquisition programs, the identification of prime contractors and subcontractors who are required to report shall be determined
during the CCDR Plan review process.  Selection of reporting subcontractors
shall be limited to high-cost and technological high-risk elements of the
contract.

5.   Unless waived by the OSD CAIG, reporting shall be required on firm
fixed-price prime contracts or subcontracts when those contracts represent a
major share of the research and development (R&D) or production of a Category
I acquisition program or component thereof.  CCDR generally will not be
required on firm fixed-price Category II contracts.

6. CCDR procedures, including instructions for the preparation and submission of the forms, are specified in the CCDR System ("Contractor Cost Data Reporting System," reference (b)) and shall be adhered to by all DoD Components.

E. INFORMATION REQUIREMENTS

1. The reporting requirements are contained in the following four CCDR forms: Cost Data Summary Report (DD Form 1921), summarizing by work breakdown structure (WBS) element all activities on a contract or proposal; Functional Cost-Hour Report (DD Form 1921-1), providing cost element breakout for selected WBS elements reported on DD Form 1921; Progress Curve Report (DD Form 1921-2), providing unit data or average unit of a lot data for selected hardware WBS elements of the contract; and Plant-Wide Data Report (DD Form 1921-3), summarizing the business base, the indirect expenses, rates, and employment, and the direct labor rates and employment. These forms (see enclosures 2 through 5) are approved by the Office of Management and Budget (OMB) (OMB No. 0704-0062). A Data Item Description (DD Form 1664) for each CCDR form is contained in reference (b).

2. For acquisition programs falling under the criteria of Category I procedures, the DoD Component concerned shall prepare and forward the proposed CCDR Plan, in accordance with Chapter 2-4, page 2-2, of reference (b) to the Chairman, OSD CAIG, at least 60 days before issuance of its RFP to industry for large advanced development prototype or full-scale development programs.

a. The WBS used in preparing the CCDR Plan shall be in conformance with MIL-STD 881A (reference (e)). This standardization is necessary to achieve comparable data among similar weapon systems to improve DoD's estimating capability. Expansion by the Military Departments for visibility on certain WBS elements shall be at level 3 or below of the structure established by reference (e). Except for high-cost or high-risk elements, the normal level of reporting detail required shall be limited to level 3 of the contract work breakdown structure (CWBS).

b. The proposed reporting contractors shall be identified by name or area of responsibility (for example, airframe prime contractor).

c. For Category I reporting, the following CCDR forms normally shall be used:

(1) DD Forms 1921 and 1921-1 shall be used in contractor responses to RFPs (Defense Acquisition Regulation, reference (f)).

(2) DD Forms 1921, 1921-1, and 1921-2 shall be used to provide actuals and estimates to complete each R&D and production contract.

(3) DD Forms 1921 and 1921-1 shall be used to provide cost projections by FY buy to complete the production program.

(4) DD Form 1921-3 shall be used to provide plantwide data; if the data already are being furnished on another contract within an applicable contractor facility, copies of that DD Form 1921-3 satisfy the requirement.

d. Reporting frequency for recurring reports shall be specified in the CCDR Plan. Generally:

(1) Reports for Category I contracts shall be submitted semi-annually for R&D and the first several production years; frequency may be reduced to annually thereafter. Reporting frequencies may be adjusted during the CCDR Plan review procedures. Contract type and contract value shall be determining factors in the DoD Component decision prescribing frequency.

(2) Cost projections may be specified (a) for source selections, (b) annually, or (c) as required during the life of the program (for example, for updated program estimates to support a scheduled DSARC review).

3. The OSD CAIG shall have 15 working days from receipt of the CCDR Plan to issue a concurrence or to provide its recommended changes. Whenever a DoD Component proposes a revision to a Category I CCDR Plan, the OSD CAIG shall be notified. For minor changes the notification can be in the form of an information copy of the CCDR Plan. Major changes shall require formal resubmittal of the CCDR Plan.

4. For acquisitions covered under Category II procedures, DoD Components shall ensure that implementation plans are reviewed and approved in time for the data requirements to be included in the RFP for the contract on which they will be implemented. The review of the plans for implementing Category II requirements shall be the responsibility of the procuring materiel command headquarters. This review shall ensure data requirements are not excessive to actual needs and are consistent and comparable for similar types of weapon systems.

a. For Category II reporting, normally only DD Forms 1921-1 and 1921-2 shall be used; however, when the financing for a Category II contract is substantial enough to require the application of a WBS in accordance with MIL-STD 881A (reference (e)), DD Form 1921 may be used at the discretion of the contracting DoD Component.

b. Reports for Category II contracts normally shall be submitted at contract completion.

c. DD Form 1921-3 normally will not be required for Category II contracts.

5. Contractually, each CCDR form shall be identified as a single line entry on the DD Form 1423, Contract Data Requirements List (CDRL), with the detailed requirements listed in the respective DD Form 1664.

6. CCDR reports shall be submitted and distributed as follows:

a. The winning contractor's completed CCDR forms in response to the RFP on Category I programs shall be forwarded to the OSD CAIG following the completion of source selection (but no later than 90 days after contract award) consistent with DoD Directive 4105.62 (reference (g)).

b. On contracts requiring submittal of CCDR reports, the reports shall be submitted by the contractor or government facility within 45 days

Mar 27, 84
7000.11

after the end of the reporting period as specified in the CCDR Plan. When
subcontractors report to the prime contractor, the prime contractor shall be
given an additional 15 days to consolidate the appropriate reports.

    c.  For Category I programs, CCDR reports shall be due in the Office
of the Director, Program Analysis and Evaluation, the Pentagon, Washington,
D.C. 20301, the executive agent of the OSD CAIG, 2 weeks after the contractor
submittal due date. Category II reports shall be forwarded to the OSD CAIG
only upon its request.

    d.  Other DoD Components desiring copies of CCDR reports on a specific
acquisition or contract shall notify the appropriate Military Department
procuring materiel command headquarters. Requests from other federal agencies
for CCDR information shall be processed through the OSD CAIG. If a DoD
Component has compelling reasons for not making CCDR information available to
other federal agencies, it promptly shall refer the matter to the OSD CAIG for
resolution.

    e.  Reports prepared by DoD Components on the accuracy or validity of
CCDR information shall be forwarded promptly to all offices receiving the
completed reports on which the evaluation was made. This does not include
audit reviews discussed in subsections E.8. and E.9., below. Requests from
higher headquarters for clarification of information in the CCDR reports shall
be addressed to the appropriate materiel command.

    f.  Each materiel command shall be responsible for storing and distrib-
uting copies of the CCDR reports.

    7.  Each DoD Component shall designate an official who shall ensure that
DoD Component policies and procedures are established for the implementation
of CCDR in accordance with this Instruction, including the storage of CCDR
data and their distribution to appropriate DoD officials. This official also
shall ensure that all Category I CCDR Plans (including any changes thereto)
are forwarded to the OSD CAIG and shall advise the OSD CAIG annually of the
status of all acquisition programs for which CCDR Plans currently are approved
for implementation, of delinquencies and deficiencies in CCDR reporting, and
of the actions being taken to correct these delinquencies and deficiencies.
The designated official (by title) and the CCDR storage locations shall be
provided to the OSD CAIG within 30 days of the effective date of this Instruction.

    8.  Requirements for field reviews of contractor implementation of CCDR
shall be made annually and, when needed, an audit report shall be requested
through the responsible administrative contracting officer (ACO).

    9.  Audit reviews of CCDR data shall be performed by the Defense Contract
Audit Agency in accordance with the Defense Contract Audit Manual (reference (h)).
Such reviews shall consist of (a) an evaluation of the effectiveness of the
contractor's policies and procedures to produce data compatible with the objectives of this Instruction and the Contractor Cost Data Reporting (CCDR)
System (reference (b)) and (b) selective tests of the reported data. Any
exceptions shall be included with appropriate comment in the audit reports
that shall be issued to the responsible ACO, with a copy to the OSD CAIG and
to the designated DoD Component official responsible for CCDR.

**F.  RESPONSIBILITIES**

1.  The <u>Chairman, OSD Cost Analysis Improvement Group</u>, consistent with DoD Directive 5000.4 (reference (d)), shall establish policy guidance pertaining to the CCDR System and shall monitor its implementation to ensure consistent and appropriate application throughout the Department of Defense.

2.  The <u>Heads of DoD Components</u> shall administer and implement the CCDR System.  This responsibility shall include ensuring that an appropriate official is designated within each DoD Component to monitor the application of the CCDR System (see subsection E.7., above).

**G.  EFFECTIVE DATE AND IMPLEMENTATION**

This Instruction is effective immediately.  Forward two copies of the implementing documents both to the Assistant Secretary of Defense (Comptroller) and to the Director, Program Analysis and Evaluation, within 120 days.


Vincent Puritano                               David S.C. Chu
Assistant Secretary of Defense                      Director
(Comptroller)                        Program Analysis and Evaluation


Enclosures - 5
   1.  References
   2.  DD Form 1921, Cost Data Summary Report
   3.  DD Form 1921-1, Functional Cost-Hour Report
   4.  DD Form 1921-2, Progress Curve Report
   5.  DD Form 1921-3, Plant-Wide Data Report

REFERENCES (Continued)

(e) Military Standard 881A, "Work Breakdown Structures for Defense Materiel Items," April 25, 1975

(f) Defense Acquisition Regulation (DAR), Part 16-206.1(c), "Contract Pricing Proposal Forms"

(g) DoD Directive 4105.62, "Selection of Contractual Sources for Major Defense Systems," January 6, 1976

(h) Defense Contract Audit Manual (CAM), "Audit Procedures--DoD Resource Management Systems," Paragraph 9-108.10[1]

---

[1] Available from the Defense Contract Audit Agency, Cameron Station, Alexandria, Virginia 22314.

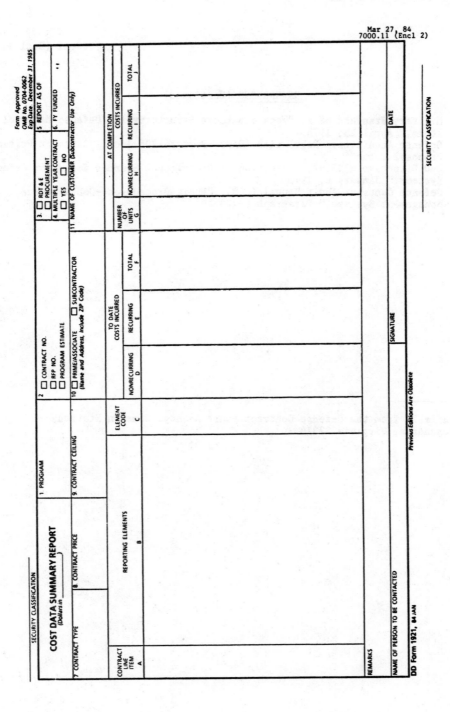

Mar 27, 84
7000.11 (Encl 3)

Form Approved
OMB No. 0704-0062
Exp Date: December 31, 1985

| SECURITY CLASSIFICATION | | | | | | |
|---|---|---|---|---|---|---|

**FUNCTIONAL COST-HOUR REPORT**   1. PROGRAM     2. REPORT AS OF

**SECTION A**

3. DOLLARS IN     4. HOURS IN     5. ☐ CONTRACT / ☐ RFP NO.     ☐ PROGRAM ESTIMATE

6. ☐ NON-RECURRING   ☐ RECURRING   ☐ TOTAL     7. ☐ RDT&E   ☐ PROCUREMENT   ☐ OTHER

8. MULTIPLE YEAR CONTRACT   ☐ YES   ☐ NO     10. ☐ PRIME/ASSOCIATE   ☐ SUBCONTRACTOR *(Name and address; include ZIP Code)*     11 NAME OF CUSTOMER *(Subcontractor Use Only)*

9. FY FUNDED

12. REPORTING ELEMENT(S)

| FUNCTIONAL CATEGORIES | ADJUSTMENTS TO PREVIOUS REPORTS A | CONTRACTOR | | SUBCONTRACT OR OUTSIDE PROD AND SERV | | TOTAL | |
|---|---|---|---|---|---|---|---|
| | | TO DATE B | AT COMPL. C | TO DATE D | AT COMPL. E | TO DATE F | AT COMPL. G |
| **ENGINEERING** | | | | | | | |
| 1  DIRECT LABOR HOURS | | | | | | | |
| 2  DIRECT LABOR DOLLARS | $ | $ | $ | $ | $ | $ | $ |
| 3  OVERHEAD | $ | $ | $ | $ | $ | $ | $ |
| 4  MATERIAL | $ | $ | $ | $ | $ | $ | $ |
| 5  OTHER DIRECT CHARGES *(Specify)* | $ | $ | $ | $ | $ | $ | $ |
| 6  TOTAL ENGINEERING DOLLARS | $ | $ | $ | $ | $ | $ | $ |
| **TOOLING** | | | | | | | |
| 7  DIRECT LABOR HOURS | | | | | | | |
| 8  DIRECT LABOR DOLLARS | $ | $ | $ | $ | $ | $ | $ |
| 9  OVERHEAD | $ | $ | $ | $ | $ | $ | $ |
| 10  MATERIALS AND PURCHASED TOOLS | $ | $ | $ | $ | $ | $ | $ |
| 11  OTHER DIRECT CHARGES *(Specify)* | $ | $ | $ | $ | $ | $ | $ |
| 12  TOTAL TOOLING DOLLARS | $ | $ | $ | $ | $ | $ | $ |
| **QUALITY CONTROL** | | | | | | | |
| 13  DIRECT LABOR HOURS | | | | | | | |
| 14  DIRECT LABOR DOLLARS | $ | $ | $ | $ | $ | $ | $ |
| 15  OVERHEAD | $ | $ | $ | $ | $ | $ | $ |
| 16  OTHER DIRECT CHARGES *(Specify)* | $ | $ | $ | $ | $ | $ | $ |
| 17  TOTAL QUALITY CONTROL DOLLARS | $ | $ | $ | $ | $ | $ | $ |
| **MANUFACTURING** | | | | | | | |
| 18  DIRECT LABOR HOURS | | | | | | | |
| 19  DIRECT LABOR DOLLARS | $ | $ | $ | $ | $ | $ | $ |
| 20  OVERHEAD | $ | $ | $ | $ | $ | $ | $ |
| 21  MATERIALS AND PURCHASED PARTS | $ | $ | $ | $ | $ | $ | $ |
| 22  OTHER DIRECT CHARGES *(Specify)* | $ | $ | $ | $ | $ | $ | $ |
| 23  TOTAL MANUFACTURING DOLLARS | $ | $ | $ | $ | $ | $ | $ |
| 24  PURCHASED EQUIPMENT | $ | $ | $ | $ | $ | $ | $ |
| 25  MATERIAL OVERHEAD | $ | $ | $ | $ | $ | $ | $ |
| 26  OTHER COSTS NOT SHOWN ELSEWHERE *(Specify)* | $ | $ | $ | $ | $ | $ | $ |
| 27  TOTAL COST LESS G & A | $ | $ | $ | $ | $ | $ | $ |
| 28  G & A | $ | | | $ | $ | $ | $ |
| 29  TOTAL COST PLUS G & A | $ | | | $ | $ | $ | $ |
| 30  FEE OR PROFIT | $ | | | $ | $ | $ | $ |
| 31  TOTAL OF LINES 29 AND 30 | $ | | | $ | $ | $ | $ |

**SECTION B**

**SECTION C**  *Cat II only*

DIRECT LABOR MAN-HOURS INCURRED THIS REPORT PERIOD

| | ENGINEERING A | TOOLING B | QUALITY CONTROL C | MANUFACTURING D |
|---|---|---|---|---|
| 1  TOTAL BEGINNING OF REPORT PERIOD | | | | |
| 2 | | | | |
| 3. | | | | |
| 4. | | | | |
| 5. | | | | |
| 6  TOTAL END OF REPORT PERIOD | | | | |

FORM CONTINUED ON REVERSE

DD Form 1921-1, 84 JAN          *Previous editions are obsolete*

SECURITY CLASSIFICATION

PLANT-WIDE LABOR AND OVERHEAD INFORMATION

| | | 1. DIRECT LABOR | | | 2. PLTWIDE OH | | 1. DIRECT LABOR | | | 2. PLTWIDE OH | | 1. DIRECT LABOR | | | 2. PLTWIDE OH | |
|---|---|---|---|---|---|---|---|---|---|---|---|---|---|---|---|---|
| | | WORK A | BASIC RATE B | EFF RATE C | IND WORK D | RATE E | WORK F | BASIC RATE G | EFF RATE H | IND WORK I | RATE K | WORK L | BASIC RATE M | EFF RATE N | IND WORK P | RATE Q |
| S E C T I O N  D . C a t  II  O n l y | 1. ENGINEERING | | | | | | | | | | | | | | | |
| | 2. TOOLING | | | | | | | | | | | | | | | |
| | A. DESIGN | | | | | | | | | | | | | | | |
| | B. FABRICATION | | | | | | | | | | | | | | | |
| | 3. QUALITY CONTROL | | | | | | | | | | | | | | | |
| | 4. MANUFACTURING | | | | | | | | | | | | | | | |
| | 5. MATERIAL | | | | | | | | | | | | | | | |
| | 6. G & A | | | | | | | | | | | | | | | |

| | | 1. DIRECT LABOR | | | 2. PLTWIDE OH | | 1. DIRECT LABOR | | | 2. PLTWIDE OH | | 1. DIRECT LABOR | | | 2. PLTWIDE OH | |
|---|---|---|---|---|---|---|---|---|---|---|---|---|---|---|---|---|
| | | WORK A | BASIC RATE B | EFF RATE C | IND WORK D | RATE E | WORK F | BASIC RATE G | EFF RATE H | IND WORK I | RATE K | WORK L | BASIC RATE M | EFF RATE N | IND WORK P | RATE Q |
| | 1. ENGINEERING | | | | | | | | | | | | | | | |
| | 2. TOOLING | | | | | | | | | | | | | | | |
| | A. DESIGN | | | | | | | | | | | | | | | |
| | B. FABRICATION | | | | | | | | | | | | | | | |
| | 3. QUALITY CONTROL | | | | | | | | | | | | | | | |
| | 4. MANUFACTURING | | | | | | | | | | | | | | | |
| | 5. MATERIAL | | | | | | | | | | | | | | | |
| | 6. G & A | | | | | | | | | | | | | | | |

REMARKS

| NAME OF PERSON TO BE CONTACTED | SIGNATURE | DATE |
|---|---|---|
| | | |

DD Form 1921-1 Reverse, 84 JAN

SECURITY CLASSIFICATION

Mar 27, 84
7000.11 (Encl 4)

Form Approved
OMB No. 0704-0062
Exp Date: December 31, 1985

| PROGRESS CURVE REPORT (Recurring Cost Only) | 1 PROGRAM | | |
|---|---|---|---|

| SECTION A | 2. DOLLARS IN | 3. HOURS IN | 5. CONTRACT NO. | 6. REPORT FOR ___ MONTHS ENDING _____ |
|---|---|---|---|---|

4. TOTAL CUMULATIVE UNITS ACCEPTED AS OF LAST REPORT

7. MULTIPLE YEAR CONTRACT  ☐ YES  ☐ NO
8. FY FUNDED

9. ☐ PRIME/ASSOCIATE  ☐ SUBCONTRACTOR (Name and address; include ZIP Code)

10. NAME OF CUSTOMER (Subcontractor Use Only)

11. REPORTING ELEMENT(S)

| ITEM | UNITS / LOTS ACCEPTED | | | | | ESTIMATE OF NEXT UNIT / LOT TO BE ACCEPTED | TO COMPLETE CONTRACT |
|---|---|---|---|---|---|---|---|
| | A | B | C | D | E | F | G |
| 1. MODEL AND SERIES | | | | | | | |
| 2. FIRST UNIT OF LOT | | | | | | | |
| 3. LAST UNIT OF LOT | | | | | | | |
| 4. CONCURRENT UNITS | | | | | | | |
| CHARACTERISTICS 5. 6. 7. | | | | | | | |
| CONTRACTOR DATA (Per Unit / Lot) | | | | | | | |
| 8. DIRECT QUALITY CONTROL MAN-HOURS | | | | | | | |
| 9. DIRECT MANUFACTURING MAN-HOURS | | | | | | | |
| 10. QUALITY CONTROL DIRECT LABOR DOLLARS | $ | $ | $ | $ | $ | $ | $ |
| 11. MANUFACTURING DIRECT LABOR DOLLARS | $ | $ | $ | $ | $ | $ | $ |
| 12. RAW MATERIAL & PURCHASED PARTS DOLLARS | $ | $ | $ | $ | $ | $ | $ |
| 13. PURCHASED EQUIPMENT DOLLARS | $ | $ | $ | $ | $ | $ | $ |
| 14. TOTAL DOLLARS | $ | $ | $ | $ | $ | $ | $ |
| SUBCONTRACT / OUTSIDE PROD. & SERV | | | | | | | |
| 15. DIRECT QUALITY CONTROL MAN-HOURS | | | | | | | |
| 16. DIRECT MANUFACTURING MAN-HOURS | | | | | | | |
| 17. TOTAL MAN-HOURS | | | | | | | |
| 18. QUALITY CONTROL DIRECT LABOR DOLLARS | $ | $ | $ | $ | $ | $ | $ |
| 19. MANUFACTURING DIRECT LABOR DOLLARS | $ | $ | $ | $ | $ | $ | $ |
| 20. RAW MATERIAL & PURCHASED PARTS DOLLARS | $ | $ | $ | $ | $ | $ | $ |
| 21. PURCHASED EQUIPMENT DOLLARS | $ | $ | $ | $ | $ | $ | $ |
| 22. TOTAL DOLLARS | $ | $ | $ | $ | $ | $ | $ |
| UNIT TOTAL ☐ AVERAGE ☐ | | | | | | | |
| 23. DIRECT QUALITY CONTROL MAN-HOURS | | | | | | | |
| 24. DIRECT MANUFACTURING MAN-HOURS | | | | | | | |
| 25. TOTAL MAN-HOURS | | | | | | | |
| 26. QUALITY CONTROL DIRECT LABOR DOLLARS | $ | $ | $ | $ | $ | $ | $ |
| 27. MANUFACTURING DIRECT LABOR DOLLARS | $ | $ | $ | $ | $ | $ | $ |
| 28. RAW MATERIAL & PURCHASED PARTS DOLLARS | $ | $ | $ | $ | $ | $ | $ |
| 29. PURCHASED EQUIPMENT DOLLARS | $ | $ | $ | $ | $ | $ | $ |
| 30. TOTAL DOLLARS | $ | $ | $ | $ | $ | $ | $ |
| 31. % SUBCONTRACT OR OUTSIDE PROD. & SERV. | | | | | | | |
| MFG FLOW TIME | | | | | | | |
| M O S O R Q T R S | 32. START | | | | | | |
| | 33. FINISH | | | | | | |
| | 34. | | | | | | |
| | 35. | | | | | | |
| | 36. | | | | | | |
| | 37. | | | | | | |
| | 38. | | | | | | |
| | 39. | | | | | | |

DD Form 1921-2, 84 JAN          Previous editions are obsolete

| ITEM : | UNITS / LOTS ACCEPTED | | | | | ESTIMATE OF NEXT UNIT / LOT TO BE ACCEPTED | TO COMPLETE CONTRACT |
|---|---|---|---|---|---|---|---|
| | A | B | .C | D | E | F | G |
| PERFORMANCE DATA *(Per Unit / Lot)* | | | | | | | |
| 40. STANDARD HOURS | | | | | | | |
| 41. VARIANCE | | | | | | | |

| SCHEDULE OF RELEASE DATES | ENGINEERING A | MATERIAL B | TOOLING C | MANUFACTURING D |
|---|---|---|---|---|
| 1. PLANNED | | | | |
| 2. ACTUAL | | | | |

REMARKS

S E C T I O N   C   . C a t   I I   O n l y .

| NAME OF PERSON TO BE CONTACTED | SIGNATURE | DATE |
|---|---|---|

**DD Form 1921-2 Reverse,** 84 JAN

4-2

Mar 27, 84
7000.11 (Encl 5)

PLANT-WIDE DATA REPORT

DD FORM 1921-3

SECURITY CLASSIFICATION

**DIRECT LABOR RATES**

| SECTION C | 1ST QUARTER | | | 2ND QUARTER | | | 3RD QUARTER | | | 4TH QUARTER | | | PAST YEAR | YEAR | YEAR |
|---|---|---|---|---|---|---|---|---|---|---|---|---|---|---|---|
| | WORKERS | BASIC RATE | EFF. RATE | WORKERS | BASIC RATE | EFF. RATE | WORKERS | BASIC RATE | EFF. RATE | WORKERS | BASIC RATE | EFF. RATE | BASIC RATE | BASIC RATE | BASIC RATE |
| 1. ENGINEERING | | | | | | | | | | | | | | | |
| 2. TOOLING | | | | | | | | | | | | | | | |
| a. DESIGN | | | | | | | | | | | | | | | |
| b. FABRICATION | | | | | | | | | | | | | | | |
| 3. QUALITY CONTROL | | | | | | | | | | | | | | | |
| 4. MANUFACTURING | | | | | | | | | | | | | | | |

REMARKS:

NAME OF PERSON TO BE CONTACTED    SIGNATURE    DATE

SECURITY CLASSIFICATION

# APPENDIX E
# The DOD JIG:
## Cost/Schedule Control
## Systems Criteria
## Joint Implementation Guide

| | |
|---|---|
| **HQ AIR FORCE SYSTEMS COMMAND PAMPHLET** | **AFSC P173-5** |
| **HQ AIR FORCE COMMUNICATIONS COMMAND PAMPHLET** | **AFCC P173-5** |
| **HQ AIR FORCE LOGISTICS COMMAND PAMPHLET** | **AFLC P173-5** |
| **HQ US ARMY MATERIEL COMMAND PAMPHLET** | **AMC- P 715-5** |
| **ASSISTANT SECRETARY OF THE NAVY (S&L) PAMPHLET** | **NAVSO P3627** |
| **DEFENSE LOGISTICS AGENCY HANDBOOK** | **DLAH 8400.2** |
| **DEFENSE CONTRACT AUDIT AGENCY PAMPHLET** | **DCAA P7641.47** |

# COST/SCHEDULE CONTROL
# SYSTEMS CRITERIA
# JOINT IMPLEMENTATION GUIDE

## 1 OCTOBER 1987

**DEPARTMENTS OF THE AIR FORCE, THE ARMY, THE NAVY,
THE DEFENSE LOGISTICS AGENCY, AND THE DEFENSE CONTRACT AUDIT AGENCY**

**DEPARTMENTS OF THE AIR FORCE, THE ARMY, THE NAVY
THE DEFENSE LOGISTICS AGENCY, AND THE DEFENSE CONTRACT AUDIT AGENCY**

| | |
|---|---|
| Headquarters Air Force Systems Command<br>Andrews Air Force Base, DC 20334-5000 | AFSC   PAMPHLET  173-5 |
| Headquarters Air Force Communications Command<br>Scott Air Force Base, IL 62225-5280 | AFCC   PAMPHLET  173-5 |
| Headquarters Air Force Logistics Command<br>Wright-Patterson Air Force Base, OH 45433-5001 | AFLC   PAMPHLET  173-5 |
| Headquarters Army Materiel Command<br>Alexandria VA 22333-0001 | AMC    PAMPHLET  715-5 |
| Assistant Secretary of the Navy (S&L)<br>Washington DC 20360-5000 | NAVSO PAMPHLET  3627 |
| Headquarters Defense Logistics Agency<br>Cameron Station, Alexandria VA 22314-6100 | DLA    HANDBOOK  8400.2 |
| Headquarters Defense Contract Audit Agency<br>Cameron Station, Alexandria VA 22304-6178 | DCAA PAMPHLET  7641.47<br>**1 OCTOBER 1987** |

**COST/SCHEDULE CONTROL SYSTEMS CRITERIA
JOINT IMPLEMENTATION GUIDE
for
DOD INSTRUCTION 7000.2, "Performance Measurement for Selected Acquisitions"**

**Purpose:** This guide provides the uniform procedures which have been approved by AFSC, AFCC, AFLC, AMC, ASN(S&L), DLA, and DCAA during planning and implementation of the DoD Cost/Schedule Control Systems Criteria (C/SCSC) and for surveillance of contractor compliance. Users of this guide are encouraged to submit recommendations for refined procedures, through channels, to appropriate DoD component focal points.

**TABLE OF CONTENTS**

|  | PARAGRAPH | PAGE |
|---|---|---|

---

Supersedes AFSCP/AFLCP 173-5, DARCOM-P715-5, NAVMAT P5240, DLAH 8315.2, 1 Oct 1980. (See signature page for summary of changes.)
OPR:        AFSC/ACC
            AFCC/ACC
            AFLC/ACC
            AMC/AMCRM-K
            ASN (S&L)/CBM
            DLA/AE
            DCAA/OPD

**Distribution:**   See inside back cover.

i

THE DEPUTY SECRETARY OF DEFENSE

WASHINGTON, D.C. 20301

10 July 1986

MEMORANDUM FOR SECRETARIES OF THE MILITARY DEPARTMENTS
                    UNDERSECRETARY OF DEFENSE FOR RESEARCH AND
                        ENGINEERING
                    ASSISTANT SECRETARY OF DEFENSE (ACQUISITION AND
                        LOGISTICS)
                    COMMANDANT, DEFENSE SYSTEMS MANAGEMENT COLLEGE

SUBJECT:  Cost/Schedule Control Systems Criteria (C/SCSC)

     A survey conducted for the Assistant Secretary of Defense
(Comptroller) on C/SCSC implementation within DoD and industry
revealed an inadequate understanding of C/SCSC and Cost
Performance Reports (CPR) by people who do not have day-to-day
involvement in those areas.  The survey report recommended that
a "white paper" be prepared, addressed both to government and
contractor program managers and their higher level managers.

     Survey findings overwhelmingly endorsed C/SCSC as a valid
concept and approach to controlling contract performance.  When
dissatisfaction was expressed, it almost universally was based
on expectations that C/SCSC could provide information it was
never designed or expected to produce, or on requirements for
excessive reporting detail.  Consequently, substantial emphasis
was placed on clarifying the objectives and purpose of C/SCSC,
and on the need for improving understanding between government
and industry.

     A copy of the paper is attached.  It is intended to achieve
better understanding of the different purposes and needs of DoD
and its contractors relative to C/SCSC, and of what C/SCSC and
the associated CPRs can and cannot do.  The paper will be
included as a preface in an upcoming revision to the C/SCSC
Joint Implementation Guide.  Please distribute the paper
widely, including all current and future programs with
contracts subject to C/SCSC, their contractors, and Defense
schools with acquisition management curricula.

                                      William H. Taft, IV

Attachment

AFSC/AFCC/AFLC-P173-5    AMC-P 715-5    NAVSO-P3627    DLAH 8400.2    DCAA-P7641.47

PREFACE

C/SCSC WHITE PAPER

**INTRODUCTION.** DoD Instruction 7000.2, "Performance Measurement for Selected Acquisitions," first issued in 1967, requires that on major contracts, contractors use management control systems meeting the Cost/Schedule Control Systems Criteria (C/SCSC or CS[2]). C/SCSC can be controversial. While many experienced program and business managers in both government and industry are sold on its benefits, other equally experienced managers consider it a burdensome requirement that generates excessive data. This paper summarizes the objectives of C/SCSC and the associated cost performance reports, and what can and cannot be expected from their use.

**C/SCSC OBJECTIVES AND PURPOSE.**
The objectives of C/SCSC are:
• For contractors to use effective internal cost and schedule management control systems, and
• For the Government to be able to rely on timely and auditable data produced by those systems for determining product-oriented contract status.
*Both objectives are essential.* However, Government managers should recognize that effective contractor management does not in itself require product-oriented cost reporting in addition to cost reporting by contractor organization. On the other hand, contractors should recognize the Government's need for such information on contracts that involve substantial cost risk to the Government. Differences arising from these divergent needs, such as the level of reporting detail required, should be discussed during contract negotiations. The criteria are not subject to negotiation, but many problems concerning timing of C/SCSC implementation and reporting requirements can be avoided or minimized through negotiation.
*C/SCSC is not a system!* It is a set of criteria designed to define an adequate contractor cost and schedule management control system. Changes to an existing system are required only to the extent that the system does not meet the criteria. The criteria do not purport to address all of a contractor's needs for day-to-day or week-to-week internal control, such as informal communications, internal status reports, reviews, and similar management tools. These management tools are important and are not intended to be replaced by C/SCSC requirements. The basic purpose is to assure that the contractor has in place, and uses, adequate cost and schedule control systems providing reliable contract status at least monthly.

**C/SCSC REQUIREMENTS.** C/SCSC improves on the budget vs. actuals (or "spend plan") management technique by requiring that actual work progress be quantified through "earned value," an objective measure of how much work has been accomplished on the contract. Without earned value, one can only compare how much has been spent with what was planned to be spent, with no objective indication of how much of the planned work was actually accomplished. C/SCSC require the contractor to plan, budget, and schedule authorized effort in time-phased "planned value" increments constituting a performance measurement baseline (time-phased budget). As work is accomplished, it is "earned" on the same budget dollar basis. Earned value compared with planned value provides a measure of work accomplishment against plan, called a schedule variance.

The contractor's accounting systems provide accumulation of actual cost of accomplished work, which is compared with earned value, providing a cost variance for the accomplished work and indicating whether the work is over, or underrunning its plan. Planned value, earned value, and actual cost data provide an objective measure of performance, enabling trend analysis and evaluation of cost estimates at completion at all levels of the contract.

In addition to earned value, C/SCSC requires thorough planning, baseline establishment and control, information broken down by product as well as by organization or function, measurement of accomplishment against the plan at relatively low levels with summarized reporting to higher management, reporting discipline, variance analysis, and corrective action. These are all desirable features of a good management control system.

AFSC/AFCC/AFLC-P173-5     AMC-P 715-5      NAVSO-P3627      DLAH 8400.2      DCAA-P7641.47

*CISCSC requirements have been over-whelmingly acknowledged by both Government and industry managers as representing good management principles.* The extent of effort needed for a contractor to meet these requirements depends on how much change, if any, is needed for the existing systems to meet the criteria.

**BASELINE IMPLEMENTATION.** An initial and critical contractor step in applying C/SCSC to a contract is establishing the baseline for performance measurement. *The work involved in establishing a baseline may be substantial, but must not be avoided or delayed because valid cost data depend on it. It should be planned during the proposal phase and completed as soon as possible after contract award.*

When the contract is awarded, internal documentation must be updated and work planned in detail. Work authorizations, schedules, and budgets must be negotiated between the contractor program office and the various functional organizations and managers who are responsible for accomplishing the work. This process can be time-consuming, but is necessary to develop a baseline that is meaningful for internal control. Some additional time also may be needed to verify the data produced after the baseline is negotiated. *The time required by the contractor to complete these tasks and be prepared to demonstrate compliance with CISCSC may be negotiated if it is likely to exceed the time specified in the standard CISCSC contract clause.*

The desired result is a timely, well planned and realistic baseline for controlling internal performance and for reporting valid contract status information to the Government.

**RELATIONSHIP TO CONTRACTUAL SCHEDULES.** The C/SCSC performance measurement baseline represents the contractor's internal work plan, the dollarized schedule for performing the contract effort, and may allow a "cushion" with respect to the contract delivery schedules. These cushion (or "setback") schedules anticipate typical problems such as late vendor deliveries and rework. If not understood, setback schedules can cause confusion because a negative schedule variance would not affect contract deliveries if the cushion can absorb the delay.

*A CISCSC schedule variance is stated in terms of dollars' worth of work and must be analyzed in conjunction with other schedule information such as provided by networks, Gantt charts, and line-of-balance.* By itself, the C/SCSC schedule variance reveals no "critical path" information, and may be misleading because unfavorable accomplishment in some areas can be offset by favorable accomplishment in others. *A CISCSC schedule variance is an "accomplishment variance" that provides an early indicator of cost problems when it shows the contractor is not meeting the internal work plan.* Further analysis must be performed to determine the effect on contract cost and schedule.

**MANAGEMENT SYSTEM ACCEPTANCE.** Contractors are required to demonstrate to the Government that their cost- and schedule management control systems comply with the criteria. A comprehensive demonstration review is required once for R&D effort and once for production; shorter subsequent application reviews (SARs) are conducted for follow-on contracts requiring compliance with C/SCSC *Because the criteria approach permits a wide variety of equally effective ways for contractors to meet the criteria, trained, experienced Government people are used to conduct the reviews and follow-on surveillance. Similarly, contractors need skilled people to develop, maintain, and monitor their systems.*

C/SCSC review reports are usually coordinated among the Military Departments, resulting in triservice acceptance (or "validation") of contractors' systems. Along with frequent meetings of the DoD component C/SCSC focal points, this coordination helps to ensure uniform criteria interpretations.

**REPORTING.** There are no explicit external reporting requirements in the C/SCSC. The criteria require that contractors have and use effective <u>internal</u> control systems. *Summary data from the internal system are reported to the Government through the Cost Performance Report (CPR), as specified on the Contract Data Requirements List.* The CPR has five formats, which provide cost and schedule performance data broken down both by product (work breakdown structure) and by contractor functional organizations; baseline information; planned vs. actual manpower usage; and problem analysis. The problem analysis section is also used to reconcile the dollar-based CPR schedule information and actual time-based schedules.

The CPR is almost always submitted monthly, and is intended to report summary information from the contractor's internal cost and schedule control system. *Summary reporting suffices because C/SCSC discipline assures that the contractor uses objective performance measurement information to manage at levels where work is performed, allowing management attention to be directed to areas where significant problems are indicated.* When a problem area surfaces in a CPR, detailed data may be requested until the problem is resolved. It is important to recognize that CPR frequency, reporting levels, variance analysis thresholds, and formats are all subject to negotiation, and any needed adjustments in these areas may be proposed by either party during contract execution.

In addition to earned value, two important CPR data elements are the estimated cost at completion (EAC) and management reserve. *The EAC is of prime interest and must be updated periodically by the contractor using approved procedures,* including evaluation of cost and schedule variance trends along with information from other management tools. *Management reserve is an amount of the contract budget set aside by the contractor for management control purposes,* such as for use in performing unanticipated tasks that are within the scope of the contract. It is not a contingency fund, and may neither be eliminated from contract prices by the Government during subsequent negotiations nor used to absorb the cost of contract changes.

**CPR TIMELINESS.** Typically, the CPR is submitted about 25 days after the close of the contractor's accounting month. That time is needed to accumulate, verify and correct data, analyze significant variances, and prepare reports. Although 25 days may appear excessive to some recipients, *the CPR is timely for its intended purposes -- to provide an objective indication of contract status, a basis for observing trends, and formal communication between contractor and Government managers.* Negotiation with the contractor may result in shorter submission time, using such techniques as submitting the data first and analysis later, or substituting contractor internal formats provided they contain adequate data in a form suitable for use by Government managers.

**USE OF CPR.** The CPR, like C/SCSC, is no substitute for day-to-day contract management or communication between the contractor and the Government program manager. *The CPR may not reveal many new problems, but within the Government program office it is valuable for confirming and quantifying the problems reported by the contractor's functional managers.* For example, a CPR would confirm a previously anticipated schedule slippage or previously known technical problem, allowing analysis of the effect on current and future contract cost and schedule.

Government program offices also use CPRs to monitor cost and schedule variance trends and to project the trends to contract completion to determine the validity of EACs and completion dates. In addition, CPRs are used to correlate contract cost performance with program financial planning by verifying funding requirements identified by contractors on the Contract Funds Status Report.

Above the Government program office level, CPRs are used as the basis for various management oversight reports. CPRs are not provided routinely above the major command level in the Military Departments, but data summarized from the CPRs are used in periodic program status reports to higher headquarters including the Office of the Secretary of Defense (OSD), and Congress. *This high-level interest reflects awareness that it is necessary to assess whether overall program schedules and budgets are reasonable.* Graphic portrayal of CPR data from contractor systems accepted under C/SCSC is a key feature of the Military Department and OSD reporting systems.

**C/SCSC IMPLEMENTATION PROBLEMS.** Typical points of contention between the Government and industry concerning C/SCSC implementation include time required to implement, levels designated for management and reporting, variance analysis thresholds, and system discipline requirements. These are not a direct result of the criteria, but can affect the cost of implementing and operating a C/SCSC compliant management system. The cost of C/SCSC, sometimes perceived to be excessive, has defied quantification because it is virtually impossible to

**AFSC/AFCC/AFLC-P173-5    AMC-P 715-5    NAVSO-P3627    DLAH 8400.2    DCAA-P7641.47**

separate the incremental C/SCSC cost from the management cost that would be incurred in any case  However, there is no dispute that improper implementation imposes an unnecessary burden on the contractor

*Reasons for improper implementation include overreaction to CISCSC and CPR requirements by contractors  as well as excessive Government contractual and review requirements. In most cases, improved communication can correct these problems.* Government C/SCSC specialists should review solicitations for appropriate work breakdown structure, C/SCSC, and cost performance reporting requirements. Contract negotiations should include discussion of implementation schedules, reporting levels, and variance analysis thresholds. When a contractor believes changes are necessary, they should be brought to the procuring agency's attention. After contract award, certain revisions can also be made. For example, variance analysis thresholds may be adjusted if they generate too much problem analysis narrative.

When a contractor has a C/SCSC implementation problem and is unable to resolve it with the procuring agency, an appeal may be made to the DoD component C/SCSC focal point. Failing resolution at that level, further appeal to the Performance Measurement Joint Executive Group is possible.

**COST/SCHEDULE STATUS REPORT.** On smaller contracts that do not require the contractor to comply with C/SCSC, the Cost/Schedule Status Report (C/SSR) approach to performance measurement may be used. *The CISSR is similar to the first format of the CPR, and like the CPR has a narrative problem analysis section, but the data required are not as extensive and the contractor is not subject to the in-depth demonstration reviews or management system acceptance associated with CISCSC.* The manner in which C/SSR data are generated is subject to negotiation and inclusion as part of the contract.

The C/SSR may be required as an alternative on large contracts for which C/SCSC compliance is not considered mandatory. In this case, the DoD component may conduct a more detailed C/SSR review, but the administrative and reporting effort both for Government and the contractor is less than with C/SCSC or CPR requirements.

**CONCLUSION.** *CISCSC provide the best tool available to assure that contractors have and use adequate cost and schedule management control systems.* They provide better overall planning and control discipline on defense contracts. The associated Cost Performance Report summarizes objective data from contractors' internal systems for contractor and Government managers The C/SCSC and CPR requirements have proved their value over many years. *Real improvements in contract management can be achieved by top-level attention to developing and using good cost and schedule management control systems and by taking timely corrective action when a problem is identified.* Problems are corrected by management decisions. A C/SCSC-compliant system can ensure that valid cost and schedule performance data are generated, easing the manager's task in making the correct decision.

**AFSC/AFCC/AFLC-P173-5          AMC-P 715-5          NAVSO-P3627          DLAH 8400.2          DCAA-P7641.47**

Chapter I

INTRODUCTION

**1-1.   Purpose:**
   **a.   Uniform Guidance.**   This pamphlet provides uniform guidance for the military departments and other Defense agencies (hereafter referred to as DoD components) responsible for implementation of the Cost/Schedule Control Systems Criteria (C/SCSC) consistent with the provisions of DoD Instruction 7000.2, Performance Measurement for Selected Acquisitions. Contents were developed jointly by AFSC, AFCC, AFLC, AMC, ASN(S&L), DCAA, and DLA. Within this guide the term "criteria" is synonymous with "C/SCSC." The term "performance" means "cost/schedule performance." Procedural guidance for surveillance of Cost/Schedule Control Systems is provided in the C/SCSC Joint Surveillance Guide (AMC-P 715-10, NAVMAT P5243, AFLC/AFSC P173-6, DLAH 8315.1, and DCAA P7641.46).
   **b.   Implementation:**
      (1) Uniform implementation of the criteria consistent with this guidance will avoid imposing multiple cost and schedule systems on contractors. When management control systems acceptable to both the contractor and DoD components are applied to Defense contracts at a given contractor's facility, the systems will provide a common source of information required by all management levels of the Government and the contractor. Supplemental instructions issued by individual DoD components to provide additional guidance will be consistent with this pamphlet.
      (2) The criteria are intended to be general, to permit their use in evaluating contractors' management control systems for development, construction, and production contracts. Since these types of contracts tend to differ significantly, it is impossible to provide detailed guidance which will apply specifically in all cases. Users of the criteria should be alert for areas in which distinctions in detailed interpretations seem appropriate or reasonable, whether or not they are specifically identified. Use of the criteria must be based on common sense, which means that the interpretations must be practical as well as sensitive to the overall requirements for performance measurement.
   **c.   Assistance to Users.** These procedures provide a basis to assist--
      (1) DoD managers in assessing the acceptability of contractors' systems in response to the criteria.
      (2) Contractors in understanding and responding to the criteria.

**1-2.   Background:**
   **a.   Management Needs.** A fundamental responsibility in the acquisition and modification of major systems is to ensure that visibility of contractors' progress is sufficient for management purposes. In carrying out this responsibility in selected contracts

within applicable Defense programs, DoD receives and reviews cost and schedule performance data. These data must--
      (1) relate time-phased budgets to specific contract tasks and/or statements of work;
      (2) indicate work progress;
      (3) properly relate cost, schedule and technical accomplishment;
      (4) be valid, timely, and auditable;
      (5) supply DoD managers with information at a practical level of summarization; and
      (6) be derived from the same internal management control systems used by the contractor to manage the contract.
   **b.   Criteria Concept.** No single set of management control systems will meet every DoD and contractor management data need for performance measurement. Due to variations in organizations, products, and working relationships, it is not feasible to prescribe a universal system for cost and schedule controls. DoD has adopted an approach which simply defines the criteria that contractors' management control systems must meet. The criteria provide the basis for determining whether contractors' management control systems are acceptable.
      (1) The responsibility for developing and applying the specific procedures for complying with these criteria is vested in the contractors. The specific management control systems they propose are subject to DoD acceptance. In instances where the contractors' systems do not meet the criteria, adjustments necessary to achieve compliance will be required by the procuring activity.
      (2) By applying criteria, rather than specific DoD prescribed management control systems, contractors have the latitude and flexibility for meeting their unique management needs. This approach allows contractors to use existing management control systems or other systems of their choice, provided they meet the criteria.
      (3) When the solicitation document (request for proposal, request for quotation, and the like) specifies application of the criteria, an element in the evaluation of proposals will be the prospective contractor's proposed systems for planning and controlling contract performance. The prospective contractor will describe the systems to be used in sufficient detail to permit their evaluation for compliance with the criteria (appendix A).
      (4) Upon award of the contract, the contractor will be required to have a comprehensive description of the management control systems and to demonstrate to a Government C/SCSC review team their effective application in planning and controlling the work under

| Typical C/SCSC Action Items (See Chapter 5) | ACTION AGENCY | |
| --- | --- | --- |
| | DoD | Contractor |
| 1. Criteria specified in solicitation  (DFARS Clause) | X | |
| 2. Description of system submitted in proposals. | | X |
| 3. Evaluation of system description in proposals. | X | |
| 4. Source Selection Evaluation Board (SSEB) considers findings of evaluation review. | X | |
| 5. Criteria requirement in contract  (DFARS Clause) | X | |
| 6. C/SCSC Review Team is organized. | X | |
| 7. Implementation visit/readiness assessment. | X | X |
| 8. Demonstrates management control systems. | | X |
| 9. Determines compliance.[1] | X | |
| 10. Official acceptance.[2] | X | |
| 11. Continuous surveillance.[2] | X | |
| 12. Continuous operation of systems meeting criteria. | | X |

NOTES:    1. After contractor corrects any deficiencies the DoD team reexamines those areas.
          2. Demonstration may be required for major changes after acceptance.

Figure 1-1 Typical Actions for C/SCSC Implementation

the contract. DoD relies on the contractor's systems when they are accepted and does not superimpose duplicative planning and control systems (appendix B).

(5) Contractors having systems previously accepted are encouraged to maintain the essential elements and disciplines of the systems if they intend to remain in the competitive environment for future defense contracts involving large acquisition programs.

c. **Typical Actions.** This guide contains general procedures which may be adapted to specific situations as they arise. Details concerning each implementation will be developed by the procuring activity responsible for the contracts and be consistent with the guidance contained here and in DoDI 7000.2. A matrix of the overall process is provided in figure 1-1

**1-3. Joint Participation:**

a. **DoD Components.** Successful application of the criteria requires the participation and coordinated efforts of various DoD components. Generally, the procuring activity is responsible for ensuring implementation of the criteria with the contractors concerned. It is mutually advantageous, however, for representatives of other interested DoD components to participate in C/SCSC reviews.

b. **Liaison.** The principal points of contact among DoD components for implementation of the criteria are identified in chapter 4. The primary functions of the representatives participating are also described. These contact points have been established to coordinate functions and monitor the activities responsible for these functions.

**1-4. Appeals.** Differences in interpretation of criteria application between Government personnel and the contractor which cannot be resolved may be appealed to the focal point (figure 4-1) for resolution. If the difference involves contractor system applications

AFSC/AFCC/AFLC-P173-5      AMC-P 715-5      NAVSO-P3627      DLAH 8400.2      DCAA-P7641.47

1-4                                                                                          1-6

concerning more than one DoD component, the appeal may be directed to the Performance Measurement Joint Executive Group (PMJEG) (figure 4-1) for resolution. Either a Government or contractor representative may initiate an appeal. Participants in the appeal have the opportunity to provide appropriate rationale, exhibits, discussion, etc., as required to support the positions. Pending resolution of appeals, the C/SCSC review team should continue to complete assessment of the contractor's compliance with the criteria or the contractor's system description as appropriate.

**1-5. Withdrawal of Acceptance.** In extreme cases, such as when a contractor has failed to maintain a previously accepted system and will not take actions to restore it to compliance with the criteria, a DoD component may consider withdrawing or suspending acceptance of the contractor's management system. When such a situation occurs, the component will advise the contractor through the cognizant Contract Administration Office that the acceptance is in jeopardy and request the contractor to "show cause" within a reasonable period of time why the acceptance should not be withdrawn, and will advise the other DoD

component focal points of its action at the same time. If the contractor disagrees with the component's position and the contractor's systems application concerns more than one DoD component, the contractor may appeal to the PMJEG. However, if the contractor does not respond satisfactorily or appeal to the PMJEG (if appropriate), the component may withdraw or suspend the acceptance after coordination with the other DoD component focal points. When an acceptance has been withdrawn or suspended, the contractor may not claim to have an accepted system until a new letter of acceptance has been issued.

**1-6. Revisions and Additions.** Persons using this guide are encouraged to submit suggestions for improvements to appropriate focal points identified in figure 4-1. Proposed revisions from outside DoD should be sent to AFSC/ACC, Andrews AFB DC 20334-5000. Proposed revisions from within DoD should be properly coordinated and approved prior to submission. Any conflict between the C/SCSC Joint Implementation and Surveillance Guides should be brought to the attention of the Performance Measurement Joint Executive Group (figure 4-1) for resolution.

AFSC/AFCC/AFLC-P173.5     AMC-P 715.5      NAVSO-P3627      DLAH 8400.2      DCAA P7641.4

Chapter 2

CRITERIA

**2-1. General Information.** When required by the contract, the system used by the contractor in planning and controlling the performance of the contract must meet the criteria set forth in paragraph 2-4. The contractor's internal systems need not be changed if they satisfy these criteria. Information required by DoD must be produced from the same system used by the contractor for internal management. DoD reporting requirements are specified separately in DD Form 1423, Contract Data Requirements List, accompanying each solicitation and in the contract (chapter 8).

**2-2. Scope:**
a. **DoD Requirements.** Compliance with the criteria as prescribed by DoDI 7000.2 is required by DoD components on significant contracts and subcontracts within major and nonmajor programs, including construction, and highly classified programs; on significant in-house activities; and on contracts executed for specialized organizations and foreign governments.
b. **DoD Component Thresholds.** Uniform contract values for mandatory application of the C/SCSC will be identified in the policies of the DoD components, as identified in figure 4-1. Application of the C/SCSC to contracts below the mandatory levels established is optional subject to the policies of the cognizant DoD component.
c. **Subcontracts.** Subcontracts will be selected for application of C/SCSC in accordance with the policies of the cognizant DoD component by mutual agreement between the prime contractor and the procuring authority, according to the criticality of the subcontract to the program (appendix B).
d. **Exceptions:**
(1) Contracts or subcontracts which are firm-fixed-price or firm-fixed-price-with-economic-price-adjustment normally will not be selected for application of C/SCSC unless fully justified on an individual basis. All other types of contracts, including fixed-price incentive, may have C/SCSC applied.
(2) There are other situations involving major contracts where the application of C/SCSC may not be necessary. In such cases, the procuring activity will forward requests for waivers, prior to releasing the request for proposal (RFP) to the DoD component focal point (figure 4-1) for approval. When waivers are granted, C/SCSC review activities will not be performed. However, contract cost performance reporting will still be required. This reporting will normally be provided via the Cost/Schedule Status Report (C/SSR) or Cost Performance Report (CPR), tailored if necessary. Examples of contractual situations where waivers of C/SCSC requirements will be considered are:
(a) Follow-on contracts within mature

production programs which are not experiencing significant cost or schedule problems and where no significant changes to the product are anticipated.
(b) Contracts to acquire items directly from production lines which currently manufacture predominantly commercial products.
(c) Contracts which consist almost entirely of level of effort (as defined in paragraph 2-3.s).
e. **Contractor Systems.** As a minimum, contractors' management control systems are expected to provide a framework for defining work, assigning work responsibility, establishing budgets, controlling costs, and summarizing, with respect to planned versus actual accomplishments, the detailed cost, schedule, and related technical achievement information for appropriate management levels. Such systems must provide for--
(1) Realistic budgets for work scheduled within responsibility assignments.
(2) Accurate accumulation of costs related to progress of the planned work.
(3) Comparison between the actual resources applied and the estimated resources planned for specific work assignments.
(4) Preparation of reliable estimates of costs to complete remaining work.
(5) Support of an overall capability for managers to analyze available information to identify problem areas in sufficient time to take remedial action.
f. **Payments.** Nothing in these criteria is intended to affect the basis on which costs are reimbursed and progress payments are made.

**2-3. Terms Explained:**
a. **Actual Cost of Work Performed (ACWP).** The costs actually incurred and recorded in accomplishing the work performed within a given time period.
b. **Actual Direct Costs.** Those costs identified specifically with a contract, based upon the contractor's cost identification and accumulation system as accepted by the cognizant Defense Contract Audit Agency (DCAA) representatives. (See Direct Costs.)
c. **Allocated Budget.** (See Total Allocated Budget.)
d. **Applied Direct Costs.** The actual direct costs recognized in the time period associated with the consumption of labor, material, and other direct resources, without regard to the date of commitment or the date of payment. These amounts are to be charged to work-in-process when any of the following takes place:
(1) Labor, material, or other direct resources are actually consumed.

AFSC/AFCC/AFLC-P173-5        AMC-P 715-5       NAVSO-P3627       DLAH 8400.2       DCAA-P7641.47
2-3d(2)                                                                                            2-3ac

(2) Material resources are withdrawn from inventory for use.

(3) Material resources are received that are uniquely identified to the contract and scheduled for use within 60 days.

(4) Major components or assemblies that are specifically and uniquely identified to a single serially numbered end item are received on a line flow basis .

e. **Apportioned Effort.** Effort that by itself is not readily divisible into short-span work packages but which is related in direct proportion to measured effort.

f. **Authorized Work.** That effort which has been definitized and is on contract plus that effort for which definitized contract costs have not been agreed to but for which written authorization has been received.

g. **Baseline.** (See Performance Measurement Baseline.)

h. **Budgeted Cost for Work Performed (BCWP).** The sum of the budgets for completed work packages and completed portions of open work packages, plus the applicable portion of the budgets for level of effort and apportioned effort.

i. **Budgeted Cost for Work Scheduled (BCWS).** The sum of the budgets for all work packages, planning packages, etc., scheduled to be accomplished (including in-process work packages), plus the amount of level of effort and apportioned effort scheduled to be accomplished within a given time period.

j. **Budgets for Work Packages.** (See Work Package Budgets.)

k. **Contract Budget Base.** The negotiated contract cost plus the estimated cost of authorized unpriced work.

l. **Contractor.** An entity in private industry which enters into contracts with the Government. In this guide, the word also applies to Government-owned, Government-operated activities which perform work on major defense programs.

m. **Cost Account.** A management control point at which actual costs can be accumulated and compared to budgeted cost of work performed. A cost account is a natural control point for cost/schedule planning and control since it represents the work assigned to one responsible organizational element on one contract work breakdown structure (CWBS) element.

n. **Direct Costs.** Any costs which can be identified specifically with a particular final cost objective. This term is explained in FAR 31.202.

o. **Estimate at Completion (EAC).** Actual direct costs, plus indirect costs allocable to the contract, plus the estimate of costs (direct and indirect) for authorized work remaining.

p. **Indirect Costs.** Costs which, because of their incurrence for common or joint objectives, are not readily subject to treatment as direct costs. This term is further defined in FAR 31.203.

q. **Initial Budget.** (See Original Budget.)

r. **Internal Replanning.** Replanning actions performed by the contractor for remaining effort within the recognized total allocated budget.

s. **Level of Effort (LOE).** Effort of a general or supportive nature which does not produce definite end products.

t. **Management Reserve.** (Synonymous with Management Reserve Budget.) An amount of the total allocated budget withheld for management control purposes rather than designated for the accomplishment of a specific task or set of tasks. It is not a part of the Performance Measurement Baseline.

u. **Negotiated Contract Cost.** The estimated cost negotiated in a cost-plus-fixed-fee contract or the negotiated contract target cost in either a fixed-price-incentive contract or a cost-plus-incentive-fee contract.

v. **Original Budget.** The budget established at, or near, the time the contract was signed, based on the negotiated contract cost.

w. **Overhead.** (See Indirect Costs.)

x. **Performance Measurement Baseline (PMB).** The time-phased budget plan against which contract performance is measured. It is formed by the budgets assigned to scheduled cost accounts and the applicable indirect budgets. For future effort, not planned to the cost account level, the performance measurement baseline also includes budgets assigned to higher level CWBS elements, and undistributed budgets. It equals the total allocated budget less management reserve.

y. **Performing Organization.** A defined unit within the contractor's organization structure, which applies the resources to perform the work.

z. **Planning Package.** A logical aggregation of work within a cost account, normally the far-term effort, that can be identified and budgeted in early baseline planning, but is not yet defined into work packages.

aa. **Procuring Activity.** The subordinate command to which the Procuring Contracting Officer (PCO) is assigned. It may include the program office, related functional support offices, and procurement offices. Examples of C/SCSC focal points/procuring activities are AFSC/ESD, AFLC/OC-ALC, AFCC/SSC, AMC/MICOM, and ASN (S&L) /NAVSEASYSCOM .

ab. **Replanning.** (See Internal Replanning.)

ac. **Reprogramming.** Replanning of the effort remaining in the contract, resulting in a new budget allocation which exceeds the contract budget base.

**ad. Responsible Organization.** A defined unit within the contractor's organization structure which is assigned responsibility for accomplishing specific tasks.

**ae. Significant Variances.** Those differences between planned and actual performance which require further review, analysis, or action. Appropriate thresholds should be established as to the magnitude of variances which will require variance analysis.

**af. Total Allocated Budget.** The sum of all budgets allocated to the contract. Total allocated budget consists of the performance measurement baseline and all management reserve. The total allocated budget will reconcile directly to the contract budget base. Any differences will be documented as to quantity and cause.

**ag. Undistributed Budget.** Budget applicable to contract effort which has not yet been identified to CWBS elements at or below the lowest level of reporting to the Government.

**ah. Variances.** (See Significant Variances.)

**ai. Work Breakdown Structure (WBS).** A product-oriented family tree division of hardware, software, services, and other work tasks which organizes, defines, and graphically displays the product to be produced as well as the work to be accomplished to achieve the specified product.

(1) Project Summary Work Breakdown Structure. A summary work breakdown structure (WBS) tailored to a specific defense material item by selecting applicable elements from one or more summary WBSs or by adding equivalent elements unique to the project in accordance with MIL-STD-881 (latest revision).

(2) Contract Work Breakdown Structure (CWBS). The complete WBS for a contract, developed and used by a contractor within the guidelines of MIL-STD-881 (latest revision) and according to the contract work statement.

**aj. Work Package Budgets.** Resources which are formally assigned by the contractor to accomplish a work package, expressed in dollars, hours, standards or other definitive units.

**ak. Work Packages.** Detailed short-span jobs, or material items, identified by the contractor for accomplishing work required to complete the contract. A work package has the following characteristics:

(1) It represents units of work at levels where work is performed.

(2) It is clearly distinguished from all other work packages.

(3) It is assignable to a single organizational element.

(4) It has scheduled start and completion dates and, as applicable, interim milestones, all of which are representative of physical accomplishment.

(5) It has a budget or assigned value expressed in terms of dollars, man-hours, or other measurable units.

(6) Its duration is limited to a relatively short span of time or it is subdivided by discrete value milestones to facilitate the objective measurement of work performed.

(7) It is integrated with detailed engineering, manufacturing, or other schedules.

**2-4. Criteria.**

The contractor's management control systems will include policies, procedures, and methods designed to ensure that they will accomplish the following:

a. **Organization:**

(1) Define all authorized work and related resources to meet the requirements of the contract, using the framework of the CWBS.

(2) Identify the internal organizational elements and the major subcontractors responsible for accomplishing the authorized work.

(3) Provide for the integration of the contractor's planning, scheduling, budgeting, work authorization and cost accumulation systems with each other, the CWBS, and the organizational structure.

(4) Identify the managerial positions responsible for controlling overhead (indirect costs).

(5) Provide for integration of the CWBS with the contractor's functional organizational structure in a manner that permits cost and schedule performance measurement for CWBS and organizational elements.

b. **Planning and Budgeting:**

(1) Schedule the authorized work in a manner which describes the sequence of work and identifies the significant task interdependencies required to meet the development, production, and delivery requirements of the contract.

(2) Identify physical products, milestones, technical performance goals, or other indicators that will be used to measure output.

(3) Establish and maintain a time-phased budget baseline at the cost account level against which contract performance can be measured. Initial budgets established for this purpose will be based on the negotiated target cost. Any other amount used for performance measurement purposes must be formally recognized by both the contractor and the Government.

(4) Establish budgets for all authorized work with separate identification of cost elements (labor, material, etc.).

(5) To the extent the authorized work can be identified in discrete, short-span work packages, establish budgets for this work in terms of dollars, hours, or other measurable units. Where the entire cost account cannot be subdivided into detailed work packages, identify the far-term effort in larger planning packages for budget and scheduling purposes.

(6) Provide that the sum of all work package budgets plus planning packages within a cost account equals the cost account budget.

(7) Identify relationships of budgets or standards in underlying work authorization systems to budgets for work packages.

(8) Identify and control level of effort activity by time-phased budgets established for this purpose. Only that effort which cannot be identified as discrete or as apportioned effort will be classed as level of effort.

(9) Establish overhead budgets for the total costs of each significant organizational component whose expenses will become indirect costs. Reflect in the contract budgets, at the appropriate level, the amounts in overhead pools that will be allocated to the contract as indirect costs.

(10) Identify management reserves and undistributed budget.

(11) Provide that the contract target cost plus the estimated cost of authorized but unpriced work is reconciled with the sum of all internal contract budgets and management reserves.

c. Accounting:

(1) Record direct costs on an applied or other acceptable basis in a formal system that is controlled by the general books of account.

(2) Summarize direct costs from cost accounts into the WBS without allocation of a single cost account to two or more WBS elements.

(3) Summarize direct costs from the cost accounts into the contractor's functional organizational elements without allocation of a single cost account to two or more organizational elements.

(4) Record all indirect costs which will be allocated to the contract.

(5) Identify the basis for allocating the cost of apportioned effort.

(6) Identify unit costs, equivalent unit costs, or lot costs, as applicable.

(7) The contractor's material accounting system will provide for--

(a) Accurate cost accumulation and assignment of costs to cost accounts in a manner consistent with the budgets using recognized, acceptable costing techniques.

(b) Determination of price variances by comparing planned versus actual commitments.

(c) Cost performance measurement at the point in time most suitable for the category of material involved, but no earlier than the time of actual receipt of material.

(d) Determination of cost variances attributable to the excess usage of material.

(e) Determination of unit or lot costs when applicable.

(f) Full accountability for all material purchased for the contract, including the residual inventory.

d. Analysis:

(1) Identify at the cost account level on a monthly basis using data from, or reconcilable with, the accounting system:

(a) Budgeted cost of work scheduled and budgeted cost of work performed.

(b) Budgeted cost of work performed and applied (actual where appropriate) direct costs for the same work.

(c) Variances resulting from the above comparisons classified in terms of labor, material, or other appropriate elements together with the reasons for significant variances.

(2) Identify on a monthly basis, in detail needed by management for effective control, budgeted indirect costs, actual indirect costs, and variances along with the reasons.

(3) Summarize the data elements and associated variances listed in (1) and (2) above, through the contractor organization and WBS to the reporting level specified in the contract.

(4) Identify significant differences on a monthly basis between planned and actual schedule accomplishment and the reasons.

(5) Identify managerial actions taken as a result of criteria items (1) through (4) above.

(6) Based on performance to date, on commitment values for material, and on estimates of future conditions, develop revised estimates of cost at completion for WBS elements identified in the contract and compare these with the contract budget base and the latest statement of funds requirements reported to the Government.

e. Revisions and Access to Data:

(1) Incorporate contractual changes in a timely manner, recording the effects of such changes in budgets and schedules. In the directed effort before negotiation of a change, base such revisions on the amount estimated and budgeted to the functional organization.

(2) Reconcile original budgets for those elements of the WBS identified as priced line items in the contract, and for those elements at the lowest level of the DoD program WBS, with current performance measurement budgets in terms of (a) changes to the authorized work and (b) internal replanning in the detail needed by management for effective control.

(3) Prohibit retroactive changes to records pertaining to work performed that will change previously reported amounts for direct costs, indirect costs, or budgets, except for correction of errors and routine accounting adjustments.

(4) Prevent revisions to the contract budget base (paragraph 2-3k) except for Government-directed changes to contractual effort.

**AFSC/AFCC/AFLC-P173-5**     **AMC-P 715-5**     **NAVSO-P3627**     **DLAH 8400.2**     **DCAA-P7641.47**
2-4e(5)                                                                                                         2-4e(6)

(5) Document internally, changes to the performance measurement baseline (paragraph 2-3x) and notify the procuring activity expeditiously through prescribed procedures.

(6) Provide the contracting officer and the contracting officer's authorized representatives with access to the information and supporting documents necessary to demonstrate compliance with the C/SCSC

**NOTE:** Paragraphs 2-2a, 2-3, and 2-4 are to be revised to achieve consistency with any revision to DoD Instruction 7000.2.

Chapter 3

CRITERIA DISCUSSION

**3-1.    General Information.** This    chapter    is devoted to a discussion of C/SCSC. The explanations and interpretations in this guide are intended to ensure a uniform and consistent  implementation of perform-ance measurement requirements.    This chapter is intended to clarify DoD requirements and objectives for defense and contractor organizations which must operate cost/schedule control systems which satisfy the criteria.  The terminology used in this guide is based on DoDI 7000.2 and is intended to be consistent with it. Contractor cost/schedule control systems may use differing terminology, but such terminology must be directly  translatable  with  relative  ease  to  the terminology of this guide in connection with Govern-ment reviews to determine C/SCSC compliance.

**3-2.    Organization.** The  organization section of the C/SCSC is concerned principally with definition of work required to  be  performed by the contractor and the assignment of tasks to  organizations responsible for performing the work.  It requires that all authorized work be defined within the framework of a CWBS. MIL-STD-881 (latest revision), Work Breakdown Structures for Defense Materiel Items, establishes guidelines governing the preparation and employment of the WBS.

   **a.    Contract Work Breakdown Structure (CWBS).** The  contractor's extension of the WBS should reflect what contract work is to be done and the way it is to be managed and performed.  It must include the levels at which required  reports are to be submitted to the Government, contract line  items (if in consonance with MIL-STD-881 (latest revision)),  major subcontractors, intermediate levels, and cost accounts.  Lower level elements should be meaningful products of  task-oriented subdivisions of a higher level element.

   (1)  **Objective.**  A WBS serves many purposes and facilitates planning by providing a formal structure for identifying the work.   It simplifies the problems of summarizing contract or  project-oriented data, and it establishes the reporting structure for Government-required management information. CWBS planning should take into consideration C/SCSC data elements, summation characteristics, scheduling systems, technical performance parameters, configuration items, and actual cost history.  Below the levels contained in MIL-STD-881 (latest revision), the CBWS should recognize and accommodate  the differences in the way work is organized and performed in  the development and production phases.

   (2)  **Flexibility.** The contractor must be provided flexibility and must   not be driven to  subdividing work down to very low levels.  Contractors may recommend, propose, and negotiate  alteration  of the preliminary contract WBS, particularly below the  levels contained in MIL-STD-881 (latest revision).   The   contractor  has complete flexibility in extending the negotiated  CWBS to reflect the approach to be used in the work. It is not necessary to extend all elements of the CWBS to the same levels.   A basic objective is to subdivide the total contractual  effort  into manageable  units of work. Large  or  complex  tasks  may  require  numerous subdivisions.  Other tasks of lesser complexity or size may require substantially fewer levels.  There is no need to use "dummy" levels to force all segments of the CWBS to a common level.  However, if this enables the contractor to use a particular data accumulation coding system more effectively, dummy levels are acceptable.

   (3)  **Effect of Phase.**    In  the establishment of the lower levels of a CWBS,  it is essential to recognize and  accommodate  the  differences      between  the organization, performance, and management control of work  in the development and production phases. System  design and development     normally  are organized and performed along the lines of the major subsystems of the overall system. The design normally is developed in progressively greater detail until it is established at the component level.  In the production or  manufacturing  phase, components    first  are fabricated or purchased and then joined together in progressively larger subassemblies and assemblies until a  complete  system  is produced.   In  addition, the production sequence normally follows a physical parts breakdown  rather  than  the  subsystem  breakdown characteristic of design.   It  may  be  impractical therefore to use the same lower levels of  the CWBS in the  production phase  as  were  used  during  the development phase.   Extension of production WBS requirements below those contained in MIL-STD-881 (latest revision) should be reviewed with the contractor to  verify  compatibility  with  the  hardware manufacturing breakdown and should be limited to those levels absolutely essential to satisfying DoD management needs.

   (4)  **Subcontract.**   The  level of  detail in a subcontract CWBS is independent of the level of detail of the prime contract CWBS and  is also independent of the level  of  the prime contract  CWBS element into which the subcontract feeds.  This means that if subcontracted work is    large  enough or complex enough to warrant  C/SCSC  flow down, then these subcontract work tasks should be broken down to the same extent as if the tasks were a prime contract. Care should be taken by the prime contractor to assure that

the subcontractor has an appropriate WBS in the subcontract.

b. **Interrelation of WBS and Organization.** The CWBS defines and organizes the work to be performed. The contractor's organizational structure reflects the way the contractor has organized the people who will accomplish the work  To assign work responsibility to appropriate organization elements, the CWBS and organizational structure must be interrelated with each other; that is, functional responsibility  must be established for identified units of work. This inter-relationship may occur at any level, but the criteria require that the integration exists at least at the level where performance of work is managed. Other natural points of integration may occur as a result of the manner in which the contractor's work authorization, budgeting, and scheduling functions interface with each other and the CWBS.

(1) CWBS hardware "legs" (e.g., breakdowns of prime mission equipment, support equipment, spare and repair parts, etc.) should not contain functional organization subdivisions at any level between the cost account level and the total contract level. This product-oriented breakdown must allow summarization and analysis by end products regardless of functional organizations working on the end products. However, as long as the contractor's WBS meets these requirements for summarization and analysis, the contractor may include intermediate summarizations (e.g., by function, by geographical area, or for some other purpose) as long as the contractor can and does summarize and analyze data by WBS hardware element.

(2) If there are hardware "leg" functional organization breakdowns within the way the contractor is summarizing or managing, they should be completely explainable and capable of being shown as in compliance with the criteria.

c. **Establishment of Cost Accounts.** The assignment of lower level CWBS elements to responsible lower level functional managers provides a key point for management control purposes and cost collection. The lowest level at which functional responsibility for individual CWBS elements exists, actual costs are accumulated, and performance measurement occurs is referred to as the cost account level.

(1) **Cost Account Level.** The cost account levels should be primarily determined by the scope of the management tasks. The proper levels should not be an arbitrary predetermination or the result of one "across-the-board" level. As an aid in determining a proper level, the size (dollar value, length, etc.) of the resulting cost accounts should be used to help indicate proper subdivision of work. While cost accounts are usually located immediately above the work package level,

they may be located at higher levels when in consonance with the contractor's method of management. In addition to its function as a focal point for collecting costs, the cost account in a performance measurement system is also the lowest level in the structure at which comparisons of actual direct costs to budgeted costs are required. This should not be construed to imply that actual costs cannot be collected at a level below the cost account. Some contractors collect costs and make comparisons at a level below the cost account. The cost collection point must be at a level which will identify the cost elements and factors contributing to cost variances. Data elements BCWS, BCWP, ACWP, and variances determined at the cost account level or below should be summarized through both the WBS and the organizational structure for reporting to higher levels of contractor management and to the Government.

(2) **Basis.** The cost account is the main action point for planning and control of contractual effort, since virtually all aspects of the system come together at this point including budgets, schedules, work assignments, cost collection, progress assessment, problem identification, and corrective actions. In addition, most management actions taken at higher levels occur on an exception basis as a result of significant problems identified at the cost account level. For these reasons the levels selected for establishment of cost accounts should be carefully considered at the outset of a new contract to ensure that the work will be properly defined into manageable units and that functional responsibilities are clearly and reasonably established. The quality and amount of visibility available during the performance of the contract will largely depend upon the level and makeup of the cost accounts.

(3) **Responsibility.** Cost accounts are normally assigned to managers with direct line authority to the performing organizations. However, a cost account may be assigned to a manager even without direct line authority to the performing organization. In this case, the responsible manager must have clearly defined authority and direct managerial responsibility.

(4) **Responsibility Assignment.** Integration of the CWBS and organizational structure at the cost account level may be visualized as a matrix with the functional organizations listed on one axis and the applicable CWBS elements listed on the other axis (figure 3-1). Each organization may then be clearly identified with the work for which it is responsible. Further subdivision of the effort into work packages may be accomplished by the appropriate organization managers by assigning work to operating units. Critical subcontractors (as determined by the prime contractor and DoD program manager) must also be separately measured and integrated into the CWBS. Figure 3-1

AFSC/AFCC/AFLC-P173.5        AMC-P 715-5        NAVSO-P3627        DLAH 8400.2        DCAA-P7641.47

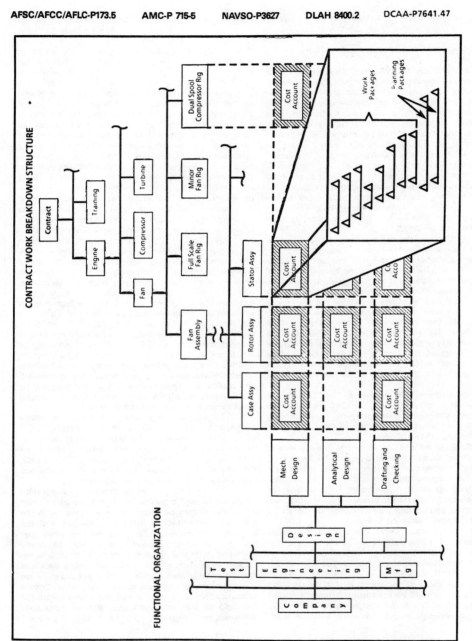

Figure 3-1. Integration of CWBS and Organizational Structure

illustrates integration of the CWBS and organizational structure for a development contract.

(5) **Number, Size, and Length.** No generalization should be made relative to the number of cost accounts versus contract size. Company size, company organization, and contract statement of work are but a few of the factors which must be considered. Attempts to standardize the number, value, or length of cost accounts from contract to contract or contractor to contractor are not appropriate. It is not appropriate to insist on cost accounts which are unnecessarily small in dollar value. Some situations with unreasonably small cost accounts may be alleviated by allowing cost accounts which cross functional lines, by allowing LOE and discrete effort to be intermingled, or by raising the level of the WBS or organizational element on which the cost account is based. The length of a cost account should be considered in determining if a cost account is "small." The contractor should be permitted to group work into cost accounts in a manner which reduces the paperwork for cost/schedule control provided there is no substantial distortion in performance measurement or reduction in cost/schedule visibility.

(6) **Crossing Functional Lines.** Potential problems may occur when an organization is assigned a cost account budget that includes tasks to be performed with nonorganizational resources. A cost account for which an organization is responsible may contain nonorganization work, if nonorganization work is minor, and segregated, and if there are procedures which provide for the responsible organization to monitor, assess, and report performance measurement (including ACWP) on nonorganizational effort.

(7) **Cost Accounts for Manufacturing.** As indicated in paragraph 3-2a(3), care should be taken to allow the contractor the flexibility to structure a production CWBS which is compatible with the manufacturing breakdown of the production hardware and accommodates any differences in the management required for the development phase and the management required for the production phase. This same need for compatibility with the manufacturing process and recognition of differences in the management of development and production, applies to the point of interface between the CWBS and the organization levels of the contractor which are selected to be the cost account and performance measurement baseline levels for production work.

(a) In general, it is more economical and effective to establish cost accounts for production at higher levels of both the CWBS and the organization structure than would be the case for comparable development effort. During the production phase, it is important for the Government to allow the contractor flexibility in the points of interface between the CWBS

and the manufacturing organization levels. Cost accounts should not be established at such a low level of the CWBS that repetitive reporting of detailed performance data would be of questionable utility.

(b) The lowest echelons of production management are primarily concerned with sustaining the required manufacturing throughput as defined by work orders and schedules issued to them. Cost and schedule management by contract or product is normally the responsibility of higher echelons of management within the contractor's production organizations. Management is typically supported by one or more production planning and control organizations which develop integrated schedules for the performance of all production work and prepare appropriate work orders. The planning and control of production typically is in terms of the major functional organizations responsible for material procurement and handling, component fabrications, and product assembly. Tooling, production engineering, quality, inspection, and testing are assigned appropriate supporting roles. Within the major functional organizations, work orders usually cover a manufacturing lot of like items and are likely to cross the boundaries of lower level organizations as the manufacturing lot is moved through the various manufacturing processes.

(c) The management of cost account work in an R&D or low rate production environment should be assigned to a single responsible organizational element. Because of the characteristics of the manufacturing process, the management planning and control of cost account work in a continuing manufacturing environment may not always be performed by a single individual. However, the cost account management function must always be fulfilled within the responsible manufacturing organization, and a single responsible individual must always be assigned from that organization to coordinate the management for each cost account. The procedures used for assigning responsibility and for the performance of the planning and control of cost account work must be documented.

(d) The selection of a low organizational level for the production cost account is likely to result in the assignment of cost and schedule management and analysis responsibilities at a level which is inappropriate for two reasons. First, it will be below the level at which cost and management capability and responsibility actually exist in the organization. Second, it is likely to result in the generation of a substantial number of additional plans, documents, and performance reports without significantly improving management control. A similar condition can arise if cost accounts are established at very low levels of the CWBS. If the two are combined (cost accounts located at low levels of both CWBS and organization), the result may be increased costs for control system operation without additional benefits. Tracing of cost and schedule data to very low levels of detail (that is, part number and performing organization) is normally not a problem in production. A satisfactory production planning and control system should have this capability, but cost accounts need not be established at that level. The establishment of cost accounts at the level of major functional departments (or comparable organizations) within the overall manufacturing organization usually results in the proper level of management.

(e) The levels of the work breakdown structure which define appropriate production cost accounts in conjunction with the organization breakdown level are related to the hardware involved. The level of CWBS appropriate for cost accounts in an electronics production contract is likely to be unsuited to an aircraft production contract. The contractor typically will have a breakdown of the hardware by assembly, subassembly, component, and part number. This breakdown normally will be aligned with the sequence of manufacturing operations followed in building the hardware. It can be of considerable use in determining the appropriate level for establishing cost accounts for production contracts. However, the lowest level of a hardware manufacturing breakdown, the individual part, is almost never the appropriate level for the cost account. Typically, the hardware subsystem, sub-subsystem, or major assembly may be suitable levels for the cost accounts, depending on the product being produced.

(8) **Indirect Cost Control.** While all direct costs are accumulated in cost accounts, the criteria do not require the recording of indirect costs (overhead) at this level. Contractors must, however, be able to identify the organizational managers responsible for controlling the indirect costs that are allocated to Government contracts. Indirect budgets should be established and assigned to the organization managers responsible for controlling such costs. Further, overhead pools and corresponding budgets must be designated and the methods used for budgeting, control, and allocation clearly defined and documented.

(9) **Classification of Effort.** At the lower levels, all work should be categorized into one of three different types of effort: (a) discrete tasks which have a specific end product or end result; (b) work which does not result in a final product ( e.g., sustaining engineering, liaison, coordination, followup, or other support type activities); and (c) factored effort which can be directly related to other identified discrete tasks ( e.g., portions of quality control or inspection). In the C/SCSC, discrete tasks are referred to as "work

packages," support type effort as "level-of-effort (LOE)," and factored effort as "apportioned effort." All work under the contract must eventually be planned as and placed in one of these categories during the performance of the contract.

d. **Work Packages.**

(1) **General.** Work packages are natural subdivisions of cost accounts and constitute the basic building blocks used by the contractor in planning, controlling, and measuring contract performance. A work package is simply a low level task or job assignment. It describes the work to be accomplished by a specific performing organization and serves as a vehicle for monitoring and reporting progress of work. Documents which authorize and assign work to a performing organization are designated by various names throughout industry. "Work package" is the generic term used in the criteria to identify discrete tasks which have definable end results. Consequently, there may be no need for a contractor to establish a new procedure or introduce new documentation to meet the work package requirement.

(2) **Work Package Documents.** It is not necessary that work package documentation contain complete, stand-alone descriptions. Supplemental documentation (such as the CWBS Dictionary, specifications, test plans, etc.) may augment the work package descriptions. However, the work package descriptions must permit cost account managers and work package supervisors to understand and clearly distinguish one work package effort from another. In the review of work package documentation, it may be necessary to obtain explanations from personnel routinely involved in the work, rather than requiring the work package descriptions to be completely self-explanatory. To be effective for planning and controlling work, work packages should have the characteristics defined in paragraph 2-3ak.

(3) **Work Package Duration.** A key feature from the standpoint of evaluating accomplishment is the desirability of having short-term work packages. This requirement is not intended to force contractors to make arbitrary cutoff points simply to have short-term work packages. Work packages should be natural subdivisions of effort planned according to the way the work will be done. However, when work packages are relatively short, little or no assessment of work-in-process is required and the evaluation of contract status is possible mainly on the basis of work package completions. The longer the work packages, the more difficult and subjective the work-in-process assessment becomes unless they are subdivided by objective indicators such as discrete milestones with preassigned budget values or completion percentages.

(a) It is recognized that work packages will

vary significantly between functions. For example, manufacturing work packages tend to be quite short and discrete as natural products of the fabrication and assembly operations. Engineering work package planning may be somewhat more difficult since the work is more dynamic in nature throughout the development phase, making it more difficult to define in discrete terms. For these reasons, the criteria do not attempt to impose specific limitations on work package duration. It should be recognized, however, that reports of contract status, such as the Cost Performance Report, are normally provided to the Government on a monthly basis.

 (b) Although reporting normally is done only for summary level items, accomplishment should be based on completed work packages plus a determination of the amount of work completed in open work packages. Work packages which extend over several reporting periods may require special evaluations to determine the amount and value of in-process work completed as of the reporting cutoff date, and an undesirable amount of subjective judgment may be used in making the determination. On the other hand, work packages which start during one reporting period and end during that period or the next, provide a more objective basis for determining status of contract work.

 (c) This does not mean that the criteria require work packages to be limited to two months duration, but it does mean that objective devices for evaluating completed work-in-process should exist for longer work packages. The use of objective indicators or milestones within such work packages is a desirable technique which should reduce the subjectivity of the work-in-process evaluation.

**(4) Composition of Manufacturing Work Packages.** A manufacturing work package is derived from the relationship between the work breakdown structure and the manufacturing organizational structure and represents a logical subdivision of this relationship. A manufacturing work package may be: a combination of several part numbers; a single part number; a combination of several shop traveler packets; a group of sequences on a shop traveler packet; a single purchase order; a purchase order item number; a subdivision of purchase order elements; or other logical product structure/manufacturing subdivisions.

 (a) A combination of part numbers may be grouped in one work package (that is, all parts going into one assembly may be a logical grouping for a work package of this type).

 (b) A part number may be a work package consisting of one or more shop releases. Each shop release or sequence or combination thereof may be considered as a work package milestone.

 (c) A shop release may be a work package. Each sequence or combination of sequences may be considered work package milestones.

 (d) Individual sequences may be work packages.

 (e) Predetermined combinations of sequences may be work packages.

 (f) A combination of purchase orders may be grouped into one work package (that is, several related purchase orders going to one vendor may be a logical grouping for a work package of this type). Each purchase order, purchase order item number, part number, or delivery date, or combination thereof may be considered work package milestones.

 (g) A purchase order consisting of one or more part numbers may be a work package. Each purchase order item number, part number, or delivery date, or combination thereof may be considered work package milestones.

 (h) A purchase order item number may be a work package. Each part number, or delivery date, or combination thereof may be considered work package milestones.

 (i) A part number (purchased) may be a work package. Delivery dates may be considered work package milestones.

 (j) A subdivision or grouping of purchase order elements such as "purchase order-part number-delivery date" may be a work package.

**(5) Considerations Concerning Manufacturing Work Packages.** In the definition and establishment of manufacturing work packages, proper recognition should be given to the characteristics of the production process as opposed to those of design and development. The most significant of these is the relative ease of measurement of most manufacturing work. Manufacturing typically produces a finite output in accordance with a detailed schedule. There are many reasonably accurate and objective techniques for measuring manufacturing performance. The normal production planning and control system usually includes several subdivisions of the manufacturing work which provide a basis for acceptable performance measurement. The objective is to select as the "work package" the work subdivision which best satisfies the requirement for performance measurement.

 (a) Since accurate measurement of in-process manufacturing is not usually a problem, the most compelling reason for the selection of the smallest (shortest duration, least value) work subdivision as the production work packages is to minimize the need to make changes to the schedules or budgets of open (in-process) work packages or packages scheduled to be started in the current accounting period, both of which are restricted by the C/SCSC in the interests of preserving a stable near-term planning and measurement baseline. However, the smallest formally-defined subdivisions of manufacturing work are, in many production control systems, scheduled with definitive dates only a short time before their start, which creates problems in satisfying the normal C/SCSC requirement for advance work package planning.

(b) In many production control systems, longer term planning of the lowest work levels is done only in terms of "schedule windows"; that is, time periods of a month or more in which the actual work performance of the "package" will consume only a fraction of the total time, or of "complete by" dates. In some control systems, the formal scheduling of the lowest level of work subdivision may not exceed this degree of precision at any point. Where systems do provide for the establishment of start and completion dates for smaller subdivisions of manufacturing work, these dates are frequently subject to in-process revision to achieve efficient day-to-day workloading of the performing organizations, and to reflect current schedule priorities.

(c) The use of large work subdivisions to satisfy the C/SCSC work package requirement does not avoid this problem, since the type of schedule changes described are still internal changes to the package when it is in process. Further, the cancellation (closing) and reissue of a new work package for each change generally does not constitute a practical or economical approach in manufacturing, particularly for contractors who have automated their production scheduling and manpower planning (and in some cases also work order preparation and issue).

(d) Under these conditions, a certain amount of rescheduling of open manufacturing work packages is appropriate and acceptable providing procedures are in existence which prevent the inadvertent invalidation of baseline schedules and budgets through these detail-level changes. The substance of such procedures should be to limit the range of rescheduling so as to maintain consistency with key production schedule dates. Key production schedule dates define the required completion dates for key elements of the manufacturing plan, are normally found on internal production schedules, and normally should not be more than three months apart. This flexibility for rescheduling applies only to manufacturing work packages. No changes may be made to BCWS in open, nonmanufacturing work packages.

(e) It is emphasized that the term "work packages" is generic and is used to identify discrete work tasks. In some production control systems involving repetitive manufacturing operations,

objective indicators reflecting groups of tasks may be used and viewed as work packages. For example, when objective indicators are used, values should be established each month based on the tasks in the group. The monthly value established for the group of tasks becomes BCWS for the month.

(f) A contractor must utilize anticipated learning when developing time-phased BCWS. Any method used to apply learning is acceptable as long as the BCWS is established to represent as closely as possible the expected ACWP that will be charged to the cost account/work package.

(g) It must be stressed that the measurement of performance of manufacturing work through the use of objective indicators does not eliminate the requirement for detailed planning and control of manufacturing work. The breakdown of manufacturing work into work/shop orders which specify the processes or assembly steps, materials, and organizations necessary to fabricate or assemble a manufacturing lot, and which have assigned schedules and budgets or values, is an accepted general practice in the management of manufacturing effort. This is essential if schedules and efficient performance are to be maintained.

(h) Examples of the use of objective indicators for measuring accomplishment of repetitive manufacturing operations may include--

1. The use of milestones with assigned or readily determinable budget values.

2. Direct measurement of accomplishment in terms of units of work; that is, some form of an earned or equivalent unit measurement system.

3. An input-output measurement system which compares planned levels and actual performance.

These indicate the principal types of manufacturing measurement systems and reflect the fact that a contractor who already has an effective means of measuring manufacturing performance should be able to satisfy the C/SCSC, providing that this means of measurement is integrated with the contractor's baseline plan for the performance of the manufacturing work.

(i) The contractor must still have a baseline plan for manufacturing work which includes time-phased budgets that are consistent with the schedules for the performance of the work. The performance measurement indicators (milestones, earned units, scheduled output, etc.) must be clearly identified and directly related to cost accounts. They must be scheduled in a sequence which supports the achievement of higher level schedules including those specified for cost accounts. These indicators (milestones, units, etc.) must clearly represent the accomplishment of an identifiable quantity of work within the cost account and be assigned a value reflecting the planned cost of that work. These values must summarize or reconcile to the total budget for the cost account. The use of a measurement base which is only generally indicative of some progress (for example, equal value milestones not related to specific work) is not acceptable.

(j) The performance measurement indicators (milestones, etc.) must be scheduled with sufficient frequency to provide a basis for accurate performance measurement. This entails provision for measurement which supports monthly reports of cost and schedule performance status at the cost account level. To do this, it is normally necessary to measure performance of tasks below the cost account in a way which accurately indicates the performance in each report period. For example, this can be done by scheduling performance measurement indicators at least bimonthly (every two months) or by providing for a means of accurately assessing "in-process" work when indicators are scheduled at greater than bimonthly intervals.

(k) The restrictions on changes to schedules for manufacturing performance measurement indicators are equivalent to those regarding changes to manufacturing work packages specified in paragraph 3-2d(5)(d). Rescheduling must be constrained so as to maintain consistency with key production schedule dates. Procedures should be established which provide the necessary constraints. There should not be changes to the budgets or values assigned to performance measurement indicators which are scheduled to occur in the current monthly accounting period. This is required in order to maintain baseline stability.

**e. Level of Effort (LOE).** LOE activity is treated differently from work-packaged effort. While work packages are discrete and accomplishment can be measured based on the completed pieces of work, LOE is "measured" through the passage of time. LOE activity must be separately identified from work packaged effort to avoid distorting that which is measurable.

(1) The amount of LOE activity will vary among performing organizations, but within each should be held to the lowest practical minimum. The criteria do not establish guidelines as to how much LOE is acceptable, but require that only work which cannot be work packaged or apportioned be designated LOE.

(2) As a minimum, LOE budgets must be separately substantiated and planned as direct labor, material/subcontract, and other costs. LOE activity should be budgeted on a time-phased basis for control and reporting purposes.

(3) LOE and discrete work are normally segregated by cost account, but in some cases may be intermingled within the same cost account. This intermingling must be minimized to preclude distortion of performance measurement. When LOE and discrete work are mixed within the same cost account, it is preferable that ACWP be collected separately for the LOE and discrete portions and the separate ACWP be used for performance analysis. When ACWP is available only at the cost account level (and not separately available within the cost account for LOE and discrete work), then the amount of LOE intermingled with discrete work must be small (strictly controlled). Intermingling of LOE and discrete work within the same cost account is not allowed when the cost account is large and the amount of both LOE and discrete work is substantial. Judgment must be used when addressing the intermingling of LOE and discrete work within small cost accounts. The splitting of a small cost account into two very small cost accounts should not be required solely to create a total segregation of discrete effort from LOE.

**f. Apportioned Effort.** Apportioned effort is dependent on or related in direct proportion to the performance of other effort. For example, quality assurance and other inspection functions are frequently treated as apportioned effort based on the amount of manufacturing effort. Apportioned effort may be included and budgeted as a part of the work package or cost account to which it relates or may be established as a separate work package with its own budget which is based on a percentage of the related work package or cost account budget. Factors established for the application of apportioned effort must be documented and applied in a formal, consistent manner. Apportioned effort should be limited to that which is genuinely related to discrete effort.

**g. Detailed Planning.** While all contractual effort eventually is planned and controlled through work packages, LOE, or apportioned effort, it may not be practicable or possible to do such detailed planning for an entire contract at the outset. Work is planned in finite but sizable increments at the outset of a contract. These planning increments (that is, cost accounts) form the basis for work authorization, budgeting, and master scheduling.

(1) As the contract work is defined, a "rolling wave" planning concept may be used. Tasks suitable for job assignment evolve naturally, and at least the near-term work is segregated into work packages, with the remaining work residing in planning packages. Planning packages have characteristics similar to work packages, but combine under one estimated budget and schedule, tasks which will be converted into several work packages with precise budgets and exact schedules when detail planning is possible. Thus, the contractual effort is progressively divided into smaller

segments as work on the contract proceeds and as responsibility is assigned to successively lower levels of management. However, such work package definition must be accomplished in sufficient time for budgets to be developed and detailed plans for work accomplishment to be completed.

(2) Detailed planning approximately six months in the future should provide for adequate planning and control. The use of "six months" is intended as a guide, and not as a rule. Each management system and contract application should be considered on its own merit. The extent of the detailed planning is determined by the nature of the work, and should be planned as far in the future as practical. Production effort is normally planned considerably longer than six months in the future. However some development projects are less readily defined and consequently detailed planning may be less than six months in advance. Once work packages have been defined and budgeted, controls should be established to minimize further changes to budgets, schedule, or scope of work, particularly in the near term (approximately 30 days).

3-3. **Planning and Budgeting.** The organization criteria establish the basic framework for defining and organizing the work to be performed. This section of the criteria deals with the requirements for program scheduling and budgeting. Generally, it requires that all authorized work be scheduled and that budgets be assigned to identified manageable units of effort.

a. **Planning.** The assignment of budgets to scheduled segments of work produces a time-phased plan against which actual performance can be compared. The establishment, maintenance, and use of this plan are extremely important aspects of performance measurement. Good planning demands thoroughness and discipline at the outset with continuing discipline required in the maintenance and operation of the plan. This does not mean that the system must be totally inflexible but that changes to the time-phased budget plan must be rigorously controlled and documented.

(1) While planning is required at all levels of management, it becomes progressively more detailed and finite at lower levels of the organizational structure and the CWBS.

(2) Usually, all of the work for a given contract cannot be planned in detail at the outset, but it can and should be initially divided into larger segments so that the entire contract requirement may be viewed as a sum of identified parts.

(3) When it is clearly impractical to plan authorized work in cost accounts, budget should be identified to effort at higher CWBS levels for further subdivision at the earliest opportunity. The budget for

this effort must be identified specifically to the work for which it is intended, be time-phased, and have controls established to ensure that it is not used in performance of other work. Eventually, all the work to be performed will be planned by specific organizational elements to the appropriate level of detail. The key point pertaining to summary level planning is that it is no substitute for early and definitive planning. Without timely and adequate work definition and budget allocation, the validity of the entire performance measurement baseline is questionable.

(4) For authorized unpriced work (relative to a proposed contract change or letter contract), it is acceptable for the contractor to plan and budget near-term effort in cost accounts, with the remaining effort and budget planned at a higher level or maintained in undistributed budget. After negotiation the remaining effort will be planned and budgeted within cost accounts as soon as practical to ensure disciplined baseline planning.

b. **Work Authorization.** Before work actually begins, the work authorization system should define and identify the work to be done and the organizational elements responsible. Schedules and budgets should be established for all work at appropriate levels within the framework of the CWBS. Task authorizations, work orders, or other appropriate means may be used for this purpose.

c. **Scheduling.** The scheduling system should provide for all specified work to the lowest defined element of the CWBS in a way compatible with contract milestones and meaningful in terms of the technical requirements of the contract. It should provide schedules so actual progress can be related. Such schedules should identify key milestones and activities which recognize significant constraints and relationships. Scheduling should interface with other planning and control systems to the extent necessary for measurement and evaluation of contract status. The scheduling system should provide current status and forecasts of completion dates for scheduled work. The contractor's summary and detailed schedules should enable a comparison of planned and actual status of program accomplishment based on milestones or other indicators used by the contractor for control purposes.

(1) The criteria do not require the use of any specific scheduling system or methodology. Various scheduling techniques are available which will satisfy these requirements. These techniques may be employed at the summary and detail level but must remain consistent with and supportive of the master schedule. Clear and adequate relationships between the various techniques employed at various levels must be maintained, including vertical traceability.

(2) Basically, the criteria require the scheduling

system to be formal, complete, and consistent. The scheduling system should contain a summary or master schedule and related subordinate schedules (intermediate and/or cost account) which provide a logical sequence and show interdependencies from the summary to the detailed work package levels. However, when adequate lower level manufacturing schedules are directly related to a higher level schedule, there might not be a need for a separate "work package schedule." If a manufacturing work package is made up of several tasks (i.e., shop releases, operation sheets, etc.) which have their own schedules that directly relate to a higher level schedule (cost account or intermediate), there is no need for the task schedules to be listed on the work package budget document or to have a document called "work package schedule."

(3) Work package documentation does not have to contain specific calendar dates; it must, however, always contain either the month, week, or day, whichever is appropriate.

d. **Budgeting.**

(1) The planning and scheduling procedures serve as the basis for developing budgets and work authorizations. As the work is progressively defined in greater detail, budgets for the planned work should be concurrently assigned. When planning packages are established within a cost account, the contractor's system should provide for sufficient control of cost account budgets to avoid a situation at the end of the cost account where there is inadequate budget remaining for the work left to be performed. This means that budgets must be related to and be part of the planning package from which the budget originated.

(2) Budgets may be stated either in dollars, man-hours, or other measurable units, although budgets for cost accounts and higher levels are normally expressed in dollars.

(3) Average (level) labor, overhead, and other rates for the life of the contract or cost account, in excess of one year in length, normally cause too much distortion in cost performance and are not acceptable. Monthly, quarterly, semi-annual, or annual rates are acceptable, and should result in a valid time-phased estimate of cost for the task(s) to be accomplished. It is desirable to use the most recent negotiated forward pricing rates, but when this is not feasible, it is acceptable to use rates that provide a valid estimate of costs for the effort to be accomplished during a particular period. At all times, BCWP must be based on the same rates as used for BCWS. Internal replanning of remaining portions of the performance measurement baseline to account for significant changes in the anticipated labor, overhead, and other rates is desirable, but not mandatory.

(4) In general, the budget systems should provide for the following:

(a) Direct budgets allocated to organizations performing the planned work identified to elements in the CWBS.

(b) Indirect budgets allocated to specific organizations having responsibility for controlling indirect costs.

(c) Identification of any management reserves and undistributed budget.

(d) Normally, the total of direct and indirect budgets, and management reserves equals the negotiated contract cost plus the estimated cost of authorized unpriced work.

(5) Since primary budget assignments may be made to functional organizations rather than to pieces of hardware or tasks, the level at which the organizational and CWBS elements are integrated may be the first point at which budgets are specifically assigned to CWBS elements. This is not always the case. Certain elements of the CWBS may be priced line items with budgets assigned at the summary level, and then subdivided as the work is broken down into manageable units of effort. Regardless of the budgeting technique, all work eventually receives a budget.

e. **Management Reserve.**

(1) In most major acquisition contracts, particularly in the development phase, there is considerable uncertainty regarding the timing, CWBS elements involved, or magnitude of future difficulties. The C/SCSC permit the use of a management reserve provided that adequate identification and controls are maintained. Management reserve budget and its use must always be accounted for at the total contract level. Normally, it is retained and controlled at this level, although in some cases it might be distributed to and controlled at lower management levels. In any event, management reserve budget is maintained separately from undistributed budget. There is no such thing as "negative management reserve." If the contract is budgeted in excess of contract budget base (the negotiated contract cost plus the estimated cost for authorized unpriced work), the provisions applicable to formal reprogramming should apply.

(2) Management reserve is not a contingency which can be eliminated from contract prices during subsequent negotiations or used to absorb the cost of contract changes. The contractor should not be required to use existing management reserve to provide funds for authorized but undefinitized work or other modifications to authorized contractual efforts. The contractor may, if the documented management system permits, use management reserve to provide temporary budgets for authorized undefinitized effort;

however, it must remain clear to both parties that the management reserve budget was derived from cost previously negotiated for the contractual effort authorized prior to the change in process. Definitization of contract changes may result in establishing a new level of management reserve reflecting the revised effort. This new level may exceed prior reserves.

f. **Undistributed Budgets.** Budgets applicable to contract effort, which cannot be specifically identified to CWBS elements at or below the level specified for reporting to the Government, are referred to as undistributed budgets.

(1) The establishment of an undistributed budget may be necessary when contract changes are authorized. For example, reporting deadlines may preclude the planning of newly authorized work prior to report preparation. However, since budgets for all authorized contract work must be accounted for, some provision for the budget applicable to contract changes must be made. In such cases, undistributed budgets identified to the specific contract changes may be established. Except as provided in (2) below, the budget should be distributed to appropriate CWBS elements and cost accounts by the end of the next reporting period.

(2) For authorized work which has not been negotiated, the contractor may maintain budgets in an undistributed budget account until negotiations have been concluded, allocating budget only to that work which will start in the interim. After negotiations, the remaining budget should be allocated appropriately. Both before and after negotiations, budgets may be allocated as additions to the scope of existing cost accounts or when appropriate allocated to separate cost accounts.

g. **Contract Budget Base.** The original budget established for those elements of the CWBS identified as priced line items in the contract should constitute a traceable basis against which contract growth can be measured. The starting point or base on which these original budgets are built is the negotiated contract cost (paragraph 2-3u). For C/SCSC purposes, this is called the contract budget base. The contract budget base increases or decreases only as a result of changes authorized by the contracting officer. For definitized changes, the contract budget base changes by the amount negotiated for those changes. For authorized work which has not been negotiated, the contract budget base changes by the amount of cost estimated by the contractor for that effort. After negotiations, the contract budget base is adjusted to reflect the negotiation results. For a letter contract the contract budget base is initially the contractor's estimated costs for authorized work. The contract budget base, therefore, is a dynamic amount, changing as the

authorized work under the contract changes; but it is controlled, as it cannot be changed by the contractor except as a result of contracting officer actions.

h. **Economic Price Adjustment (EPA).** For those contracts which recognize abnormal escalation by use of price adjustment clauses, the amounts related to these clauses can be treated in essentially the same manner as undefinitized changes.

(1) If it can be foreseen that economic conditions will apparently result in contract cost revision under the economic price adjustment clause, the contractor may estimate the amount of the adjustment anticipated at the end of the specified economic price adjustment period or other period agreed to by the contracting parties and may include that amount in the contract budget base. Distribution of the estimate should be made to management reserve and the performance measurement baseline or both.

(2) As the contract proceeds, and amounts applicable to EPA are definitized, the contract budget base is adjusted to reflect these changes and also to reflect the contractor's latest estimated cost adjustment for the next period. At all times, the economic price adjustment estimate should be identified to contract specified periods and reflect actual experience, current trends, and a reevaluation of future conditions. Thus, the performance measurement baseline can reflect the economic price adjustment conditions contained in the contract, and performance can be measured against a more realistic plan.

(3) At the contract level, estimates for economic price adjustment will be identified and reported separately from estimates for unnegotiated changes. No matter what period is chosen for inclusion of the estimate in the contract budget base, the estimated and definitized values should be specifically identified and reported by the time periods specified in the economic price adjustment clause. The purpose is to identify properly what was definitized versus what was estimated. This is necessary for estimate tracking, for tracing adjustments to management reserve, and to the budgets for remaining work.

i. **Performance Measurement Baseline.** As the contract effort is defined within the CWBS and identified to responsible organizational elements, the basis for budget assignments to identified tasks is provided. Eventually, each work package will have a budget. Since all work packages cannot normally be planned at the beginning of a contract, initial planning may consist of larger segments of work assigned to designated organizational elements. These organizational work assignments frequently serve as cost accounts in addition to their role in the planning function. Budgets assigned to cost accounts are time-phased according to the schedule for performing that work, thus forming the major portion of the time-phased budget baseline; that is, the performance measurement baseline which is used in the measurement of both task and organizational performance. Further budget assignments to work packages are made as detailed planning proceeds. When all work packages are planned within a cost account, the sum of the assigned budgets plus LOE and apportioned effort should equal the total cost account budget.

**(1) Cost Account Budgets.** All cost accounts must contain a budget, schedule, and scope of work and should realistically represent the manner in which work is assigned and budgeted to the organizational units. The cost account budget should include all direct costs for the total of work with separate identification of cost elements (labor, material, other direct costs). Establishing and maintaining control at the cost account level permits flexibility in the management of resources at the lower detail levels through work package replanning.

**(2) Cost Account Length.** Since cost account budgets and schedules also establish the constraints required for baseline control, cost accounts should not be exorbitantly long, or additional controls are needed. When cost accounts average about a year in length replanning within cost accounts can be accommodated without the need for rigid constraints. It is not intended to limit cost accounts to one year in length, but to ensure that budgeting procedures prohibit budget planned for far-term work from being used in the near term. Therefore, cost accounts which exceed a year in length must be disciplined by budget allocation constraints and/or procedures that prohibit the premature use of budget planned and required for far-term effort within these accounts.

**(3) Cost Account Replanning.** Replanning of work packages within cost accounts is sometimes necessary to compensate for internal conditions which affect the planning and scheduling of remaining work. Such replanning should, however, be accomplished within the constraints of the previously established cost account schedule and budget. When more extensive replanning of future work is necessary and the total cost account budget must be changed, management reserves may be used to increase or decrease the cost account budgets if done in a formal, documented manner.

(a) If replanning requires that work and associated budget be transferred between cost accounts, this transfer must also be documented. Except for correction of errors and accounting adjustments, no retroactive changes will be made to budgets for completed work. Replanning actions designed to reduce costs, improve or reflect improved efficiency of operations, or otherwise enhance the completion of the contract, are encouraged.

(b) Replanning actions which significantly affect the time-phasing of the performance measurement baseline should be clearly auditable by review of contractor records and should be shown in applicable reports to the DoD procuring activity. Maintenance of a performance measurement baseline is required to ensure that deviations from plan are visible and can be examined to determine their causes (paragraph 3-6d). Reschedule of manufacturing work packages is discussed in paragraph 3-2d(5).

**(4) Relation to Negotiated Contract Cost.** After contract negotiations are completed, the total allocated budget used to report contract performance to the DoD must always represent an amount which is formally recognized by both parties. This is to force recognition of contractual requirements and to preclude undisciplined changes to the performance measurement baseline. The initial establishment of the performance measurement baseline should be tied to the negotiated contract cost (paragraph 3-3g). As new work is authorized on the contract, the negotiated contract cost and the performance measurement baseline are increased accordingly. Normally, the total allocated budget (the performance measurement baseline plus management reserve) should not exceed the negotiated contract cost plus the estimated cost of authorized but unpriced work (the contract budget base).

**(5) Internal Operating Budgets.** Nothing in the criteria prevents the contractor from establishing an internal operating budget which is less than or more than the total allocated budget. However, there must be controls and procedures to ensure that the performance measurement baseline is not distorted.

(a) Operating budgets are sometimes used to establish internal targets for rework or added in-scope effort which is not significant enough to warrant formal reprogramming. Such budgets do not become a substitute for the cost account budgets in the performance measurement baseline, but should be visible to all levels of management as appropriate. Cost account managers should be able to evaluate performance in terms of both operating budgets and cost account budgets to meet the requirements of internal management and reporting to the Government.

(b) Establishment and use of operating budgets should be done with caution. Working against one plan and reporting progress against another is undesirable and the operating budget should not differ significantly from the cost account budget in the performance measurement baseline. Operating budgets are intended to provide targets for specific

3-12

elements of work where otherwise the targets would be unrealistic. They are not intended to serve as a completely separate work measurement plan for the contract as a whole.

**(6) Baseline Greater Than Contract Budget Base.**

(a) Any increase which results in a total allocated budget in excess of the contract budget base constitutes formal reprogramming and must be formally submitted by the contractor and formally recognized by the procuring activity. This includes documented reconciliation from the old baseline. It should be clearly understood that such changes are not acceptable on a frequent basis, such as quarterly or semi-annually, but may be expected to occur only once or twice during the life of a multiyear contract. One would not expect such an adjustment, for instance, on a contract that covers a single year.

(b) When a contractor formally notifies the procuring agency of a total allocated budget in excess of the contract budget base and the revised plan is accepted for reporting performance to the Government, then it should also be recognized that this condition may be an indicator to the Administrative Contracting Officer (ACO) that progress payments, liquidation rates, or cost reimbursement fee vouchers may require review for appropriate adjustment.

**3-4. Accounting.** The contractor's accounting system must provide for adequately recording all direct and indirect costs applicable to the contract. Such costs must be directly summarized from the level at which they are applied to the contract through both the WBS and functional organization structures according to procedures acceptable to DCAA.

a. **Cost Accounts.** Ordinarily, cost accounts are established by the contractor at the lowest level in the CWBS at which actual costs are recorded and compared with budgeted costs. As the natural control point for cost/schedule planning and control, the cost account provides a logical point for cost collection and evaluation (paragraphs 3-2c and 3-3i(1).

b. **Direct Costs.** The criteria require the contractor to record direct costs on an applied or other acceptable basis for performance measurement and unit costing purposes. Direct labor costs are normally applied to work-in-process on an as-used (applied) basis. Direct material costs should also be recorded in the same manner; however, there may be cases where it is not logical to make this a uniform requirement. In these cases, if existing contractor systems provide the fundamental elements for cost and schedule performance measurement and for determining unit or lot cost as appropriate, they may be accepted even though they do not record material as a direct cost at the point of usage.

c. **Material Accounting System.**

(1) To be acceptable, contractor material accounting systems should have the following characteristics:

(a) An accurate cost accumulation system which assigns material cost to appropriate cost accounts in a manner consistent with the budget.

(b) Recognized costing techniques acceptable to DCAA.

(c) Capability to establish material price variances and cost variances attributed to material usage where appropriate.

(2) Little need be said of the first two characteristics since these are the province of the DCAA personnel in their normal activities and they are participants in the review.

(3) With regard to material accounting, the contractor should be able to account for all material subcontracted items and purchased parts which, by their value and significance, warrant such attention. It is not cost effective to require individual identification of such things as small hardware, miscellaneous wiring materials, and other items of a similar nature. Accurate recording of transfers between contracts is required in the material accounting system.

(4) Material price variance is an essential element of material cost control. This can be determined early in the cycle of ordering materials, at which point the price of the materials can be compared with the amount budgeted for that material. Accumulation of these differences represents the total material price variance. Various routines can be used to calculate this variance, but the system should readily provide such data. When it becomes known that material costs will vary from the amounts planned, the contractor should show these differences in the estimates of final costs.

(5) Material usage variance is an important cost factor on repetitive large volume, production-type jobs, but may be of marginal significance on single copy R&D equipment. Final material usage variances are not available until the work is completed. However, acceptable cost accounting techniques for analyzing and determining current and projected usage variances should be expected to provide continuing internal measurement when the value and nature of the material warrant. The criteria contain a requirement that contractors' systems be capable of formally planning and tracking the cost of material usage. For most contractors, purchases of material in excess of bill of material requirements are standard practice for many categories of material. Planning for material usage allowance to cover scrap, test rejections, unanticipated test quantities, and the like, is a practical

necessity and the contractor should have records of such provisions. The more uncertain the expected usage, the more important it is to have a good plan and to keep track of performance against it particularly for contract peculiar materials or materials which require long procurement leadtimes.

(6) There are two preferred methods for budgeting for unanticipated excessive scrap (although other methods may be acceptable ):

(a) Management reserve may be used to increase the budget for the replacement lot (or increased subsequent lot size) which was required due to unusually large scrap; or

(b) Negative BCWP can be assigned in the current period to recognize BCWP which had previously been overstated due to significant scrap. (Negative BCWP which appears on the Cost Performance Report should be explained in Format 5 of the CPR).

(7) In those instances where the contractor maintains separate stores inventory areas, actual or applied direct cost of "store" material or components will be removed from the inventory account and charged as actual direct cost on the contract when issued. Normally, all unused material should be returned to stores for disposition. Actual direct material cost includes the materials in the final product, scrap, damaged materials, and so forth, plus any material purchased for the contract but not used, for which an alternate use cannot be found. However, unit cost projections for follow-on procurements would be expected to include material consumed plus material requirements for schedule assurance based on waste and spoilage trends determined from an appropriate phase of the contract performance.

(8) Work progress is determined on the basis of completion of individual segments of work or the attainment of specific milestones. Each such segment of work or milestone is assigned a budget for the resources estimated as necessary to perform that work. Actual resources expended must be recorded on the same basis as resource budgets were assigned if meaningful comparisons are to be made.

(a) The definition of applied direct costs takes into consideration the different types of material involved in a contract. Not all material items are processed through inventory accounts. High-dollar value items such as major components or assemblies are frequently scheduled for delivery in accordance with the assembly line schedule. Items of this type are not usually scrapped if found defective, but are returned to the supplier for rework or repair. Under the applied direct cost approach, the costs of such items may be considered as applied direct material costs at the time they are received provided they are either scheduled for use within 60 days or are specifically identified to a unique, serially-numbered end item.

(b) If a contractor's system is qualified on other than an "applied cost" basis, actual direct costs may be recorded upon receipt of material, or upon payment, as appropriate under the system.

(9) Neither the applied direct cost approach nor any acceptable alternate should be interpreted to relieve the contractor of the need to maintain records of contract commitments for material.

(10) Material BCWS and BCWP are intended to permit measurement of events which reflect progress in contract performance, not for measurement of administrative or financial events (e.g., booking of actual costs or invoice payment). Therefore, BCWS should normally be scheduled in accordance with a contract event and BCWP should be earned when the event occurs.

(a) To avoid distortion, actuals should be recorded when BCWP is earned. In situations where BCWP is earned and the invoice has not been paid, estimated actual cost may be incorporated into ACWP from purchase order information.

(b) Administrative or financial events may be used as indicators for contract events when such indicators occur in the same reporting period as the contract events. However, it is not generally acceptable to use administrative or financial events as indicators when they would depict performance past the actual material use or need dates.

d. **Indirect Costs.** The contractor should charge indirect costs to appropriate overhead pools by methods acceptable to DCAA.

(1) Controls of indirect costs are required and should include--

(a) Establishment of realistic time-phased budgets or forecasts by organization; for example, department or cost center.

(b) Placement of responsibility for indirect costs in a manner commensurate with a person's authority.

(c) Variance analyses and appropriate action to eliminate or reduce costs where feasible.

(d) Review of budgets at least annually and when major unforeseen variations in workload or other factors affecting indirect costs become known.

(2) After indirect costs are accumulated and allocated to contracts, they are applied at the level selected by the contractor. There is no requirement in the criteria to apply indirect costs at either the work package or the cost account levels, although some contractors may choose to do so. However, it must be possible to summarize indirect costs from the applied level to the contract level without the need for further divisions.

e. **Level of Effort.** LOE costs are normally

AFSC/AFCC/AFLC-P173-5          AMC-P 715-5          NAVSO-P3627          DLAH8400.2          DCAA-P7641.47
3-4e                                                                                                            3-5c(3)

segregated from costs of discrete effort at the cost account level to permit an evaluation of the measurable effort before it is combined with the support effort. This segregation is intended to prevent distortion of measurable activity until at least one comparison of BCWP versus ACWP has been made.

f. **Apportioned Effort.** Cost should be directly related to the discrete work packages or cost accounts to which the cost pertains. Factors and methods used to apply apportioned effort should be formally defined in established procedures with such costs accumulated on the same basis as budgets are allocated.

**3-5. Analysis.** The C/SCSC do not require the submission of data or reports from the contractor to the Government. The criteria only set forth characteristics which contractors' systems must possess, and specify the type of data which should be derived from the systems. Five basic data elements are identified in the criteria: ACWP, BCWS, BCWP, Budget at Completion (BAC) and Estimate at Completion (EAC). ACWP (direct and indirect) was discussed previously under Accounting (paragraph 3-4). BAC was discussed in paragraph 3-3i. This section discusses BCWS, BCWP, EAC, and analyses of variances resulting from comparisons of these five basic elements.

a. **Budgeted Cost for Work Scheduled.** BCWS represents the time-phased budget plan against which performance is measured. For the total contract, BCWS is normally the negotiated contract cost plus the estimated cost of authorized but unpriced work (less any management reserve). It is time-phased by the assignment of budgets to scheduled increments of work.

(1) For any given time period, BCWS is determined at the cost account level by totaling the budgets for all work packages scheduled to be completed, plus the budget for the portion of in-process work (open work packages) scheduled to be accomplished, plus the budgets for LOE and apportioned effort scheduled to be completed during the period.

(2) A contractor must utilize anticipated learning when developing the time-phased BCWS. Any recognized method used to apply learning is acceptable as long as the BCWS is established to represent as closely as possible the expected ACWP that will be charged to the cost account/work package.

(3) In developing BCWS, consideration should be given to the methods planned for taking credit for BCWP (b below).

b. **Budgeted Cost for Work Performed.** BCWP consists of the budgeted costs for all work actually accomplished during a given time period. At the cost account level, BCWP is determined by totaling the

budgets for work packages actually completed, plus the budget applicable to the completed in-process work within open work packages, plus the budgets for LOE and apportioned effort associated with completed work.

(1) The major difficulty encountered in the determination of BCWP is the evaluation of in-process work (work packages which have been started but have not been completed at the time of cutoff for the report). As discussed previously in paragraphs on the organization criteria, the use of short-span work packages or establishment of discrete value milestones within work packages will significantly reduce the work-in-process evaluation problem and procedures used will vary depending on work package length. For example, some contractors prefer to take no BCWP credit for a short-term work package until it is completed, others take credit for 50 percent of the work package budget when it starts and the remaining 50 percent at completion. Some contractors use formulae which approximate the time-phasing of the effort, others use earned standards, while still others prefer to make physical assessments of work completed to determine the applicable budget earned. For longer work packages many contractors use discrete milestones with preestablished budget or progress values to measure work performance.

(2) The criteria do not specify any particular method as the technique used will largely depend on work package content, size, and duration. The use of arbitrary formulae, as described above, should be limited to very short work packages (paragraph 3-2d(3). At all times BCWP must be computed using the same labor, overhead, and other rates as for BCWS.

c. **Data Analyses:**

(1) Comparisons of BCWS with BCWP relate work completed to work scheduled during a given period of time. While this provides a valuable indication of schedule status, in terms of dollars worth of work accomplished, it may not clearly indicate whether or not scheduled milestones are being met since some work may have been performed out of sequence or ahead of schedule. A formal time-phased scheduling system must, therefore, provide the means of determining the status of specific activities and milestones.

(2) Comparisons of BAC with EAC are required internally at the cost account level and provide estimated variances expected at the completion of the contract. Cost account managers need to be constantly alert to circumstances which will cause the estimate at completion and, therefore, the variance at completion, to change. Such changes must be reported monthly (paragraph 3-5g).

(3) Comparisons of BCWP and ACWP will clearly

AFSC/AFCC/AFLC-P173-5        AMC-P 715-5        NAVSO-P3627        DLAH8400.2        DCAA-P7641.47
3-5c(3)                                                                                                    3-5d(2)

show whether completed work has cost more or less than was planned for that work. Analysis of these differences should reveal the factors contributing to the variances, such as poor initial estimate for the task, technical difficulties requiring application of additional resources, the cost of labor or materials different than planned, personnel efficiency different than planned, or a combination of these or other reasons.

(4) Comparisons of BCWP with BCWS and with ACWP are required at the cost account level. Cost accounts consist of an aggregation of work packages which are the responsibility of a single organization. Managerial authority and responsibility for corrective action should exist at this point making the cost account a key management control point in the system. It is important that the performance measurement baseline be maintained at this level since comparisons of planned versus actual performance are of little value if the measurement base is subject to uncontrolled fluctuation and change. Since higher level management information consists of direct summaries of the results of such comparisons, there is less need for further calculations at high levels to determine program status.

(5) When a subcontractor is required to comply with the C/SCSC and provide a Cost Performance Report (CPR), subcontractor data will be provided to the prime contractor for performance measurement purposes. If a subcontractor is not required to comply with the criteria, the prime contractor should establish procedures which tie the planned and actual accomplishment of the subcontractor to valid indicators, such as the proposed payment schedule or completion of identified work segments. The Cost/Schedule Status Report (C/SSR) may be used for obtaining the data from a subcontractor when the CPR is not needed.

(a) In all other cases if a subcontract (including firm fixed price) is $1M or more, has at least six months between the beginning of work and the first significant delivery, and is scheduled to receive progress payments, then the prime contractor will normally be expected to measure in-process performance of that subcontractor prior to receipt by the prime of the product(s) being produced by that subcontractor. The prime contractor should establish procedures which tie the planned and actual performance of the subcontractor to valid indicators (such as milestones, completion of identified work segments, or proposed payment schedules where directly related to accomplishment).

(b) While the foregoing approach is preferred, other procedures for determining and reporting subcontract progress may be acceptable (for subcontracts which do not have a CPR or C/SSR requirement) provided that the procedures furnish:

1 Adequate indicators of progress including progress prior to delivery of subcontracted items;

2 Identification, cause, and impact of the subcontract schedule or technical problems;

3 Reporting in CPR Format 5 (Problem Analysis) of the impact of such subcontract problems as are causing (or are expected to cause) impact on the performance of the prime contract;

4 Reporting in CPR Formats 1 and 2, the appropriate increased EACs reflecting these problems;

5 Reporting in CPR Formats 1 and 2, the proper BCWS, BCWP, and ACWP at the appropriate point (between receipt and consumption).

d. Summarization. BCWS, BCWP, ACWP, and associated variances should be summarized directly into both the WBS and organizational structure from the appropriate level (cost account or below) to provide both contract status and organizational performance at all levels of management. Because favorable variances in some areas are offset by unfavorable variances in other areas, higher level managers will normally see only the most significant variances at their own level. However, the accumulation of many small variances which may be adding up to a large overall cost problem not attributable to any single major difficulty will also be evident. The same is true of the information to be reported to the Government.

(1) If required by the contract, the Cost Performance Report provides data to the Government at a summary level, normally the third level of the contract WBS or higher. Functional cost information will be reported at the total contract level for major functional categories which reflect the contractor's organizational structure, such as engineering, manufacturing, tooling, material, subcontract, etc. While only problems having significant cost or schedule impact on the contract will appear on this report due to the wash-out effect of favorable and unfavorable variances, all significant variances should be explained in the problem analysis portion of the report. The reason for reporting only summary level information to the Government is that as long as contract performance is proceeding according to plan, there should be no need to report additional detail. If actual performance begins to deviate from the plan, the contractor's system should provide the capability for tracing the variances to their source to isolate the causes of the deviation.

(2) It should be recognized that this method of performance measurement is only one of the management tools available to contractors and DoD project managers. Many major problems are disclosed through methods other than monthly cost reports. For example, failure to meet closely monitored schedule,

3-16

AFSC/AFCC/AFLC-P173-5        AMC-P 715-5        NAVSO-P3627        DLAH8400.2        DCAA-P7641.47
3-5d(2)                                                                                    3-5g

manpower, or technical achievement plans and requirements should promptly alert contractor management that a problem exists. However, the contractor's internal cost performance reports and the Cost Performance Reports to the Government should indicate the overall cost impact of such problems on the contractor.

**e. Significant Variances.** It is important to establish reasonable variance thresholds that will cause problem analyses and narrative reports to be prepared. Careful selection of these thresholds is necesssary to prevent unnecessary work associated with preparing an excessive number of analyses. The analysis of every cost and schedule variance is usually unnecessary and unproductive. Therefore the contractor should establish internal cost and schedule variance thresholds and analyze only those variances which are significant; that is, those which exceed the thresholds. These thresholds may vary with respect to the level of the WBS element, the level of the organizational element, the amount of work remaining, etc. It is essential that these internal variance thresholds be so established that all significant variances will be analyzed while at the same time avoiding an excessive number of variance analyses.

(1) Generally, thresholds are established requiring a variance analysis for any cost or schedule variance that exceeds a certain percentage of BCWS or BCWP and/or exceeds an established dollar minimum (for example, ± _____ % of cum BCWS, or $_____ ,whichever is greater). When initially establishing the thresholds, it may be advisable to provide for tightening these thresholds as the contract progresses, in view of the increased cumulative values of BCWS, BCWP, and ACWP.

(2) Another approach is to establish the thresholds as a percentage of the Budget at Completion (BAC) rather than as a percentage of BCWS and BCWP (for example, $100(BCWP-ACWP) \div BAC$ for cost variance threshold; $100(BCWP-BCWS) \div BAC$ for schedule variance threshold). This results in a threshold which becomes a progressively smaller percentage of cumulative BCWS and BCWP as the contract progresses. Since this type of variance threshold may be relatively loose early in the contract, the threshold for early variances may be limited by adding a threshold based on a percentage of cumulative BCWS (for example, ± _____ % of BAC, or ± _____ % of cumulative BCWS, whichever is less).

(3) Whenever a variance exceeds the prescribed threshold, analysis and explanation are required. Consideration should be given to establishing higher thresholds for underrun or ahead-of-schedule conditions to minimize the generation of analyses and explanations of variances that do not have potential for adverse impact.

(4) The selection of thresholds should avoid the explanation of variances that are unimportant, while not missing variances that are significant. It should be recognized that no particular approach or set of thresholds is "best" for all circumstances. It may be appropriate to use different thresholds for different levels of management, for different organizational elements, and for reporting to the customer. Whenever, during the performance of a contract, it becomes apparent that the thresholds are no longer appropriate, they should be revised. Too few or too many variance analyses in relation to the performance status of the contract may indicate improperly set thresholds which require adjustment.

**f. Technical Achievement.**

(1) The key to meaningful correlation of technical achievement with cost and schedule control is the proper organization and supervision of effort. If a CWBS matches the specification tree and also reflects the manner in which the contractor actually does the work, the problem of correlation is greatly simplified. In correlating cost, schedule, and technical achievement, it is apparent that unfavorable cost or schedule conditions are usually caused by technical difficulties. Therefore, quantitative information as to technical status is desirable and should be supplemented by narrative reports.

(2) As work on a contract progresses, the contractor determines the adequacy and quality of the work performed by making inspections, tests, or other types of technical measurements. If the results are satisfactory and no corrective action is required, the work is then allowed to proceed further. If, on the other hand, deficiencies are found, the contractor considers various alternatives for corrective action; for example, redesign, scrap and remake, rework, etc. When considering these alternatives, the impact on cost and schedule must be weighed in addition to the technical considerations. After one of the alternatives is selected as the desired course of action to correct the deficiencies, it becomes necessary to plan the additional work in terms of new work packages or additions to existing unopened work packages and to change the schedules affected. In some cases the contractor may choose to provide additional budget to the responsible organization. Thus, there is a close relationship between technical achievement (that is, inspection and test) and its impact on cost and schedule.

**g. Estimate at Completion.** C/SCSC also require the contractor periodically to develop comprehensive estimates of costs at contract completion. In developing estimate at completion, the contractor should use all available information to arrive at the best possible estimate of costs for all authorized contract effort.

AFSC/AFCC/AFLC-P173-5      AMC-P 715-5      NAVSO-P3627      DLAH8400.2      DCAA-P7641.47
3-5g(1)
    3-6b(2)

(1) The procedure should be systematically and consistently used from period to period, with adequate consideration given to performance to date. The EAC procedures should provide for the formulation or updating of an estimate of cost to completion, time-phased to the extent necessary to reflect projected rates. This is necessary to ensure that resource requirements are realistic and phased in accordance with projected performance. In addition, the estimate at completion should be examined monthly for accuracy as a routine cost management function and should be updated, as warranted. Such an examination is required to ensure reliable and timely EAC status reporting consistent with contractor reporting requirements.

(2) The EAC process focuses on the cost account manager, but it should also provide for regular input from production control, industrial engineering, material management, finance, and other functions which develop information which may impact cost.

(3) Both the comprehensive EACs and the monthly updates are essential as a basis for management decision making by both the contractor and DoD managers. While no specific time period for developing the comprehensive EAC is established by the criteria, it is expected that a comprehensive estimate will be prepared on an annual basis as a minimum, usually in support of the business plan update, or more frequently when performance indicates that the current estimate is invalid. The estimated cost at completion submitted to the Government on the Cost Performance Report should be reconcilable with internal cost reports and the contractor's latest statement of funds requirements reported on DD Form 1586, Contract Funds Status Report (CFSR), or its equivalent. EACs should be established without regard for contract ceilings.

**3-6. Revisions.** The final section of the criteria pertains to revisions to planning which are necessitated either by contractual change or by internal conditions which require replanning within the scope of the contract. It also deals with maintaining the validity of the performance measurement baseline.

**a. Contract Changes.** Government-directed changes to the contract can impact virtually all aspects of the contractor's internal planning and control system, such as work authorizations, budgets, schedules, and estimated final costs. Revisions required to incorporate authorized changes to contractual effort should be made in a timely manner.

(1) Where the change has been negotiated, budget revisions are based on the negotiated cost of the change. Where work is authorized before negotiations, appropriate change order planning will be accomplished and budgets will be established based on the contractor's cost estimate for the change.

(a) The adjustment of budgets to reflect negotiations is normally accomplished by revising undistributed budgets, management reserves, budgets established for work not yet started, or a combination of these. The use of undistributed budgets or management reserve generally has the least impact since it does not change budgets already issued and agreed to by the responsible organization.

(b) Because budgets associated with near-term work should be well-planned, retroactive changes to budgets for completed work associated with the change should not be necessary.

(c) The formal negotiation of completed tasks may result in an agreed-upon value different from that used to establish BCWS for these tasks. In this situation, it may be appropriate to adjust BCWS and BCWP retroactively to reflect the negotiated values of the completed tasks.

(2) Adequate records of all budgeting changes should be maintained to provide the basis for reconciliation with original budgets at the priced line item level and for subsidiary budgets at the lowest level of the DoD project summary WBS as a minimum.

**b. Internal Replanning.** It may be necessary to perform other replanning actions within the scope of the authorized contract to compensate for cost, schedule, technical problems, which have caused the original plan to become unrealistic; require a reorganization of work or people to increase efficiency of operations; or require different engineering or manufacturing approaches than originally contemplated.

(1) Due to the importance of maintaining a valid baseline for performance measurement, such changes should be accomplished in a systematic and timely manner and must be carefully controlled. Many such changes can be handled within the budget and schedule constraints of cost accounts. Other changes may require the application of management reserves to cost accounts to cover additional costs anticipated as a result of the changes. All changes which affect cost account budgets or include significant schedule revisions, which impact on the time-phasing of the performance measurement baseline, should be brought to the attention of the DoD procuring activity in applicable contractually required reports. This requirement is not intended to reduce contractors' flexibility in the management of their resources, but is intended to assist all users of the data produced from the management systems in understanding and interpreting these data correctly.

(2) If the contractor proposes a change to budgets for completed or in-process work, the contract administration office (CAO), in conjunction with the

AFSC/AFCC/AFLC-P173-5        AMC-P 715-5        NAVSO-P3627        DLAH8400.2        DCAA-P7641.47
3-6b(2)                                                                                                    3-6d

procuring activity, should promptly and thoroughly evaluate the proposed change and its effect on performance measurement. This review should occur before the procuring activity approves the change. The agreement with the contractor should address the specific adjustments to be made and the time period during which the change will be implemented (paragraph 3-6d(7).

(3) It is unusual to close work packages prior to their being completed. However, if closure is authorized, then the only acceptable method of closing uncompleted work packages is to set the BCWS equal to the BCWP earned to date (never vice versa); and subtract that amount from the work package's budget at completion (BAC) to determine the remaining budget which is then handled in accordance with normal replanning guidance. (paragraph 3-3 (i) 3).

(4) When labor, overhead and other rates change, it may be necessary to perform a replanning action. Internal replanning of remaining portions of the performance measurement baseline to account for significant changes in the anticipated rates is desirable, but not mandatory.

c. Formal Reprogramming:

(1) During the life of a contract, situations may arise whereby available contract budgets for the remaining work are decidedly insufficient. Consequently, performance measurement against the available budgets becomes unrealistic. Under these circumstances, a requirement may exist for the total allocated budget to exceed the contract budget base, and formal reprogramming may be necessary. As appropriate, formal reprogramming by the contractor may entail: replanning future work; replanning in-process work; or adjusting variances (that is, cost or schedule or both). Such reprogramming allows the contractor to increase the amount of budget for the remaining work to a more realistic amount, adequate to provide reasonable budget objectives, work control, and performance measurement.

(2) A thorough analysis of contract status requiring full coordination between the Government program manager and the contractor is necessary before the implementation and recognition of a total allocated budget in excess of the contract budget base. The contractor must perform a detailed estimate of all costs necessary to complete the contract. Factors to consider in developing the estimate are: the amount of authorized work remaining, the estimated cost of the resources required to accomplish the remaining work and the budget (including management reserve, if any) available for reallocation to the remaining work. If the difference between the estimated cost to complete and the remaining budget is significant, the contractor will notify the procuring activity of the need to increase the

remaining budgets and measure subsequent performance against a total contract goal higher than the contract budget base.

(3) Before making a decision as to whether to recognize a baseline over the contract budget base, the procuring activity should consider the following:

(a) The primary consideration should be an analysis of the work remaining and the budget remaining. The fact that a contract is overrun to date and is projecting an overrun at completion is not the most important factor in the decision. Changing a baseline merely to compensate for variances already experienced is inappropriate.

(b) The contract should have at least six months of substantial work remaining after reprogramming.

(c) Reprogramming should not be done more frequently than annually and preferably no more frequently than once during the life of the contract.

(4) If the procuring activity is satisfied that the new baseline represents a reasonable plan for completing the contract, the new goal may be accepted as a basis for future performance measurement. Timeliness is essential in making this determination. Therefore, the procuring activity should take immediate action to evaluate the--

(a) Impact on contract status reporting, such as the effect on cost and schedule variances and the change in the relationship of BCWP to the contract value.

(b) Method to be employed by the contractor in implementing the change; for example, adjustment to variances applicable to completed work, and/or adjustments to work-in-process.

(c) Estimated amount of time required to accomplish the reprogramming and the guidelines for performance measurement during that time.

(d) Effect on other contractual requirements; for example, the status of contractually specified program milestones, the contract share ratio, and the liquidation rates for progress payments.

(5) In formal reprogramming, the changes to baseline budgets must be fully documented and traceable. Internal records and reports should be revised expeditiously and provide appropriate visibility to account for the manner in which contract budgets were changed. If variances are adjusted, the BCWS and BCWP values before adjustment will be retained to ensure traceability. Establishment of management reserve for the reprogrammed effort is acceptable in most circumstances. If deemed necessary, guidance may be obtained from the appropriate focal points identified in figure 4-1.

d. Baseline Maintenance. To maintain the validity of the performance measurement baseline, contractor

AFSC/AFCC/AFLC-P173-5    AMC-P 715-5    NAVSO-P3627    DLAH8400.2    DCAA-P7641.47
3-6d                                                                  3-6d(8)

discipline is mandatory throughout the organization, particularly in regard to budgetary control. Contractors' written internal procedures should clearly delineate acceptable and unacceptable budget practices. These should include the following:

(1) Budgets are assigned to specific segments of work (CWBS elements, cost accounts, planning packages, and work packages).

(2) Work responsibility should not be transferred from one performing organization to another, or from one cost account to another without transferring the associated budget.

(3) A budget assigned to future specific tasks should not be used to perform another task, regardless of the CWBS level involved.

(4) When management reserves are used, records should clearly indicate when and where they were applied.

(5) When undistributed budgets exist, records should clearly identify their amount, purpose, and level at which held.

(6) Budgets which are assigned to work packages should not be changed once they are started unless the scope of work is affected by contractual change, or other reasons agreed to by the contracting parties.

(7) Retroactive changes to budgets or costs for completed work or to schedules are not made except for correction of errors or normal accounting adjustments, (including revisions to budgets to reflect the formal negotiated value of completed tasks.)

(8) Retroactive adjustments to BCWP based on substantiated work status to reflect more correctly the actual accomplishment may be appropriate. (However, widespread use of such adjustments due to erroneous BCWP would indicate unacceptable problems in the contractor's planning and control methods. Such widespread adjustments will require the contractor to review internal techniques for establishing BCWS and BCWP to minimize future requirements for such adjustments.)

AFSC/AFCC/AFLC-P173-5      AMC-P 715-5      NAVSO-P3627      DLAH 8400.2      DCAA-P7641.47

Chapter 4

**DOD COMPONENT RELATIONSHIPS**

**4-1.    General Information.** As noted in paragraph 1-3, representatives of various DoD components participate in C/SCSC implementation. Besides major organizations within the military departments, DCAA and DLA/DCAS are included.  This chapter explains responsibilities of various representatives concerned with implementation of the criteria contained in chapter 2 and discussed in chapter 3.  Implementation procedures are explained in chapter 5.    Chapter 6 describes contract administration and audit functions.

**4-2.    Terms Explained.** Several terms are used with reference to various activities responsible for criteria implementations.    When applied to specific efforts, these terms are intended to describe functions rather than organizations.    Each DoD component may assign different  designations  consistent  with  internal operations to accomplish responsibilities associated with these terms.  For example, figure 4-1 indicates which  organizations  usually  perform  functions described in this publication.  Significant terms used for this purpose are described below.

**a.  DoD Component.** The overall responsibility for implementation  of  the  criteria  within  each  DoD component is assigned to the designated focal point for C/SCSC responsibility; for example, AMC, ASN (S&L), AFSC.  When two or more DoD components have collateral interest in application of criteria by a specific contractor facility, one is designated as the lead to organize C/SCSC review activities and provide liaison with DCAA and DCAS as well as other applicable DoD components through focal points described in **c** below. Various factors considered in designation are--

(1) When a new contractual requirement involving criteria implementation exists or is imminent, the component responsible for the applicable procuring activity is the lead.

(2) When no new contractual requirement exists or is imminent, the major component having cognizance for contract administration will function as the lead.

(3) When there is any question about designation of the lead component regarding a specific contractor facility, the designation will be accomplished by mutual agreement through established focal points.

**b.  Procuring Activity.** This term usually identifies the subordinate organization where the procuring contracting office is located. It includes the program office and related functional support offices. Examples of C/SCSC focal points and procuring activities are AFSC/ASD;  AFCC/ASPO;  AFLC/OCALC;  AMC/MICOM; and  ASN(S&L)/NAVSEASYSCOM.

**c.  Focal Points.** DoD components have established focal points to serve as the principal points of contact

for coordination and exchange of information on implementation of the criteria.  The focal point is concerned at a policy level  with establishment of contract  provisions,  the  memorandum  of understanding,  the  letter  of  acceptance,  and surveillance of procuring command implementation of policy guidance.  Usually, focal points within the lead organization are directly responsible for--

(1) Directing the overall organization of teams, scheduling reviews, and maintaining liaison with other DoD component focal points.

(2) Reviewing and approving  major changes (that is, those requiring interpretation of the criteria) to accepted systems.

**d.  Executive Group.** The Performance Measurement Joint Executive Group provides uniform policy guidance  and  a forum to arbitrate any matters concerning C/SCSC reviews and other C/SCSC matters that cannot be resolved amicably through established focal points. This group is expected to solve problems before they reach such magnitude that they would be referred to the Joint Logistics Commanders individually or collectively. Officials designated to serve on the group represent the following:

(1) Chief  of  the  Contract  Cost  Performance Division,  Deputy  Chief  of  Staff  for  Resource Management, HQ Army Materiel Command.

(2) Head, Contracts and Business Management, Assistant  Secretary  of  the  Navy  (Shipbuilding  & Logistics).

(3) Director of Cost (ACC), DCS/Comptroller, HQ Air Force Systems Command.

(4) Appropriate DoD components or program representative when a program is involved which is not under the staff supervision of AMC, ASN (S&L), or AFSC.

(5) HQ DCAA and DLA/DCAS as appropriate.

(6) Office of the Assistant Secretary of Defense (Comptroller), (Ex-officio).

**e.  Contract Administration Office.** This is the cognizant office which is assigned to administer contractual activities at a specific facility. It is a general term  and  includes  AFPROs,  NAVPROs,  SUPSHIPs, ARPROs, DCASRs, DCASMAs, DCASPROs, and CACOs. The cognizant CAO may be part of the procuring activity or may be part of DLA when DCAS is assigned responsibilities for plant cognizance. The focal point in DLA concerning criteria implementation is the Systems and Engineering Division, Executive Director for Contract Management, Defense Logistics Agency. Additional guidance regarding CAO functions is provided in paragraph 6-2.

**f.  Contract Auditor.** This is the representative of the cognizant audit office designated by the DCAA for conducting audit reviews of the contractor's accounting

4-1

AFSC/AFCC/AFLC-P173-5        AMC-P 715-5          NAVSO-P3627        DLAH 8400.2      DCAA-P7641.47
4-2f                                                                                                    4-3a(2)

| Function | Army | Navy | Air Force |
|---|---|---|---|
| DoD Component* | AMC | ASN(S&L) | AFSC<br>AFCC<br>AFLC |
| Procuring Activity | Major subordinate commands | NAVSYSCOMS | Major subordinate commands |
| C/SCSC Focal Point** | AMCRM-K[1] | ASN(S&L) CBM[2] | AFSC/ACC[3] |
| Performance Measurement Joint Executive Group | AMCRM-K[1] | ASN(S&L) CBM[2] | AFSC/ACC[4] |
| Contract Administration Office (CAO) | DCAS/ARPRO/NAVPRO/SUPSHIPS/AFPRO/AFCMC | | |

*    One Service focal point will serve as lead during a C/SCSC review.
**   In DLA the focal point is DLA-AE.  The cognizant audit office maintains liason for DCAA.

[1]   Chief of Contract Cost Performance Division, Deputy Chief of Staff for Resource Management,
      HQ Army Materiel Command.
[2]   C/SCSC Focal Point Office, Acquisition Oversight Division, Contracts and Business Management
      Directorate, Assistant Secretary of the Navy (Shipbuilding & Logistics).
[3]   Directorate of Cost, Headquarters Air Force Systems Command.  Overall Air Force coordination/liason
      is provided by AFSC/ACC.
[4]   HQ Air Force Systems Command/ACC serves as the overall Air Force focal point.

Figure 4-1.  Functional Responsibilities of Selected Organizations.

system policies and procedures for compliance with the criteria. The auditor participates in demonstration reviews as well as subsequent surveillance. In DCAA the focal point is DCAA, Audit Programs Division.

**4-3.   C/SCSC Review Teams.** The procuring activity of the lead component will organize a team of qualified individuals to conduct in-plant reviews of the contractor's management control systems. The purpose of these reviews is to verify that the contractor is operating systems which meet the criteria.

a.  **Team Composition.** The DoD component focal point will approve the apppointment of  the review director and team chief, and will inform other DoD component focal points of those appointments; and, in cases where it is appropriate, will request them to identify representatives with pertinent qualifications to serve as team members. As soon as a review schedule is developed the lead DoD component  will apprise all participants. The team functions are--

(1) Review Director. The director is usually located in the component focal point office. The director will supervise    team efforts in collaboration with representatives from systems commands, major subordinate commands, field activities , and other DoD components selected to work with each C/SCSC review team. The director may be concerned with more than one team simultaneously, and will furnish policy, guidance,   liaison with other focal points,   and interpretation of the criteria to the team chief and team members.

(2) Team Chief. The team chief is usually selected or designated from within a lead component subordinate organization (for example, MICOM for AMC; NAVSEASYSCOM or NAVAIRSYSCOM for ASN (S&L); ASD or SD for AFSC; SSC  for AFCC.) The team chief will organize the team and lead team members in reviewing the application of the criteria by a specific contractor. The team chief reports to the review director, and seeks liaison with other DoD components

through the review director.

(3) **Team Members.** Teams will be composed of qualified representatives from DoD component focal point offices or from applicable major subordinate organizations; particularly, the office of the program manager, applicable functional offices, as well as the cognizant CAO, and the cognizant resident or branch audit office. The team chief supervises assigned members during the course of the C/SCSC reviews. The assigned auditor will obtain technical advice from the audit supervisor as necessary.

b. **Operation of Team.** The team is responsible for a rigorous assessment of the contractor's compliance with the criteria. Such assessment should include review of management control techniques used by contractor organizational elements which perform work on the contract. Additional guidance is contained in chapters 5 and 7.

(1) Members will be responsible to the team chief for the completion of their assignments. To the extent possible, the team chief assigns tasks consistent with background qualifications of team members. However, the team chief will retain the prerogative, with the approval of the review director, to select and use any professional skills and methods considered necessary to accomplish an assignment adequately.

(2) Members should be full-time participants during C/SCSC reviews. However, the team may be augmented with functional specialists to assist in specific aspects of a review.

(3) Team size and types of expertise of members will be determined by the requirements; for example, the type of review, contract size, contractor characteristics, and program characteristics.

c. **Qualifications of Members.** Normally, members should possess one or more of the following qualifications:

(1) Knowledge of the technical content of the program or contract.

(2) Knowledge of the principal engineering design and test requirements of the activity under review.

(3) General industrial engineering/production control background.

(4) Accounting/auditing knowledge.

(5) Program planning and control experience.

(6) Management analysis and/or cost/price analysis experience.

(7) Contract negotiation or administration experience.

d. **Training.** All members should receive specialized training, dealing with management control systems concepts and performance requirements and interpretations before participating as team members. Formal training, such as that given in the Air Force Institute of Technology (AFIT) Course 362, Cost/Schedule Control Systems Criteria is a requirement that normally will not be waived. Such training should be supplemented by additional instruction to ensure the fullest comprehension of the task to be performed during the demonstration review. On-the-job training will be provided, when feasible, to enlarge upon background experience and classroom training for members without prior demonstration review participation.

**4-4. Review Techniques:**

a. **Checklist.** Appendix E provides a checklist for use by the team members in the examination of the contractor's management control systems to ensure conformance. The checklist includes a restatement of criteria followed by specific questions or areas to be addressed by the review team.

b. **Formats.** To clarify checklist items, formats should be developed as illustrations during the review. Appendix F provides typical formats for displaying team findings and supporting conclusions drawn.

**4-5. Coordination:**

a. **Advance Planning.** The focal point in the leading DoD component will inform focal points in other DoD components as far in advance as possible concerning the starting date and estimated duration of the review. Applicable focal points will then inform the lead component focal point for coordination as to whether they intend to participate in the review. If so, they will identify their representatives for the review team.

b. **Administration:**

(1) The team chief will make all necessary arrangements ensuring availability of team members for the time required for preliminary indoctrination and each review for which a team member is needed. Members will be administratively responsible to the team chief during the period of the review.

(2) If another review is necessary to determine the correction of observed deficiencies, or to cover another phase of the program, the same members should be reassembled if possible.

A⁻SC/AFCC/A          ᴸMC-P 715-5      NAVSO-P3627       DLAH 8400.2      DCAA-P7641.47

## Chapter 5

### JLE CONTROL SYSTEMS CRITERIA IMPLEMENTATION PROCEDURES

**5-1.   General In**

a.   **Policy.** It is          al policy of DoD procuring activities to require--

(1) Application ᴏⁱ the C/SCSC to programs that are within the scope outlined in paragraph 2-2.

(2) No changes to contractors' existing management control systems except those necessary to meet the criteria.

(3) The contractor to use data from its own management control system(s) in reports   to the Government.

b.   **Circumstances.** When it has been determined that the criteria will be applied to a specific major system acquisition, generally it will be as--

(1) A requirement within a new contract(s), usually first   expressed in a solicitation document (paragraph 5-2a), or

(2) A requirement of an existing contract(s), subject to bilateral agreement between the contractor and the Government.

c.   **Review Type.** In determining the type of C/SCSC review        (development or    production) to be accomplished, the       following issues should be evaluated:

(1) The type of funding should be considered, but it should not override other considerations.

(2) If the manufacturing effort in the contract is not true manufacturing (e.g., model shop work) and there is no major difference in the way cost data are collected from the method used for the engineering effort, then the C/SCSC review can be based on the application of a development system.

(3) If the preponderance of discrete effort in the contract is identified as either engineering or manufacturing, then the   identification of the C/SCSC review as development   or production should be self-evident.

(4) If there is little or no manufacturing effort (e.g.,contracts for long-lead items, engineering services, or   production planning), the contractor can apply either an   accepted development or an accepted production system regardless of funding.

d.   **Phasing.** Since the contractor's management control   systems utilized during development and during production are usually significantly different from each other, normally   separate demonstration reviews will usually be required for the development phase and production phase.   The contractor may request a simultaneous review of the systems used for both   development and production contracts (or a contractor may have one system for both development and production contracts), thus obviating the necessity for successive reviews. However, the production system demonstrated to gain acceptance should be of such extent that its review will demonstrate its applicability to production contracts that warrant the imposition of the C/SCSC.

e.   **Review Cycle.** The checklist and guidance in this guide   will be used by DoD representatives for evaluation of contractors' proposals concerning C/SCSC implementation and   for conducting an in-plant demonstration review of a contractor's management control systems after a contract is awarded.  They may also serve as   references   for the contractors in preparing descriptions of the   management control systems.   Contractors are encouraged to follow the criteria and checklist when preparing descriptions so as to provide for more effective   assessment by DoD representatives.   The phases of a typical   review cycle include evaluations preliminary to contract award (paragraph 5-2c), an implementation visit after contract award   (paragraph 5-4a(1), readiness assessment after the implementation visit (paragraph 5-4a(2), and the in-plant demonstration   review leading to official acceptance (paragraph 5-4b).   A   redemonstration review may be scheduled when it is necessary to examine any changes made by the contractor after deficiencies are identified (paragraph 5-4d).   After acceptance, the review process continues as a surveillance function (paragraph 6-1c(2), 6-2a(3), and 6-3b).   Figure 5-1 shows   typical phases of C/SCSC implementation.

**5-2.   Preaward Actions.** Preaward   acquisition documents should be reviewed to ensure that C/SCSC and related   reporting are properly included when appropriate.

a.   **Solicitation.** When it is determined that the criteria will  be implemented on a new contract, they will be included as a   requirement in the solicitation document.   The DFARS clause used for this purpose is in appendix A.

b.   **Proposal.** In response to the solicitation, each contractor's proposal should include a description of the management control systems to   be used to meet the requirements of the   criteria under contract.   The contractor may propose to use the   existing systems which in the contractor's judgment meet the  criteria. Upon receipt of notification in the proposal that the contractor will apply the accepted system to a pending contract,  the procuring activity will inform the DoD component C/SCSC focal point  of the contractor's proposal response.

(1) The description of the contractor's management  control system must be presented in sufficient detail to  describe compliance with the criteria, and to permit adequate surveillance of  the operational systems by the   cognizant DoD components.   The

| Evaluation of Proposals (Preaward) | Implementation Visit (After Contract Award) | Readiness Assessment | Demonstration Review | Acceptance | Surveillance : Phase II |
|---|---|---|---|---|---|
| | Surveillance: Phase I | | | | |

**Figure 5-1. Typical Phases of C/SCSC Implementation.**

contractor must also clearly show how the systems meet each of the criteria in chapter 2. While the contractor's system description is not required to follow the evaluation/demonstration review checklist (appendix E) the description must address all items in the checklist. The contractor should correlate checklist items with applicable portions of the system description to ensure adequate coverage (appendix A).

(2) When a contractor chooses to keep the C/SCSC system description general, and rely on cross-referencing to internal procedures or policy manuals for a discussion of the details, the procedures and policy documents are to be referenced in and considered a part of the system description, from a control and revision standpoint. In specific instances only portions of the referenced documents may be C/SCSC related from a control and revision standpoint. In these cases, the contractor and the local Contract Administration Office (CAO) may develop control procedures that will permit changes to the non-C/SCSC related portions of those documents without submittal to the CAO for approval. This will require the contractor to identify, in the system description those specific sections or portions of the internal documents that are related to the contractor's cost/schedule control system and require ACO approval of any change or deletion.

(3) A contractor proposing to use management control systems previously accepted may satisfy the criteria requirement in the solicitation document by citing in the proposal the memorandum of understanding (paragraph 5-6) or notification of acceptance.

c. **Evaluation.** Normally, for a new program the evaluation review is accomplished as a part of precontract award procedures. It is the process of evaluating proposed or existing systems and methods by which the contractor plans to comply with the criteria. The review is basically an analysis of the contractor's management control systems proposed in response to the criteria prescribed in the solicitation. The review will include use of applicable parts of the checklist (appendix E). If a contractor has proposed to use a previously accepted system, the cognizant CAO and resident auditor will furnish a report stating whether or not the contractor's system still meets the criteria.

d. **Onsite Examination.** Normally, an onsite examination of the contractor's systems in operation

will not be required during the evaluation review. However, when any part of the system is not clearly understood, an onsite examination of that part may be necessary to clarify the contractor's intent. If an onsite review is necessary, approval of the activity responsible for source selection will be obtained. The procuring activity will formally notify the cognizant CAO and the resident auditor of the requirement as far in advance as possible. The CAO and DCAA will each provide a representative to assist in the onsite review. The lead command focal point should provide advice and assistance as required. Care should be exercised during the entire evaluation review process to ensure that the contractor and DoD have the same understanding of the system described in the contractor's proposal. Data examples using actual data in the case of existing systems, should be provided to illustrate systems procedures and data flow.

e. **Coordination.** During an onsite evaluation, if it is found that the contractor's proposed system is in use under a contract with another command, coordination with the other command should be maintained during the evaluation review process. If it becomes necessary to review actual plans and reports of the other command's contract, concurrence of the other command should be obtained.

f. **Proprietary Information.** Care must be exercised to avoid improper disclosure of information obtained from contractors, especially in competitive situations, when an onsite evaluation is being made in which the degree of compliance with performance measurement criteria is a factor in contract award.

g. **Evaluation Report.** Following the evaluation review, a written report will be prepared by the evaluation review team which will attest whether or not the contractor's system description in the proposal adequately describes compliance with the criteria. If not, the report will identify specific deficiencies. The reports will be provided to the Source Selection Evaluation Board.

**5-3. Contracts:**

a. **Provisions.** The contract will require that the contractor's systems comply with the criteria throughout performance of the contract. The applicable DFARS clause is in appendix B. It covers the requirements of the criteria and other conditions as follows:

(1) Requires the contractor to establish, demonstrate, and use management control systems which meet the criteria.

(2) Requires the contractor to obtain approval of changes affecting the accepted management system description before implementation.

(3) Provides for Government access to pertinent records and data associated with the management control systems.

(4) When mutually agreed to by the procuring activity and the prime contractor, the criteria will be applied to selected subcontractors, based upon such factors as criticality to program. In these cases, the prime contractor will contractually require subcontractors to comply with the criteria. Subcontracts selected for application of the criteria should be identified in the prime contract.

(a) After a prime contractor has reviewed and accepted a subcontractor's management control system, the prime contractor should provide the subcontractor a written statement that documents the acceptance. Such acceptance does not constitute DoD acceptance and does not apply to DoD contracts or subcontracts from prime contractors on other DoD programs.

(b) Review and acceptance of these selected subcontractors' management control systems may be performed by the procuring activity in coordination with the prime contractor when requested by either the prime contractor or subcontractor. Such review and acceptances will be accomplished in accordance with paragraph 5-4.

b. **Prior Acceptance.** Contractors whose management control systems were accepted for application to another contract of the same type (for example, development or production) at the same facility will not be required to undergo a demonstration review on a new contract unless significant modifications have been made to the previously accepted systems, or surveillance reveals that the accepted systems have not been operated as contractually agreed to in the prior contract. Prior acceptance will be withdrawn if deficiencies are not corrected. This applies to all accepted systems, whether or not covered by a memorandum of understanding (paragraph 5-6).

c. **Subsequent Application Review.** When a contractor has a previously accepted system, a subsequent application review should be conducted in conjunction with a newly awarded contract with a C/SCSC requirement in the same facility. The contractor is expected to be ready for this type review within 90 days after contract award. This type of review is to determine that the contractor has properly applied the previously accepted management control system to the new contract. The team composition and duration for the subsequent application review should be minimized. See chapter 7 for specific guidance.

d. **Extended Subsequent Application Review.** When a contractor has a previously accepted system but wishes to extend it from one program phase to another (development to production or production to development) or from one facility to another, or when the contractor has accomplished an extensive revision to the system description, an extended subsequent application review may be deemed appropriate by the DoD component focal point. The contractor is expected to be ready for this type of review within 90 days after contract award. This type review is to determine that the contractor has properly extended the previously accepted management control system in accordance with the criteria and is applying a criteria-compliant system to the new contract. Team composition and duration for the extended subsequent application review should be minimized. See chapter 7 for specific guidance.

**5-4. Demonstrations:**

a. **Preliminary Actions:**

(1) **Implementation Visit.** As soon as possible after contract award, preferably within 30 days, representatives of the C/SCSC review team should visit the contractor's plant and review the contractor's plans for implementing the C/SCSC. Areas of noncompliance or potential problems will be identified. This visit provides an early dialogue between the lead command and the contractor relative to the C/SCSC review process. During this preliminary review the contractor will usually make presentations to reflect the systems' design and operation and explain applicable reports. The team will examine selected documents and procedures proposed by the contractor. During the visit, the schedule will be developed for the readiness assessment and full-scale demonstration review.

(2) **Readiness Assessment.** The readiness assessment is a meeting or series of meetings, usually three to five days duration, held by representatives of the team with the contractor before the full-scale demonstration review. Without involving the time and expense of the full Government and contractor teams, it provides an opportunity to review contractor progress toward implementing the criteria, to clear up misunderstandings, and to assess the contractor's readiness to demonstrate a fully integrated management control system. It assists in the Government's preparation for the full-scale demonstration review by familiarizing key team members with the fundamentals of the contractor's systems. Any discrepancies should be identified to the contractor for correction. Team members should not design or recommend changes to systems to meet the criteria. The contractor will be afforded an opportunity to correct deficiencies.

b. **Demonstration by the Contractor.** When a demonstration review is required, it will begin as soon as practicable following the contractor's implementation of the management systems pertinent to the contractual effort. The C/SCSC review team will examine the contractor's working papers and documents to ascertain compliance and document its findings. For this purpose, the contractor will be required to make available to the team the documents used in the contractor's management control systems; for example, budgeting, work authorization, accounting, and other functional documents which apply to the specific contracts being reviewed. The documentation must be current and accurate.

(1) The contractor will demonstrate to the team how the management control systems are structured and used in actual operation. The contractor will make available all appropriate internal planning and control documentation required for an indepth analysis of the adequacy of the system in relation to the criteria and the work under contract.

(2) The contractor should have current written descriptions available which describe the management control systems. Applicable portions of the systems descriptions and operating procedures must also be available at the contractor's operating levels. Detailed operating procedures should delineate the following: Responsibilities of operating personnel, limitations on action, and internal authorization required.

c. **Compliance with Criteria.** The burden of proof for demonstrating compliance with the criteria necessarily rests with the contractor. The C/SCSC review team will assess compliance with the criteria.

d. **Corrective Actions.** If the contractor's systems are not acceptable, corrective actions to achieve compliance with criteria must be initiated by the contractor. Areas to be reexamined will be clearly identified to the contractor. A schedule for developing solutions and for a subsequent demonstration review to determine acceptability will be agreed upon by the contractor and review director.

e. **Review Process:**

(1) The team will follow the evaluation/demonstration review checklist (appendix E) to assist members in completing an orderly, comprehensive and conclusive review. The team may employ sampling techniques when it is not practical to review entire systems. Generally, the team will proceed in any given area until conclusive findings are reached. Based upon the best judgment and counsel available, the team chief will identify the cutoff point in any test after sufficient evidence has been obtained on which to base conclusive findings.

(2) The evaluation of a contractor's indirect cost control system is within the purview of the cognizant plant representative and the DCAA; the responsibility for ensuring that these systems are in compliance with the C/SCSC is normally assigned to

their representatives on the demonstration · review team. If the DCAA auditor has accomplished a recent evaluation of the indirect cost control system that verifies compliance with the criteria, a second investigation during the demonstration review is normally not required. Conversely, if the DCAA has not recently evaluated the indirect cost control system, this must be done as part of the demonstration review.

(3) The prime contractor is responsible for the review and acceptance of each subcontractor's management control system that requires application of C/SCSC unless the Government has accepted the responsibility as a result of a request from either the prime or subcontractor for the Government to perform that review. When the prime still maintains that responsibility, the Government may hold open the review of the prime for the failure of the prime to review and accept the subcontractor's management control system adequately. A service focal point may choose to close out the review of the prime, even though the prime has not reviewed and accepted the subcontractor's management system for reasons such as "subcontract not defined" or "not enough work completed to date to evaluate the subcontractor's system." In these cases, the Government team must determine, as a minimum, that the prime's procedures for review of subcontractor's cost/schedule control systems are adequate and that the plan for subcontractor C/SCSC compliance is adequate. The Government CAO may then be required to confirm later that the prime has properly determined subcontractor C/SCSC compliance as a Phase II surveillance item, or a follow-up review by the Government team may be planned.

f. **Acceptance.**

(1) **Formal Report.** At the conclusion of the demonstration review, a formal C/SCSC review report will be prepared and submitted to the review director within 15 working days after completion and approval of all corrective actions. Appendix C discusses in detail the format and content of the report.

(a) Preparation of the demonstration review report is the responsibility of the team chief.

(b) The report will state whether the contractor's system complies with the criteria. If it does not comply, the report will identify the areas of noncompliance in detail.

(c) Requirements and deadlines for preparing drafts of various sections of the report may be delegated to individual team members. A draft of the report should be made available for review by team members.

(d) Any significant disagreements on the final wording or content of the report will be referred through appropriate channels for resolution, as described in paragraphs 1-4, 4-2c, and 4-2d.

AFSC/AFCC/AFLC-P173-5          AMC-P 715-5          NAVSO-P3627          DLAH 8400.2          DCAA-P7641.47
5-4g                                                                                                              5-6a(7)

g. **Procedures.** The demonstration review report will be the basis for acceptance of the contractor's management control systems by the DOD components.

(1) All demonstration review reports will be subject to review by the lead component focal point for coordination with the C/SCSC component focal point responsible for conducting the demonstration review. C/SCSC review reports will be offered by the lead service to the other military service focal points for coordination before release.

(2) The appropriate contracting officer will inform the contractor regarding acceptance or nonacceptance of the systems and provide the contractor with copies of the report when released by the review director.

(3) The contractor will provide a description of the accepted management systems according to appendix B, paragraph (b). A memorandum of understanding (paragraph 5-6) may be used to satisfy the requirements of describing accepted systems.

h. **Report Distribution.** The lead focal point for coordination will control the issuance and distribution of the reports. When applicable, the cover page of each report will contain a statement indicating that the report contains contractor proprietary data, and that distribution of copies will be limited. Contents will not be disseminated outside DoD, in whole or in part, without the express permission of the cognizant service focal point and the contractor.

**5-5.    Compliance after Acceptance:**

a. Acceptance of a contractor's management control systems as meeting the criteria is not intended to inhibit continuing innovations and improvement of its systems. However, contractors are contractually obligated to maintain their systems in a state which satisfies the criteria.

b. Surveillance to ensure that contractors properly maintain their systems is a DoD management responsibility which will be accomplished by the cognizant CAO and DCAA auditor. Indications that a contractor's system is failing to comply with any part of the criteria can be cause for scheduling another demonstration review and may result in revocation of prior acceptance. Specific discrepancies discovered as a result of the demonstration review or normal surveillance procedures should be corrected immediately. Surveillance responsibilities are described in chapter 6 and in more detail in the C/SCSC Joint Surveillance Guide.

c. Contractor-proposed changes to accepted management control systems will be submitted to the cognizant CAO in accordance with the C/SCSC Joint Surveillance Guide.

**5-6.    Memorandum of Understanding:**

a. **General.** After demonstration and acceptance of a contractor's management control systems, the contractor's system description should be updated as necessary to describe accurately the system as accepted. Since complete descriptions may be voluminous, consideration should be given to preparing them in a format which may be referenced or summarized for use in related documents. A memorandum of understanding (referencing the description of the accepted systems) may then be executed relative to the application of those accepted systems to contracts which require compliance with the C/SCSC. Pertinent features of the memorandum of understanding (appendix D) are described below:

(1) The memorandum of understanding is not a contract clause, but it may be incorporated in any contract by appropriate reference when the contract includes a requirement for compliance with the criteria.

(2) This document serves to clarify intent of the contractor and DoD components relative to implementation of the criteria. It contains reference to a description of accepted systems and subsystems; it identifies facilities and locations; and provides for Government access to pertinent contractor records and data for surveillance purposes. Provision is also made to permit changes to accepted systems.

(3) A memorandum of understanding may be executed after the contractor's management control systems are applied to a single contract containing the criteria requirement or it may be developed without an existing or pending contractual requirement when requested by the contractor or DoD, provided that a demonstration review is accomplished through mutual agreement.

(4) If a request for a memorandum of understanding is processed without an existing or pending contractual requirement, it will be necessary to designate the lead command (paragraph 4-2a). Applicable demonstration reviews may involve any contract in the facility where performance measurement systems are applied, provided that the contracts selected will ensure that a representative appraisal of the contractor's system is made.

(5) When a memorandum of understanding is to be consummated between the DoD components and the contractor, such a memorandum will be prepared and executed by the appropriate ACO, based upon the demonstration review report and letter of acceptance.

(6) A memorandum of understanding will normally be limited for application to a single contractor facility as defined for the purpose of contract administration and may be limited as to application to development or production contracts.

(7) A contractor may respond to solicitations for potential contracts by citing the memorandum of understanding in the proposal. Procuring activities may evaluate the current status of implementation of criteria by the contractor to ensure themselves that

applicable systems are acceptable without requesting a full-scale demonstration review (paragraph 5-3c).

    b.  **Procedures.** In the execution of a memorandum of understanding, the following procedures will apply:

    (1) A contractor desiring a memorandum of understanding will direct a written request to the cognizant CAO.

    (2) The CAO will forward the request to the lead component focal point for coordination.

    (3) A contractor requesting a memorandum of understanding subsequent to acceptance under an existing or previous DoD contract will make this known to the CAO. The CAO will coordinate the request with the lead component focal point. The other military departments will be asked to review the contractor's system either through review of the C/SCSC demonstration review report or a joint service subsequent application review. Following agreement, a memorandum of understanding will be executed as set forth above.

    (4) The memorandum of understanding should be distributed to each military department, CAO, DCAA, contractor, and other appropriate addressees.

AFSC/AFCC/AFLC-P173-5     AMC-P 715-5     NAVSO-P3627     DLAH 8400.2     DCAA-P7641.47

Chapter 6

CONTRACT ADMINISTRATION AND AUDIT

**6-1.    General Information:**

**a.    Scope.** This chapter describes the responsibilities of the cognizant CAO and the resident DCAA auditor for the review and surveillance of C/SCSC management control systems (paragraphs 6-2 and 6-3). With the commencement of contract performance, contractors are expected to operate management systems which have been proposed and evaluated prior to contract award. Surveillance is a DoD management responsibility to be carried out at each contractor's facility to ensure the contractor complies with the requirements of the executed contract. Uniform guidance for the DoD components performing this surveillance is contained in the C/SCSC Joint Surveillance Guide.

**b.    Time Span.** Following award of the contract, the contractor's management control systems may be in various stages of implementation. The surveillance function will begin immediately following contract award. Continuing surveillance will be directed toward the procedures and functions of the contractor's management control systems. During surveillance, if the description of the systems identified in the contract is found to differ from the contractor's practices, the procuring activity must be promptly informed.

**c.    Phases of Surveillance.** Surveillance consists of two phases. The first is applicable immediately after contract award, the second following the demonstration review (figure 5-1).

**(1)  Phase I.** This phase is directed to assisting the procuring activity and monitoring the progress of the contractor to ensure satisfactory implementation of the contractor's management control systems. The cognizant CAO and contract auditor will provide team members for the C/SCSC reviews and assist the DoD procuring activity in monitoring remedial actions to meet the criteria. During this period, even though the contractor's systems have not yet been accepted, it is necessary that the procuring activity make decisions based upon contractor reports derived from the currently operating management control systems. Thus, it is necessary to verify that the data contained in the reports submitted are in accordance with contractual requirements and are valid and complete.

**(2)  Phase II.** Immediately following acceptance of the contractor's management control systems, surveillance should be formalized to include a comprehensive program covering the complete scope of the criteria. Such a program should provide for verifying, tracing, and evaluating the information contained in the reports submitted to DoD procuring components. It also should ensure that the contractor's management control system continues to operate as accepted and that any proposed or actual changes comply with the criteria and are reflected in the contractor's system description.

**6-2.    CAO Functions and Responsibilities.** The cognizant CAO will--

**a.    During Phase I--**

(1) Provide a C/SCSC review team member to assist the DoD procuring activity by monitoring contractor progress during the implementation process.

(2) Consummate a memorandum of agreement with the Government program office to ensure all participants understand their surveillance responsibilities.

(3) Prepare a surveillance plan, using the written description of the systems provided by the contractor and referenced in the contract. The assistance of the contract auditor should be obtained in respect to that part of the program concerning financial data. The written surveillance program plan will be submitted by the cognizant CAO to the DoD procuring activity for concurrence.

**b.    During Phase II--**

(1) Implement the surveillance plan which will assess continuity and consistency in the operation of the contractor's systems.

(2) Evaluate any formal or informal changes in the management systems to determine whether such systems continue to comply with the criteria and contract provisions. The purpose is to detect and appraise alterations which are not in accord with the criteria.

(3) Perform recurring evaluations of the effectiveness of the contractor's policies and procedures, selective tests of the contractor's internal data flow, and validations of external reports submitted to the Government.

(4) Forward to the contract auditor a list of all reports submitted in response to DD Form 1423, Contract Data Requirements List, which require audit verification of financial data.

(5) Verify that the contractor's systems continue to comply with the criteria and contract provisions.

(6) Apprise the contractor and DoD components of any deficiencies in the contractor's management control systems. Determine whether corrective actions taken have remedied such deficiencies.

(7) Advise the contractor and the concerned DoD procuring activity of any uncorrected deficiencies which affect the overall acceptability of contractor's systems.

**6-3.    DCAA Functions and Responsibilities.** The cognizant DCAA audit office will provide an auditor who will--

a.  During Phase I--
    (1) Serve as a C/SCSC review team member for the review of the accounting system and related financial areas, including budgeting, direct and indirect costs, variance analysis, and forecasting.
    (2) Participate in monitoring contractor progress in assigned areas during C/SCSC implementation.
b.  During Phase II--
    (1) Perform reviews of the contractor's accounting system policies and procedures for compliance with performance measurement criteria and contract provisions.

    (2) Perform periodic reviews, on a selective basis, of the financial data contained in the various reports prepared by the contractor to determine whether they accurately reflect the information in the contractor's books and records.
    (3) Perform periodic evaluations of the contractor's financial policies and procedures.
    (4) Prepare audit reports incorporating deficiencies, disclosed during surveillance reviews that cannot be resolved with the contractor. Such reports should be addressed to the procuring activity through the cognizant CAO.

AFSC/AFCC/AFLC-P173-5    AMC-P 715-5    NAVSO-P3627    DLAH 8400.2    DCAA-P7641.47

Chapter 7

POST- ACCEPTANCE REVIEWS OF COST/SCHEDULE CONTROL SYSTEMS

**7-1. General Information:**
a. **Purpose.** This chapter provides guidance on conduct of reviews of lesser magnitude that follow the demonstration review, as well as guidance in the preparation for and performance of these post- acceptance reviews. The reviews include the subsequent application review, the extended subsequent application review, and the baseline review.
b. **Importance.** The C/SCSC subsequent application review and the extended subsequent application review are major means of assuring continued use of a C/SCSC compliant management system. Although not as comprehensive as the initial demonstration review, the subsequent reviews are of equal importance to the continued successful implementation of the C/SCSC approach and its credibility. Post-acceptance review findings and recommendations are of consequence to the Army, Navy, and Air Force, as well as to other DoD components that may be doing business with a particular contractor. Uniformity of application and consistency of interpretation are advantageous both to DoD and to the contractor.

**7-2. Subsequent Application Review:**
a. **Definition.** A C/SCSC subsequent application review is a formal review performed in lieu of a C/SCSC demonstration review when compliance with the DoD Cost/Schedule Control Systems Criteria is a requirement in a contract (DFARS 52.234-7001) at a facility where the management control system has been accepted for the same type of contract (e.g., development or production). Because the intent of conducting a subsequent application review is to minimize unnecessary repetition of work previously performed in the demonstration review, the length and scope of a subsequent application review are limited.
b. **Objective.** The objective of a subsequent application review is to ensure that, on a new contract, the contractor is properly and effectively using the accepted system, revised in accordance with approved changes. It is not the purpose of the review to reassess the contractor's previously accepted system.
c. **Basis for Application.** At the same facility subsequent application reviews will normally be required in connection with new contracts which require C/SCSC where the work is to be performed at a facility whose management control system has previously been accepted on another contract of the same type (that is, development, production). Where there is a production option on a development contract, a subsequent application review (or a demonstration review if there is no accepted production system) will normally be required when work on the production option begins. Where the contract is a follow-on contract for the same (or almost the same) item at the same facility, the subsequent application review requirement may be waived on recommendation to the contracting officer by the focal point.
d. **Contractual Requirement.** DFARS Clause 52.234-7001 Cost/Schedule Control Systems, requires that the contractor be prepared to demonstrate that the contractor's management control system meets the criteria (C/SCSC). The clause also provides that "If the contractor...is utilizing Cost/Schedule Control Systems which have previously been accepted,...the Contracting Officer may waive all or part of the provisions concerning..demonstration and review" (See DFARS clause, appendix B).
e. **Policy.**
(1) The subsequent application review will be performed in lieu of a complete C/SCSC demonstration review when--
(a) A contractor or subcontractor is contractually required to apply C/SCSC and is using a management control system which has been previously accepted.
(b) The C/SCSC surveillance monitor in the contract administration office (CAO) confirms that the accepted system has been or is being operated as contractually agreed to in the prior or current contract.
(2) A subsequent application review is normally not considered appropriate--
(a) When an accepted system is being transferred from one facility to another and simultaneously to a different program phase; i.e., development to production or production to development.
(b) When there are major changes to the system description of the accepted system (in the case of its extension to either another program phase or another facility).
(3) When a contractor's facility has an accepted system for the proper acquisition phase, a demonstration review will be required only when determined necessary by the DoD component focal point.
f. **Responsibilities.** The DoD component focal point has the authority and responsibility concerning the subsequent application review for selection of the review director; approval of type, scope, and extent of the review; and approval of team recommendations.
g. **Common Elements of the Subsequent Application Review and the Extended Subsequent Application Review.** For a discussion of elements common to the two types of reviews see paragraph 7-4.

**7-3. Extended Subsequent Application Review.**
a. **Definition.** A C/SCSC extended subsequent application review is a formal review performed in lieu

AFSC/AFCC/AFLC-P173-5      AMC-P 715-5      NAVSO-P3627      DLAH 8400.2      DCAA-P7641.47
7-3a                                                                                          7-4b(1)

of a C/SCSC demonstration review when compliance with the DoD Cost/Schedule Control Systems Criteria is a requirement in a contract (DFARS 52.234-7001). This type review extends a previously accepted system. The extension includes such factors as extending the system from one program phase to another, from one contractor facility to another, or it can extend the validation of a previously accepted system description to a revised system description.

b. **Objectives.** The primary objectives of extended subsequent application reviews are to--

(1) extend the coverage of existing accepted system descriptions; and

(2) assess rewritten or extensively revised and updated system descriptions; and

(3) assure the application of the accepted systems with approved changes.

c. **Basis for Application.** The extended subsequent application review may be conducted under the following conditions:

(1) A previously accepted system is applied in the contractor's facility to a different program phase (e.g., a system previously accepted for development contracts is applied to production, or a system previously accepted for production is applied to development).

(2) A previously accepted system is applied to a different facility of the same contractor for the same program phase (e.g., development or production).

(3) The contractor has accomplished an extensive rewrite or revision of the accepted system description.

d. **Contractual Requirement.** DFARS Clause 52.234-7001 Cost/Schedule Control Systems Criteria requires that the contractor be prepared to demonstrate that the contractor's management control system meets the criteria (C/SCSC). The clause also provides that "if the contractor...is utilizing Cost/Schedule Control Systems which have previously been accepted...the Contracting Officer may waive all or part of the provisions concerning demonstration and review." (See DFARS clause, appendix B).

e. **Policy.** The intent of conducting an extended subsequent application review is to minimize unnecessary repetition of work previously performed in the demonstration review. Its length and scope are limited. The extended subsequent application review will be performed in lieu of a complete C/SCSC demonstration review under circumstances described in paragraph 7-2.c above when--

(1) A contractor or subcontractor is contractually required to apply C/SCSC and is using a management control system which has been previously accepted.

(2) The C/SCSC surveillance monitor in the contract administration office (CAO) confirms that the accepted system has been or is being operated as contractually agreed to in the prior or current contract.

f. **Determination.** When a contractor facility has an accepted system for the proper acquisition phase, a demonstration review will be required only when determined necessary by the service focal point. The DoD component focal point will make the final recommendation to the contracting officer as to whether an extended subsequent application review or a demonstration review will be required of the contractor, considering such relevant factors as--

(1) Assessment of CAO and DCAA surveillance findings.

(2) Current and prior experience of other Government program offices requiring C/SCSC application by the contractor.

g. **Responsibilities.** The DoD component focal point has the authority and responsibility concerning the extended subsequent application review for selection of the review director; approval of type, scope, and extent of the review; and approval of team recommendations. The areas of review to be emphasized must be established by the review director at the outset of the review.

h. **Triservice.** The choice of an extended subsequent application review in lieu of a demonstration review must be coordinated among the services.

**7-4. Common Elements of the Subsequent Application Review and the Extended Subsequent Application Review:**

a. **Selection and Composition of Team.** Team members for either the subsequent application review or the extended subsequent application review must meet the same standards as demonstration review team members (chapter 4). The members should be experienced and understand the C/SCSC. Knowledge of both the program and the contract is desirable. Formal training, such as that given in AFIT courses 361 and 362 (Surveillance of Cost/Schedule Control Systems Criteria and Cost/Schedule Control Systems Criteria) is a requirement that normally will not be waived. The review director, team chief, and members will be formally assigned to the team. The team composition will normally be as indicated for demonstration review teams (paragraph 4-3a), although the number of team members will normally be fewer. The C/SCSC surveillance monitor in the CAO may be selected as team chief, or as an assistant team chief (paragraph 4-3).

b. **Pre-Award Process:**

(1) A contractor proposing to apply a management control system previously accepted may satisfy the C/SCSC requirements of the solicitation document by citing in the proposal the formal notice of prior acceptance of the management system and/or the memorandum of understanding by which the con-

AFSC/AFCC/AFLC-P173-5          AMC-P 715-5          NAVSO-P3627          DLAH 8400.2          DCAA-P7641.47
7-4b(1)                                                                                                      7-4e(1)

tractor has agreed to apply the accepted system to all contracts requiring C/SCSC.

(2) Upon receipt of notification in the proposal that the contractor will apply the accepted system to a pending contract, the procuring activity will inform the DoD component focal point (through subordinate command channels) of the contractor's C/SCSC proposal response.

(3) Based upon information available from the contractor's proposal, the CAO and DCAA surveillance findings from other procuring activities, and from other services' C/SCSC experience with the given contractor, a determination will be made as to the nature and extent of the required review. The procuring activity will be responsible for this appraisal and will forward its recommendation to the DoD component focal point. The focal point will review the recommendation, and will notify the procuring activity of its approval or disapproval.

c. Preparation for the Review:

(1) Team Preparation. After contract award and prior to formal review activities with the contractor, the review team chief should ensure that the team members receive briefing on the program, the content and status of the contract, and the findings of the CAO and DCAA C/SCSC surveillance activities. The team members should also review the contractor's management control system description, demonstration review report upon which the current acceptance was based, subsequent application review reports, and recent Cost Performance Reports.

(2) Implementation Visit. When the review director and/or team chief consider it to be necessary, an implementation visit should be made to the contractor's plant to discuss plans and actions associated with the subsequent application review and to ensure that the anticipated scope of the review is understood. Coordination by telephone or correspondence may be used in lieu of an implementation visit whenever practicable.

(3) Contractor Preparation. Prior to the start of the review, it is desirable (but not mandatory) that--

(a) The principal contract tasks have been definitized.

(b) The contractor has developed schedules and a complete set of performance measurement baseline budgets for the definitized work under the contract.

(c) The contractor has completed at least two complete monthly accounting periods of performance against baseline budgets and schedules, and has submitted Cost Performance Reports (CPR) for these two periods.

(d) Each subcontractor required to comply with the C/SCSC or to provide Cost /Schedule Status Reports (C/SSR), has submitted at least one CPR or C/SSR to the prime contractor.

(e) Obvious significant deficiencies in the contractor's management control system operation on the new contract (possibly evident from the quality of the reports, on-site progress reviews, or C/SCSC surveillance) have been identified to the contractor and corrected.

d. Conduct of the Review:

(1) Subsequent Application Review. The contractor is expected to be ready for the subsequent application review 90 days after contract award. This is to assure that the previously accepted management control system is being properly applied on the new contract. The team composition and the duration of the review should be the minimum necessary to complete the task. Usually a three to five day visit to the contractor's facility by a team composed of fewer members than a demonstration review team will suffice. The review is normally conducted by the office which conducts demonstration reviews and includes participation by the Government program management office, the cognizant CAO, and Defense Contract Audit Agency (DCAA) representatives. The review director assigned by the DoD component focal point is expected to provide consistency of C/SCSC interpretation, and maintain the depth of review at a reasonable level.

(2) Extended Subsequent Application Review. The contractor is expected to be ready for the extended subsequent application review within 90 days after contract award to assure that the previously accepted management control system is being applied properly on the current contract(s). The team composition and the duration of the review should be the minimum necessary to accomplish the task. Normally ten workdays should be sufficient for the extended subsequent application review. The review is normally conducted by the office which conducts demonstration reviews and includes participation by the Government program management office, and by the cognizant CAO and Defense Contract Audit Agency (DCAA) representatives. Because of the nature of an *extended* subsequent application review, the nature of the extension of the previously accepted system must be clearly understood. Portions of the management control system designated for review to assure that the extension meets the criteria must be described at the start of the review.

e. Procedure for the Subsequent Application Review and the Extended Subsequent Application Review.

(1) Subsequent Application Review . The basic review routine is similar to that of a C/SCSC demonstration review. However, the direct use of the Evaluation/Demonstration Review Checklist for C/SCSC, appendix E, to the C/SCSC Joint Implementation Guide, is not appropriate unless used on an exception basis and in abbreviated form. The level of detail resulting

from strict application would otherwise be too great and would result in a full reevaluation of the contractor's management control system.

(a) The review will consist of five basic activities. These are--

1. An overview briefing by the contractor to familiarize the review team with the accepted management control system identifying any changes which have occurred since the management system was last subjected to a demonstration review or subsequent application review.

2. A review, on a sample basis, of the documentation which establishes and records changes to the contractor's baseline plan for the contract. This will include work authorizations, schedules, budgets, resource plans, and change records (including management reserve and undistributed budget logs). The purpose is to verify that the contractor has established and is maintaining a valid, comprehensive integrated baseline plan for the contract.

3. A review, on a sample basis, of the reporting of cost and schedule performance against the baseline plan, along with appropriate analyses of problems and projection of future costs. Also, a tracing of the summarization of cost/schedule performance data from the lowest level of formal reporting to the Cost Performance Report. The purpose of this activity is to verify the accuracy of reported information.

4. Interviews with a selected sample of contractor managers to verify that the contractor's previously accepted control systems are fully implemented and are being used in the management of the contract.

5. An exit briefing by the review team covering the team's findings. During this briefing any open system discrepancies should be discussed along with the agreed upon corrective action plan which establishes responsibility and a time-frame for corrective action.

NOTE: In all of the foregoing activities, the sample actually reviewed should be relatively small so as to limit the duration of the review. However, samples should be carefully selected to focus on the areas of greatest cost, activity, and, if possible, risk. If significant problems are found, the sample size and, if necessary, the duration of the review should be extended sufficiently to determine their extent.

(2) **Extended Subsequent Application Review.** The basic review routine is similar to that of a C/SCSC demonstration review. The direct use of the Evaluation/Demonstration Review Checklist for C/SCSC, appendix E, is appropriate here. However, it is not intended to be pursued to the extent that it would result in a full reevaluation of the contractor's management control system.

(a) The review will consist of the following basic activities:

1. An overview briefing by the contractor to familiarize the team with the accepted management control system, identifying any changes which have occurred since the system was last reviewed, especially those changes which provide for the requested extension of the system.

2. A review of the system to establish that it is in fact the accepted system.

3. A review, on a sample basis, of the documentation which establishes and records changes to the contractor's baseline plan for the contract. This will include work authorizations, schedules, budgets, resource plans, and change records (including management reserve and undistributed budget logs). The purpose is to verify that the contractor has established and is maintaining a valid, comprehensive integrated baseline plan for the contract.

4. A review, on a sample basis, of the reporting of cost and schedule performance against the baseline plan, along with the appropriate analyses of problems and projection of future costs. Also a tracing of the summarization of cost performance data from the lowest level of formal reporting to the Cost Performance Report. The purpose of this activity is to verify the accuracy of reported information.

5. Interviews with a selected sample of contractor managers to verify that the contractor's previously accepted control systems are implemented fully and are being used in the management of the contract. The system description manual should also be evaluated both before and during the review to assure that the management control systems being applied to the contract are accurately and completely described within the manual.

6. An exit briefing by the review team covering its draft of findings. During this briefing any open system discrepancies should be discussed along with the agreed upon corrective action plan which establishes responsibility and schedule for corrective action.

NOTE: In all of the foregoing activities, the sample actually reviewed should be sufficient to meet the intent of the review. Samples should be carefully selected to focus on the areas of greatest cost activity, complexity, and if possible, risk. Care should be taken to assure that the criteria are satisfied if the extended subsequent application review is for a phase different from that originally accepted. Identification of significant problems may require a follow-up visit to complete the review.

f. **Review Results.**

(1) **Conclusion of the Review.** It is expected that the subsequent application review and the extended subsequent application review will result in approval after one review. However, there can be no

approval until all significant discrepancies have been corrected. Significant discrepancies should be brought to the attention of the contractor by the review director or team chief. A schedule to correct deficiencies should be agreed upon during the review. This should include the corrective action plan, persons responsible for correction of deficiencies, and a timeframe for accomplishment.

(2) Uncorrected Discrepancies. Outstanding discrepancies resulting from either a subsequent application review or an extended subsequent application review will be corrected within a reasonable time period (normally 30 days) as specified by the procuring activity performing the review. Failure to do so can result in termination of the memorandum of understanding and withdrawal of prior acceptance of the contractor's system.

(3) Further Review. Where it is necessary to verify that deficiencies have been corrected, the review director should determine whether this can be accomplished by the CAO or whether it will be necessary to reassemble all or part of the review team for a follow-up review. This determination should be based upon an evaluation of the nature of the corrective action required and the contractor's plan and schedule for corrective action. Follow-on reviews must be approved by the DoD component focal point and will be scheduled by the team chief. The contractor's corrective actions prior to the follow-up review will be monitored by the C/SCSC surveillance monitor and reported to the team chief.

(4) Deficiencies in the Previously Accepted System. At the time of either the subsequent application review or the extended subsequent application review, there is a mutual presumption that the contractor's management system is in compliance with the C/SCSC as accepted by DoD. In those instances when the review team determines that the contractor's accepted management system does not meet C/SCSC requirements, the contractor and ACO should be promptly notified. The information provided must detail the specific area of deviation. The procuring activity and the focal point should be notified of major discrepancies and advice should be obtained from all parties regarding items of major disagreement including the lead service involved in acceptance of the system. If during the review the team discovers problems which require changes to the contractor's accepted system, the following procedures should be used:

(a) If the contractor agrees with the problems and proposes an acceptable change to the system, the normal ACO approval procedures for system description changes will apply as provided in both the Joint Implementation and Surveillance Guides.

(b) If the contractor disagrees that there is a problem and does not propose an acceptable change

to the system, the procedures outlined in paragraph 1-4 of the Joint Implementation Guide will apply. In those cases where problems cannot be resolved by the team, the discrepancy will be elevated to the focal point. In exceptional cases, particularly when more than one military department is involved, the Performance Measurement Joint Executive Group should be convened to adjudicate outstanding issues.

g. Reports for the Subsequent Application Review and the Extended Subsequent Application Review.

(1) Subsequent Application Review Report. A formal report of the subsequent application review will be prepared by the team chief and forwarded to the DoD component focal point within ten workdays after completion of the review. It should document overall findings, problems, conclusions, and recommendations (see Appendix C for review report format). Specifically, the report should identify the contractor facility and contract reviewed, the dates of the review, and the review team members. It should state the significant findings including any significant discrepancies and any agreements with the contractor regarding their correction. Also, it should specify what further review is required, if any, and recommend responsible activities (CAO, review team, etc.).

(a) Abbreviated reports will be prepared for any follow-up reviews required to assess corrective action. They will be forwarded to the DOD component focal point within seven workdays after completion of the follow-up review.

(b) Upon review and approval of the report and its recommendations, the contractor will be notified through the procuring activity and the CAO, with a copy furnished to the DoD component focal point. The team chief will coordinate plans for the follow-up review with the review director and the contractor.

(2) Extended Subsequent Application Report. A draft report of the extended subsequent application review will be prepared by the team chief prior to departure from the contractor's facility. It should document overall findings, problems, conclusions, and recommendations (see appendix C for required format). Specifically the report should identify the contractor's facility, the source of the previously accepted system, its phase, the contract reviewed, the dates of the review, and the review team members. It should state the significant findings, including any significant discrepancies and any agreements with the contractor regarding their correction. Also, it should specify what further review is required, if any, and recommend the responsible activities (CAO, review team, etc.). After approval of corrective actions, the finalized formal report will be forwarded by the team chief to the appropriate focal point within 20 workdays after completion of corrective actions.

(a) **Minimum Requirements.** The extended subsequent application review report requirements are reduced from those of a demonstration review and are as follows:

1. The same general requirements as for a subsequent application review except that when the accepted system is being applied to a different program phase at the same facility, each of the 35 Cost/Schedule Control Systems Criteria items must be addressed.

2. Any differences between the previously accepted system and the system being reviewed must be addressed at the checklist question level (not just at the criteria level).

3. Exhibits must include as a minimum, Formats 1, 2, 3, 4, 5, 6, 7, and 12 of appendix F, and a schedule trace.

(b) **Review and Approval.** Following approval by the review lead component focal point, the report is forwarded to other Service C/SCSC focal points for concurrence with the team recommendations. Upon review of and concurrence with the report and its recommendations, the procuring activity will be advised of action to be taken.

**7-5. Baseline Review:**

a. **Basis for Application.** A baseline review is conducted to determine on a very limited sampling basis that a contractor is continuing to use the previously accepted performance measurement system and is properly implementing a baseline on the contract or option under review. A baseline review is particularly applicable to follow-on contracts, where key C/SCSC knowledgeable contractor personnel are retained from previous efforts. The baseline review is not intended to be a routine replacement for more comprehensive reviews. It should be utilized only where there is a firm basis (e.g., historical evidence) to propose that a more comprehensive review is not warranted. A request coordinated with the cognizant CAO must be processed by the procuring activity to the applicable focal point to conduct such a review. Requests are normally considered when --

(1) The baseline review is to be scheduled within one year of an original performance measurement system acceptance;

(2) The baseline review is to be scheduled within one year of either a successful extended subsequent application review or a subsequent application review;

(3) Otherwise justified by the procuring activity and approved by the applicable focal point.

(4) There are no significant outstanding CAO

C/SCSC discrepancies existing at the time of the review.

b. **Scope.** The review is primarily a data review. The majority of the interface will be with the contractor's cost/schedule performance measurement personnel and key contractor management personnel in the program/project management organization.

c. **Conduct of the Baseline Review:**

(1) **Review Duration.** The baseline review should be conducted at the contractor's facility and should normally take no longer than three days.

(2) **The Review Team.** The Government team will typically consist of four or more people: A team chief, a program/project office representative, a local CAO representative (normally the C/SCSC surveillance monitor), and a DCAA representative. Additional team members may be utilized at the discretion of the team chief to investigate areas of special interest or concern. A review director may also participate.

d. **Preparation for the Baseline Review.** Prior to proceeding with a baseline review, the Government team must be familiar with the contractor's cost/schedule performance measurement system description, the applicable C/SCSC demonstration report and any other previous C/SCSC reports. It is also important that the contractor be notified prior to the baseline review of the scope of the review and the required documentation.

e. **Baseline Review Methodology.** The baseline review is intended to concentrate on selected criteria checklist items of the C/SCSC Joint Implementation Guide. These items are selected to assure that the baseline is in place and current. Among the items which might be selected are: responsibility assignment matrix, the hierarchy of schedules, a schedule trace, management reserve and undistributed budget logs, work authorization documents and flows, cost account/work package documentation, selected performance measurement element traces through internal reports, material acquisition and subcontract reviews, earned value techniques, statusing, estimate at completion calculations, verification of authorized changes to the baseline, and reconciliation of external with internal reports.

f. **Results of Baseline Review:**

(1) Significant discrepancies should be brought to the attention of the contractor by the team chief. Corrective actions and/or a schedule for correction of deficiencies should be agreed upon during the review.

(2) **Uncorrected discrepancies.** Outstanding discrepancies resulting from a baseline review will be corrected within a reasonable time period (normally 30 days).

AFSC/AFCC/AFLC-P173-5     AMC-P 715-5     NAVSO-P3627     DLAH 8400.2     DCAA-P7641.47

## Chapter 8

## DATA REQUIREMENTS

**8-1. General Information:**

**a. Specification.** The contractor is required to use data from the operative management control systems in making reports to DoD components. The inclusion of the criteria in a solicitation document or contract is not of itself a requirement for delivery of data. Data requirements must be specified in the solicitation and contract in the Contract Data Requirements List (CDRL), DD Form 1423.

(1) DD Form 1660, Management Systems Summary List, identifying appropriate systems from the DoD Acquisition Management Systems and Data Requirements Control List (AMSDL).

(2) The Department of Defense Federal Acquisition Regulations Supplement (DFARS), formerly Defense Acquisition Regulations (DAR).

**b. Performance Measurement.** Normally the Cost Performance Report (CPR), latest revision of data item DI-F-6000,will be required. Regardless of the reporting formats required, all reported performance measurement information must be derived from the contractor's internal systems. To provide a sound basis for responsible decision making by both contractor management and DoD managers, contractors' management control systems must provide timely data which effectively relate cost, schedule, and technical accomplishment within the framework of the CWBS. As a minimum, a contractor's systems must be capable of providing, at least monthly, such information as--

(1) BCWS, BCWP, and ACWP.

(2) Actual indirect costs and budgeted indirect costs.

(3) Budgeted cost at completion and estimated cost at completion.

(4) Significant variances resulting from the analysis of these data. These variances should be identified in terms of labor rate and efficiency variances, material price and usage variances, and deviations from overhead budgets, together with the reasons for the variances and the impact on the CWBS and organizational elements to which resources have been allocated.

(5) The time-based schedule, significant differences between the planned and actual achievements, and the reasons for the differences.

(6) Appropriate managerial actions taken or proposed as a result of variances and differences reported.

(7) Baseline changes and reasons.

(8) Management reserve changes and reasons.

**8-2. Data Elements.** A CWBS which has been prepared in accordance with guidance provided in MIL-STD-881 (latest revision), constitutes the basic framework against which the data elements selected are to be reported. Even though reported cost and schedule data may be required only at summary levels, all such data must consist of traceable accumulations which account for work performed and resources expended at appropriate lower levels.

**8-3. Cost Performance Report.**

**a. Specify Data Item.** When required by the contracting activity, the Cost Performance Report will be obtained from the contractor by specifying data item DI-F-6000 (latest revision) on DD Form 1423. DI-F-6000 (latest revision) is listed in the DoD 5000.19L, Volume II, Authorized Management Systems and Data Requirements Control List (AMSDL). The AMSDL may be requisitioned from the Naval Publications and Forms Center, 5801 Tabor Avenue, Philadelphia PA 19120.

**b. CWBS and Variance Thresholds.** When the DD Form 1423 specifies DI-F-6000, the DD 1423 item should state the WBS items to be reported on and should state the variance thresholds (quantitative or by exception) beyond which cost and schedule variances must be discussed in the problem analysis section (Format 5) of the report.

**c. Discontinuance of Cost Performance Reporting When Costs Reach Ceiling.** Performance measurement reporting should not be discontinued unless appropriate waivers have been granted and the Government CAO and Program Office no longer need the data .

**AFSC/AFCC/AFLC P-173-5          AMC-P 715-5          NAVSO-P3627          DLAH 8400.2          DCAA-P7641.47**

**APPENDIX A**

**DOD FEDERAL ACQUISITION REGULATIONS SUPPLEMENT**

**SOLICITATION PROVISION**

52.234-7000 Notice of Cost/Schedule Control Systems. As prescribed at 34.005-71, insert the following provision:

**NOTICE OF COST/SCHEDULE CONTROL SYSTEMS  (AUG 1985)**

(a) The Offeror shall submit a comprehensive plan for compliance with the attached criteria (DoDI 7000.2 Performance Measurement for Selected Acquisitions) for the internal Cost/Schedule Control Systems which are or will be operational for any contract resulting from this solicitation, and which includes the C/SCSC clause set forth at 52.234-7001 of the DoD FAR Supplement. The Offeror shall identify the Offeror's existing management systems separately from proposed modifications to meet the criteria. The plan shall:

    (i)    describe the management systems and their application in all major functional cost areas such as engineering, manufacturing and tooling, as related to development of the work breakdown structure, planning, budgeting, scheduling, work authorization, cost accumulation, measurement and reporting of cost and schedule performance, variance analysis, and baseline control;

    (ii)   describe compliance with each of the criteria, preferably by cross-referencing appropriate elements in the description of systems with the items in the checklist for C/SCSC contained in AFSC/AFCC/AFLC-P173-5, AMC-P 715-5, NAVSO-P3627, DLAH 8400.2, DCAA-P7641.47, Cost/Schedule Control Systems Criteria Joint Implementation Guide.

    (iii)  Identify the major subcontractors, or major subcontracted effort in the event major subcontractors have not been selected, planned for application of the criteria;

    (iv)  describe the proposed procedure for administration of the criteria as applied to subcontractors.

(b) If the contractor is utilizing Cost/Schedule Control Systems which have been previously accepted, or is operating such systems under a current Memorandum of Understanding, evidence of such may be submitted in lieu of the comprehensive plan mentioned above. In such event, the Contracting Officer will determine the extent to which such systems shall be reviewed to assure continued compliance with the criteria.

(c) The Offeror shall provide information and assistance as requested by the Contracting Officer for evaluation of compliance with the cited criteria.

(d) The Offeror's plan for Cost/Schedule Control Systems will be evaluated prior to contract award. Upon acceptance of the Cost/Schedule Control Systems a description of the accepted systems will be referenced in the contract.

(e) Subcontractor selection for application of the C/SCSC will be by agreement between the prime contractor and the Government. The prime contractor will contractually require the selected subcontractors to comply with the criteria. However, demonstrations and reviews of these selected subcontractors' management systems may be performed by the procuring authority when requested by either the prime or subcontractor.

(End of provision)

A-1

**AFSC/AFCC/AFLC-P173-5      AMC-P 715-5      NAVSO-P3627      DLAH 8400.2      DCAA-P7641.47**

**APPENDIX B**

**DOD FEDERAL ACQUISITION REGULATIONS SUPPLEMENT**

**CONTRACT CLAUSE**

52.234-7001 Cost/Schedule Control Systems.  As prescribed at 34.005-71 insert the following clause:

**COST/SCHEDULE CONTROL SYSTEMS (AUG 1985)**

(a)  The Contractor shall establish, maintain and use in the performance of this contract Cost/Schedule Control Systems meeting the attached criteria (DoDI 7000.2 Performance Measurement for Selected Acquisitions).  Prior to acceptance by the Contracting Officer and within ninety (90) (or as otherwise agreed to by the parties) calendar days after contract award, the Contractor shall be prepared to demonstrate the operation of the Contractor's systems to the Government to verify that the proposed systems meet the established criteria set forth above.  As a part of the demonstration review and acceptance procedure, the Contractor shall furnish the Government a description of the Cost/Schedule Control Systems applicable to this contract in such form and detail as indicated by the AFSC/AFCC AFLC-P173-5  AMC-P 175-5  NAVSO-P3627  DLAH 8400.2  DCAA-P7641.47, Cost/Schedule Control Systems Criteria Joint Implementation Guide hereinafter referred to as the guide, or required by the Contracting Officer.  The Contractor agrees to provide access to all pertinent records, data and plans as requested by representatives of the Government for the conduct of the review.

(b)  The description of the management systems accepted by the Contracting Officer, identified by title and date, shall be referenced in the contract.  Such systems shall be maintained and used by the Contractor in the performance of the contract.

(c)  Contractor changes to the accepted systems shall be submitted to the Contracting Officer for review and approval.  The Contracting Officer shall advise the Contractor of the acceptability of such changes within sixty (60) days after receipt from the Contractor.  When systems existing at time of contract award do not comply with the criteria, adjustments necessary to assure compliance will be effected at no change in contract price or fee .

(d)  The Contractor agrees to provide access to all pertinent records and data requested by the Contracting Officer or duly authorized representative for the purpose of permitting Government  surveillance to ensure continuing application of the accepted systems to this contract.  Deviations from accepted systems discovered during contract performance shall be corrected as directed by the Contracting Officer.

(e)  The Contractor shall require that each selected subcontractor, as mutually agreed to between the Government and the Contractor and as set forth in the schedule of this contract, shall meet the Cost/Schedule Control Systems criteria as set forth in the guide and shall incorporate in all such subcontracts adequate provisions for demonstration, review, acceptance and surveillance of subcontractors' systems, to be carried out by the Government when requested by either the prime or subcontractor.

(f)  If the Contractor or subcontractor is utilizing Cost/Schedule Control Systems which have been previously accepted or is operating such systems under a current Memorandum of Understanding, the Contracting Officer may waive all or part of the provisions hereof concerning demonstration and review.

(End of Clause)

APPENDIX C

C/SCSC REVIEW REPORTS

**DEMONSTRATION REVIEW REPORT.** Primary consideration must be given to the fact that reports (particularly the findings) must provide a basis for effective review by others with limited or no knowledge of the specific management system. The quality of the report is usually taken as a direct reflection of the nature and quality of the review and as such is the vehicle for obtaining acceptance from other DoD components. The following is a format for a typical C/SCSC demonstration review report:.

**1.   Table of Contents.**

**2.   Index to Exhibits.**

**3.   General.**  Introductory comment:

   **a.  Background.**  Briefly describe the events relating to the contractor's implementation of C/SCSC and the Government's reviews relating thereto.   Identify the contract purpose, type, duration, amounts (total, ceiling price, target cost, etc.), the program being supported, and the cognizant DoD component. Also indicate other work in the contractor's facility that has the contractual requirement for compliance with C/SCSC.
   **b.  Contractual Requirement.**  Identify the specific contract requirement for the C/SCSC.

**4.   Purpose.**  Identify the purpose of the review. Normally, it will be for the demonstration review (or redemonstration review(s) if applicable) of the performance measurement system operated in a specific contract effort.

**5.   Scope.**  This section should identify the specific contractual entity which is the subject of this review; for example, division, company, plant, and the functional organizations such as engineering, manufacturing, quality assurance, etc., included in the review. Also, discuss whether the review is related to development or production contracts and if the system is restricted to the specific contract or is used throughout the facility.

**6.   Review Process.**  Describe the extent of the review, indicate the approach taken.  Areas not investigated should be discussed and reasons provided; for example, when review of the method of implementing contract changes could not be done because no contract changes had been executed. Identify the methodology used in conducting the review indicating such items as range of interviews, depth of review, documentation examined, and traces accomplished.    Team members and  their associated responsibilities should be identified in this section.

**7.   Findings.**   Organize this section according to the major categories of the criteria; for example, organization, planning and budgeting, accounting, analysis, and revisions. Address each of the five basic areas reviewed in narrative of sufficient depth to explain system compliance.     State each criterion, describe how the management  system complies with that criterion, and support responses  by exhibits to illustrate  and prove the compliance.
   a.   State each checklist question, and reference the contractor's system description  paragraph numbers. Findings  must explain how the system satisfies or does not satisfy the checklist question by going into sufficient depth to clearly establish compliance or noncompliance.
   b.   The narrative may be supported by or relate to exhibits.   However, the narrative must explain the exhibit so that it  would not be necessary for the reviewer to turn to the exhibit  to understand why it is there and what it portrays.  The  narrative should be able to stand by itself, but exhibits cannot  stand alone. The narrative in the Findings section should state explicitly what the reader should look for on each exhibit and   how the exhibit proves that the requirement is met.

**8.   Conclusions.**  This section should include the overall evaluation of the systems reviewed as to their compliance with the criteria.  Reference should be made, when applicable, to the supporting evidence in the Findings section. This portion of the report must contain a conclusion concerning the acceptability of the contractor's system as to its compliance with the C/SCSC. The acceptance statement should specifically identify the system demonstrated and whether it is used for development, production, or construction .

**9.   Recommendations.**  This section should recommend necessary corrective actions to achieve acceptability or compliance.      The recommendations should not delineate specific corrective   methods to correct deficiencies but should identify areas  requiring improvement. Suggested improvements to enhance  the system can be noted here but should be identified separately from corrective actions necessary to comply with the criteria. If applicable, include a recommendation of the necessity for a redemonstration review.

**10. Redemonstration Reviews.** When it is necesssary to conduct redemonstration reviews because of deficiencies found and not corrected during the demonstration review,  the following guidance applies:
   a.  The deficiencies existing at the conclusion of the demonstration review are to be cited in the findings associated  with the specific criteria items.  These

C-1

deficiencies then become the basis for the redemonstration review and are addressed in this section of the report. The report will have separate sections to address the findings of each redemonstration review.

b. The redemonstration review section will be presented in the same format as the demonstration review section. Only those events applicable to the redemonstration will be addressed. However, do not restate the deficiency in the Findings section unless necessary for understanding the new findings.

### 11. Exhibits:

a. The exhibits will include as a minimum those exhibits, formats, and procedures called for in the Evaluation/Demonstration Review Checklist for C/SCSC. Exhibit 1 will be a reproduced checklist marked to show, for each question, the compliance or noncompliance of the management system. The criterion block will be left blank and all N/As will be placed in the "No" column. ("No" answers should be explained in the Findings.)

b. The remarks column of the checklist may be used to show the page and paragraph in the contractor's system description where the question is discussed.

c. In preparing exhibits it is important that--

(1) Exhibits be completely legible. Do not reduce them merely to avoid foldouts. Foldouts are entirely acceptable when they provide clearer, more legible exhibits.

(2) Exhibits be annotated and marked to highlight the specific element(s) of information and to identify the trail in support of the related narrative.

(3) Exhibits be placed at the end of the report and numbered consecutively without regard to the category of criteria to which they relate.

(4) Exhibit numbers be placed in the lower outside corner.

(5) Exhibits be from the same time frame and, where feasible, from the same leg of the WBS. The Government team shall not redraw the CWBS or any of the exhibits in order to eliminate intermediate summarizations (e.g., geographical, functional, etc.).

(6) Exhibits supporting the Analysis section of the Findings be provided for both direct and indirect cost variances. Indirect cost variances must be analyzed from the standpoint of the manager responsible for their control; that is, the point at which they were incurred.

NOTE: The following precautions should be observed in report preparation to produce concise and meaningful reports :

a. An executive summary is not required. (It is optional).

b. The narrative content must adequately explain how the system complies with the related criteria. There is a strong tendency to refer to contractor documents without an adequate description of the nature and function of the document. However, do not quote at length from the system description, but instead, synopsize the portion of the system description involved.

c. Elements elected for trace should be stated in the narrative. Selected trace elements should be consistently used in reporting on the various categories of the criteria.

d. Exhibits must be legible and complete. In many cases, handwritten exhibits cannot be deciphered. Required reconciliations, such as reconciliation of internal to external reports, are frequently omitted.

e. Exhibits must identify the specific areas to which attention is directed; that is, they must be marked to highlight the items of interest, or an explanatory note superimposed to make clear exactly what the exhibit illustrates.

f. Exhibits must portray "live data," except when used to reproduce a part of directives, procedures, or forms.

g. Include only the pertinent pages (appropriate excerpts) of multipage exhibits (such as WBS Dictionary, CPRs, Schedules, etc.).

h. After stating each checklist question, do not repeat it in a positive statement. It is enough to say "Yes" or "No" or "Yes. Not demonstrated," and follow with appropriate remarks.

i. For each checklist question:

(1) State what the system description requires.

(2) Refer to the applicable procedures or subsection of the system description documentation.

(3) Describe briefly what the team did for verification using the exhibit section as applicable.

j. Each checklist answer does not have to have an exhibit.

k. "Yes. Not demonstrated" checklist items should also be highlighted in the recommendation/conclusion area.

l. "N/A" will only be used when the system does not provide compliance and never will have to comply (e.g., provide higher level CWBS budgets above the cost account level).

m. Answers to checklist questions may be combined or cross referenced rather than repeating narrative discussions found elsewhere.

AFSC/AFCC/AFLC-P173-5      AMC-P 715-5      NAVSO-P3627      DLAH 8400.2   DCAA-P7641.47

**EXTENDED SUBSEQUENT APPLICATION REVIEW REPORT.** The requirements of this report are reduced from those of a demonstration review. A draft report of the review will be prepared by the team chief prior to departure from the contractor's facility. After approval of corrective actions the finalized formal report will be forwarded by the team chief to the appropriate focal point within 20 working days after completion of corrective actions. The minimum requirements for reports of the extended subsequent application review are as follows:

1. Table of Contents

2. Index to Exhibits

3. **General.** Introductory comment:
    a. **Background** Discuss why the extended subsequent application review was selected as the appropriate type C/SCSC review (see Chapter 5-3.d). Briefly describe the events relating to the contractor's prior system acceptance and any subsequent reviews. Identify the contract purpose, type, duration, amounts (total, ceiling price, target cost, etc.), the program being supported, and the cognizant DoD component. Also list other work in the contractor's facility to which application of the C/SCSC is a contractual requirement.
    b. **Contractual Requirement.** Identify the specific contract requirement for the C/SCSC.

4. **Purpose.** Identify the purpose by describing how the system demonstrated during this review extends the applicability of the previously accepted system.

5. **Scope.** Identify the specific contractual entity which is the subject of this review; for example, division, company, plant, and the functional organizations such as engineering, manufacturing, quality assurance, etc., included in the review. Discuss whether the review is related to development or production contracts and if the system is restricted to the specific contract or is used throughout the facility.

6. **Review Process.** Describe the extent of the review, such as whether or not the entire system was demonstrated, or merely parts applicable to the extension of the system. Areas not investigated should be discussed and reasons provided. Indicate the approach taken; that is, "criteria category," "functional," or other. Identify the methodology used in conducting the review, indicating such items as range of interviews, depth of review, documents examined, and traces conducted. Team members and their associated responsibilities should be identified in this section.

7. **Findings.** Organize this section according to the major categories of the criteria; for example, organization, planning and budgeting, accounting, analysis, and revisions. Address each of these in narrative of sufficient depth to explain C/SCSC compliance of the contractor's system.
    a. Each of the 35 criteria should be addressed, with a description of how the management system complies with each criterion. Support responses with appropriate exhibits to illustrate and prove criteria compliance.
    b. Any differences between the previously accepted system and the system being reviewed must be addressed at the checklist question level (not just at the criteria level).

8. **Exhibits.** Exhibits must include, as a minimum, Formats 1, 2, 3, 4, 5, 6, 7, and 12 of the Joint Implementation Guide appendix F, and a schedule trace. Exhibits must be explained within the narrative by telling why the exhibit has been entered and what it illustrates or proves.

9. **Conclusions.** This section should include the overall evaluation of the systems reviewed as to their compliance with the criteria. Reference should be made, when applicable, to the supporting evidence in the Findings section. This portion of the report must contain a conclusion concerning the acceptability of the contractor's system as to its compliance with the C/SCSC, and the acceptability of extending the contractor's previously accepted management control system as proposed. The acceptance statement should specifically identify the system demonstrated and whether it is used for development or production.

10. **Recommendations.** This section should recommend necessary corrective actions to achieve acceptability or compliance. The recommendations should not delineate specific corrective methods to correct deficiencies but should identify areas requiring improvement. Suggested improvements to enhance the system may be noted here but should be identified separately from corrective actions necessary to comply with the criteria. If applicable, include a recommendation for further review.

C-3

AFSC/AFCC/AFLC-P173-5          AMC-P 715-5          NAVSO-P3627          DLAH 8400.2   DCAA-P7641.47

**SUBSEQUENT APPLICATION REVIEW REPORT.** This report should be prepared by the team chief and forwarded to the DoD component focal point within 10 working days after completion of the review. Abbreviated reports will be prepared for any follow-up reviews required to assess corrective action. They will be forwarded to the DoD component focal point within 7 working days after completion of the follow-up review. The report will be prepared according to the following outline:

**1. Introduction:**

a. Summarize type and scope of contract.

b. Give basis of acceptance of contractor's system as C/SCSC compliant.

c. Identify any other in-plant contracts requiring C/SCSC compliance.

d. Identify team members and their organizations.

**2. Scope of Review.** Identify contractor organizations and data samples reviewed.

**3. Findings.**

a. Organize findings in paragraph form under each of the major criteria groups; that is, organization, planning and budgeting, accounting, analysis, and revisions.

b. Each criterion need not be addressed. Determine data samples and manager interviews by the critical aspects of the contractual statements of work. As a minimum, the findings should address:

(1) WBS subdivision and integration with the contractor's organizational structure.

(2) Schedule subdivision and integration with cost account/work package schedules.

(3) Work package identification.

(4) Baseline establishment and maintenance.

(5) BCWP determination.

(6) Identification of management reserves and undistributed budgets.

(7) Establishment of internal budgets which add up to the contract budget base.

(8) Material measurement.

(9) Estimated cost at completion determination and reasonableness.

(10) Identification of variance analysis thresholds and quality of analysis.

(11) Contractor manager knowledge and use the system.

(12) Contractual change incorporation.

**4. Conclusions and Recommendations.**

a. The contractor has (or has not) properly implemented the system.

b. Deficiencies found and corrective action taken.

c. Remaining deficiencies with assigned responsibility and schedule for accomplishment of corrective action.

d. Recommendation for a second review if necessary.

e. Recommended items for CAO surveillance.

**BASELINE REVIEW REPORT.** A draft report of the baseline review will be prepared by the team chief prior to departure from the contractor's facility. After approval of corrective actions the finalized report will be forwarded by the team chief to the appropriate service focal point within 10 workdays. If a follow-up review is required to assess corrective action, an abbreviated report will be prepared and forwarded to the DoD component focal point within 7 workdays after completion of the follow-up review. Specifically the baseline review report should do the following:

a. Identify the contractor's facility, the program phase, the contract reviewed, dates of the review, contract performance measurement status, and review team members.

b. State significant findings, including any significant discrepancies and any agreements with the contractor regarding their correction.

c. Specify whether or not further review is required, and recommend the responsible activities (CAO, DCAA, or review team).

AFSC/AFCC/AFLC-P173-5      AMC-P 715-5      NAVSO-P3627      DLAH 8400.2      DCAA-P7641.47

**APPENDIX D**

**EXAMPLE OF MEMORANDUM OF UNDERSTANDING FOR C/SCSC**

This Memorandum of Understanding entered into as of _____ establishes a mutual agreement between the Department(s) of the (Army-Navy-Air Force, as appropriate) and (insert contractor's full name, including facility and location) regarding the implementation and maintenance of management control systems conforming to the criteria established by Department of Defense Instruction 7000.2, Performance Measurement for Selected Acquisitions, and as implemented by AFSC/AFCC/AFLC-P173-5, AMC-P 715-5, NAVSO-P3627, DLAH 8400.2, DCAA-P7641.47.

WHEREAS, the contractor has demonstrated certain management control systems and subsystems as identified and defined in (contractor's system description dated _____ ), and

WHEREAS, the Department(s) of the (Army-Navy-Air Force, as appropriate), by letter dated _____ ), based on demonstration review report dated _____ , did validate such systems and subsystems then.

BE IT UNDERSTOOD AND AGREED that such systems and subsystems which have been validated as indicated above, together with approved changes thereto, shall apply to future (specify type of contract; for example, RDT&E, production, or both) contracts entered into between the contractor and the Department(s) of the (Army-Navy-Air Force, as appropriate) which require compliance with the C/SCSC; and

BE IT FURTHER UNDERSTOOD AND AGREED THAT:

(1) Contractor-proposed changes to those validated systems and subsystems will be submitted to the cognizant CAO for review and approval or disapproval by the ACO.

(2) The contractor agrees to provide access to pertinent records and data in order to permit adequate surveillance of the validated systems and subsystems.

This Memorandum of Understanding will remain in force indefinitely, subject to modification by mutual agreement or termination by either party.

_____              _____
(Administrative Contracting Officer)                                    (Contractor)

D-1

AFSC/AFCC/AFLC-P173-5     AMC-P 715-5     NAVSO-P3627     DLAH 8400.2     DCAA-P7641.47

APPENDIX E

| EVALUATION/DEMONSTRATION REVIEW CHECKLIST FOR C/SCSC | | | |
|---|---|---|---|
| CHECKLIST ITEMS | YES | NO | REMARKS |
| **I.   ORGANIZATION** | | | |
| 1.   DEFINE ALL THE AUTHORIZED WORK AND RELATED RESOURCES TO MEET THE REQUIREMENTS OF THE CONTRACT, USING THE FRAMEWORK OF THE CWBS. | | | |
| a.  Is only one CWBS used for the contract (attach copy of CWBS)? | | | |
| b.  Is all contract work included in the CWBS? | | | |
| c.  Are the following items included in the CWBS (annotate copy of CWBS to show elements below): | | | |
| (1)   Contract line items and end items (if in consonance with MIL-STD-881 latest edition)? | | | |
| (2)   All CWBS elements specified for external reporting? | | | |
| (3)   CWBS elements to be subcontracted, with identification of subcontractors? | | | |
| (4)   Cost account levels? | | | |
| 2.   IDENTIFY THE INTERNAL ORGANIZATIONAL ELEMENTS AND THE MAJOR SUBCONTRACTORS RESPONSIBLE FOR ACCOMPLISHING THE AUTHORIZED WORK. | | | |
| a.  Are all authorized tasks assigned to identified organizational elements?  (This must occur at the cost account level as a minimum.   Prepare exhibit showing relationships.) | | | |
| b.  Is subcontracted work defined and identified to the appropriate subcontractor within the proper WBS element? (Provide representative example.) | | | |
| 3.   PROVIDE FOR THE INTEGRATION OF THE CONTRACTOR'S PLANNING, SCHEDULING, BUDGETING, WORK AUTHORIZATION, AND COST ACCUMULATION SYSTEMS WITH EACH OTHER, THE CWBS, AND THE ORGANIZATIONAL STRUCTURE. (Reference format 1.) | | | |
| a.  Are the contractor's management control systems listed above integrated with each other, the CWBS, and the organizational structure at the following levels: (Use matrix to illustrate the relations.) | | | |
| (1)   Total contract? | | | |
| (2)   Cost account? | | | |

AFSC/AFCC/AFLC-P173-5        AMC-P 715-5        NAVSO-P3627        DLAH 8400.2        DCAA-P7641.47

**Appendix E-continued**

| CHECKLIST ITEMS | YES | NO | REMARKS |
|---|---|---|---|
| 4.    IDENTIFY THE MANAGERIAL POSITIONS RESPONSIBLE FOR CONTROLLING OVERHEAD (INDIRECT COSTS) | | | |
| a. Are the following organizational elements and managers clearly identified: | | | |
| (1)  Those responsible for the establishment of budgets and assignment of resources for overhead performance? | | | |
| (2)  Those responsible for overhead performance control of related costs? | | | |
| b. Are the responsibilities and authorities of each of the above organizational elements or managers clearly defined? | | | |
| 5.    PROVIDE FOR INTEGRATION OF THE CWBS WITH THE CONTRACTOR'S FUNCTIONAL ORGANIZATIONAL STRUCTURE IN A MANNER THAT PERMITS COST AND SCHEDULE PERFORMANCE MEASUREMENT FOR CWBS AND ORGANIZATIONAL ELEMENTS.  (Provide matrix showing integration.) | | | |
| a. Is each cost account assigned to a single organizational element directly responsible for the work and identifiable to a single element of the CWBS? | | | |
| b. Are the following elements for measuring performance available at the levels selected for control and analysis: | | | |
| (1)  Budgeted cost for work scheduled? | | | |
| (2)  Budgeted cost for work performed? | | | |
| (3)  Actual cost of work performed? | | | |
| II. PLANNING AND BUDGETING | | | |
| 1.    SCHEDULE THE AUTHORIZED WORK IN A MANNER WHICH DESCRIBES THE SEQUENCE OF WORK AND IDENTIFIES THE SIGNIFICANT TASK INTERDEPENDENCIES REQUIRED TO MEET THE DEVELOPMENT, PRODUCTION, AND DELIVERY REQUIREMENTS OF THE CONTRACT. | | | |
| a. Does the scheduling system contain (Prepare exhibit showing traceability from contract task level to work package schedules.)-- | | | |
| (1)  A master program schedule? | | | |
| (2)  Intermediate schedules, as required, which provide a logical sequence from the master schedule to the cost account level? | | | |

AFSC/AFCC/AFLC-P173-5     AMC-P 715-5     NAVSO-P3627     DLAH 8400.2     DCAA-P7641.47

**Appendix E-continued**

| CHECKLIST ITEMS | YES | NO | REMARKS |
|---|---|---|---|
| (3) Detailed schedules which support cost account and work package start and completion dates/events? | | | |
| b. Are significant decision points, constraints, and interfaces identified as key milestones? | | | |
| c. Does the scheduling system provide for the identification of work progress against technical and other milestones, and also provide for forecasts of completion dates of scheduled work? | | | |
| d. Are work packages formally scheduled in terms of physical accomplishment by month, week, or day as appropriate? | | | |
| 2. IDENTIFY PHYSICAL PRODUCTS, MILESTONES, TECHNICAL PERFORMANCE GOALS, OR OTHER INDICATORS THAT WILL BE USED TO MEASURE OUTPUT. | | | |
| a. Are meaningful indicators identified for use in measuring the status of cost and schedule performance? (Provide representative samples.) | | | |
| b. Does the contractor's system identify work accomplishment against the schedule plan? (Provide representative examples.) | | | |
| c. Are current work performance indicators and goals relatable to original goals as modified by contractual changes, replanning, and reprogramming actions? (Provide exhibit showing incorporation of changes to original indicators and goals.) | | | |
| 3. ESTABLISH AND MAINTAIN A TIME-PHASED BUDGET BASELINE AT THE COST ACCOUNT LEVEL AGAINST WHICH CONTRACT PERFORMANCE CAN BE MEASURED. INITIAL BUDGETS ESTABLISHED FOR THIS PURPOSE WILL BE BASED ON THE NEGOTIATED TARGET COST. ANY OTHER AMOUNT USED FOR PERFORMANCE MEASUREMENT PURPOSES MUST BE FORMALLY RECOGNIZED BY BOTH THE CONTRACTOR AND THE GOVERNMENT. (Reference formats 2 and 8.) | | | |
| a. Does the performance measurement baseline consist of the following: | | | |
| (1) Time-phased cost account budgets? | | | |
| (2) Higher level CWBS element budgets (where budgets are not yet broken down into cost account budgets)? | | | |
| (3) Undistributed budgets, if any? | | | |

**Appendix E-continued**

| CHECKLIST ITEMS | YES | NO | REMARKS |
|---|---|---|---|
| (4)   Indirect budgets, if not included in the above? | | | |
| b.  Is the entire contract planned in time-phased cost accounts to the extent practicable? | | | |
| c.  In the event that future contract effort cannot be defined in sufficient detail to allow the establishment of cost accounts, is the remaining budget assigned to the lowest practicable CWBS level elements for subsequent distribution to cost accounts? | | | |
| d.  Does the contractor require sufficient detailed planning of cost accounts to constrain the application of budget initially allocated for future effort to current effort? (Explain constraints.) | | | |
| e.  Are cost accounts opened and closed based on the start and completion of work contained therein? | | | |
| 4.   ESTABLISH BUDGETS FOR ALL AUTHORIZED WORK WITH SEPARATE IDENTIFICATION OF COST ELEMENTS (LABOR, MATERIAL, ETC.).  (Reference formats 2, 3, and 4.) | | | |
| a.  Does the budgeting system contain--   (Provide exhibit.) | | | |
| (1)   The total budget for the contract  (including estimates for authorized but unpriced work)? | | | |
| (2)   Budgets assigned to major functional organizations? (See checklist Item II, 9ab.) | | | |
| (3)   Budgets assigned to cost accounts? | | | |
| b.  Are the budgets assigned to cost accounts planned and identified in terms of the following cost elements: (Reference Formats 3 and 4.) | | | |
| (1)   Direct labor dollars and/or hours? | | | |
| (2)   Material and/or subcontract dollars? | | | |
| (3)   Other direct dollars? | | | |
| c.  Does the work authorization system contain-- (Prepare sample exhibit.) | | | |
| (1)   Authorization to proceed with all authorized work? | | | |

AFSC/AFCC/AFLC-P173-5     AMC-P 715-5     NAVSO-P3627     DLAH 8400.2     DCAA-P7641.47

**Appendix E-continued**

| CHECKLIST ITEMS | YES | NO | REMARKS |
|---|---|---|---|
| (2) Appropriate work authorization documents which subdivide the contractual effort and responsibilities within functional organizations? | | | |
| 5. TO THE EXTENT THE AUTHORIZED WORK CAN BE IDENTIFIED IN DISCRETE, SHORT-SPAN WORK PACKAGES, ESTABLISH BUDGETS FOR THIS WORK IN TERMS OF DOLLARS, HOURS, OR OTHER MEASURABLE UNITS. WHERE THE ENTIRE COST ACCOUNT CANNOT BE SUBDIVIDED INTO DETAILED WORK PACKAGES, IDENTIFY THE FAR TERM EFFORT IN LARGER PLANNING PACKAGES FOR BUDGETING AND SCHEDULING PURPOSES: (Reference format 6.) | | | |
| a. Do work packages reflect the actual way in which the work will be done and are they meaningful products or management-oriented subdivisions of a higher level element of work? (Provide representative sample.) | | | |
| b. Are detailed work packages planned as far in advance as practicable? | | | |
| c. Is work progressively subdivided into detailed work packages as requirements are defined? | | | |
| d. Is future work which cannot be planned in detail subdivided to the extent practicable for budgeting and scheduling purposes? (Provide sample.) | | | |
| e. Are work packages reasonably short in time duration or do they have adequate objective indicators/milestones to minimize subjectivity of the in-process work evaluation? | | | |
| f. Do work packages consist of discrete tasks which are adequately described? (Provide representative sample.) | | | |
| g. Can the contractor substantiate work package and planning package budgets? | | | |
| h. Are budgets or values assigned to work packages and planning packages in terms of dollars, hours, or other measurable units? | | | |
| i. Are work packages assigned to performing organizations? | | | |
| 6. PROVIDE THAT THE SUM OF ALL WORK PACKAGE BUDGETS PLUS PLANNING PACKAGES WITHIN A COST ACCOUNT EQUALS THE COST ACCOUNT BUDGET. (Reference format 2.) | | | |
| a. Does the sum of all work package budgets plus planning packages within cost accounts equal the budgets assigned to those cost accounts? | | | |

AFSC/AFCC/AFLC-P173-5    AMC-P 715-5    NAVSO-P3627    DLAH 8400.2    DCAA-P7641.47

**Appendix E-continued**

| CHECKLIST ITEMS | YES | NO | REMARKS |
|---|---|---|---|
| 7.  IDENTIFY RELATIONSHIPS OF BUDGETS OR STANDARDS IN UNDERLYING WORK AUTHORIZATION SYSTEMS TO BUDGETS FOR WORK PACKAGES. | | | |
| a. Where engineering standards or other internal work measurement systems are used, is there a formal relationship between these values and work package budgets? (Provide samples showing relationships.) | | | |
| b. Where "learning" is used in developing underlying budgets is there a direct relationship between anticipated learning and time-phased budgets? | | | |
| 8.  IDENTIFY AND CONTROL LEVEL OF EFFORT ACTIVITY BY TIME-PHASED BUDGETS ESTABLISHED FOR THIS PURPOSE.  ONLY THAT EFFORT WHICH CANNOT BE IDENTIFIED AS MEASURED EFFORT OR AS APPORTIONED EFFORT WILL BE CLASSED AS LOE. (Reference format 6.) | | | |
| a. Are time-phased budgets established for planning and control of level of effort activity by category of resource;  for example, type of manpower and/or material? (Explain method of control and analysis.) | | | |
| b. Is work properly classified as measured effort, LOE, or apportioned effort and appropriately separated? | | | |
| 9.  ESTABLISH OVERHEAD BUDGETS FOR THE TOTAL COSTS OF EACH SIGNIFICANT ORGANIZATIONAL COMPONENT WHOSE EXPENSES WILL BECOME INDIRECT COSTS.  REFLECT IN THE CONTRACT BUDGETS AT THE APPROPRIATE LEVEL, THE AMOUNTS IN OVERHEAD POOLS THAT WILL BE ALLOCATED TO THE CONTRACT AS INDIRECT COSTS. (Reference DCAA Audit Manual and FAR 31.203 (Reference format 7.)) | | | |
| a. Are overhead cost budgets (or projections) established on a facility-wide basis at least annually for the life of the contract? | | | |
| b. Are overhead cost budgets established for each organization which has authority to incur overhead costs? | | | |
| c. Are all elements of indirect expense identified to overhead cost budgets of projections? | | | |
| d. Are overhead budgets and costs being handled according to the disclosure statement when applicable, or otherwise properly classified (for example, engineering overhead, IR&D)? | | | |
| e. Is the anticipated (firm and potential) business base projected in a rational, consistent manner? (Explain.) | | | |
| f. Are overhead costs budgets established on a basis consistent with anticipated direct business base? | | | |

AFSC/AFCC/AFLC-P173-5      AMC-P 715-5      NAVSO-P3627      DLAH 8400.2      DCAA-P7641.47

Appendix E-continued

| CHECKLIST ITEMS | YES | NO | REMARKS |
|---|---|---|---|
| g. Are the requirements for all items of overhead established by rational, traceable processes? | | | |
| h. Are the overhead pools formally and adequately identified? (Provide a list of the pools.) | | | |
| i. Are the organizations and items of cost assigned to each pool identified? | | | |
| j. Are projected overhead costs in each pool and the associated direct costs used as the basis for establishing interim rates for allocating overhead to contracts? | | | |
| k. Are projected overhead rates applied to the contract beyond the current year based on- | | | |
| (1) Contractor financial periods; for example, annual? | | | |
| (2) The projected business base for each period? | | | |
| (3) Contemplated overhead expenditure for each period based on the best information currently available? | | | |
| l. Are overhead projections adjusted in a timely manner to reflect- | | | |
| (1) Changes in the current direct and projected base? | | | |
| (2) Changes in the nature of the overhead requirements? | | | |
| (3) Changes in the overhead pool and/or organization structures? | | | |
| m. Are the WBS and organizational levels for application of the projected overhead costs identified? | | | |
| 10. IDENTIFY MANAGEMENT RESERVES AND UNDISTRIBUTED BUDGET. | | | |
| a. Is all budget available as management reserve identified and excluded from the performance measurement baseline? | | | |
| b. Are records maintained to show how management reserves are used? (Provide exhibit.) | | | |
| c. Is undistributed budget limited to contract effort which cannot yet be planned to CWBS elements at or below the level specified for reporting to the Government? | | | |

AFSC/AFCC/AFLC-P173-5      AMC-P 715-5      NAVSO-P3627      DLAH 8400.2      DCAA-P7641.47

**Appendix E-continued**

| CHECKLIST ITEMS | YES | NO | REMARKS |
|---|---|---|---|
| d. Are records maintained to show how undistributed budgets are controlled? (Provide exhibit.) | | | |
| 11. PROVIDE THAT THE CONTRACT TARGET COST PLUS THE ESTIMATED COST OF AUTHORIZED BUT UNPRICED WORK IS RECONCILED WITH THE SUM OF ALL INTERNAL CONTRACT BUDGETS AND MANAGEMENT RESERVES. (Reference formats 3, 4, and 5.) | | | |
| a. Does the contractor's system description or procedures require that the performance measurement baseline plus management reserve equal the contract budget base? | | | |
| b. Do the sum of the cost account budgets for higher level CWBS elements, undistributed budget, and management reserves reconcile with the contract target cost plus the estimated cost for authorized unpriced work? (Provide exhibit.) | | | |
| III.  ACCOUNTING | | | |
| 1. RECORD DIRECT COSTS ON AN APPLIED OR OTHER ACCEPTABLE BASIS CONSISTENT WITH THE BUDGETS IN A FORMAL SYSTEM THAT IS CONTROLLED BY THE GENERAL BOOKS OF ACCOUNT. | | | |
| a. Does the accounting system provide a basis for auditing records of direct costs chargeable to the contract? | | | |
| b. Are elements of direct cost (labor, material, and so forth) accumulated within cost accounts in a manner consistent with budgets using recognized acceptable costing techniques and controlled by the general books of account? | | | |
| 2. SUMMARIZE DIRECT COSTS FROM THE COST ACCOUNTS INTO THE WBS WITHOUT ALLOCATION OF A SINGLE COST ACCOUNT TO TWO OR MORE WBS ELEMENTS. (Reference format 3.) | | | |
| a. Is it possible to summarize direct costs from the cost account level through the CWBS to the total contract level without allocation of a lower level CWBS element to two or more higher level CWBS elements? (This does not preclude the allocation of costs from a cost account containing common items to appropriate using cost accounts.) | | | |

AFSC/AFCC/AFLC-P173-5          AMC-P 715-5          NAVSO-P3627          DLAH 8400.2          DCAA-P7641.47

**Appendix E-continued**

| CHECKLIST ITEMS | YES | NO | REMARKS |
|---|---|---|---|
| 3. SUMMARIZE DIRECT COSTS FROM THE COST ACCOUNTS INTO THE CONTRACTOR'S FUNCTIONAL ORGANIZATIONAL ELEMENTS WITHOUT ALLOCATION OF A SINGLE COST ACCOUNT TO TWO OR MORE ORGANIZATIONAL ELEMENTS. (Reference format 4.) | | | |
| a. Is it possible to summarize direct costs from the cost account level to the highest functional organizational level without allocation of a lower level organization's cost to two or more higher level organizations? (This does not preclude the allocation of costs from a cost account containing minor non-organizational work to the appropriate functional organizations.) | | | |
| 4. RECORD ALL INDIRECT COSTS WHICH WILL BE ALLOCATED TO THE CONTRACT. | | | |
| a. Does the cost accumulation system provide for summarization of indirect costs from the point of allocation to the contract total? | | | |
| b. Are indirect costs accumulated for comparison with the corresponding budgets? | | | |
| c. Do the lines of authority for incurring indirect costs correspond to the lines of responsibility for management control of the same components of costs? (Explain controls for fixed and variable indirect costs.) | | | |
| d. Are indirect costs charged to the appropriate indirect pools and incurring organization? | | | |
| e. Are the bases and rates for allocating costs from each indirect pool consistently applied? | | | |
| f. Are the bases and rates for allocating costs from each indirect pool to commercial work consistent with those used to allocate such costs to Government contracts? | | | |
| g. Are the rates for allocating costs from each indirect cost pool to contracts updated as necessary to ensure a realistic monthly allocation of indirect costs wihout significant year-end adjustments? | | | |
| h. Are the procedures for identifying indirect costs to incurring organizations, indirect cost pools, and allocating the costs from the pools to the contracts formally documented? | | | |

AFSC/AFCC/AFLC-P173-5        AMC-P 715-5        NAVSO-P3627        DLAH 8400.2        DCAA-P7641.47

**Appendix E-continued**

| CHECKLIST ITEMS | YES | NO | REMARKS |
|---|---|---|---|
| 5.   IDENTIFY THE BASIS FOR ALLOCATING THE COST OF APPORTIONED EFFORT. | | | |
| a. Is effort which is planned and controlled in direct relationship to cost accounts or work packages identified as apportioned effort? | | | |
| b. Are methods used for applying apportioned effort costs to cost accounts applied consistently and documented in an established procedure? | | | |
| 6.   IDENTIFY UNIT COSTS, EQUIVALENT UNIT COSTS, OR LOT COSTS AS APPLICABLE. | | | |
| a. Does the contractor's system provide unit costs, equivalent unit or lot costs in terms of labor, material, other direct, and indirect costs? (Describe procedure.) | | | |
| b. Does the contractor have procedures which permit identification of recurring or nonrecurring costs as necessary? | | | |
| 7.   THE CONTRACTOR'S MATERIAL ACCOUNTING SYSTEM WILL PROVIDE FOR:   ACCURATE COST ACCUMULATION AND ASSIGNMENT OF COSTS TO COST ACCOUNTS IN A MANNER CONSISTENT WITH THE BUDGETS USING RECOGNIZED, ACCEPTABLE COSTING TECHNIQUES;   DETERMINATION OF PRICE VARIANCES BY COMPARING PLANNED VERSUS ACTUAL COMMITMENTS;   COST PERFORMANCE MEASUREMENT AT POINT IN TIME MOST SUITABLE FOR THE CATEGORY OF MATERIAL INVOLVED, BUT NO EARLIER THAN THE TIME OF ACTUAL RECEIPT OF MATERIAL;   DETERMINATION OF COST VARIANCES ATTRIBUTABLE TO THE EXCESS USAGE OF MATERIAL;   DETERMINATION OF UNIT OR LOT COSTS WHEN APPLICABLE;   AND FULL ACCOUNTABILITY FOR ALL MATERIAL PURCHASED FOR THE CONTRACT INCLUDING THE RESIDUAL INVENTORY. | | | |
| a. Does the contractor's system provide for accurate cost accumulation and assignment to cost accounts in a manner consistent with the budgets using recognized acceptable costing techniques? | | | |
| b. Are material costs reported within the same period as that in which BCWP is earned for that material? | | | |
| c. Does the contractor's system provide for determination of price variance by comparing planned vs actual commitments? | | | |
| d. Is cost performance measurement at the point in time most suitable for the category of material involved, but no earlier than the time of actual receipt of material? | | | |
| e. Does the contractor's system provide for the determination of cost variances attributable to the excess usage of material? | | | |

AFSC/AFCC/AFLC-P173-5       AMC-P 715-5       NAVSO-P3627       DLAH 8400.2       DCAA-P7641.47

**Appendix E-continued**

| CHECKLIST ITEMS | YES | NO | REMARKS |
|---|---|---|---|
| f. Does the contractor's system provide unit or lot costs when applicable? | | | |
| g. Are records maintained to show full accountability for all material purchased for the contract, including the residual inventory? | | | |

**IV. ANALYSIS**

1. IDENTIFY AT THE COST ACCOUNT LEVEL ON A MONTHLY BASIS USING DATA FROM, OR RECONCILABLE WITH, THE ACCOUNTING SYSTEM; BCWS AND BCWP; BCWP AND APPLIED (ACTUAL WHERE APPROPRIATE) DIRECT COSTS FOR THE SAME WORK; VARIANCES RESULTING FROM THE ABOVE COMPARISONS CLASSIFIED IN TERMS OF LABOR, MATERIAL, OR OTHER APPROPRIATE ELEMENTS, TOGETHER WITH THE REASONS FOR SIGNIFICANT VARIANCES.

| | | | |
|---|---|---|---|
| a. Does the contractor's system include procedures for measuring performance of the lowest level organization reponsible for the cost account? (Provide typical example.) | | | |
| b. Does the contractor's system include procedures for measuring the performance of critical subcontractors? | | | |
| c. Is cost and schedule performance measurement done in a consistent, systematic manner? | | | |
| d. Are the actual costs used for variance analysis reconcilable with data from the accounting system? | | | |
| e. Is budgeted cost for work performed calculated in a manner consistent with the way work is planned? (For example, if work is planned on a measured basis, is budgeted cost for work performed calculated on a measured basis using the same rates and values ?) | | | |
| f. Does the contractor have variance analysis procedures and a demonstrated capability for identifying (at the cost account and other appropriate levels) cost and schedule variances resulting from the system (provide examples) which- | | | |
| (1) Identify and isolate causes of favorable and unfavorable cost and schedule variances? | | | |
| (2) Evaluate the impact of schedule changes, workaround, etc.? | | | |
| (3) Evaluate the performance of operating organizations? | | | |
| (4) Identify potential or actual overruns and underruns? | | | |

AFSC/AFCC/AFLC-P173-5        AMC-P 715-5        NAVSO-P3627        DLAH 8400.2        DCAA-P7641.47

**Appendix E-continued**

| CHECKLIST ITEMS | YES | NO | REMARKS |
|---|---|---|---|
| 2. IDENTIFY ON A MONTHLY BASIS, IN THE DETAIL NEEDED BY MANAGEMENT FOR EFFECTIVE CONTROL, BUDGETED INDIRECT COSTS, ACTUAL INDIRECT COSTS, AND VARIANCES, ALONG WITH THE REASONS. (Reference format 7.) | | | |
| a. Are the variances between budgeted and actual indirect costs identified and analyzed at the level of assigned responsibility for their control (indirect pool, department, etc.)? | | | |
| b. Does the contractor's cost control system provide for capability to identify the existence and causes of cost variances resulting from-- | | | |
| (1) Incurrence of actual indirect costs in excess of budgets, by element of expense? | | | |
| (2) Changes in the direct base to which overhead costs are allocated? | | | |
| c. Are management actions taken to reduce indirect costs when there are significant adverse variances? | | | |
| 3. SUMMARIZE THE DATA ELEMENTS AND ASSOCIATED VARIANCES LISTED IN ITEMS 1 AND 2 ABOVE THROUGH THE CONTRACTOR ORGANIZATION AND WBS TO THE REPORTING LEVEL SPECIFIED IN THE CONTRACT. (Reference formats 2, 3, 4, 5.) | | | |
| a. Are data elements (BCWS, BCWP, and ACWP) progressively summarized from the detail level to the contract level through the CWBS? (Provide exhibit.) | | | |
| b. Are data elements summarized through the functional organizational structure for progressively higher levels of management? (Provide exhibit.) | | | |
| c. Are data elements reconcilable between internal summary reports and reports forwarded to the Government? | | | |
| d. Are procedures for variance analysis documented and consistently applied at the cost account level and selected WBS and organizational levels at least monthly as a routine task? (Provide examples.) | | | |
| 4. IDENTIFY ON A MONTHLY BASIS SIGNIFICANT DIFFERENCES BETWEEN PLANNED AND ACTUAL SCHEDULE ACCOMPLISHMENT TOGETHER WITH THE REASONS. | | | |
| a. Does the scheduling system identify in a timely manner the status of work? (Provide representative examples.) | | | |

AFSC/AFCC/AFLC-P173-5      AMC-P 715-5      NAVSO-P3627      DLAH 8400.2      DCAA-P7641.47

**Appendix E-continued**

| CHECKLIST ITEMS | YES | NO | REMARKS |
|---|---|---|---|
| b  Does the contractor use objective results, design reviews, and tests to trace schedule performance? (Provide examples.) | | | |
| 5    IDENTIFY MANAGERIAL ACTIONS TAKEN AS A RESULT OF CRITERIA ITEMS 1 THROUGH 4 ABOVE | | | |
| a  Are data disseminated to the contractor's managers timely, accurate, and usable? (Provide examples.) | | | |
| b. Are data being used by managers in an effective manner to ascertain program or functional status, to identify reasons for significant variance, and to initiate appropriate corrective action? (Provide examples.) | | | |
| c. Are there procedures for monitoring action items and corrective actions to the point of resolution and are these procedures being followed? | | | |
| 6    BASED ON PERFORMANCE TO DATE, ON COMMITMENT VALUES FOR MATERIAL, AND ON ESTIMATES OF FUTURE CONDITIONS, DEVELOP REVISED ESTIMATES OF COST AT COMPLETION FOR WBS ELEMENTS IDENTIFIED IN THE CONTRACT AND COMPARE THESE WITH THE CONTRACT BUDGET BASE AND THE LATEST STATEMENT OF FUNDS REQUIREMENTS REPORT TO THE GOVERNMENT. (Reference formats 2, 3, 4, 5, 10, and 11.) | | | |
| a. Are estimates of costs at completion based on- | | | |
| (1) Performance to date and material commitment? | | | |
| (2) Actual costs to date? | | | |
| (3) Knowledgeable projections of future performance? | | | |
| (4) Estimates of the cost for contract work remaining to be accomplished considering economic escalation? | | | |
| b. Are the overhead rates used to develop the contract cost estimate to complete based on- | | | |
| (1) Historical experience? | | | |
| (2) Contemplated management improvements? | | | |
| (3) Projected economic escalation? | | | |
| (4) The anticipated business volume? | | | |

E-13

AFSC/AFCC/AFLC-P173-5        AMC-P 715-5        NAVSO-P3627        DLAH 8400.2        DCAA-P7641.47

**Appendix E-continued**

| CHECKLIST ITEMS | YES | NO | REMARKS |
|---|---|---|---|
| c. Are estimates of cost at completion generated with sufficient frequency to provide identification of future cost problems in time for possible corrective or preventive actions by both the contractor and the Government program manager? | | | |
| d. Are estimates developed by program personnel coordinated with those responsible for overall plant management to determine whether required resources will be available according to revised planning? | | | |
| e. Are estimates of cost at completion generated by knowledgeable personnel for the following levels: | | | |
| (1)   Cost accounts? | | | |
| (2)   Major functional areas of contract effort? | | | |
| (3)   Major subcontracts? | | | |
| (4)   WBS elements contractually specified for reporting of status to the Government (lowest level only)? | | | |
| (5)   Total contract (all authorized work)? | | | |
| f. Are the latest revised estimates of costs at completion compared with the established budgets at appropriate levels and causes of variances identified? | | | |
| g. Are estimates of costs at completion generated in a rational, consistent manner? Are procedures established for appropriate aspects of generating estimates of costs at completion? | | | |
| h. Are estimates of costs at completion utilized in determining contract funding requirements and reporting them to the Government? | | | |
| i. Are the contractor's estimates of costs at completion reconcilable with cost data reported to the Government? | | | |
| **V.   REVISIONS AND ACCESS TO DATA** | | | |
| 1.   INCORPORATE CONTRACTUAL CHANGES IN A TIMELY MANNER, RECORDING THE EFFECTS OF SUCH CHANGES IN BUDGETS AND SCHEDULES. IN THE DIRECTED EFFORT BEFORE NEGOTIATION OF A CHANGE, BASE SUCH REVISIONS ON THE AMOUNT ESTIMATED AND BUDGETED TO THE FUNCTIONAL ORGANIZATIONS. | | | |
| a. Are authorized changes being incorporated in a timely manner? | | | |

AFSC/AFCC/AFLC-P173-5      AMC-P 715-5      NAVSO-P3627      DLAH 8400.2      DCAA-P7641.47

Appendix E-continued

| CHECKLIST ITEMS | YES | NO | REMARKS |
|---|---|---|---|
| b. Are all affected work authorizations, budgeting, and scheduling documents amended to properly reflect the effects of authorized changes? (Provide examples.) | | | |
| c. Are internal budgets for authorized, but not priced changes based on the contractor's resource plan for accomplishing the work? | | | |
| d. If current budgets for authorized changes do not sum to the negotiated cost for the changes, does the contractor compensate for the differences by revising the undistributed budgets, management reserves, budgets established for work not yet started, or by a combination of these? | | | |
| 2. RECONCILE ORIGINAL BUDGETS FOR THOSE ELEMENTS OF THE WBS IDENTIFIED AS PRICED LINE ITEMS IN THE CONTRACT, AND FOR THOSE ELEMENTS AT THE LOWEST LEVEL OF THE DOD PROJECT SUMMARY WBS, WITH CURRENT PERFORMANCE MEASUREMENT BUDGETS IN TERMS OF CHANGES TO THE AUTHORIZED WORK AND INTERNAL REPLANNING IN THE DETAIL NEEDED BY MANAGEMENT FOR EFFECTIVE CONTROL. (Reference formats 8 and 9.) | | | |
| a. Are current budgets resulting from changes to the authorized work and/or internal replanning, reconcilable to original budgets for specified reporting items? | | | |
| 3. PROHIBIT RETROACTIVE CHANGES TO RECORDS PERTAINING TO WORK PERFORMED THAT WILL CHANGE PREVIOUSLY REPORTED AMOUNTS FOR DIRECT COSTS, INDIRECT COSTS, OR BUDGETS, EXCEPT FOR CORRECTION OF ERRORS AND ROUTINE ACCOUNTING ADJUSTMENTS. | | | |
| a. Are retroactive changes to direct costs and indirect costs prohibited except for the correction of errors and routine accounting adjustments? | | | |
| b. Are direct or indirect cost adjustments being accomplished according to accounting procedures acceptable to DCAA? | | | |
| c. Are retroactive changes to BCWS and BCWP prohibited except for correction of errors or for normal accounting adjustments? | | | |
| 4. PREVENT REVISIONS TO THE CONTRACT BUDGET BASE EXCEPT FOR GOVERNMENT-DIRECTED CHANGES TO CONTRACTUAL EFFORT. | | | |
| a. Are procedures established to prevent changes to the contract budget base (see definition) other than those authorized by contractual action? | | | |

**AFSC/AFCC/AFLC-P173-5      AMC-P 715-5      NAVSO-P3627      DLAH 8400.2      DCAA-P7641.47**

**Appendix E-continued**

| CHECKLIST ITEMS | YES | NO | REMARKS |
|---|---|---|---|
| b. Is authorization of budgets in excess of the contract budget base controlled formally and done with the full knowledge and recognition of the procuring activity? Are the procedures adequate? | | | |
| 5. DOCUMENT, INTERNALLY, CHANGES TO THE PERFORMANCE MEASUREMENT BASELINE AND, ON A TIMELY BASIS, NOTIFY THE PROCURING ACTIVITY THROUGH PRESCRIBED PROCEDURES. | | | |
| a. Are changes to the performance measurement baseline made as a result of contractual redirection, formal reprogramming, internal replanninng, application of undistributed budget, or the use of management reserve, properly documented and reflected in the Cost Performance Report? | | | |
| b. Are procedures in existence that restrict changes to budgets for open work packages, and are these procedures adhered to? | | | |
| c. Are retroactive changes to budgets for completed work specifically prohibited in an established procedure, and is this procedure adhered to? | | | |
| d. Are procedures in existence that control replanning of unopened work packages, and are these procedures adhered to? | | | |
| 6. PROVIDE THE CONTRACTING OFFICER AND DULY AUTHORIZED REPRESENTATIVES ACCESS TO ALL OF THE FOREGOING INFORMATION AND SUPPORTING DOCUMENTS. | | | |
| a. Does the contractor provide access to all pertinent records to the C/SCSC Review Team and surveillance personnel? | | | |

AFSC/AFCC/AFLC-P713-5        AMC-P 715-5        NAVSO-P3627        DLAH-8400.2        DCAA-P7641.47

APPENDIX F

C/SCSC REVIEW WORKSHEETS AND EXHIBITS

**1. Instruction for Selected Exhibits.**

a. **Responsibility Assignment Matrix.** With the contractor's extended work breakdown structure on one axis and the contractor's organization down to the cost account manager's organization on the other axis, all levels of the organization should be shown. A dollarized matrix is preferred where dollars are identified at each level of the horizontal and vertical axis. (Reference criteria checklist item I-5). It is advisable that this be accomplished during the readiness assessment and updated accordingly during the demonstration review.

b. **Schedule Trace.** This involves identifying a master schedule, various levels of intermediate schedules (if any) and detail schedules down to the work package level. Interdependencies should be identified. Live data will be used. (Reference criteria checklist items II-1).

c. **Material Flow.** This identifies: (1) the authorizing, requisitioning, and purchasing cycle, (2) the receipt, storage and issue cycle, and (3) the accounting cycle. The determination point of BCWS, BCWP, and ACWP will be highlighted along with price and usage variance, variance analysis, and EAC. Actual documents should be used. (Reference criteria checklist items II-4, III-6, and III-7.)

**2. Worksheet Formats.**

a. **Typical Formats.** On the following pages are typical formats for performing data reconciliations and evaluating cost account and work package characteristics. It is recognized that the formats may require modification to meet the requirements of different organizations and contract work breakdown structures. The team members assigned responsibilities applicable to these formats should include them as exhibits in the review report. Worksheets needed to develop the data arrayed on the formats should be developed in conjunction with the contractor. Contractor internal reports may replace formats and exhibits wherever possible.

b. **Accomplishment of the Formats.** The following must be considered:

(1) Formats should include effort which has significant portions of measured effort (including material work packages, if separate), apportioned (factored) effort, and LOE.

(2) Data must be evaluated for consistent application of standards or targets, planned ratios and bases, factors, rates, and methods.

(3) Accomplishment indicators (for example, realization factors, milestones) must be consistent for computing BCWP.

(4) Derivation of the data elements used in the sample formats must be substantiated.

(5) The selected CWBS level should be interpreted as the lowest CWBS element on which the selected cost account is based. (Formats 2, 3, 4, and 8.)

c. **Instructions and Definitions.** Formats listed below should be accomplished using the instructions and definitions appearing thereon:

(1) Subsystem Integration Major Organization (for example, Engineering) and Associated Documentation.

(2) Reconciliation of Internal Data--Cost Account Data.

(3) Reconciliation of Internal Data--CWBS Data.

(4) Reconciliation of Internal Data--Organization Data.

(5) Reconciliation of Internal Data--Summary Level Data.

(6) Evaluation of Cost Accounts/Work Packages

(7) Contractor Indirect Cost Evaluation.

(8) Performance Measurement Baseline Change Traceability--Cost Account Level.

(9) Reconciliation of Internal Data (Budget Revision)-- at Total Contract Level.

(10) Reconciliation of External Reports to Internal Data (CWBS).

(11) Reconciliation of External Reports to Internal Data (Major Internal Organizations).

(12) Reconciliation of External Reports.

AFSC/AFCC/AFLC-P173-5     AMC-P 715-5     NAVSO-P3627     DLAH 8400.2     DCAA-P7641.47

## SUBSYSTEM INTEGRATION
## MAJOR ORGANIZATION (FOR EXAMPLE: ENGINEERING) AND
## ASSOCIATED DOCUMENTATION
## SAMPLE FORMAT 1

| CWBS LEVEL (1) CONTRACT | ORGANIZATION LEVEL (2) | SCHEDULING (3) | BUDGETING (4) | WORK AUTHORIZATION (5) | PERFORMANCE MEASUREMENT (6) |
|---|---|---|---|---|---|
| | | | | | |
| | | | | | |
| | | | | | |
| | | | | | |
| | | | | | |
| | | | | | |
| | | | | | |
| COST ACCOUNT | | | | | |
| WORK PACKAGE | | | | | |

NOTES:

1. Column 1 - Identify a representative element (name & number) for each level of the CWBS from the total contract level to the cost account and work package level.

2. Column 2 - Where applicable, identify a representative responsible/performing element by name and/or number for each level of the organization from the corporate/division level to the cost account and work package level.

3. Columns 3, 4, 5, and 6 - Identify the appropriate document title associated with the column heading for each CWBS level (column 1) and internal organization level (column 2).

4. Prepare format for each major organization or subdivision that differs.

5. There need not be a different type of document used for each CWBS and organization level.

6. Reference criteria checklist item I-3.

F-2

AFSC/AFCC/AFLC-P173.5    AMC-P 715-5    NAVSO-P3627    DLAH 8400.2    DCAA-P7641.47

## RECONCILIATION OF INTERNAL DATA
## COST ACCOUNT DATA
## SAMPLE FORMAT 2

AS APPLICABLE (CUMULATIVE TO DATE DATA)

| | TOTAL BUDGET | LABOR - HOURS | | | LABOR $ | | | | MATERIAL $ | | | | ODC $ | | | | OVERHEAD $ | | | | TOTAL $ | | |
|---|---|---|---|---|---|---|---|---|---|---|---|---|---|---|---|---|---|---|---|---|---|---|
| | | BCWS | ACWP | EAC | BCWS | BCWP | ACWP | EAC | BCWS | BCWP | ACWP | EAC | BCWS | BCWP | ACWP | EAC | BCWS | BCWP | ACWP | EAC | BCWS | BCWP | ACWP | EAC |

COST ACCOUNT
ORGANIZATION
WORK PACKAGE/ PLANNING PACKAGE

CA Name / No.
ORG. Name / No.
WP/PP No.

SELECTED COST ACCOUNT TOTAL

NOTES:

1. Overhead $ need not be at work package or cost account level. Include these $ at the level where contractor allocates them.

2. Summarization to contract level continues on sample formats 3, 4, 5.

3. ACWP and EAC need not be at the work package level.

4. A separate format will be prepared for each trace element selected.

5. The contractor's internal reports may be used wherever possible provided they contain all the required data.

6. Reference criteria checklist items II-3, II-4, II-6, IV-3, and IV-6.

F-3

AFSC/AFCC/AFLC-P173-5    AMC-P 715-5    NAVSO-P3627    DLAH 8400.2    DCAA-P7641.47

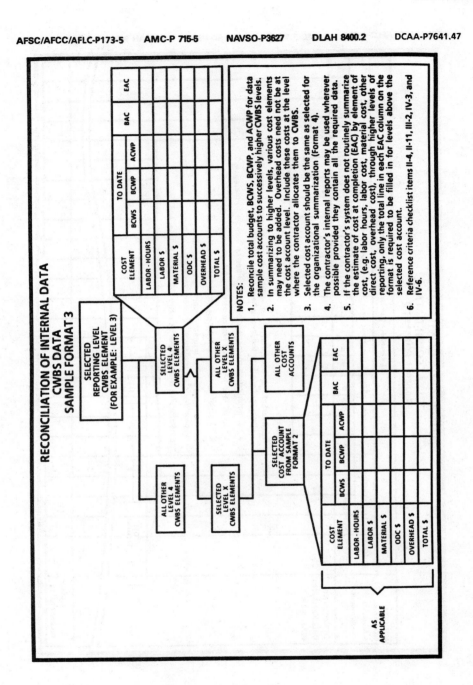

RECONCILIATION OF INTERNAL DATA
CWBS DATA
SAMPLE FORMAT 3

NOTES:

1.  Reconcile total budget, BCWS, BCWP, and ACWP for data sample cost accounts to successively higher CWBS levels.

2.  In summarizing to higher levels, various cost elements may need to be added. Overhead costs need not be at the cost account level. Include these costs at the level where the contractor allocates them to CWBS.

3.  Selected cost account should be the same as selected for the organizational summarization (Format 4).

4.  The contractor's internal reports may be used wherever possible provided they contain all the required data.

5.  If the contractor's system does not routinely summarize the estimate of cost at completion (EAC) by element of cost, (e.g. labor hours, labor cost, material cost, other direct cost, overhead cost), through higher levels of reporting, only the total line in each EAC column on the format is required to be filled in for levels above the selected cost account.

6.  Reference criteria checklist items II-4, II-11, III-2, IV-3, and IV-6.

AFSC/AFCC/AFLC-P173-5     AMC-P 715-5     NAVSO-P3627     DLAH 8400.2     DCAA-P7641.47

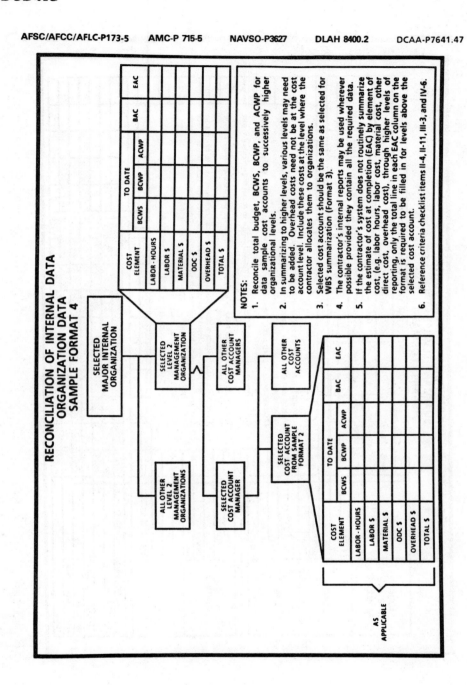

RECONCILIATION OF INTERNAL DATA
ORGANIZATION DATA
SAMPLE FORMAT 4

NOTES:

1. Reconcile total budget, BCWS, BCWP, and ACWP for data sample cost accounts to successively higher organizational levels.

2. In summarizing to higher levels, various levels may need to be added. Overhead costs need not be at the cost account level. Include these costs at the level where the contractor allocates them to organizations.

3. Selected cost account should be the same as selected for WBS summarization (Format 3).

4. The contractor's internal reports may be used wherever possible provided they contain all the required data.

5. If the contractor's system does not routinely summarize the estimate of cost at completion (EAC) by element of cost, (e.g. labor hours, labor cost, material cost, other direct cost, overhead cost), through higher levels of reporting, only the total line in each EAC column on the format is required to be filled in for levels above the selected cost account.

6. Reference criteria checklist items II-4, II-11, III-3, and IV-6.

AFSC/AFCC/AFLC-P173-5　　　　AMC-P 715-5　　　　NAVSO-P3627　　　　DLAH 8400.2　　　DCAA-P7641.47

## RECONCILIATION OF INTERNAL DATA
## SUMMARY LEVEL DATA
## SAMPLE FORMAT 5

| MAJOR INTERNAL ORGANIZATIONS | DATA ELEMENT | REPORTING LEVEL CWBS ELEMENTS | | | | | | | | | | | | | | | | | | |
|---|---|---|---|---|---|---|---|---|---|---|---|---|---|---|---|---|---|---|---|---|
| | | CWBS ELEMENT _____ | | | | | | CWBS ELEMENT _____ | | | | | | TOTAL | | | | | |
| | | CUMULATIVE | | | | | | CUMULATIVE | | | | | | CUMULATIVE | | | | | |
| | | BCWS | BCWP | ACWP | BAC | EAC | | BCWS | BCWP | ACWP | BAC | EAC | | BCWS | BCWP | ACWP | BAC | EAC | |
| ENG | LABOR | | | | | | | | | | | | | | | | | | |
| | MATERIAL | | | | | | | | | | | | | | | | | | |
| | ODC | | | | | | | | | | | | | | | | | | |
| | OVERHEAD | | | | | | | | | | | | | | | | | | |
| | TOTAL | | | | | | | | | | | | | | | | | | |
| MFG | LABOR | | | | | | | | | | | | | | | | | | |
| | MATERIAL | | | | | | | | | | | | | | | | | | |
| | ODC | | | | | | | | | | | | | | | | | | |
| | OVERHEAD | | | | | | | | | | | | | | | | | | |
| | TOTAL | | | | | | | | | | | | | | | | | | |
| OTHER | LABOR | | | | | | | | | | | | | | | | | | |
| | MATERIAL | | | | | | | | | | | | | | | | | | |
| | ODC | | | | | | | | | | | | | | | | | | |
| | OVERHEAD | | | | | | | | | | | | | | | | | | |
| | TOTAL | | | | | | | | | | | | | | | | | | |
| SUBTOTAL | LABOR | | | | | | | | | | | | | | | | | | |
| | MATERIAL | | | | | | | | | | | | | | | | | | |
| | ODC | | | | | | | | | | | | | | | | | | |
| | OVERHEAD | | | | | | | | | | | | | | | | | | |
| | TOTAL | | | | | | | | | | | | | | | | | | |
| OVERHEAD NOT INCLUDED IN ABOVE | | | | | | | | | | | | | | | | | | | |
| COST OF MONEY | | | | | | | | | | | | | | | | | | | |
| G&A | | | | | | | | | | | | | | | | | | | |
| UNDISTRIBUTED BUDGET | | | | | | | | | | | | | | | | | | | |
| SUBTOTAL | | | | | | | | | | | | | | | | | | | |
| MANAGEMENT RESERVE | | | | | | | | | | | | | | | | | | | |
| TOTAL | | | | | | | | | | | | | | | | | | | |

NOTES:

1. Accomplish at summary WBS levels and undistributed budget.

2. Management reserve - identify and add to internal budgets to reconcile to negotiated contract cost.

3. Discrepancies - document, identify levels where occurred, and dollar amount; include cause if known.

4. One of the reporting level CWBS elements and major internal organizations will correlate to formats 3 and 4, respectively.

5. The contractor's internal reports may be used wherever possible provided they contain all the required data.

6. If the contractor's system does not routinely summarize the estimate of cost at completion (EAC) by element of cost (i. e. labor cost, material cost, other direct cost, overhead cost) to higher levels of reporting, only the total line of each EAC column on the format is required to be completed.

7. Accomplish at level 2 or lower level.

8. Reference criteria checklist items II-11, IV-3, and IV-6.

AFSC/AFCC/AFLC-P173-5     AMC-P 715-5     NAVSO-P3627     DLAH 8400.2     DCAA-P7641.47

## EVALUATION OF COST ACCOUNTS/WORK PACKAGES
## SAMPLE FORMAT 6

### COST ACCOUNTS

| | NUMBER | LONGEST CA | SHORTEST CA | MEAN DURATION | MEDIAN DURATION | TOTAL VALUE | LARGEST CA | SMALLEST CA | MEAN VALUE | MEDIAN VALUE |
|---|---|---|---|---|---|---|---|---|---|---|
| TOTAL | | | | | | | | | | |
| MEASURED | | | | | | | | | | |
| APPORTIONED | | | | | | | | | | |
| LEVEL OF EFFORT | | | | | | | | | | |
| TOTAL | | | | | | | | | | |

### WORK PACKAGES

| TYPE OF MEASUREMENT | NUMBER | LONGEST WP | SHORTEST WP | MEAN DURATION | MEDIAN DURATION | TOTAL VALUE | LARGEST WP | SMALLEST WP | MEAN VALUE | MEDIAN VALUE |
|---|---|---|---|---|---|---|---|---|---|---|
| MILESTONED | | | | | | | | | | |
| OBJECTIVE INDICATORS | | | | | | | | | | |
| EARNED UNITS | | | | | | | | | | |
| 50 - 50 | | | | | | | | | | |
| OTHER | | | | | | | | | | |
| PLANNING PACKAGES | | | | | | | | | | |
| TOTAL | | | | | | | | | | |

**NOTES:**

1.  Use data from total contract or a representative sample (basis of sample should be explained).
2.  Under type of measurement, list all methods used by the contractor to measure work package performance.
3.  Reference criteria checklist items II-5 and II-8.

F-7

AFSC/AFCC/AFLC-P173-5     AMC-P 715-5      NAVSO-P3627      DLAH 8400.2     DCAA-P7641.47

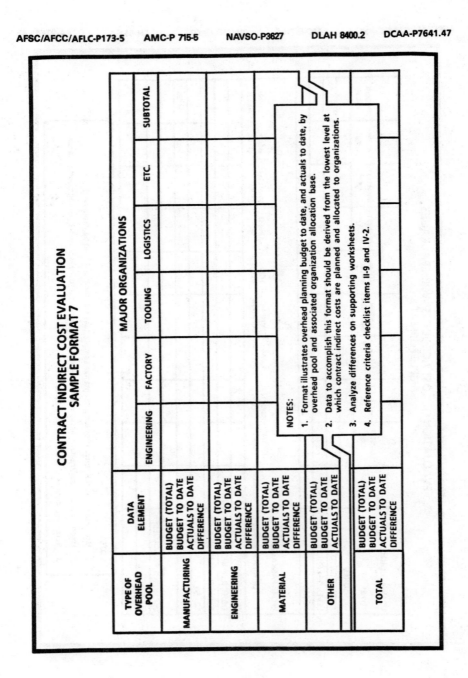

CONTRACT INDIRECT COST EVALUATION
SAMPLE FORMAT 7

| TYPE OF OVERHEAD POOL | DATA ELEMENT | MAJOR ORGANIZATIONS | | | | | | |
|---|---|---|---|---|---|---|---|---|
| | | ENGINEERING | FACTORY | TOOLING | LOGISTICS | ETC. | SUBTOTAL |
| MANUFACTURING | BUDGET (TOTAL) BUDGET TO DATE ACTUALS TO DATE DIFFERENCE | | | | | | |
| ENGINEERING | BUDGET (TOTAL) BUDGET TO DATE ACTUALS TO DATE DIFFERENCE | | | | | | |
| MATERIAL | BUDGET (TOTAL) BUDGET TO DATE ACTUALS TO DATE DIFFERENCE | | | | | | |
| OTHER | BUDGET (TOTAL) BUDGET TO DATE ACTUALS TO DATE | | | | | | |
| TOTAL | BUDGET (TOTAL) BUDGET TO DATE ACTUALS TO DATE DIFFERENCE | | | | | | |

NOTES:

1. Format illustrates overhead planning budget to date, and actuals to date, by overhead pool and associated organization allocation base.

2. Data to accomplish this format should be derived from the lowest level at which contract indirect costs are planned and allocated to organizations.

3. Analyze differences on supporting worksheets.

4. Reference criteria checklist items II-9 and IV-2.

F-8

AFSC/AFCC/AFLC-P173-5   AMC-P 715-5   NAVSO-P3627   DLAH 8400.2   DCAA-P7641.47

PERFORMANCE MEASUREMENT BASELINE CHANGE TRACEABILITY
COST ACCOUNT LEVEL
SAMPLE FORMAT 8

| COST ACCOUNT NUMBER | ORIGINAL BUDGET | SOURCE AND AMOUNT OF CHANGES (AS APPLICABLE) | | | | SUBTOTAL (2,3, 4, 5, & 6) | CURRENT BUDGET | DIFFERENCE (8 MINUS 7) | EXPLANATION OF DIFFERENCE |
| | | CONTRACT CHANGE | HIGHER LEVEL CWBS | UNDIS BUDGET | MGMT RESERVE | | | | |
|---|---|---|---|---|---|---|---|---|---|
| (1) | (2) | (3) | (4) | (5) | (6) | (7) | (8) | (9) | (10) |
| | | | | | | | | | |
| | | | | | | | | | |
| | | | | | | | | | |
| CWBS ELEMENT SUBTOTAL | | | | | | | | | |

NOTES:

1. For the selected CWBS element format reconciles current cost account budget to original budgets for baseline control. (Refer to contractor internal control logs.)

2. Analyze differences on supporting worksheets.

3. Reference criteria checklist items II-3 and V-2.

AFSC/AFCC/AFLC-P173-5      AMC-P 715-5      NAVSO-P3627      DLAH 8400.2      DCAA-P7641.47

## RECONCILIATION OF INTERNAL DATA (BUDGET REVISION)
## AT TOTAL CONTRACT LEVEL
## SAMPLE FORMAT 9

| (1) | ORIGINAL BUDGET (2) | SOURCE AND AMOUNT OF CHANGES (AS APPLICABLE) | | | | | SUBTOTAL 2,3,4,5,&6 (7) | CURRENT BUDGET (8) | DIFFERENCE (8 MINUS 7) (9) | EXPLANATION OF DIFFERENCE (10) |
| | | CONTRACT CHANGE (3) | HIGHER LEVEL CWBS (4) | UNDIS BUDGET (5) | MGMT RESERVE (6) | | | | |
|---|---|---|---|---|---|---|---|---|---|---|
| TOTAL OF ALL COST ACCOUNTS | | | | | | | | | | |
| TOTAL OF HIGHER LEVEL CWBS ELEMENTS NOT BROKEN DOWN TO COST ACCOUNTS | | | | | | | | | | |
| OVERHEAD NOT INCLUDED IN ABOVE | | | | | | | | | | |
| COST OF MONEY | | | | | | | | | | |
| G&A | | | | | | | | | | |
| UNDISTRIBUTED BUDGET | | | | | | | | | | |
| PERFORMANCE MEASUREMENT BASELINE | | | | | | | | | | |
| MANAGEMENT RESERVE | | | | | | | | | | |
| TOTAL ALLOCATED BUDGET | | | | | | | | | | |

NOTES:

1. Reconcile current contract budgets to original budgets and compare values to contract target cost. (Refer to contractor internal control logs.)

2. Analyze differences on supporting worksheets.

3. Reference criteria checklist item V-2.

F-10

AFSC/AFCC/AFLC-P173-5    AMC-P 715-5    NAVSO-P3627    DLAH 8400.2    DCAA-P7641.47

## RECONCILIATION OF EXTERNAL REPORTS TO INTERNAL DATA (CWBS)
## SAMPLE FORMAT 10

| CWBS | DATA ELEMENTS | | | | | | | |
| | CURRENT PERIOD | | | CUMULATIVE TO DATE | | | BAC | EAC |
| | BCWS | BCWP | ACWP | BCWS | BCWP | ACWP | | |
|---|---|---|---|---|---|---|---|---|
| **AIR VEHICLE** COST PERFORMANCE REPORT (FORMAT # 1) | | | | | | | | |
| CONTRACTOR INTERNAL REPORT (SPECIFY) | | | | | | | | |
| DIFFERENCE | | | | | | | | |
| **TEST** COST PERFORMANCE REPORT | | | | | | | | |
| CONTRACTOR INTERNAL REPORT (SPECIFY) | | | | | | | | |
| DIFFERENCE | | | | | | | | |
| **SYSTEM ENGINEERING** COST PERFORMANCE REPORT | | | | | | | | |
| **OTHER** | | | | | | | | |
| **TOTAL CWBS ELEMENTS** COST PERFORMANCE REPORT | | | | | | | | |
| CONTRACTOR INTERNAL REPORT | | | | | | | | |
| DIFFERENCE | | | | | | | | |

NOTES:

1. Reports to be compared should cover identical periods.

2. Items shown in the first column are for illustrative purposes. Use applicable WBS reporting level items.

3. Analyze differences on a separate worksheet, trace each difference to its origin, and explain.

4. Reference criteria checklist items IV-3 and IV-6.

F-11

AFSC/AFCC/ AFLC-P173.5     AMC-P 715-5     NAVSO-P3627     DLAH 8400.2     DCAA-P7641.47

## RECONCILIATION OF EXTERNAL REPORTS TO INTERNAL DATA
### (MAJOR INTERNAL ORGANIZATIONS)
### SAMPLE FORMAT 11

| MAJOR INTERNAL ORGANIZATION | DATA ELEMENTS | | | | | | | | |
| | CURRENT PERIOD | | | CUMULATIVE TO DATE | | | BAC | EAC |
| | BCWS | BCWP | ACWP | BCWS | BCWP | ACWP | | |
| ENGINEERING COST PERFORMANCE REPORT (FORMAT # 2) | | | | | | | | |
| CONTRACTOR INTERNAL REPORT (SPECIFY) | | | | | | | | |
| DIFFERENCE | | | | | | | | |
| MANUFACTURING COST PERFORMANCE REPORT (SPECIFY) | | | | | | | | |
| CONTRACTOR INTERNAL REPORT (SPECIFY) | | | | | | | | |
| DIFFERENCE | | | | | | | | |
| OTHER COST PERFORMANCE REPORT (SPECIFY) | | | | | | | | |
| CONTRACTOR INTERNAL REPORT (SPECIFY) | | | | | | | | |
| TOTAL COST PERFORMANCE REPORT | | | | | | | | |
| CONTRACTOR INTERNAL REPORT | | | | | | | | |
| DIFFERENCE | | | | | | | | |

NOTES:

1. Reports to be compared should cover identical periods.

2. Items shown in the first column are illustrative. Use applicable contractor organizational structure.

3. Analyze differences on a separate worksheet, trace each difference to its origin, and explain.

4. Reference criteria checklist items IV-3 and IV-6.

F-12

AFSC/AFCC/AFLC-P173-5      AMC-P 715-5      NAVSO-P3627      DLAH 8400.2      DCAA-P7641.47

## RECONCILIATION OF EXTERNAL REPORTS
## SAMPLE FORMAT 12

| REPORT | DATE OF REPORT | ESTIMATED PRICE | ESTIMATED COST AT COMPLETION | EXPLANATION OF DIFFERENCES |
|---|---|---|---|---|
| COST PERFORMANCE REPORT | | | | |
| DD FORM 1586, CONTRACT FUNDS STATUS REPORT (Col. 11g) | | | ///// | |
| DIFFERENCE | ///// | | | |

NOTES:

1. Ascertain that reports conform to current contractual requirements. (Ensure the estimated price includes contractor fee sharing participation, when required.)

2. Reports to be compared should cover identical periods.

3. Analyze differences on a separate worksheet, trace each difference to its origin, and explain.

4. Reference criteria checklist item IV-6.

F-13

AFSC/AFCC/AFLC-P173-5      AMC-P 715-5      NAVSO-P3627      DLAH 8400.2      DCAA-P7641.47

## GLOSSARY

The following acronyms or abbreviations appear within the C/SCSC Joint Implementation Guide:

| | |
|---|---|
| ACO | Administrative Contracting Officer |
| ACWP | Actual Cost of Work Performed |
| AFCC | Air Force Communications Command |
| AFIT | Air Force Institute of Technology |
| AFLC | Air Force Logistics Command |
| AFPRO | Air Force Plant Representative Office |
| AFSC | Air Force Systems Command |
| ARPRO | Army Plant Representative Office |
| AMC | Army Materiel Command |
| ASN (S&L) | Assistant Secretary of the Navy (Shipbuilding & Logistics) |
| BAC | Budget at Completion |
| BCWP | Budgeted Cost for Work Performed |
| BCWS | Budgeted Cost for Work Scheduled |
| CA | Cost Account |
| CACO | Corporate Administrative Contracting Officer |
| CAO | Contract Administration Office |
| C/SCSC | Cost/Schedule Control Systems Criteria |
| C/SSR | Cost/Schedule Status Report |
| CWBS | Contract Work Breakdown Structure |
| DAB | Defense Acquisition Board |
| DCAA | Defense Contract Audit Agency |
| DCAS | Defense Contract Administration Services |
| DCASMA | Defense Contract Administration Services Management Area |
| DCASPRO | Defense Contract Administration Services Plant Representative Office |
| DCASR | Defense Contract Administration Services Region |
| DID | Data Item Description |
| DLA | Defense Logistics Area |
| EAC | Estimate at Completion |
| ESAR | Extended Subsequent Application Review |
| LOE | Level of Effort |

**AFSC/AFCC/AFLC-P173-5      AMC-P 715-5      NAVSO-P3627      DLAH 8400.2      DCAA-P7641.47**

**Glossary - continued**

| | |
|---|---|
| **MR** | Management Reserve |
| **NAVPRO** | Navy Plant Representative Office |
| **NAVSO** | Navy Secretarial Office |
| **PCO** | Procuring Contracting Officer |
| **PMB** | Performance Measurement Baseline |
| **PP** | Planning Package |
| **SAR** | Subsequent Application Review |
| **SSC** | Standard Systems Command |
| **SUPSHIP** | Superintendent of Shipbuilding, Conversion, and Repair, USN |
| **UB** | Undistributed Budget |
| **WBS** | Work Breakdown Structure |
| **WP** | Work Package |

AFSC/AFCC/AFLC-P173-5   AMC-P 715-5   NAVSO-P3627   DLAH 8400.2   DCAA-P7641.47

## INDEX

INDEX 1

AFSC/AFCC/AFLC-P173-5   AMC-P 715-5   NAVSO-P3627   DLAH 8400.2   DCAA-P7641.47

Index - continued

AFSC/AFCC/AFLC-P173-5   AMC-P 715-5   NAVSO-P3627   DLAH 8400.2   DCAA-P7641.47

AFSC/AFCC/AFLC-P173-5   AMC-P 715-5   NAVSO-P3627   DLAH 8400.2   DCAA-P7641.47

AFSC/AFCC/AFLC-P173-5   AMC-P 715-5   NAVSO-P3627   DLAH 8400.2   DCAA-P7641.47

AFSC/AFCC/AFLC-P173-5    AMC-P 715-5    NAVSO-P3627    DLAH 8400.2    DCAA-P7641.47

AFSC/AFCC/AFLC-P173-5   AMC-P 715-5   NAVSO-P3627   DLAH 8400.2   DCAA-P7641.47

AFSC/AFCC/AFLC-P173-5   AMC-P 715-5   NAVSO-P3627   DLAH 8400.2   DCAA-P7641.47

AFSC/AFCC/AFLC-P173-5   AMC-P 715-5   NAVSO-P3627   DLAH 8400.2   DCAA-P7641.47

# APPENDIX F
# C/SCSC Forms

| PROJECT/PROGRAM | WORK BREAKDOWN STRUCTURE DICTIONARY (STATEMENT OF CONTENT) | WBS _____ | |
|---|---|---|---|
| CONTRACT NO. | | DATE | |
| | | PAGE | OF |

| WBS LEVEL | | | | | | ELEMENT TITLE | MPC CODE |
|---|---|---|---|---|---|---|---|
| 1 | 2 | 3 | 4 | 5 | 6 | | |
| | | | | | | | |

**WBS DICTIONARY**

| EFFORT REQUIRED | FSD | | PRODUCTION | | ASSOCIATED LOWER LEVEL ELEMENTS | | |
|---|---|---|---|---|---|---|---|
| | NR | R | NR | R | WBS NO. | LEVEL | TITLE |
| | YES NO | YES NO | YES NO | YES NO | | | |
| ENGR DESIGN | | | | | | | |
| ENGR TEST | | | | | | | |
| INTEG LOG SUP | | | | | | | |
| GRAPHICS | | | | | | | |
| TOOLING | | | | | | | |
| MFG ENGR | | | | | | | |
| MANUFACTURING | | | | | | | |
| MFG SUPPORT | | | | | | | |
| QUALITY ASSUR | | | | | | | |
| MATERIEL | | | | | | | |
| FACILITIES | | | | | | | |
| DATA PROCESS | | | | | | | |

FSD – FULL-SCALE DEVELOPMENT; NR – NONRECURRING, R – RECURRING

**COST ACCOUNT PLAN (CAP)**

PAGE 1 OF

| PROGRAM | NUMBER | TITLE | TYPE OF CAP | TYPE OF EFFORT |
|---|---|---|---|---|
| | | | ☐ DISCRETE | ☐ RECURRING |
| SUMMARY COST ELEMENT | | | ☐ LEVEL OF EFFORT | ☐ NONRECURRING |
| | | | ☐ APPORTIONED | ☐ PROVISIONING |

| SALES ORDER | | | EARNED VALUE CRITERIA (DIRECT ONLY) | | |
|---|---|---|---|---|---|
| | | | ☐ STANDARDS  ☐ % COMPLETION | ☐ DIRECT |
| DEPARTMENT | | | ☐ BAR CHARTS  ☐ LEVEL OF EFFORT APPORTIONED BASE _____ | ☐ INDIRECT |
| | | | ☐ MILESTONES | |

| SCHEDULES START DATE | SCHEDULED COMPLETE DATE | PREPARED BY | DEPT | DATE |
|---|---|---|---|---|
| | | | | |

| BUDGETED COST OF WORK (BCW) | HOURS | DOLLARS |
|---|---|---|
| | | |

**STATEMENT OF WORK**

COST ACCOUNT PLAN
(S.O.W.)

**APPROVALS**

| ISSUE | COST ACCOUNT MGR | DATE | CONTROLLER | DATE | PROGRAM OFFICE | DATE |
|---|---|---|---|---|---|---|
| ORIGINAL | | | | | | |
| REV | | | | | | |
| REV | | | | | | |
| REV | | | | | | |
| REV | | | | | | |
| REV | | | | | | |
| REV | | | | | | |

COST ACCOUNT PLAN TASK SCHEDULE

PAGE 1 OF

| PROGRAM | NUMBER | TITLE | EARNED VALUE CRITERIA | BUDGETED COST OF WORK (BCW) |
|---------|--------|-------|-----------------------|------------------------------|

EARNED VALUE CRITERIA

1 APPORTIONED BASE

2 PERCENT COMPLETE
3 LEVEL OF EFFORT
4 MILESTONES

BUDGETED COST OF WORK (BCW)

HOURS.

DOLLARS.

SUMMARY COST ELEMENT

SALES ORDER

PREPARED BY.        DEPT:        DATE.

DEPARTMENT

| ISSUE | COST ACCOUT MGR | DATE | CONTROLLER | DATE | PROGRAM OFFICE | DATE |
|-------|-----------------|------|------------|------|----------------|------|
| ORIG  |                 |      |            |      |                |      |
| REV   |                 |      |            |      |                |      |

WORK PACKAGE

$ / Hr

BCW HOURS

COST ACCOUNT PLAN (SCHEDULE)

BCWS MONTHLY
BCWS CUMULATIVE
BCWP MONTHLY
BCWP CUMULATIVE

**BUDGET TRANSFER REQUEST**

| ORIGINATOR | | DEPT NO. | ZONE | EXT | DATE |
|---|---|---|---|---|---|

| FROM | TO |
|---|---|
| DEPARTMENT | DEPARTMENT |
| SALES ORDER NO. | SALES ORDER NO. |
| SUMMARY COST ELEMENT NO. | SUMMARY COST ELEMENT NO. |

| MANAGEMENT RESERVE ☐ | INTERDEPARTMENT ☐ | ECP/CP ☐ |
|---|---|---|

DESCRIPTION OF TASK

BUDGET TRANSFER

| HOURS (ALLOCATED) | DOLLARS (UNBURDENED) |
|---|---|
| | |

| APPROVAL SIGNATURES | |
|---|---|
| TRANSFERING MANAGER | PERFORMING MANAGER |
| PROGRAM CONTROLLER | BASELINE: | REVISED CAP DUE: |

# C/SCS PROBLEM ANALYSIS REPORT

① PROGRAM

⑦ PAR REV NO.

⑧ DATE

⑨ AS OF

② CAP

③ SO

④ WBS

⑤ CAP MGR

⑥ DEPT

| D |
| L |

⑩ IMPACT:

| | SCHEDULE (HRS/$) | % | COST (HRS/$) | % |
|---|---|---|---|---|
| CAP CUM VARIANCE TO DATE | — | | — | |
| CAP EST VARIANCE AT COMP | X | | — | |

⑬ DEPARTMENTAL PROGRAM IMPACT:

| | RECOVERABLE | | IRRECOVERABLE | |
|---|---|---|---|---|
| | SCH | COST | SCH | COST |
| | □ | □ X | □ | □ |

PROBLEM ANALYSIS

⑪ PROBLEM/REASON: (IDENTIFY SPECIFIC COST/SCHEDULE ITEMS)

⑫ CORRECTIVE ACTION: (WHAT, BY WHOM AND WHEN)

## PLAN OF ACTION:

| REPORT DATE | | CUM TO DATE | CUMULATIVE BY MONTH | | | | | | | |
|---|---|---|---|---|---|---|---|---|---|---|
| COST | BCWP ◊ FORECAST | | | | | | | | | |
| | ACWP ◊ FORECAST | | | | | | | | | |
| | VARIANCE | | | | | | | | | |
| SCHEDULE | BCWS (PER CAP) | | | | | | | | | |
| | BCWP ◊ FORECAST | | | | | | | | | |
| | VARIANCE | | | | | | | | | |

⑭ PREPARED BY

⑮ APPROVED BY

**CSCS PROBLEM ANALYSIS**

| CONTRACTOR: | CONTRACT NO. | PROGRAM NAME/NUMBER | AUTHORIZED SIGNATURE/TITLE/DATE |
|---|---|---|---|
| LOCATION. | ☐ RDT & E    ☐ PRODUCTION | | |

ANALYSIS REPORT (ELEMENT)

| WORK BREAKDOWN STRUCTURE ITEM/FUNCTION | CONTRACT BUDGET | ITEMS CREATING CHANGES TO ___ EAC | | | | | | EAC |
|---|---|---|---|---|---|---|---|---|
| | | BURDEN RATES | LABOR RATES | LABOR | MATERIAL | PREMIUM | OTHER | SUBTOTAL | |

( ) = UNDERRUNS

(ALL ENTRIES IN 000'S OF DOLLARS THRU G & A)

# APPENDIX G
# Glossary of C/SCSC Terms

**AACE**—*See* "American Association of Cost Engineers."

**ACO**—*See* "Administrative Contracting Officer."

**Activity**—Something that occurs over time, and generally consumes resources. Also referred to as a Task.

**Actual Cost**—A cost sustained in fact, on the basis of costs incurred, as distinguished from forecasted or estimated costs.

**Actual Cost of Work Performed (ACWP)**—The costs actually incurred and recorded in accomplishing the work performed within a given time period.

**Actual Direct Costs**—Those costs specifically identified with a contract, based upon the contractor's cost identification and accumulation system as accepted by cognizant auditing representatives. (*See also* Direct Costs).

**ACV**—*See* "At Completion Variance."

**ACWP**—*See* "Actual Costs of Work Performed."

**Administrative Contracting Officer (ACO)**—The official primarily responsible for monitoring contract performance and negotiating certain contract modifications.

**Advanced Material Release (AMR)**—A document typically used by engineering organizations to release long-lead time or time critical material requirements prior to the formal release of a design. AMRs are used to start the procurement process without waiting for the design of something to be completed.

**AFCMD**—Air Force Contract Management Division.

**AFIT**—Air Force Institute of Technology.

**AFPRO**—*See* "Air Force Plant Representative Office."

**AFSC**—Air Force Systems Command.

**Air Force Plant Representative Office (AFPRO)**—Air Force Contract Administration Offices located at major defense contractors and installations throughout the U.S. where the USAF has been assigned plant cognizance. They are responsible for contract administration and other subsidiary functions.

**Allocated Budget**—*See* "Total Allocated Budget."

**AMC**—Army Material Command.

**American Association of Cost Engineers (AACE)**—A professional organization which exists for the advancement of the science and art of cost engineering.

**American Production and Inventory Control Society (APICS)**—A professional organization which focuses on manufacturing and inventory control issues.

**AMETA**—Army Management Engineering Training Activity.

**AMR**—*See* "Advanced Material Release."

**APICS**—*See* "American Production & Inventory Control Society."

**Applied Direct Costs**—The actual direct costs recognized in the time period associated with the consumption of labor, material, and other direct resources, without regard to their date of commitment or their date of payment. These amounts are to be charged to the appropriate work-in-progress when any of the following takes place:

**1.** When labor, material, and other direct resources are actually consumed.

**2.** Material resources are withdrawn from inventory for use.

**3.** Material resources are received that are uniquely identified to the contract and scheduled for use within sixty days.

**4.** Major components or assemblies that are specifically and uniquely identified to a single serially numbered end-item are received on a line flow basis.

**Apportioned Effort**—Effort that by itself is not readily divisible into short span work packages, but which is related in direct proportion to some other measured effort.

**Army Plant Representative Office (ARPRO)**—Army contract administrative offices located at defense contractors and installations throughout the U.S. where the U.S. Army has plant cognizance. They are responsible for contract administration and its numerous subsidiary functions.

**ARPRO**—*See* "Army Plant Representative Office."

**Association of Project Managers (APM)**—A professional organization in the United Kingdom which aims to foster the efficiency and well-being of project management.

**At Completion Variance (ACV)**—The difference between the Budget at Completion (BAC) and Estimate at Completion (EAC). At any point in time, it represents a forecast of budget overrun or underrun.

**Authorized Unpriced Work (AUW)**—The effort for which definitized contract costs have not been agreed to, but for which written authorization has been received by the contractor.

**Authorized Work**—That effort which has been definitized and is on contract, plus that for which definitized contract costs have not been agreed to but for which written authorization has been received.

**AUW**—*See* "Authorized Unpriced Work".

**BAC**—*See* "Budget at Completion".

**Baseline**—*See* "Performance Measurement Baseline" and also "Contract Budget Base."

**Baseline Review (BR)**—A customer review conducted to determine with a limited sampling that a contractor is continuing to use the previously accepted performance system and is properly implementing a baseline on the contract or option under review. A baseline review is particularly applicable to follow-on contracts, where key C/SCSC knowledgeable contractor personnel are retained from previous efforts.10

**BCWP**—*See* "Budgeted Costs for Work Performed."

**BCWS**—*See* "Budgeted Costs for Work Schedules."

**Bid and Proposal (B&P)**—The effort associated with the preparation and submittal of cost bids and technical proposals.

**Bill of Material**—A listing of all the sub-assemblies, parts and raw materials that go into a parent assembly showing the quantity of each required to make an assembly. There are a variety of formats of Bill of Material, including Single Level, Indented, Modular (planning), Transient, Matrix, Costed, and so on.

**Booking Rates**—Rates used during the course of a year to record estimated actual indirect costs to a project. The overhead booking rates are applied to direct labor, materials and other direct costs.

**Bottom Up Cost Estimate**—*See* Engineering Cost Estimate.

**BR**—*See* "Baseline Review."

**Budget**—A plan of operations for a fiscal period in terms of: **(a)** estimated costs, obligations, and expenditures; **(b)** source of funds for financing including anticipated reimbursements and other resources; and **(c)** history and workload data for the projected programs and activities.

**Budget at Completion (BAC)**—The sum of all budgets (BCWS) allocated to the contract. It is synonymous with the term Performance Measurement Baseline (PMB).

**Budgeted Cost for Work Performed (BCWP)**—The sum of the budgets for completed work packages and completed portions of open work packages, plus the appropriate portion of the budgets for level of effort and apportioned effort. Also known as "Earned Value."

**Budgeted Cost for Work Scheduled (BCWS)**—The sum of the budgets for all work packages, planning packages, etc., scheduled to be accomplished (including in-process work packages) plus the amount of level of effort and apportioned effort scheduled to be accomplished within a given time period.

**Budgeting**—The process of translating approved resource requirements into time-phased financial requirements.

**Budgets for Work Packages**—*See* Work Package Budgets.

**Burden**—*See also* Indirect Cost.

**Burden**—Overhead expenses not conveniently chargeable directly to a specific job order, and therefore distributed over the appropriate direct labor and/or material base.

**CA**—*See* Cost Account.

**CAIG**—*See* "Cost Analysis Improvement Group."

**CAM**—*See* "Cost Account Manager."

**CAO**—*See* "Contract Administration Office."

**CAP**—Cost Account Plan, a term typically used by firms to describe a "Cost Account." *See* Cost Account.

**CBB**—*See* "Contract Budget Base."

**CCDR**—*See* "Contractor Cost Data Reports."

**CDRL**—*See* "Contractor Data Requirements List."

**CFSR**—*See* Contract Funds Status Report."

**Chart of Accounts**—A formally established and controlled identification of accounting cost elements.

**Commitment**—A binding financial obligation in the form of a purchase order, or as used in the military, the amount administratively reserved for future obligation against available funds based upon firm requisitions.

**Concurrent**—Two or more tasks that are done at the same time or at times which overlap. Also called Parallel.

**Constraint**—Things that cannot happen until something else happens first. Also referred to as a Dependency or Restraint.

**Contract Administration Office (CAO)**—The activity assigned by the DOD to perform contract administration responsibilities for the government, including the offices of the AFPRO, ARPRO, NAVPRO, and DCAS.

**Contract Budget Base (CBB)**—The negotiated contract cost plus the estimated cost of authorized but unpriced work.

**Contract Data Requirements List (CDRL)**—A listing of data requirements specified for a contract.

**Contract Funds Status Report (CFSR)**—A DOD report which provides information to forecast contract funding requirements.

**Contract Line Item Number (CLIN)**—The number used to identify a specific contract deliverable item.

**Contract Target Cost (CTC)**—The negotiated cost for the original definitized contract and all contractual changes which have been definitized, but excluding the estimated cost of any authorized, unpriced changes. The CTC equals the value of the BAC plus management reserve, when there is no authorized, unpriced work.

**Contract Target Price (CTP)**—The negotiated estimated cost (CTC) plus profit or fee.

**Contract Work Breakdown Structure (CWBS)**—The CWBS is a customer prepared family tree sub division of a program which:

**1.** Subdivides an entire program into all its major hardware, software, and service elements.

**2.** Integrates a customer and contractor effort.

**3.** Provides a framework for planning, control and reporting from the lowest levels to the total contract level.

**Contractor**—An entity in private industry which enters into contracts with the Government. The term also applies to Government-owned, Government-operated activities which perform work on major defense programs.

**Contractor Cost Data Report (CCDR)**—A report developed to provide the DOD components with a means by which contract cost and related data can be collected to aid in acquisition management. It is designed to collect data on defense material items in a standard format in carrying out cost estimating, programming, budgeting and procurement responsibilities.

**Cost Account (CA)**—An identified level at the natural intersection point of the work breakdown structure (WBS) and organizational breakdown structure (OBS) at which functional responsibility for work is assigned, and actual direct labor, material, and other direct costs are compared with earned value budget for management control purposes. Cost accounts are the focal point of cost/ schedule control.

**Cost Account Manager (CAM)**—A member of a functional organization responsible for task performance detailed in a cost account and for managing the resources authorized to accomplish such tasks.

**Cost Accounting Standards (CAS)**—Standards established under public law intended to achieve uniformity and consistency in cost accounting practices of government contractors.

**Cost Analysis Improvement Group (CAIG)**—An OSD/DOD advisory body established to perform cost analysis of current and future weapon systems. The CAIG also develops common cost estimating procedures for the DOD.

**Cost Breakdown Structure**—A system for subdividing a program into (a) hardware elements and sub-elements; (b) functions and subfunctions; and (c) cost categories to provide for more effective management and control of the program.

**Cost Center**—A subdivision of an activity or a responsibility center, for which identification of costs is desired and which is amenable to cost control through one responsible supervisor.

**Cost Control**—Any system of keeping costs within the bounds of budgets or standards based upon work actually performed; applicable at any level of management.

**Cost Element**—Typical elements of cost are: direct labor; direct material; other direct costs, and indirect costs.

**Cost Estimate**—A result or product of an estimating procedure which specifies the expected dollar cost required to perform a stipulated task or to acquire an item. A cost estimate may constitute a single value or a range of values.

**Cost Incurred**—A cost identified through the use of the accrued method of accounting and reporting or otherwise actually paid. Cost of direct labor, direct materials, and direct services identified with and necessary for the performance of a contract, and all properly allocated and allowable indirect costs as shown by the books of the contractor.

**Cost of Money**—A form of indirect cost incurred by investing capital in facilities employed on government contracts.

**Cost Overrun**—The amount by which a contractor exceeds the estimated cost and/or the final limitation (ceiling) of a contract.

**Cost Performance Index (CPI)**—The value earned for every measurable unit of actual cost expended.

**Cost Performance Report (CPR)**—A monthly DOD report generated by the contractor to obtain cost and schedule status information for program management. The CPR is intended to provide early identification of problems having significant cost impact, effects of management actions and program status information for use in making and validating management decisions.

**Cost Reimbursement Contracts**—A category of contracts whose use is based on payment by the government to a contractor of allowable costs as prescribed by the contract. Normally only "best efforts" of the contractor are involved, and includes: **(1)** cost; **(2)** cost sharing; **(3)** cost-plus-fixed fee; and **(4)** cost-plus-incentive fee contracts.

**Cost/Schedule Control Systems Criteria (C/SCSC)**—Government established standards which a contractor's internal management system must meet in order to insure the government of effective planning and control of contract work.

**Cost/Schedule Planning and Control Specification (C/SPCS)**—The Air Force forerunner of C/SCSC.

**Cost/Schedule Status Report (C/SSR)**—The scaled down C/SCSC requirement generally imposed on contracts smaller than would warrant a full DODI 7000.2 application.

**Cost to Complete Forecast**—A forecast spread by time periods for indicated remaining costs for the completion of contractual tasks. This term refers to the contractor's estimate of the cost-to-complete remaining tasks. Synonymous with Estimate to Complete.

**Cost Variance (CV)**—The numerical difference between earned value (BCWP) and actual costs (ACWP).

**CPI**—*See* "Cost Performance Index."

**Critical Path**-A sequential path of activities in a network schedule which represents the longest duration of a contract. Any slippage of the tasks in the critical path will increase the duration of a contract.

**Critical Subcontractor**-A contractor performing a complex portion of a contract which requires a flow down of C/SCSC or C/SSR requirements and integration, reviews, acceptance and control of subcontractor system and reporting. Critical subcontractors are designated as a result of customer negotiation or by management direction.

**CTC**—*See* "Contract Target Cost."

**CTP**—*See* Contract Target Price."

**CV**—*See* "Cost Variance."

**CWBS**—*See* "Contractor Work Breakdown Structure."

**DCAA**—*See* "Defense Contract Audit Agency."

**DCAS**—*See* "Defense Contract Administration Services."

**Defense Contract Administration Services (DCAS)**—Government offices located at numerous contractor facilities throughout the United States. These units are roughly equivalent to Army, Navy and Air Force Plant Representative Offices and their primary function is that of contract administration.

**Defense Contract Audit Agency (DCAA)**—A government agency that provides accounting and financial services on DOD contracts.

**Delta**-Net funding changes or differences.

**Demonstration Review (DR)**—The formal review of a contractor's management control system to determine whether or not it satisfies the requirements of the 35 C/SCS Criteria.

**Dependency**—Also called a Constraint.

**Design to Cost (DTC)**—A process utilizing unit cost goals as thresholds for managers and design parameters for engineers normally in terms of a single cumulative "average flyaway cost." This cost represents what the government has determined it can afford to pay for a unit of military equipment which meets established and measurable performance requirements at a specified production quantity and rate during a specified period of time.

**Design to Cost Goal**—A specific cost established as a goal for a specific configuration, established performance characteristics and a specific number of systems at a defined production rate.

**Detailed Cost Estimate**—*See* Engineering Cost Estimate.

**Direct Costs**-Those costs (labor, material, etc.) which can be reasonable and consistently related directly to service performed on a unit of work. Charged directly and finally to the contract, without distribution to an overhead unit.

**Direct Labor Standard**—A specified output or a time allowance established for a direct labor operation.

**Discrete Effort**—Tasks which have a specific end product or end result.

**Discrete Milestone**-A milestone which has a definite, scheduled occurrence in time, signaling the finish of an activity, such as "release drawings," "pipe inspection complete," and/or signaling the start of a new activity. Synonymous with the term objective indicator.

**Dog and Pony Show**—A briefing which uses a number of viewgraph slides, flip charts, or other graphic aids. Sometimes this term is used to simply indicate that someone is to be briefed.

**DOD**—Department of Defense.

**DOE**—Department of Energy.

**DR**—*See* "Demonstration Review."

**DSMC**—Defense Systems Management College.

**DTC**—*See* "Design to Cost."

**EAC**— *See* "Estimate at Completion."

**Earned Hours**—The time in standard hours credited to a workman or group of workmen as a result of their completion of a given task or group of tasks.

**Earned Value**—What you got for what you spent; performance measurement; the Budgeted Cost of Work Performed (BCWP).

**Economic Lot Size**—That number of units of material or a manufactured item that can be purchased produced within the lowest unit cost range. Its determination involves reconciling the decreasing trend in preparation unit costs and the increasing trend in unit costs of storage, interest, insurance, depreciation, and other costs incident to ownership, as the size of the lot is increased.

**Efficiency Factor**—The ratio of standard performance time is actual performance time, usually expressed as a percentage.

**End-Item**—The final production product when assembled, or completed, and ready for issue or deployment.

**Engineering Cost Estimate**—An estimate derived by summing detailed cost estimates of the individual work packages and adding appropriate burdens. Usually determined by a contractor's industrial engineering, price analysis and cost accountants.

**ESAR**—*See* "Extended Subsequent Applications Review."

**Escalation**—Use of a price index to convert past to present prices or of converting present to future prices; increases due to inflation.

**Estimate at Completion (EAC)**—A value (expressed in dollars and/or hours) developed to represent a realistic appraisal of the final cost of tasks when accomplished. It is the sum of direct and indirect costs to date plus the estimate of costs for all authorized work remaining. The EAC = Cumulative Actuals + the Estimate-to-Completion.

**Estimate to Completion (ETC)**—The value (expressed in dollar and/or hours) developed to represent a realistic appraisal of the cost of the work still required to be accomplished in completing a task.

**ETC**—*See* "Estimate to Completion"

**Event**—Something that happens at a point or moment in time.

**Expenditure**—A charge against available funds. It is evidenced by a voucher, claim, or other document approved by competent authority. Expenditure represents the actual payment of funds.

**Extended Subsequent Applications Review (ESAR)**—A formal review performed in lieu of a full C/SCSC demonstration review when contractor conditions have changed: **(1)** when programs change from *one phase to another* (e.g., R & D into production); **(2)** when contractors move programs from *one facility to another*; **(3)** when contractors make significant *changes to their C/SCSC systems description.*

**FAR**—*See* "Federal Acquisition Regulation."

**Federal Acquisition Regulation (FAR)**—The regulations which govern all Federal procurements. Formerly referred to as Defense Acquisition Regulations (DAR) and earlier as the Armed Services Procurement Regulations (ASPR).

**Fiscal Year**—United States Government: 01 October to 30 September (12 months).

**Fixed Costs**—Costs that do not vary with the volume of business, such as property taxes, insurance, depreciation, security, and minimum water and utility fees. Cost which does not fluctuate with variable outputs in the relevant range.

**Fixed Price Contracts**—A category of contracts whose use is based on the establishment of a firm price to complete the required work. Includes: **(a)** firm-fixed price, **(b)** fixed price with escalation, **(c)** fixed price re-determinable, and **(d)** fixed price with incentive provisions contracts.

**Formal Reprogramming**—*See* "Reprogramming."

**Forward Pricing**—Use of progressively escalated labor rates to convert direct labor hours to direct labor dollars and progressively escalated direct material and subcontract dollars to develop an escalated estimate. Contrasted with "constant dollar pricing", which uses a single un-escalated set of labor rates and does not escalate direct material and subcontract dollars to develop an un-escalated estimate.

**Front Loading**—An attempt by a contractor to provide adequate budget in the near-term budget baseline, at the expense of the far-term effort. It is an attempt to delay an acknowledgement of a potential overrun condition, in the hope that the contractor can "get well" through changes in the contract statement of work. Front loading is often the result of inadequate or unrealistic negotiated contract target costs.

**Functional Division**—Manufacturing, Engineering, Material, Business Management, Quality, and so on.

**Functional Organization**—An organization or group of organizations with a common operational orientation such as Quality Control, Engineering, or Turbine Area Engineer, Inspection, and so on.

**Funding Profile**—An estimate of program funding requirements usually displayed in columnar spread sheet format by years, starting with previous year through the current year and out-years.

**Gantt Chart**—A graphic representation used as an aid to effective scheduling and control by setting up graphically on a time scale when certain events are to take place or where deadlines occur, a sophisticated bar chart.

**General and Administrative (G&A)**—A form of indirect expenses incurred in the direction, control, and administration of the company (including selling expenses). These expenses are spread over the total direct and burden cost at a negotiated rate.

**Government Furnished Equipment/Property/Material (GFE/GFP/GFM)**—Property purchased by the government which is supplied to a contractor normally in accordance with the contract for use or incorporation in the final product.

**ICA**—*See* "Institute of Cost Analysis."

**Idle Time**—A time interval during which either the workman, the equipment, or both do not perform useful work.

**IDWA**—*See* "Interdivisional Work."

**Implementation Review/Visit**—An initial visit by selected members of the customer C/SCSC review team to a contractor's plant, to review the contractor's plans for implementing C/SCSC on a new contract. Such visits should take place within 30 days after contract award.

**Independent Cost Analysis**—An analysis of program cost estimates conducted by an impartial body disassociated from the management of the program.

**Independent Cost Estimate**—An estimate of program cost developed outside normal advocacy channels by a team which generally includes representation from cost analysis, procurement, production management, engineering and program management.

**Independent Government Cost Estimate**—An estimate of the cost for goods and/or estimate of services to be procured by contract. Such estimates are prepared by government personnel, i.e., independent of contractors.

**Indirect Cost**—Resources expended which are not directly identified to any specific product or service.

**Indirect Cost Pools**—A grouping of indirect costs identified with two or more cost objectives but not specifically identified with any final cost objective.

**Institute of Cost Analysis (ICA)**—A professional organization dedicated to improving the effectiveness of cost and price analysis in government and industry.

**Interdivisional Work**—Any portion of a contract which is performed by another segment of the same company having overall responsibility for management of the prime contract. Commonly refereed to as IDWA, Inter Divisional Work Authorization, and sometimes as IOTs, Interorganizational Transfers.

**Internal Replanning**—Replanning actions performed by the contractor for remaining effort within the scope of the budget that is remaining. The contractor is required to notify the government of all internal replanning actions.

**Internet-The International Association of Project Management**—A world wide professional body which seeks to advance the concept of project management.

**IOT**—*See* "Interdivisional Work."

**Labor Rate Variances**—Difference between planned labor rates and actual labor rates. Labor rate variances are derived by subtracting from actual hours x planned rates, the actual hours x actual rates.

**Labor Standards**—A compilation of time study of standard time for each element of a given type of work.

**Latest Revised Estimate (LRE)**—*See* "Estimate at Completion."

**LCC**—*See* "Life Cycle Costs."

**Learning/Improvement Curves**—A mathematical way to explain and measure the rate of change of cost (in hours and dollars) as a function of quantity.

**Level of Effort (LOE)**—Work that does not result in a final product, e.g., liaison, coordination, follow-up, or other support activities, and which cannot be effectively associated with a definable end product process result. It is measured only in terms of resources actually consumed within a given time period.

**Life Cycle Cost (LCC)**—The total cost to the government of acquisition and ownership of that system over its useful life. It includes the cost of development, acquisition, support, and where applicable, disposal.

**Line of Balance (LOB)**—A graphic scheduling technique for controlling production type efforts.

**LOB**—*See* "Line of Balance."

**LOE**—*See* "Level of Effort."

**LRE**—Latest Revised Estimate, *see* "Estimate at Completion."

**Make or Buy**—The classification of components on a contract as to whether they will be produced by the contractor (Make) or obtained from an outside source (Buy).

**Management Control Systems**—The planning, scheduling, budgeting, estimating, work authorization, cost accumulation, performance measuring, and so on. Systems used by a contractor to plan and to control the cost and scheduling of work.

**Management Reserve (MR)**—A portion of the Contract Budget Base that is held for management control purposes by the contractor to cover the expense of unanticipated program requirements. It is not a part of the Performance Measurement Baseline.

**Management Reserve Budget**—*See* Management Reserve (MR).

**Manufacturing Resource Planning (MRP II)**—A method for the effective planning of all resources of a manufacturing company. Ideally, it addresses operational planning in units, financial planning in dollars, and has simulation capability to answer "what if" questions. It is made up of a variety of functions, each linked together: business planning, production planning, master production scheduling, material requirements planning (MRP), capacity requirements planning, and the execution support systems for capacity and material. Output from these systems would be integrated with financial reports such as the business plan, purchase commitment report, shipping budget, inventory projections in dollars, and so on. Manufacturing Resource Planning (MRP II) is a direct outgrowth and extension of closed-loop MRP, Material Requirements Planning.

**Master Program Schedule (MPS)**—The highest summary level schedule for a major program depicting overall program phasing and all major interfaces, contractual milestones, and program elements.

**Material**—Property which may be incorporated into or attached to an end item to be delivered under a contract or which may be consumed or expended in the performance of a contract. It includes, but is not limited to raw and processed material, parts, components, assemblies, fuels and lubricants and small tools and supplies which may be consumed in normal use in the performance of a contract.

**Material Requirements Planning (MRP)**—A set of techniques which uses bills of material, inventory data and the master production schedule to calculate requirements for materials. It makes recommendations to release replenishment orders for material. Further, since it is time-phased, it makes recommendations to reschedule open orders when due dates and need dates are not in phase. Originally seen as merely a better way to order inventory, today it is thought of as primarily a scheduling technique, i.e., a method for establishing and maintaining valid due dates on orders.

**Memorandum of Agreement (MOA)**—A document which establishes mutual agreement between the cognizant on-site agency and the government program offices in order to ensure adequate surveillance. The MOA delineates the responsibilities of both the procuring agency and the cognizant government office and should be explicit as to surveillance activities, frequency of audits and reports, depth and detail of analysis, notification of deficiencies and other special problems that may be unique to that contract.

**Memorandum of Understanding (MOU)**—A document between the DOD procuring activity concerned and the contractor regarding the implementation and maintenance of its management control systems. The MOU clarifies the intent of the contractor and the DOD components relative to implantation of the criteria and its application on a plant-wide basis for all contractual activities in that facility.

**Midpoint Pricing**—The use of a set of rates that are the average of a specific time period in lieu of progressively escalated rates to develop an escalated price estimate.

**Milestone**—An event, usually of particular importance, i.e., a big event.

**MOA**—*See* "Memorandum of Agreement."

**MOU**—*See* "Memorandum of Understanding."

**MPS**—*See* "Master Program Schedule."

**MR**—*See* "Management Reserve."

**MRP**—*See* "Material Requirements Planning."

**MRP II**—*See* "Manufacturing Resource Planning."

**National Contract Management Association (NCMA)**—A professional organization devoted to fostering the advancement of professionalism in contract management.

**NAVPRO**—*See* "Navy Plant Representative Office."

**Navy Plant Representative Office (NAVPRO)**—A Navy Contract Administration Office established at defense contractor's plants. They are equivalent to the AFPRO or DCAS organizations.

**NCMA**—*See* "National Contract Management Association."

**Negotiated Contract Cost**—(*See also* Contract Target Cost). The estimated cost negotiated in a Cost-Plus-Fixed-Fee Contract or the negotiated contract target cost in either a Fixed Price-Incentive Contract or a Cost-Plus-Incentive-Fee Contract.

**Network**—A logic flow diagram in a prescribed format consisting of the activities and events which must be accomplished to reach program objectives, which show their planned sequence and interrelationships.

**Nonrecurring Costs**—Expenditures against specific tasks that are expected to occur only once on a given program. Examples are such items as preliminary design effort, qualification testing, initial tooling and planning, and so on.

**Objective Indicator**—*See* "Discrete Milestone."

**OBS**—*See* "Organizational Breakdown Structure."

**ODC**—*See* "Other Direct Costs."

**Organizational Breakdown Structure (OBS)**—A functionally oriented pyramid-like structure indicating organizational relationships and used as the framework for the assignment of work responsibilities. The highest level of the OBS is the top level of management for a weapon system. The organizational structure is progressively detailed downward to the lowest level of management. The OBS relates to the WBS in that compatible or corresponding levels of each structure normally have similar degrees of authority and work responsibility.

**Original Budget**—The budget established at or near the time the contract was signed, based on the negotiated contract cost.

**OTB**—*See* "Over Target Baseline."

**Other Direct Costs (ODC)**—A group of accounting elements which can be isolated to specific tasks, other than labor and material. Included in ODC are such items as travel, computer time, and services.

**Output Standard**—Specifies the number of items or amount of services that should be produced in a specific amount of time by a specific method.

**Over Target Baseline (OTB)**—A baseline which results from formal reprogramming with the approval of the customer.

**Overhead**—Costs incurred in the operation of a business which cannot be directly related to the individual products or services being produced. *See also* Indirect Cost.

**Overrun**—Costs incurred in excess of the contract target cost on an incentive contract, or the estimated cost on a fixed fee contract.

**PAR**—See "Problem Analysis Report."

**Parametric Cost Estimate**—A cost estimating methodology using statistical relationships between historical costs and other program variables such as system physical or performance characteristics, contractor output measures, manpower loading, and so on. Also referred to as a "top-down" estimating approach.

**PD**—See "Program Directive."

**Performance Management Association (PMA)**—A professional organization dedicated to promoting high standards in performance measurement, with particular emphasis on C/SCSC.

**Performance Measurement Baseline (PMB)**—The time-phased budget plan against which project performance is measured. It is formed by the budgets assigned to scheduled cost accounts and the applicable indirect budgets. For future effort, not planned to the cost account level, the Performance Measurement Baseline also included budgets assigned to higher level CWBS elements. The PMB equals the total allocated budget less management reserve.

**Performance Measurement Joint Executive Group (PMJEG)**—A group composed of the individuals in HQ AMC, HQ NMC, and HQ AFSC directly responsible for supervising the application of C/SCSC to major defense acquisitions. The group considers major policy aspects of C/SCSC and provides high-level interpretation of C/SCSC requirements.

**Performing Organization**—The organizational element expending resources to accomplish a task.

**Period of Performance**—The time interval of contract performance that includes the effort required to achieve all significant contractual schedule milestones.

**PERT**—Program Evaluation and Review Technique.

**Planned Value for Work Accomplished (PVWA)**—An early C/SCSC term meaning BCWP.

**Planned Value for Work Scheduled (PVWS)**—An early C/SCSC term meaning BCWS.

**Planning Account**—Tasks which have been detailed to the greatest extent practicable, but which cannot yet be subdivided into detailed tasks. Planning accounts can exist at any level above the task level.

**Planning Package**—A logical aggregation of far term work within a cost account that can be identified and budgeted but not yet defined into work packages. Planning packages are identified during the initial baseline planning to establish the time phasing of the major activities within a cost account and the quantity of the resources required for their performance. Planning packages are placed into work packages consistent with the rolling wave concept prior to the performance of the work.

**PM**—*See* "Program/Project Manager."

**PMA**—*See* "Performance Management Association."

**PMB**—*See* "Performance Measurement Baseline."

**PMI**—*See* "Project Management Institute."

**PMJEG**—*See* "Performance Measurement Joint Executive Group."

**Price Variance (PV)**-Difference between the planned cost of a purchased item and its actual cost. Price variance is derived by subtracting from actual quantity x planned cost, the actual quantity x actual cost.

**Privity of Contract**—The legal relationship between two parties of the same contract. The government has "privity of contract" with the prime contractor. The prime contractor has "privity of contract" with the subcontractor. Therefore, the government's relationship with subcontractors is indirect in nature. Government involvement with subcontractors is channeled through prime contractor directed activities: only the prime contractor is authorized to direct the subcontractor.

**Problem Analysis Report (PAR)**—A report made by the responsible manager to explain a significant cost/schedule variance, its probable impact on the program, and the corrective actions taken to resolve the problem(s).

**Program Directive (PD)**—A document which gives specific contract operational instructions. A PD may be issued to inform functional organizations of program requirements, selected control system options, place responsibilities, direct corrective actions, and to authorize or limit lines of authority. Often PDs are of a limited, short-term duration, but if they are of a permanent nature, are frequently superceded by regular company procedures.

**Program (Project) Manager (PM)**—The person assigned the prime responsibility for overall management of a program.

**Program Risk Analysis**—The system that provides a continuous analysis of identified risks, with respect to their impact on program cost, schedule, and technical performance.

**Progress Payments**—Payments made to a contractor during the life of a fixed-price type contract on the basis of a percentage of incurred total cost or total direct labor and material cost.

**Project Management Institute (PMI)**—A nonprofit professional organization dedicated to advancing the state of the art in project management.

**Project Manager**—An official who has been assigned responsibility for accomplishing a specifically designed unit of work effort or group of closely related efforts established to achieve stated or designated objectives, defined tasks, or other units of related effort on a schedule for performing the stated work funded as part of the project. The project manager is responsible for the planning, implementing, controlling, and reporting on a project.

**Purchase Order**—An order issued by a functional organization (usually material) to purchase any parts from a source outside the prime contractor.

**Purchased Labor**—A type of labor used to relieve shop overload and/or to take advantage of special processing skills or fabricating facilities possessed by a supplier.

**Purchased Parts**—Details or small subassemblies that are purchased or subcontracted to an outside source. The parts/subassemblies consist of parts that are not normally within the prime contractor's capability to make.

**PV**—See "Price Variance."

**PVWA**—Planned Value Work Accomplished, see new term Budgeted Costs for Work Performed (BCWP).

**PVWS**—Planned Value Work Scheduled, see new term Budgeted Costs for Work Scheduled (BCWS).

**Rate Cost Curves**—A mathematical way of explaining and measuring the impact of changing production rates on a program's total cost.

**RDT&E or R&D**—Research, Development, Test & Evaluation.

**Readiness Assessment**—A meeting or series of meetings by selected members of the customer C/SCSC review team to a contractor's plant, to review contractor plans and progress in implementing C/SCSC in preparation for a full demonstration review. Such visits are expected to happen about 30 days after the initial implementation review/visit, or about 60 days after contract award.

**Realization Factor**—The ratio of actual performance time to standard performance time, usually expressed as a decimal number.

**Recurring Costs**—Expenditures against specific tasks that would occur on a repetitive basis. Examples are sustaining engineering, production of operational equipment, tool maintenance, and so on.

**Replanning**—A change in the original plan for accomplishing authorized contractual requirements; there are two types of replanning effort:

**1. Internal Replanning**—A change in the original plan that remains with in the scope of the authorized contract. It is caused by a need on the part of the contractor to compensate for cost, schedule, or technical problems which have made the original plan unrealistic.

**2. External Replanning**—(Government directed changes to the contract) can be in the form of a definitized change order or an unpriced change order that calls for a change in the original plan. While this change may remain within the scope of the original contract it most often exists as a change in the scope of the contract in terms of cost, schedule, technical parameter or a combination thereof.

**Reprogramming**—A comprehensive replanning of the effort remaining in the contract resulting in a revised total allocated budget which may exceed the current contract budget base.

**Request for Proposal (RFP)**—An official procurement document that requests proposals from potential contractors.

**Request for Quote (RFQ)**—An official document requesting a cost estimate for the performance of work.

**Responsible Organization**—A defined unit within the contractor's organization structure which is assigned responsibility for accomplishing specific tasks.

**RFP**—*See* "Request for Proposal."

**RFQ**—*See* "Request for Quote."

**Risk Management**—The manipulation of risk factors in the interest of desired objectives.

**Rolling Wave Concept**—The progressive refinement of detailed of work definition by continuous subdivision of downstream activities into near-term tasks.

**Rubber Baselining**—An attempt by a contractor to take far-term budget baseline and move it into the current period in an attempt to disguise current cost problems. The attempt will be to move budget without a corresponding equal amount of work tasks, to cover current cost difficulties. It is an indicator of a likely overrun condition.

**SAIMS**—Selected Acquisition Information Management System.

**SAR**—*See* "Subsequent Application Review" and/or "Selected Acquisition Report."

**Schedule**—A time plan of goals or targets which serve as the focal point for management actions.

**Schedule Variance (SV)**—The numerical difference between Earned Value (BCWP) and the Budget Plan (BCWS).

**Scheduling**—The act of preparing and/or implementing schedules.

**Scrub (Budget)**—A review of a budget with the eye toward reducing or reprogramming of funding to meet current priorities.

**SEAC**—*See* "Statistical Estimate at Completion."

**Selected Acquisition Reports (SAR)**—Standard, comprehensive, summary status reports on DOD systems for management within the DOD. Required for periodic submission to the Congress, in accordance with DODI 7000.3.

**Sequential**—Things that are done in a sequence, serial, or series; one thing after another.

**Should-Cost Estimate**—An estimate of contract price which reflects reasonably achievable economy and efficiency. Its purpose is to develop a realistic price objective for negotiation purposes.

**Significant Variances**—Those differences between planned and actual performance which require further review, analysis, or action. Appropriate thresholds should be established as to the magnitude of variances which will require variance analysis.

**SOW**—*See* "Statement of Work."

**SPO**—*See* "System Program Office."

**Standard**—A term applied in work measurement to any established or accepted rule, model, or criterion against which comparisons are made.

**Standard Cost**—The normal expected cost of an operation, process, or product including labor, material, and overhead charges, computed on the basis of past performance costs, estimates, or work measurement.

**Standard Time**—The amount of time allowed for the performance of a specific unit of work.

**Statement of Work (SOW)**—A description of a product or services to be procured under a contract; a statement of requirements.

**Statistical Estimate at Completion (SEAC)**—A statistically computed forecast based on performance to date and the mathematical projection of this performance to derive the estimated contract cost value by the BCWP cost performance index.

**Subcontract**—A contractual document which defines the effort of providing services, data, parts, components, assemblies or other hardware which a company commits to perform on behalf of another firm.

**Subsequent Application Review (SAR)**—A visit by government personnel (and/or prime contractor and/or both) to a contractor's facility to determine whether the contractor has properly applied the management control system which had been previously accepted as meeting the requirements of C/SCSC, to a *new contract*.

**Surveillance**—A term used in C/SCSC to mean the monitoring of continued compliance with an approved/validated management control system.

**Surveillance Monitor**—The individual in the CAO who is responsible for coordinating C/SCSC surveillance functions with other members of the CAO organization and with the auditor to assure that the surveillance objectives are accomplished.

**Surveillance Plan**—A document in concert with a formal Memorandum of Agreement which establishes the procedures for accomplishing C/SCSC surveillance.

**SV**—*See* "Schedule Variance."

**SWAG**—The addition of the word "scientific," to a WAG (a "wild-ass guess").

**System Program Office (SPO)**—The office of the program manager and the single point of contact with industry, Government agencies and other activities participating in the system acquisition process.

**TAB**—*See* "Total Allocated Budget."

**Target Cost**—*See* Contract Target Cost and/or Contract Budget Base.

**Task**—Also called an activity, something that takes place over a period of time, which generally consumes resources.

**TCPI**—*See* "To Complete Performance Index."

**Thresholds**—Monetary, time, or resource points, placed on something, which are used as a guideline, which if breached, cause some type of management review to happen.

**To Complete Performance Index (TCPI)**—The projected value to be earned for every measurable unit to be expended in the future.

**Total Allocated Budget (TAB)**—The sum of all budgets allocated to a contract. Total allocated budget consists of the performance measurement baseline and all management reserve. The total allocated budget will reconcile directly to the contract budget base.

**Touch Labor**—Defined as production labor which can be reasonably and consistently related to a unit of work being manufactured, processed, or tested.

**UB**—*See* "Undistributed Budget."

**Undistributed Budget (UB)**—Budget applicable to contract effort which has not yet been identified to CWBS elements at or below the lowest level of reporting to the government.

**Unit Cost**—Total labor, material, and overhead cost for one unit of production, i.e., one part, one gallon, one pound, and so on.

**Unpriced Changes**—Authorized but unnegotiated changes to the contract.

**USA**—United States Army.

**USAF**—United States Air Force.

**Usage**—The number of units or dollars of an inventory item consumed over a period of time.

**Usage Variance (UV)**—The UV is the difference between planned quantity of materials and actual quantity used, expressed in dollars. UV is derived by subtracting from planned quantity times planned unit cost, the actual quantity times planned unit cost.

**USN**—United States Navy.

**UV**—*See* "Usage Variance."

**VAC**—*See* "Variance at Completion."

**Validation**—A term used in C/SCSC to mean "approval" or compliance with the criteria.

**Variable Cost**—A cost that changes with the production quantity or the performance of services. This contrasts with fixed costs that do not change with production quantity or services performed.

**Variance**—The difference between the expected/budgeted/planned and the actual results.

**Variance at Completion (VAC)**—Variance at Completion is the algebraic difference between Budget at Completion and Estimate at Completion (VAC = BAC - EAC).

**Variance Threshold**—The amount of variance beyond which a Problem Analysis Report is required, as agreed to between the contractor and the customer. Variance parameters will differ depending on the function, level and stage of the project.

**WBS**—*See* "Work Breakdown Structure."

**What If Analysis**—The process of evaluating alternative strategies.

**Work Breakdown Structure (WBS)**—The WBS is a product-oriented family tree division of hardware, software, services and program unique tasks which organizes, defines, and graphically displays the product to be produced, as well as the work to be accomplished to achieve the specified product. There are several types of WBSs, including these two major categories:

**1. Project Summary WBS (PSWBS)**—A summary WBS tailored to a specific defense material item by selecting applicable elements from one or more summary WBSs or by adding equivalent elements unique to the project in accordance with government defined WBS requirements.

**2. Contract WBS (CWBS)**—The complete WBS for a contract, developed and used by a contractor within the guidelines of government defined WBS requirements and the contract statement of work.

**Work Breakdown Structure Dictionary**—A document which describes the tasks of WBS elements in product-oriented terms, and relates each element to the direct cost charging practices of the program.

**Work Breakdown Structure Element**—A discrete portion of a WBS. A WBS element may be an identifiable product, a set of data, or a service.

**Work Package Budgets**—Resources which are formally assigned by the contractor to accomplish a work package, expressed in dollars, hours, standards or other definitive units.

**Work Packages (WP)**—Detailed short-span jobs, or material items, identified by the contractor for accomplishing work required to complete a contract.

**WP**—*See* "Work Packages."

# Index

In addition to this Index, there is a subject Index contained in the DOD Joint Implementation Guide, Appendix E to this book.

# About the Author

Quentin W. Fleming is employed by a major aircraft contractor in the greater Los Angeles area. He has held various domestic and overseas management positions with that firm since he joined it in 1968. He is presently a subcontract manager on a major subcontract, where he also functions as the cost account manager in the flow-down of C/SCSC.

On a leave of absence from his current employer, he accepted an appointment with the United States Government. He and his family moved initially to Washington, D.C., and then to Tehran, Iran, where he became the seventh and final Peace Corps Director in that country. Peace Corps closed its mission to Iran in 1976. Concurrently, he directed the Peace Corps program on the small island nation of Bahrain, on the south shore of the Arabian/ Persian Gulf. He rejoined his firm in 1976.

He is the author of three published business books:

1. *A Guide to Doing Business on the Arabian Peninsula,* published by the American Management Associations, AMACOM division, NY: 1981.
2. *Put Earned Value (C/SCSC) Into Your Management Control System*, Publishing Horizons, Inc., Columbus, OH: 1983.
3. *Project and Production Scheduling*, Probus Publishing Company, Chicago, IL: 1987. Co-authored with John W. Bronn and Gary C. Humphreys.

He holds the degrees of B.S. and M.A. in management, and an L.L.B. He is a member of the Performance Management Association, the Institute of Cost Analysis, and the National Contract Management Association. He and his wife reside in Southern California.